INFORMATION TECHNOLOGY OUTSOURCING

Advances in Management Information Systems

INFORMATION TECHNOLOGY OUTSOURCING

SUZANNE RIVARD
BENOIT A. AUBERT
EDITORS

AMIS

ADVANCES IN MANAGEMENT INFORMATION SYSTEMS
VLADIMIR ZWASS SERIES EDITOR

M.E.Sharpe
Armonk, New York
London, England

Library of Congress Cataloging-in-Publication Data

References to the AMIS papers should be as follows:

Barthélémy, J. Population-level learning and the evolution of IT outsourcing decisions. S. Rivard and B.A. Aubert, eds., *Information Technology Outsourcing,* Volume 8 (Armonk, NY: M.E. Sharpe, 2008), 25–35.

ISBN 978-0-7656-1685-2
ISSN 1554-6152

Printed in the United States of America

The paper in this publication meets the minimum requirements of American National Standards for Information Sciences Permanence of Paper for Printed Library Materials, ANSI Z 39.48-1984.

∞

BM (c) 10 9 8 7 6 5 4 3 2 1

ADVANCES IN MANAGEMENT INFORMATION SYSTEMS

AMIS Vol. 1: Richard Y. Wang, Elizabeth M. Pierce, Stuart E. Madnick, and Craig W. Fisher
Information Quality
ISBN 978-0-7656-1133-8

AMIS Vol. 2: Sergio deCesare, Mark Lycett, and Robert D. Macredie
Development of Component-Based Information Systems
ISBN 978-0-7656-1248-9

AMIS Vol. 3: Jerry Fjermestad and Nicholas C. Romano, Jr.
Electronic Customer Relationship Management
ISBN 978-0-7656-1327-1

AMIS Vol. 4: Michael J. Shaw
E-Commerce and the Digital Economy
ISBN 978-0-7656-1150-5

AMIS Vol. 5: Ping Zhang and Dennis Galletta
Human-Computer Interaction and Management Information Systems: Foundations
ISBN 978-0-7656-1486-5

AMIS Vol. 6: Dennis Galletta and Ping Zhang
Human-Computer Interaction and Management Information Systems: Applications
ISBN 978-0-7656-1487-2

AMIS Vol. 7: Murugan Anandarajan, Thompson S.H. Teo, and Claire A. Simmers
The Internet and Workplace Transformation
ISBN 978-0-7656-1445-2

AMIS Vol. 8: Suzanne Rivard and Benoit A. Aubert
Information Technology Outsourcing
ISBN 978-0-7656-1685-2

Forthcoming volumes of this series can be found on the series homepage.
www.mesharpe.com/amis.htm

Editor in Chief, Vladimir Zwass (zwass@fdu.edu)

CONTENTS

SERIES EDITOR'S INTRODUCTION

VLADIMIR ZWASS, EDITOR-IN-CHIEF

It is, in a sense, natural for an enterprise to seek market power and attempt to gain economies of scale and scope through size and direct control of resources. Internal corporate growth, with corporate hierarchies submitting large swaths of economic activities to their plans, was the predominant business trend during much of the past century (Chandler, 1977). Vertical integration and the internalization of business functions and processes are features of such expansion, still practiced today by a number of major corporations. As an iconic illustration of this line of managerial thinking, Ford Motor Company owned a rubber plantation in Brazil in the past century, the better to supply its own tire plants (Dempsey, 1994).

Over the past five decades, the advancing technologies of transportation, communication, coordination, and control have brought the ability not only to disperse corporate operations around the globe, but also to externalize them to advantage. In particular, advanced information and communication technologies have made it advantageous for many firms to organize their activities around their core competencies, the activities they do best, and to go to the market for their noncore business processes. Of course, externalizing business processes is based on long-term relationships with the process suppliers. As in any such relationships, discernment in the selection of vendors (or partners, as some choose to perceive them) has to be followed by great care in contracting and by well-honed regimes of governance and monitoring.

The deployment of modern information technologies (IT) has lowered the transaction costs of market access, that is, the nonproduction costs of searching for a supplier, contracting, monitoring performance, and coordinating interorganizational activities. In many industries, a shift has occurred toward specialization, with the aim of developing the capabilities to operate and innovate in narrower marketplaces (Hagel and Brown, 2005). With strategic outsourcing, companies concentrate their resources on the activities in which they can "achieve definable preeminence and provide unique value for customers" (Quinn and Hilmer, 1994, 43). The appropriate use of external suppliers of business processes has become attractive in overall organizational governance. Clemons, Reddi, and Row (1993) have shown that the use of IT lowers coordination costs while not increasing transaction risks when a carefully selected small set of long-term suppliers is involved. As a consequence, we see the emergence of networks of cooperating firms, often concentrated around a hub company (such as Intel, for example), and of process specialists (such as FedEx in logistics). Business value is delivered to the customers by a virtual supplier, made up of the firms whose actions are coordinated by a focal firm with the heavy use of IT.

Speed is a major factor. The resources owned by an individual firm are very often not sufficient to address a marketplace opportunity within the time window that goes with it. Building up world-class capabilities in logistics, processing of financial transactions, or IT management takes years. The speed of action, both paced and enabled by IT, necessitates collaboration across corporate boundaries to rapidly combine the competencies to create the requisite customer value.

Firms that are unable to mobilize the resources of others in a common effort lose in the competitive marketplace. This speed imperative extends to innovation, with the ever-shorter product cycles and ever more time-driven business processes. To thrive is this business environment, Procter & Gamble, for instance, has adopted the strategy of open innovation, in effect going to the market for much of its research and development (Huston and Sakkab, 2006).

The progressing development of information economies, characterized by the ever-greater digitization of products and by the preponderance of knowledge work with digital tools and media, has accelerated the trend. The political and economic liberalization affecting large spans of the world during the last decade of the twentieth century has fostered an overlapping trend toward offshoring, which is transferring corporate business processes abroad, often (but certainly not always) on an outsourced basis. The proliferation of the Internet–Web compound has further facilitated the outsourcing of business functions, as they become universally built around Web-enabled systems. In a more profound way, spreading uniform enterprise systems and other platform IT foster greater uniformity in work practices and business processes around the world. World-class processes are available worldwide, often in regions with superior capabilities or lower cost structures, and they can be incorporated into global supply chains and webs owing to the Internet–Web infrastructure.

Outsourcing, the transfer of an organization's business function to an external vendor, has become a broad business development. IT is both the means of outsourcing and, as this *Advances in Management Information Systems (AMIS)* volume analyzes thoroughly, its object. IT outsourcing is an important part of the global trend, as it both determines the governance of a vital organizational function and influences the processes of exploitation and exploration in all other functions of an enterprise. In dissecting IT outsourcing, the editors of the present volume of *AMIS*, Suzanne Rivard and Benoit A. Aubert, have admirably fulfilled the mission of the series. They have framed the domain of research and practice broadly, and assembled and guided an outstanding team of authors. They present to the reader not only the most recent research work and actionable conclusions but also research methods that will serve to generate new results in the future. Indeed, the volume brings out the complexities of IT outsourcing. Beyond that, the authors bring to bear a great variety of theoretical perspectives that undoubtedly will be taken up in the future by the researchers who will build on this work.

Although the contracting of various information system (IS) subfunctions to external vendors has always been a part of organizational IT provisioning, the momentous decision of Eastman Kodak Company in 1989 to outsource its large IS function has focused our field on the potential, and on the pitfalls, of outsourcing. Indeed, by considering the role of IT in outsourcing and of outsourcing in IS governance, our discipline has over the years produced many important results. To indicate the scope of work in the area, I will mention only some of them here. The readers of the volume will, of course, gain a far deeper and more extensive view.

The motivations for IT outsourcing vary. Yet, they most frequently center on cost containment and managerial control, financial infusion into the company shedding its IT owing to the transfer of resources (such as data centers) to the outsourcer, and attempts to gain access to superior IT expertise and management skills (Loh and Venkatraman, 1992). A great variety of outsourcing scopes and contracting practices has been identified (Lacity and Willcocks, 1998). New outsourcing modes are emerging, such as use-based services of utility providers, including application service providers and business service providers. Further progress may be expected with service-oriented architectures, relying on Web-accessible standardized software components for the support of business functions.

Since the outsourcer incurs significant front-end costs, contractual arrangements are generally long-term, affording the outsourcer an opportunity to recoup expenditures. Long-term contracting has to be done skillfully, combining guarantees with flexibility across potential major technological discontinuities (imagine a ten-year outsourcing contract signed in 1990!). The term and structure of the outsourcing arrangement have a significant effect on its success (Lee, Miranda, and Kim, 2004). The management of the outsourcing relationship, including such factors as information sharing, trust- and commitment-building, and incentive alignment, are crucial factors of success (Lee and Kim, 1999). Offshore outsourcing requires special care in structuring to spread the risks, avoid excessive costs owing to micromanagement, and protect intellectual property (Rottman and Lacity, 2006).

By its very nature, outsourcing carries significant risks, as it resorts to the vagaries of the market, as opposed to the internal management of IT by a firm. A great measure of decision making is being transferred to the outside supplier. The risks may be classified as strategic, operational, geopolitical, and those attendant on the atrophy of a vital function (Aron, Clemons, and Reddi, 2005). Equity markets are quite discerning in identifying certain classes of risks incurred by client companies and in acting accordingly when valuating them (Oh, Gallivan, and Kim, 2006). Although a variety of risk-containment measures are employed, ranging from specialized contracting processes through continuing quality assurance and managerial and professional oversight, inherent risks remain. Comprehensive risk-management policies are successfully deployed by various firms (Aubert, Patry, and Rivard, 2005). From the organizational learning and innovation perspectives, firms that are strategically dependent on information systems run a danger of falling behind in understanding and exploiting the intricate interdependence among IT-based and other functional processes. For companies strategically dependent on the deployment of IS, it is vitally important to consider outsourcing governance and monitoring on the strategic corporate level (Nolan and McFarlan, 2005). The major outsourcing alternatives should be undertaken with considerations that go well beyond short-term cost savings, and with a view toward the long-term competitiveness of the enterprise.

All told, the study of IT outsourcing is the study of major options in organizational IT service delivery. The profusion of alternatives and the complexity of outsourcing relationships make IT outsourcing a truly important field of study within the IS discipline. Emerging technologies increase the complexity of this delivery and bear ever-new options. Beyond that, it is to be noted that the studies of IT outsourcing published here can cross-pollinate the research work on general business-process sourcing and on strategic alliances in the era of globalization. The work of the editors and the authors of the present volume is a worthy contribution to this research.

REFERENCES

Aron, R.; Clemons, E.K.; and Reddi, S. 2005. Just right outsourcing: Understanding and managing risk. *Journal of Management Information Systems*, 22, 2 (Fall), 37–55.

Aubert, B.A.; Patry, M.; and Rivard, S. 2005. A framework for information technology outsourcing risk management. *Data Base for Advances in Information Systems*, 36, 4 (Fall), 9–28.

Chandler, A.D. 1977. *The Visible Hand: The Managerial Revolution in American Business.* Cambridge, MA: Harvard University Press.

Clemons, E.K.; Reddi, S.P.; and Row, M.C. 1993. Information technology and the organization of economic activity: The "move to the middle" hypothesis. *Journal of Management Information Systems*, 10, 2 (Fall), 9–35.

Dempsey, M.A. 1994. Fordlandia, *Michigan History* (July–August). Available at www.michiganhistorymagazine.com/extra/fordlandia/fordlandia.html (accessed July 28, 2006).

Hagel, J., III and Brown, J.S. 2005. *The Only Sustainable Edge: Why Business Strategy Depends on Productive Friction and Dynamic Specialization.* Boston: Harvard Business School Press.

Huston, L. and Sakkab, N. 2006. Connect and develop: Inside Procter & Gamble's new model for innovation. *Harvard Business Review*, 84, 3 (March), 58–66.

Lacity, M. and Willcocks, L.P. 1998. An empirical investigation of information technology sourcing practices: Lessons from experience. *MIS Quarterly*, 22, 3 (September), 363–408.

Lee, J. and Kim, Y. 1999. Effects of partnership quality on IS outsourcing success: Conceptual framework and empirical validation. *Journal of Management Information Systems*, 15, 4 (Spring), 7–28.

Lee, J.; Miranda, S.; and Kim, Y. 2004. IT outsourcing strategies: Universalistic, contingency, and configurational explanations of success. *Information Systems Research*, 15, 2 (June), 110–131.

Loh, L. and Venkatraman, N. 1992. Determinants of information technology outsourcing: A cross-sectional analysis. *Journal of Management Information Systems*, 9, 1 (Summer), 7–24.

Nolan, R. and McFarlan, F.W. 2005. Information technology and the board of directors. *Harvard Business Review*, 83, 10 (October), 96–106.

Oh, W.; Gallivan, M.J.; and Kim, J.W. 2006. The market's perception of the transactional risks of information technology outsourcing announcements. *Journal of Management Information Systems*, 22, 4 (Spring), 271–303.

Quinn, J.B. and Hilmer, F.G. 1994. Strategic outsourcing. *Sloan Management Review*, 35, 4 (Summer), 43–55.

Rottman, J. and Lacity, M. 2006. Proven practices for effectively offshoring IT work. *Sloan Management Review*, 47, 3 (Spring), 56–63.

ACKNOWLEDGMENTS

We are grateful to Vladimir Zwass, editor-in-chief of the *Advances in Management Information Systems* (AMIS) series, for having invited us to become editors of this monograph. We also wish to thank Heather Smith for her valuable assistance in preparing this introductory chapter. Finally, our warmest thanks go to the authors for their generosity and efficiency throughout the process. Because of their expertise in the field, we are confident of the quality of this volume. Because of their enthusiasm, the preparation of the monograph was a most pleasurable endeavor.

Information Technology Outsourcing

CHAPTER 1

INFORMATION TECHNOLOGY OUTSOURCING

An Introduction

SUZANNE RIVARD AND BENOIT A. AUBERT

In the late 1980s, when the term *information-systems* (IS), or *information-technology* (IT), outsourcing was a neologism, some believed the phenomenon itself was a fad that would soon fall into oblivion. Yet some two decades after the first major IT outsourcing agreement was announced, the number of firms that decide to transfer their IT assets and services to external suppliers continues to increase. In terms of science, fifteen years is indeed a short period of time. Yet, during that period, the quantity and variety of studies on IT outsourcing have been impressive. There are two explanations for this situation. First, IT outsourcing is a multifaceted phenomenon that can be viewed from a variety of theoretical perspectives, for example, transaction cost theory, agency theory, resource-based theory, institutional analysis, and risk management, to name a few. Second, the phenomenon itself changes, raising new research questions. For instance, a decade ago application service provisioning was not even considered as an outsourcing alternative, and we heard very little about offshore outsourcing. They are now common options offered to organizations, and they raise new research issues.

This abundant and varied research falls into two broad streams: studies that aim at understanding and explaining the outsourcing decision and studies that focus on the management of the outsourcing relationship. Studies in the first stream of research are aimed at providing a better understanding of the antecedents of an outsourcing decision (be they economic, political, or institutional), of sourcing alternatives (insourcing, total outsourcing, selective sourcing, offshore outsourcing, ASP, and the like), or of the decision process itself. Studies that belong to the second stream aim at understanding the management of outsourcing relationships. Some propose models that depict the evolution of IT outsourcing relationships while others attempt to identify drivers for successful relationship management, be they success factors or management mechanisms.

The main objective of this volume is to encapsulate current knowledge and contribute to the building of a cumulative research tradition in the domain of IT outsourcing. To do so, the volume has been divided into four parts. The first examines past and current research and suggests new approaches for better understanding this phenomenon. The second and third parts explore the IT sourcing decision and the management of outsourcing relationships, respectively. The fourth and final part presents chapters that adopt a holistic perspective to analyze IT outsourcing and look at future trends in outsourcing research.

Part I. Taking Stock of IT Outsourcing Research

The field of IT outsourcing research is an evolving one, not only because of new practices but also because our methodologies for studying this phenomenon are becoming more refined over time. To date, academics have taken a fairly focused approach to the factors involved, concentrating largely on the economics of sourcing (i.e., costs, risks, and resources), types of outsourcing arrangements (e.g., total outsourcing, partial outsourcing), and the types of outsourcing contracts (e.g., detailed, general) as well as the relationship itself. Today, looking back on fifteen years of IT sourcing research, we are coming to recognize that we have just scratched the surface of our understanding of these methods.

IT outsourcing is a worthwhile research topic for three reasons. First, it is of intrinsic interest in and of itself. It is a new and different means of delivering organizational products and services and therefore valuable to understand. The chapters in this section introduce the reader to novel perspectives on the shape and meaning of IT outsourcing in organizations. In Chapter 2, Jérôme Barthélémy explores the question of whether or not an entire population of organizations can learn how to manage outsourcing better over time. In Chapter 3, Benoit A. Aubert and Anne-Marie Croteau explore how firm strategy affects key outsourcing issues. Chapter 4, by Teresa Marcon and Abhijit Gopal, introduces us to how language shapes our understanding of the world of outsourcing. This section invites consideration of new ways of viewing the outsourcing phenomenon, not by denigrating what has been done to date but by widening the scope of what is involved and by training new lenses on our current understanding of this topic.

Second, IT outsourcing is also a "field within a field" in that it is part of the larger arena of IT management, and like this broader subject, it is changing rapidly as technology enables new ways of working, creates entirely new products and services, and changes the competitive landscape. As a subset of this larger topic, outsourcing research can therefore illuminate new and fruitful ways of looking at and understanding the whole field, particularly its dynamics, which are both exciting to observe and frustrating to pin down. This section presents some challenging and provocative ideas for studying IT outsourcing that also have applicability to research in the broader field of IT management. Chapter 2 takes us to a new level of analysis—the entire population of organizations. Chapter 3 incorporates new theoretical perspectives and introduces us to the dynamic nature of this field. Chapter 4 shows us how the very language we use drives our practices.

Third, IT outsourcing represents the vanguard of some new organizational models, characterized by more open and porous boundaries, interorganizational collaboration and learning, and increasing globalization. What is learned about studying this phenomenon can inform and guide our understanding of the changes in store for organizations as a whole and how they can navigate through potential difficulties to achieve successful outcomes. Learning, strategy, and language have not typically been studied in outsourcing, yet each of these chapters shows how one of these concepts can and should affect the nature and trajectory of outsourcing in organizations and possibly other new organizational trends. These chapters encourage academics to expand their methodological bases of organizational research and better understand how new knowledge is produced. They also point the way to new levels of analysis and different ways of studying organizational dynamics. Chapter 2 illustrates how population-level learning can be studied and shows how this level of analysis can inform us in new ways. Chapter 3 demonstrates how multiple theoretical perspectives can be integrated in a research model and suggests how dynamics can be studied. Finally, Chapter 4 introduces new ways to interpret a multiplicity of stakeholder perspectives and illustrates ways in which the role of language can be productively researched.

Chapter 2: Population-Level Learning and the Evolution of IT Outsourcing Decisions

Can an entire population of organizations "learn" as a group? This is the question Jérôme Barthélémy sets out to explore in Chapter 2 of this volume. Theory suggests that populations of organizations can learn from experience in one of three ways. First, individual organizations can each learn from their direct experience with a phenomenon, for example, outsourcing. Second, they can learn from imitating what they know of other organizations' experiences (i.e., interorganizational learning), or, third, a set of organizations (e.g., in an industry or geographic region) can learn from another set of organizations.

While this premise is theoretically compelling, the little empirical research that has been done in this area has yielded mixed results. One of the reasons for this, Barthélémy contends, is that these studies have focused on whether or not productivity gains can be transferred from one firm to another, not on what was learned or how it was learned. As he points out in this chapter, organizations can and do sometimes learn the wrong things from others' experiences, particularly if the learning is from indirect sources, such as the trade press or consultants, which often tend toward optimistic reports or concentrate on the wrong reasons for success.

Research on IT outsourcing is not typically done at this level of analysis, yet it has the potential to yield significant insights not only into outsourcing as a phenomenon but also into organizational behavior in general. The 1989 contract between Kodak and its partners—IBM, DEC, and Businessland Inc.—is widely accepted as a tipping point in the use of outsourcing in organizations in that it legitimated the practice among large firms. Barthélémy's goal in this chapter is to show not only that IT outsourcing has gained wider acceptance since this date, but also that organizations' understanding of how best to undertake it has been progressively refined since then. While this proposition appears intuitively obvious, it has never been demonstrated.

Using the population of organizations that outsource all or part of their IT as the unit of analysis, this chapter presents and tests four propositions on what organizations have learned about outsourcing over time. These examine which activities organizations choose to outsource, how they select vendors, how contracts are developed, and finally, the overall success of the outsourcing effort. Barthélémy's findings show that the outsourcing vendor-selection process and contracting processes have indeed evolved to become more elaborate, demonstrating that population-level learning took place over the ten-year period surrounding the 1989 watershed point. He also shows that organizations were more successful in outsourcing when they waited until a sufficient stock of knowledge about it was accumulated by the population as a whole.

This chapter's conclusions are significant for two reasons. First, it convincingly demonstrates the importance and value of studying organizational learning at this unit of analysis, not only in the field of IT outsourcing, but also in other areas in which organizations learn from each other. Understanding the population of organizations is becoming increasingly vital as boundaries become more porous and open to new ideas from the outside and as organizational partnerships for learning become the norm rather than the exception. Second, it provides evidence that first movers in outsourcing have not seemed to enjoy advantages over later movers. This not only has implications for companies seeking to innovate in the outsourcing arena (e.g., global sourcing), but also suggests the accepted wisdom that innovation in IT yields a competitive advantage needs to be more carefully studied.

Chapter 3: Strategic Profiles and Information Technology Outsourcing

This chapter looks at another neglected dimension of the nature and dynamics of outsourcing decisions—organizational strategy. Although strategy is the element that distinguishes one organization from another and guides both an organization's structure and performance, the influence of strategic characteristics has largely been ignored in outsourcing research. To date, studies have explored IT outsourcing largely from the perspective of the characteristics of outsourcing transaction costs or how outsourced resources are to be used.

Benoit A. Aubert and Anne-Marie Croteau suggest that a firm's strategic position should affect two key outsourcing questions: Which IT activities should be outsourced? and how should IT outsourcing contracts be structured? In addition, outsourcing decisions must be dynamic they postulate, because as firms and industries mature, strategies also change, thereby influencing the nature and type of outsourcing desired. The authors examine several ways in which different strategic choices might affect these organizational decisions.

Current outsourcing research suggests that outsourcing activities are comparable between organizations. The authors feel that our understanding of outsourcing decisions could be improved by considering the strategic type of an organization. They illustrate their proposition by examining two fundamentally distinct strategies—defenders and prospectors—that could affect outsourcing behavior.

Aubert and Croteau postulate that these strategic profiles will also be associated with different types of outsourcing. Defenders will tend to choose more traditional outsourcing contracts that are more predictable and stress economies of scale and lower prices. Prospectors, will be more inclined to sign partnership contracts, which will have a higher level of incompleteness.

This chapter makes two important contributions to outsourcing research. First, it presents a theoretical foundation for addressing an organization's strategic profile when studying outsourcing decisions and makes a case for looking at outsourcing from a higher level of analysis than earlier transaction-based research. In doing so, it also recognizes that sourcing has become an important variable in how different firms pursue their business strategies. Second, it proposes a dynamic model for understanding how and why an organization will change its sourcing decisions over time as its strategic position within an industry changes and as an industry matures.

Chapter 4: Information Technology Outsourcing: Questions of Language

The final chapter in this section explores another largely untapped avenue of research into IT outsourcing, that is, how language shapes our understanding of this phenomenon. Authors Teresa Marcon and Abhijit Gopal, note that language is used to create and construct societal awareness, and does not simply mirror an objective reality. They suggest that not only does our language name objects and concepts, it is also a way of understanding the world that excludes other views of it and helps shape our practices. The relationship between language and practices is particularly vital to understand in fields where new practices are developing and new language is being created.

Neologisms, that is, new words or expressions, are a particular feature of the world of information technology, of which outsourcing is a significant part. Marcon and Gopal point out that the creation and evolution of these words is a reflection of current practices and concerns. They argue that the constant interplay between language and practice can be a lens through which the outsourcing phenomenon may be studied. However, researchers in this field have not yet adopted the more nuanced methodologies that the study of language offers. Therefore, these represent an opportunity to bring new perspectives to old problems. Such approaches to research will not lead to predictive models, but can offer a new form of generalizability based on readers' interpretations.

To illustrate this methodological approach, the authors reanalyze an ethnographic case study of outsourcing in a Fortune 500 company completed in 2000. At this firm, work activities were classified either as a "commodity" or as "value-adding." All commodity work was targeted for outsourcing. Marcon and Gopal show that distinguishing between these two types of work (as opposed to classifying work in other ways) helped shape the perceptions of those doing it and affected how the work itself was accomplished. For example, commodity work was assigned to contractors, while value-added work was given to internal employees.

Interestingly, the contractors did not agree that their work was a commodity and they actively sought ways to avoid involvement in routine work and to develop practices that would enhance their status as consultants and professionals. This led to struggles between employees and contractors over the work they were expected to do and also shaped how contractors made choices about their daily practices and career development.

The authors suggest that language can be used to help better understand some of the challenges companies encounter in IT outsourcing and demonstrate a new approach for analyzing this and other organizational phenomena. While traditional wisdom in outsourcing research suggests that success derives from effective contracts and relationships, the authors propose that language can be used to tease out some of the deeper complexities and challenges facing organizations and new approaches to addressing them.

The chapter calls for increasing methodological sophistication and new directions for inquiry in IT outsourcing research. Such nuanced approaches have not yet been used in this field. Yet these have the ability to much better interpret the multiplicity of voices—their positions, interests, and concerns—involved in outsourcing. A linguistic approach also enables researchers to better theorize and understand change, which is essential to understanding an activity as dynamic as outsourcing. Finally, the authors suggest that linguistic sensitivity will help researchers deconstruct the knowledge-production process whereby consultants, the trade press, and researchers themselves create new categories of understanding, which in turn affect how we act in the world. Marcon and Gopal's appeal for reflexivity in outsourcing research implies that our understanding in this area has reached yet another tipping point. We have come to a place where academics cannot merely act as a mirror to reflect a preconstructed view of the world. We can now begin to understand how language and practices interact to create new versions of reality.

Part II. The Sourcing Decision

Deciding whether or not to outsource all or part of an IT activity is an important managerial function, and several studies have been devoted to better understanding the antecedents of this decision. To date, these studies have been grounded in theories from industrial organization, mainly transaction cost theory and agency theory. While this theoretical grounding continues to be important in helping to explain outsourcing decisions, the chapters of this section demonstrate how new and important perspectives contribute to broaden our understanding of how and why sourcing decisions are made.

All of the chapters argue that our theories and conceptualizations need to be refined and enhanced. In Chapter 5, William R. King tells us that what has traditionally been seen as a binary yes/no decision is today being fragmented into several different types of sourcing options, each of which is appropriate for a particular type of IT activity. In Chapter 6, Pankaj Nagpal and Kalle Lyytinen show how macro- and micro-organizational theory (i.e., institutional theory and role-based theory) can be used together to shed light on why similar organizations choose different sourcing arrangements. Wonseok Oh demonstrates in Chapter 7 that several key organizational characteristics affect how much outsourcing a firm chooses to use. In Chapter 8, Bouchaib Bahli and Suzanne Rivard expand the notion of IT outsourcing risk using resource-based theory, and introduce the notion of a capability gap in resources as a key element of risk. Finally, in Chapter 9, Ebrahim Randeree, Rajiv Kishore, and H. Raghav Rao examine the role of trust and privacy in outsourcing decisions and suggest ways that these can be integrated into current theory and more carefully conceptualized.

Some of these chapters also extend our understanding of the sourcing phenomenon to include some of its newer dimensions. In Chapter 5, for example, King presents a framework for distinguishing among four different sourcing options—outsourcing, insourcing, strategic alliances, and internal markets. This reflects the fact that sourcing is becoming a more complex decision that is taking on strategic implications. Echoing this, Chapter 8 looks specifically at the dimensions and risks involved in strategic outsourcing specifically to better understand how this might affect an organization's competitive advantage. In the final chapter of this section, Randeree, Kishore, and Rao look at the decision to use an application service provider (ASP) and at the factors that are important in doing so.

This section offers many fruitful new avenues of research into sourcing decision making. The chapters also provide practitioners with a more thorough understanding of the factors that contribute to effective decisions and provide useful guidance concerning some of the implications and risks of these decisions. In reading them, both researchers and practitioners will develop a new appreciation for the complexity of sourcing decision making and the value of thoroughly thinking through the concepts, risks, and scope involved.

Chapter 5: A Methodology for IT Sourcing Decisions

In this chapter, William R. King outlines a practical framework for making sourcing decisions in IT. Based on his experiences as a consultant and drawing extensively from best practices in the literature, he provides a guideline for choosing between four broad sourcing alternatives: outsourcing, insourcing, internal markets, and strategic alliances. While it does not make the sourcing decision easy or straightforward, this framework has been designed to ensure that all relevant aspects of a sourcing decision are addressed and documented before it is made.

The first important point to note about this chapter is that it looks at sourcing decisions not outsourcing decisions. Sourcing has now become a much more elaborate and granular process in many companies and is moving away from the "to outsource or not to outsource" question to how and where IT resources and services should properly be deployed. The key question, now is to assess whether or not a particular IT activity might currently be, or has the potential to be, a core competence or a critical success factor (CSF) for the organization.

King then clarifies these two complex concepts on which the sourcing decision is to be made and discusses the relationship between them. While ideally an IT activity would clearly be a core competence and/or a CSF, in reality, they are not. As the author reiterates several times in this chapter, the sourcing decision is rarely clear. This is why it is best made by a group of business and IT executives working together over time. Joint decision making tends to lead to better and more well-thought-out sourcing decisions. Rather than being a checklist, the framework should be used as a guide to stimulate thinking about the issues involved and to examine paths that might otherwise go unexplored. This highlights a second important point about the sourcing decision—that it is a judgment call by managers and must be related to the company's strategy and capabilities. For example, even where a strategic alliance is desirable, as in the case of an IT activity that is both a potential core competency and a potential CSF, the organization may not have the ability to develop and sustain this choice. Thus, different organizations could make different judgments in similar conditions.

The five-step methodology outlined is the third, and by no means the least important, contribution of this chapter to our understanding of sourcing decisions. King notes that each step typically requires more than a yes/no answer. For example, the first step is to identify an IT activity that is a candidate for sourcing. Doing this involves developing a deep understanding of how the target activity contributes to the organization's current and future strategic capability. Following this approach to sourcing has several dimensions that may not initially be appreciated by either executives or researchers, and identifying these underlines the true business value of making appropriate sourcing decisions. Use of a sourcing framework forces executives to be more thorough in the process and to fully identify the implications of their decision and other potential problems that may arise. Furthermore, it can identify activities that are vital to the organization's current and future success and in which further investments need to be made. Finally, because the methodology focuses attention on the organizational model of the future, it tends to shed new light on the value of IT activities and create new understanding about organizational strategy in the minds of executives. In providing managers a guideline, and not a cookie-cutter formula, for making sourcing decisions, King illustrates the multiplicity of factors that contribute to deriving true business value from sourcing.

Chapter 6: Institutional and Individual Antecedents of Information Technology Sourcing Arrangements

This chapter explores the sourcing decision from a very different perspective than the previous one. Pankaj Nagpal and Kalle Lyytinen ask the question: Why do similar IT activities in firms become subject to different sourcing arrangements? Like other authors in this volume, they note that most current theory on outsourcing cannot account for these differences. Different IT sourcing arrangements have been observed in practice but the reasons for these organizational decisions have been inadequately theorized.

To address this gap between theory and practice, the authors adopt two different but complementary lenses with which to explore the IT sourcing decision. The first, institutional theory, suggests that different organizational choices are influenced by internal and external forces that lead managers to unintentionally make their organizations similar to others. This theory suggests that IT sourcing choices will vary according to the cost and noncost pressures on the organization. These pressures include such factors as: the degree of IT complexity, maturity of the technology, availability of economic benchmarks, participation of executives in interorganizational learning opportunities, dependence on the finance function, and budgetary restrictions. Nagpal and Lyytinen then examine how these elements might be expected to influence an organization's choice of one of two contrasting sourcing models: a cost-center model designed to achieve efficiency and a service-center design created to improve user satisfaction. They present a series of propositions as to how such institutional influences could be expected to affect the choice of outsourcing model. In summary, they suggest that greater uncertainty, more outside learning opportunities and less dependence on finance will be associated with service-center sourcing models.

The theoretical lens is then reversed to explore how role theory might influence sourcing decisions, by looking at how the degree of role autonomy of the IT manager could influence the model selected. Using the same two contrasting sourcing models, the authors postulate how the degree of influence of other internal functions on the IT manager, the manager's length of tenure, and the strength of an organizational culture could affect the freedom an IT manager will have to make sourcing decisions. They anticipate that greater role autonomy will be associated with service-center sourcing models.

While each of these lenses is interesting in that it suggests new ways of thinking about the sourcing decision, Nagpal and Lyytinen, then integrate their thoughts to show how macro- and micro-level theorizing might be combined into a more comprehensive view of sourcing practices. They suggest that greater role autonomy will be associated with more flexible sourcing structures and that these, in turn, will be linked to greater sourcing success. Importantly, the authors note that such a rich, multitiered approach to theorizing about sourcing decisions will help future researchers move beyond the relatively unidimensional approaches others have taken in the past (i.e., cost-related criteria in low-uncertainty environments). They correctly point out that as the attention of practitioners and researchers moves toward achieving a greater understanding of the business value of IT, there is a need for future sourcing research to recognize and theorize about more realistic and complex scenarios. It is only when these are available that better metrics of sourcing effectiveness will be able to be developed.

Chapter 7: Firm Characteristics and Allocation of IT Budget to Outsourcing

This chapter, by Wonseok Oh, provides a clear and thorough discussion of the theory and empirical research that have been done to date to address the question of why some firms spend proportionally more of their IT budgets on outsourcing than others. As such, it will be a useful resource for others who wish to understand how previous researchers have examined this question and the theories on which their work is based.

Oh suggests that there is still a multitude of larger organizational factors, which both drive and constrain sourcing choices, that are still not well understood. He notes the huge variation in how much Fortune 500 organizations spend proportionally on IT outsourcing—ranging from 6 percent to 80 percent in the late 1990s. Such large differences cannot be explained by a single variable but are much more likely to arise from numerous factors working in conjunction with each other. Drawing from multiple theoretical streams, he examines a number of these factors and presents propositions as to how they might affect a firm's propensity to outsource more or less of its IT services.

He postulates that two sets of organizational factors will influence an organization's IT outsourcing intensity. Organizational risk, which incorporates uncertainty, agency risk (i.e., the conflict of interest between an organization's shareholders and management), and operational inefficiency, is discussed first in detail. Then, the size of a firm's technological resources (as reflected in its research and development [R&D] intensity and its IT intensity) and their relationship to the amount of outsourcing done are examined. For each variable, Oh hypothesizes how IT outsourcing intensity will be affected.

Following this careful reasoning, Oh then tests the effect of his model against a database of 128 firms. After controlling for the number of IT employees, firm size, and industry, he demonstrates that four out of these five organizational variables are related to the degree of IT outsourcing intensity. Only IT intensity, that is, the proportional amount an organization spends on IT, is unrelated. Together, the independent variables in this model explain 37 percent of the variance in IT outsourcing intensity. Interestingly, a firm's willingness to invest in R&D and operational inefficiencies are positively related to IT outsourcing intensity, while uncertainty and agency costs are negatively related to this variable.

Oh's study convincingly illustrates the importance of better understanding firm characteristics in IT outsourcing research. He notes that more diverse theoretical foundations are needed to better explore this phenomenon and help managers make optimal sourcing decisions for their firms. His careful operationalization of his variables demonstrates clearly how researchers can empirically explore new perspectives in IT outsourcing. His study also stresses the importance of determining an optimal balance between outsourcing and insourcing and highlights the need to better understand how firms can attain this. While transaction cost economics continues to be an important foundation for research in this area, Oh concludes that because each firm is different in its ability to optimize the benefits and minimize the risks associated with IT outsourcing, firm characteristic variables are important for understanding and ultimately guiding sourcing decisions.

Chapter 8: Information Technology Outsourcing Risk: A Resource-Based Perspective

This chapter focuses on a particular but very significant aspect of the sourcing decision—the risk involved. Even though outsourcing is now widely used in organizations, approximately 30 percent of contracts are terminated, while another 25 percent are renegotiated within two years of their inception. Authors, Bouchaib Bahli and Suzanne Rivard note that while the notion of risk exposure is broadly used in the research, it has been inadequately conceptualized. As a result, there is a need to clarify the concepts involved in outsourcing risk exposure. This would not only facilitate empirical research but also establish a foundation that could be a base for refining our theoretical and practical understanding of the nature of outsourcing risk. A key gap in our understanding relates to the risk of outsourcing strategic IT activities.

The authors define risk exposure as the intersection of the probability that an undesirable outcome (e.g., major contractual amendments) will occur and the consequences (e.g., financial loss) of such an occurrence. They briefly outline the four major risk scenarios that have been identified for outsourcing to date. These negative events are not "acts of God" but are within the client's control. Therefore, risk mitigation mechanisms can be adopted to reduce the likelihood that a particular scenario will occur.

The majority of this chapter then builds on these fundamental concepts of risk exposure and risk mitigation. Extending the concept of risk exposure to the outsourcing of strategic IT activities, Bahli and Rivard apply resource-based theory to explain how firms create competitive advantage through building organizational and IT capabilities. An organization's ability to assemble, integrate, and deploy valued resources is enhanced through its routines, activities, and processes. Competitive advantage occurs when others are not able to use their resources in the same way or to the same extent to exploit an opportunity or neutralize a threat.

To exploit their strategic resources, companies must develop and isolate them. Often, this involves acquiring complementary resources and capabilities that they do not have in-house. Outsourcing allows organizations to fill gaps in their resources and capabilities through partnerships and contracts. How firms acquire and leverage both internal and external IT resources and the complementarity between them is significantly related to firm performance. The risks of mismanaging capability gaps are therefore important to understand and mitigate. However, our current understanding of the risks involved is unclear and confused. Bahli and Rivard note two distinct scenarios that could occur when outsourcing strategic resources. First, a firm may lose some of its capabilities through outsourcing. Second, outsourcing increases the risk that a competitor will gain access to these capabilities. Clearly, transferring strategic resources to a third party carries a high risk of loss of competitive advantage. The authors then examine possible mitigating mechanisms that could be adopted to isolate the resource and reduce the risk involved, such as restrictive rules or keeping some resources in-house. Both practitioners and academics have yet to fully explore these mechanisms.

By extending our understanding of outsourcing risk exposure to strategic resources, the authors have made two important contributions to research. First, they clarify the concepts needed to create a risk assessment framework in this area. Second, they identify and describe the concept of a capability gap, which helps us better understand the nature of risk exposure in strategic outsourcing. Taken together, these suggest ways in which the new phenomenon of strategic outsourcing can be better managed and studied.

Chapter 9: Investigating Trust in Outsourcing: A Study in the Health Care Industry

The final chapter in this section, by Ebrahim Randeree, Rajiv Kishor, and H. Raghav Rao, focuses on a particular type of outsourcing in a particular industry. It explores both theoretically and empirically the use of applications service provisioning in the Canadian health care industry. In addition to examining the drivers behind the selection of an ASP, it also looks at the elements of trust and privacy and their importance in this sourcing decision.

This study is groundbreaking for a number of reasons. First, because IT outsourcing in the health care industry has not been well researched, the authors' efforts attempt to rectify this omission. Second, ASPs are among the newer models of sourcing so this work contributes to our general understanding of this field and of the factors that influence the decision to use an ASP. Third, it investigates the role of trust and privacy in this choice—both significant concerns in any outsourcing relationship, but particularly in health care. Fourth and finally, it presents and tests a new staged model of ASP adoption that has significant potential for the future study of IT sourcing in general.

The authors introduce this chapter with a well-rounded discussion of their research arena, that is, the use of ASPs in health care, and the obstacles that have prevented their more widespread adoption, particularly as they relate to trust. They then comprehensively explore the theory and research done to date on the nature of trust in the outsourcing relationship, both prior to the finalization of this relationship and afterward.

The research model itself looks at the influence of production costs (i.e., the cost of hardware, software, and personnel); the availability of slack resources; transaction costs (i.e., coordination, monitoring, negotiation, and governance); asset specificity (i.e., the uniqueness of a firm's IT); and supplier presence (i.e., the availability of reputable vendors with track records) on the decision to choose an ASP to deliver IT products and services. It then further explores the effect of trust and privacy considerations, both directly on the ASP selection decision and indirectly as a moderating influence on transaction and production costs.

Data were derived from a mail survey of hospital executives and yielded a small sample (eighty-nine responses). Interestingly, the researchers applied a seven-stage adoption model to their data analysis. The model's stages included: awareness, interest, evaluation, trial and reject, commitment, limited deployment, and general deployment. Respondents replied with their concerns based on their current stage of adoption. This enabled a richer analysis of results than would have been possible with a simple binary adoption variable.

The results show that high transaction costs negatively affect the decision to select an ASP. High asset specificity positively affects transaction costs while the presence of reputable vendors with track records is seen to lower transaction costs. Interestingly, production costs did not affect the decision to use an ASP. When the direct influence of privacy and trust were examined, it was found that the presence of trust had a slight positive influence on this sourcing decision, while privacy concerns did not influence it at all, nor did they have a moderating influence.

The authors conclude that privacy and trust need to be more fully conceptualized in future sourcing research. For example, it may be that current legislation forces vendors to ensure privacy concerns are fully addressed prior to adoption. Or, governance mechanisms built into contracts may adequately address trust issues. They note that their findings suggest that the maturing outsourcing model may have shifted the focus of organizations from make-versus-buy questions to the issue of transaction costs. They conclude that the decision to use an ASP appears to follow an adoption pattern similar to more traditional forms of outsourcing. Overall, this research is valuable both for what it found and what it did not find about this form of sourcing; its methodological contribution to the study of sourcing; and the greater light it sheds on the role of trust and privacy in making the sourcing decision.

Part III. Managing the Outsourcing Relationship

Following a decision to outsource some or all of its IT function, both the client organization and the vendor(s) involved must structure and manage their relationship to successfully achieve their mutual and specific objectives. As all of the chapters in this section point out, building and maintaining a successful outsourcing relationship is the result of much hard work on the part of both parties. In early outsourcing research and practice, it was expected that the legal and economic conditions built into the contract would be adequate for a successful outcome. As the chapters in this section point out, while these are certainly important prerequisites for success, there are many additional factors that contribute toward ensuring that this relationship achieves expected business goals.

The chapters presented here make a number of contributions toward our understanding of this new and complex relationship. First, they simply examine it as an international phenomenon. The research studies come from Australia, Asia, Europe, and North America and demonstrate the global nature of the outsourcing trend. Second, they apply numerous theoretical lenses to the relationship. The first and last chapters examine the need for control and coordination in outsourcing. Kim Langfield-Smith and David Smith use control theory to explore whether or not control is different in an outsourcing relationship than in an in-house one. Antti Nurmi, Petri Hallikainen, and Matti Rossi apply a different but complementary lens, coordination theory, to better understand the formal and informal dynamics of the outsourcing relationship.

The other two chapters also use a variety of theoretical perspectives but, in addition, demonstrate how multiple lenses can be applied together to produce a more integrated picture of the outsourcing relationship. In Chapter 11, Matthew Swinarski, Rajiv Kishore and H. Raghav Rao adopt new views from both economic-based theories and the interorganizational relationship literature to examine the influence of client power over a vendor and partnership quality on vendor commitment to the outsourcing relationship. And in Chapter 12, Erik Beulen and Pieter Ribbers integrate strategic, economic, and social/organization theories to better conceptualize the factors that lead to IT outsourcing success.

Another strength of this section is the examination of the IT outsourcing relationship from a number of methodological perspectives. Chapters 10 and 12 adopt a comparative case study methodology; chapter 11 uses an experimental approach; and chapter 13 uses a longitudinal case study. Also interesting are the different dimensions of the IT outsourcing phenomenon studied. Several chapters, notably chapters 11 and 12 incorporate the vendor perspective in their understanding of what makes a successful outsourcing relationship. The vendor point of view has been largely unstudied by researchers to date. Finally, the last three chapters look at newer and more complex outsourcing relationships (chapters 13 and 14) and at the ASP outsourcing relationship (chapter 12).

Taken together, these chapters shed new light on how best to manage the IT outsourcing relationship. While they extend our understanding of this phenomenon, they also point out new areas for research, introduce new concepts and methodologies, and enhance existing conceptualizations. In addition, they provide useful and practical insights for practitioners into new ways that organizations can make their outsourcing relationships more successful.

Chapter 10: Managing the IS Outsourcing Relationship

This chapter provides a comprehensive look at the relationship between the organization and the outsourcer. Authors Kim Langfield-Smith and David Smith conducted case studies on the issues that arise in this relationship in three public sector firms in Australia. In particular, they investigated how outsourcing relationships in IS can be managed to achieve control. They note that there has been limited research to date in this aspect of outsourcing, although it has long been known to be a significant risk factor.

While much study has been done of the sourcing decision itself, less is known about the successful management of the outsourcing relationship or about how to achieve effective control. In their case studies, the authors examine whether the management aspects and control issues of this relationship are different for outsourced IS functions than in-house ones. Because outsourcing extends organizational boundaries, a new organizational form is created in the process. This model more closely resembles a partnership than a traditional customer–supplier relationship. This analogy is more true of IS outsourcing relationships than it is of others, given the high degrees of uncertainty, large costs, speed and flexibility, and heterogeneity of activities involved. These factors create complex interdependencies between an organization and outsourcer.

Through detailed interviews with the managers involved in each outsourcing contract and examination of company documents and media reports, Langfield-Smith and Smith first describe each firm's motivation for outsourcing and the criteria involved in the sourcing decision. They then turn to the key issues that arose in effectively managing this relationship. They identify a range of issues that appear to be common to all three firms, though in different ways and in different degrees. These include:

- Inadequate contract specification
- Unrealistic initial expectations of performance improvements
- Different organizational cultures
- The loss of skills and knowledge
- Ineffective communication and information-sharing processes
- Inadequate performance measures and incentives
- An absence of trust, and
- Adverse reactions of employees

Of these, the first three, as well as ineffective communication, appear to be the most significant challenges in the outsourcing relationship for both organizations and outsourcers. For each issue, the authors outline possible causes and examine the approaches that were used to address them.

Interestingly, as organizations wrestle with these issues, they are using precisely the same types of skills that should be applied to managing in-house IS functions, according to the managers interviewed. It was because of the corporate boundaries involved in establishing and maintaining an outsourcing relationship that the need for improved controls quickly became apparent in all three organizations. As a result of the effort put into managing these issues, their organizations appeared ultimately to end up with greater control over IT, and not less control, as has been previously supposed. Furthermore, the formal controls and systems for increased accountability that were implemented were more rigorous than the ones used in-house. The authors therefore suggest that their research raises a new question about the nature of control in the outsourcing relationship, that is, why are organizations better able to enforce controls when outsourcing and not in-house?

Chapter 11: Vendor Commitment in an ASP Outsourcing Context: A Comparative Evaluation of the Roles of Power and Partnership

In this chapter, researchers Matthew Swinarski, Rajiv Kishore, and H. Raghav Rao also examine the duality of the outsourcing relationship. Their study of vendor commitment in this relationship seeks to more completely understand the factors that contribute to full vendor commitment to a client. De-escalation of vendor commitment has been previously shown to undermine the economic and technical benefits of outsourcing. Earlier research has found that client–vendor economics and client dependence on a vendor are important factors in the relationship but has generally ignored the relational dynamics involved. As a result, we have only a limited view of how best to manage IT outsourcing relationships.

This research examines two further reasons for vendor commitment that are largely under the control of the client—power and partnership. Using a single model, it compares both to understand which one better explains vendor commitment to the outsourcing relationship. It also integrates and synthesizes what we know from competing theoretical frameworks to provide deeper insights into this important relationship.

The first influence on vendor commitment studied is vendor perceptions of the client's power over them. In many newer forms of outsourcing, where fewer companies are seeking services (e.g., as in ASPs), a service provider may be highly dependent on a client because the organization represents a substantial portion of its business. Where this is the case, vendor commitment to the relationship would likely be high. The second source of vendor commitment explored is vendor perceptions of the quality of the client–vendor partnership. Partnership quality is based on mutual trust, satisfaction, communication, and cooperation. Where a service provider's perception of partnership quality is high, vendor commitment to the outsourcing relationship is also likely to be high.

The research team conceptualized commitment to the relationship as having three distinct dimensions: willingness to invest capital and effort in it; positive beliefs about the relationship; and the expectation that the relationship will continue. They selected the ASP arena in which to study these factors because it is a new form of outsourcing, and therefore an area in which client power over a vendor might be important. In addition, there have been very few studies of partnership in the ASP outsourcing context.

Unusually, the authors chose an experimental design with which to test their theories, using a role-play exercise where subjects acted as account managers for an ASP company. Manipulation of the two variables involved—partnership quality and power—was accomplished by providing the subjects (MBA students and senior undergraduates) with a letter describing different dimensions of these variables either favorably or unfavorably. Subjects were provided with a list of items (presented as recommendations) corresponding to each aspect of the commitment construct. They were asked to indicate how much they agreed or disagreed with each.

Their results show that 42 percent of the variance in the vendor commitment to the outsourcing relationship is explained by these two variables. Interestingly, the researchers found that partnership quality had a much stronger influence on commitment to the relationship than client power. The interaction between power and partnership was also important. They particularly noted the size of the effect of partnership quality on vendor commitment, given that the study's definition of partnership deliberately did not include any economic components.

This chapter makes a number of contributions to research and practice. First, it examines new dimensions of the client–vendor outsourcing relationship, that is, partnership quality, client power, and vendor commitment. Second, it looks specifically at the ASP model of outsourcing, which has been little studied. Third, it integrates alternative theoretical perspectives and shows how this approach can increase our understanding of the outsourcing relationship. Fourth, it introduces an interesting methodological approach, a laboratory experiment, to outsourcing research. Finally, it suggests noneconomic ways that clients can increase vendor commitment to their organizations.

Chapter 12: Governance of Complex IT Outsourcing Partnerships

In another look at the duality of the IT outsourcing relationship, Erik Beulen and Pieter Ribbers's study of governance practices in complex IT outsourcing partnerships explores the role of these practices in achieving success. This chapter is rich with insights into the factors that contribute to a successful relationship and more fully characterizes these elements for both the client and the supplier. Based on case studies in a variety of European organizations, the chapter fleshes out the relatively limited research that has been done to date and presents several building blocks necessary for developing a sound IT outsourcing relationship.

Governance in IT outsourcing is designed to ensure that the IT services delivered add value to the business and that any IT risks are mitigated. Because two organizations are involved, both have goals they wish to achieve, which may not be aligned. Governance assists in ensuring that both clients and suppliers are better able to meet their goals and thus, have a successful relationship. Following a discussion of IT governance and the client–supplier relationship, the authors describe the nature of complex IT outsourcing relationships. These are defined as multisite, multivendor partnerships involving multiple services and a high contract value. The authors then introduce several elements from three different theoretical approaches—strategy, economic, and social/organizational—to help them identify relevant governance factors.

Ten factors were identified from these theories and were combined into a conceptual model of the client–supplier relationship. Some factors were relevant to the outsourcing company; others to the supplier company. Several factors affecting the relationship itself were also determined. To explore their importance to the success of complex IT outsourcing partnerships, Beulen and Ribbers completed case studies in fourteen firms all using a single outsourcer, conducting interviews, and analyzing documents and archival data. Of particular interest are the criteria they established for determining a successful IT outsourcing relationship. These are much more comprehensive than other measures of success and include five quantitative and five qualitative metrics. To be deemed a success, an outsourcing partnership had to meet at least eight of the ten criteria.

The balance of the chapter examines the importance of the ten governance factors that they identified from the literature and supports their significance in the IT outsourcing relationship with evidence from their case studies. The authors found that the presence of two governance factors in the client firm is important—IT strategy and information management. They note that neither of these is outsource-able and both were present in all cases. From the supplier point of view, a well-defined IT strategy and an adequate contract and account management capability are seen as prerequisites to success.

Six governance factors are important to the relationship between the partners. Properly structured contracts and success metrics are the foundation of all successful partnerships. However, this study found that contracts are often not able to reflect and deal with the dynamics of these relationships. Contract flexibility will be key to future success, they predict. Other success factors include regular reporting and communication at the strategic, tactical, and operational levels of the partner organizations. Annual audits should be built into governance as well. Interestingly, the researchers identify both trust and experience in managing IT outsourcing partnerships as critical to a successful relationship. While trust has been explored in the contract negotiation phase, it is also necessary for maintaining relationships, they note. And an important element of trust is equality between the partners. Lack of experience on both sides of the relationship was identified as a serious threat to its success.

The descriptive framework presented in this chapter identifies many of the elements necessary for a successful partnership. The authors conclude that managing complex IT outsourcing partnerships is not an easy job. They also note that success is seriously inhibited by the limited experience of the partners and also by the growing list of national laws and regulations that aim to regulate governance and accountability.

Chapter 13: Coordination of Complex Information System Development Projects: A Case Study of Finnish Universities

In the final chapter of this section, researchers Antti Nurmi, Petri Hallikainen, and Matti Rossi describe the coordination mechanisms used in a complex, multistakeholder outsourcing project. Their work is a detailed, longitudinal case study of the efforts over ten years of multiple Finnish universities to develop a common student record. The authors focus particularly on how coordination theories can help us understand the management of dependencies over time in this highly complex relationship.

Since information systems change and evolve during their life cycles, it is reasonable to suppose that different methods and tools would be needed to manage them in different stages and circumstances. Coordination theory suggests that four different coordination mechanisms are possible: standards (the rules about performing a task), plans (the goals to be achieved), formal mutual adjustment, and informal mutual adjustment. The first two mechanisms are more structured and prescribed than the last two. The authors note that coordination mechanisms have not been examined for either internal or outsourced systems development projects. Theory also suggests that coordination mechanisms evolve over time. An event will trigger a change in the attributes of a project, which will, in turn, trigger a change in the coordination mechanisms needed to manage it.

The outsourcing relationship described in this case is a complex one in that it involves many clients and many vendors, some of whom changed over the course of the project. As a result, the researchers believe the outcome of the project was likely influenced by the context in which the relationships took place. The researcher set out to answer three questions: What were the coordination mechanisms used in this case? What issues have had an effect on the mechanisms used? And, how did coordination evolve over the different phases of system development?

The project studied began in 1995 with a group of five universities and two vendors and has continued until the present. Over time, eight more universities joined the group and the vendors involved changed. Coordination between the vendors and the universities was managed by a mediating consortium, whose primary responsibility was this systems development project. Through interviews and document analysis, the authors describe what happened in each of the six stages of system development, the issues faced by the consortium in dealing with both the vendors and the university partners, and the mechanisms employed to ensure coordination. They also looked for key events that might have changed the project's attributes, and hence, its coordination mechanisms.

This research shows that coordination mechanisms do indeed change over time. The project began with informal mutual adjustment mechanisms (e.g., meetings) but these gradually matured and more formal mechanisms (i.e., standards and plans) began to be used. Furthermore, coordination became more important as the number of stakeholders increased and their relationships became more complex.

Two important new findings have emerged from this research. First, the research team identified a new concept—the need to compromise—which is characteristic of all stages in this type of system development and which affects the number of coordination mechanisms used and the need for coordination. Second, this study demonstrates the importance of the concept of dependence in the coordination mechanisms selected. As the project developed, stakeholder dependence on each other decreased and the goals of the partners diverged. This led to the necessity of establishing more formal coordination mechanisms to hold the partnership together. This case opens new theoretical avenues with which to explore increasingly complex outsourcing relationships. It also suggests a framework for better understanding of how the outsourcing relationship will change over time and the factors that are necessary to keep it successful.

Part IV. Holistic View of IT Outsourcing

This section takes a step back from specific aspects of the IT outsourcing relationship and looks at how IT outsourcing is evolving and at some of the factors that may be important to understanding it in the future. The three chapters in this section recognize that IT outsourcing is a dynamic field and that our understanding and response to it must become increasingly sophisticated. Whether at a project level or an IT function level, there are new trends and considerations that must be taken into account by both managers and academics.

We are only just beginning to understand the role and importance of social and intellectual capital in developing organizational capabilities and sustaining competitive advantage. In Chapter 14, Rajiv Saberwahl provides an in-depth analysis of how these two factors can both promote the successful delivery of an outsourced IS project and have longer-term benefits to the firm. He points out that as our appreciation of the value of social and intellectual capital grows, we can expect to see managers and organizations make decisions about outsourcing project management using a much broader set of criteria than in the past.

At the IT functional level, in Chapter 15, Christine Koh and Soon Ang present an expanded view of the contractual elements involved in IT outsourcing incorporating both hierarchical governance mechanisms and psychological contract obligations into a framework for IT outsourcing success. They suggest that organizations are increasingly recognizing these elements as vital to future outsourcing performance. Firms must therefore seek to find ways to better address both in their outsourcing contracts and at all levels of the outsourcing relationship—strategic, tactical, and operational.

At a different level of analysis, Beena George and Rudy Hirschheim suggest—in Chapter 16—that offshore outsourcing is a trend that is here to stay. They examine the reasons behind this trend and the challenges that remain in building a successful offshore outsourcing partnership. More important, however, they believe that offshoring signals a broader change in how organizations perform IT work. They call for a greater recognition by both managers and practitioners of the implications of these trends.

Identifying trends and predicting their trajectories is a difficult task. These chapters successfully manage this by grounding their conclusions solidly in existing research. Nevertheless they all suggest that our understanding of the outsourcing phenomenon is by no means complete. Chapter 14 argues for a deeper appreciation of the complex feedback mechanisms involved in outsourced IT projects. Chapter 15 contends that future organizations will need a much more nuanced approach to outsourced relationships that reflect a more complex understanding of the factors that motivate flexibility and agility. Chapter 16 calls for a redesign of the IS discipline altogether. While only time will tell if these trends are as significant as suggested, this section leaves the reader and researcher with much food for reflection.

Chapter 14: Management of Outsourced IS Development Projects: The Role of Social Capital and Intellectual Capital

In this chapter, Rajiv Sabherwal reflects on what he has learned from the in-depth analysis of eighteen large outsourced information systems development (OISD) projects around the world. He suggests that as outsourcing of these projects is becoming more frequent in organizations and more critical to their success, our understanding of the factors that help them achieve "project deliverables" needs to become more refined. Indeed, how we define project deliverables needs to be reexamined to include more than short-term, "on time, on budget" considerations. His proposed emergent model of the relationship between project management mechanisms and project deliverables therefore includes integrating the roles that social and intellectual capital play over time.

In all information systems development (ISD) projects, project management mechanisms are important to ensuring project performance. These have been characterized as mechanisms of control, that is, those that help ensure that individuals act consistently with the objectives being pursued, and coordination, that is, those that help ensure that work is not done redundantly and it gets handed off expeditiously. Coordination is especially difficult on OISD projects because teams tend to be comprised of diverse individuals across two or more organizations, with each organization having its own goals, shared language, and belief systems. These concepts are complementary and can be supported through similar mechanisms.

Sabherwal then explores the effect of these mechanisms on project performance, which is defined as both long- and short-term project deliverables. He also suggests that shifting project management mechanisms can lead to either increased or decreased social and intellectual capital and consequently, to greater or reduced project effectiveness. Social capital describes the active connections between people. Positive social capital suggests that trust, mutual understanding, and shared values and behaviors exist on a team. Building social capital is especially important on OISD projects, which bring together individuals who are total strangers, who may never meet, and who are expected to work in a high-stress environment. Sabherwal then outlines the ways that social capital can be expected to improve both project efficiency and effectiveness, supporting his reasoning with examples from case studies.

Intellectual capital describes the knowledge and knowing capability that reside across the organizations involved in a project. It too can facilitate project performance in that the distinctive thought world, unfamiliar language, and disparate verbal skills of the participants represent obstacles to success. Gaps in intellectual capital can lead to multiple, conflicting interpretations of specifications and the system development process. Sabherwal goes on to note the ways that different project management mechanisms can promote or inhibit the development of intellectual capital.

As well as introducing strong evidence for the importance of social and intellectual capital in the OISD relationship, the author explores a number of other interactions that affect the relationship between project management mechanisms and project deliverables. He examines the relationship between social capital and intellectual capital and the importance of feedback paths. Understanding reverse effects in every dimension of this relationship is important. For example, successfully demonstrating interim deliverables can affect trust, knowledge sharing, and the emphasis that is placed on project control and coordination. Finally, he examines the role of four contingency factors (project complexity, criticality, relationship structure, and interorganizational differentiation) on the selection of project management mechanisms.

In addition to providing readers with a better understanding of the factors involved in ensuring an OISD project's success, Sabherwal describes new ways in which "success" should be viewed by organizations in an outsourcing relationship. Both social and intellectual capital can lead to additional benefits for the organization in both the short and long term. This broader view will provide managers with insights into ways they can embed the development of these elements within their normal project management practices. It also points to a new need to balance short- and long-term objectives because of their future impacts on capabilities. Interestingly, it suggests viewing project management mechanisms as a portfolio of practices that can be used dynamically as needs and project deliverables dictate. Finally, this chapter documents the importance of feedback paths and models and illustrates how they work in an OISD project. Sabherwal's research paints a clear picture of how our understanding of OISD is evolving toward more sophisticated management of and research on these projects.

Chapter 15: Contracting in IT Outsourcing: Hierarchical and Psychological Contractual Elements as Key Managerial Governance Mechanisms

In Chapter 15, researchers Christine Koh and Soon Ang explore the importance of the contract in IT outsourcing success. However, unlike past research, which has largely focused on the legal structures involved (e.g., product and service specifications, pricing, payment schedules, and contract duration), their research focuses on the other complementary elements that are essential for a successful outsourcing relationship. Furthermore, while existing research is essentially one-sided, Koh and Ang call for a more balanced understanding of this relationship—one that considers the needs of both the client and the vendor involved.

The authors suggest, based on their own previous empirical research, that outsourcing success is not only the result of the analysis and legal contracting that goes into the relationship but also involves two additional sets of factors. The first, collectively called hierarchical elements, addresses the governance mechanisms that, if incorporated into a contract, assist in the control and coordination of the relationship. Five elements are important: command structures and authority systems, rule-based incentive systems, standard operating procedures, non–market-based pricing systems (to accommodate uncertainties), and informal dispute resolution mechanisms. Together, these elements can help a firm achieve flexibility, effective risk management, and control. Failure to incorporate these elements has been shown to contribute to outsourcing failures.

The second set of factors relates to the two parties' unspoken or psychological contract. Koh and Ang point out that not all outsourcing obligations are made explicit in a written contract. There are also many implicit obligations in an outsourcing relationship that exist only in the minds of the people involved. These drive their behavior, regardless of what is written in the legal contract. There are a number of reasons why this is the case—most relating to the fact that because of the complexity of the relationship and the multiple stakeholders involved, formal contractual provisions tend to differ from their day-to-day execution. The authors cite their own recent research, which shows the critical role this psychological contract plays in a successful IT outsourcing relationship.

The researchers identify six vendor obligations and six client obligations that must be fulfilled if the relationship is going to be successful. For example, clients expect vendors to assign high quality staff to work on a project and to minimize staff turnover. For their part, vendors expect clients to understand and articulate explicitly and comprehensively the requirements for the services covered by the project. The concept of a psychological contract is important because it draws our attention to the fact that not all promises are incorporated into a typical legal contract. Thus, the more organizations work on clarifying these unwritten promises and making them explicit, the greater the likelihood that there will be a successful relationship.

Hierarchical and psychological factors tend to overlap in some ways but are not synonymous. Instead, they complement each other. The authors contend that both should be incorporated into an integrated conceptual framework of the factors that contribute to IT outsourcing success. Such a framework makes several contributions toward research and practice. First, it incorporates the vendor's perspective in the outsourcing relationship, which has been largely missing from research to date. Second, it better represents conceptually the factors that are important to a successful relationship. This lays the groundwork for designing better and more comprehensive governance mechanisms for IT outsourcing contracts. Finally, it opens the door to future research and better understanding of the role of these elements in IT outsourcing success.

Chapter 16: The Offshore Outsourcing Landscape: Historical Development and Challenges for the IS Discipline

The final chapter in this volume examines the newest and potentially most disruptive form of IT outsourcing to date, that is, the trend to offshore outsourcing. Authors Beena George and Rudy Hirschheim look briefly at the history of outsourcing in general—from its roots in Roman times until the present—and then more closely examine offshore outsourcing. They believe the trend toward outsourcing in different global locations is "inexorable" but brings a unique set of challenges to all parties involved.

By way of introducing these challenges, George and Hirschheim describe the growth and evolution of IT outsourcing and its primary drivers. In the late 1980s, outsourcing arrangements tended to be fairly simple. One vendor would provide a single basic function to a customer, for example, facilities management. Over time, more complex arrangements have developed involving multiple vendors and multiple clients and more sophisticated partnerships and alliances. Companies are also becoming more selective in what they outsource. Interestingly, as long as the impacts were limited to the client and vendor firms, outsourcing was barely noticed by the public press.

This situation has changed with the growth in offshore outsourcing. As with earlier forms of outsourcing, a primary driver of this trend is the need to cut costs. However, companies are also facing increasing pressures from globalization and the lack of trained professionals at home. In addition, the authors note the "bandwagon effect" that has prompted other companies to explore this option. As a result, in the United States, offshore outsourcing is growing at a faster pace than other forms.

George and Hirschheim then describe how India came to be the dominant force in this market. India's capabilities in this field have been recognized since the 1980s but the current wave of offshore outsourcing got its impetus from two factors. The Y2K phenomenon and the lack of IT professionals to complete the remediation work involved led many organizations to look offshore. At the same time, improvements in telecommunications reached a level where it was practical and cheaper to do this work elsewhere.

Several factors have contributed to India's sustained success in this field. The authors note that the country's competitive advantage lies in the effectiveness and efficiency of its cultural, economic, and social institutions. Their success, in turn, is based on the capabilities of individuals and their strong emphasis on formal education. Key individuals with far-reaching vision and entrepreneurial spirit have played a significant role in India's present position. Expatriates have helped to create and sustain linkages between client companies and vendors.

There are still many challenges in using offshore outsourcing successfully. There are four major categories of concern. Cultural factors lead to differences in practices and communication between clients and vendors. Geographical distance can result in additional costs and coordination problems across multiple time zones. The quality of the infrastructure available and ensuring security in vendor locations can also be a concern. Finally, organizations may face employee resistance and negative publicity when moving IT work offshore.

The authors believe that offshore outsourcing is a trend that is here to stay. They note that few researchers and practitioners have fully considered the implications of this trend. This chapter suggests that IT as a discipline will have to evolve in response and may evolve differently in Western and Eastern countries. Western organizations and universities might do well to focus on differentiating themselves, for example, by concentrating on enabling business processes, contract management, and IT strategy. Eastern ones may take leadership in software development and management. Such trends cannot be ignored by our institutions if they want to play a leadership role in the changes that are occurring in this field.

CONCLUSION

As the reader will find, much can be learned from the chapters that make up this monograph. First, several of the chapters introduce the reader to novel perspectives on the shape of IT outsourcing arrangements, whether this is application service provision and offshoring or hierarchical and psychological contracting. Second, several of the chapters contribute to our better understanding of the outsourcing decision by identifying an array of sourcing alternatives—outsourcing, insourcing, internal markets, and strategic alliances—along with a framework for choosing among the alternatives, analyzing the decision through a risk-management lens or by taking into account the critical notion of trust between the parties. Third, the chapters in the monograph analyze IT outsourcing through several conceptual lenses—population-level learning, strategic management, institutional theory, transaction cost, and agency theory, to name a few—providing a multifaceted, hence richer, portrayal of the phenomenon. Last, but not least, the variety of methodological approaches—from historical analysis to experimentation, from language-centered approach to survey, and from content analysis of qualitative data to structural equation modeling—contributes to richness in understanding that no single method could provide.

PART I

TAKING STOCK OF IT OUTSOURCING PRACTICE AND RESEARCH

CHAPTER 2

POPULATION-LEVEL LEARNING AND THE EVOLUTION OF IT OUTSOURCING DECISIONS

JÉRÔME BARTHÉLÉMY

Abstract: *This chapter contends that there has been a progressive refinement of information technology (IT) outsourcing since the mid-1980s. Specifically, it is proposed that the evolution and progressive refinement of IT outsourcing practices can be attributed to "population-level learning." Population-level learning is a learning phenomenon that occurs at the level of a population of organizations through mechanisms such as selective imitation and inferential learning. Four features of IT outsourcing are studied in detail: (1) outsourcing scope, (2) vendor selection, (3) outsourcing contract, and (4) outsourcing outcome.*

Keywords: *Information Technology, IT Outsourcing, Population-Level Learning*

INTRODUCTION

Information technology (IT) outsourcing can be defined as "the significant contribution by external vendors in the physical and/or human resources associated with the entire or specific component of the IT infrastructure in the user organization" (Loh and Venkatraman, 1992, 356). IT outsourcing is not a new phenomenon. "Time sharing," which involves purchasing computer time, was very popular in the 1960s and 1970s. From the mid-1980s on, however, a new type of IT outsourcing started spreading. There are at least four differences between this new type of IT outsourcing and more traditional IT outsourcing (Cheon, Grover, and Teng, 1995). First, outsourcing is no longer restricted to small and medium-sized firms that do not possess their own IT infrastructure. Second, firms outsource an increasingly large range and depth of services. Third, personnel and equipment are frequently transferred to the vendor. Fourth, the nature of the relationship with the vendor evolves toward partnerships.

Outsourcing has received a lot of attention from the IT literature. The first stream of research investigates the determinants of the IT outsourcing decision. Indeed, why do firms outsource IT at such an unprecedented rate when IT has never been more critical to firm performance? The major determinants include the gap between actual and desired IT performance (Teng, Cheon, and Grover, 1995), transaction costs and production costs considerations (Ang and Straub, 1998), interactions between economic and institutional factors (Ang and Cummings, 1997) and competing insights from the transaction cost, knowledge-based, agency and measurement literatures (Poppo and Zenger, 1998). The second stream of research focuses on vendor management. Several papers have explored the implications of partnerships on outsourcing success (Grover, Cheon, and Teng, 1996; Lee, 2001; Lee and Kim, 1999). The impact of transaction costs on the terms and management of the contract has also been investigated (Aubert, Rivard, and Patry, 1996).

Figure 2.1 **IT Outsourcing and Population Level Learning Model**

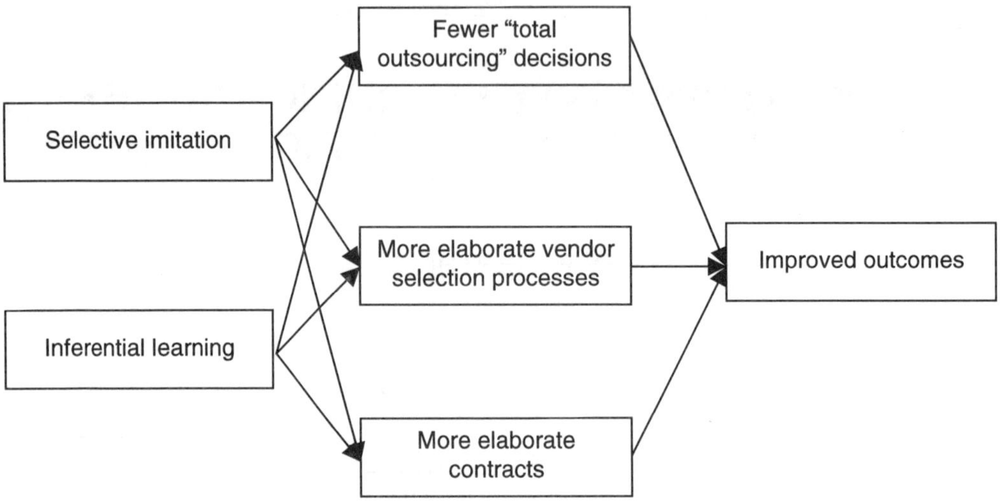

While the IT outsourcing phenomenon started developing in the mid-1980s, it really took off after the very much heralded contract between Kodak and its vendors (IBM, DEC, and Businessland Inc.) in 1989. Loh and Venkatraman (1992) found that this landmark deal legitimized the practice of IT outsourcing among Fortune 500 firms (i.e., the "Kodak effect"). In other words, the adoption rate of this new business practice quickly increased after Kodak had announced its deal. My aim is to build on the work of Loh and Venkatraman (1992) and to show that IT outsourcing has not only gained wider acceptance but also has been progressively refined over time.

This idea has occasionally been hinted at in the IT outsourcing literature. For instance, DiRomualdo and Gurbaxani (1998, 68) suggested that: "The motivations for outsourcing are evolving from a primary focus on cost reduction to an emerging emphasis on improving business performance." However, the progressive refinement of IT outsourcing practices has never been really elaborated on. In a study of U.S. and U.K. firms, Lacity and Willcocks (1998) observed that the outcome of IT outsourcing efforts improve over time. Two explanations were offered for this empirical observation. First, richer markets (i.e., a larger number of IT suppliers) may have helped remove small-number bargaining problems (Williamson, 1996). Second, customers may have become increasingly proficient with outsourcing. However, Lacity and Willcocks (1998, 365) do not really explain why "customers are learning to make better decisions and negotiate more favorable deals." A potentially valuable tool for examining why and how IT outsourcing practices have refined since the mid-1980s is "population level learning" (Miner and Haunschild, 1995).

The chapter is organized as follows. First, I present the population-level learning concept. Second, I derive propositions regarding the impact of population-level learning on four key dimensions of IT outsourcing: (1) outsourcing scope, (2) vendor selection, (3) outsourcing contract, and (4) outsourcing outcome (see Figure 2.1). Third, I present some preliminary evidence of "population level learning" using a secondary database of sixty-one outsourcing efforts. The implications of the findings are discussed in the fourth section.

THEORETICAL BACKGROUND

The Concept of Population-Level Learning

The literature generally distinguishes three levels of learning. First, authors such as Argyris and Schön (1978) contend that only individuals can learn (i.e., individual learning). Second, authors such as Cyert and March (1963) argue that organizations are also learning entities (i.e., organizational learning). The terms *collective minds* (Weick and Roberts, 1993) and *organizational minds* (Sanderlands and Stablein, 1987) have been used to describe organizations as learning entities. Third, entire populations of organizations may learn. Though authors such as Levinthal and March (1993) and Levitt and March (1988) have noted the potential for population-level learning, there has been limited theoretical and empirical work on this topic.

According to Miner and Haunschild (1995, 118), population-level learning can be defined as a "systematic change in the nature and mix of organizational action routines in a population of organizations, arising from experience." Three different processes can lead to outcomes at the population level as population-level learning "can arise from the experience of organizations and populations as a whole." (Miner and Haunschild, 1995, 119). First, organizations in the population may learn on their own (i.e., organizational learning). "Learning by doing" (Arrow, 1962) is a classic way for organizations to learn by themselves, through direct experience. Second, organizations in the population may learn by imitating other organizations (interorganizational learning). Learning by watching others, through indirect experience, is a phenomenon known as vicarious learning (Huber, 1991). Third, an entire population of organizations may collectively learn by imitating another population. A classic example of such collective learning is the SEMATECH research consortium, which resulted from the American semiconductor industry's observation of Japanese research consortia.

Two major theoretical approaches use population of organizations as their unit of analysis: population ecology (Hannan and Freeman, 1977) and neoinstitutional theory (DiMaggio and Powell, 1983). While population-level learning is related to both, it also has distinct features. Contrary to population ecology, population-level learning focuses on changes in routines rather than on the survival of one type of organization at the expense of others. Institutional theory contends that organizations replicate common routines to gain legitimacy rather than to achieve technical results. Contrary to neoinstitutional theory, population-level learning postulates complex learning mechanisms in which the efficiency and effectiveness of routines also determine whether they will be subsequently adopted by organizations. According to Miner and Haunschild (1995, 150): "Because of its important and distinct role in emphasizing institutional rationality, neoinstitutional theory has downplayed the occurrence of (such) technical rationality and its ongoing interaction with institutional rationality. . . . Population level learning confirms and draws on institutional research, but takes as a primary concern the interaction of institutional and technical rationalities over time."

On the empirical side, few studies document the outcome of population-level learning. Argote, Beckman, and Epple (1990) found that shipyards that began production late were more productive than those who started earlier. However, once production began, they did not appear to benefit from the experience accumulated at other yards. While Darr, Argote, and Epple (1995) found that pizza stores benefited from production experience at other stores (provided they were owned by the same franchisee), Joskow and Rose (1985) found no evidence of industry experience transfer in the case of coal-burning power-station construction. In a recent study of the hard disk drive industry, McKendrick (2001) found that—through a process of selective imitation—firms from the same country initially adopted similar global strategies. However, practices within this industry tended to converge over time.

As can be seen above, empirical results are mixed. Moreover, most of these empirical studies examine whether productivity gains resulting from experience can be transferred from one firm to another. They do not focus on what was learned and how it was learned. Only the most recent one (i.e., McKendrick, 2001) describes what was actually learned through population-level learning.

Population-Level Learning Processes

In this section, I study the major processes through which population-level learning occurs: selective imitation and inferential learning. I also describe the mechanisms through which knowledge actually diffuses within a population of organizations: contact transmission and broadcast transmission (Miner and Haunschild, 1995).

Selective Imitation and Inferential Learning

Selective imitation means copying only the routines that are thought to have been successful in other organizations. Through selective imitation of the best routines, significant improvements can arise at the population level. An example in IT outsourcing is the "best of breed" approach initially developed by British Petroleum Exploration (BPX). In the early 1990s, BPX outsourced to three vendors simultaneously, using Sema Group to manage its data centers and commercial engineering applications, Science Applications International Corporation to manage its distributed computer services and scientific applications, and Syncordia to manage its telecommunications network. As this practice apparently turned out to be successful, it was subsequently adopted by firms such as DuPont and J.P. Morgan, for instance (DiRomualdo and Gurbaxani, 1998). In other words, these firms selectively copied a successful practice pioneered by BPX when they devised their own IT outsourcing strategy.

It is important to note that selective imitation is not necessarily immune from superstitious learning. Superstitious learning has been defined by Levitt and March (1988) as copying routines thought to have successful outcomes while they had nothing to do with the observed outcomes. For instance, the notion that outsourcing vendors are partners and that contracts should play only a minor role was popularized by the landmark deal between Kodak and its three vendors (IBM, DEC, and Businessland Inc.). As the relationships between Kodak and its vendors were both cooperative and based on loose contracts, it was wrongly inferred that tight contracts were not necessary in IT outsourcing. However, a good contract is essential because it helps establish a balance of power between the client and the vendor (Lacity and Hirschheim, 1993a and 1993b). In sum, organizations may copy routines that appear desirable but are unrelated to the outcomes they expect.

Beyond simply copying allegedly successful routines, firms may use the experience of others as a substitute for their own "learning by doing." According to Miner and Haunschild (1995, 126): "In inferential organizational learning, the organization uses the experience of other organizations as a natural experiment, and draws conclusions from which it both adopts and avoids routines." For instance, many early IT outsourcing operations entailed the transfer of the entire IT department to an outside vendor. As most of these "total outsourcing" efforts failed, companies that outsourced later could easily derive from these failures that keeping a sufficient level of expertise within the firm was necessary (Lacity, Willcocks, and Feeny, 1996). In sum, firms may develop "best practices" using not only the experience of successful firms, but also the experience of less successful ones. While successful IT outsourcing cases suggest what should be done, less successful ones suggest what should be avoided.

Contact and Broadcast Transmission

The diffusion of routines among organizations occurs through two main mechanisms: contact transmission and broadcast transmission (Miner and Haunschild, 1995).

With contact transmission, the potential user of a routine directly acquires new knowledge from a prior user. Contact transmission frequently occurs through interpersonnel contact. An example in IT outsourcing is when a chief information officer (CIO) offers face-to-face advice to another CIO about the benefits of drafting a detailed contract rather than accepting the vendor's standard contract.

On the other hand, broadcast transmission does not require direct contact between organizations. With broadcast transmission, learning occurs through observation of successful organizations. Information can be obtained from a wide range of media including conferences and articles in the trade press or the managerial literature. Consulting firms also play an important role in developing and disseminating "best practices." Thus, the imitation of "best practices" can take place without interpersonal contact. This phenomenon is known as "observational learning" (Greve, 1998).

Finally, it is important to note that broadcast transmission is more likely than contact transmission to lead to superstitious learning. For instance, the trade press is generally overly optimistic about IT outsourcing because operations are reported during the "honeymoon period" (i.e., just after the contract has been signed) (Lacity and Hirschheim, 1993b). A face-to-face conversation with a CIO often leads to a more balanced assessment of the situation than an article in the press.

THE IMPACT OF POPULATION-LEVEL LEARNING ON IT OUTSOURCING

In this section, I develop propositions regarding the impact of population-level learning on IT outsourcing practices and outcomes. Contrary to most empirical studies (see, for instance, Argote, Beckman and Epple [1990]; Darr, Argote and Epple [1995]; Epple, Argote and Devadas, [1991]), I study the content of learning and not only its impact on productivity. As my unit of analysis is a population of organizations, I do not deal with firm-level issues such as the impediments to "best practices" transfer within firms (Szulanski, 1996).

If the premise is that population-level learning is the cause of changes in IT outsourcing practices, it is important to have a clear definition of what a population of organizations actually means. In this chapter, the population is composed of the organizations that outsource all or part of their IT. While these organizations do not necessarily belong to the same industry or geographic area, they have one important thing in common: they use external vendors to manage all or part of their IT.

Outsourcing Scope

Firms that contemplate outsourcing their IT have two basic options. First, they may outsource their entire IT activity, a practice usually referred to as *total outsourcing*. Second, they may outsource only part of their IT activity. Lacity, Willcocks, and Feeny (1996) have coined the expression "selective outsourcing" to describe this practice. Firms may also set up their own IT subsidiary instead of contracting with a vendor. This situation, which is referred to as *quasi-outsourcing* by Barthélémy and Geyer (2005), is outside the scope of this chapter.

IT is a highly heterogeneous function. While some components are commodities (e.g., data centers, telecommunications networks, and PCs), some others are more specific (e.g., applications development, system design, and systems integration) (Teng, Cheon, and Grover, 1995). Selective IT outsourcing has been reported to have higher success rates than total IT outsourcing due to this heterogeneity. Specific IT activities should not be outsourced because vendors may standardize them to the extent that the unique needs of the client are no longer met (Ang and Cummings, 1997). Outsourcing specific IT activities is also dangerous because it creates a dependence situation that may be exploited by the vendor (Williamson, 1996). On the other hand, "selective outsourcing meets customers' needs while minimizing the risks associated with total outsourcing approaches" (Lacity, Willcocks, and Feeny, 1995, 13).

Through population-level learning and inferential learning from total IT outsourcing failures, it should become increasingly clear that this practice must be avoided. This should eventually result in a decreasing proportion of total IT outsourcing efforts over time.

Proposition 1: Population-level learning should result in fewer total IT outsourcing efforts.

Vendor Selection Process

Selecting a good vendor, with a proper fit, is crucial for IT outsourcing success. The easiest option is to accept the offer of a vendor without any request for proposal. A more refined way consists in requiring formal bids from several vendors and comparing them with internal IT costs. An even more refined way consists in asking the internal IT department to develop a formal bid along with potential outside vendors (Lacity and Willcocks, 1998).

Through population-level learning and selective imitation of the most successful organizations, the vendor selection process should become increasingly elaborate over time. Though devising an elaborate vendor selection process is costly, it helps avoid even more costly problems later, such as having to switch vendors because of poor performance (Barthélémy, 2001). To bring in the necessary expertise, legal and technical experts may be used. It may also be worth hiring people who have been involved in IT outsourcing management. Though this experience is rarely stated in résumés, firms may look for people with experience in managing joint ventures or leading cross-functional teams (Useem and Harder, 2000). Thanks to population-level learning and selective copying of "best practices," I expect elaborate vendor selection processes to become increasingly common.

Proposition 2: Population-level learning should result in more elaborate vendor selection processes.

Outsourcing Contract

The contract is a key element in IT outsourcing relationships as it helps protect the client from potential opportunism by the vendor. Indeed, it may be "the only mechanism that establishes a balance of power in the outsourcing relationship" (Lacity and Hirschheim, 1993a, 24). The major issue with any contract is that it will never be able to anticipate all potential contingencies. Thus, the vendor may take advantage of the incompleteness of the contract to engage in opportunistic behavior.

There are two ways to deal with the incompleteness of IT outsourcing contracts. First, short-term contracts may be used, which makes it possible to use up-to-date information when the contract is renewed. However, the use of short-term contracts can also lead to vendor opportunism. This is highly likely when specific assets have been engaged, making the client vulnerable to the threat of nonrenewal (Williamson, 1996). Second, contract incompleteness may be minimized by incorporating elaborate clauses, which will eventually make it more difficult for vendors to engage in opportunistic behavior. While drafting an elaborate contract is costly, additional time and expense early on helps avoid costly problems later, such as having to renegotiate the contract or constantly monitor the vendor to get the needed performance (Barthélémy, 2001).

Thanks to population-level learning and contact transmission, I expect contractual expertise to spread among the population of organizations that outsource their IT. Legal experts should contribute to the diffusion of "best practices" within the population by interacting with their clients' internal legal departments (Lacity and Hirschheim, 1993b).

> Proposition 3: Population-level learning should result in more elaborate contracts.

Outsourcing Outcome

As population-level learning occurs, "best practices" regarding outsourcing scope, vendor selection process, and outsourcing contract should become increasingly common. If population-level learning leads to the selection of the best routines, overall satisfaction with IT outsourcing operations at the population level should improve. In other words, IT outsourcing should increasingly live up to the expectations that firms have when they make their decision. These expectations fit into three broad categories: economic, technological, and strategic. Economic motivations refer to the possibility of lowering costs through accessing the economies of scale enjoyed by specialized vendors. Technological motivations refer to accessing the vendor's more advanced technology. Strategic motivations refer to using outsourcing to help focus resources on the core business.

> Proposition 4: Population-level learning should result in more successful IT outsourcing efforts.

PRELIMINARY EVIDENCE OF POPULATION-LEVEL LEARNING

To provide preliminary evidence of population-level learning, I use a secondary database of 61 IT sourcing decisions made in the United States and in the United Kingdom between 1984 and 1994. These data were collected by two prominent IT researchers through face-to-face interviews with 145 business executives in 40 organizations (mainly Fortune 500 and Financial Times European 1,000 firms). They focus on the dawn of today's IT outsourcing (immediately before and after the 1989 deal between Kodak and its vendors). Thus, they can help us explore the extent to which IT outsourcing not only gained wider acceptance, but also refined after this landmark deal (Loh and Venkatraman, 1992).

Outsourcing Scope

Lacity and Willcocks (1998) distinguish three types of sourcing: (1) total outsourcing, (2) total insourcing, and (3) selective outsourcing. Here, I focus on the forty-six total outsourcing and selective outsourcing efforts contained in the database. Contrary to my expectations, the chi-square analysis shows no significant difference between the scope of IT outsourcing efforts before 1989 and after 1989 ($x^2 = 0.01, p > 0.05$). Thus, selective outsourcing does not seem to be more widespread after 1989 than it was before 1989.

Table 2.1

Outsourcing Scope

	Before 1989	After 1989	Total
Selective outsourcing	9	23	32
Total outsourcing	4	10	14
Total	13	33	46

($\chi^2 = 0.01, p = 0.975$)

Table 2.2

Vendor Selection Process

	Before 1989	After 1989	Total
No formal bid	7	4	11
Compare vendor bid with current costs	10	31	41
Compare vendor bid with internal bid	2	7	9
Total	19	42	61

($\chi^2 = 6.62, p = 0.036$)

Vendor Selection Process

In their database, Lacity and Willcocks (1998) measure the extent to which the bidding procedure is sophisticated using three categories: (1) no formal bid, (2) vendor bid compared with current costs, and (3) vendor bid compared with internal bid. The chi-square analysis shows that there is a significant difference between the types of bids used before 1989 and after 1989 ($x^2 = 6.62, p < 0.05$). Hence, the vendor selection process seems to become increasingly elaborate after 1989.

Outsourcing Contract

Lacity and Willcocks (1998) distinguish the following types of IT outsourcing contracts: (1) standard/loose contracts; (2) detailed contracts; and (3) mixed contracts (i.e., requirements are fully specified but only for the beginning of the contract). The chi-square analysis of the forty-six outsourcing efforts shows that there is a significant difference between pre-1989 and post-1989 contracts ($x^2 = 7.45, p < 0.05$). Thus, there is some evidence that detailed and mixed contracts become more common after 1989.

Outsourcing Outcome

Lacity and Willcocks (1998) use the variable "expected cost savings achieved" as a heuristic to evaluate the success of sourcing operations. Their rationale is that cost reduction is the most important motivation for IT outsourcing. Indeed, cost reduction was cited as a motivation in 80 percent of the cases they studied. Given the large amount of missing data, the size of the sub-sample is only thirty-three and the results are very tentative. The chi-square analysis shows that there is a significant difference between the pre-1989 period and the post-1989 period ($x^2 = 6.19,$

Table 2.3

Outsourcing Contract

	Before 1989	After 1989	Total
Standard and loose	4	1	5
Mixed	2	6	8
Detailed	7	26	33
Total	13	33	46

($\chi^2 = 7.45, p = 0.024$)

Table 2.4

Outsourcing Outcome

	Before 1989	After 1989	Total
Cost reduction not achieved	6	3	9
Cost reduction achieved	5	19	24
Total	11	22	33

($\chi^2 = 6.19, p = 0.013$)

$p < 0.01$). Overall, the proposition that IT outsourcing operations become more successful after 1989 seems to be supported.

DISCUSSION AND CONCLUSIONS

In this chapter, I contend that population-level learning resulted in the progressive refinement of IT outsourcing practices since the mid 1980s. Empirical tests provide some preliminary support for this proposition. First, the vendor selection process is evolving toward a more elaborate state. Through population-level learning, even firms that have never before outsourced have become increasingly aware of the importance of elaborate bidding procedures. Second, contractual expertise seems to spread. Standard and loose contracts have become increasingly rare over time. On the other hand, detailed fee-for-service and mixed contracts have become more common. Third, and thanks to those "best practices," more recent IT outsourcing efforts seem to be more successful than older ones. Through population-level learning, firms new to IT outsourcing seem to be able to benefit from the knowledge accumulated by firms that outsourced before them. This may have happened both through selective imitation (i.e., copying only the best routines of experienced firms) and inferential learning (i.e., drawing lessons from the experience of not only successful but also less successful firms).

One important implication of this study is that waiting until IT outsourcing "best practices" emerged was apparently a better strategy than being an innovator. "First movers" frequently enjoy advantages over "late movers" (Lieberman and Montgomery, 1988). In the case of IT outsourcing, large benefits seem to accrue to "late movers." "Late movers" are the firms that choose to wait until a sufficient stock of common knowledge about IT outsourcing has emerged. While the major challenge for "first movers" is to innovate, the challenge for "late movers" is to appropriate the knowledge available on IT outsourcing.

In this chapter, I used variables such as the type of contract and vendor selection process to proxy for learning. However, the data did not allow me to directly measure population-level mechanisms. As a next step, these mechanisms (i.e., selective imitation, inferential learning, contact transmission, and broadcast transmission) should be operationalized and the ideas presented in this chapter properly tested using longitudinal data.

REFERENCES

Ang, S. and Cummings, L. 1997. Strategic response to institutional influences on information systems outsourcing. *Organization Science,* 8, 235–255.

Ang, S. and Straub, D. 1998. Production and transaction economies and IT outsourcing: A study of the US banking industry. *MIS Quarterly,* 535–548.

Argote, L.; Beckman, S.; and Epple, D. 1990. The persistence and transfer of learning in industrial settings. *Management Science,* 36, 2, 140–154.

Argyris, C. and Schön, D. 1978. *Organizational Learning,* Reading. MA: Addison-Wesley.

Arrow, K. 1962. The implications of learning by doing. *Review of Economic studies,* 29, 166–170.

Aubert, B.; Rivard S.; and Patry, M. 1996. A transaction cost approach to outsourcing behavior: Some empirical evidence. *Information & Management,* 30, 51–64.

Barthélémy, J. 2001. The hidden costs of IT outsourcing. *MIT Sloan Management Review* (Spring), 60–69.

Barthélémy, J. and Geyer, D. 2005. An empirical investigation of IT outsourcing vs. quasi-outsourcing in France and Germany. *Information & Management,* 42, 533–542.

Cheon, M.; Grover, V.; and Teng, J. 1995. Theoretical perspectives on the outsourcing of information systems. *Journal of Information Technology,* 10, 4, 209–220.

Cyert, R. and March, J. 1963. *A Behavioral Theory of the Firm.* Englewood Cliffs, NJ: Prentice Hall.

Darr, E.; Argote, L.; and Epple, D. 1995. The acquisition transfer and depreciation of knowledge in service organizations: Productivity in franchises. *Management Science,* 4, 1750–1762.

DiMaggio, P. and Powell, W. 1983. The iron cage revisited: Institutional isomorphism and collective rationality in organizational fields. *American Sociological Review,* 48, 147–160.

DiRomualdo, A. and Gurbaxani, V. 1998. Strategic intent for IT outsourcing. *Sloan Management Review* (Summer), 67–80.

Epple, D.; Argote, L.; and Devadas, R. 1991. Organizational learning curves: A method for investigating intra-plants transfer of knowledge acquired through learning by doing. *Organization Science,* 2, 1, 58–70.

Greve, H. 1998. Managerial cognition and the mimetic adoption of market positions: What you see is what you do. *Strategic Management Journal,* 19, 10, 967–988.

Grover, V.; Cheon, M.; and Teng, J. 1996. The effect of service quality and partnership on the outsourcing of information systems functions. *Journal of Management Information Systems,* 12, 4 , 89–116.

Hannan, M. and Freeman, J. 1977. The population ecology of organizations. *American Journal of Sociology,* 82, 929–964.

Huber, G. 1991. Organizational learning: The contributing processes and the literatures. *Organization Science,* 2, 1, 88–115.

Joskow, P. and Rose, N. 1985. The effect of technological change, experience and environmental regulation on the construction cost of coal-burning generating units. *Rand Journal of Economics,* 16, 1–27.

Lacity, M. and Hirschheim, R. 1993a. *Information Systems Outsourcing.* Chichester, UK: Wiley.

———. 1993b. The information systems outsourcing bandwagon. *Sloan Management Review* (Fall), 73–86.

Lacity, M. and Willcocks, L. 1998. An empirical investigation of information technology sourcing practices: Lessons from experience. *MIS Quarterly* (September), 363–408.

Lacity, M.; Willcocks, L.; and Feeny, D. 1995. IT outsourcing: Maximize flexibility and control. *Harvard Business Review* (May–June), 84–93.

———. 1996. The value of selective IT outsourcing. *Sloan Management Review* (Spring), 13–25.

Levinthal, D. and March, J. 1993. The myopia of learning. *Strategic Management Journal,* 14, 95–112.

Levitt, B. and March, J. 1988. Organization learning. *Annual Review of Sociology,* 14, 319–340.

Lee, J.-N. 2001. The impact of knowledge sharing, organizational capability and partnership quality on IS outsourcing success. *Information & Management,* 38, 323–335.

Lee, Y. and Kim, J.-N. 1999. Effect of partnership quality on IS outsourcing: Conceptual framework and empirical validation." *Journal of Management Information Systems,* 15, 4, 29–52.

Lieberman, M. and Montgomery, D. 1988. First mover advantages. *Strategic Management Journal,* 9, 41–58.

Loh, L. and Venkatraman, N. 1992. Diffusion of Information Technology outsourcing: Influence sources and the Kodak effect. *Information Systems Research,* 3, 4, 337–378.

McKendrick, D. 2001. Global strategy and population-level learning: The case of hard disk drives. *Strategic Management Journal,* 22, 307–334.

Miner, A. and Haunschild, P. 1995. Population level learning. *Research in Organizational Behavior,* 17, 115–166.

Poppo, L. and Zenger, T. 1998. Testing alternative theories of the firm: Transaction cost, knowledge-based and measurement explanations for make-or-buy in information services. *Strategic Management Journal,* 19, 853–877.

Sanderlands, L. and Stablein, R. 1987. The concept of organizational mind. *Research in Sociology of Organizations,* 5, 135–161.

Szulanski, G. 1996. Exploring internal stickiness: Impediments to the transfer of best practice within the firm, *Strategic Management Journal* (Winter Special Issue), 27–43.

Teng, J.; Cheon, M.; and Grover, V. 1995. Decisions to outsource systems functions: Testing a strategy-theoretic discrepancy model. *Decision Science,* 26, 75–103.

Useem, M. and Harder, J. 2000. Leading laterally in company outsourcing. *Sloan Management Review* (Winter), 25–36.

Weick, K. and Roberts, K. 1993. Collective minds in organizations: Heedful interrelating on flight decks. *Administrative Science Quarterly,* 38, 357–381.

Williamson, O. E. 1996. *The Mechanisms of Governance.* Oxford: Oxford University Press, 1996.

CHAPTER 3

STRATEGIC PROFILES AND INFORMATION TECHNOLOGY OUTSOURCING

BENOIT A. AUBERT AND ANNE-MARIE CROTEAU

Abstract: *This chapter investigates the links between outsourcing and strategy. Traditional outsourcing literature has done little investigation on the effect of a firm's strategic profile on outsourcing. This chapter explores this effect. Using Miles and Snow's typology, it is posited that prospectors will display higher usage of outsourcing to manage IT operations than analyzers. These, in turn, will rely more on outsourcing than defenders. The chapter also investigates the contract type that each group is likely to use. Analyzers and defenders are more likely to rely on complete contracts than are prospectors, who will tolerate incomplete contracts.*

Keywords: *Information Technology, IT Outsourcing, Strategic Profile, Strategy*

INTRODUCTION

The objective of this chapter is to underline the impact of strategy on the level and type of information technology (IT) outsourcing used by an organization. Past research in IT outsourcing has focused mainly on the transaction itself, without investigating the strategic characteristics of the organization. When observing organizations, one cannot avoid noticing that those of similar size, dealing in the same markets, can make very different decisions with respect to IT outsourcing. Since major organizational decisions should reflect a company's strategy, there is a need for scrutinizing the decisions to outsource IT activities and evaluating how aligned these decisions are with the strategy. Therefore, this study investigates the characteristics of organizations with regard to their strategy, their outsourced IT activities, and the structure of IT outsourcing contracts.

This chapter draws on the fields of economics, strategy, and management information systems. It seeks to explore the extent to which outsourcing is linked with strategic profile. It lays out the theoretical background and presents the hypotheses. Future research avenues are presented. This research focuses on IT operations, not on IT projects. IT operations are more homogeneous from one organization to another than IT projects. Operations include mainframe and server operations, maintenance activities, operation of software systems, telecommunication activities, and so on. The relative comparability of IT operations from one organization to another should make possible the identification of different outsourcing behaviors, and hopefully their association with different strategic types. Expected results should contribute to a better understanding of how performing organizations outsource their IT activities and how they adjust their outsourcing portfolio to their strategy. Subsequent results coming from this stream of research should provide practitioners with guidelines to better select the IT activities that should be outsourced and to negotiate performing IT outsourcing contracts, taking into account their strategy.

THEORETICAL BACKGROUND

The IT outsourcing phenomenon has been expanding over the past decade, and this growth is likely to continue (Tettelbach, 2000). The relationships implied in IT outsourcing arrangements are increasingly complex. For example, while as client and supplier, Xerox and Electronic Data Systems were engaged in a legal battle on some aspects of their agreement, as business partners they were collaborating on ventures such as the state of Connecticut's $1 billion outsourcing deal (Madden, 1999). Two key questions arise when studying the IT outsourcing phenomenon: Based on their strategic characteristics, which IT activities should be outsourced? And how should IT outsourcing contracts be structured? The following paragraphs briefly review both streams of research.

Outsourced IT Activities

An important strand of research has examined the make-or-buy decision using transaction costs theory. Its foundation was laid by Coase (1937) who positioned the market and the firm as alternative mechanisms that could be chosen to conduct a transaction. The theory has been refined and used extensively in the past twenty years. According to the transaction costs theory, the decision to use the market or the firm to regulate a transaction depends primarily on four variables (Milgrom and Roberts, 1992; Williamson, 1985): specificity of the assets required to produce the good or service; uncertainty and measurement problems surrounding the transaction; origin of the most important investment; and frequency of the transaction. These considerations constitute deviations from the ideal situation of a perfectly competitive spot market transaction where all goods are available, all information is public knowledge, and all transactions are performed instantly (Williamson, 1985).

Asset specificity has received a lot of attention from researchers (Williamson, 1985). When the value of the next-best use of an asset is less than the value associated with its primary use, it creates a lock-in situation between the parties as well as a risk associated with this investment. The role of asset specificity has been supported by studies in many fields: auto parts (Monteverde and Teece, 1982; Walker and Weber, 1984), aerospace (Masten, 1984), and aluminum (Hennart, 1988). However, results have been ambiguous in the IT field (Aubert, Patry, and Rivard, 2004; Nam et al., 1996).

A fundamental assumption of transaction costs theory is that the parties ought to be able to measure the quality and the quantity of the goods exchanged in order to complete a transaction. Empirical studies have shown that uncertainty plays a key part in the choice of a governance mode (Anderson, 1985; Masten, 1984; Walker and Weber, 1984), and interacts with asset specificity (Murray and Kotabe, 1999). Recently, empirical studies have also supported the agency proposition that the measurability of the transactions strongly increases the probability of outsourcing decisions by reducing the cost of using market mechanisms (Aubert, Patry, and Rivard, 2004; Poppo and Zenger, 1998).

Accepting that all possible contingencies are impossible to foresee, the parties can decide to allocate to one of the contracting parties the ability to decide ex post what the appropriate actions should be. This is exactly what happens when a company buys a supplier. Grossman and Hart (1986) demonstrated that the party making the most important investment for the success of the transaction should be awarded the decision rights. Supporting this argument, Aubert et al. (2004) showed that companies were more likely to outsource IT activities requiring less technical skills and to keep in-house activities with higher organizational skills. These results were in line with

Pisano's (1990) results, suggesting that companies with less experience in specific areas were better off relying on outsourcing for activities in these areas because the supplier could bring the investment and expertise they lacked.

Finally, organizing a transaction inside a firm implies creating a governance structure, which means incurring important and irreversible costs. If a transaction is known to be unique, the firm will prefer to bear the risk associated with specific assets or uncertainty rather than to invest in order to internalize a single transaction. Internal organization is efficient only for recurrent transactions (Williamson, 1985). This is why companies will outsource IT activities that they do not conduct on a regular basis (Aubert, Rivard, and Patry 1996). This variable is not often studied extensively in IT since most IT operations are recurrent and therefore have a high frequency. However, frequency would be relevant for software development activities, which can be conducted more or less often in organizations.

IT Outsourcing Contracts

The second question is related to how a company, once it has decided to outsource its IT activities, decides to structure the contract. An organization can put more or less effort into contract design to cover all contingencies. Firms can increase their protection against contractual hazards by reducing their contract incompleteness until the marginal cost of risk exposure equals the marginal benefit associated with a reduction in risk exposure. For instance, in order to reduce the probabilities of negative consequences or sometimes reduce the impact of these events, the parties can include contingencies for different outcomes, arbitration mechanisms, termination conditions, sequential contracting mechanisms, or other contract clauses to reduce their risk exposure. All these clauses are costly to negotiate, implement, and manage (Williamson, 1985). Therefore, parties will have to compromise between the level of risk they are supporting and the level of completeness of the contract they intend to aim for. Using the same theoretical background as transaction theory, incomplete contracting predicts that as asset specificity increases, as uncertainty and measurement problems rise, as business skills become more important, and as technical skills lose importance, the contract will become more difficult to write. This increase in difficulty means that the party will settle for a more incomplete contract because increasing completeness would be too costly.

Transaction characteristics have been measured in a few studies and several aspects of contract completeness were indeed confirmed by Crocker and Masten (1991), Crocker and Reynolds (1993), Adler et al. (1998), and Saussier (2000). One study addressing the level of completeness of outsourcing contracts was specific to the IT industry (Aubert et al., 2003).

Another type of research analyzing IT outsourcing contracts stems from the "resource-based view." This view analyzes the resources available in an organization and their strategic value in order to explain strategic advantage. When applied to outsourcing contracts, it makes it possible to define whether companies should enter into partnerships or use regular outsourcing forms (Roy and Aubert, 2002). Regular forms can be described as arms-length transactions while partnership contracts imply significant exchange of information and expertise. The key variables considered are the strategic value of the resources and their availability in the organization.

Strategy

All these studies relying on transaction costs, while providing several insights into organization behavior, have ignored organizations' intrinsic properties. The transaction costs model considers only the characteristics of the transaction itself. It does not take into account, for instance, any of the managers' preferences or the organization's intent. While ignoring these differences did not prevent transaction costs theory from explaining outsourcing patterns, taking into account these unique organizational properties would increase our understanding of IT outsourcing. A similar concern arises with the resource-based view. Its analysis remains more focused on the resource level, not on the organization level, although it considers the historical path of the organization and the configuration it generated (Barney, 1999).

Strategy is a key organizational element that distinguishes one organization from another. It corresponds to the outcome of decisions made to guide an organization with respect to its environment, structure, and processes that influence its organizational performance. In other words, it represents the means taken by an organization to reach its goals conditional upon environmental events (MacCrimmon, 1993).

As indicated by Venkatraman (1989), there is a three-level categorization of the strategy concept: corporate, business, and functional. The corporate strategy is more concerned with the set of businesses an organization is engaged in and overviews the various business activities that constitute a business profile (Bowman and Helfat, 2001; Grant, 1995; Venkatraman, 1989). This level of strategy addresses the decisions related to the resource allocation among the various business units and provides guidelines with regard to the establishment of potential partnerships (merger, venture, alliance) with other companies (Jelassi and Enders, 2005).

A business unit strategy is concerned with the way an organization decides to compete within a chosen product-market segment (Bowman and Helfat, 2001). The major goal related to this level is to provide the proper directives for reaching the right balance between the external opportunities and threats, on one hand, and the internal resources available and capabilities of the organization, on the other hand (Venkatraman, 1989). As per Porter (1980), it is at the business unit level that decisions are made to gain or maintain a competitive advantage. Finally, the functional level strategy focuses on the means needed to make each function effective and is usually derived from the business unit-level strategy.

Approaches to identifying a strategy can be textual, multivariate, or typological (Hambrick, 1980). The typological approach is recognized as creating a better understanding of the strategic reality of an organization, since all types of strategy are viewed as having particular characteristics but a common strategic orientation. While several typologies have been proposed by Ansoff and Stewart (1967), Freeman (1974), Miles and Snow (1978), and Porter (1980), the most frequently used in empirical research is Miles and Snow's (1978) (Smith, Guthrie, and Chen, 1989; Zahra and Pearce, 1990), which has been quoted more than 1,000 times (ISI Web of Knowledge, 1989–2004). The principal strength of this typology is the simultaneous consideration of the structure and processes necessary for the realization of a given type of strategy. Miles and Snow's (1978) typology reflects a complex view of organizational and environmental processes, as well as the attributes of product, market, technology, organizational structure, and management characteristics (Smith, Guthrie, and Chen, 1989). Also, this typology reflects a broader and more holistic perspective than does Porter's (1980) other most popular typology (MacCrimmon, 1993).

Miles and Snow's Typology

As per MacCrimmon (1993), Miles and Snow's typology is probably the only classification that not only provides indications related to the means chosen by a company to reach its goals, but also takes into account some of its environmental conditions. This typology makes it possible to evaluate factors qualifying a corporate strategy such as the scope of the firm, planning and control activities, organizational structure and climate, core competencies, and corporate management (Bowman and

Figure 3.1 **Adaptive Cycle**

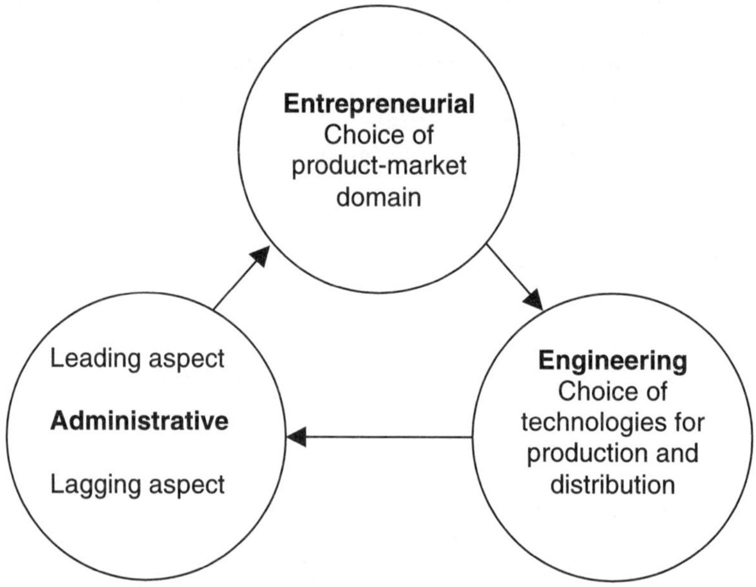

Source: Miles and Snow (1978), p. 24. Reprinted with permission.

Helfat, 2001). It also addresses the business unit's strategic decisions related to the product-market domain a company wants to penetrate and covers how its resources are deployed, including those related to technology. Indeed, Miles and Snow illustrate the process by which organizations continually adjust to their environments by developing the concept of the "adaptive cycle."

Assuming the relationships and interdependence among an organization's strategy, structure, and process exists, the adaptive cycle explains how organizations have an effect on their environments The cycle demonstrates how the choice of a given strategy (entrepreneurial phase) demands a particular portfolio of technologies and capabilities (engineering phase). And this choice, in turn, affects the design of organizational structures and processes (administrative phase). Finally, the choice of structure and process would influence and constrain future strategic decisions. The adaptive cycle with its main phases and their respective significance is shown in Figure 3.1.

Miles and Snow's typology is defined with four types of strategy: prospector, analyzer, defender, and reactor. Firms choose one type rather than another according to their perception of their environment. The first three types are expected to enhance organizational performance and share a continuum where the prospector strategy is at one end, the defender strategy is at the other, and the analyzer strategy stands in the middle. The reactor strategy is excluded from the continuum since it represents an organization with no specific identified strategy, which is likely to impede organizational performance.

Organizations supporting the prospector strategy try to reach the largest possible market. They repeatedly make efforts to innovate and bring about change in their industry. Organizations choosing the defender strategy have a restricted market. They emphasize production efficiency, the excellence of their products, the quality of their services, and their lower prices. Organizations implementing the analyzer strategy share both prospector and defender characteristics, but in moderation. They try to be the first to introduce new products, yet remain in second place with certain products for which they offer a good quality/price ratio. Finally, organizations supporting the reactor strategy do not have the capacity to take over new opportunities or maintain markets already acquired.

Several empirical studies have used Miles and Snow's (1978) typology (Abernethy and Guthrie, 1994; Auger, 2003; Conant, Mokwa, and Burnett, 1989; Croteau and Bergeron, 2001; Croteau, Raymond, and Bergeron, 2001; Hambrick, 1983; Julien et al., 1996; Karimi, Gupta, and Somers, 1996; Moore, 2003; Namiki, 1989; Parry and Parry, 1992; Sabherwal and Chan, 2001; Shortell and Zajac, 1990; Smith, Guthrie, and Chen, 1989; Snow and Hrebiniak, 1980; Tavakolian, 1989; Thomas, Litschert, and Ramaswamy, 1991). Some variations among the four strategic types have been observed depending upon the industry, the sample size, or other organizational constructs. Organizational performance has been regularly used in evaluating the impact of strategy based on this typology.

More specifically, the link between this typology and IT activities has been studied in various works. One study indicates that the structure of IT function is related to the strategic types, it provides some insight into the decision-making process and how IT activities are managed. For instance, the structure of the IS department of defenders is usually centralized, whereas the opposite is also true for prospectors, who usually privilege a decentralized structure for their IT function (Tavakolian, 1989).

Findings also indicate that each type of strategy deploys and uses IT in a different manner, which leads us to believe that IT outsourcing activities will vary according to each strategic type. For example, it was found that prospectors use IS to enhance their market flexibility and make quick strategic decisions whereas analyzers use IS to conduct strategic scanning, and therefore improve their comprehension of the other organizations' behaviors (Croteau and Bergeron, 2001; Croteau, Raymond, and Bergeron, 2001; Sabherwal and Chan, 2001). When it comes to defenders, they deploy their IS to create operational efficiencies (Tan, 1997), and improve their business performance by enhancing the strategic role of the IS department, maintaining an open information technology architecture, conducting strategic scanning, and constantly evaluating their information systems' performance (Croteau and Bergeron, 2001).

LINKING STRATEGY AND OUTSOURCING

The discussion above indicates how complex the concept of strategy is, and, moreover, how difficult it can be to classify one firm within one type of strategy and be able to compare it to another one. Therefore, it is agreed that a typology approach such as the one proposed by Miles and Snow can enable a finer analysis of outsourcing. This typology allows one to capture the pattern of decisions made by a company in relation to the selection of businesses it wants to be in or plans to be in, its long-term objectives, and its resource allocation priorities, taking into account its own capabilities and resources available to address external opportunities and threats (MacCrimmon, 1993).

While common wisdom has often suggested that strategic activities should be kept inside the firm, research has avoided the analysis of outsourcing taking into account specific strategic characteristics of the organization. Activities were deemed comparable from one organization to another. While this approach is not false, it may be improved. A given activity might be managed very differently depending on the strategic type of an organization. The three phases of the adaptive cycle offer some insights into the propensity of different firms to outsource. To simplify the text, emphasis will be put on defenders and prospectors. Analyzers, being in the middle, should present behavior in between the two extremes.

Entrepreneurial Phase

When analyzing the product-market domain and the paths toward growth, it is possible to anticipate outsourcing behavior. Defenders concentrate their efforts on narrower markets, focusing on efficiency and deep penetration of their market. Therefore, their growth is incremental. Prospectors, on the other hand, thrive on innovation. They tend to focus on the introduction of new products, new markets, and horizontal growth. Their growth is less predictable and less stable than that of the defenders.

These characteristics suggest different usage of outsourcing between organizations of different strategic types. The relative stability enjoyed by defenders should make internal operations (and their optimization) easier than is the case in the more volatile environment of prospectors. Prospectors might not have the time to develop IT services to adjust constantly to their entrepreneurial ventures. The use of outsourcing services would facilitate the constant adjustment of IT activities with product or market innovations. Attitudes toward risk also come into play. Prospectors are the risk takers in Miles and Snow's typology whereas defenders are the risk adverse. Entering into an outsourcing contract entails changes and contractual risks (Aubert, Patry, and Rivard, 2002; Earl, 1996). This means that prospectors would be more willing to enter into an outsourcing relationship than defenders, who normally avoid contractual risks.

Engineering Phase

The preferences associated with the engineering phase also provide insights into the behavior of different strategic types. Defenders are often technology-driven. They tend to develop one (or a few) specific technologies to enhance efficiency and will be very protective of their know-how. This is facilitated by vertical integration because it saves them from revealing information to business partners. Prospectors, on the other hand, will foster innovation as long as it is associated with the development of markets. They are more people-driven and will use many different core technologies. This suggests the use of multiple providers, often external, since the pace at which innovations can be introduced on the market is dependent on the pace at which resources are made available.

The information from the engineering phase offers suggestions aligned with the entrepreneurial phase. Protective attitudes of defenders would prevent outsourcing contracts. Prospectors, focusing more on people than technology, would be less reticent about spinning off their IT services.

Administrative Phase

The characteristics of defenders vary from those of prospectors when reaching the administrative phase. For instance, defenders tend to be more functional whereas prospectors tend to be organized by products. Defenders are usually more centralized than prospectors.

The features of the different strategic profiles at this stage do not necessarily suggest a distinctive outsourcing strategy. For example, the higher level of centralization enjoyed by defenders might make outsourcing easier, since the IT activities would already be regrouped. However, their grouping also means that companies might already be enjoying economies of scale, which makes outsourcing less attractive. Defenders, relying on a functional organization, probably have an IT function, fostering the development of the required IT skills. Prospectors, organized by products, might not have the same possibilities to develop and keep IT skills. This would increase the likelihood of outsourcing.

Figure 3.2 **Outsourcing and Profiles**

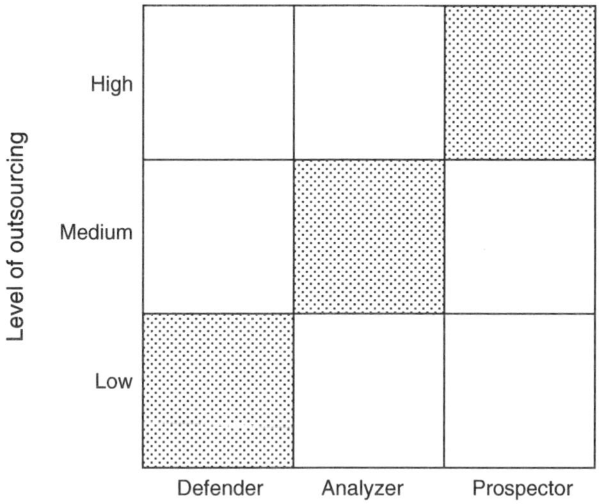

Therefore, taking into account the previous discussion, we can anticipate the relationship between the strategic type and the level of outsourcing observed. Defenders would be the most cautious users of IT outsourcing while prospectors, being the most prone to change and innovation, would be the highest users of IT outsourcing. Analyzers would be between the two groups (see Figure 3.2).

In order to formally test this relationship, we must control for variations in the IT operation characteristics. The strategic profile will not explain all the variations between outsourcing profiles. Transaction cost variables should be used as control variables. This leads to the evaluation of the following:

H_1: Prospectors should have a higher propensity to outsource than analyzers.
H_2: Analyzers should have a higher propensity to outsource than defenders.

If the hypotheses are true, defenders will tend to carry out more of their operations in-house, analyzers will make moderate use of IT outsourcing, and prospectors will be the greatest users of IT outsourcing.[1]

LINKING STRATEGY AND CONTRACT TYPE

As mentioned at the beginning of the chapter, companies deciding to outsource IT activities can use different contracting strategies. Contract incompleteness is often used to characterize the contracts. Contracts vary with respect to their level of detail, the extent to which they plan for every possible contingency, the extent to which they specify every activity that the supplier has to perform, and so on; the more complete a contract, the more expensive it is to write. However, a more complete contract is often seen as an insurance policy for the client. A complete contract is reputed to protect the concerned parties since there is less room for haggling over unanticipated events.

Based on their characteristics, defenders and analyzers will tolerate very limited levels of incompleteness. While defenders will put less effort into analyzing and defining their contract than analyzers, they will be involved in simpler, smaller contracts. Analyzers will tackle more complex contracts but will invest more effort in completing them. This leads us to suppose that both groups

Figure 3.3 **Contract Incompleteness and Profiles**

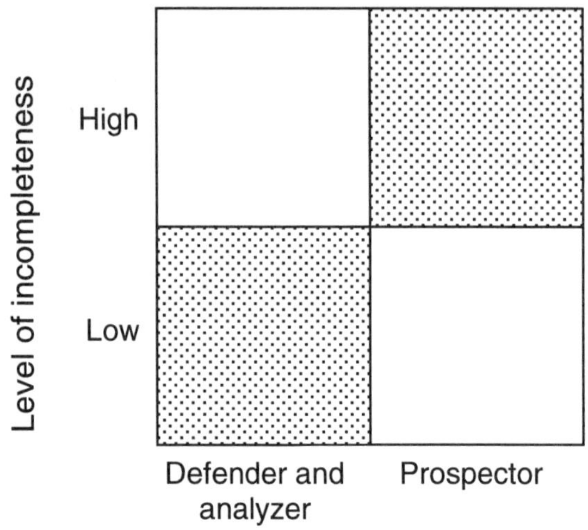

will end up with contracts that show comparable levels of incompleteness. However, prospectors will tolerate higher levels of incompleteness than both defenders and analyzers.

Finally, the contract type (arms-length transaction vs. partnership) should also depend on the strategic type and influence the level of incompleteness. Defenders, trying to maximize efficiency, will aim at arms-length transactions, trying to benefit from economies of scale and lower prices. These contracts should be "traditional" outsourcing contracts. Traditional contracts are more predictable and easier to write in a complete form. On the other end of the scale, prospectors should be more inclined to sign partnership contracts. Because they repeatedly make efforts to innovate and bring about change in their industry, they will need changing capabilities, flexibility, and a large variety of different resources. This should generate more alliances and more strategic outsourcing. Analyzers should be in the middle.

Partnerships are generally very incomplete contracts. Parties rely on the alignment of goals (rather than the contract) to ensure efficient collaboration. A similar analysis can be done to predict the contract type. The initial incompleteness model would take the form presented in Figure 3.3. Again, one should control for traditional transactional variables when testing this model.[2]

H_3: Defenders and analyzers will show the same level of contract incompleteness in their outsourcing arrangements.

H_4: Prospectors will show a higher level of contract incompleteness in their outsourcing arrangements than analyzers (or defenders).

MANAGERIAL IMPLICATIONS

The inclusion of strategic profile in the outsourcing model has several implications for practitioners. It suggests that even when IT activities are similar, conducted by firms in the same industry, they still might be (should be) managed differently by companies pursuing different strategies. Rivard et al. (2004) suggested that the organization could be seen as a puzzle, where all the pieces have to be adjusted together to fit. The main pieces are strategy, technology, structure, and leadership. Outsourcing falls

Table 3.1

Outsourcing and Strategic Profile

	Defender	Analyzer	Prospector
Main focus	Price	Careful investigation of market opportunities	Innovation
Tactics	Economies of scale	Cautious diversification of activities	Diversification
Structural choices	Centralization, internalization	Probably mostly centralized	Project orientation
Outsourcing	Little outsourcing	Careful analysis of outsourcing opportunities	Series of loose contracts for numerous projects

Table 3.2

Outsourcing and Strategic Transition

	Defender **Analyzer**	**Prospector**
Transition	Increased formal analysis of internal processes challenge in-house status quo.	High set-up cost (and time) required to establish services in-house for new ventures impedes innovation.
Transition	Rationalization of products or services offered increases economies of scale and facilitates concentration of skills on a limited set of activities.	Increase care in exploration (or maintenance) of business lines reduces the number of contracts and create a stable portfolio of contracts—hence it is easier to reduce incompleteness.

under the structure piece. This means that, depending on the strategy adopted by an organization, the outsourcing profile has to be adjusted. Analogously, the decision to outsource an activity previously done in-house, because it changes the structure of the organization, should be accompanied by adjustments to the company's strategy. Table 3.1 illustrates the major differences among the types.

The analysis of the relationship between the strategic profile and the outsourcing strategy also suggests transitional events or behaviors from one strategic profile to another. If we accept the idea of a continuum proposed by Miles and Snow, this means that companies can move from one strategic type to another with time, along this continuum. Doing so, they will change their outsourcing strategy. Table 3.2 illustrates these changes.

Defenders moving toward the analyzer behavior will begin to investigate its processes more thoroughly. Doing so, they might find that some activities conducted in-house will benefit from outsourcing. This formal analysis will also help analyzers to write nearly complete contracts. When analyzers move forward to become prospectors, they start to have more and more projects at the same time. Each project brings a new need to be met by IT services. The fact that there are numerous projects means that these services have to be constantly set up (and folded when a venture is terminated). The time and costs required to do so will rise exponentially. By outsourcing the IT services, companies adopting a prospective strategy will increase their agility.

Conversely, prospectors changing their strategy toward that of analyzers would see their portfolio of contracts decrease. Therefore, it would become easier to create a stable portfolio of activities and to research them carefully (with respect to governance mode). This would lead to more complete contracts, for a narrower range of activities. Some activities would be repatriated in-house. As analyzers move toward a defensive strategy, the number of activities undertaken becomes more limited, and can be conducted with greater efficiency. The need to develop higher control over the activities could lead to further internalization decisions. The limited number of activities that would remain outsourced would still be tightly integrated within the firm's activities, hence the propensity of defenders toward complete contracts.

CONCLUSION

As discussed by Miles and Snow (1986), many companies in the same industry can have different strategies. More specifically, prospectors would play the role of the designer, being the one innovating and suggesting new approaches to gain market share or to develop a product. At the opposite side, defenders would be the ones producing the goods. Analyzers would be in the middle and performing the marketing/distribution and information broker role. To maintain its long-term viability, the whole industry must balance the needs of innovation and efficiency, therefore requiring a certain mix of organizations in each of the strategic profiles.

Another observation made by Miles and Snow (1986) is that an industry can see some adjustments made over time by its companies. In an emerging industry, there is usually a good balance between the proportion of prospectors, analyzers, and defenders, whereas in a mature industry, the tendency is to have more defenders than any other types to prevent the decline of that industry. This implies that some companies that were prospectors in the beginning may decide to shift their focus and move closer to the defender type.

Consequently, several IT outsourcing strategies can be found within the same industry and the strategic evolution observed over time within a same industry might be observed with respect to the outsourcing profile. Companies in mature industries will become more similar. With time, the portfolios of activities that they decide to outsource should also increase in likeness.

Another observation stemming from this line of work is that outsourcing strategies might vary over time, even if the activities do not change much, and even if the environment is relatively stable. A company deciding to modify its strategy will adjust its outsourcing portfolio. This gives more "internal will" to the companies when analyzing outsourcing decisions. They will assess their governance (structure) options at the same time as their strategic ones. Even if Chandler established the importance of the link between strategy and structure more than forty years ago, too little attention has been given to strategy when analyzing outsourcing decisions. Strategy cannot be separated from structure. When strategy is modified, structure must be adjusted (Chandler, 1962).

Different strategies will lead to different governance choices, even if the activities are comparable between organizations in a same industry. Considering the strategic profile of the organizations (not only the characteristics of the activities) enables us to explain why similar activities are not managed in a uniform way from one organization to another. It offers a better understanding of outsourcing behavior.

Several avenues can be pursued to validate the proposed hypotheses and the relationship between strategy and outsourcing. Longitudinal case studies will enable the identification of shifts in strategies and corresponding decisions about structure. This approach would enable the identification of links between variables and rich information from managers would provide key insights into apparent causality. Another approach would be to conduct a survey. Many measures already exist to assess the strategic profile of an organization. Measures also exist to identify contract types. A survey would provide static information but the number of observations would enable a formal test of the hypotheses.

Another interesting extension to the chapter would be to consider IT projects. This might be a challenging task. Unlike IT operations, software projects are quite disparate from one organization to another. There would be no guarantee that organizations of different strategic types would launch similar IT projects, therefore making comparisons difficult. In-depth case studies might be an appropriate methodology to investigate this problem. For instance, a legitimate hypothesis when looking at IT projects could be that there might not be any detectable difference between prospectors, analyzers, and defenders in the use of outsourcing. What would differentiate them is the type of projects undertaken. Defenders and analyzers would engage mainly in routine projects, while prospectors would take on more innovative ones.[3] In this case, when looking at contract completeness, it would be difficult to determine whether the completeness level is related to the type of project undertaken or to the strategic type.

This chapter offers several promising research avenues. First, the interaction between the strategic profile of an organization and IT outsourcing, which has never been investigated before, is examined. This leads to a set of testable hypotheses. It provides an explanation for IT outsourcing behavior that relies on both transactional characteristics and intrinsic organizational properties. This also provides us with some explanations as to why different governance decisions are made for similar activities within the same industry. This line of research should enrich outsourcing literature and provide interesting insights for literature related to strategy.

ACKNOWLEDGMENT

This research project is supported by the SSHRC (Social Sciences and Humanities Research Council of Canada).

NOTES

1. Formally, we posit that the *IT outsourcing level* $= \Sigma\, b_i X_i + \varepsilon$, where X_1, X_2, and X_3 are dummies for defenders, analyzers, and prospectors, respectively, and X_4 is the level of uncertainty and measurement problems, X_5 is the level of business skills, X_6 is the level of technical skills, and X_7 is the asset specificity. Since our default is the reactor, we can hypothesize that $0 < b_1 < b_2 < b_3$.

2. Written more formally, we can anticipate that *Incompleteness Level* $= c_i X_i + \varepsilon$, where X_1, X_2, and X_3 are dummies for defenders, analyzers, and prospectors, respectively, and X_4 is the level of uncertainty and measurement problems, X_5 is the level of business skills, X_6 is the level of technical skills, and X_7 is the asset specificity. We can hypothesize that $c_1 = c_2 < c_3$.

3. We are grateful to an anonymous reviewer for this insight.

REFERENCES

Abernethy, M.A. and Guthrie, C.H. 1994. An empirical assessment of the "fit" between strategy and management information system design. *Accounting and Finance*, 34, 2, 49–66.

Adler, T.; Scherer, R.; Barton, S.; and Katerberg, R. 1998. An empirical test of transaction cost theory: Validating contract typology. *Journal of Applied Management Studies*, 7, 2, 185–200.

Anderson, E. 1985. The salesperson as outside agent or employee: A transaction cost analysis. *Marketing Science*, 4, 3, 234–254.

Ansoff, H.I. and Stewart, J.M. 1967. Strategies for a technology-based business. *Harvard Business Review*, 45, 6, 71–83.

Aubert, B.A.; Patry, M.; and Rivard, S. 2002. Managing IT outsourcing risk: Lessons learned. In R.A. Hirschheim, A. Heinzl, and J. Dibbern, eds., *Information Systems Outsourcing in the New Economy: Enduring Themes, Emergent Patterns and Future Directions.* New York: Springer-Verlag, pp. 155–176.

———. 2004. A transaction cost model of IT outsourcing. *Information & Management*, 41, 921–932.

Aubert, B.A.; Rivard, S.; and Patry, M. 1996. A transaction cost approach to outsourcing behavior: Some empirical evidence. *Information & Management*, 30, 2, 51–64.

Aubert, B.A.; Houde, J.-F.; Patry, M.; and Rivard, S. 2003. Characteristics of outsourcing contracts. Paper presented at the thirty-sixth Annual Hawaii International Conference on System Sciences (HICSS '03). Maui, HI: Organizational Systems and Technology Track, IEEE Computer Society Press.

Auger, P. 2003. An empirical investigation of the Miles and Snow typology for small online businesses. *International Journal of Internet and Enterprise Management*, 1, 3, 245–264.

Barney, J. 1999. How a firm's capabilities affect boundary decisions. *Sloan Management Review*, 40, 3, 137–145.

Bowman, E.H. and Helfat, C.E. 2001. Does corporate strategy matter? *Strategic Management Journal*, 22, 1–23.

Chandler, A. 1962. *Strategy and Structure: Chapters in the History of the Industrial Enterprise*. Cambridge: MIT Press.

Coase, R.H. 1937. The nature of the firm. *Economica*, 4, 386–405.

Conant, J.S.; Mokwa, M.P.; and Burnett, J.J. 1989. Pricing and performance in health maintenance organizations: A strategic management perspective. *Journal of Health Care Marketing*, 9, 1, 25–36.

Crocker, K.J. and Masten, S.E. 1991. *Pretia ex machina*? Prices and process in long-term contracts. *Journal of Law and Economics*, 34, 69–100.

Crocker, K.J. and Reynolds, K.J. 1993. The efficiency of incomplete contracts: An empirical analysis of Air Force engine procurement. *Rand Journal of Economics*, 24, 1, 126–146.

Croteau, A.-M. and Bergeron, F. 2001. An information technology trilogy: business strategy, technological deployment and organizational performance. *Journal of Strategic Information Systems*, 20, 2, 77–99.

Croteau, A.-M.; Raymond, L.; and Bergeron, F. 2001. Comportements stratégiques, choix et gestion des systèmes d'information: Contribution à la performance. *Systèmes d'Information et Management*, 4, 2, 5–17.

Earl, M.J. 1996. The risks of outsourcing IT. *Sloan Management Review*, 26–32.

Freeman, C. 1974. *The Economics of Industrial Innovation.* Harmondsworth, UK: Penguin.

Grant, R. M. 1995. *Contemporary Strategy Analysis*, 2nd ed, Basil Blackwell: Oxford, UK.

Grossman, S. and Hart, O. 1986. The costs and benefits of ownership: A theory of vertical and lateral integration. *Journal of Political Economy*, 94, 4, 691–719.

Hambrick, D.C. 1980. Operationalizing the concept of business-level strategy in research. *Academy of Management Review*, 5, 4, 567–575.

———. 1983. Some tests of the effectiveness and functional attributes of Miles and Snow's strategic types. *Academy of Management Journal*, 26, 1, 5–26.

Hennart, J.-F. 1988. Upstream vertical integration in the aluminum and tin industries: A comparative study of the choice between market and intrafirm coordination. *Journal of Economic Behavior & Organization*, 9, 3, 281–299.

Jelassi, T. and Enders, A. 2005. *Strategies for e-Business: Creating Value through Electronic and Mobile Commerce.* London: Financial Times/Prentice Hall.

Julien, P.-A.; Raymond, L.; Jacob, R.; and Ramangalahy, C. 1996. Patterns and determinants of technological scanning: An empirical investigation of manufacturing SMEs. In D. Reynolds D. et al., eds., *Frontiers of Entrepreneurship Research.* Babson Park, MA: Babson College, 584–598.

Karimi, J.; Gupta, Y.P.; and Somers, T.M. 1996. Impact of competitive strategy and information technology maturity on firms' strategic response to globalization. *Journal of Management Information Systems*, 12, 4, 55–88.

MacCrimmon, K.R. 1993. Do firm strategies exist? *Strategic Management Journal*, 14, 113–130.

Madden, J. 1999. EDS locks horns with Xerox. *eWEEK*, February 5.

Masten, S. 1984. The organization of production: Evidence from the aerospace industry. *Journal of Law and Economics*, 27, 2, 403–418.

Miles. R.E. and Snow, C.C. 1978. *Organizational Strategy, Structure, and Process.* New York: McGraw-Hill.

Miles, R.E. and Snow, C.C. 1986. Organizations: New concepts for new forms. *California Management Review*, 28, 3 62–73.

Milgrom, P. and Roberts, J. 1992. *Economics, Organization, and Management.* Englewood Cliffs, NJ: Prentice Hall.

Monteverde, K. and Teece, D.J. 1982. Supplier switching costs and vertical integration in the automobile industry. *Bell Journal of Economics*, 206–213.

Moore, M. 2003. Towards a confirmatory model of retail strategy types: An empirical test of Miles and Snow. *Journal of Business Research*, 1–9.

Murray, J. and Kotabe, M. 1999. Sourcing strategies of U.S. service companies: A modified transaction-cost analysis. *Strategic Management Journal*, 20, 9, 791–809.

Nam, K.; Rajagopalan, S.; Rao, H.R.; and Chaudhury, A. 1996. A two-level investigation of information systems outsourcing. *Communications of the ACM*, 39, 7, 37–44.

Namiki, N. 1989. Miles and Snow's typology of strategy, perceived environmental uncertainty, and organizational performance. *Akron Business and Economic Review*, 20, 2, 72–88.

Parry, M. and Parry, A.E. 1992. Strategy and marketing tactics in nonprofit hospitals. *Health Care Management Review*, 17, 1, 51–61.

Pisano, G.P. 1990. The R&D boundaries of the firm: An empirical analysis. *Administrative Science Quarterly*, 35, 1, 153–176.

Poppo, L. and Zenger, T. 1998. Measurement explanations for make-or-buy decisions in information services. *Strategic Management Journal*, 19, 9, 853–877.

Porter, M.E. 1980. *Competitive Strategy: Techniques for Analyzing Industries and Competitors.* New York: Free Press.

Rivard, S.; Aubert, B.A.; Paré, G.; Patry, M.; and Smith, H. 2004. *Information Technology and Organizational Transformation: The Management Puzzle* Butterworth-Heinemann, UK.

Roy, V. and Aubert, B.A. 2002. A resource-based analysis of IT sourcing. *Database*, 33, 2, 29–40.

Sabherwal, R. and Chan, Y.E. 2001. Alignment between business and IS strategies: A study of prospectors, analyzers, and defenders. *Information Systems Research*, 12, 1, 11–33.

Saussier, S. 2000. Transaction costs and contractual incompleteness: The case of Électricité de France. *Journal of Economic Behavior & Organization*, 42, 2, 189–206.

Shortell, S.M. and Zajac, E.J. 1990. Perceptual and archival measures of Miles and Snow's strategic types: A comprehensive assessment of reliability and validity. *Academy of Management Journal*, 33, 4, 817–832.

Smith, K.G.; Guthrie, J.P.; and Chen, M.J. 1989. Strategy, size, and performance. *Organizational Studies*, 10, 1, 63–81.

Snow, C.C. and Hrebiniak, L.G. 1980. Strategy distinctive competence and organizational performance *Administrative Science Quarterly*, 25, 2, 317–336.

Tan, F.B. 1997. Strategic type, information technology, and performance: AA study of executive perceptions. *Proceedings of the Third American Conference on Information Systems*, Indianapolis.

Tavakolian, H. 1989. Linking the information technology structure with organizational competitive strategy: A survey. *MIS Quarterly*, 13, 3, 309–317.

Tettelbach, B. 2000. CIO update: How measurement can help in evaluations of IT outsourcing. *Gartner Group document #IGG05032000–04*, 3.

Thomas, A.S.; Litschert, R.J.; and Ramaswamy, K. 1991. The performance impact of strategy-manager coalignment: An empirical examination. *Strategic Management Journal*, 12, 7, 509–522.

Venkatraman, N. 1989. Strategic orientation of business enterprises: The construct dimensionality and measurement. *Management Science*, 35, 8, 942–962.

Walker, G. and Weber, D. 1984. A transaction costs approach to make-or-buy decisions. *Administrative Science Quarterly*, 29, 3, 373–391.

Williamson, O. 1985. *The Economic Institutions of Capitalism.* New York: Free Press.

Zahra, S.A. and Pearce, J.A., II. 1990. Research evidence on the Miles-Snow typology. *Journal of Management*, 16, 4, 751–768.

CHAPTER 4

INFORMATION TECHNOLOGY OUTSOURCING

QUESTIONS OF LANGUAGE

TERESA MARCON AND ABHIJIT GOPAL

Abstract: *A theoretical and methodological sensitivity to language has fruitfully been put to use in social science and management research but has rarely found its way into research on information technology outsourcing. In this chapter, we argue that language matters and that attending to language can enhance our understanding of the IT outsourcing phenomenon. We explore the potential for insight that a language-centered approach offers and illustrate its applicability to the study of information technology outsourcing.*

Keywords: *Discourse, IT Outsourcing, Language Effects, Methodology*

Questions of language are increasingly of interest in social science and management research (e.g., Alvesson and Karreman, 2000a; Chia, 2000; Tsoukas, 2005). An interest in language stems from the displacement of a representational view of language in favor of a constructionist understanding of how language shapes social reality. Rather than considering language simply as a means to represent the world or as a medium for communication, a growing body of management research brings into relief the revelatory or world-disclosing (Lafont, 1999) function of language as the means through which we collectively give shape to the world and come to understand our reality. We act in the world on the bases of such understandings, with significant consequences for how we conduct human affairs.

In this chapter, we take the position that language *matters;* that is to say that language is important because it has concrete or material effects. We suggest that taking account of language can enhance our understanding of the information technology (IT) outsourcing phenomenon. Following an introduction to different ways of thinking about language and their methodological implications, we make use of an existing empirical study of IT outsourcing to explore some of the ways in which we might understand the intricacies of language use and the material effects language has on the outsourcing enterprise. By these means, we hope to illustrate the potential of a language-centered approach to contribute to understanding and open new directions for inquiry into IT outsourcing.

WHY LANGUAGE MATTERS

Language is fundamental to human experience. Though we might imagine a time when humans had yet to invent language, the individual we encounter in society is already, almost without exception, a person who speaks (Benveniste, 1971). It is perhaps only too obvious that human beings make frequent use of language. Though it is sometimes possible to communicate with others or perform activities without speaking, for example, through the use of gestures or the manipulation of objects, it is difficult to imagine how people could accomplish many tasks without language. For example, how could an outsourcing contract detailing vendor and client responsibilities be negotiated or specified without words?

The use of language through speaking and writing is so commonplace in fact that it might easily escape close examination. A scholarly enterprise that pursues a rigorous understanding, however, must in some way ground itself on a foundation that includes, as part of its onto-epistemological bases, a theoretical understanding of what language is and how it functions. A rich assortment of reflections and explorations on language can be found in domains such as philosophy (e.g., Austin, 2001; Wittgenstein, 1968), literature (e.g., Bakhtin, 1986) and linguistics (e.g., Chomsky, 1965; Culler, 1976). We can begin to appreciate the insights gained through this collective engagement and their implications for IT outsourcing research by considering two broad conceptualizations of language: the representational and the constructionist.

LANGUAGE AS REPRESENTATION: THE MIRROR

A concern with human beings as users of language can be traced to the early writings of Greek philosophers. Indeed, the predominant view of language up to the twentieth century was Aristotelian (Specht, 1969). According to this view, we come to know objects in the world independently of language. People apprehend objects through the senses and the intellect and subsequently associate them with specific terms. Language, whether written or spoken, simply expresses the thoughts of a conscious subject. In the words of John Locke (1959 [1825]), words are "signs of internal conceptions" (p. 106). They serve as "marks for the ideas within [a person's] mind whereby they might be made known to others and the thoughts of man's mind might be conveyed from one to another" (ibid.). Understanding the world of nature or ideas therefore begins with a living, thinking human who acquires a knowledge of these domains through the senses and the intellect and uses language to communicate with others.

An Aristotelian view thus ascribes a *representational* role to language. Here language is a set of symbols (signs) that are associated with referent objects or ideas (signifieds) and used by people to describe reality; language reflects or serves as a *mirror* for the world and for our thoughts (Alvesson and Karreman, 2000a). If we accept this view of language, words such as *computer* or *programmer* are simply pointers to objects that exist and can be apprehended independently of the terms used to describe them. Using different terms to denote these objects would serve our purpose equally well, as long as we agreed to do so. The terms *outsourcing* and *insourcing* similarly simply capture different ways of managing the IT function. We can argue about whether particular business activities (e.g., alliances or partnerships) should be considered instances of outsourcing or insourcing or question the adequacy of our definitions, but the language we use is assumed to have a passive role: it does not in any way shape or alter the actual activities that a firm undertakes. It simply describes them, more or less accurately.

A representational view of language has an ancient lineage and is still in use today. This view implicitly underlies knowledge production in many domains of science and social science where it is rarely discussed. Kuhn (1996), for example, has little to say about the use of language. Within this enterprise, language serves a communicative function by linking a word (a sign) to an object or idea (a signified).[1] As language simply represents, it is in large part ancillary to a scientific enterprise that seeks to uncover regularities in an objective reality conceived as largely independent of the observer and his/her use of language. Nevertheless, a representational view of language implicitly guides research practices and leads to certain concerns. A theoretical understanding of language as representation, for example, underlies attempts to arrive at precise definitions, a matter that is far from simple, as illustrated by the proliferation of definitions of IT outsourcing currently in use—see Dibbern et al. (2004) for a summary. Further concerns might include the design of unambiguous questionnaires, interview protocols or methods for analyzing textual materials. In these cases, the researcher's interest is in ensuring that language provides an adequate mirror for the objects it points to or the ideas it seeks to convey.

Though such concerns are by no means unimportant, they are predicated on a particular view of language. Questions of language take a different form if the function of language is understood along other lines. During the twentieth century a rethinking on matters of language took place among philosophers and linguists.[2] This rethinking challenged a representational view of language by inquiring into just *how* human beings are able to make language (a system of signs) intelligible or meaningful. As a consequence of this questioning, an understanding of language as a collection of signs that stand in a largely unproblematic relation to the ideas or objects they point to has been displaced in favor of an understanding of the way the meaning of objects and ideas is collectively constructed through an ongoing process of negotiation that is predicated on the use of language.

LANGUAGE AS CONSTRUCTION: THE LENS

A constructionist view emphasizes the revelatory or world-disclosing (Lafont, 1999) function of language. Rather than positing a subject who apprehends the world and subsequently articulates his/her perceptions in language, a constructionist view begins with a subject whose thoughts and perceptions are already shaped by language (Wittgenstein, 1968). Language directs our attention along particular lines and permits us to apprehend the world in a meaningful way. The function of language is not merely to reflect but to reveal or disclose a world of meaningful objects by providing a structure for organizing our encounter with the world and arriving at meaning (Eco, 2000).

That language plays a role in this process is perhaps most evident when we attempt to translate words from one language to another. To make use of a well-known example, the English word for snow can be translated into at least a dozen Inuit words that distinguish between different types of *snow* (e.g., "snow for drinking water," "small snow layer on the water of a fishing hole," or "snow drift made by the North East wind") (Elements, 2005). The collection of words for *snow* available in the Inuit language attunes the competent speaker to fine distinctions that might well escape an English speaker. It allows one to see snow as a source of drinking water rather than merely precipitation of a particular kind or as a covering that hides an opening in the ice that should be circumnavigated or used for fishing. Language therefore does not merely provide a way of pointing to objects whose meaning is transparent to us. Rather language is a structure that enables us to see particular objects *as something.*

If the mirror serves as a useful metaphor for a representational view, then the metaphor of the *lens* captures a constructionist perspective on language. A lens is a filter we look through that colors what we see and shapes our understanding of the world. Our ability to recognize objects *as particular kinds of things* is predicated on the existence of vocabularies that are endowed with meaning.

How does a word (a symbol or sign) come to be endowed with meaning? Words acquire meaning through a historical process of construction that brings ways of seeing into being and makes them available for use. The ability to think about what outsourcing means, for example, is predicated on the availability of ideas such as a world in which some things are *inside* and some *outside* such that it is possible to conceive of firms in this manner (e.g., Coase, 1937). The ideas of an *inside* and an *outside* in turn are only available to us through a language that is the outcome of an ongoing process of construction. We take such ideas for granted in our everyday lives, of course, but it is quite possible to imagine an isolated society in which there are no words to represent these concepts nor any perceived need for them. It is equally possible to imagine that this hypothetical society could over time develop such concepts and words to represent them in response to particular practices or events such as contact with a different cultural group. Languages and the ways of seeing that they allow are subject to successive alterations within a historical process of construction that renders the world meaningful for us in different ways at different times and places.[3]

Against a representational view that posits a subject who conceptualizes the world in thought and articulates ideas in language, a constructionist approach thus implicates language in how reality comes into being. Here language takes an active, rather than passive, role. Language *does things:* it is "performative" or "a mode of action" (Austin, 2001).[4] Language articulates ways of understanding the world and in the process "produces a particular version of social reality to the exclusion of other possible worlds" (Chia, 2000, pp. 513–514).

That language constructs social reality is not merely an ontological concern.[5] Language stands in a mutually constitutive relation to human practices: alterations in how we articulate our reality discursively in language at times change human activities, and vice versa (Tsoukas, 2005). To understand the connection between language and practice, we can begin by noting that language constructs ways of understanding that serve as the basis for action and shape our practices: it permits us to envision and conduct human affairs in particular ways and not in others. Recall here the example we offered earlier about how our ability to outsource IT is predicated on the possibility of regarding organizations as having an *inside* and an *outside,* a way of thinking that is made possible by a historically constructed language. Practices, for their part, at times alter our understanding and engender transformations in language. Consider, for example, the recent proliferation of terms for international outsourcing that include *nearshoring* and *farshoring*. These terms are neologisms (new words or expressions) that suggest a particular way of thinking about choosing an international destination for outsourcing. Most obviously, perhaps, they invite consideration of geographical distance and its practical implications such as differences in time zones and travel times. Less obviously, they carry additional meanings that associate nearshore with reduced opportunities for cost savings and farshore with maximum economic benefits (e.g., Mazzawl, Munsif, and Stark, 2003). In some cases, they also signal differences in cultural distance (e.g., Foster, 2004). Their emergence is a reflection of current outsourcing practices and the concerns these entail. This is a manifestation of the constant interplay between language and practices that gives shape to what we hold to be real and true in our present and therefore appropriate as a basis for action. It is in this manner that language acquires a materiality, or a concreteness, that engenders effects and implicates it in the world beyond the level of description. This materiality is not equivalent to that of an object but rather something that emerges through human practices (Foucault, 1982).

We began this chapter with the claim that language *matters;* that is, that language has concrete or material effects. To show how it is possible to conceive of language in this way, we have presented two different ways of thinking about language (Table 4.1). When language is merely a mirror for the world, it is difficult to see how language might *matter.* Viewed as a lens, however, language takes an active hand in human affairs and becomes an interesting site for analysis. In the next section, we explore how we might go about putting an active view of language to work in IT outsourcing research.

Table 4.1

Language as Representation and Construction

	Representation	Construction
Metaphor	mirror	lens
Function	reflects	reveals/discloses
	passive	active
Relations	thought → language	language → thought
	sign → signified	sign ~ meaning to receiver ~ signified
Research interest	ancillary	site of analysis

LANGUAGE IN ACTION

Different theories about language entail different concerns and invite different methodologies.[6] When the function of language is to represent rather than construct, language can for the most part be taken for granted. We might be concerned with ensuring adequate representations through precise definitions and robust instruments but we need not inquire into *just how* language works to achieve such ends. Our choice of methodology can be made without particular attention to language.

When language actively constructs the world, however, we are invited to inquire into how language functions as an integral part of the investigation. Because language is an act that has material consequences (Foucault, 2002), it cannot simply be taken for granted. Here, we are in need of a methodology that is sensitive to language and allows us to investigate language in action: as it is put into play by social actors in a domain of practice through the structures that language provides, the multitude of voices, and the contest over meaning.

Methodologies that take an interest in language are concerned with how language functions to achieve meaning in order to understand the effects that ensue. Because meaning is the outcome of an ongoing process of construction, methodological approaches that take an interest in language generally proceed on the basis of an ontology of *becoming* (Chia, 1995) that views reality as constantly in flux and responsive to local conditions. As such, they do not lead to deterministic theories or predictive models but rather to theoretically nuanced accounts of human practices that contribute to knowledge at the level of understanding and permit a different kind of generalizability by providing a theoretical lens that can be transposed to similar settings by the reader (Klein and Meyers, 1999).

To assist us in putting an active view of language to work, we have at our disposal a range of methodologies that accord primacy to language, to a greater or lesser extent. Ethnomethodological (Garfinkel, 1967) and Foucauldian (Foucault, 2002) approaches, for example, push language (or discourse) forcefully into the foreground, taking a radical view of language as constitutive of both what we hold to be real and also the subject him/herself as a conscious being. Organizational research conducted in these modes views language as inseparable from the process through which our inner and outer realities are constituted (Alvesson and Karreman, 2000b). Other approaches that are concerned with language and the question of meaning direct attention to the role of

Table 4.2

Selected Methodologies

Methodology	Basic interest in language	Selected references
Discourse analysis	Language as a social practice that is constitutive of the social world and/or structures of domination	Alvesson and Karreman, 2000b; Chia, 2000; Fairclough, 1993
Deconstruction	Reality is a text that can be read by studying the relations between what is said and what is not said	Cooper, 1989; Kilduff, 1993
Dramatism	Human activities as narratives that have an underlying dramatic structure	Jackson, 1999, 2000
Ethnomethodology	How meaning is achieved through language in social interaction	Maynard and Clayman, 1991; Ross and Chiasson, 2005
Genealogy	The historical constitution of the "real" through discourse	Kendall and Wickham, 1999; Miller and Napier, 1993
Hermeneutics	The rules that guide the interpretation of texts	Phillips and Brown, 1993; Prasad, 2002
Narrative analysis	How stories or narratives function to construct understanding	Boje, 1991; Boje, 1995
Semiotics	How meaning is achieved through the underlying structure of language	Fiol, 1989; Mick, 1986
Symbolism	How symbols, archetypes, or myths are read, produced, and reproduced, lending meaning to human activities	Bowles, 1997; Strati, 1998

symbols (e.g., Hirschheim and Newman, 1991; Mick, 1986), myths (e.g., Aredal, 1986; Bowles, 1997) or story-telling (e.g., Boje, 1991, 1995). Here, language, as the basis for socially embedded processes of interpretation, serves as a conduit for the articulation and rearticulation of identities and organizational reality.[7]

It is not possible to do justice to the multiplicity of available perspectives in the space available in this chapter. Each methodology makes available a theoretical vocabulary (or a set of concepts) that reflects nuanced onto-epistemological commitments and provides a frame for understanding. The choice of methodology guides the investigation in particular directions that may be more or less useful, depending on the research questions and the interests of the researcher. By way of introduction, Table 4.2 provides a brief overview of some methodologies that accord particular attention to understanding language in action.

To attempt to illustrate the potential for insight of attending to language in a more concrete manner, in the next section we provide an example of how employing a linguistically sensitive methodology might contribute to our understanding of IT outsourcing.

THEORIZING LANGUAGE IN IT OUTSOURCING

To the best of our knowledge, there are no studies of IT outsourcing that take advantage of the opportunities a linguistically sensitive methodology may afford. An exploration of the tensions between space and place by Schultze and Boland (2000), however, is set in an IT outsourcing context and makes use of a methodology that allows us to theorize the role of language (Bourdieu, 1991). We attempt to give concrete form to our argument in favor of a linguistic approach to the study of IT outsourcing by reanalyzing the findings reported by Schultze and Boland (2000), with our own particular interests in mind.[8]

Schultze and Boland's investigation explores the social construction of space and place by outsourced system administrators in the context of emerging organizational forms that rely on extended networks (e.g., partnerships, alliances, outsourcing). In contrast, our own particular interest is in bringing into visibility how language can be an act that has material effects and how an active view of language might usefully contribute to our understanding of IT outsourcing. As we cannot point to any existing studies of how language is woven into practices in an outsourcing setting, we take advantage of the detailed account of organizational life provided by Schultze and Boland to illustrate how we might investigate the reciprocal relation between language and practices in an IT outsourcing context and to suggest what we might learn from such efforts.

Schultze and Boland report on an ethnographic study of the practices of systems administrators working as contractors at U.S. Company, a Fortune 500 manufacturer. As part of a restructuring process to change U.S. Company into an entrepreneurial organization, work activities were classified as either commodity or value-adding. All commodity work, including systems administration and development, was targeted for outsourcing. This was intended to allow U.S. Company employees to focus on value-adding activities with a potential to impact the strategy and competitive position of the organization.

Like Schultze and Boland, we frame our exploration within Pierre Bourdieu's (1998) theory of practice. A Bourdieun lens posits a reciprocally constitutive relation between the dispositions of agents (their habitus) and social structures. Within this theoretical framework, the categories of commodity and value-added work are structures that contractors and U.S. Company employees internalize and enact through practices. These same practices in turn function so as to either reproduce existing structures or create new ones in an ongoing struggle over the definition of the real.

From Schultze and Boland's account, we thus single out for analysis (1) the categories of commodity and value-added work that were put into play at this organization, (2) the contest over the meaning of outsourced work that ensued, and (3) the relation of this struggle to the practices of outsourced computer systems administrators.

COMMODITY AND VALUE-ADDED WORK

Pierre Bourdieu (1985) has noted that "the social world can be uttered and constructed in different ways. It may be practically perceived, uttered, constructed, according to different principles of vision and division" (p. 726). That is to say that it is possible to articulate distinctions regarding human affairs in multiple ways as the result of a collective process of social construction. Categories articulated in language that may seem to merely describe and distinguish types of activities such as commodity and value-added work function as "principles of vision and division" (ibid.) by focusing attention in particular ways and drawing distinctions between groups.

At U.S. Company, the distinction between commodity and value-added work operated in this way (Schultze and Boland, 2000). It directed attention to the commodity and value-adding aspects of IT work, emphasizing a particular way of analyzing work (or a way of seeing) in relation to strategic goals and the competitiveness of the organization. This way of seeing work is only one among many. It would be quite possible, for example, to analyze work based on the level of skill required for its performance or the physical location entailed in the delivery of a service or in many other ways. This would result in a different classification and accord different roles to U.S. Company employees and contract workers. While focusing on the distinction between commodity and value-added work was only a particular (i.e. arbitrary) way of drawing distinctions, it was not merely a matter of choosing one nomenclature over another: the categories of commodity and value-added work provided the basis for distinctions between groups. When applied to individuals and groups, categories shape perceptions of self and others and become implicated in practices and processes of identity formation.

THE CONTEST OVER THE MEANING OF OUTSOURCED WORK

At U.S. Company work was assigned to internal employees or contractors depending on how it was classified. Having particular activities classified as commodity shaped the understanding of both U.S. Company employees and contractors, though in different ways. While the work of systems administrators was considered a commodity by U.S. Company employees, this view was not shared by the contractors who saw their work as value-adding. Systems administrators did not refer to themselves as "contractors" or "commodity workers" but as "consultants" who "added value and gained capital by adopting the objective stance of an outsider" (Schultze and Boland, 2000, p. 201). Here the meaning of value-added work is redefined by the contractors: while U.S. Company sought to signal the strategic potential of value-added work, contractors related value to their status as professionals and the objectivity they brought to their work.

Schultze and Boland document the struggle between contractors and U.S. Company employees over the definition of what constituted the contractors' responsibility. U.S. Company employees accorded contractors the consideration due to commodity workers as performers of routine, nonstrategic activities and often requested assistance with routine tasks. When contractors were unresponsive to such requests, U.S. Company employees evaluated their performance negatively. Contractors, on the other hand, contested the classification of their work as commodity, sought to avoid involvement in routine work, and constituted their identities as consultants and professionals through a variety of daily practices.

CONTRACTORS' PRACTICES

Schultze and Boland's (2000) analysis of the work practices of IT contractors at this organization details the manner in which constructing work as either commodity or value-adding was implicated in the daily practices of systems administrators. The contractors' work practices reflected the attempt to "align themselves with value adding knowledge" (p. 207) by concentrating on the development of documentation and resisting involvement in routine support work. Contractors were reluctant to help users solve problems on their local machines, for example, preferring to provide users with documentation that would allow them to resolve routine troubles independently. Moreover, systems administrators sought out assignments to develop competencies that would make them valuable to organizations, rather than interchangeable commodities. They saw little benefit in achieving certification in particular technologies, for example, in spite of the positive way in which this was regarded by the vendor who employed them, as this tended to limit rather than expand their choice of assignments. Through their practices, contractors struggled to construct their career paths and identities as value-adding workers.

Recognition of the importance of systems of classification and their contested nature points to the mutually constitutive relation between language and practices (Tsoukas, 2005). While language provides categories for understanding that shape practices in particular ways (though not necessarily as intended), practices in turn entail the constant production, reproduction, and, at times, transformation of systems of classification in the particularity of their meanings. As Bourdieu (1985) notes "[t]his work of categorization, i.e. of making explicit and of classification, is performed incessantly, at every moment of ordinary existence, in the struggles in which agents clash over the meaning of the social world and their position in it" (p. 729). The struggle between contract workers and U.S. Company employees reflects this ongoing process of negotiation over the meaning of commodity and value-added work. It highlights the multiplicity of meanings that may be ascribed to particular activities by different individuals or groups in confrontation with linguistic structures and the manner in which the existence of conflicting views is embroiled in practices including the contractors' practices of documentation.

FROM LANGUAGE TO INFORMING RESEARCH AND PRACTICE

An active view of language accords a complex function to linguistic structures. Categories that differentiate one type of work from another and, by implication, distinguish between groups in the organizational settings thus are more than labels that merely describe self-evident aspects of organizational life. The categories of commodity and value-added work put into play as a result of organizational restructuring engendered particular effects as they were taken up by U.S. Company employees and outsourced systems administrators. Contractors contested the definition of their work as commodity and attempted to align themselves with value-added work and transform its meaning. Alterations of meaning are embedded in material practices. The contractors attempted to reformulate the meaning of their work by engaging in some practices rather than others: they favored the development of documentation over direct assistance to users and avoided the pursuit of professional certifications that might constrain their mobility as employees of the vendor company. Contractors thus oriented their practices to the categories of commodity and value-added work, in the process attempting to construct through their material practices a particular version of what value-added work and their own work was *really* about.

Attending to categories and the contest over meaning that is played out in practice helps us to understand some of the challenges related to IT outsourcing that U.S. Company encountered and informs our understanding of IT outsourcing at a broader level by suggesting an explanatory schema for coming to conclusions about similar phenomena. Our rereading of Schultze and Boland's (2000) study, for example, begins to suggest the kind of considerations that may deserve attention from researchers who might take an interest in further explicating service-level issues in IT outsourcing arrangements. At U.S. Company, the practices of IT contractors met contract specifications yet were not always positively regarded as they failed to meet the needs of some users. Traditional wisdom in IT outsourcing research would suggest that resolution of such issues would flow from robust contracts and service-level agreements (e.g., Lacity and Willcocks, 2001; Willcocks, Fitzgerald, and Lacity, 1996) and from managing the client–vendor relationship (e.g., Heckman, 1999; Marcolin and McLellan, 1998). Our rereading of this case study suggests that what might be at issue here is the relationship with vendor employees on the front lines. In particular, the events that Schultze and Boland (2000) recount suggest that, at least in some settings, questions of contractors' identity might be important in teasing out the complexities of managing a client–vendor relationship to achieve a satisfactory level of service. It further suggests that questions of identity might usefully be explored in the context of organizational discourses, the categories for understanding they put into play, and the transformations in meanings that these may be subject to in particular contexts.

The practical implications for organizations that might flow from this kind of analysis cannot be articulated in the form of prescriptions. We cannot conclude from this kind of exploration, for example, that vendors should recruit employees whose psychological makeup is well suited to commodity work. Given the methodological lens taken here, we regard commodity work and individual psychology (or identity) as ways of understanding the world and ourselves that are constantly in flux, subject to an ongoing process of construction and potential transformation. Rather, our rereading of the case study informs business practices by inviting readers to explore, in their own organizational setting, the applicability of the theoretical concepts presented here (Klein and Meyers, 1999): the idea of categories of work as structures that people orient to, the way these may be contested and reinterpreted by organizational members, and the way they may be connected to the adoption of particular work practices and thus engender intended or unintended outcomes.

We have argued that our attempts to contribute to a scholarly understanding of IT outsourcing are predicated on a theory of what language is and how it functions. We have offered two different conceptualizations of the function of language and pointed to their implications for how we approach research. In our rereading of the organizational reality described by Schultze and Boland (2000), we have attempted to illustrate in concrete terms how attending to the reciprocal relations of language and practices might fruitfully illuminate the IT outsourcing phenomenon and inform research and practice. In the remainder of this chapter, we single out some aspects of IT outsourcing where our understanding might perhaps be most fruitfully illuminated by a linguistic approach. We further suggest that placing language at center stage may open new directions for inquiry in the IT outsourcing domain.

BRINGING LANGUAGE IN

A constructionist view of language invites into the IT outsourcing domain a range of theoretically nuanced methodologies that have not yet been engaged by researchers in this field. The richness of explanation or the process of "causal multiplication" (Foucault, 1991, p. 76) that these methodologies allow contributes to our understanding of IT outsourcing through a layering of theoretically nuanced accounts of human practices that do not lead to predictive models but rather to a form of generalizability that rests with the reader. As we attempted to illustrate through an example, alternative methodologies bring new perspectives to old problems. They provide a different set of explanations that can enrich our present understanding and inform further investigations. If we accept that every methodology is a lens that inevitably obscures as well as reveals (Heidegger, 1993a), then expanding the methodological bases of IT outsourcing research in itself might be sufficient reason for advocating a turn to language in IT outsourcing research.

Beyond the benefits of methodological pluralism, a linguistic sensitivity that attends to the negotiation of meaning attunes us to the multitude of voices that participate in the ongoing construction of organizational realities. The ability to account for multiple stakeholders—their positions, interests, and concerns—would seem to be particularly relevant to a domain of practice that crosses organizational boundaries and brings multiple stakeholder groups into play. The methodologies that a linguistic perspective invites are well suited to this challenging task and may facilitate engagement in multistakeholder research in IT outsourcing beyond the relatively small body of work that has appeared to date (e.g., Lacity and Willcocks, 2000; McAulay and Doherty, 2002; Palvia, 1995).

Further, attention to language may help us to theorize and understand change. The IT outsourcing landscape is dynamic. Outsourcing practices, for example, take different forms and often evolve over the course of client–vendor relationships (e.g., Klepper, 1995; Robinson and Kalakota, 2004; Willcocks and Kern, 1998). We might go so far as to state that change and dynamism, rather than stasis, characterize IT outsourcing practices (cf., Chia, 2000). In the context of studying organizational change, Grant et al. (2005) have noted the considerable promise of a linguistically sensitive approach that attends to the negotiation of meaning and its effects, as "organizational discourses related to change do not simply start out in possession of 'meaning'" (p. 8). Similarly, the evolution of IT outsourcing practices, from arms-length contracts to partnerships (Robinson and Kolakota, 2004), for example, or from outsourcing to backsourcing (Hirschheim, 1998), is likely to entail the negotiation of new meanings and new ways of understanding through the interplay of language and practices. Bringing language into the picture in studying the evolution of IT outsourcing in organizations may help us understand how and why IT outsourcing practices may change over time or unfold differently in particular settings.

Methodologies provide ways of thinking. As such, they may prompt not only new ways of illuminating existing questions but also new directions for inquiry. A linguistic sensitivity that attends to the multiplicity of voices invites the questions: who is speaking? And with what effects? Questions such as these suggest consideration of power relations and the differential ability of various stakeholders to effect change in the field of play through language and practices. We might then ask, along with Bourdieu (1991), whether the act of naming—of designating and differentiating—does not acquire its force from outside language, from the authority invested in some speakers and not others. These are old questions, of course, and important ones in our view, though they are not often addressed by research on IT outsourcing (exceptions are Allen, Kern, and Mattison, 2002; Peled, 2001; and Silva, 2002).

From a perspective that accords privilege to language, we might, however, explore the field of power in new directions by attending to expert discourses or "knowledges" (Foucault, 1980) with a view to understanding their effects. We are accustomed to consider expert discourses, those of industry analysts or think tanks, for example, to assess the validity of their claims to truth. The truthfulness of the discourse of IT offshoring as a win-win proposition (McKinsey Global Institute, 2003), for example, may be asserted or brought into question by supporters and by detractors as well as by researchers. When language is an act, however, it enjoins us to ask not whether a discourse is true or false but what effects it produces. We need not then decide whether those who favor IT offshoring are right or whether truth rests with the critics. Our task instead is to uncover the effects engendered by a discourse that makes a claim to truth (Foucault, 1980).

Expert discourses are not only read and evaluated but also used (Prior, 2003). They are put into circulation at a societal level through the permanence of the written word: they are cited, referred to, or called upon to support particular claims or discredit others. The discourse of IT offshoring as a "win-win proposition" (McKinsey Global Institute, 2003), for example, puts categories for understanding offshoring into circulation. These categories find their way into written texts (e.g., articles in the popular press) and organizational discourses, where they may be reproduced, contested, or transformed in the interplay between language and practices and where they may engender both intended and unintended consequences.

An active view of language gives us some useful tools to bring the production of knowledge by experts such as industry analysts, consultants, governments, and interest groups into contact with practices to account for its participation in the ongoing construction of what we hold to be real and true (Foucault, 1997) in the matter of IT outsourcing. It encompasses knowledge production within the circle of inquiry on IT outsourcing and extends our interests beyond current boundaries. Moreover, an active view of language enjoins us to account for how the discourses we as researchers produce may also contribute to the collective process of construction that gives shape to IT outsourcing and puts into play "a particular version of social reality to the exclusion of other possible worlds" (Chia, 2000, pp. 513–514). A call to language thus entails also a call to reflexivity (Bourdieu, 1988) on our own enterprise and its connection to the world of practice.

CLOSING REMARKS

In this chapter, we have sought to highlight the relevance of questions of language to IT outsourcing research. We have argued that language *matters,* that is, that language has concrete effects on human practices such as IT outsourcing. As such, language deserves careful consideration from the research community. Yet, unlike other domains of organizational research that have pursued the kind of questions that an active view of language entails for some time (e.g., Boje, 1991; Fairclough, 1993), research in the IT outsourcing domain has not engaged in this kind of inquiry to date.

In our view, a linguistic approach holds considerable promise for the study of IT outsourcing. In an attempt to direct the attention of the research community to this potential, we have sought to provide an introduction to how we might think about language and its consequences. To make our point in concrete terms, we applied Pierre Bourdieu's (1998) theory of practice, of one among several linguistically sensitive theoretical lenses at our disposal, to the IT outsourcing domain by reanalyzing the findings of Schultze and Boland's (2000) study. We further engaged in reflection on how taking account of language in IT outsourcing research might contribute to the pursuit of knowledge in this domain. In particular, we argued that employing theoretical approaches that accord a central role to how language functions may offer new insights into the IT outsourcing phenomenon through methodological pluralism, support for multistakeholder research, and the ability to account for change. Finally, we have suggested that such perspectives allow us to account for the process of knowledge production in IT outsourcing, calling for an expansion of the domain of inquiry and for reflexivity on our own enterprise as producers of knowledge.

In the IT outsourcing domain, language has largely been taken for granted as a means to represent or communicate. Alternatively, as we have suggested, paying careful attention to the use of language through a theoretically informed linguistic sensitivity can contribute to our knowledge of the IT outsourcing phenomenon and open new directions for inquiry.

ACKNOWLEDGMENTS

We are grateful to the anonymous reviewer who provided insightful comments and suggestions to guide the preparation of this chapter. We also wish to thank the anonymous reviewer for capturing our argument in the statement that language "matters." We found this elegant play on words useful in our presentation.

NOTES

1. Scientists and other researchers are, of course, aware that achieving a precise language completely devoid of ambiguity is very difficult. Heisenberg (cited in Styhre, 2004), for example, has remarked on the multiple interpretations that language permits and on the difficulties of transferring a concept by analogy from one domain to another. Similarly, Kuhn (1996) refers to Wittgenstein (1968) in noting the role that language plays in arriving at a shared set of assumptions, concepts, and methods within a scientific paradigm. While using language to communicate clearly entails more than establishing a simple relation between a sign and a signified, a representational view of language is in large part still accepted as an adequate, if imperfect, foundation for scientific investigations.

2. Given space constraints, we do not attempt to provide an overview of the multiple challenges launched against a representational view by linguists (e.g., Culler, 1976) and philosophers (e.g., Austin, 2001; Heidegger, 1993b; Wittgenstein, 1968). Useful discussions of these developments are provided by Alvesson and Karreman (2000a) and Lafont (1999).

3. While it may be tempting to regard alterations as corrections that bring us closer to a truthful understanding, within a constructionist ontology and epistemology, all understandings, including the present one, must be regarded as equally arbitrary (Foucault, 1980). This is not equivalent to saying that we could construct the world in any way whatsoever, as in a kind of naive nonrealism. It is merely to note that there are many ways to construct a knowledge of the world none of which can make an unequivocal claim to truth (Kuhn, 1996).

4. The concept of *performativity* was introduced by Austin (2001) around 1955 in the context of the philosophy of everyday language. Austin states that "to say is to do," it is an act. Consider, for example, the statement "I promise" or the well-known phrase "I do," which, in certain settings, is not a description but

an act. Speech act theory (Searle, 1969) is perhaps the most well-known translation of the concept of the performative into social theory though others (e.g., Butler, 1997; Foucault, 2002) have pushed this line of thinking along different lines.

5. At this point, the objection may be raised that this is perhaps only an ontological concern (i.e., a concern with what things really are). Can we not simply recognize our understanding of the world as constructed through language and attempt to uncover regularities that, while particular to this historical time, can be assumed to hold until proven otherwise? While it is possible to proceed in this fashion, to do so is to basically return to a representational view of language and miss the opportunity for insight offered by a linguistic approach.

6. Though theory and method are usually treated separately in the functionalist tradition, this separation is viewed as untenable from other onto-epistemological positions. Methods are not ontologically and epistemologically neutral but rather colored by onto-epistemological assumptions. Following the conventions in "qualitative" or alternative research traditions (Prasad, 2005), we use the term *methodology* to denote a combination of both theory and method.

7. This is by no means a complete list of methodological approaches that accord a central function to language. For example, we have omitted mention of rhetorical and metaphorical analysis, perspectives that clearly accord a central place to linguistic practices. It should also be noted that the function of language is theorized somewhat differently across methodologies. The role of language with respect to the autonomy of individuals, for example, varies in nuanced ways that reflect a range of possible positions (see Alvesson and Karreman [2000b] for a more complete discussion).

8. We do not provide a full account of Schultze and Boland's (2000) findings here but merely highlight selected aspects that are particularly useful for our purposes. Our analysis is necessarily speculative and partial and offered only as a means to explicate the insights that a linguistic perspective might permit. The reader is referred to the original article for a more complete account.

REFERENCES

Allen, D.; Kern, T.; and Mattison, D. 2002. Culture, power and politics in ICT outsourcing in higher education institutions. *European Journal of Information Systems*, 11, 2, 159–173.

Alvesson, M. and Karreman, D. 2000a. Taking the linguistic turn in organizational research: Challenges, responses, consequences. *Journal of Applied Behavioral Science*, 36, 2, 136–158.

———. 2000b. Varieties of discourse: On the study of organizations through discourse analysis. *Human Relations*, 53, 9, 1125–1149.

Aredal, A. 1986. Procrustes: A modern management pattern found in a classical myth." *Journal of Management*, 12, 36, 403–414.

Austin, J.L. 2001. *How to Do Things with Words.* The William James Lectures Delivered at Harvard University in 1955. Cambridge, MA: Harvard University Press, 2001.

Bakhtin, M.M. 1986. *Speech Genres and Other Late Essays.* Austin: University of Texas Press.

Benveniste, E. 1971. Subjectivity in language. In *Problems in General Linguistics.* Coral Gables, FL: University of Miami Press, 223–238.

Boje, D.M. 1991. The storytelling organization: A study of story performance in an office-supply firm. *Administrative Science Quarterly*, 36, 106–126.

———. 1995. Stories of the storytelling organization: A postmodern analysis of Disney as "Tamara-Land." *Academy of Management Journal*, 38, 4, 997–1035.

Bourdieu, P. 1985. The social space and the genesis of groups. *Theory and Society*, 14, 723–744.

———. 1988. *Homo Economicus.* Cambridge, UK: Polity Press in association with Basil Blackwell.

———. 1991. *Language and Symbolic Power.* Cambridge, MA: Harvard University Press, 1991.

———. 1998. *Practical Reason. On the Theory of Action.* Stanford, CA: Stanford University Press, 1998.

Bowles, M. 1997. The myth of management: Direction and failure in contemporary organizations. *Human Relations*, 50, 7, 779–803.

Butler, J. 1997. *Excitable Speech. A Politics of the Performative.* New York: Routledge.

Chia, R. 1995. From modern to postmodern organizational analysis. *Organization Studies*, 16, 4, 579–604.

———. 2000. Discourse analysis as organizational analysis. *Organization*, 7, 3, 513–518.

Chomsky, N. 1965. *Aspects of the Theory of Syntax.* Cambridge, MA: M.I.T. Press.

Coase, R.H. 1937. The nature of the firm. *Economica* (November), 386–405.

Cooper, R. 1989. Modernism, post modernism, and organizational analysis 3: The contribution of Jacques Derrida. *Organization Studies*, 10, 4, 479–502.

Culler, J. 1976. Saussure's theory of language. In J. Culler, *Saussure*, ed. Hassocks, UK: Harvester Press, 18–52.

Dibbern, J.; Goles, T.; Hirschheim, R.; and Jayatilaka, B. 2004. Information systems outsourcing: A survey and analysis of the literature. *DATABASE for Advances in Information Systems*, 35, 4, 6–102.

Eco, U. 2000. *Kant and the Platypus. Essays on Language and Cognition.* London: Vintage.

Elements. 2005. Available at www.elements.nb.ca/kids/snow/snoword.htm (accessed October 15, 2005).

Fairclough, N. 1993. Critical discourse analysis and the marketization of public discourse. *Discourse and Society*, 4, 133–159.

Fiol, C.M. 1989. A semiotic analysis of corporate language: Organizational boundaries and joint venturing. *Administrative Science Quarterly*, 34, 277–303.

Foster, S. 2004. Canada ranks "relatively low" on global IT pay scale. *Computing Canada*, 30, 10, 25.

Foucault, M. 1980. Two lectures. In Colin Gordon, ed. *Power/Knowledge. Selected Interviews and Other Writings 1972–1977.* New York: Pantheon Books, pp. 78–108.

———. 1982. The subject and power. *Critical Inquiry*, 8, 4, 777–795.

———. 1991. Questions of method. In G. Burchell, C. Gordon, and P. Miller, eds. *The Foucault Effect. Studies in Governmentality with Two Lectures and an Interview with Michel Foucault.* Chicago: University of Chicago Press, 73–86.

———. 1997. *The Politics of Truth.* New York: Semiotext(e).

———. 2002. *The Archaeology of Knowledge.* London: Routledge Classics.

Garfinkel, H. 1967. *Studies in Ethnomethodology.* Englewood Cliffs, NJ: Prentice Hall.

Grant, D.; Michelson, G.; Oswick, C.; and Wailes, N. 2005. Guest editorial: Discourse and organizational change. *Journal of Organizational Change Management*, 18, 1, 6–15.

Heckman, R. 1999. Organizing and managing supplier relationships in information technology procurement. *International Journal of Information Management*, 19, 2, 141–155.

Heidegger, M. 1993a. The question concerning technology. In D.F. Krell, ed., *Martin Heidegger: Basic Writings.* New York: HarperCollins, 283–317.

———. 1993b. Letter on humanism. In D.F. Krell, ed. *Martin Heidegger. Basic Writings.* New York: HarperCollins, 213–266.

Hirschheim, R. 1998. *Backsourcing: An Emerging Trend?* Outsourcing Center, Everest Partners, L.P.

Hirschheim, R. and Newman M. 1991. Symbolism and information systems development: Myth, metaphor and magic. *Information Systems Research*, 2, 1, 29–62.

Jackson, B.G. 1999. The goose that laid the golden egg? A rhetorical critique of Stephen Covey and the effectiveness movement. *Journal of Management Studies*, 36, 3, 353–377.

———. 2000. A fantasy theme analysis of Peter Senge's learning organization. *Journal of Applied Behavioral Science*, 36, 2, 193–209.

Kendall, G. and Wickham, G. 1999. *Using Foucault's Methods.* London: Sage.

Kilduff, M. 1993. Deconstructing organizations. *Academy of Management Review*, 18, 1, 13–31.

Klein, H.K. and Meyers, M.D. 1999. A set of principles for conducting and evaluating interpretive field studies in information systems. *MIS Quarterly*, 23, 1, 67–94.

Klepper, R. 1995. The management of partnering: Development in I/S outsourcing. *Journal of Information Technology*, 10, 249–258.

Kuhn, T.S. 1996. *The Structure of Scientific Revolutions.* 3d ed. Chicago: University of Chicago Press.

Lacity, M.C. and Willcocks, L.P. 2000. Relationships in IT outsourcing: A stakeholder perspective. In R.W. Zmud, ed., *Framing the Domains of IT Management: Projecting the Future Through the Past.* Cincinnati, OH: Pinnaflex Information Resources, 355–384.

———. 2001. *Global Information Technology Outsourcing. In Search of Business Advantage.* Chichester, UK: Wiley.

Lafont, C. 1999. *The Linguistic Turn in Hermeneutic Philosophy.* Cambridge, MA: MIT Press.

Locke, J. 1959 [1825]. *An Essay Concerning Human Understanding. Vol. II.* New York: Dover.

Marcolin, B.L. and McLellan, K. 1998. Effective IT outsourcing arrangements. In *Thirty-first Annual Hawaii International Conference on System Sciences.* Hawaii: IEEE, 654–665.

Maynard, D.W., and Clayman, S.E. 1991. The diversity of ethnomethodology. *Annual Review of Sociology*, 17, 385–418.

Mazzawl, E.; Munsif, S.; and Stark, R. 2003. Sun rises on "rightshore." *Business Strategy Review*, 14, 3, 4–6.

McAulay, L. and Doherty, N. 2002. The stakeholder dimension in information systems evaluation. *Journal of Information Technology*, 17, 241–255.

McKinsey Global Institute. 2003. *Offshoring: Is It a Win-Win Game?* San Francisco: McKinsey & Company.

Mick, D.G. 1986. Consumer research and semiotics: Exploring the morphology of sings, symbols and significance. *Journal of Consumer Research*, 13 (September), 196–213.

Miller, P. and Napier, C. 1993. Genealogies of calculation. *Accounting, Organization and Society*, 18, 7/8, 631–647.

Palvia, P.C. 1995. A dialectic view of information-systems outsourcing—pros and cons. *Information & Management*, 29, 5, 265–275.

Peled, A. 2001. Outsourcing and political power: Bureaucrats, consultants, vendors and public information technology. *Public Personnel Management*, 30, 4, 495–514.

Phillips, N. and Brown, J.L. 1993. Analyzing communication in and around organizations: A critical hermeneutic approach. *Academy of Management Journal*, 36, 6, 1547–1576.

Prasad, A. 2002. The contest over meaning: Hermeneutics as an interpretative methodology for understanding texts. *Organizational Research Methods*, 5, 1, 12–33.

———. 2005. *Crafting Qualitative Research. Working in the Postpositivist Traditions.* Armonk, NY: M.E. Sharpe.

Prior, L. 2003. *Using Documents in Social Research.* London: Sage.

Robinson, M. and Kalakota, R. 2004. *Offshore Outsourcing. Business Models, ROI and Best Practices.* Alpharetta, GA: Mivar Press.

Ross, A. and Chiasson, M.W. 2005. A call to (dis)order: An ethnomethodological study of information technology "disruptions" in the courtroom. *Information and Organization*, 15, 203–227.

Schultze, U. and Boland, R.J.J. 2000. Place, space and knowledge work: A study of outsourced computer systems administrators. *Accounting, Management and Information Technologies*, 10, 187–219.

Searle, J.R. 1969. *Speech Acts: An Essay in the Philosophy of Language.* London: Cambridge University Press.

Silva, L.O. 2002. Outsourcing as an improvisation: A case study in Latin America." *Information Society*, 18, 2, 129–138.

Specht, E.K. 1969. *The Foundations of Wittgenstein's Late Philosophy.* New York: Barnes and Noble.

Strati, A. 1998. Organizational symbolism as a social construction: A perspective from the sociology of knowledge. *Human Relations*, 51, 11, 1379–1402.

Styhre, A. 2004. Rethinking knowledge: A Bergsonian critique of the notion of tacit knowledge. *British Journal of Management*, 15, 177–188.

Tsoukas, H. 2005. Afterword: Why language matters in the analysis of organizational change. *Journal of Organizational Change Management*, 18, 1, 96–104.

Willcocks, L.; Fitzgerald, G.; and Lacity, M. 1996. To outsource IT or not? Recent research on economics and evaluation practice. *European Journal of Information Systems*, 5, 3, 143–160.

Willcocks, L.P. and T. Kern. 1998. IT Outsourcing as strategic partnering: The case of the UK inland revenue. *European Journal of Information Systems*, 7, 1, 29–45.

Wittgenstein, L. 1968. *Philosophical Investigations.* Oxford, UK: Blackwell.

PART II

THE SOURCING DECISION

CHAPTER 5

A METHODOLOGY FOR IT SOURCING DECISIONS

WILLIAM R. KING

Abstract: *An IT sourcing framework is presented that relies on concepts from the resource-based theory of the firm and from industrial economics. The framework may be used by a group of executives to guide them in deciding among the broad alternatives of outsourcing, insourcing, internal markets, and strategic alliances as sourcing options. The framework requires a team to assess an activity in terms of its criticality (critical success factor) and its core nature (core competence) in two different temporal contexts. Once this has been done, the framework serves to identify a "working option" that is appropriate for the situation and also the inevitable consequences (which are sometimes unrecognized) and the likely issues that will materialize if the working option is selected (which often are unrecognized). By working through this framework, a management group can identify a sourcing option in terms of the most salient criteria, understand the option better and identify costs, issues, and payoffs that may otherwise be difficult to foresee.*

Keywords: *Core Competence, Critical Success Factor, Insourcing, Internal Markets, Outsourcing, Strategic Alliances*

A sourcing decision for any information technology (IT) activity must be based on the answer to a key question: Is the activity that is being considered for a change in sourcing an element of an IT capability that might currently be, or have the potential to be, a core competence and/or a critical success factor for the organization?

This is a simply stated but complex criterion involving two constructs—critical success factor (CSF) and core competence (CC)—and both current and predicted temporal contexts.

In applying this criterion, as suggested here, a group of executives should begin the sourcing decision process by taking an activity that is being considered for a sourcing decision, and make judgments concerning the degree to which it is, or may become, an organizational critical success factor as well as the degree to which it is, or may become, an organizational core competence. This chapter provides a framework that builds on such judgments by suggesting an appropriate "working option" as well as the sometimes-unrecognized inevitable consequences of selecting that option and the issues that are likely to arise if it is chosen. Thus, the framework requires managers to make specific key judgments and then directs them on a path of thinking that will enable them to fully explore the consequences of these judgments.

The framework provides guidance to managers, but it does not provide "answers." If the consequences and issues raised by using the framework make the working option undesirable, the framework can be used to consider other options as well. It is meant to stimulate thinking along paths that might otherwise go unexplored, and in so doing, provide the basis for a clearer and more comprehensive formulation of the sourcing decision. It makes use of many "academic" concepts and relationships; however, it has been developed in a series of real-world contexts by the author during his work as a consultant.

AN IT SOURCING FRAMEWORK

Table 5.1 provides the framework for guiding executives in making an IT sourcing decision. It anticipates that an organization's relevant managers will develop an initial evaluation of the activity being considered for a change in sourcing in terms of the two key constructs—CSF and CC—at both a present and predicted future time. Then, the row of the table corresponding to that preliminary assessment should be entered.

The various columns of the table for the row that is designated by the preliminary judgment concerning CSF and CC in the two temporal contexts indicates a "working option" for a sourcing approach as well as a rationale for, and salient consequences of, choosing the option. This working option is the one that logically follows from the preliminary judgments that have been made concerning the activity's current and potential criticality and its current and potential core nature. The working option, its rationale, and these consequences should be carefully analyzed, discussed, and considered before a final sourcing decision is made.

When this approach has been used in practice, it has been done with a group of information systems (IS) and non-IS executives meeting regularly. Typically, using the table as a guide, as a stimulant for discussion, and as a preliminary source of issues, such a group develops a broader and deeper set of possible ramifications and consequences of their decision. Then, the group can do studies or convene other groups to consider these issues before arriving at an overall judgment on a best sourcing option.

Sometimes, this process has led to a reevaluation of the initial judgment that was made in terms of CSFs and CCs, and therefore to the identification of a new working sourcing option. More typically, when the initial judgment has been rendered carefully, it leads to a rich set of issues and potential problems that can be useful both in selecting the best sourcing option and in pursuing its successful implementation.

To explain the framework of Table 5.1 in detail, we first develop a specification of the salient constructs—core competencies and critical success factors—and then specify the nature of the alternatives to outsourcing that various rows of the table suggest should be considered. Finally, we give a detailed exposition of each row of the table in order to explain its use.

Core Competencies

The notion of a core competency is fundamental to the resource-based view of the firm (Wernerfelt, 1984), but it is more widely discussed than it is understood (Quinn and Hilmer, 1994). Barthélémy and Adsit (2003) argue that core competencies are the resources and capabilities of the organization that are valuable, difficult to imitate, and difficult to substitute. In particular, to qualify as a core competency, a strategic capability—one that is closely related to the strategy that the organization is pursuing—should do the following (King, 1994, 1995a, 1995b):

- have evolved slowly through collective learning and information sharing;
- be incapable of being readily enhanced through additional investment;
- be synergistic with other capabilities;
- not be readily duplicable by others;
- not be readily transferable to others;
- play a role in creating a competitive advantage.

Table 5.1

Framework for Information System (IS) Sourcing Decision Process

If an IS activity is assessed to be:	"Working" option to be considered	Rationale for suggested option	Implications (actions required)	Other issues
Not currently or potentially a core competence or a critical success factor (CSF)	• Outsource	• Why do it?	• Develop contract negotiations and management capability • Need for baseline and benchmark measures • Need for vendor monitoring	• Loss of control • Loss of expertise • Create a competitor • Create a technological ceiling • Risk • Develop a "partner" relationship
Currently a CSF *and* a core competence	• Insource	• Preserve • Continue to improve/develop	• Invest • Cost/benefit (C/B) and risk assessment	• Feasibility of improving through reengineering, new incentives, and so on • C/B assessment
Currently a critical success factor and *not* currently a core competence	• Use insourcing or any other option to develop	• Mandatory development	• Integrate into strategic capabilities architecture • Investment required	• Feasibility and C/B assessment • Risk of other-than-insourcing strategies • Viability of the business
Currently a core competence and a *potential* CSF	• Internal markets	• Refine capability • Continue to improve/develop • Develop necessary scale	• Develop internal markets infrastructure • Develop plan for transformation to internal markets	• Feasibility • Fit with culture • Fit with incentives

(continued)

Table 5.1 *(continued)*

If an IS activity is assessed to be:	"Working" option to be considered	Rationale for suggested option	Implications (actions required)	Other issues
Potential core competence *and potential* CSF	• Strategic alliance	• Secure complementary skills for development	• Develop project management system	• Impact on the culture • Risk • Potential for losses to exceed gains of expertise and information
	(or) • Internal markets	• Provide scale for development • Develop plan for transformation	• Develop internal markets infrastructure • Fit with culture and incentive system	• Feasibility
	(or) • Monitor	• Obtain further information	• Secure and develop sources of information and perform timely reassessment	• Cost/benefit of waiting to decide

Source: Adapted from King (2001).

Clearly, the conventional "CC" view of activity sourcing is that if an activity meets these criteria, it is a core competence and should not be outsourced. If it is a "commodity"—loosely speaking, something that does not meet any, or most, of the core competency criteria—it may be considered for outsourcing (Hancox and Hackney, 2000; Insinga, 2000; King, 2001; Quinn and Hilmer, 1994).

However, today's information technologies are so integrated into business processes that it may not be possible to clearly distinguish between what is core and what is not core (Earl, 1996). Also, most IS functions have some elements that belong to the core and some that do not (Barthélémy and Adsit, 2003). Thus, it may not be a simple exercise to separate core from noncore activities when deciding about the "outsourcability" of any IS activity. As a result, various studies have suggested that at times organizations may tend to outsource broad IT activities, part of which may happen to be a core competency (Hancox and Hackney, 2000; McLellan, Marcolin, and Beamish, 1995).

Critical Success Factors

Loosely speaking, critical success factors are those attributes that generally lead to success in a business. The notion is imprecise, but it has long been recognized that there are generally a small number of activities that, if exhibited or performed well, will create the opportunity for success (Rockart, 1979). Conversely, organizations that do not possess these attributes or perform these functions well will often not be successful.

More precisely, CFSs are necessary, but not sufficient, for success in a particular business context. Success at a CSF, or a set of CSFs, enables an enterprise or unit to compete for the prize, but it does not guarantee that it will win it.

The CSF notion has been widely used in IS contexts, such as IS strategic planning (Bullen, 1995; Pollalis and Grant, 1994; Rockart and Earl, 1996). Here, it is applied in the context of IS sourcing.

Because CSFs may be identified at the industry, market, business, or organizational levels, in this framework, criteria that are based on the CSF notion offer the opportunity for the inclusion of external factors that transcend the internally oriented resource-based view.

Core Competencies and Critical Success Factors

Although the notions of a core competency and a critical success factor emanate, respectively, from the resource-based and industrial economics views of business, they are not mutually exclusive in their application.

First, although CCs have an internal focus that CSFs may not, they can coincide—for example, a core competence may be a critical success factor. Indeed, this may be thought of as an important goal of management—that is, to create core competencies that are, or can be, critical success factors.

This relationship between the two criteria forms the basis for the initial phase of the process and the use of the framework.

SOURCING OPTIONS

The options that are dealt with in the methodology of using Table 5.1 require some explanation. The broad alternatives that are considered are outsourcing, insourcing, strategic alliances, and internal markets. Although each of these may have a range of possible forms, this set is sufficiently diverse to offer a rich basis for making a strategic choice.

Outsourcing

Outsourcing is the use of external agents to perform activities; usually those that were previously performed within the organization. Because IS is the third largest corporate expense category and about 50 percent of U.S. capital expenditures by business are in IS/IT, the potential for IT outsourcing is huge.

IS outsourcing is generally done for cost savings (Loh and Venkatraman, 1992), to achieve a better focus on "core" businesses (Grover and Teng, 1993), or because the internal IS function is considered to be inefficient, ineffective, or technically not fully competent (Lacity and Hirschheim, 1993).

The primary rationale for outsourcing is based on the antithetical concepts of "commodity" versus "core competency." If an IS activity can be considered to be a commodity—something that is widely available and more or less the same from whomever it is purchased—it is argued that there is little justification for performing the activity internally. In such a case, a specialist vendor may normally be able to provide the service, perhaps at a higher level of quality, a lower level of cost, or both (Quinn and Hilmer, 1994).

As the argument for outsourcing goes, the business enterprise should outsource "commodity" activities and focus its attention and energy on its "core competencies"—a notion that is intuitively appealing, but is often only imprecisely defined.

In many enterprises, IS has historically been thought of as a service activity rather than a core competency; so it is often considered to be a prime candidate for outsourcing.

Insourcing

Insourcing, as the term is used here, simply means that the enterprise performs the function internally, thereby incurring all of the relevant fixed and administrative costs in addition to the variable costs of the activity. When IS is insourced, it is often handled on a "charge back" basis to the user organization with somewhat arbitrary transfer prices being applied (King, 1995b). In an era in which the reduction of investment and fixed-cost levels is a way of managerial life and in which employee benefits are viewed as exorbitantly expensive, there is great appeal to the idea of trading the fixed and variable costs of conducting an activity internally and the contentiousness that is often associated with transfer pricing, for the presumably lower, fixed, and readily predictable costs of a long-term outsourcing contract.

However, the choice of the insourcing option need not be associated with the status quo. The reengineering of development processes should be considered in assessing this option as should the providing of new incentives to departments and groups to conduct their activities more productively.

Strategic Alliances

Strategic alliances are activities conducted jointly by two or more organizations. There are various formal/legal ways in which this may be done, such as through a joint venture. The primary basis for a strategic alliance is the ability of one "partner" to provide a capability, asset, or service that complements those provided by the other partner, and the simultaneous inability, or lack of desire, of each enterprise to provide or develop the complementary capabilities on their own.

Strategic alliances, if well conceived, designed, and implemented can be classic "win-win" situations for both partners, because the joint activity can operate at a high level of effectiveness and efficiency because of the synergies among the complementary activities and capabilities of the participants. The parties to the alliance can also moderate their investment and risk versus those that would be required to perform the activity internally.

The potential problems associated with strategic alliances have to do with the difficulties in administering a complex activity involving participants from two or more cultures and the possibility that more information and knowledge will be taken away by the partner than will be gained.

Although some outsourcing ventures are often referred to as "alliances," true alliances involve the creation of a joint, focused activity rather than a vendor–client relationship such as is the norm in conventional IT outsourcing.

Internal Markets

Internal markets are organizational structures within which activities such as IS operate to provide services both within the enterprise and outside it (King, 1995b). By having a unit sell its services on the open market, it is expected that it will be forced to provide a competitive level of quality and price—something that is difficult to ensure when the unit is operating internally and providing services only internally on a noncompetitive basis.

The internal markets approach is a way of allowing external market forces to operate within the enterprise, so that a unit such as IS must effectively compete or go "bankrupt," much as a business enterprise is forced to do (Ackoff, 1993; Halal, 1993).

One of the major appeals of this approach is that many of the arbitrary and subjective aspects of evaluating and rewarding an internal unit are avoided, because each is rewarded on the basis of the revenues and profits that it can generate. The unit need not suffer the derogatory opinions that managers often hold concerning the quality of in-house service providers. Managers who are unhappy with the price or service level that they are getting from an internal unit in an internal markets situation are free to look elsewhere for the service. Similarly, the service provider is not forced to agree to an arbitrary transfer price for services; rather, the unit can price at the market levels at which it can attract internal and external clients.

USING THE METHODOLOGY TO SUPPORT A SOURCING DECISION

The framework for selecting an IS sourcing strategy is outlined in Table 5.1. The process that supports the framework is one in which a group of managers judgmentally makes a series of evaluations. The evaluations may be made on the basis of consensus judgment, analysis of data, or both. In implementations of the framework and process, it has been typical that the group discussions adjourn from time to time so that additional data may be collected and analyses performed. Thus, the framework provided in Table 5.1 supports and guides a judgmental decision-making process that involves five steps.

Identify and Make a Preliminary Assessment of the Activity Under Consideration

The first step of the process is performed to identify an IS activity that is at issue—for example, one that is not performing adequately or one that has been proposed for outsourcing—and to preliminarily assess the activity in terms of a key question: Is the activity, in and of itself, or in terms of the role that it plays in a broader organizational capability, a current or potential critical success factor and/or a current or potential core competence?

The preliminary assessment of an element is made in terms of the two criteria—CC and

CSF—each at one of three levels: "not currently or potentially," "currently," or "not currently, but potentially." In other words, each element may be assessed to be either "not currently or potentially a core competence," "currently a core competence," or "not currently, but potentially, a core competence." It should also be assessed as being either "not currently or potentially a CSF," "currently a CSF," or "not currently, but potentially, a CSF."

Nine theoretical possibilities may result from this preliminary assessment. However, four of them are illogical or infeasible and are not considered in the framework.

In taking the resource-based view that is necessary for the core competence element of the preliminary assessment, the following questions should be addressed:

- Is the activity in question itself a strategic capability?
- If not, is it a component of an existing strategic capability?
- If not, is it likely to be required as a component of a future strategic capability?
- Is it, or should it be, a core competence?

As previously noted, these questions are not amenable to simple "yes or no" answers. In some instances, firms have taken the core competency criteria outlined earlier and used them as items in an overall core competency measure—for instance, by associating seven-point scales with each criterion and having a variety of people rate the activity in terms of the criteria. Finally, they are either aggregated into an overall "score" or depicted as a profile of the mean and range of scores for each criterion.

The initial assessments of whether an activity is a current or potential CSF provides a broader industrial economics-based perspective on an activity's current and potential importance. The key questions in this phase are as follows. What have been the CSFs in this business/industry/market? What changes are likely in the array of CSFs for the foreseeable future? In many instances, these questions are more susceptible to "yes or no" answers than those that are used to address the CC concept, but there will invariably be extensive discussion needed in order to arrive at a consensus.

These questions motivate the participating executives to analyze the business and what is important for success in it, rather than to simply dismiss a "service" area such as IS on a casual historical basis as has so often been done in making outsourcing decisions.

These preliminary assessments will typically require considerable discussion and some data gathering and analysis. Once the preliminary assessment has been made, the relevant row of Table 5.1 is identified and the table comes directly into play.

Use the Framework to Identify the Sourcing Option to Be Initially Considered

Once a preliminary assessment has been made and used to identify a row in Table 5.1, the framework identifies a prime candidate, or "working" option, that is consistent with the assessment. For instance, if the assessment is that the activity is "currently a core competence and potentially a CSF," which corresponds to the fourth row of Table 5.1, the entry in the second column suggests that the initial focus should be on the "internal markets" working option.

Use the Framework to Guide the Development of a Rationale for the "Working" Sourcing Choice

The third step is to use Table 5.1 to develop the initial statement of a rationale for the "working" sourcing choice. Very brief rationales that are meant to be suggestive are provided in the third column of the table. For instance, in column 3 of row 4 the rationale for the "internal markets" strategy suggests the need to refine the capacity and to continue to improve and develop it. The logic of this rationale is that the activity is clearly important to the organization because it is a core competence, and that it could become critical in the future because it is a potential CSF. Thus, logic suggests that although it does not require mandated ("full speed ahead") development, it would be prudent to continue its evolutionary development in a cost-effective fashion. The internal markets approach is such a cost-effective approach since it leads to a new revenue stream and to new internal pricing that allows prudent investment and development.

If the suggested option brief and rationale makes sense to the group that is participating, the group will often create a more elaborate and sophisticated statement of the rationale as a means of focusing their thinking and communicating to others.

Consider the Organizational Implications of the Working Sourcing Option

The fourth step in the process is to use the framework to suggest the *nearly certain organizational implications* of the working strategy. These implications emanate from "lessons learned" in a variety of circumstances in which this sourcing strategy has been adopted. For instance, in row 4, the working sourcing option is "Internal markets," and the fourth column of the table suggests the need to develop an internal markets infrastructure (King, 1995b). The organization implications in this column are the direct and certain consequences of selecting this sourcing strategy. Others may be suggested by the group that are reflective of the client firm's unique situation.

Use the Framework to Suggest Other Issues That May Arise

The fifth step in implementing the framework is reflected in the fifth column of Table 5.1. For instance, if the fourth row is the one that has been entered, this column also identifies "lessons learned" from the choice of the internal markets strategy in various firms. The issues in this column are different from those in the previous one in that they represent possibilities that *may* ensue if this sourcing strategy is selected. In this case, the issues relate to the feasibility of the working strategy and its "fit" with the organization's existing culture and incentives.

Alternatively, if the first row is the one that has been entered, the fourth column suggests that the "outsource" option will create the need for the contract negotiation and management capability, the need for baseline and benchmark measures and measurement processes, and the need for vendor monitoring. The fifth column in this row identifies some issues that may need to be addressed—such as the possible loss of control, loss of expertise, and risk.

SUMMARY OF USING THE METHODOLOGY

Table 5.1 thereby provides the basis for a five-step framework for identifying an option and for testing and exploring the implications of the preliminary assessment of an activity that is being considered for a new sourcing choice. At any phase of the process, it may be determined that the working option is inappropriate; in which case, another preliminary assessment should be made or another row of the table should be considered. When this occurs, there is great value in developing a statement, similar to that which represents the rationale for the working strategy. In the rare cases in which this has been done, such a statement—basically, one that argues why the initial working option is not the best one—is very useful in bringing a group to consensus and in communicating with others. Most often, the consideration of the various issues that are raised as the group proceeds across a row may serve to validate the working strategy to be both feasible and desirable.

Detailed Description of the Framework

Table 5.1 represents the overall framework that guides the process just described. The rows of the table, which reflect various preliminary assessments of an activity that is being reviewed, will now be described. Each row is referred to by its associated working strategy or some other familiar term. However, each row is, in fact, identified by the assessment of its status as a core competency and CSF, as is indicated parenthetically.

The Outsourcing Working Option (Not Currently or Potentially a Core Competence or a CSF)

In the first row, the IS activity at issue is shown to have been preliminarily assessed to be neither a current CSF nor a core competency—that is, it is neither necessary to business success nor something that is a core element of business competence. In addition, it is assessed as not likely to become either in the foreseeable future.

The second column of the first row shows the prime candidate, or "working," sourcing option that is suggested for consideration, given this assessment of the activity. In the case of an IS activity that is so viewed, the first row suggests that outsourcing is the prime candidate for consideration.

The third column shows the succinct rationale for the suggested choice. Because the activity has been preliminarily assessed to be neither a current or potential core competence nor a current or potential CSF, the rationale is simply stated as, "Why do it?" which means that the activity can probably be procured externally at a higher level of quality or a lower cost than can be achieved internally. (The importance of this succinct rationale will be made clear later as more expansive use of the framework is illustrated.)

The fourth column shows the direct implications of the tentative choice. For instance, in the first row, the implication is described as "develop contract negotiations and management capability." This is an essential implication of the choice of outsourcing because the firm choosing this option will necessarily become engaged in managing an outsourcing contract. Most IS outsourcing contracts are large in financial terms and most involve many complexities, such as the procedures for, and costing of, the transfer of software licenses, so that active contract management is required. Most long-term contracts also involve updating and changes over time. Such changes must be actively managed in terms of ongoing requirements, cost, and performance assessments of the vendor (King, 1994).

The "need for baseline and benchmark measures" is also indicated as an implication of choosing this option since effective contract management will require that existing (baseline) service levels and realistic goals (benchmark levels) be established in advance. This will enable the vendor's service level to be measured and monitored over time.

The first row of the framework thereby initially confirms the "commodities should be outsourced" conventional wisdom as something to be considered, but it goes beyond that to show the consequences of this selection. It may be that the need to develop a contract management capability could result in the rethinking of the tentative choice of outsourcing. Are the savings to be expected from outsourcing worth the costs that must be incurred in creating a new contract management function, for instance? Because getting out of the IS "business" means getting into the contract management "business," is there really much to be gained or are the savings promised by the outsourcing vendor likely to be overshadowed by the costs and complexities of a new activity?

Alternately, an awareness of the need for baseline and benchmark measures and for a monitoring system could result in a postponing of the sourcing decision until such measures are developed.

Other possible unintended consequences of the preliminary choice are suggested in the last column of Table 5.1. For the (first row) outsourcing option, for instance, the "other issues" illustrated are as follows:

- Will there be a significant loss of control? What will be the implications of this?
- Will there be a loss of critical IS expertise that will preclude us from ever doing anything but outsourcing this activity even if it were to become more critical to us?
- Is there the risk of creating a competitor by allowing a vendor to perform this activity for us?
- Will outsourcing of IS create a technological "ceiling" that will limit us in the future?
- What risks are involved in choosing this option?
- Will we need to develop a partner relationship with the vendor? How difficult/desirable will this be?

These issues are derived from research results and "lessons learned" from outsourcing. They are meant to be a starting point of the identification of other issues that should be developed by the organizational participants, perhaps using "brainstorming" or another similar process (Schweiger, Sandberg, and Ragan, 1986) or by studying the increasing body of published experiences with outsourcing (Caldwell, 1995; Caldwell and McGee, 1996; DeRose, 1997; Due, 1992; Kaiser and Hawk, 2004; Kotabe and Murray, 2004).

Based on the preliminary assessment that is made in terms of an activity's current and prospective role as a CSF or core competency, each row of Table 5.1 thereby provides the decision makers with a prime candidate option and simple rationale, and places them in a position to ratify the suggested choice or to conclude that the implementation requirements and the possible unintended consequences and derivative issues are so serious that the prime candidate should be reconsidered. In effect, it identifies some of the considerations that go beyond the simple rationale for the alternative, thus, allowing the decision makers to make a more sophisticated and comprehensive judgment than would otherwise be possible.

The Insourcing Working Option (Currently a CSF and a Core Competence)

Insourcing is the working strategy to be considered, according to the second row of Table 5.1, when an activity is preliminarily assessed to be both a current core competence (according to the criteria given previously) and a current critical success factor.

In this instance, the insourcing alternative is the prime candidate that is suggested based on the need to preserve and to continue to improve and to develop the activity. Insourcing is preliminarily indicated to offer the best opportunity to conduct the activity within the confines of the organization so that unique or critical expertise will not inadvertently be shared with others and so that critical professional competence can be developed to the fullest extent and under organizational control.

Among the actions that are implied by the suggested insourcing alternative is the need to make further investments in the activity, so that it can be improved and further developed, the need to do a cost/benefit and risk assessment of the investment options, and the need to integrate the activity into an architecture of strategic capabilities, because this is the best way to defend it against duplication by competitors (King, 1995a).

The issues derived from lessons learned from insourcing that are suggested for the insourcing option in the second row involve the feasibility of improving and further developing the activity, such as through the use of reengineering or new incentive systems, and the cost/benefit assessment of doing so. In some instances, it may be the case that the activity has been so highly developed and refined that further improvements are extremely costly. In such an instance, the desirability of the preliminarily suggested insourcing option might be questioned.

The Mandatory Development Working Option (Currently a CSF but Not Currently a Core Competence)

The third row of Table 5.1 deals with the situation in which the activity in question is assessed to be a current CSF, but not a current core competence.

This preliminary assessment suggests "Mandatory development," probably through insourcing as the prime candidate. However, the framework indicates that any available strategy should be employed to develop the activity, making whatever investment is required. This is the case because success in the underlying business is, by definition, problematic unless the activity is more fully developed. Although insourcing is the preferred prime candidate for all of the reasons previously discussed for the situation in the second row of the table, further development of the activity is so critical that any potential strategy must be considered, however risky it may be.

Because investment, perhaps massive in scale, is indicated in this case, the primary issue is the feasibility of developing the capability to the required level in the timeframe that is contemplated. If the insourcing option is not feasible, the risk involved in other options needs to be considered. Since they are of secondary importance for this situation, these risks will be further discussed below where they are of greater importance.

If feasibility is deemed to be uncertain regardless of the option chosen, some basic decisions may be dictated concerning the desirability of being in a "business" in which one's ability to succeed, in terms of CSFs, is questionable.

The Internal Markets Working Option (Currently a Core Competence and a Potential CSF)

The fourth row of Table 5.1 deals with the preliminary assessment of an activity to be a current core competence, and a potential (but not current) critical success factor.

This is likely to be the situation for some IS activities in many firms in which IS has moved from a pure service function to being a more integral element of business operations. For instance, some firms have integrated IS with their products in terms of warranty and service systems, automatic product problem-diagnosis systems, and training systems. IS may be assessed to have the potential to be a CSF in such instances because the integration of IS may change the nature of the product or the basis for competition.

The "internal markets" organizational option is suggested as the prime candidate in this situation because there is the need to refine, improve, and further develop the activity. However, there is no imperative to massively invest. The internal markets approach offers the opportunity for development without great investment. In effect, in this circumstance, external market opportunities would be pursued to generate greater scale for the activity, more resources for its further development, and a broader scope of experience with it.

The action implied by this choice is the development of an internal markets infrastructure that is at least adequate to support a single, perhaps prototypical, activity that is being managed in this fashion (King, 1995b). Also critical to the success of this option is the development of a plan for the transformation to the internal markets mode of doing business.

The issues suggested by this alternative reflect the impact on the culture and the existing incentive systems in the organization. For instance, is the change and the planned pace of change feasible? Can the established culture accommodate to the radically different management styles and processes that are inherent in internal markets? Can the leadership of the activity become more entrepreneurial? Can the incentives that are required for an entrepreneurial internal markets situation coexist with the organization's existing incentive systems?

The "Potential" Working Option (Potential Core Competence and Potential CSF)

The last row of Table 5.1 describes the most complex situation in which IS is preliminarily assessed to be both a potential CSF and a potential core competence. Because this is the least certain of all of the circumstances, it is not surprising that several options need to be preliminarily considered. The general circumstance is one in which the enterprise would not wish to unduly commit resources because of the level of uncertainty; yet, it wishes to further develop the activity because of its future potential as both a CSF and a core competency.

The first sourcing option that should be considered for this case is the one in which a strategic alliance would be developed to provide complementary resources, skills of funding to facilitate future development of the activity. In this instance, the development of a project management system (Cleland and King, 1988) will be required to manage the joint effort.

A resultant issue of considering the impact on the organizational culture is identified because project management is a radically different management process from traditional hierarchical management. Also, assessing the risks that are inherent in any strategic alliance, such as that of greater loss than gain of information and expertise, is indicated.

The second working option to be considered in the case of this preliminary assessment is that of internal markets. This option would serve to provide sufficient scale for the development of the IS activity with modest investment. The remaining columns of the table for this working strategy are the same as those for the internal markets strategy that emanates from another preliminary assessment (row 4).

The last working option for consideration under this preliminary assessment is the one in which the uncertainty is deemed to be so great that a "wait-and-see" approach is suggested. In this case, a firm would be waiting to obtain additional information that will resolve some of the uncertainty inherent in the "potential" of the activity that is both a core competence and a CSF. The action indicated is to ensure that mechanisms are in place for obtaining and assessing these data so that a choice can be made as soon as it is indicated.

The issue that has been identified from "lessons learned" in this latter instance is the need to actually obtain the required information and reconsider the cost/benefit assessment in a timely fashion. Because deferring a choice is such an "easy" way to resolve a difficult issue, it may be wise to allow some time to pass and then to formally reconsider the choice of this "procrastination" option once it has been preliminarily adopted. Otherwise "wait-and-see" may become a "hide-one's-head-in-the-sand-and-hope-it-will-go-away" reality.

THE BENEFITS OF USING THE FRAMEWORK AND PROCESS

The framework and process may be used to support the judgment of an individual decision maker. However, it has been found to be most valuable as a guide to decision making in a group or team setting. In such an instance, the initial judgments may be approached jointly and systematically. When this is done, it is often the case that preconceived notions about such concepts as core competencies and CSFs may be called into question, since the explication and questioning of implicit assumptions often demonstrate that long-held "truths" are no longer valid.

IS activities are more likely to be assessed positively as the criteria are delved into in depth, because in many organizations IS does not constitute a strategic capability, or even a key component of a strategic capability. However, there are many organizations in which it may well be critical to an evolving or future strategic capability.

This has been found to be one of the primary benefits of using the process and framework, because it focuses attention on the future rather than on the past and on the desired "architecture" of strategic capabilities for the organization (King, 1995a). These assessments, when addressed in an open and creative forum, have been found to shed new light on the role and value of IS activities and to create new understandings in the minds of the participating executives.

Once a preliminary judgment has been made in terms of the activity's role as a CSF and core competence, the appropriate row in Table 5.1 should be identified. The rationale suggested in the third column of the table reflects the logic of the assessment. However, the validity of the rationale that is presented should be tested in the group decision process before it proceeds further. For instance, the preliminary strategy statement and rationale may call the results of the previous step into question and the group may decide to revisit the criteria of core competency and CSF to make reassessments in light of the stated rationale.

This reflects the values of the framework and process in that they represent a combination of the following:

- judgments that must be made in terms of specific, well-defined criteria;
- both certain and possible implications of those judgments that are provided by the framework;
- opportunities for reassessment of previously made judgments;
- suggestions for beginning a creative process of attempting to identify uncertain and unforeseen consequences of a tentatively chosen action.

The latter benefit primarily relates to the items presented in the last column of the table. Once the direct implications of the choice of the working strategy have been considered, the "other issues" that represent less certain and perhaps unintended consequences of the strategy should be considered and used as a starting point for developing a more comprehensive list of such issues. Once such a list has been created, even though each item on the list is speculative, it represents a "picture" of the risk profile of the strategy. As such, it may be factored into the final selection of a sourcing strategy.

One simple but important element presented by the framework is the rationale for the working strategy. The development of a simple explanation, or rationale, for the preliminarily chosen strategy is consistent with the management adage that "anything that requires a complex justification is probably not well understood." However, an important reason for having the rationale, whether it is the one provided in the framework or some other version of it, is to record the basis for the preliminary selection of this alternative. Such a record may be necessary because some committed people may be prone to ignoring the basis for their choice as time passes. For instance, when unintended consequences are identified that may call into question the reasons that the preliminary choice was made, advocates of that strategy may be prone to shifting their argument to some other rationale. This is a well-known decision-making phenomenon (Hammond, Keeney, and Raiffa, 1998), and it may be readily addressed through the simple device of having everyone initially commit to a stated rationale for the preliminary strategy option.

This is one reason that the very brief rationale given in the table should be expanded on, if only minimally. This provides an "ownership" of the rationale that makes it more difficult to switch away from it later.

The significance of the judgments that are involved in identifying the requirements and implications of that preliminary choice—in the last two columns of Table 5.1—should be readily understood. Those that are listed in Table 5.1 are derived from "lessons learned" in instances in which the working option has been adopted. Nonetheless, they represent only illustrations that should drive the discussion and identification of other possible requirements and implications. Collectively, these requirements and implications can serve to verify that the working strategy is the correct choice, or they can call into question the merits of proceeding with an option that may preliminarily be indicated. In this latter case, the benefit is clear, since many such options that initially appear to be "no brainers" have turned out badly.

REFERENCES

Ackoff, R.L. 1993. Corporate perestroika: The internal markets economy. In W.E. Halal, A. Geranmayeh, and J. Pourdehnad, eds. *Internal Markets: Bringing the Power of Free Enterprise INSIDE Your Organization*. New York: Wiley, 15–26.

Barthélémy, J. and Adsit, D. 2003. The seven deadly sins of outsourcing. *Academy of Management Executive*, 17, 2, 87–100.

Bullen, C.V. 1995. Reexamining productivity CSFs: The knowledge worker challenge. *Information Systems Management*, 12, 3, 13–18.

Caldwell, B. 1995. Outsourcing megadeals. *InformationWeek*, 552, 34–52.

Caldwell, B. and McGee, M.K. 1996. DuPont goes outside. *InformationWeek*, 610, 14–16.

Cleland, D.I. and King, W.R. 1988. *Project Management Handbook*, 2d ed. New York: Van Nostrand-Reinhold.

DeRose, L.J. 1997. The downside to outsourcing. *Electronic Buyer News*, July, 14.

Due, R.T. 1992. The real costs of outsourcing. *Information Systems Management*, 9, 1, 78–81.

Earl, M.J. 1996. The risks of outsourcing IT. *Sloan Management Review*, 37, 3, 26–32.

Grover, V. and Teng, J.T.C. 1993. The decision to outsource information systems functions. *Journal of Systems Management*, 44, 11, 34–37.

Halal, W. E. 1993. The transition from hierarchy to . . . what? Market systems are the paradigm of information age. In W.E. Halal, A. Geranmayeh, and J. Pourdehnad, eds. *Internal Markets: Bringing the Power of Free Enterprise INSIDE Your Organization*. New York: Wiley, 27–51.

Hammond, J.S.; Keeney, R.L.; and Raiffa, H. 1998. The hidden traps in decision making. *Harvard Business Review*, 76, 5, 47–48, 50.

Hancox, M. and Hackney, R. 2000. IT outsourcing: Frameworks for conceptualizing practice and perception. *Information Systems Journal*, 10, 3, 217–238.

Insinga, R.C. 2000. Linking outsourcing to business strategy. *Academy of Management Executive*, 14, 4, 58–70.

Kaiser, K.M. and Hawk, S. 2004. Evolution of offshore software development: From outsourcing to cosourcing. *MIS Quarterly Executive*, 3, 2, 69–81.

King, W.R. 1994. Strategic outsourcing decisions. *Information Systems Management*, 11, 4, 58–61.

———. 1995a. Creating a strategic capabilities architecture. *Information Systems Management*, 12, 1, 67–69.

———. 1995b. Creating internal markets. *Information Systems Management*, 12, 2, 61–63.

———. 2001. Developing a sourcing strategy for IS: A behavioral decision process and framework. *IEEE Transactions on Engineering Management*, 48, 1, 15–24.

Kotabe, M. and Murray, J.Y. 2004. Global sourcing strategy and sustainable competitive advantage. *Industrial Marketing Management*, 33, 1, 7–14.

Lacity, M.C. and Hirschheim, R. 1993. *Information Systems Outsourcing: Myths, Metaphors and Realities*. Chichester, UK: Wiley.

Loh, L. and Venkatraman, N. 1992. Determinants of information technology outsourcing: A cross-sectional analysis. *Journal of Management Information Systems*, 9, 1, 7–24.

McLellan, K.; Marcolin, B.L.; and Beamish, P.W. 1995. Financial and strategic motivations behind IS outsourcing. *Journal of Information Technology*, 10, 4, 299–321.

Pollalis, Y. and Grant, J.H. 1994. Information resources and corporate strategy development. *Information Strategy: The Executive's Journal*, 11, 1, 12–28.

Quinn, J.B. and Hilmer, F.G. 1994. Strategic outsourcing. *Sloan Management Review*, 35, 43, 43–55.

Rockart, J.F. 1979. Chief executives define their own data needs. *Harvard Business Review*, 57, 2, 81–93.

Rockart, J.F. and Earl, M.J. 1996. Eight imperatives for the new IT organization. *Sloan Management Review*, 38, 1, 43–55.

Schweiger, D.M.; Sandberg, W.R.; and Ragan, J.W. 1986. Group approaches for improving strategic decision making: A comparative analysis of dialectical inquiry, devil's advocacy, and consensus. *Academy of Management Journal*, 29, 1, 51–71.

Wernerfelt, B. 1984. A resource-based view of the firm. *Strategic Management Journal*, 5, 2, 171–180.

CHAPTER 6

INSTITUTIONAL AND INDIVIDUAL ANTECEDENTS OF INFORMATION TECHNOLOGY SOURCING ARRANGEMENTS

PANKAJ NAGPAL AND KALLE LYYTINEN

Abstract: *In this chapter, we build on the extant research on sourcing of information technology (IT) by exploring the question: Why do similar IT activities in firms become subject to different sourcing arrangements? This question also has a bearing on empirical observations that selective sourcing is a more certain recipe for success. We seek to explain the observed variation in sourcing arrangements by exploring institutional forces that channel organizations to alternative and/or selective sourcing arrangements. We draw on institutional theories based on macro-level explanations, and examine the role of IT managers as boundary spanners at the micro level. Cost and service centers are proposed as diametrically opposite structural contexts that lead to divergent sourcing arrangements, which are a result of both institutional forces and the behavior of managers. The institutional and individual antecedents are key elements in the success of selective sourcing and other novel arrangements. Alternative relationships with IT vendors follow under cost and service center strategies.*

Keywords: *Boundary Spanner, Institutional Theory, IT Sourcing Arrangement*

INTRODUCTION

Information Technology (IT) outsourcing can be defined as "the delegation, through a contractual arrangement, of all or any part of the technical resources, human resources, and the management responsibilities associated with providing IT services to an external vendor" (Clark, Zmud, and McGray, 1995). Information system (IS) discipline has seen a large and growing body of research on this topic, with an increasing emphasis on explanation and prediction. The significance of outsourcing research has been catalyzed by the announcements of multibillion-dollar multiyear contracts, where the original Kodak arrangement with its three vendors—IBM, DEC, and Businessland Inc.—is the most well known. The role and nature of factors that influence such decisions has remained unclear and has not necessarily followed predictions offered by the extant literature.

The development of varying sourcing practices has been paralleled by researchers' interest in, and search to better understand, this complex phenomenon. As a result, outsourcing has been approached through multiple theoretical lenses from a number of reference disciplines (Hui and Beath, 2001). The most popular approaches have been the resource-based view (RBV), transaction cost economics (TCE), and agency theory. Although there has been work on the development of constructs (Aubert, Rivard, and Patry, 1994), there is limited explanation (Nagpal, 2004) of sourcing phenomena. While interest in sociological approaches is more recent, IS researchers have expanded their scope of theoretical analysis to social/relational, exchange, institutional, and power theories to understand the impact of relationships between IS and business managers or the significance of the social context (Ye and Agarwal, 2003) in explaining outsourcing arrangements and their outcomes. Overall, there has been less interest in investigating the role of institutional environments and fields (Tolbert and Zucker, 1983) in shaping sourcing practices.

It is widely believed that the Kodak outsourcing contract—announced in 1989—was a watershed event. In this contract, Kodak's IT operations were taken over by three vendors: IBM, DEC, and Businessland Inc. Given the size and reputation of Kodak, other firms considering outsourcing were strongly influenced by the signal this contract communicated, thus creating the so-called Kodak effect[1] (Loh and Venkatraman, 1992). Since then, the explanations as to why and under what conditions managers commit themselves to different types of sourcing relations has varied. In this chapter we seek to answer the following question: Why do similar IT activities in firms become subject to different sourcing arrangements? This is contrary to what would be expected from explanations offered by the extant literature. The key explanations offered are differentiating pressures behind IT sourcing practices within institutional contexts, and the role of actors in different organizational environments in seeking information and proposing solutions to nagging organizational problems. In addressing this question, we also shed light on why selective sourcing is rare in spite of its success (Willcocks and Lacity, 1998). In wide-ranging studies of sourcing (Lacity and Hirschheim, 1993; Lacity and Willcocks, 1996), success rates were highest for selective sourcing—which involves outsourcing only some selected systems—versus success rates for total insourcing or outsourcing.

The chapter improves our understanding of IS outsourcing decisions by using the lens of institutional theories and the literature on boundary spanning. We will first examine the use of. institutional theory in the IS sourcing[2] literature, where scholars have studied the impact of imitative pressures (Ang and Cummings, 1997; Jayatilaka, 2002) on the buyer firms. The existing work is reviewed, and propositions put forward for future research. This constitutes a macro view of the sourcing process restricted to institutions, where the role of individual actors is not taken into consideration. Next the institutional view is complemented by micro-level analysis of actors who can influence opinions during the sourcing process. This analysis draws on the concept of boundary spanning, which examines the roles and behaviors of actors in cross-boundary contexts. A micro-level theoretical lens is added to gain greater understanding.

Institutional and boundary behaviors refer to two complementary levels of social analysis: structure and agency (Giddens, 1986). Institutional and role theories are proposed as complementary lenses to understand the interactions between structure and agency, respectively, in sourcing decisions. Forces that act in concert or opposition can show different effects depending on the context (structure). One context is characterized as a "service center" and the other, as a "cost center." Ot is more difficult to understand the behavior of actors in the setting of service centers than in the simpler "cost" centers that have been researched using economic theories. In these situations, role autonomy of the actors is subject to institutional pressures at the firm and functional levels while the individual and functional levels influence boundary-spanning behavior. We do not apply structuration theory as such,[3] but as Giddens did, we observe that the homogenizing forces of social institutions owe their genesis to structuration processes (DiMaggio and Powell, 1983).

In this chapter, we briefly review institutional theory, focusing on its analysis of isomorphic effects, and study its application to IT sourcing. We then look at the role of individuals in the sourcing process. While business and IT managers are the two broad groups emphasized in previous research, more understanding will be gained from focusing on variations in organizational structures within the IT function. We expect that "boundary spanner" IT buyer managers under different structures will adopt different roles, which will have an impact on their interactions with IT vendors. In this way, we benefit from looking at agents that have limited maneuverability, while in the institutional view the influence is limited to macro-level "straitjackets." Propositions that serve as the basis for future empirical research are presented. We also look at anecdotal and practitioner evidence to support our propositions with the available evidence.

THEORETICAL BACKGROUND

Theoretical Preliminaries

Institutional theory is based on the assumption that "the major factors that organizations must take into account are other organizations" (Aldrich, 1979). While this could also be said of neoclassical economics, what is different about institutional theory is the way organizations affect each other, that is, *through normative isomorphism as well as competition in markets.* The institutional literature has emphasized normative isomorphism while economics has focused on the competition in markets. Therefore institutional theorists look for "organizational fields" or even society as the unit of analysis in which specific isomorphisms result as an outcome of institutional forces or processes. Thus, institutional theorists explain significant organizational change as decision makers' responses to institutional pressures whereby managers unintentionally make their organizations more similar to other organizations by imitating organizations that are viewed as successful. The conditions under which imitation takes place and the types of isomorphisms have been theorized (DiMaggio and Powell, 1983) to result from three major sources: normative, mimetic, and coercive processes. These refer to influences of professionalization, "standardized responses," and regulatory pressures, respectively. They have significant implications for goal ambiguity, technical uncertainty, and the perceived role of technology in business decisions. Analysis of these processes can be expected to increase understanding of IT sourcing choices.

Application of Institutional Theory to Sourcing

A review of the IT sourcing literature reveals several schools of thought that have used ideas from institutional theory. Some studies emphasize empirical modeling (Hu, Saunders, and Gebelt, 1997; Loh and Venkatraman, 1992) that uses archival data to show how influences are shaped. More direct applications of institutional theory (Ang and Cummings, 1997; Jayatilaka, 2002) are reported where significant antecedents to sourcing outcomes are modeled after institutional theory. Given the small number of studies conducted, each paper is discussed briefly before we offer an overall summary of the impact of institutional theory in explaining sourcing behaviors. The first two papers, by Loh and Venkatraman (1992) and Hu, Saunders, and Gebelt (1997), used sophisticated modeling techniques derived from the diffusion of innovation literature. Internal, external, and mixed (both internal and external) influences were modeled separately, and the "best" fit in explaining the data was tested, using significance tests between model parameters. Loh and Venkatraman (1992) discuss their results in light of institutional theory, using imitative behavior as a theoretical basis. Hu, Saunders, and Gebelt (1997) rely on more sophisticated modeling and larger datasets to critique previous work. They conclude that internal as well as external effects are at work in diffusing the knowledge of outsourcing practices. These refer to imitative behavior (internal effect) and "external influences" such as mass media.

Ang and Cummings (1997) studied regulatory and peer-firm institutional factors, moderated by economic effects. The effects of peers and federal regulators on outsourcing were corroborated empirically. In general, coercive pressures were moderated to a lesser extent by cost/financial aspects than by mimetic ones. This moderating effect was observed for mimetic as well as coercive regulatory pressures. The authors concluded that the unbounded, discretionary strategic choice assumed in strategic thinking is limited by institutional forces. Using a two-step survey, Jayatilaka (2002) studied changes in sourcing contracts over time. Cost was an important initial criterion when buyers had limited knowledge of sourcing. However, it was generally overtaken in later stages by firm-specific criteria that resulted from learning related to sourcing arrangements. These included the need for expertise, innovation, and creation of new IS practices among vendors.

To summarize, external as well as internal pressures are important in sourcing decisions. However, it has been difficult to tease out the relative effects of internal and external influences in different contexts. The findings align well with general hypotheses derived from institutional theory, which draw upon the literature on institutional practices, and managerial insights into the phenomenon. In line with the other literature the findings particularly stress the importance of mimetic forces (Mizruchi and Fein, 1999), although the impact of both normative and coercive elements have been observed.

Propositions from Institutional Theory

Coercive, mimetic, and normative pressures, although theorized to be different, overlap significantly in empirical observations (DiMaggio and Powell, 1983). Their interplay subjects the firm to a vector of multiple and diverse pressures. In this chapter, we propose that IT organizations will differ in the major type of pressures they face depending on the context in which they face those pressures. Given the dominant effect *in that context*, it is possible to hypothesize the result with respect to IT outsourcing decisions for the firm.

We propose that IT functions will differ to the extent to which they face institutional (noncost) and economic (cost) pressures, and how they react to them. Based on this observation, IT functions can be localized into a continuum where specific institutional or economic pressures dominate. The hypothesized extremes (Figure 6.1) range from a cost-center to a service-center approach. Further, we theorize that in more complex and turbulent environments IT is more likely to be organized as a service center. Industries with higher IT investment (as a percentage of revenue or capital) are more often organized using a service-center model. Below, we present the typical characteristics of cost and service centers, drawing on anecdotal evidence. Service centers generally follow user satisfaction metrics to help assess performance. IT function will also have a service orientation in solving business needs and making itself valuable to the firm. Service centers are likely to report to top management through a chief information officer (CIO), in contrast to cost centers that would likely go through a finance function, or chief financial officer (CFO).

Given these characteristics, cost and service centers will differ in their strategies for outsourcing. Cost centers will be subject to simpler and stricter criteria largely based on comparative efficiency. These have been studied using the economic concepts of production and transaction costs (Ang and Straub, 1998) in the IS literature. However, more complex conditions to evaluate performance in service centers are underresearched. In service centers, the lack of strict measures makes IT managers more amenable to imitative pressures. At the same time, using such effects as a baseline for action and legitimacy, service centers will be shielded from being evaluated by simplistic cost-only criteria. These bases of legitimacy might be culturally supported, legally sanctioned, or morally governed (Scott, 2001). The resulting influences are mimetic, coercive, and normative. These different legitimacy concerns can also explain why firms comply differently with the needs

Figure 6.1 **Institutional Organization of Information Technology Function**

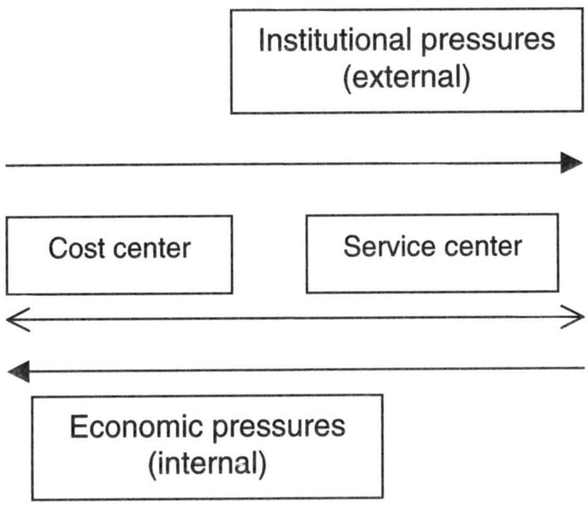

of arranging their IT services, thereby clarifying the logic of choosing their sourcing arrangements in a specific organizational field. Here, the organizational field is loosely defined as a set of IT vendors, (buyer) IT managers, and finance managers, who form key actors in the institutional life of sourcing arrangements. Although there have been examples of using well-defined institutions as a baseline to define an organizational field in the IS literature (Purvis, Sambamurthy, and Zmud, 2001), another view holds that the structure of such an organizational field is defined only empirically (Scott, 2001) for a given context. A detailed analysis of the structure and evolution of organizational fields associated with IT sourcing is beyond the scope of this chapter. Next, we will characterize the impact of each major institutional force in shaping IT sourcing arrangements under the service- versus the cost-center approach.

Mimetic Influences

In the service-center approach, the IT function is assumed to be subject to strong imitative pressures. Given the extant status of outsourcing, it implies increased pressure to outsource the "right" type of IT functions. This will hold regardless of evidence that, in fact, any efficiency gains would result from outsourcing. The need for external (to IT function) legitimation, rather than actual realization of efficiency gains, becomes important. In general, institutional pressures are driven by uncertainties about how to connect "means to ends" (DiMaggio and Powell, 1983). This uncertainty leads one to imitate similar organizations that are seen to be successful. The imitation is necessarily limited, as "actual" efficiencies are not known. Instead, imitators rely on indirect sources to form views and select their responses. Therefore, IT functions in firms where the role of technology is highly complex and not well understood (service center) will be subject to higher institutional (imitative) pressures.

Proposition 1: The more uncertain the relationship between investments in IT resources and their value to the firm, the more likely the IT function will be subject to mimetic pressure, that is, organized as a service center.

Figure 6.2 **Institutional Antecedents of Information Technology (IT) Governance**

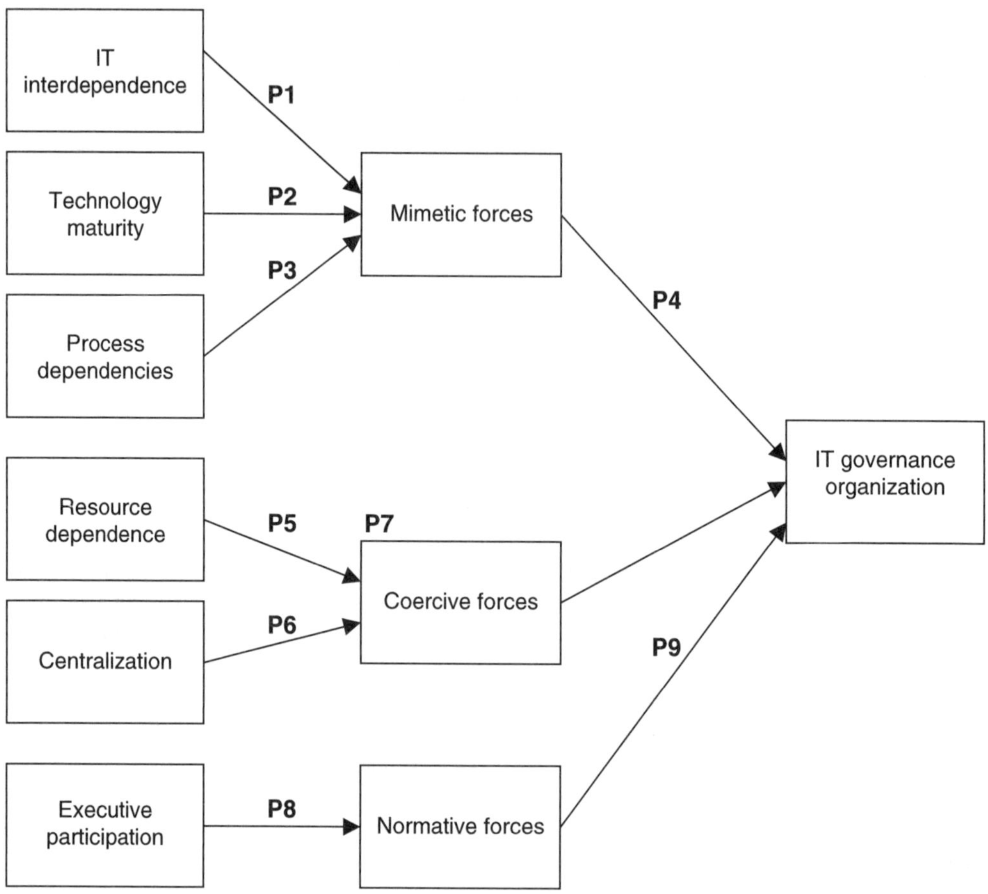

In contrast, where the relationship between input and output is well understood, the IT function is more easily held accountable for the costs. In these cases, it is more likely that the IT function will be subject to sheer cost pressure, which also drives outsourcing decisions. This would be true generally for mature technologies, where economic benchmarks are easily available and well known in the industry.

Proposition 2a: The more novel the technologies used, the more likely the IT function will be subject to mimetic pressure, that is, organized as a service center.

The more ambiguous the role of IT organization, the greater will be the mimetic pressure. In this situation, IT function will likely pursue the creation of a legitimate appearance. In general, some dependencies between IT function and the firm's activities will remain, and these are not clear with respect to the other functions. Industries in which IT has a greater role in product delivery and service configuration, such as financial services, are likely to demonstrate these behaviors.

Proposition 2b: The higher the availability of economic benchmarks and the better understood the technology, the more likely the IT function will be subject to cost pressures, that is, organized as a cost center.

In general, for new or complex technologies, it is unlikely for impact metrics to be available. As technologies diffuse, more refined benchmarks will follow, giving rise to well-known metrics of cost and usage levels and/or impact. The early deployments of a technology involve a variety of dissimilar features, which makes direct benchmarking difficult. These technologies are also used in different ways, which makes comparisons across firms difficult.

Proposition 3: The less clear the dependencies between IT and other firm processes, the more likely the IT function will be subject to mimetic pressure, that is, organized as a service center.

The above propositions indicate that higher mimetic pressures will be accompanied by a service-center style of governance in most organizational fields. The taken-for-granted nature of shared understanding among actors follows the logic of orthodoxy (Scott, 2001). In the initial stages of technology availability, a high level of ambiguity surrounds use and adoption behaviors. Accordingly, isomorphic forces move the governance mechanism toward service centers.

Proposition 4: The greater the extent of mimetic pressures, the more likely that the IT function will be organized as a service center.

Coercive Influences

Institutional pressures are a result of tight dependency relationships across organizations (DiMaggio and Powell, 1983) that control access to resources. In the following discussion, we will consider the resource controllers and dominant actors who shape these dependencies (Teo, Wei, and Benbasat, 2003). We argue that reporting relationships in the firm and the centralization of IT function can lead to different coercive pressures. In turn, the nature of these influences makes either cost or service centers more likely. The reporting relationship of the IT function with finance, other things being equal, is important here. Finance is a key function that commonly has oversight of IT investment, with the IT head reporting to the finance equivalent. The typical actors are the chief financial officer or controller and the chief information officer. In IT functions that have the CIO reporting to the CFO, there is likely to be greater pressure to follow practices that serve the interests of the finance function. It will be more difficult to justify allocation of resources, if the CIO does not follow the interests and the rationales of the finance function.

Proposition 5: The higher the dependence of the IT function on the finance function, the more likely it will be subject to coercive pressure, that is, organized as a cost center.

The centralization of IT function will also have a bearing on the coercive pressures that are exerted. The centralized organization of IT is likely to be accompanied by dependency relationships with the finance function. With an arms-length relationship between IT organization and the "user" business units in a large firm, finance function is likely to use policies such as chargeback (Ross, Vitale, and Beath, 1999) to monitor resources used in the firm. In contrast, decentralized

IT units will likely report to the business unit leadership. In this structure, they have a lower likelihood of having to justify their actions to the business managers in "cost only" terms. In a direct contact, service-related metrics will be vital to the business, and easily made visible to the divisional customers.

Proposition 6: The greater the extent of centralization of the IT function, the more likely it will be subject to coercive pressure, that is, organized as a cost center.

Coercive influences have a strong economic component that is illustrated by resource dependence and centralization structures. The logic of instrumentality, in terms of conforming to rules set by an external authority, is vital to these arrangements. The instrument is typically in the form of budgetary constraints, which are associated with incentives and sanctions. These instruments are accompanied by legitimizing elements such as audits that act as a "third party" constraint on the IT function. However, conflicts of interest are likely to weaken the effectiveness of IT function in creating long-term value.

Proposition 7: The greater the extent of coercive pressures, the more likely the IT function will be organized as a cost center.

Normative Influences

The level of similarity of behaviors within an industry is strongly influenced by organizations that spread "best practices." These shared norms are shaped by relationships that IT employees have in their specialization and industry. Professional organizations and trade bodies act as vehicles for transferring the knowledge of the latest practices in the industry. A number of new business periodicals and consortia dedicated to outsourcing can act as supporters of new outsourcing initiatives. Consulting firms that offer a large number of services also have a role in making their successes highly salient to the executives involved in decision making.

Proposition 8: The higher the participation of executives in associations and consortia, the more likely that IT function will be subject to normative pressures.

Normative influences strongly derive from "what is right" in a given situation, and hence depend on external accreditation/certification. The influence on governance type depends on the "organizational field" even more than in case of the mimetic or coercive forces. These institutional elements are somewhat fickle, and can change with time. Hence, the direction of the pressure in terms of whether it will emphasize cost or service centers will depend on the dominant mode in the industry. So it is more difficult to theorize the direction of this "hype related" effect (Fichman, 2004). Fads also rise and fall in line with what is fashionable at a given time (Abrahamson and Fairchild, 1999) with early arrangements somewhat skewed toward service centers.

Proposition 9: Depending on what is seen as appropriate in a given field at a given time, the IT function will be organized as either a cost or service center.

The propositions, in many ways, parallel the hypotheses in DiMaggio and Powell (1983). The above propositions assume that other conditions, for example, financial resources and firm size, remain constant. Other *ceteris paribus* conditions[4] are also important in conducting empirical work. These include an individual company's history, the structure of the industry, and the dynamics of the overall business environment. An important moderator is the organization's experience and learning with sourcing practices, as the pressures will differ across user firms with different learning environments. More seasoned buyers of IT services will have their own experience base to enable a more individualistic strategy, and will be less subject to isomorphic pressures. At the industry level, normative effects differ depending on the structure and history of the industry. We also assume a certain cultural milieu in terms of what is "in" so that it forms the basis for a comparative static analysis, insofar as the overall hype on outsourcing is not stationary. The dynamic effects of institutional forces are more complex to handle.

KEY INFLUENCERS

In the institutional setup, the treatment of agents is assumed to be comparatively uniform. This leaves little scope for any discrimination among the roles of actors. We feel that this is not the case in practice, and that institutional analysis will thus be accompanied by a more detailed micro-level analysis. We propose boundary-spanning behavior as another theoretical lens to complement the structural approaches emanating from institutional analysis. In doing so, we adopt a micro-level view of actors' roles under different institutional setups in shaping the final sourcing decisions. The leeway that the actors have in enacting their boundary roles has implications for the resource acquisition of information technologies. In enacting their roles differently, these key agents have an impact on the range of sourcing arrangements that are feasible in a given setup. In this view, we do not assume that structural elements solely determine micro-level behavior. The micro- and macro-level behaviors are mutually constituted in a dynamic way (Giddens, 1986).

Alternative behaviors associated with cost and service centers are mediated by key actors. We define these actors as IT managers in the buyer firm responsible for sourcing. While these managers might not make the final decision, they are key influencers. Though cost and service centers work differently—even in similar institutional environments—the actors have different roles by virtue of their agency, and this influences the final sourcing outcome.

Theoretical Assertions

Boundary-spanning roles are suggested as the main theoretical link between the organization and its environment at the level of individual behaviors (Aldrich and Herker, 1977). Individuals in these roles act as links by processing external information, and serve as representatives of the firm to other organizations, while simultaneously representing those organizations internally within the firm. Given the competing expectations (and interests) of organizations, role ambiguity leading to stress and conflict has been widely discussed in association with these roles. Roles constrain behavior, and are also institutionalized. Different organizational contexts affect individual behavior through roles (Shapiro, 1987). However, agent behavior being dictated by roles has been challenged by Perrone, Zaheer, and McEvily (2003), who argue that roles affect the level of trust called forth by agents. Focusing on buyer–supplier relationships, role autonomy is seen to influence the level of trust placed in the boundary spanner. *Role autonomy* is defined as "the degree of freedom role incumbents have in balancing the diverse expectations from their role set by devising appropriate actions and behaviors" (Perrone, Zaheer, and McEvily, 2003). Such role autonomy is subject to organizational as well as individual influences. Therefore, the latter can be used as controls to study organizational effects.

In an organizational setting, role autonomy among boundary spanners is seen in the discretion they need to enact their role. Role autonomy is conceptualized in three dimensions: functional influence, tenure, and clan culture (Perrone, Zaheer, and McEvily, 2003). These dimensions collectively lead to more innovative and active roles, where agents are relatively free to maneuver while satisfying the boundary organizations. Furthermore, autonomy will be used to demonstrate trustworthy behaviors toward suppliers, as compared with those boundary spanners who are constrained through monitoring. Role autonomy is seen as more important for contingencies and adjustments that arise among industrial buyer–seller relationships (Williamson, 1985). Buyer managers can exhibit discretionary behaviors by working on the spirit (rather than the letter) of contracts when conditions change, as is commonly the case in technology-related contracts. There is also greater scope to make independent decisions without having to check with the contacts external to the IT function. This becomes more important under dynamic conditions.

Functional influence is the level of influence that other functions (internal to the organization) have on boundary spanners' discretionary role. *Tenure* includes the level of experience, competence, and power accumulated over time in similar roles in the organization. *Internalization* (or clan culture) of collective goals and values takes place through socialization or an "organizational culture" that connotes clear norms. Through "shared values, beliefs, and goals, appropriate behaviors are rewarded." *Role autonomy* is the degree of freedom incumbents have in balancing the diverse expectations from their role set by devising appropriate actions and behaviors (Perrone, Zaheer, and McEvily, 2003). While functional influence is negatively related to role autonomy, tenure and internalization are positively related.

Application of Theory

In the context of IT sourcing, both vendors and firms have managers acting in boundary-spanning roles. While similar arguments could be applied on either side, the focus here is on the institutional effects on the buyers' IT organization. In this section, the dimensions of role autonomy and trust are considered with reference to "buying" information technology services. The dimensions (Figure 6.3) are applied to IT sourcing in cost and service centers. IT managers' role autonomy is considered, and its relation to trust placed by vendors in the managers.

Functional Influence

Differing organization of IT will result in different influences on the IT manager responsible for sourcing activities. Under conditions of change in the technologies being sourced, buyers need higher levels of role autonomy to respond and to effectively manage the supplier's expectations of their organization. Strong constraints, implied by a cost-center approach and financial controls, would suggest lower levels of autonomy. In contrast, IT managers in service centers will be less pressured by such controls, as they are directly in touch with users. The managers' understanding of institutional pressures will help them draw legitimate justifications for supplier actions.

> Proposition 10: Lower functional influence in service centers (versus cost centers) will be related to greater role autonomy for IT managers.

Tenure

Length of tenure is seen as associated with informal power and greater working knowledge of the organization. While these are not strictly related to a cost- or service-center approach it is likely

Figure 6.3 **Role Autonomy of IT Managers**

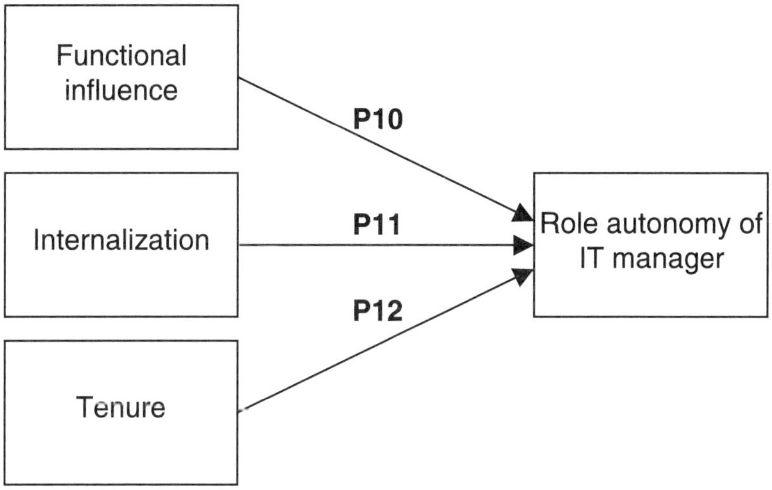

for the latter to have longer-tenured IT managers. Given the general complexity of requirements there would be some value of on-the-job learning. Cost centers, where selection criteria are drawn by finance, are likely to see some level of "interchangeability" or even attrition among managers, thus reducing the average tenure.

> Proposition 11: Higher levels of tenure in service centers (versus cost centers) will be related to greater role autonomy for IT managers.

Internalization

Strong organizational cultures and higher levels of socialization are used to orient individuals in "clan cultures" (Ouchi, 1980). Given the difficulty of estimating individual performance, low-powered incentives would be used. These would mesh with characteristics of service centers, in terms of having a "techie" culture and promotions from within the function. IT managers would have a higher level of discretion due to more ambiguous definitions of tasks or activities. Under the domination of finance function, cost centers are less likely to show such strong cultures. Relatively high-powered incentives and focus on tasks and activities will constrain the sourcing manager.

> Proposition 12: Higher levels of internalization in service centers (versus cost centers) will be related to greater role autonomy for IT managers.

The role of the "boundary spanner" IT manager is important in sourcing arrangements, as vendor information is channeled through this manager. Vendor representatives' trust in the IT manager is related to the degree of autonomy (or leeway) that the manager has in enacting his/her role (Perrone, Zaheer, and McEvily, 2003).

The discretionary behaviors that are enabled by role autonomy will characterize the level of trust placed in (buyer) managers. In this formulation, trust is seen as the expectation of being treated fairly by a manager.

INSTITUTIONAL AND INDIVIDUAL LEVELS

We argue that the sourcing arrangement will be strongly related to influences at the macro and micro levels. These influences include governance type, whether cost or service center, and the role autonomy of IT managers. In Figure 6.4, we synthesize the two levels to demonstrate the effect on sourcing arrangement.

IT governance arrangements in different institutional environments will be strongly related to sourcing arrangements. Service centers will be important antecedents to dynamic, adaptive arrangements. In contrast, lower levels of trust in cost centers is likely to lead to less adaptive arrangements such as "total outsourcing." We have theorized on the vector[5] of mimetic, coercive, and normative forces acting on the IT governance organization. IT governance structure will depend on the combination of institutional forces in a given context. While stronger mimetic forces will be related to service centers, and coercive forces to cost centers, normative forces might tilt the balance to either a cost- or service-center organization. The combined effect of these forces will be related to the sourcing arrangement in a given context.

> Proposition 13: IT governance organization (cost or service center) will be positively related to adaptive sourcing arrangements.

Given the complexity of the technology services being bought, we propose that higher levels of role autonomy for the IT manager will be associated with more adaptive behaviors. The autonomy of this key actor implies a greater range of options, for example, selective sourcing instead of total outsourcing. These manifestations of flexibility among IT managers have been seen in sourcing practices such as creative multivendor strategies (Lacity and Willcocks, 1996). High trust relationships with vendors are prerequisites for such novel arrangements, which are recommended by research (Willcocks and Lacity, 1998), although there has been limited explanation of the conditions under which such complex arrangements might arise. We propose that higher role autonomy of IT managers is a necessary condition for such arrangements. The allied mechanisms of joint teams will facilitate the exploration of hybrid arrangements with vendors as a result of adaptive practices.

> Proposition 14: Greater role autonomy among IT managers will be positively related to adaptive sourcing arrangements.

We propose that the higher role autonomy of IT managers coexisting with service centers is an additional condition. IT governance will have a strong nexus with role autonomy. This emphasis on structure is seen in literature that considers roles emerging from structures. "Institutions are embodied in individual experience by means of roles . . . the institution, with its assemblage of *programmed* actions, is like the unwritten libretto of a drama. The realization of the drama depends on the reiterated performance of its prescribed roles by living actors" (Berger and Luckmann, 1967).

> Proposition 15: IT governance organization (cost or service center) will be positively related to role autonomy.

However, it is possible to have service centers, with lower levels of role autonomy among IT managers. In this case, the institutional and individual levels are not symbiotic, and will thus hinder the adaptive sourcing arrangements.

Figure 6.4 **Antecedents of Sourcing Arrangements**

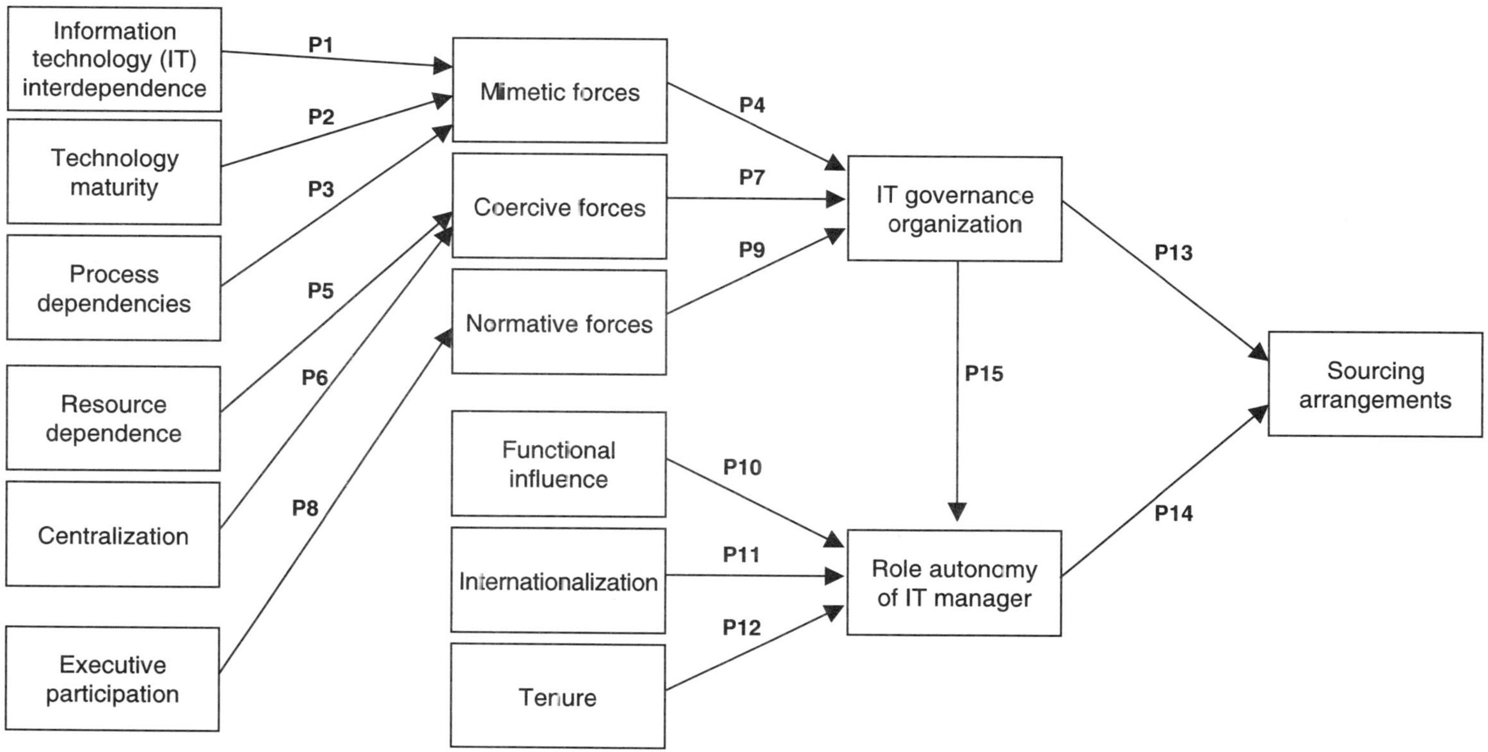

We speculate that adaptive sourcing practices would be associated with higher sourcing effectiveness. This would take place due to dynamic management of contracts, as business and/or technology conditions change during the length of a contract. Higher levels of trust are seen to coexist with "voice" relationships (Helper, MacDuffie, and Sabel, 2000). The value of flexibility inherently lies in better dynamic handling of uncertainty (Kulatilaka, 1988). Less flexible arrangements such as total outsourcing have been seen to lower success (Lacity and Willcocks, 1996). Therefore, service centers will tend to show higher effectiveness in sourcing, on a number of metrics. These are necessarily a wider range of metrics than "cost only" criteria. There is some evidence that in dynamic environments, the value of the sourcing arrangement increasingly depends on future flexibility for the buyer organization more than on the current monetary value.

CONTRIBUTION, IMPLICATIONS, AND LIMITATIONS

We have used institutional theory to characterize different influences on the IT organization with regard to sourcing, and examined how boundary-spanning roles can explain how organizational influences eventually lead to different sourcing relationships with vendors. The propositions give some direction as to how more successful IT sourcing arrangements arise. This situation has been observed in practice but not theorized adequately. The complementary lenses of institutional theory and boundary spanning help us better understand complex environments under which the sourcing decision makers operate under the influence of different forces. Our key contribution is in theorizing the vector of forces as a key antecedent to the adaptive behaviors and practices seen in dynamic business environments. We also draw attention to the rich research possibilities in the development of IT sourcing effectiveness as a construct, which needs to move beyond cost-related criteria rooted in quiescent environments. In these low-uncertainty environments, flexibility has little (if any) value. With an underlying focus on the business value of IT, it is important that future research in sourcing recognize and theorize on more realistic, complex scenarios.

This chapter also has managerial implications. IT managers, to realize business value, need to be aware of the institutional contexts of IT sourcing. When senior managers endeavor to design governance organizations akin to service centers, there is also a need to ensure high role autonomy at the individual level to allow successful execution. The mutual effect of institutional environment and individual roles is the key to success of adaptive sourcing strategies. In the extreme, however, there might be a tendency for service centers to develop insular and "cliquish" cultures that essentially love technology for technology's sake, lose touch with business needs, and have low accountability for their activities. It is under such extreme conditions that corporate executives easily justify a move to cost centers, which look "viable" as a short-term solution. In highly ambiguous environments for business and technology, IT managers need to experiment selectively to generate digital options (Sambamurthy, Bharadwaj, and Grover, 2003). We argue that the variety and complexity of actions that can arise from adaptive sourcing practices are the true measure of sourcing effectiveness. If these are low, IT managers risk being drawn to a "technology as cost" motif, which frequently manifests itself in total outsourcing.

The main limitations have to do with the rudimentary modeling of institutional and economic influences (Figure 6.1). While these are negatively correlated in the proposed model, it is possible to theorize many combinations, for example, both influences being low, low economic and high institutional pressures, and so on. The treatment is cross-sectional, as we consider the influences at a given time. The focus is on mimetic processes even though other structures and activities are recognized in the literature (Scott, 2001). We have not distinguished the environment and organization levels (Zucker, 1987), as we are trying to relate these macro levels (in combination) to micro-level behaviors. We also need better definitions of the organizational field and its institutions. This could come from case study research or case modeling of power and resource dependencies among IT organizations. We study the "majority" of IT organizations as they strive to follow successful examples, and not the organizations (or behaviors) that shape organizational fields, sometimes in the face of institutional resistance. In the future, some instrument must be developed to convert the propositions into testable hypotheses. Some propositions might need to be developed into multiple hypotheses, amenable to statistical testing. In order to do empirical research, we need longitudinal data and studies of large populations, as is the general practice in institutional theory. We could also consider the role of service providers such as IBM in mobilizing bias as well as the role of big consulting firms in rationalizing this behavior in understanding the role of fashions.

ACKNOWLEDGMENTS

We would like to thank the anonymous reviewers, including those of the Hawaii International Conference on System Sciences (HICSS) Organizational Systems and Technology Track, for which an earlier version of this chapter was accepted, and Susan Helper and Julie Rennecker at Case Western Reserve University, for their comments on earlier versions.

NOTES

1. While the Kodak effect remains a popular belief, the differences among diffusion regimes (pre and post Kodak) as regards the role of internal and external factors were reconsidered in later research by Hu, Saunders, and Gebelt (1997).
2. *Sourcing* and *outsourcing* are used synonymously, though sourcing is currently "politically correct."
3. We thank the anonymous reviewer for clarification on the application of structuration.
4. Thanks to anonymous reviewers of the HICSS Conference for suggesting these conditions.
5. For simplicity, we assume independent action of these forces.

REFERENCES

Abrahamson, E. and Fairchild, G. 1999. Management fashion: Lifecycles, triggers, and collective learning processes. *Administrative Science Quarterly*, 44, 4, 708–740.

Aldrich, H.E. 1979. *Organizations and Environments*. Englewood Cliffs, NJ: Prentice Hall.

Aldrich, H.E. and Herker, D. 1977. Boundary spanning roles and organization structure. *Academy of Management Review*, 2, 2, 217–230.

Ang, S. and Cummings, L. L. 1997. Strategic response to institutional influences on information systems outsourcing. *Organization Science*, 8, 3, 235–256.

Ang, S. and Straub, D.W. 1998. Production and transaction economies and IS outsourcing: A study of the U.S. banking industry. *MIS Quarterly*, 22, 4, 535–552.

Aubert, B.A.; Rivard, S.; and Patry, M. 1994. Development of measures to assess dimensions of IS operation transactions perspective. *Proceedings of the International Conference on Information Systems*. Vancouver, BC, 13–26.

Berger, P. and Luckmann, T. 1967. *The Social Construction of Reality.* New York: Doubleday Anchor.

Clark, T.D.; Zmud, R.W.; and McGray, G.E. 1995. The outsourcing of Information services: Transforming the nature of the business in the Information industry. *Journal of Information Technology*, 8, 1, 5–13.

DiMaggio, P.J. and Powell, W.W. 1983. The iron cage revisited: Institutional isomorphism and collective rationality in organizational fields. *American Sociological Review*, 48, 2, 147–160.

Fichman, R.G. 2004. Going beyond the dominant paradigm for IT innovation research: Emerging concepts and methods. *Journal of the Association for Information Systems*, 5, 8, 314–355.

Giddens, A. 1986. *The Constitution of Society: Outline of the Theory of Structuration.* Berkeley: University of California Press.

Helper, S.; MacDuffie, J.P.; and Sabel, C. 2000. Pragmatic collaborations: Advancing knowledge while controlling opportunism. *Industrial & Corporate Change*, 9, 443–488.

Hu, Q.; Saunders, C.; and Gebelt, M. 1997. Research report: Diffusion of information systems outsourcing: A reevaluation of influence sources. *Information Systems Research*, 8, 3, 288–301.

Hui, P. and Beath, C. 2001. The IT sourcing process: A framework for research. Working paper, University of Texas at Austin.

Jayatilaka, B. 2002. IT sourcing: A dynamic phenomenon: Forming an institutional theory perspective. In R. Hirschheim, A. Heinzl and J. Dibbern, eds., *Information Systems Outsourcing in the New Economy.* Berlin: Springer-Verlag, 100–130.

Kulatilaka, N. 1988. Valuing the flexibility of flexible manufacturing systems. *IEEE Transactions on Engineering Management*, 35, 4, 250–257.

Lacity, M. and Hirschheim, R. 1993. *Information Systems Outsourcing: Myths, Metaphors, and Realties.* Chichester, UK: Wiley.

Lacity, M. and Willcocks, L. 1996. Best practices in information technology sourcing. Oxford Executive Research Briefings, Templeton College.

Loh, L. and Venkatraman, N. 1992. Diffusion of information technology outsourcing: Influence sources and the Kodak effect. *Information Systems Research*, 3, 4, 334–358.

Mizruchi, M.S. and Fein, L.C. 1999. The social construction of organizational knowledge: A study of the uses of coercive, mimetic, and normative isomorphism. *Administrative Science Quarterly*, 44, 4, 653–683.

Nagpal, P. 2004. Use of TCE framework to study IT sourcing: Over-application or under-theorizing? *Proceedings of the Americas Conference on Information Systems.* New York, 3995–4005.

Ouchi, W.G. 1980. Markets, bureaucracies, and clans. *Administrative Science Quarterly*, 25, 1, 129–141.

Perrone, V.; Zaheer, A.; and McEvily, B. 2003. Free to be trusted? Organizational constraint on trust in boundary spanners. *Organization Science*, 14, 4, 422–439.

Purvis, R.L.; Sambamurthy, V.; and Zmud, R.W. 2001. The assimilation of knowledge platforms in organizations: An empirical investigation. *Organization Science*, 12, 2, 117–135.

Ross, J.W.; Vitale, M.R.; and Beath, C.M. 1999. The untapped potential of IT chargeback. *MIS Quarterly*, 23, 2, 215.

Sambamurthy, V.; Bharadwaj, A.; and Grover, V. 2003. Shaping agility through digital options: Reconceptualizing the role of information technology in contemporary firms. *MIS Quarterly*, 27, 2, 237–263.

Scott, W.R. 2001. *Institutions and Organizations*, 2d ed. Thousand Oaks, CA: Sage.

Shapiro, S.P. 1987. The social control of impersonal trust. *American Journal of Sociology*, 93, 3, 623.

Teo, H.H.; Wei, K.K.; and Benbasat, I. 2003. Predicting intention to adopt interorganizational linkages: An institutional perspective. *MIS Quarterly*, 27, 1, 19–49.

Tolbert, P.S. and Zucker, L.G. 1983. Institutional sources of change in the formal structure of organizations: The diffusion of civil service reform, 1880–1935. *Administrative Science Quarterly*, 28, 1, 22–39.

Willcocks, L. and Lacity, M. 1998. The sourcing and outsourcing of IS. In L. Willcocks and M. Lacity, eds., *Strategic Sourcing of Information Systems.* Chichester, UK: Wiley, 1–44.

Williamson, O.E. 1985. *The Economic Institutions of Capitalism.* New York: Free Press.

Ye, F. and Agarwal, R. 2003. Strategic information technology partnerships in outsourcing as a distinctive source of information technology value: A social capital perspective. *Proceedings of the International Conference on Information Systems.* Seattle, WA, 304–315.

Zucker, L.G. 1987. Institutional theories of organization. *Annual Review of Sociology*, 13, 443–464.

CHAPTER 7

FIRM CHARACTERISTICS AND ALLOCATION OF IT BUDGET TO OUTSOURCING

WONSEOK OH

Abstract: *The conventional benefits (i.e., cost reduction, the ability to focus on core competence, technological leadership, etc.) and risks (i.e., vendor opportunism, lock-ins, contractual difficulties, etc.) of information technology (IT) outsourcing are extensively documented in the literature. Nevertheless, because each firm is different in terms of its ability to leverage the potential benefits and mitigate the inherent risks associated with IT outsourcing, firm characteristic variables should be taken into account for understanding outsourcing-related decisions. This study provides new insight into the broader organizational factors that may influence a firm's propensity to outsource IT. More specifically, we assess how firm characteristic variables (i.e., a firm's uncertainty, agency cost, innovativeness, IT intensity, and operational inefficiency) play a role in making outsourcing-related decisions. The results indicate that a firm's uncertainty and agency cost negatively influence the propensity to outsource, while a firm's innovativeness and operational inefficiency are positively associated with the extent of IT outsourcing. No significant relationship was observed between IT intensity and the degree of outsourcing intensity.*

Keywords: *Firm Characteristics, Firm Innovativeness, Outsourcing Determinants, Outsourcing Intensity*

INTRODUCTION

Despite the ongoing debate over its business benefits and risks, information technology (IT) outsourcing[1] has become a widespread organizational practice, which has grown briskly in recent years (Ang and Straub,1998, 2002; Aubert, Rivard, and Patry, 2004; Oh and Gallivan, 2004). According to a report by the Gartner Group (March 9, 2004), overall spending in IT outsourcing in the United States reached $177 billion in 2003 and is predicted to rise to $236 billion in 2007. Given the harbinger of IT doom as reflected in companies' tightened IT budgets in recent years, the anticipated upward swing in outsourcing spending is surprising. At the fore of this burgeoning trend are offshore outsourcing and application service provider (ASP)-based outsourcing arrangements. These new waves of outsourcing practice have radically changed the competitive landscape of the outsourcing industry, while concurrently providing businesses with more cost-effective service. According to *InformationWeek* (Caldwell, 1998), 92 percent of major corporations in the United States outsource their IT operations instead of developing IT in-house. As such practice becomes ubiquitous, the manager's dilemma appears to have shifted from whether or not to outsource to deciding the extent to which his/her firm should outsource within the IT budget.

Over the past several years, the literature on IT outsourcing has tapped into a variety of issues, including the business performance impact of IT outsourcing (Cross, Earl, and Sampler, 1997; Loh and Venkatraman, 1992a; Palvia, 1995), transactional risks inherent to outsourcing arrangements (Ang and Cummings, 1997; Ang and Straub, 2002; Aubert, Rivard, and Patry, 2004; Oh and Gallivan, 2004), relationship issues between clients and vendors (Ho, Ang, and Straub, 2003; Kern, 1997; Kern and Willcocks, 2002; Lee and Kim, 1999; Willcocks and Choi, 1995), contract management (Ang and Beath, 1993; Ang and Endeshaw, 1997; DiRomualdo and Gurbaxani, 1998), and the determinants of IT outsourcing (Ang and Straub,1998; Aubert, Rivard, and Patry, 2004; Lacity and Willcoks, 2000; Smith, Mitra, and Narasimhan, 1998; Teng, Cheon, and Grover, 1995).

However, little is known about the larger organizational factors that influence a firm's propensity to outsource IT resources *for their given IT budget.* As IT outsourcing becomes a more pervasive organizational phenomenon, the multitude of driving and constraining forces should be understood in a larger organizational context. More specifically, it could be asked: Why do some firms spend a greater portion of their IT budget on IT outsourcing, while others rely mostly on internal development or insourcing? For example, in the late 1990s, Safeway Inc., a large U.S. food retailer, spent only 10 percent of its IT budget on outsourcing IT activities, while Pathmark Inc., one of Safeway's competitors, allocated 80 percent of its IT budget to outsourcing during the same period (Hayes, 1997). Similarly, what accounts for the significant difference between Ryder Inc. (80 percent) and Fed Ex (6 percent) in terms of their allocation of IT budget to outsourcing? Can the traditional corporate governance framework (i.e., markets versus hierarchies) alone explain this stark inequality in the intensity of IT outsourcing?

The main purpose of this chapter is to shed some light on this issue in conjunction with an examination of the broader organizational contextual variables that may influence a firm's propensity to outsource IT. The specific questions we attempt to answer include: To what extent do firm uncertainty and agency risk affect outsourcing decisions? Do innovative firms that invest heavily in research and development (R&D) outsource IT more aggressively than firms that make smaller R&D investments? Do a firm's IT intensity (as measured by a proportion of IT budget divided by firm revenue) and operational efficiency significantly influence the propensity to outsource? Although other organizational variables, such as top management decisions and political power, may affect a firm's outsourcing-related decision, special attention has been paid to the factors that determine a firm's characteristics (Oh and Kim, 2001). Drawing from multiple theoretical underpinnings, including resource-based views (e.g., Barney, 1986) and agency costs (e.g., Jensen, 1986), we identify such organizational factors and assess how they influence a firm's propensity to outsource.

This chapter makes several contributions to the growing literature on IT outsourcing, the body of which has been of enduring concern to many information systems (IS) researchers and practitioners. Borrowing from multiple streams of research, we present an integrated framework by which the sourcing decision can be explained in light of a larger organizational context that goes beyond the governance-based explanation. In addition to the well-publicized motivations for outsourcing and insourcing activities (e.g., cost reduction, technological leadership, transactional risks), a new insight is provided with respect to the determinants of IT outsourcing. The results reported in this study serve as a fresh vantage point from which to understand the new opportunities and challenges that IT outsourcing creates.

RELATED STUDIES

Researchers have examined the determinants of IT outsourcing decisions from different theoretical and empirical perspectives. Loh and Venkatraman (1992b) find that an outsourcing decision is positively dependent on both business and IT cost structures, but negatively associated with a firm's IT performance. However, none of the other variables inherent to their model—such as business performance, financial leverage, business size, and industry—were found to have a significant association with outsourcing expenditure. Nam and colleagues (1996) show that asset specificity, tacit IT knowledge, and decision analysis efforts have a significant strategic impact on a firm's differentiation effort, but that these variables do not appear to affect cost reduction efforts. They also identify four types of outsourcing relationships (i.e., reliance, alliance, support, and alignment) based on the two criteria, namely, the strategic impact of IS applications and the extent of substitution by vendors. This classification scheme was used to predict the possibility that a client will continue a relationship with the same vendor. Their results indicate that an outsourcing relationship is likely to be sustained when either the strategic impact of outsourced resources or the extent of substitution by vendors is high. Interestingly, however, the relationship is likely to be terminated when both criteria are simultaneously high.

Ang and Straub (1998) examine the economic determinants of IT outsourcing, and they find that production cost advantage, transaction cost, and firm size are significantly associated with the degree of IS outsourcing, as perceptually measured by a survey instrument. Contrary to their expectations, the degree of financial slack resource was not found to have a significant bearing on an outsourcing decision. Smith, Mitra, and Narasimhan (1998) explore the specific financial characteristics of the firms that enter into large-scale IT outsourcing arrangements. They test empirically the general motives for IT outsourcing as identified in the literature, including cost reduction, cash generation, profitability, organizational focus on core competencies, and access to technical expertise. Among these potential motivators, only cost reduction and cash generation were found to be main drivers in the decision to outsource IT. Recently, Lee, Miranda, and Kim (2004) used a holistic approach with the configurational, universalistic, and contingency perspectives in explicating the relationship between IT outsourcing strategies and outsourcing success, as measured by strategic competence, cost efficiency, and technology catalysis. The results indicate that the configuration approach is superior to the other two alternatives in explaining outsourcing success.

In summary, these studies focus primarily on a firm's financial characteristics (i.e., financial credit, debt, leverage, etc.) in order to identify the determinants for IT outsourcing. In this study, however, we pay attention to other critical organizational dimensions in which firms differ fundamentally with respect to their investment behavior, such as level of uncertainty (Fama and French, 1992), agency risk (Jensen, 1986), operational efficiencies (Banker, Kauffman, and Morey, 1990), the degree of a firm's level of innovation (Cohen and Levin, 1989), and IT intensity (Harris and Katz, 1991). The literature suggests that these factors may have a profound impact on a firm's corporate investment decisions.

In addition, in contrast to the previous studies, the present study operationalizes the intensity of IT outsourcing as a proportion of IT budget allocated to IT outsourcing. Earlier studies rely mostly upon survey-based outsourcing measures (e.g., Ang and Straub, 1998; Nam et al., 1996) as proxies that represent outsourcing intensity. These methods indicate a firm's overall outsourcing budget, but do not necessarily illustrate the ratio of outsourcing to insourcing. For example, a report saying that a firm spends *x* percent of its revenue on outsourcing does not convey much information about its outsourcing strategy because the ratio merely conveys the total amount spent on outsourcing, and not the proportion of outsourcing versus insourcing. Our dependent variable reflects the importance of outsourcing within a firm's IS strategy, showing the proportion of IT budget allocated to outsourcing activities.

FIRM CHARACTERISTICS AND OUTSOURCING PROPENSITY

Several organizational researchers (e.g., Koberg, 1987) have investigated a firm's key strategic investment decision from the perspectives of a firm's risk management and resource availability. Following this framework, we identify two dimensions of firm characteristics—corporate risk and technological resources and capability—in assessing the propensity to outsource IT. Such well-accepted theoretical underpinnings as resource dependency (Pfeffer and Salancik, 1978), transaction cost economics (Williamson, 1979), and agency costs (Jensen, 1986) posit the existence of various organizational hazards that influence a firm's key strategic decisions. To understand the interplay between these corporate risks and a firm's decision to outsource IT, we explore the extent to which uncertainty, agency risk, and operational inefficiencies influence the propensity to outsource IT functions.

Drawing from a resource-based view of strategic management (Amit and Schoemaker, 1993; Barney, 1986; Dierickx and Cool, 1989; Oliver, 1997; Wernerfelt, 1984), which denotes that the extent to which a firm possesses resources and capabilities determines its strategic decisions and subsequently the level of economic rents, we investigate how a firm's technological resources reflected in innovative capabilities and IT resource intensity influence a firm's decision making in outsourcing IT operations.

Uncertainty

Viewed as a key variable in explaining firm behavior (March and Simon, 1958) and in making strategic decisions (Porter, 1980), uncertainty is one of the most important constructs in organizational theory. Although transactional uncertainty has been studied in the past as a key determinant of IT outsourcing (Aubert, Rivard, and Patry, 2004), little attention has been paid to the possible impact of environmental and firm-specific uncertainty on the propensity to outsource IT. Uncertainty is "dysfunctional in maintaining equilibrium and to satisfactory performance" (Jauch and Kraft, 1986, p. 777). Although a firm's action is limited in terms of controlling environmental uncertainty, it can proactively react to firm-specific uncertainty (Cyert and March, 1963; Jauch and Kraft, 1986) and manage risk through either a "buffering" or "smoothing" practice (Lev, 1975). Buffering activities subsume inventory holding, preventive maintenance, training, and so on, while smoothing practices refer to more aggressive organizational interventions, such as capital investments, dividend adjustments, and the like. The ability to manage this risk varies from firm to firm (ibid.).

There have been two different schools of thought regarding the potential smoothing role of IT investments in decreasing uncertainty (Hunter, Kobelsky, and Richardson, 2003; Oh, Kim, and Richardson, 2005). One perspective suggests that IT investments are a *source* of uncertainty (Craine, 1989), whereas another considers IT a *solution* to uncertainty (Galbraith, 1977; Gurbaxani and Whang, 1991). According to the formal perspective, IT departments are viewed as cost centers, and IT projects bear a high risk of failure; as a result, uncertainty increases rather than decreases. The literature on real option approaches to measuring the business value of IT (Benaroch and Kauffman, 1999, 2000; Taudes, Feurstein, and Mild, 2000; Schwartz and Zozaya-Gorostiza, 2003) generally supports the view that IT inherently embodies high uncertainty, and real option approaches are therefore more appropriate in estimating the true business value of IT.

Conversely, the information-processing view of a firm (Galbraith, 1977) argues that IT investments enable firms to reduce uncertainty by helping them react more actively and responsively to both external and internal risks. IT investments facilitate increased information processes and operational efficiencies, provide firms with growth opportunities and the components necessary to stabilize a firm's operation, and also generate future cash flow (Mukhopadhyay, Kekre, and Kalathur, 1995). IT outsourcing can therefore be seen as a smoothing practice by which a firm can reduce its own firm-specific uncertainty.

Two competing models may explain the possibility that the IT governance mode can moderate the smoothing role of IT investments and affect a manager's decision to outsource IT resources. Resource dependence theory (Pfeffer and Salancik, 1978) asserts that when facing uncertainties, firms tend to seek out external linkages in an effort to "share" the risks. This theory has been empirically validated in studies of joint ventures (Pfeffer and Nowak, 1976) and corporate mergers (Pfeffer, 1972). In the presence of uncertainties, companies may more aggressively outsource their IT functions to secure more external resources, which may in turn buffer the risks created by environmental shocks (Boyd, 1990). Such an external adaptation and dependence lead to a "system equilibrium" (Jauch and Kraft, 1986) under which uncertainties are distributed across the parties that share resources. Outsourcing can also produce "social capital" in the form of knowledge sharing and learning through which firms can increase their ability to cope with uncertainties (Ye and Agarwal, 2003).

The transaction costs economics (TCE) perspective (Williamson, 1979), in contrast, suggests that when firms face uncertainties, they are likely to adopt vertical integration as an effective governance mode. This argument has been supported by numerous empirical studies, including those of John and Weitz (1988), Anderson (1985), and Walker and Weber (1987). To a certain extent, TCE asserts that creating external linkages will lead to a "system disequilibrium" in which the risks systematically increase, rather than decrease, for firms that depend on such resources. Consistent with this view, internal IT development, rather than external outsourcing, was found to serve as a more suitable governance structure by which uncertainties are mitigated (Malone, Yates, and Benjamin, 1987; Walker and Weber, 1984). Market-based outsourcing contracts may create additional uncertainty due to the high transactional risks involved (Aubert, Rivard, and Patry, 2004; Malone, Yates, and Benjamin, 1987). Moreover, when uncertainties increase, it becomes more costly to manage interorganizational linkages created by outsourcing arrangements (Hill and Hoskisson, 1987).

Despite the parallel manifested in the two competing theoretical insights (system equilibrium versus system disequilibrium) with regard to the influence of external linkages on the level of firm uncertainties, the TCE appears more convincing in the outsourcing context, especially as the business and technological environments become more turbulent and unpredictable. Creating external linkages and producing social capital may indeed enhance a firm's long-term "health" in terms of managing uncertainties, but only in the absence of all the major risks articulated by TCE theory. Consequently, firms facing great uncertainty are predicted to rely heavily on a hierarchical governance mode through internal development.

Hypothesis 1: There is a negative relationship between a firm's uncertainty and the propensity to outsource IT.

Agency Risk

A firm's capital structure (e.g., debt, investment, etc.) in response to market imperfection has been the center of interests in corporate finance and strategic management research (Harris and Raviv, 1991; Kochhar, 1996; Myers, 1984). Agency theory (Jensen, 1986; Jensen and Meckling, 1976), which is essentially concerned with the hazards arising from the separation of control from ownership in large corporations, provides a viable framework for understanding a firm's behavior in determining capital structure. In addition to the traditional factors (e.g., information asymmetry, moral hazards, etc.), agency problems arise when parties (principals and agents) have conflicting goals and different risk preferences (Jensen and Meckling, 1976). Such a conflict of interest is prevalent between shareholders and management when they determine the optimal capital structure (i.e., the amount of free cash flow [FCF] discretionarily available to managers) (Jensen, 1986).

FCF has been widely used in finance and strategy to substantiate the agency cost between shareholders and management. Generally, managers retain cash flow when profitable investment opportunities are not present (Howton, Howton, and Perfect, 1998). Ideally, managers are expected to reinvest excessive cash into new profit-generating projects in order to maximize shareholder value. Nevertheless, they may retain free cash when new project opportunities cannot offer returns above the market rates. A firm's low growth option, inefficient cost structure, or the absence of adequate management skills may be sources for a lack of positive investment opportunities.

The free cash flow hypothesis (Jensen, 1986) asserts that to increase bargaining power against shareholders, managers tend to allocate more resources under their control, and limit dividend payments to shareholders. At an extreme, agents may even invest in negative net present value (NPV) projects to minimize dividend payouts and increase their control. Therefore, if managers withhold a substantial amount of free cash without distributing it to investors (via dividends or by investing it in other value-creating projects), the agency costs increase severely. Dewan, Michael, and Min (1998) demonstrate that to avoid dividend payments, firms with high levels of FCF tend to make excessive IT investments, because of the ease with which they can justify them. As a result, overinvestments in IT are a likely consequence that adds little value to firm performance, but rather empowers managers by putting more resources under their control.

Assuming that an IT budget comes from the previous year's FCF, firms with high levels of free cash are likely to develop IT systems internally rather than rely on external vendors in order to increase their power against shareholders (Oh and Kim, 2001). From the agency-cost perspective, outsourcing IT from external vendors is likely to diminish their influence and control over the project, and thus result in "poaching" (Clemons, 2000). When outsourcing IT resources, a smaller amount of resources—both human- and capital-based resources—is likely to be under the manager's control, and a form of power transfer will occur (Kern, Willcocks, and Heck, 2002; Oh and Kim, 2001). In addition, various types of transactional risks inherent to IT outsourcing (e.g., opportunism, shirking, lock-ins, etc.) (Aubert, Rivard, and Patry, 2004) may further reduce the manager's control and power, and limit his or her "sphere of influence" within the organization. Consequently, even when outsourcing is considered a better strategic option for the firm, managers may be more inclined to keep the IT development in-house, because doing so will increase his or her control and bargaining power against shareholders. Accordingly, a negative relationship is expected between a firm's agency cost and the propensity to outsource.

Hypothesis 2: There is a negative relationship between a firm's agency cost and the propensity to outsource IT.

Operational Inefficiencies

Traditionally, IT has been conceived as an "efficiency driver" that plays a key role in reducing a firm's operating cost (Bakos and Treacy, 1986; Banker, Kauffman, and Morey, 1990; Barua, Kriebel, and Mukhopadhyay, 1995; Barua & Lee, 1997; Clemons & Row 1991; Harris and Katz, 1991; Thatcher and Oliver, 2001). Such large-scale information systems as enterprise resource planning (ERP), supply management systems (SCM), and electronic data interchange (EDI) allow firms to streamline value chain activities and facilitate internal operations in a far more efficient fashion, resulting in substantial cost savings. Firms that successfully implement and use IS are therefore expected to garner greater operational efficiency. Conversely, high operational inefficiency may reflect underdevelopment or the inappropriate utilization of IS (Banker, Kauffman, and Morey, 1990).

Smith, Mitra, and Narasimhan (1998) examine the cost efficiency metric prior to outsourcing. Based on a sample of twenty-nine companies, they find that firms that enter into outsourcing arrangements—compared with other firms in the same industry who do not outsource—have lower overhead costs as measured by the amount of selling, general, and administrative expenses (SG&A) divided by sales. This result is interesting, given that twenty-six of the twenty-nine firms that the authors investigated indeed state cost reduction as a primary objective of outsourcing.

Whereas Smith, Mitra, and Narasimhan (1998) focus on the cost efficiency structure between firms that outsource and those that do not, we focus our attention on the impact of operational efficiency in determining the level of outsourcing in the subsequent period. More specifically, we seek to identify the impact of *ex ante* cost structure on outsourcing propensity, and argue that firms that experience significant overheads may pursue outsourcing more aggressively by allocating a large portion of their IT budget on hiring external vendors. Firms with high operational inefficiency are less likely to have competent IT resources or agile capabilities (Banker, Kauffman, and Morey, 1990; Barua and Lee, 1997), and as a result, effective internal IT development may not be feasible. In addition, these firms may desperately seek to reduce IT costs through outsourcing arrangements, in which the vendor can often provide the same level of service as in-house expertise, but at lower costs (Arnett and Jones, 1994; Lacity, Hirschheim, and Willcocks, 1994; Palvia, 1995).

Hypothesis 3: There is a positive relationship between a firm's operational inefficiency and the propensity to outsource IT.

Innovative Capabilities

A firm's level of innovation is an important organizational variable that determines the firm's investment decisions (Cohen and Levin, 1989). Some firms devote themselves to enhancing their innovative capabilities more than others; in the process, they may allocate massive amounts of financial and human resources to research and development in order to develop new products or processes. Through making R&D investments, firms build and maintain technological infrastructures that enable them to keep abreast of the latest technologies, as well as "develop the ability to identify, assimilate and exploit knowledge from the environment" (Cohen and Levin, 1989). Organizations commit themselves to R&D in the pursuit of creating competitive advantages through product or process innovations rather than through licensing agreements (e.g., purchasing ideas or properties that have already been developed by someone else). Organizations that make substantial R&D investments typically anticipate long-term, strategic gains, even at the expense of short-term operational losses.

Developing and managing IT in-house may be seen as an act that is tantamount to making an R&D investment. An internal IT development strategy serves as a corporate platform that is often characterized as risky and focused on the long term. Moreover, IT insourcing requires substantial amounts of time in terms of planning, developing, and implementing information systems that best meet the needs of the organizations involved, not to mention the difficulty of maintaining those systems. In the presence of these challenges, some organizations may simply make contracts with external IT vendors, similar to licensing agreements. Therefore, there is a similarity between these two types of key corporate investments with respect to governance modes.

Innovative firms, through aggressive R&D investments, proactively anticipate changing environments and internally nurture *dynamic capabilities* defined as a subset of corporate competences and capabilities that allow firms to competently develop new products and processes (Teece and Pisano, 1994). These firms seek long-term profits, and aggressively carry out risky initiatives to meet that end. Therefore, they are likely to develop IT systems internally to produce dynamic and distinctive capabilities rather than purchase them through the market as a matter of convenience.

Another key reason why innovative firms may want to keep their IT operation in-house is that outsourcing typically involves a great amount of knowledge transfer (Earl, 1996). When creating external linkages through outsourcing arrangements, an opportunistic exploration of tacit knowledge can occur (Williamson and Ouchi, 1981). The transfer of tacit knowledge poses a great threat to innovative firms when they engage in partnerships and other forms of interfirm corporations (Clemons, 2000; Dutta and Weiss, 1997; Teece, 1988). Given that recent outsourcing trends shift toward more complex arrangements involving multiple vendors and clients (Gallivan and Oh, 1999)—with clients often becoming IT contractors themselves (Ho, Ang, and Straub, 2003)—protecting the transfer of such tacit knowledge accumulated through extensive R&D spending is a daunting task. Examining 120 manufacturing firms that invest heavily in R&D, Dutta and Weiss (1997) found that technologically innovative firms tend, in fact, to form partnerships in ways that reduce the transfer of tacit knowledge. However, they show that a full prevention of tacit knowledge transfer is extremely difficult to accomplish when engaging in a partnership relationship. Consequently, organizations that are more aggressive in their R&D spending have a higher propensity to develop and manage IT systems in-house than do organizations that are less aggressive in making such long-term and risky investments.

Hypothesis 4: There is a negative relationship between a firm's R&D intensity and the propensity to outsource IT.

IT Intensity

Over the past several decades, numerous conceptual models and empirical manifestations have been documented in support of the business value of IT. Nonetheless, no consensus has been made regarding an optimal level of IT investment that yields maximum economic returns. Similar to the case seen in R&D investments, some organizations aggressively pursue an IT strategy and spend more on IT than do others. Accordingly, IT intensity[2]—which is highly contingent on corporate vision and support—differs dramatically from firm to firm.

Previous studies have shown that IT intensity significantly influences a firm's performance (Harris and Katz, 1991). A firm's IT intensity may influence the degree to which it outsources IT. Intuitively, firms that spend relatively more on IT accumulate a greater amount of IT capital and labor—both of which, in turn, promote an internal development. More important, firms with high IT intensity may more readily recognize the strategic value of IT and leverage it to gain and sustain competitive advantages. Despite recent heated debates on its strategic value, IT remains an opportunity for gaining competitive advantages.

According to the resource-based view (Barney, 1991; Mata, Fuerst, and Barney, 1995), however, IT is most likely to provide firms with competitive advantages when it is unique and inimitable. In an environment where firms can purchase IT as a commodity through market-based outsourcing arrangements, creating and sustaining competitive advantages through market-based governance modes is an extremely difficult task. Even when firms successfully develop unique and nonimi-

Figure 7.1 **The Research Model**

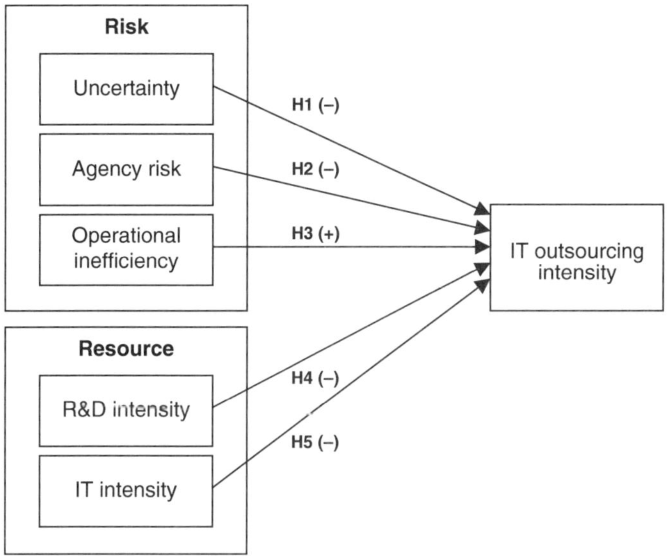

Control variables:
- Industry
- Firm size
- IT staff

table systems, there is always a potential risk that service providers may use the knowledge they obtained from the client to develop competitors' systems. Under the market-based outsourcing governance mode, IT is more likely to be viewed as a commodity, and a form of knowledge transfer is therefore likely to occur. As a result, firms that have a high level of IT intensity may keep their IT development in-house in order to sustain their competitive advantages.

Hypothesis 5: There is a negative relationship between a firm's IT intensity and the propensity to outsource IT.

Figure 7.1 shows the research model in which relationships between outsourcing intensity and the five organizational contextual variables are specified schematically.

RESEARCH METHODS

Data

Our primary data source for IT-related variables is *InformationWeek*, a magazine that publishes key IT spending data on a yearly basis. Several earlier studies (e.g., Brynolfsson and Hitt, 1996; Santhanam and Hartono, 2003) have also used *InformationWeek* as their primary data source. In the late 1990s, the magazine issued special reports that ranked 500 of the most innovative IT organizations, providing specific information about the size of the IT budget, the number of IT employees, the proportion of the IT budget spent on outsourcing, and so on. Of the top 500 firms, 169 are included in the final sample used in the study. Over 300 firms were excluded from the study either because they are not public firms whose stocks are traded at major exchanges (NYSE and NASDAQ), or insufficient IT data was provided by *InformationWeek.* More specifically, of the 500 firms surveyed, *InformationWeek* detailed specific IT data for only 256 firms, 87 of which are identified as private firms whose stocks are not publicly listed. Therefore, 169 (or 256 – 87) firms are identified as public firms whose IT data were available in *InformationWeek.* However, specific data on outsourcing intensity measured by the percentage of IT budget (not revenues) allocated to outsourcing was available for 128 of 169 companies. Ultimately, a sample of 128 companies was used in the study.

To obtain information about firm characteristics, we used COMPUSTAT and the University of Chicago's Center for Research in Security Prices (CRSP), which supply financial data only for public companies. In addition, because *InformationWeek* provides detailed IT information for selected firms, we had to remove those firms for which outsourcing and IT budget information was not fully available.

Variables

Outsourcing intensity was used as the dependent variable, while uncertainty, agency risk (FCF), operational inefficiency (SGA/sales), R&D intensity, and IT intensity constituted the independent variables for our model. In addition, three control variables (the number of IT employees, firm size, and industry) were added in order to control for their potential effects. Table 7.1 presents the variables used in the study in greater detail, with a precise description and measurement for each variable. *Outsourcing intensity was measured based on the percentage of a company's IT budget, not the percentage of the company's revenue allocated to outsourcing IT.* This study is concerned with the balance between IT outsourcing and insourcing, rather than the total amount spent on IT outsourcing, the operationalization used in Loh and Venkatraman (1992a). The dependent variable used reflects a firm's outsourcing intensity within its IT strategy, showing the equilibrium of outsourcing and insourcing. The operationalization of outsourcing intensity measured by the amount of revenues allocated to outsourcing does not accurately represent the significance of outsourcing within a firm's IS strategy.

Uncertainty and agency costs were calculated based on data from the CRSP at the University of Chicago and COMPUSTAT, respectively. Building on the work by Bloom and Reenen (2002) and Leahy and Whited (1998), we calculated the standard deviation of stock returns for one year[3] and used it as a proxy for uncertainty. Agency costs were measured according to the procedures specified in the accounting literature (Fama and French, 1992); that is, the amount of discretionary cash flow a business has at its disposal at any given time, after deducting operating costs, interest payments on bank loans and bonds, salaries, and other fixed costs. In accordance with Smith, Mitra, and Narasimhan (1998), operational inefficiency was measured by SGA divided by sales. SGA refers to expenses and costs not linked to the production of specific goods, but includes all selling, general company expenses, and administrative expenses. IT intensity and R&D intensity were operationalized through the normalization of the total amount allocated to each investment by the size of each company. Finally, data on the number of IT employees and firm size were obtained directly from *InformationWeek* and COMPUSTAT, respectively. Based on our literature review, manufacturing and health care were identified as the industries that were relatively less active in adopting IT, while the rest of the industries (financial, insurance, retail, etc.) were classified as heavy users of IT.

Table 7.1

Variable Description and Measurement

Variables	Data source	Description	Measurement
Outsourcing intensity	*InformationWeek* (*IW*) (1997)	A firm's intensity toward information technology (IT) outsourcing	Percentage of company's IT budget spent on outsourced projects (*IW*)
Uncertainty	CRSP (1996)	The degree of instability with respect to a firm's ability to produce cash flow in the future	Standard deviation of stock returns for one year (1996)
Agency costs (free cash flow)	COMPUSTAT (1996)	The amount of free cash flow available for reinvestment or dividend payment	The amount of discretionary cash flow that a business has at its disposal at any given time, after deducting operating costs, interest payments on bank loans and bonds, salaries, research and development (R&D), and other fixed costs
R&D intensity	COMPUSTAT (1996)	A firm's intensity toward innovation	Percentage of revenues spent on R&D
IT intensity	COMPUSTAT, *IW* (1996)	A firm's intensity toward IT investment	Percentage of revenues spent on IT budget
Operational inefficiency	COMPUSTAT (1996)	A firm's operational inefficiency measured by selling, general administrative (SGA) expenses, which represent the costs associated with selling and the general expenses of running the business.	The amount of SGA divided by sales
IT employee	*IW* (1997)	The number of IT staff hired by the company (Outsourced IT staff members were not included in the count.)	The number of IT employees
Firm size	COMPUSTAT (1997)	The size of a firm	The number of total employees
Industry	*IW* (1997)	The industry in which a firm operates	Manufacturing and health care are coded as 0 and the rest are coded as 1

Control Variables

Industry (Loh and Venkatraman, 1992b), firm size (Ang and Straub, 1998; Loh and Venkatraman, 1992b), and the number of IT staff within the firm were included to control for their potential effects on the propensity to outsource IT. Dummy codes were used in order to separate the industries that traditionally have been less active in adopting and using IT (e.g., manufacturing and health care) from those industries that have been characterized as more IT-intensive (e.g., financial, insurance, service, retail, etc.) (Brynjolfsson and Hitt, 1996). The industries less inclined to use IT are predicted

Table 7.2

Descriptive Statistics

	N	Minimum	Maximum	Mean	Standard deviation
Outsourcing intensity (%)	128	0.00	90	16.67	18.70
Uncertainty	135	0.0064	0.04	0.02	0.01
Agency costs (free cash flow, millions of dollars)	137	–936	3,465	58.55	352.49
Operational inefficiency	104	0.04	1.64	0.252	0.237
Research and development intensity (%)	87	0.0000	0.17	0.03	0.03
Information technology (IT) intensity (%)	153	0.002	0.14	0.03	0.02
IT employee	149	12	13,000	1,082	1,578
Firm size	123	698	647,000	54,975	94,038
Industry	169	0.00	1.00	0.69	0.47

to be more dependent on IT outsourcing than those that are active, because the former are not as likely to have the IT capabilities and experience necessary to develop their own IT systems.

The size of a firm has been considered a potential determinant that moderates IT buy-or-make decisions. Ang and Straub (1998) found that firm size is negatively related to the propensity to outsource.[4] Developing IT internally requires resources and expertise that are not readily available in small firms. Compared to their larger counterparts, small firms generally have a lower IT adoption rate, accumulate limited IT knowledge and expertise, underutilize their IT applications, and lack infrastructural integration (Iacovou, Benbasat, and Dexter, 1995). Financial limitations also result in a shortage of management staff, which restricts a small firm's ability to develop innovative and sophisticated IT applications (Markland, 1974). In contrast, larger firms are typically not as limited by the availability of financial resources, and have more expertise in developing and managing IT than small firms do (Delone, 1981). In addition, tangible and intangible assets are relatively more ubiquitous in large firms, making it easier for them to develop applications that are tailored to their specific needs (Ang and Straub, 1998).

RESULTS

Descriptive Statistics

Table 7.2 shows the descriptive statistics for the variables in the model, including average and standard deviation. The average for outsourcing intensity is about 17 percent, indicating that our sample firms spent 17 percent of their IT budgets on outsourcing. A wide range of variation was observed with respect to the degree of outsourcing intensity, with a minimum of 0 percent and a maximum of 90 percent. IT intensity indicates a percentage of IT spending standardized by firm revenues. The results show that the firms in our sample spend, on average, 2.6 percent of their revenues on IT, which is similar to the ratio found in other studies. The average for uncertainty is 0.017, which was calculated based on the standard deviation of stock returns during a one-year period. The amount of free cash flow, a proxy that reflects agency costs, ranges from –$936 million to $3,465 million. A striking difference was seen in terms of SGA/sales, with the minimum being

Table 7.3

OLS Regression Results

	Model 1	Model 2
(Constant)	7.14** (36.46)	6.75** (16.46)
IT employee	–3.15E-05 (–0.22)	–2.63E-04 (–1.35)
Firm size	3.18E-07 (0.15)	1.65E-07 (0.08)
Industry	–1.13E-02 (–0.05)	0.37 (1.39)
Uncertainty		–44.00* (–2.21)
Agency costs		–2.17E-03** (–3.00)
Research and development intensity		12.85** (2.56)
IT intensity		16.28 (1.21)
Operational inefficiency		1.70* (2.33)
Adjusted R^2	–0.040	0.37
F-value	0.02	3.90

$^{**}p < 0.01$
$^{*}p < 0.05$

0.04 and the maximum 1.64. The average was 0.25. Firms spend 3.3 percent of their revenues on R&D, which is a little higher than the proportion allocated to the IT budget. The average number of IT employees for the firms in our sample is just over 1,000, which is about 2 percent of the total number of employees in the sampled firms. Approximately 30 percent of the firms in our sample can be classified as falling within either the manufacturing or health care industries, while the rest are in finance, insurance, retail, and so on.

OLS Results

We began by creating a base model (Hair, 1998), which consists of the control variables that may have significant effects on the dependent variable (Table 7.3). After regressing the firm size, the number of IT employees, and industry dummy on the propensity of outsourcing (model 1), we found that none of the control variables of our choosing yielded a significant model. Model 2 shows the results of the full model, which is composed of both independent and control variables. Following this procedure, we can understand the additional explanatory power beyond the base model, through a comparison the R^2 of the two models (Hair, 1998).

The OLS regression results of the full model indicate that the *F*-value of the model is significant ($F = 3.9$, $p < 0.01$). The adjusted R^2 is 0.37, indicating that 37 percent of the variance in the dependent variable can be explained by the independent variables in our model. The control variables collectively increased the explanatory power of the model by a significant margin (0.43 or 16/37). The diagnostic test reveals that neither multicollinearity nor heteroscedascity is present in the model. The results suggest that a firm's propensity to outsource IT resources for its given IT budget is positively associated with R&D intensity ($p < 0.01$) and operational inefficiency ($p < 0.05$), while a significant negative relationship was observed for uncertainty ($p < 0.05$) and agency risk ($p < 0.01$) (Table 7.3). In contrast, our hypothesis for IT intensity is not supported by the data.

As hypothesized, our results suggest that uncertainty has a negative impact on a firm's decision to outsource IT resources. In the presence of uncertainty, organizations tend to vertically integrate their operations and extend their hierarchies by developing IT systems in-house, while minimizing the market-based outsourcing arrangements. Despite the potential benefits (e.g., risk-buffering), when faced with uncertainties, managers still perceive IT outsourcing to be a risky initiative and prefer an internal governance mode to avoid any detrimental consequences. With regard to the two competing theoretical explanations, our results indicate that the TCE perspective concerned with a firm's boundaries of choice appears to account more convincingly for the behavior of managers in making their outsourcing decisions than does resource dependency theory. Resource dependency theory (Pfeffer and Salancik, 1978) suggests that in the presence of uncertainty firms are likely to actively engage in creating external linkages in order to secure more resources and share the risk. We did not find strong support for this theoretical argument in the context of IT outsourcing.

As predicted, when there is high agency conflict between managers (agents) and shareholders (principals), the management of the firm allocates a greater proportion of the IT budget to internal development than to outsourcing. A manager has strong incentive to control the distribution of resources through in-house development in order to increase his command and authority within the company. Outsourcing IT projects to external vendors is likely to require some degree of "power transfer," which diminishes the manager's organizational control. Our results show that certain managers may behave opportunistically and choose insourcing in pursuit of their own "interests," even though outsourcing is considered a better alternative, one that uses core competencies and reduces operational costs. If such opportunistic behaviors prevail, internal IT development is likely to result in suboptimal consequences, primarily due to the inefficient allocations of resources and poor management.

IT intensity does not seem to significantly affect the propensity to outsource IT resources ($p > 0.1$). From the resource-based view, we predicted that firms with high IT intensity see IT as a valuable strategic initiative rather than a commodity that is easily duplicable, and, therefore, they insource their IT functions more aggressively. However, this hypothesis is not supported by our data. One speculation for this result is that IT intensity, measured by the percentage of revenues spent on the IT budget, is relatively high in small and growing firms, many of which may have limited resources and capacities to internally develop their IT systems (Harris and Katz 1991). Another possibility is that due to rapid technological changes and increased sophistication, even firms with high IT intensity rely heavily on outsourcing arrangements. These factors may confound the positive relationship, as hypothesized.

One of the intriguing results obtained from this study is that R&D intensity is positively associated with outsourcing intensity ($p < 0.01$), not negatively as hypothesized. We expected that firms that invest heavily in R&D would pursue innovation, seek long-term profits, and aggressively undertake risky initiatives, and would therefore be likely to develop IT systems internally rather than purchase them through the market. More importantly, due to the potential hazards involved in the transfer of tacit knowledge, innovative firms are assumed to be less active in outsourcing arrangements with external vendors. The results indicate exactly the opposite; that is, the greater the intensity in R&D, the higher the propensity to outsource IT.

We have speculated about the potential causes of this puzzling result. In our conceptual development, we considered R&D and IT investments separately, and argued that a firm's R&D decision process is similar to the way in which IT investment strategy is established and implemented. We focused on the structural similarity between these two types of investments, and developed the hypothesis accordingly. It is possible that our argument, which assumed that investment similarity was the main driver of outsourcing decisions, may need to be reconsidered. IT may not indeed be independent of R&D, but may constitute a significant element of all of the R&D processes that involve new product/process developments. Assuming dependency between the two types of corporate investments, firms may seek to acquire some flexibility in their IT operations in order to manage their R&D operations successfully. Similar to IT investments, realizing tangible benefits from R&D requires a substantial amount of time during which rapid technological changes are likely to occur. Therefore, developing IT internally in parallel with R&D may be risky, and potentially inhibit a firm's ability to fully leverage IT for generating innovative products or processes.

Conversely, IT outsourcing may provide R&D-intensive firms with some technological flexibility through which they can capitalize on the latest technologies in order to develop innovative products or processes. Scott and Pascoe (1987) suggest that innovative firms engage in "purposive diversification" in order to exploit technological complementarities. Outsourcing may offer a dynamic and flexible option by which a firm can enhance its innovative capabilities—that is, it may provide firms with opportunities to expand their innovative capacity by deploying and coordinating different organizational resources and processes (Teece, Pisano, and Shuen, 1997). Outsourcing can therefore be seen as an attractive venue to acquire such technological complementarities for firms that aggressively undertake R&D. As has been well publicized, one prominent advantage of IT outsourcing is the provision of the best breed of technologies, which are critical components for the successful implementation of R&D. Recently, the emergence of intriguing and nascent outsourcing phenomena, such as ASP and utility-based outsourcing,[5] has provided dynamic technological flexibilities by which firms can shorten the life cycle necessary to produce innovative products, and reduce uncertainty in R&D payoffs. This may be one of the reasons that R&D-intensive firms outsource IT more aggressively, rather than insourcing their IT needs.

IMPLICATIONS AND FUTURE STUDIES

The general benefits and costs of IT outsourcing are well documented in the literature; cost reduction, the ability to focus on core competence, technological leadership, and so on, are some of the driving forces of IT outsourcing, while transactional risks, such as opportunism, lock-ins, contractual difficulties, and the like, constitute reasons not to outsource IT. Nevertheless, such benefits and costs are less likely to affect firms' outsourcing decisions equally, since each firm has its own strengths and weaknesses and makes decisions that maximize the outcome, given its resources and capabilities (Lawrence and Lorsch, 1969). Our study aims to explore such organizational factors that may determine a firm's outsourcing decision.

A firm's capital investment decision may be contingent on the level of uncertainties it faces. Such decisions may also be greatly influenced by systematic corporate vulnerabilities, such as agency conflicts and operational inefficiencies. Moreover, a firm's capital structure should be understood in the broader context in which its resources (e.g., IT resources) and capacities (e.g., innovativeness) are fully factored into the decision-making equation. Researchers should pay more attention to the contingent nature of capital investment decisions, which often deviate from the normative prescriptions of economic theory. In terms of theory development in outsourcing research, more conceptual frameworks are needed to understand the complex nature of such capital investment. For many years, TCE has been a fundamental aspect of the outsourcing framework. However, the emergence of diverse theoretical foundations will further advance this stream of research, theoretically and empirically. Resource dependence, social capital, institutional theory, and a contingency framework can open up a new fresh theoretical vantage point from which to further the understanding of outsourcing practice.

Our study yields several implications for practitioners. Managers often tend to focus more on investment consequences than on causes or processes, making capital decisions based on past performance. However, prior to making outsourcing decisions, a full understanding of the firm's characteristics is essential in order to elicit optimal consequences. In so doing, managers should investigate a priori their managerial, technological, and environmental resources and capabilities, and make the decision accordingly. In addition to the transactional risks identified in the literature, a failure to incorporate these contingencies into investment decision making is likely to lead to unfavorable results.

The recent trends in outsourcing, such as offshore sourcing and component-based outsourcing, have made outsourcing far more affordable and manageable. As these cost-effective options become more pervasive and viable, a new responsibility arises for managers: How are they to balance or integrate outsourcing and internal IT development? On the one hand, when two different governance modes exist, synergistic benefits (e.g., knowledge transfer from outsourced IT functions to other internal IT developments) may accrue. On the other hand, combining and integrating the two heterogeneous structures in one firm may create many problems (i.e., managerial and technological coordination, cultural differences, etc.) that do not exist otherwise. Moreover, it will be a daunting task to determine what should be outsourced, the extent to which it should be outsourced, and which functions should be insourced.

This study has several limitations that can be addressed by future studies. We used only public firms to assess the pattern of outsourcing intensity due to the ease of collecting financial data that characterize the companies used in the study. The results of the study could be more generalizable if nonpublic firms were also added to the sample. Interestingly, our results suggest that firm size is not a key factor determining the propensity to outsource. Nevertheless, a future study is necessary to understand the extent to which small firms allocate their IT budgets to outsourcing.

Our model is based on several key organizational variables that influence a firm's capital structure and IT governance decisions. The independent variables in the model collectively explained approximately 40 percent of the variance in the balance between outsourcing and insourcing, which suggests that factors unidentified in this study may also significantly govern a firm's decision to allocate its IT budget to outsourcing. Future research should elaborate further in this area, and also identify the equilibrium under which firms can optimize the benefits from IT investments. Similar to the issues seen in finance regarding the optimal proportion of debts versus credits in relation to a firm's financial health, future research should explore the outsourcing equilibrium where firms can maximize their IT health to the full capacity.

Finally, due to rapid technological changes and the emergence of alternative forms of outsourcing arrangements in recent years, the dynamics inherent in outsourcing decisions may evolve over time. New theoretical vocabularies and practical insights are therefore needed to better understand the evolutionary nature of outsourcing decisions. Future studies should investigate changes seen over time in the outsourcing equilibrium, the results of which may better capture the impact of firm characteristics on outsourcing decisions.

CONCLUSION

Transaction cost economics has been widely used as a general conceptual framework from which researchers have drawn primary determinants of IT outsourcing. In this chapter, we provide new insights into such a research area in conjunction with firm characteristics variables. We identify several organization factors (i.e., uncertainty, agency cost, innovativeness, IT intensity, and operational inefficiency) that have been found to influence significantly a firm's investment decisions, and assess how each factor influences a firm's allocation of IT budget to outsourcing. With the exception of IT intensity, the rest of the firm characteristic variables significantly influence a firm's outsourcing-related decisions. Capital investment decisions are complex and require a profound understanding of the various contingencies that are seemingly present both within and outside a firm. The transaction cost economics view lays a solid theoretical base for understanding the boundaries of firms in conjunction with the alternatives between markets and hierarchies in determining capital investments. However, because each firm is different in terms of its ability to leverage the potential benefits and mitigate the inherent risks associated with IT outsourcing, firm characteristic variables should be taken into account for understanding outsourcing-related decisions.

ACKNOWLEDGMENT

The author thanks McGill University's research center for providing financial resources essential for the completion of this work.

NOTES

1. *IT outsourcing* is defined as a "significant contribution by external vendors in the physical and/or human resources associated with the entire or specific components of the IT infrastructure in the user organization" (Loh & Venkatraman, 1992b).
2. Following Harris and Katz (1991), we define *IT intensity* as the ratio of IT investment to a firm's revenue.
3. To calculate uncertainty and FCF, we used 1996 data. The IT budget, including the IT outsourcing budget is established at the beginning of the year (1997), so we used the previous year's data.
4. Note that our operationalization of IT outsourcing propensity is different from that used by Ang and Straub (1998).
5. *Utility-based outsourcing* refers to a usage-oriented outsourcing pricing model in which IT infrastructure is paid only when it is used. For example, a recent arrangement between IBM Global and American Express was based on utility pricing, allowing American Express to save millions of dollars by transforming its fixed IT costs to variable costs (http://techupdate.zdnet.com, April 8, 2002).

REFERENCES

Amit, R. and Schoemaker, P. 1993. Strategic assets and organizational rent. *Strategic Management Journal*, 14, 1, 33–46.

Anderson, E. 1985. The salesperson as outside agent or employee: A transaction cost analysis. *Marketing Science*, 4, 3 , 234–253.

Ang, S. and Beath, C.M. 1993. Hierarchical elements in software contracts. *Journal of Organizational Computing*, 3, 3, 329–361.

Ang, S. and Cummings, L. 1997. Strategic response to institutional influence on information systems outsourcing. *Organization Science*, 8, 3, 235–256.

Ang, S. and Endeshaw, A. 1997. Legal case analysis in IS research: Failures in employing and outsourcing for IT professionals. In A.S. Lee, J. Liebenau, and J.I. DeGross, eds., *Information Systems and Qualitative Research*. London: Chapman & Hall, 497–523.

Ang, S. and Straub, D.W. 1998. Production and transaction economies and IS outsourcing: A study of the U.S. banking industry. *MIS Quarterly*, 22, 4, 535–552.

Ang, S. and Straub, D.W. 2002. Costs, transaction specific investments and vendor dominance of the marketplace: The economics of IS outsourcing. In R. Hirschheim, A. Heinzl, and J.Dibbern, eds., *Information Systems Outsourcing: Enduring Themes, Emergent Patterns and Future Directions*. Berlin: Springer Verlag, 47–76.

Arnett, K. and Jones, M. 1994. Firms that choose outsourcing: A profile. *Information and Management*, 26, 4, 79–188.

Aubert, B.; Rivard, S.; and Patry, M. 2004. A transaction cost model of IT outsourcing. *Information and Management*, 41, 7, 921–932.

Bakos, Y. and Treacy, M. 1986. Information technology and corporate strategy: A research perspective. *MIS Quarterly*, 10, 2, 107–119.

Banker, R.; Kauffman, R.; and Morey, R. 1990. Measuring gains in operational efficiency from information technology: A study of the positran deployment at Hardee's Inc. *Journal of Management Information Systems*, 7, 2, 29–55.

Barney, J. 1986. Strategic factor markets: Expectations, luck, and business strategy. *Management Science*, 32, 10, 1231–1241.

Barney, J.B. 1991. Firm resources and sustained competitive advantage. *Journal of Management*, 17, 1, 99–120.

Barua, A.; Kriebel, C.; and Mukhopadhyay, T. 1995. Information technologies and business value: An analytic and empirical investigation. *Information Systems Research*, 6, 1, 3–23.

Barua, A. and Lee, B. 1997. An economic analysis of the introduction of an electronic data interchange system. *Information Systems Research*, 8, 4, 398–423.

Bloom, N. and Reenen, J. 2002. Patents, real options and firm performance. *Economic Journal*, 112, 478, 97–116.

Benaroch, M. and Kauffman, R. 1999. A case for using real options pricing analysis to evaluate information technology project investment. *Information Systems Research,* 10, 1, 70–86.

———. 2000. Justifying electronic banking network expansion using real options analysis, *MIS Quarterly*, 24, 2, 197–226.

Boyd, B. 1990. Corporate linkages and organizational environment: A test of the resource dependence model. *Strategic Management Journal*, 11, 6, 419–430.

Brynjolfsson, E. and Hitt, L. 1996. Paradox lost? Firm-level evidence on the returns to information systems. *Management Science*, 42, 4, 541–558.

Caldwell, B. 1998. Partners: Genesis of a new service era. *InformationWeek*, 44–70.

Clemons, E. 2000. The build/buy battle. *CIO Magazine*, December 1, www.cio.com/archive/120100/ea.html. Accessed June 2005.

Clemons, E. and Row, M. 1991. Information technology at Rosenbluth travel. *Journal of Management Information Systems*, 8, 2, 53–79.

Cohen, W. and Levin, R. 1989. Empirical studies of innovation and market structure. In R. Schmalensee and R. Willig, eds., *Handbook of Industrial Organization*. Amsterdam: North Holland, 1059–1107.

Craine, R. 1989. Risky business: The allocation of capital. *Journal of Monetary Economics*, 23, 2, 201–218.

Cross, J.; Earl, M.; and Sampler, J. 1997. Transformation of the IT function at British petroleum. *MIS Quarterly*, 21, 4, 401–423.

Cyert, R and March, J. 1963. A behavioral theory of the firm. Englewood Cliffs, NJ: Prentice Hall.

Delone, W.H. 1981. Small size and the characteristics of computer use. *MIS Quarterly*, 5, 4, 65–77.

Dewan, S.; Michael, S.; and Min, C. 1998. Firm characteristics and investments in information technology: Scale and scope effects. *Information Systems Research*, 9, 3, 219–231.

Dierickx, I. and Cool, K. 1989. Asset stock accumulation and sustainability of competitive advantage. *Management Science*, 35, 12, 1504–1511.

DiRomualdo, A. and Gurbaxani, V. 1998. Strategic intent for IT outsourcing. *Sloan Management Review*, 39, 4, 67–80.

Dutta, S. and Weiss, A. 1997. The relationship between a firm's level of technological innovativeness and its pattern of partnership agreements. *Management Science*, 43, 3, 343–356.

Earl, M.J. 1996. The risks of outsourcing IT. *Sloan Management Review*, 37, 3, 26–32.

Fama, E. and French, K. 1992. The cross section of expected stock returns. *Journal of Finance*, 47, 2, 427–465.

Galbraith, J.K. 1977. *Age of Uncertainty.* Boston: Houghton Mifflin.

Gallivan, M. and Oh, W. 1999. Analyzing IT outsourcing relationships as alliances among multiple clients and vendors. *Proceedings of the Thirty-second Hawaiian Internal Conference on System Science*, Maui.

Gurbaxani, V. and Whang, S. 1991. The impact of information systems on organizations and markets. *CACM*, 34, 1, 59–73.

Jauch, L. and Kraft, K. 1986. Strategic management of uncertainty. *Academy of Management Review*, 11, 4, 777–790.

John, G. and Weitz, B. 1988. Forward integration into distribution: An empirical test of transaction cost analysis. *Journal of Law, Economics and Organization*, 4, 337–355.

Hair, J., Jr.; Anderson, R.; Tatham, R.; and Black, W. 1998. *Multivariate Data Analysis*. Upper Saddle River, NJ: Prentice Hall, 1998.

Harris, M. and Raviv, A. 1991. The theory of capital structure. *Journal of Finance*, 46, 297–355.

Harris, S.E. and Katz, J.L. 1991. Organizational performance and information technology investment intensity in the insurance industry. *Organizational Science*, 2, 3, 263–296.

Hayes, M. 1997. Retail: Facing the millennium. *InformationWeek*, http://i.cmpnet.com/infoweek/649/graphics/retail.pdf. Accessed August 2004.

Hill, C. and Hoskisson, R. 1987. Strategy and structure in the multi-product firm. *Academy of Management Review*, 12, 2, 331–341.

Ho, V.; Ang, S.; and Straub, D. 2003. When subordinates become IT contractors: Persistent managerial expectations in IT outsourcing. *Information Systems Research*, 14, 1, 66–86.

Howton, D.; Howton, W.; and Perfect, S. 1998. The market reaction to straight debt issues: The effects of free cash flow. *The Journal of Financial Research*, 21, 2, 219–228.

Hunter, S.; Kobelsky, K.; and Richardson, V.J. 2003. Volatility and dispersion of earnings following IT expenditures. Baylor University Working Paper.

Iacovou, C.; Benbasat, I.; and Dexter, A. 1995. Electronic data interchange and small organizations: Adoption and impact of technology. *MIS Quarterly*, 19, 4, 465–485.

Jauch, L. and Kraft, K. 1986. Strategic management of uncertainty. *Academy of Management Review*, 11,4, 777–790.

Jensen, M. 1986. Agency costs of free cash flow, corporate finance, and takeovers. *American Economic Review*, 76, 2, 323–329.

Jensen M. and Meckling, W. 1976. Theory of the firm: Managerial behavior, agency costs and ownership Structure. *Journal of Financial Economics*, 3, 305–360.

Kern, T. 1997. The gestalt of an information technology outsourcing relationship: An exploratory analysis. *Proceedings of the Eighteenth International Conference on Information Systems*, Atlanta, Georgia, 37–58.

Kern, T. and Willcocks, L. 2002. Exploring relationships in information technology outsourcing: The interaction approach. *European Journal of Information Systems*, 11, 1, 3–19.

Kern, T.; Willcocks, L.; and Heck, E. 2002. The winner's curse in IT outsourcing: Strategies for avoiding relational trauma. *California Management Review*, 44, 2, 47–69.

Koberg, C. 1987. Resource scarcity, environmental uncertainty, and adaptive organizational behavior. *Academy of Management Journal*, 30, 4, 798–807.

Kochhar, R. 1996. Explaining firm capital structure: The role of agency theory vs. transaction cost Economics. *Strategic Management Journal*, 17, 713–728.

Lacity, M. and Willcocks, L. 2000. Survey of IT outsourcing experiences in U.S. and U.K. organizations. *Journal of Global Information Management*, 8, 2, 5–23.

Lacity, M.; Hirschheim, R.; and Willcocks, L. 1994. Realizing outsourcing expectations. *Information Systems Management*, 11, 4, 7–18.

Lawrence, P and Lorsch, J. 1969. *Organization and Environment*. Homewood, IL: Irwin.

Leahy, J. and Whited, T. 1998. The effects of uncertainty on investment: Some stylized facts. *Journal of Money Credit and Banking*, 28, 64–83.

Lee, J. and Kim, Y. 1999. Effect of partnership quality on IS outsourcing success: Conceptual framework and empirical validation. *Journal of Management Information Systems*, 15, 4, 29–61.

Lee, J.; Miranda, L.; and Kim, Y. 2004. IT outsourcing strategies: Universalistic, contingency, and configurational explanations of success. *Information Systems Research*, 15, 2, 110–131.

Lev, B. 1975. Environmental uncertainty reduction by smoothing and buffering: An empirical verification. *Academy of Management Journal*, 18, 4, 164–171.

Loh, L. and Venkatraman, N. 1992a. Diffusion of IT outsourcing: Influence sources and the Kodak effect. *Information Systems Research*, 3, 4, 334–358.

———. 1992b. Determinants of information technology outsourcing: A cross-sectional analysis. *Journal of Management Information Systems*, 9, 1, 7–24.

Malone, T.; Yates, J.; and Benjamin, R. 1987. Electronic markets and electronic hierarchies: Effects of new information technologies on market structures and corporate strategies. *CACM*, 30, 6, 484–497.

March, J. and Simon, H. 1958. *Organizations*. New York: Wiley.

Markland, R.E. 1974. The role of the computer in small business management. *Journal of Small Business Management*, 12, 1, 21—26.

Mata, F.J.; Fuerst, W.L.; and Barney, J.B. 1995. Information technology and sustained competitive advantage: A resource-based analysis. *MIS Quarterly*, 19, 4, 487–505.

Myers, S. 1984. The capital structure puzzle. *Journal of Finance*, 39, 3, 575–592.

Mukhopadhyay, T.; Kekre, S.; and Kalathur, S. 1995. Business value of information technology: A study of electronic data interchange. *MIS Quarterly*, 19, 2, 137–156.

Nam, K.; Rajagopalan, S.; Rao, H.; and Chaudhury, A. 1996. A two level investigation of information systems outsourcing. *CACM*, 39, 7, 37–44.

Oh, W. and Gallivan, M. 2004. An empirical assessment of transactional risks of IT outsourcing arrangements: An event study. *Proceedings of the Thirty-seventh Hawaiian International Conference on System Science*, Honolulu.

Oh, W. and Kim, J. 2001. The effects of firm characteristics on investor reaction to IT investment announcements. *Proceedings of the International Conference on Information Systems*, New Orleans, LA.

Oh, W.; Kim, J.; and Richardson, V. 2005. The moderating effect of context on the market reaction to IT Investments. *AAA-IS Section Mid-Year Conference*, New Orleans, LA.

Oliver, C. 1997. Sustainable competitive advantage: combining institutional and resource-based views. *Strategic Management Journal*, 18, 9, 697–713.

Palvia, P.C. 1995. A dialectic view of information systems outsourcing: Pros and cons. *Information & Management*, 29, 5, 265–275.

Pfeffer, J. 1972. Merger as a response to organizational interdependence. *Administrative Science Quarterly*, 17, 3, 382–394.

Pfeffer, J. and Nowak, P. 1976. Joint ventures and interorganizational interdependence. *Administrative Science Quarterly*, 21, 3, 398–418.

Pfeffer, J. and Salancik, G. 1978. *The External Control of Organizations: A Resource Dependence Perspective.* New York: Harper and Row.

Porter, M. 1980. *Competitive Strategy*. New York: Free Press.

Santhanam, R. and Hartono, E. 2003. Issues in linking information technology capability to firm performance. *MIS Quarterly*, 27, 1, 125–153.

Scott, J.T. and Pascoe, G. 1987. Purposive diversification of R&D in manufacturing. *Journal of Industrial Economics*, 36, 2, 193–205.

Schwartz, E., and Zozaya-Gorostiza, C. 2003. Investment under uncertainty in IT: Acquisition and development projects. *Management Science*, 49, 1, 57–70.

Smith, A.; Mitra, S.; and Narasimhan, S. 1998. Information systems outsourcing: A study of pre-event firm characteristics. *Journal of Management Information Systems*, 15, 2, 61–93.

Taudes, A., Feuerstein, M. and Mild, A. 2000. Option analysis of software platform decisions: A case study. *MIS Quarterly*, 24, 2, 227–243.

Teece, D.J. 1988. Capturing value from technological innovation: Integration, strategic partnering, and licensing decisions. *Interfaces*, 18, 3, 46–61.

Teece, D. and Pisano, G. 1994. The dynamic capabilities of firms: An introduction. *Industrial and Corporate Changes*, 3, 3, 537–556.

Teece, D.; Pisano, G.; Shuen, A. 1997. Dynamic capabilities and strategic management. *Strategic Management Journal*, 18, 7, 509–533.

Teng, J.; Cheon, M.; and Grover, V. 1995. Decisions to outsource information systems functions: Testing a strategy theoretic discrepancy model. *Decision Sciences*, 26, 1, 75–103.

Thatcher, M. and Oliver, J. 2001. The impact of technology investments on a firm's production efficiency, product quality, and productivity. *Journal of Management Information Systems*, 18, 2, 17–46.

Walker, G. and Weber, D. 1984. A transaction cost approach to make-or-buy decisions. *Administrative Science Quarterly*, 29, 3, 373–391.

Wernefelt, B. 1984. A resource-based view of the firm. *Strategic Management Journal*, 5, 171–180.

Willcocks, L. and Choi, C.J. 1995. Cooperative partnership and total IT outsourcing: from contractual obligation to strategic alliance. *European Management Journal*, 13, 1, 67–78.

Williamson, O.E. 1979. Transaction cost economics: The governance of contractual relations. *Journal of Law and Economics*, 22, 2, 233–261.

Williamson, O.E. and Ouchi, W. 1981. The markets and hierarchies program of research: Origins, implications, prospects. In A. Van de Ven and W. Joyce, eds., *Perspectives on Organization Design and Behavior*. New York: Wiley, 347–370.

Ye, F. and Agarwal, R. 2003. Strategic information technology partnerships in outsourcing as a distinctive source of information technology value: A social capital perspective. *Proceedings of the International Conference on Information Systems*, Seattle, WA.

CHAPTER 8

INFORMATION TECHNOLOGY OUTSOURCING RISK

A Resource-Based Perspective

BOUCHAIB BAHLI AND SUZANNE RIVARD

Abstract: *Firms can obtain numerous benefits outsourcing some of their information systems services. This mode of governance, however, also entails risks that can lead to significant negative consequences. Although the literature proposes a number of risk assessment frameworks and risk management strategies for information technology (IT) outsourcing, little attention has been paid to the gap differential in organizational capabilities that can result from IT outsourcing. This chapter focuses on the issue of outsourcing strategic IT activities and proposes a conceptual framework that draws on the resource-based theory (RBT) of the firm. To this end, the chapter begins with a synthesis of the existing literature on IT outsourcing risk. It then presents the main elements of the RBT of the firm and proposes a conceptual framework of risk in the outsourcing of strategic IT activities.*

Keywords: *Firm Competencies, IT Outsourcing, Resource-Based Theory, Risk*

INTRODUCTION

The decision to outsource information technology (IT)-related activities, be they operational, system development, or business process activities, has three main objectives: to reduce costs, to improve service quality, and to place greater focus on core business activities. Despite the numerous benefits that can result from outsourcing, this mode of governance also entails risks, and, sometimes, can have significant negative consequences on business performance. The information systems (IS) literature has documented several cases of IT outsourcing failure. Recently, *McKinsey Quarterly* (2002) researched thirty-five large outsourcing agreements and found that in two out of three instances, companies failed to achieve all or part of the expected benefits. Approximately 30 percent of the contracts had to be terminated and another 25 percent were renegotiated within two years in order to change critical elements such as scope, service level requirements, and price.

A number of authors have called for the adoption of a risk management approach to IT outsourcing and have proposed IT outsourcing risk factors, risk assessment frameworks, and risk management strategies (Aubert, Patry, and Rivard, 1998, 2005; Bahli and Rivard, 2003; Earl, 1996; Willcocks, Lacity, and Kern, 1999). In the recent past, outsourcing has evolved, moving from the outsourcing of noncore business to outsourcing strategic IT activities (Roy and Aubert,

2002). This move may come with a heavy price. If such a high proportion of organizations do not meet their cost-cutting or service-quality objectives when they outsource noncore activities, outsourcing strategic IT activities may entail even more risk and have disastrous consequences. Indeed, by outsourcing strategic IT activities, an organization may put itself at risk of creating a gap differential in its capabilities, and, ultimately, of losing its competitive advantage.

The IS literature has been rather silent on this issue. This chapter aims to examine, in a formal manner, the concept of risk in the outsourcing of strategic IT activities and to propose a conceptual framework based on the resource-based theory (RBT) of the firm. To this end, the chapter begins with a synthesis of the existing literature on IT outsourcing risk. It then presents the main elements of the RBT of the firm and proposes a conceptual framework of risk in the outsourcing of strategic IT activities.

IT OUTSOURCING RISK: A SYNTHESIS OF THE EXISTING LITERATURE

Although the term "risk" is frequently used in the literature, its conceptualization differs from one discipline to the next and even from one researcher to another. The terms "risk," "risk exposure," "perceived risk," and "risk factor" are often used interchangeably, leaving no standard for these constructs.

In IS research, several authors have used the notion of risk exposure, which is a function of the probability of occurrence of an undesirable outcome and the loss due to the consequences of such an occurrence (Aubert et al., 2001; Aubert, Patry, and Rivard, 1998, 2005; Barki, Rivard, and Talbot, 1993; Boehm, 1989). This conceptualization of risk exposure calls for an estimation of both the loss due to the occurrence of an undesirable outcome and the probability of such an occurrence. In certain cases, probabilities can be estimated on the basis of the past performance of the object under study. When such an assessment is not feasible, several risk assessment methods adopt the approach of estimating the probability of occurrence of an undesirable outcome by identifying and assessing the characteristics of a situation that are likely to influence this occurrence. These characteristics are labeled risk factors.

In the context of IT outsourcing risk, Aubert and colleagues (1998, 2001, 2005) proposed a risk assessment framework based on this conceptualization of risk exposure. As shown in Table 8.1, the proposed risk assessment framework is anchored in IT outsourcing literature as well as in transaction cost theory and agency theory.

Borrowing from Kaplan and Garrick's (1981) well-known conceptualization of risk, Bahli and Rivard (2003) expanded the risk assessment framework proposed by Aubert, Patry, and Rivard (1998, 2001).

Kaplan and Garrick (1981) criticize what they consider the rather limited definitions of risk often used in various fields. First, they deplore the fact that risk definitions often take into account the sole probability of occurrence of an undesirable event. Second, they consider the expected-consequence representation of risk—that is, risk exposure—inappropriate, since it assumes a risk-neutral decision maker. According to Kaplan and Garrick, most people would judge a low-probability/high-consequence scenario as more undesirable than a high-probability/low-consequence scenario, even if the level of risk exposure of the two events is equal. In other words, concepts like frequency-severity diagrams have the undesirable property that very different situations get mapped into identical diagrams, even though a rational risk-adverse decision maker might well have a clear preference between them. Kaplan and Garrick argued for addressing three questions when assessing risk:

Table 8.1

Components of IT Outsourcing Risk Exposure

Undesirable outcomes	Factors leading to outcome
Unexpected transition and management costs (Cross, 1995; Earl, 1996; Nelson et al., 1996)	• Lack of experience and expertise of the client with the activity (Earl, 1996; Lacity et al., 1995, Sappington, 1991) • Lack of experience of the client with outsourcing (Earl, 1996) • Uncertainty about the legal environment
Switching costs (including lock-in, repatriation, and transfer to another supplier)	• Asset specificity (Williamson, 1985) • Small number of suppliers (Nam et al., 1996) • Scope • Interdependence of activities (Langlois and Robertson, 1992)
Costly contractual amendments (Earl, 1996)	• Uncertainty (Alchian and Demsetz, 1972; Barzel, 1982) • Technological discontinuity (Lacity et al., 1995) • Task complexity
Disputes and litigation (Aubert et al., 1997; Lacity and Hirschheim, 1993)	• Measurement problems (Alchian and Demsetz, 1972; Barzel, 1982) • Lack of experience and expertise of the client and/or of the supplier with outsourcing contracts (Earl, 1996; Lacity et al., 1995) • Uncertainty about the legal environment • Poor cultural fit
Service debasement (Lacity and Hirschheim, 1993)	• Interdependence of activities (Aubert et al., 1997; Langlois and Robertson, 1992) • Lack of experience and expertise of the supplier with the activity (Earl, 1996) • Supplier size (Earl, 1996) • Supplier financial instability (Earl, 1996) • Measurement problems (Alchian and Demsetz, 1972; Barzel, 1982) • Task complexity
Cost escalation (Lacity and Hirschheim, 1993; Lacity et al., 1995)	• Lack of experience and expertise of the client with contract management (Earl, 1996; Lacity et al., 1995) • Measurement problems (Alchian and Demsetz, 1972; Barzel, 1982) • Lack of experience and expertise of the supplier with the activity (Earl, 1996)
Loss of organizational competency (Dorn, 1989; Earl, 1996; Lacity et al., 1995)	• Scope of the activities • Proximity to the core competency (Prahalad and Hamel, 1990) • Interdependence of activities (Langlois and Robertson, 1992)
Hidden service costs (Lacity and Hirschheim, 1993)	• Complexity of the activities • Measurement problems (Alchian and Demsetz, 1972) • Uncertainty (Barzel, 1982)

Source: Aubert, Patry, and Rivard (2005), 13. Reprinted with permission.

1. What can happen?
2. How likely is this outcome?
3. If it does occur, what are the consequences?

They proposed a general definition of risk as a set of triplets involving scenarios, the likelihood of each scenario, and the consequences or an evaluation measure of each scenario (i.e., a measure of the potential damage). To answer the three questions, one has to make a list of outcomes or

Table 8.2

Bahli and Rivard's (2003) IT Outsourcing Risk Assessment Framework

Scenarios	Risk factors	Consequences	Mitigation mechanisms
Lock-in	• Asset specificity • Small number of suppliers • Client's degree of expertise in outsourcing contracts		• Mutual hostaging • Dual sourcing
Costly contractual amendments	• Uncertainty		• Sequential contracting • Contract flexibility
Unexpected transition and management costs	• Uncertainty • Client's degree of expertise in IT operations • Client's degree of expertise in outsourcing contracts • Relatedness	Cost escalation and service debasement	• Clan mechanisms • Procurement of expertise
Disputes and litigation	• Measurement problems • Supplier's degree of expertise in IT operations • Supplier's degree of expertise in outsourcing contracts		• Alternative methods of dispute resolution • Clan mechanisms • Procurement of external expertise

Source: Bahli and Rivard (2003), 213. Reprinted with permission.

"scenarios" that correspond to the following triplet:

p_i, s_i, x_i

Where

s_i is the scenario,
p_i is the probability of that scenario, and
x_i is the consequence.

Bahli and Rivard (2003) argued that in IT outsourcing, the scenarios, which are similar to the undesirable outcomes identified by Aubert, Patry, and Rivard (1998), are not "acts of God," but rather fall within the client's limits of control. They thus suggested that risk mitigation mechanisms exist that can be used to reduce the likelihood of occurrence of scenarios and that such mechanisms ought to be part of any risk assessment framework. They then expanded Kaplan and Garrick's definition of risk by adding a fourth component, defining risk as the quadruplet s_i, p_i, x_i, m_i, where m_i is the risk mitigation mechanism. They proposed an IT outsourcing risk assessment framework corresponding to this conceptualization of risk (Table 8.2).

As shown in Tables 8.1 and 8.2, Aubert, Patry, and Rivard (2005) and Bahli and Rivard (2003) based their IT outsourcing risk assessment frameworks on transaction cost theory and the measurability and uncertainty dimensions of agency theory. From this analysis, four risk scenarios were identified: lock-in, costly contractual amendments, unexpected transition and management costs, and disputes and litigations. Bahli and Rivard have suggested that all four scenarios lead to the same consequence: cost escalation and service debasement. The risk factors included sources of risk related to the principal (the client, the agent), the vendor, and the transaction. Risk mitigation mechanisms were comprised of contractual arrangements and governance mechanisms that would include screening, bonding, signaling, and monitoring mechanisms.

While these frameworks form sound theoretical foundations and have practical relevance, this chapter argues, in agreement with Duncan (1998), that the conceptualization and measurement of IT outsourcing risk may be further refined by taking into account the strategic value of the resources targeted for outsourcing. The next section provides a brief presentation of the RBT of the firm, and the rest of the chapter presents the argument for including the strategic value of resources.

RESOURCE-BASED THEORY

Defining Key Concepts

RBT is a theory of organizational competitive advantage that builds on the assumption that some resources possessed by a firm can be used to formulate and implement competitive strategies (Barney, 1991). Resources are defined as the rent-generating assets of an organization, such as knowledge, capabilities, and organizational processes that enable the firm to conceive and implement strategic decisions (ibid.). Resources can be either tangible or intangible. Tangible resources possess two key attributes: ownership and value. Ownership can be legal in terms of title deeds to land, property, or equipment, or can be in intellectual property such as patents, trademarks, licenses, or trade secrets. The firm may also possess intangible resources such as reputation, business process, and knowledge (Ray, Barney, and Muhanna, 2004).

More specifically, most resources belong to one of the following categories: physical, human, or organizational. Physical resources include tangible assets such as plant, equipment, land, inventories, production technology, and financial reserves as well as intangible assets such as reputation, brand name, copyright, and patent. Human resources include the education and training, experience, abilities, personal relationships, skills, and intelligence of individuals in a firm. Organizational resources include corporate culture; organizational structure; procedures; guidelines; management information systems; internal systems for research, planning, and motivation and the processes or routines that support these systems; and a firm's relationships with external institutions.

It is fruitful to distinguish between property-based and knowledge-based resources (Miller and Shamsi 1996). The former are likely to make the largest contribution to performance in stable and predictable settings, whereas the latter will be of the greatest utility in uncertain—changing and unpredictable—environments. Examples of property-based resources are enforceable long-term contracts that monopolize scarce factors of production, embody exclusive rights to a valuable technology, or tie up channels of distribution. Knowledge-based resources cannot be imitated by competitors because they are subtle and difficult to understand—they involve talents that are elusive and whose connection to results is difficult to discern. Thus, tacit know-how, skills, and technical and managerial systems not protected by patents all fall into this category. In short, as these resources are not productive on their own, the analysis also needs to consider a firm's organizational capabilities to assemble, integrate, and manage these bundles of resources.

While resources serve as the basic unit of analysis, firms create competitive advantages by assembling resources that work together to create organizational and IT capabilities. Capabilities therefore refers to an organization's ability to assemble, integrate, and deploy valued resources (Bharadwaj, 2000). These capabilities are developed by combining and using resources with the aid of organizational routines. An organizational routine is a particular way of doing something;

this way of doing has been developed by the organization and learned by its members, and the organization performs the routine very efficiently and effectively, to the point that it becomes almost automatic, a "natural" reflection of the organization's "way of being" (Ray, Barney, and Muhanna, 2004). Routines embed organizational knowledge acquired through learning (Grant, 1991); consequently, they have a strong tacit dimension that makes them difficult to imitate and change (Andreu and Ciborra, 1996). Unlike resources, capabilities are based on developing, carrying, and exchanging information through the firm's human capital (Amit and Schoemaker, 1993). Consequently, developing capabilities requires organizational learning—learning how to combine and use resources, and also the learning already embedded in the organizational routines employed. Capabilities are built through the coordination and integration of activities and processes, and are the product of collective learning of individual assets. As an example, Kodak's capabilities in imaging applications have not been developed overnight, but through learning, accumulated over time, about how to bundle different types of resources, skills, and knowledge to effect a desired end of imaging potential (Hafeez, Zhang, and Malak, 2002).

Kodak, like many other firms that achieve a competitive advantage through IT, has learned to combine effectively their IT resources to create overall IT capabilities. For example, a flexible IT infrastructure, when combined with strong human IT skills, becomes a potent organizational capability (Bharadwaj, 2000). Thus, a firm's IT capability is defined as its ability to mobilize and deploy IT-based resources in combination or simultaneously with other resources and capabilities. The following section discusses the conditions necessary to arrive at such a competitive advantage. RBT has suggested that resource attributes may play a significant role in how organizations achieve this goal.

Conditions Necessary for Competitive Advantage

A firm is said to have a competitive advantage when it implements a value-creating strategy that is not simultaneously being implemented by any current or potential competitor. A firm is said to have a sustained competitive advantage when it is implementing a value-creating strategy that is not simultaneously being implemented by any current or potential competitor and when other firms are unable to duplicate the benefits of this strategy (Barney, 1991). The potential to confer sustained competitive advantage is not inherent in all resources, but, rather, in only those that meet certain conditions (Barney, 1991). According to RBT, in order for a resource to provide sustained competitive advantage to a firm, it must meet four criteria: value, rareness, imperfect imitability, and nonsubstitutability (Barney, 1991). In other words, for a resource to have strategic value to the firm, it must be unique or rare among an organization's current or potential competitors, it must not be easily imitated or copied in a perfect fashion, and competing organizations must be unable to use another resource as a substitute for it. The theory posits that an organization's competitive position depends on its ability to achieve and defend advantageous positions when it comes to resources characterized by these criteria.

For a resource to be valuable, it must provide an opportunity to exploit some environmental opportunity or neutralize some threat. Resources are considered valuable when they enable a firm to conceive of or implement strategies that improve the firm's efficiency or effectiveness. A firm that does not possess valuable resources is said to be at a competitive disadvantage. The second condition is resource heterogeneity. When a resource is valuable but is possessed by several firms, it can be a source of competitive parity but cannot be a source of competitive advantage (Mata, Fuerst, and Barney, 1995). If a valuable resource is heterogeneously distributed across firms, it can at least provide temporary competitive advantage. The conditions for continuous competitive advantage are met when the resource is characterized by imperfect mobility and inimitability. When resources are easily traded between competitors, no competitive advantage can be maintained. Imperfectly mobile resources include those that are idiosyncratic to the firm (Williamson, 1985) or those for which property rights are not well defined. The imperfect mobility of resources is a critical factor, as human resources often represent key assets, and their high mobility frequently results in the loss of accounts and the emergence of new competitive threats (e.g., when personnel move to other firms). Finally, for an advantage to be sustained, resources must be imperfectly imitable (Barney, 1991) or provide some *ex post* limits to competition. That is, subsequent to a firm gaining a superior position and earning returns, forces must exist that limit competition for those returns. Thus, for a firm to be in a position to exploit a valuable and rare resource there must be a resource position barrier preventing imitation by other firms. Sustaining a competitive advantage over a period of time requires the presence of isolating mechanisms that prevent imitation. Inimitability is a central argument of RBT; a firm can obtain unusual returns only when other firms are unable to imitate its resources.

One of the first scholars to discuss RBT was Rumelt (1984). He suggested that, in addition to resource attributes and their allocation by the firm, one should analyze how a firm's resources are internally linked as well as the relationship between such linkage and above-normal returns. Over time, firms add activities that are related to some aspect of their existing activities. They build laterally on what they have achieved. New product lines bear certain technological and market similarities with older ones. More precisely, a firm exhibits coherence when its lines of business are related, in the sense that there are certain technological and market characteristics common to each. A firm's coherence increases as the number of common technological and market characteristics found in each product line increases. Coherence is thus a measure of relatedness. A corporation fails to exhibit coherence when common characteristics are allocated randomly across a firm's lines of business (Teece, Pisano, and Shuen, 1997). In fact, the assumption is that activities that are more closely related should be combined within the same corporation. Otherwise, if outsourced to a third party, the client firm may incur risks such as dependence on its service provider, discrepancies between its own goals and the service provider's orientations, loss of flexibility, and loss of competitiveness (in the case where a service provider is unable to constantly maintain the coherence of activities).

RBT is concerned not only with the deployment of existing resources but also with their development. To both fully exploit existing resources and further develop competitive advantages, a firm must proceed with the acquisition of complementary resources and those capabilities that it does not already have—or cannot efficiently produce—in-house (Grant, 1991). This external acquisition, or outsourcing, is referred to in the strategic management literature as filling gaps in resources and capabilities (Stevenson, 1976). A firm's outsourcing strategy thus allows for the filling in of gaps of resources and capabilities through partnerships and contracts with other organizations, thereby extending and augmenting the firm's competitive advantage (Grant, 1991).

THE RESOURCE-BASED THEORY PERSPECTIVE IN IT RESEARCH

Several researchers have adopted a resource-based perspective to address the issue of IT's contribution to business value (Melville, Kraemer, and Gurbaxani, 2004; Wade and Hulland, 2004), conceptualizing IT resources in various ways. Wade and Hulland (2004) identified eight IT resources that they classified into three categories: outside-in resources, inside-out resources, and spanning resources. Outside-in resources—external relationship management and market responsiveness—are externally oriented and pertain to establishing relationships with business partners and understanding competitors. Inside-out resources—infrastructure, technical skills, system development, and cost-effective operations—are used inside the firm to meet market requirements. Finally, spanning resources—IS business partnerships and IS planning and change management—involve both internal and external analysis capabilities.

A few empirical studies have examined the relationship between IS resources and firm performance. Bharadwaj (2000) compared the performance of firms that had been recognized by the magazine *InformationWeek* as IT leaders in their industry with the performance of a control group. She found that the high IT capabilities group outperformed the control group. Using the same sample, Santhanam and Hartono (2003) compared the performance of these firms with that of two control groups, and confirmed Bharadwaj's results.

Most authors who have adopted a resource-based view of IT contribution to firm performance examined the relationships between the IT resources themselves and business performance. Some researchers have argued, however, that this view was limited in that "it assumes that resources are always applied to their best uses, saying little about how this is done" (Melville, Kraemer, and Gurbaxani, 2004). Rather, it has been argued that overall performance is influenced by *how* firms leverage their IT resources. For instance, Clemons and Row (1991, p. 289) posit that "benefits resulting from an innovative application of information technology can be more readily defended if the system exploits unique resources of the firm." This argument, referred to as the strategic necessity hypothesis, was supported by Powell and Dent-Micallef (1997), who found that IT resources alone do not provide competitive advantages; rather, firms can gain competitive advantage by leveraging complementarity between business and human resources. Espousing the same argument, Ravichandran and Lertwongsatien (2002) found support for the relationship between IS support for core competencies and firm performance. Similarly, Rivard, Raymond, and Verreault (in press) found a significant relationship between IT support for firm assets and profitability.

IT OUTSOURCING RISK FROM THE PERSPECTIVE OF RESOURCE-BASED THEORY

Analyzing outsourcing with RBT shows that, depending on a given firm's situation in terms of IT resources, outsourcing may have two opposite effects on the firm's capabilities. On the one hand, when a firm does not possess a sufficient amount of competitively advantageous resources to implement a plan of action, outsourcing may be a means of filling the resource gap. In this view, outsourcing would be a strategic decision that would help bridge the gap between current and desired capabilities and strategic resources. On the other hand, when a firm decides to outsource resources that, when combined, create a set of capabilities that have the potential of providing sustained competitive advantage, it may fall into a capability gap.

By integrating the risk framework developed by Bahli and Rivard (2003) with the main components of RBT, we propose the framework shown in Figure 8.1.

The Capability Gap Risk Scenario and Associated Risk Factors

RBT suggests that IT outsourcing may result in the loss of strategic competitiveness. Capabilities are not created overnight; they are developed over a long period of time. A service provider may need a certain amount of time to at least preserve these capabilities. During that time, the firm's competitors may take advantage of the capability gap and erode the client's competitive advantage. Conversely, if the outsourced resources are neither valuable nor rare, they are good candidates for outsourcing. An analogy with the suggestions of transaction cost theory is valid here (Williamson,

Figure 8.1 **Framework of a Resource-Based View of IT Outsourcing**

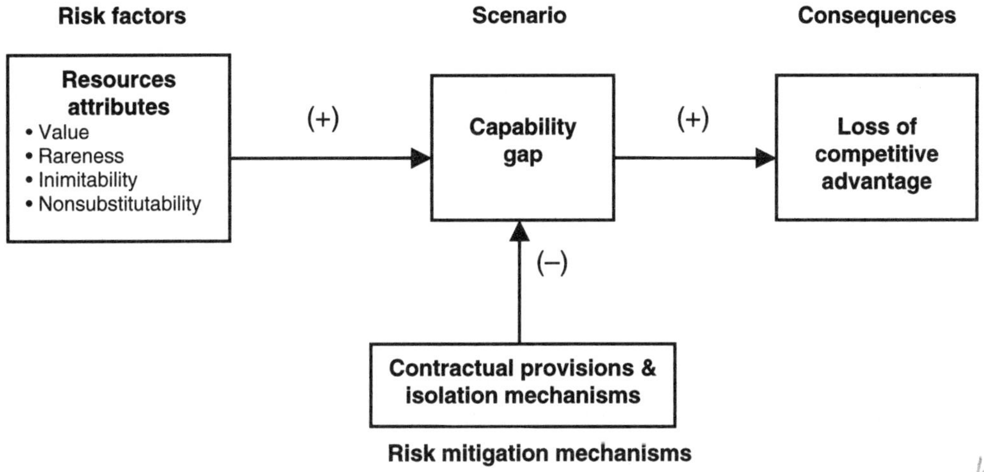

1985). Assets that are specific, that are characterized by high uncertainty, and for which there are few suppliers should not be outsourced (Bahli and Rivard, 2003).

This capability gap scenario is associated with four risk factors. The first is resource value. Resources are considered valuable when they enable a firm to conceive or implement strategies that improve its efficiency or effectiveness (Barney, 1991). Outsourcing such a resource will hinder the firm's competitive advantage, since the client will lose control of its value (Duncan, 1998). The value of resources can be viewed as the degree to which these resources have an impact on the growth and prosperity of the organization (Spanos and Lioukas, 2001). The second risk factor is resource rareness. Outsourcing a resource that is rare to a third party may expose the resource to trading between competitors, in which case the competitive advantage could not be maintained (Mata, Fuerst, and Barney, 1995). The third risk factor is the resource's imperfect imitability. Outsourcing IS people, when they are key assets, will create high mobility of these resources in the marketplace, and this frequently results in the loss of accounts and the emergence of new competitive threats from competing firms (Pereira, 1999). Finally, the fourth risk factor is resource nonsubstitutability. Outsourcing such a resource to a third party may expose the resource to substitution with another resource by competing firms (Barney, 1991).

Roy and Aubert (2002) suggest that the value of a given resource can be conceived only through the activities to which it contributes, and, by extension, through the products emanating from these activities. In other words, the strategic value of a company's resource is reflected in the value it adds to the product. In the case of IT resources, for instance, the high cost associated with implementing and managing an enterprise resource planning (ERP) system makes it extremely valuable to firms (Pereira, 1999).

To contribute to a competitive advantage, a resource must be characterized by rareness. Firms possessing unique bundles of skills and resources can attain a sustainable competitive advantage. Here again, in spite of the degree of competitiveness of the IT vendor, strong competition in the IS field makes it hard to attain this objective. ERP skills are durable to the extent that the system can be upgraded to a more complex implementation and the skills that were previously developed are largely transferable to a more complex implementation.

Resources possessed by a large number of competing firms will not be a source of competitive advantage. IT organizational skills cannot be easily replicated (imperfect imitability), because it takes considerable time to train personnel. In addition, IT personnel who have spent several years working in the mainframe environment in specific settings are difficult to replace (nonsubstitutability).

These resource attributes cannot be examined in isolation, and this has been widely discussed in the strategic management literature. Teo and Ranganathan (2003) suggest that IT resources can act in tandem with complementary business and human resources, leading to superior firm performance. Business resources include IT planning and integration with strategic planning, IT-based process redesign, flexible organization, a cross-functional orientation, and IT-driven interorganizational relationships. Human resources include top management's commitment to IT, managerial IT knowledge and skills, and IT training. The underlying premise is that although firms can have very similar IT resources, it is the mechanisms for combining and utilizing these resources that create an enduring benefit for the firm. Outsourcing such resources may hinder the firm's capabilities, creating what Cheon, Grover, and Teng (1995) called "gaps of capabilities" (i.e., the difference between desired capabilities and actual capabilities). The authors did not elaborate on this important scenario. In the next section, we will discuss how outsourcing resources or a combination of resources to a third party can create a capability differential that, in turn, leads to the loss of a competitive advantage. The conceptual and operational definitions of resource attributes are provided in Table 8.3.

Loss of Competitive Advantage as a Negative Consequence

The literature on RBT refers to the concept of competitive advantage in a variety of ways. Some of the most notable definitions utilized in relation to this concept include: return on assets, sustained competitive advantage, and competitive advantage (see Table 8.4). In a relatively stable environment, the bulk of management's efforts go toward creating competitive advantages for the firm. Since the environment changes little, any advantage they create is likely to be sustained over time (Miller and Shamsie, 1996). By contrast, in a dynamic environment, any advantages are likely to be short-lived, as competitive and environmental pressures seek to undermine any resource value or heterogeneity (Foss, 1998). Thus, the challenge for management in a dynamic environment shifts from creating an advantage to sustaining it.

The literature has suggested that outsourcing resources that possess the attributes of value, rareness, imperfect imitability, and nonsubstitutability to a third party may lead to a capability gap and therefore to a loss of competitive advantage (Cheon, Grover, and Teng, 1995). Indeed, when such resources are outsourced, the client organization may be exposed to reduced internal capabilities, resulting in the deterioration of its ability to generate a competitive advantage (Ray, Barney, and Muhanna, 2004). For example, computer hardware and software (tangible resources and capabilities with limited potential for competitive advantage) may be bundled with an organization's commitment to customer service (an intangible resource and capability with the potential to generate such advantages) to enable the delivery of customer service, an important business process for at least some firms (Ray, Barney, and Muhanna, 2004).

Risk Mitigation Mechanisms

Attenuating the consequences of the capability gap scenario and sustaining a competitive advantage over a period of time requires contractual provisions and the presence of isolating mechanisms that prevent imitation, substitutability, loss of resource value, and uniqueness (Pereira, 1999).

Table 8.3

Sample of Studies Defining Resource Attributes

Construct	Conceptual definition	Operational definition	Authors
Value	Asset stocks are valuable to the extent that they are nontradable, nonimitable, and nonsubstitutable	N/A	Dierickx and Cool, 1989
	Resources are considered valuable when they enable a firm to conceive of or implement strategies that improve the firm's efficiency or effectiveness	N/A	Barney, 1991
	The more firm-specific, durable, and scarce strategic assets are, the more valuable their deployment can be to the firm	N/A	Amit and Schoemaker, 1993
	Firm-specific information technology (IT) resources classified as IT infrastructure, human IT resources, and IT-enabled intangibles	N/A	Bharadwaj, 2000
Rareness	If valuable resources are possessed by a large number of competitors or potential competitors, they no longer represent a source of competitive advantage	N/A	Barney, 1991
	The condition where the resource is not simultaneously available to a large number of firms	N/A	Amit and Schoemaker, 1993
	Scarcity is related to the ease of identification of the bundle of factors that creates or constitutes the resource	N/A	Black and Boal, 1994
Imperfect imitability	The complexity of the relationships between a firm and its key stakeholders makes them difficult to imitate	N/A	Barney, 1991
	The strategic value of a firm's resources and capabilities is enhanced as it becomes more difficult to imitate them	N/A	Amit and Schoemaker, 1993; Collis and Montgomery, 1995
	Firm human resource-specific experience is difficult to imitate	N/A	Hatch and Dyer, 2004
	Resources are strategic to the extent that they are nonimitable by competing firms	N/A	Dierickx and Cool, 1989
Substitutability	A resource has low substitutability if there are few, if any, strategically equivalent resources that are themselves rare and inimitable	N/A	Amit and Schoemaker, 1993
	Low tradability refers to invisible assets such as tacit knowledge, which cannot be easily transferred or traded	N/A	Amit and Schoemaker, 1993
	A tradable resource is one that can be specifically identified and given a monetary value	N/A	Black and Boal, 1994
	Resources are strategic to the extent that they are nonsubstitutable by competition	N/A	Dierickx and Cool, 1989

Table 8.4

IT and Competitive Advantage

Authors	Construct	Operational definition	Independent variables
Kearns and Lederer, 2003a	Information technology (IT) competitive advantage	Five items measuring the extent to which IT is used to create a competitive advantage	Strategic IT alignment
Kearns and Lederer, 2003b	IT competitive advantage	Five items measuring the extent to which IT is used to create a competitive advantage	IT focus
Davis, Dehning, and Stratopoulos, 2003	Return on assets, total return, risk adjustment cumulative total return, market-adjusted cumulative total return, Sharpe performance index, Treynor performance index	Market data performance measures	IT-enabled strategy
Mata, Fuerst, and Barney, 1995	Sustained competitive advantage	N/A (conceptual paper)	Capital requirements, proprietary technology, technical IT skills, managerial IT skills
Kettinger et al., 1994	Sustained competitive advantage	Sustainability variables and measures	Foundation factors, action strategies
Sethi and King, 1994	Competitive advantage provided by an IT application	Seven variables assess the various constructs: primary activity efficiency, support activity efficiency, resource management functionality, resource acquisition functionality, threat, preemptiveness, and synergy	N/A (measurement development paper)

Grover, Cheon, and Teng (1996) state that, according to RBT, "insourcing" represents a strategic decision that can be used to fill the gap between the firms' current and desired IT capabilities. Grant (1991) argues that "insourcing" not only maintains a firm's stock of resources and capabilities, but also augments resources and capabilities in order to buttress and extend positions. However, filling gaps in resources and capabilities through an external sourcing strategy can inhibit the development of IT capabilities in the firm. A client firm that outsources its valuable resources to a third party would eventually lose them because they are not located and embedded in the firm. In other words, the firm has little or no control over them, which breaches the principle of resource ownership advocated by RBT at its core.

The loss of competitive advantage due to a capability gap can have two sources. First, the client firm may not possess the same capabilities as it had before it outsourced part or all of its valuable resources. Second, it is not a problem per se if these capabilities are outsourced to a third party who might be capable of providing the same or better service to the client firm. The risk lies in the supplier disseminating these capabilities to the competition.

In this case, the capability gap can be attenuated by several isolating mechanisms. First, a client organization may simultaneously safeguard against the hazards of imitation by actively protecting organizational secrets. Liebeskind (1998) suggests that in cases where the reach of law is limited, client organizations may utilize, for example, restrictive rules (such as limiting access to certain types of data, employees, processes, etc.). Additionally, causal ambiguity (Lippman and Rumelt, 1982) and time compression diseconomies (Dierickx and Cool, 1989) may protect a capability position from quick erosion. In other words, a client organization may keep some resources and capabilities in-house when they have some complementarities with the outsourced ones. This creates a causal ambiguity that prevents any type of imitation by competitors or knowledge on the part of the outsourcer.

Whereas these mitigation mechanisms may help prevent a potential loss of competitive advantage by attenuating the capability gap scenario, the risk of outsourcing valuable resources is not eliminated. It is important to note that these mitigation mechanisms are not only costly in terms of management costs, but also undermine the potential benefits sought in outsourcing these resources.

CONCLUSION

The general contribution of this chapter is to provide an additional perspective on the role of resources in outsourcing arrangements. The study elucidates the components of underlying risk suggested by RBT and integrates them into a concise model of resource characteristics, capability gap, and loss of competitive advantage. While the literature is not always clear on how to conceptualize RBT's constructs, this study has attempted to do so. First, we formulated and described a general risk framework that postulates what can happen (i.e., scenarios); how likely the scenarios are (risk factors); if a scenario occurs, what its consequences are (i.e., negative consequences); and, finally, what risk mitigation mechanism can be used to attenuate or avoid these scenarios. Second, we began addressing this issue by identifying the needed constructs and clarifying the conceptual definitions for RBT constructs, including resource, resource attributes, capability, and competitive advantage. Third, we developed a risk assessment framework for outsourcing IT strategic resources. The essence of this framework is that four conditions underlie competitive advantage, all of which must be met. These include resources that are valuable, rare, inimitable, and nonsubstitutable (risk factors) to a third party. This framework assesses the outsourcing implications of resources by evaluating their characteristics. Outsourcing such resources may expose the client firm to a capability gap (scenario). Since these resources or the combination of these resources create the firm's set of capabilities, this in turn generates a competitive advantage. These capabilities cannot be created rapidly; they require a long period of development. A service provider may need a certain amount of time to at least preserve these capabilities, let alone improve them. During that period of time, the client's competition may take advantage of this capability gap and act to erode the competitive advantage (negative consequence) that the client had enjoyed when these resources were in-house. In addition, the capability gap scenario may be attenuated by isolation mechanisms put in place by the client firm before outsourcing IT strategic activities.

The study brought to light constructs that are not always well defined, either on their own or in their nomological network. Our literature review did not find any study that conceptualizes these RBT constructs in a risk assessment and management framework for IT outsourcing. This study sought to develop such a framework. However, while we evaluated resources from a stand-alone perspective as singular distinct items, we acknowledge the importance of dynamic aspects, including the degree of variability of resources over time, how resources are nested and configured with respect to each other, and the nature of relationships between them. By taking into account these different aspects, the capability gap may also be seen to fluctuate over time, as does the degree of competitive advantage. This line of inquiry is at an early stage of development, but it establishes groundwork for future development in the area of IT outsourcing risks.

REFERENCES

Alchian, A.A. and Demsetz, H. 1972. Production, information cost and economic organization. *American Economic Review,* 62, 777–795.

Amit, R. and Schoemaker, P.J.H. 1993. Strategic assets and organizational rent. *Strategic Management Journal*, 14, 1, 33–46.

Aubert, B.A.; Patry, M.; and Rivard, S. 2003. Tale of two outsourcing contracts: An agency-theoretical perspective. *Wischaftsinformatik*, 45, 2, 181–190.

———. 1998. Assessing the risk of IT outsourcing. In *Proceedings of the Thirty-first Hawaii International Conference on System Sciences,* vol. 6. Washington, DC: IEEE Computer Society, p. 685.

———. 2005. A framework for information technology outsourcing risk management. *DataBase*, 36, 4, 9–28.

Aubert, B.A.; Patry, M.; Rivard, S.; and Smith, H. 2001. IT outsourcing risk management at British Petroleum. In *Proceedings of the Thirty-fourth Hawaii International Conference on Systems Sciences*, vol. 8. Washington, DC: IEEE Computer Society, p. 8076.

Andreu, R. and Ciborra, C. 1996. Organizational learning and core capabilities development: The role of IT. *Journal of Strategic Information Systems*, 5, 2, 111–127.

Bahli, B. and Rivard, S. 2003. The information technology outsourcing risk: A transaction cost and agency theory-based perspective. *Journal of Information Technology*, 18, 3, 211–221.

Barki, H.; Rivard, S.; and Talbot, J. 1993. Toward an assessment of software development risk. *Journal of Management Information Systems*, 10, 2, 203–225.

Barney, J. 1991. Firm resources and sustained competitive advantage. *Journal of Management*, 17, 1, 99–120.

Barzel, Y. 1982. Measurement cost and the organization of markets. *Journal of Law and Economics,* 25, 27–48.

Bharadwaj, A.S. 2000. A resource-based perspective on information technology capability on firm performance: An empirical investigation. *MIS Quarterly*, 24, 1, 169–196.

Black, J.A. and Boal, K.B. 1994. Strategic resources: Traits, configurations and paths to sustainable competitive advantage. *Strategic Management Journal*, 15, Special issue, 131–148.

Boehm, B.W. 1989. *Software Risk Management: Tutorial.* Los Alamitos, CA: IEEE Computer Society Press, 1989.

Cheon, M.J.; Grover, V.; and Teng, J.T.C. 1995. Theoretical perspectives on the outsourcing of information systems. *Journal of Information Technology*, 10, 4, 209–219.

Clemons, E.K. and Row, M.C. 1991. Sustaining IT advantage: The role of structural differences. *MIS Quarterly*, 15, 3, 275–292.

Collis, D.J. and Montgomery, C.A. 1995. Competing on resources: Strategy in the 1990s. *Harvard Business Review*, 73, 4, 118–128.

Cross, J. 1995. IT outsourcing: British Petroleum's competitive approach. *Harvard Business Review*, 73, 3, 95–102.

Davis, L.; Dehning, B.; and Stratopoulos, T. 2003. Does the market recognize IT-enabled competitive advantage? *Information & Management*, 40, 7, 705–716.

Dierickx, I. and Cool, K. 1989. Asset stock accumulation and sustainability of competitive advantage. *Management Science*, 35, 12, 1504–1513.

Dorn, P. 1989. Selling One's Birthright. *Information Week*, 241, 52.

Duncan, N. 1998. Beyond opportunism: A resource-based view of outsourcing risk. In *Proceedings of the Thirty-first Hawaii International Conference on System Sciences*, vol. 6. Washington, DC: IEEE Computer Society. p. 675.

Earl, M.J. 1996. The risks of outsourcing IT. *Sloan Management Review*, 37, 3, 26–32.

Foss, N.J. 1998. Resources and strategy: A brief overview of themes and contributions. In N.J. Foss, ed., *Resources, Firms, and Strategies: A Reader in the Resource-Based Perspective.* Cambridge: Oxford University Press, 3–20.

Grant, R.M. 1991. The resource-based theory of competitive advantage: Implications for strategy formulation. *California Management Review*, 33, 3, 114–135.

Grover, V.; Cheon, M.J.; and Teng, J.T.C. 1996. The effect of service quality and partnership on the outsourcing of information systems functions. *Journal of Management Information Systems*, 12, 4, 89–116.

Hafeez, K.; Zhang, Y.; and Malak, N. 2002. Core competence for sustainable competitive advantage: A structured methodology for identifying core competence. *IEEE Transactions on Engineering Management*, 49, 1, 28–35.

Hatch, N.W. and Dyer, J.H. 2004. Human capital and learning as a source of sustained competitive advantage. *Strategic Management Journal*, 25, 12, 1155–1178.

Kaplan, S. and Garrick, B.J. 1981. On the quantitative definition of risk. *Risk Analysis*, 1, 1, 11–27.

Kearns, G.S. and Lederer, A.L. 2003a. A resource-based view of strategic IT alignment: How knowledge sharing creates competitive advantage. *Decision Sciences*, 34, 1, 1–29.

———. 2003b. The impact of industry contextual factors on IT focus and the use of IT for competitive advantage. *Information & Management*, 41, 7, 899–919.

Kettinger, W.J.; Grover, V.; Guha, S.; and Segars, A.H. 1994. Strategic information systems revisited: A study in sustainability and performance. *MIS Quarterly*, 18, 1, 31–58.

Lacity, M.C. and Hirschheim, R. 1993. *Information Systems Outsourcing*. New York: Wiley.

Lacity, M.C.; Willcocks, L.P.; and Feeny, D.F. 1995. IT outsourcing : Maximize flexibility and control. *Harvard Business Review*, May–June, 84–93.

Langlois, R.N. and Robertson, P.L. 1992. Networks and innovation in a modular system: Lessons from the microcomputer and stereo component industries. *Research Policy*, 21, 297–313.

Liebeskind, J. 1998. Ownership, governance and incentives in human-capital-intensive firms: Evidence from the biotechnology industry. Working paper presented at the Strategic Management Society 18th Annual Conference, Orlando, FL (November 1–4).

Lippman, S.A. and Rumelt, R. 1982. Uncertain imitability: An analysis of interfirm differences in efficiency under competition. *Bell Journal of Economics*, 13, 2 , 418–438.

Mata, F.J.; Fuerst, W.L.; and Barney, J.B. 1995. Information technology and sustained competitive advantage: A resource-based view. *MIS Quarterly*, 19, 4, 487–505.

McKinsey Quarterly. 2002. The other side of outsourcing. 1, 53–63.

Melville, N.; Kraemer, K.; and Gurbaxani, V. 2004. Information technology and organizational performance: An integrative model of IT business value. *MIS Quarterly*, 28, 2, 283–322.

Miller, D. and Shamsie, J. 1996. The resource-based view of the firm in two environments: The Hollywood film studios from 1936 to 1965. *Academy of Management Journal*, 39, 3, 519–543.

Nam, K.; Rajagopalan, S.; Rao, H.R.; and Chaudhury, A. 1996. A two-level investigation of information systems outsourcing. *Communications of the ACM*, 39, 7, 37–44.

Nelson, P.; Richmond, W.; and Seidman, A. 1996. Two dimensions of software acquisition. *Communications of the ACM*, 39, 7, 29–35.

O'Leary, M. 1990. The mainframe doesn't work here anymore. *CIO*, 6, 6, 77–79.

Pereira, R.E. 1999. Resource view theory analysis of SAP as a source of competitive advantage for firms. *DATA BASE for Advances in Information Systems*, 30, 1, 38–46.

Powell, T.C. and Dent-Micallef, A. 1997. Information technology as competitive advantage: The role of human, business, and technology resources. *Strategic Management Journal*, 18, 5, 375–405.

Prahalad, C.V. and Hamel, G. 1990. The core competence of the corporation. *Harvard Business Review*, May–June 1990, 79–91.

Ravichandran, T. and Lertwongsatien, C. 2002. Impact of information systems resources and capabilities on firm performance: a resource-based perspective. In L. Applegate, R. Galliers, and J.I. DeGross, eds., *Proceedings of the Twenty-third International Conference on Information Systems*, Barcelona, Spain, 577–582.

Ray, G.; Barney, J.B.; and Muhanna, W.A. 2004. Capabilities, business processes, and competitive advantage: Choosing the dependent variable in empirical tests of the resource-based view. *Strategic Management Journal*, 25, 23–37.

Rivard, S.; Raymond, L.; and Verreault, D. 2006. Resource-based view and competitive strategy: An integrated model of the contribution of information technology to firm performance, *Journal of Strategic Information Systems*, 15, 29–50.

Roy, V. and Aubert, B. 2002. A resource-based analysis of IT sourcing. *Database for Advances in Information Systems*, 33, 2, 29–40.

Rumelt, P. 1984. Towards a strategic theory of the firm. In R Lamb, ed., *Competitive Strategic Management*. Englewood Cliffs, NJ: Prentice Hall, 566–570.

Santhanam, R. and Hartono, E. 2003. Issues in linking information technology capability to firm performance. *MIS Quarterly*, 27, 1, 125–153.

Sappington, D. 1991. Incentives in principal-agent relationships. *Journal of Economic Perspectives*, 5, 2, 45–68.

Sethi, V. and King, W.R. 1994. Development of measures to assess the extent to which an information technology application provides competitive advantage. *Management Science*, 40, 12, 1601–1627.

Spanos, Y.E. and Lioukas, S. 2001. An examination into the causal logic of rent generation: Contrasting Porter's competitive strategy framework and the resource-based perspective. *Strategic Management Journal* 22, 10, 907–934.

Stevenson, H.H. 1976. Defining corporate strengths and weaknesses. *Sloan Management Review*, 17, 3, 51–68.

Teece, J.; Pisano, G.; and Shuen, A. 1997. Dynamic capabilities and strategic management. *Strategic Management Journal*, 18, 7, 509–533.

Teo, T.S.H. and Ranganathan, C. 2003. Leveraging IT resources and capabilities at the housing and development board. *Journal of Strategic Information Systems*, 12, 3, 229–249.

Wade, M. and Hulland, J. 2004. Information systems research: Review, extension, and suggestions for future research. *MIS Quarterly*, 28, 1, 107–142.

Willcocks, L.P.; Lacity, M.C.; and Kern, T. 1999. Risk mitigation in IT outsourcing strategy revisited: Longitudinal case research at LISA. *Journal of Strategic Information Systems*, 8, 3 (September), 285–314.

Williamson, O.E. 1985. *The Economic Institutions of Capitalism*. New York: Sage Press.

CHAPTER 9

INVESTIGATING TRUST IN OUTSOURCING

A Study in the Health Care Industry

EBRAHIM RANDEREE, RAJIV KISHORE, AND H. RAGHAV RAO

Abstract: *Trust is an important consideration prior to the adoption of outsourcing options and subsequently during the management of the outsourcing relationship. Understanding the antecedents to the adoption of information technology is important both to technology firms that provide services and to policy analysts who study the effects of technology adoption and information technology success. The first part of this chapter examines the role trust plays in the outsourcing relationship. Trust is discussed as both an antecedent to adoption and a critical part of the relationship post adoption. The second part of the chapter examines a conceptual model of trust and privacy that is tested using partial least squares. The empirical study uses a transactional cost approach to investigate the role of trust and privacy, both as direct effects and as moderators in the adoption of application service providers (ASPs) as a new form of information technology outsourcing. The study focuses on the health care industry. The model results indicate that trust plays a minimal role in the adoption of ASPs. Limitations of the research are discussed; implications are reviewed;and future research areas are identified.*

Keywords: *Outsourcing, Partial Least Squares, Privacy, Transaction Costs, Trust*

INTRODUCTION

Outsourcing has matured since its inception in the early 1990s and has become an established solution within the business community (Aubert, Rivard, and Patry, 2004; Choudhury and Sabherwal, 2003; Walsh, 2003). Firms initially looked to outsourcing as a method to lower costs, gain access to skills not found internally, or refocus on core activities; outsourcing is now becoming a growth-oriented strategic tool (Goo, Kishore, and Rao, 2000). Development of the industry has allowed firms to select options for outsourcing that range from arms-length contracts to strategic partnerships and long-term alliances. The form and function of outsourcing choices continue to evolve; they may include insourcing (hierarchical governance), outsourcing (market governance), or hybrid mechanisms (Kishore, Agarwal, and Rao, 2005). The new areas for growth are in offshore outsourcing and application service provider (ASP)-based outsourcing arrangements (Oh, 2005).

For much of this study, the focus is the health care industry. While outsourcing is not new to the health care industry, health care is one of the fields that lacks adequate up-to-date research concerning technology adoption and its use (Hikmet and Chen, 2003). The turbulent health care market (Lee and Alexander, 1999; Madden, 1999) has been inundated by declining margins, increased patient demands, restrictive legislation, and constant revisions to current legislation, which has resulted in confounding factors that influence the adoption and diffusion of innovations in the health care setting (Friedman, Goes, and Orr, 2000). Innovative hospitals have previously outsourced janitorial services, food services, and nursing contracts. The health care industry increasingly views information technology (IT) as a fundamental asset in providing health-related information services and decision support on demand, as well as in managing rising costs and changing organizational needs, improving the quality of health services and patient care, and fighting illness while promoting wellness (Raghupathi and Tan, 2002). With shrinking federal and state support for health care institutions, hospitals are forced to invest only in proven technologies, and risk aversion has become an underlying obstacle to new technology adoption. IT represents a substantial investment for most corporations and constitutes a significant aspect of organizational work (Agarwal and Karahanna, 2000).

Application service providers have begun to provide outsourcing services to the health care industry. An ASP is defined as an information systems vendor that manages and distributes software-based services and solutions to customers across a wide area network (either using the Internet or a private network) from a central data center. Interestingly, the ASP model is a return to the "shared services via a mainframe" approach of the previous decade, where offsite hosting of software and data is managed by a third party. ASPs offering web-enabled software applications on a subscription (pay-as-you-go) basis revisits the traditional service bureau model of outsourcing, and promises additional business benefits of economies of scale, increased scope of business applications, and enterprise application integration (Currie, 2003a).

While ASPs are a "shared service" derivative, they offer less expensive options to cash-strapped organizations that seek to embrace current technologies; therefore, hospitals are an appealing market for the ASP industry (Serva, Sherer, and Sipior, 2003). ASPs provide shorter implementation and deployment times; the scalability and ease of entry appeals to hospitals that have unpredictable financial outlooks and that are continually forced to make difficult choices. The ASP model ensures that the client has access to the technical expertise that is too costly to employ in-house; organizations are able to avoid new investments in hardware and software (Chen and Soliman, 2002). Organizations with multiple information technology systems and various platforms are looking to external providers such as ASPs to streamline their operations and reduce noncompliance liability. Recent legislation has increased the IT demands on hospitals and has placed more emphasis on patient privacy concerns.

The ASP model has obstacles that have prevented its rapid industry-wide adoption. The ASP model puts the control of IT resources outside of the hospital's control, thus raising issues of trust, data security, privacy, and governance. Controls for outcomes and behaviors evolve over the outsourced projects (Choudhury and Sabherwal, 2003). Further, the nascent ASP industry is unable to provide evidence of a sustainable business model. Not all applications have Web interfaces, forcing ASP adopters to run two or more models. Access to outsourced applications may be subject to influences beyond the hospital's control (heavy Internet traffic, lack of Web tone, hacking, ASP mergers). The application software may not be industry specific and ASP applications may not integrate with internal systems. Also, service options and expectations are in the embryonic stage, requiring hospitals to pay more attention to details in their service level agreements. There is little formal literature that helps to demonstrate the distinctions between different ASP–client relationships and how they are managed (Kavan, Miranda, and O'Hara, 2002).

Trust is an important part of any exchange or transactional relationship; risk that is inherent in exchange transactions is mitigated by trust. Trust is vital to IT project success and deserves more discussion in outsourced projects (Natovich, 2003). Defining trust is confusing (McKnight, Cummings, and Chervany, 1998; Ring and Van de Ven, 1994); previous research has investigated trust using single dimensional constructs, but trust can also be viewed as a multidimensional construct combining specific beliefs that influence relevant behavioral intentions either directly or through an overall assessment of trust (Gefen, 2002). Trust has been defined in many different ways, often reflecting the paradigms of the particular academic discipline of the researcher (Grabner-Kräuter and Kaluscha, 2003). Trust is defined as the expectation that neither party in the exchange will act opportunistically; trust is evident when vulnerability exists (Meyer and Goes, 1988), especially when forming new organizational relationships (McKnight, Cummings, and Chervany, 1998).

Outsourcing involves two parties, the vendor and the client. For our research, trust can be defined as the willingness of a party to be vulnerable to the actions of another party based on the expectation that the other will perform a particular action important to the trustor, irrespective of the ability to monitor or control that other party. This definition of trust is applicable to a relationship with another identifiable party who is perceived to act and react with volition toward the trustor (Mayer, Davis, and Schoorman, 1995). Vulnerability implies risk and trust mitigates that risk. Trust is crucial in the health care industry. The confidentiality and security of a patient's health information have always been important, even more so with the ease of electronic access (Huston, 2001).

THE ROLE OF TRUST BEFORE ADOPTION

Trust is important prior to adoption and during the management of the outsourcing relationship. The role of trust has been investigated previously as a basis for a strong relationship that prevents opportunistic behavior (Lander et al., 2004; Zaheer, McEvily, and Perrone, 1998). Trust can play a role in lowering the transaction costs associated with adoption risks (Uzzi, 1997). Trust can reduce complexity, especially when important decisions and new technology are being considered (Gefen, 2002; Paul and McDaniel, 2004). Understanding the antecedents to the adoption of information technology outsourcing is critical to its long-term success. Vendor trust has previously been identified as an antecedent in exchange relationships that involve risks and vulnerabilities (Barthélémy, 2003; Hart and Saunders, 1998; Sabherwal, 1999) and is often the most-cited inhibiting factor (Heart and Pliskin, 2001) to the adoption of technology. Vendor trust is an important aspect of interorganizational relationships (Hart and Saunders, 1998). Due to the difficulties in monitoring the opportunistic behavior of agents, risk associated with outsourced activity may make the firm vulnerable (Oh and Gallivan, 2003). Risks can be lowered with the presence of vendor trust. In alliances between companies, trust can lower the fear associated with opportunistic partners (Gulati, 1998). Trust is difficult to develop in an outsourced project because of a lack of prior relationship (Natovich, 2003).

With respect to the relationship between transaction costs and adoption, trust may play two roles: trust may directly affect the adoption or it can play a moderating role. This can be explained by looking at the definition of transaction costs. Negotiation and monitoring costs can be lowered in the presence of vendor trust. Similarly, long-term governance will be reduced and trust may actually increase over time to minimize the transaction costs. With respect to production costs, seeking vendors in the market to produce the services required exposes the organization to risk. The organization will be more likely to engage in external contracts in the presence of high trust. The management of the relationship builds trust that allows for other data security issues to be resolved.

Trust may emanate from the reputation and capability of the vendor. Organizations need to be reassured that in turbulent times, the vendors that they contract with can guarantee that they will not disappear or renege on service-level agreements. The availability of reputable and trustworthy external IT providers in the market can also be a concern to firms seeking to adopt new technologies (Susarla, Barua, and Whinston, 2003). Vendor reputation is an antecedent to trust (Heart, Pliskin, and Tractinsky, 2004). The lack of reputable vendors was previously found to dissuade the adoption of new technologies (Ang and Straub, 1998).

Early research in outsourcing portrayed the external vendor relationship as adversarial in nature. It suggested that clients avoid partnership talk, refuse to sign incomplete contracts, hire outsourcing experts, measure everything, and include a termination clause (Lacity and Hirschheim, 1995). In the initial stages, the costs involved and the complexity of the exchanges require detailed contractual agreements; beyond contracts, trust is required (Hoecht and Trott, 2006). Reliance on trust may serve as a substitute for, or a complement to, more formal governance structures (Arino, Torre, and Ring, 2001). Trusting relationships are difficult to develop under tight governance structures (Sabherwal, 1999).

THE ROLE OF TRUST IN THE RELATIONSHIP AFTER ADOPTION

While the empirical study that follows in this chapter focuses on pre-adoption trust, a discussion of post-adoption trust is included to present a more complete analysis of trust in outsourcing. Future studies should look at longitudinal impacts of trust in the relationship. Trust is at the heart of all relationships (Gefen, Karahanna, and Straub, 2003; Ring and Van de Ven, 1994). The most important factor affecting the success of outsourcing appears to be a mutual understanding between clients and their service providers (Kishore et al., 2003). The management of the relationship builds trust. Outsourcing success requires that both the vendor and the client engage in active management of the relationship to ensure success. Previous research has examined why a client would adopt and address the concerns of the client (Koh, Ang, and Straub, 2004). Trust in an organizational setting reduces complexity when new technology concerns emerge; trust is especially important in health care delivery (Paul and McDaniel, 2004). Interorganizational trust mitigates the information asymmetries inherent in interfirm exchange by allowing for more open and honest sharing of information (Zaheer, McEvily, and Perrone, 1998). Trust permits greater flexibility in the selection of governance mechanisms, resulting in closer relationships with less need for detailed contracts (Jeffries and Reed, 2000).

Outsourcing should be considered more as a management of relationships between service providers than as a simple subcontract for information systems (IS) commodities (Kishore et al., 2003). The relationship between the client and vendor evolves (Ilie and Parikh, 2004). The supply-side of IT outsourcing remains underresearched in the academic literature (Seltsikas and Currie, 2002). Research on the other side of the equation (vendor focus) (Levina and Ross, 2003) and the ongoing management of the outsourcing relationship is minimal (Hu, Saunders, and Gebelt, 1997). Successful relationships increase trust and willingness to contract out services, and unsuccessful relationships can poison the partnership and lead to termination. Previous research has shown that these relationships change and evolve over time due to changes in the external environment and in clients' internal requirements (Kishore et al., 2003). Long-term relationships were found to be more successful than short-term arms-length relationships (Lee, Miranda, and Kim, 2004).

The key to achieving benefits from outsourcing is to maintain positive client–supplier relationships (Alborz, Seddon, and Scheepers, 2004). Prior relationships with vendors can also affect adoption behavior. Trust can be increased if successful prior relationships exist while perceived risks can be lowered and existing relationships can be strengthened. A user's satisfaction with an ASP is the result of the evaluation of the ASP's services in comparison with prior experiences (Susarla, Barua, and Whinston, 2003). Prior relationships that include positive outcomes and equitable treatment increase the chances of developing longer relationships (Ho, Ang, and Straub, 2003). Relationship experience combines previous and current experiences with vendors to create a level of willingness within firms to use outsourced services. Relational quality (the extent to which partners feel comfortable with each other) is a function of past experiences and trust (Arino, Torre, and Ring, 2001).

THEORETICAL FRAMEWORK

Prior research in information technology outsourcing has shown that a primary reason for using external providers is the potential for cost savings (Ang and Cummings, 1997; Aubert, Rivard, and Patry, 1996; Lacity and Hirschheim, 1993; Lacity and Willcocks, 1998). In the classic "buy" or "build" decision from transaction costs theory (Coase, 1937; Williamson, 1991, 1996), organizations have to weigh the costs of creating and supporting their own IT structure and applications versus using ASPs to provide the services. The level of integration is determined by the relative costs of using the markets or employing resources within the firm (Rasheed and Geiger, 2001). ASPs have been projected to reduce production costs in pure monetary terms for factors such as hardware, software, and personnel costs. The transaction cost approach has been the basis of previous research in the outsourcing of technology (Ang and Straub, 1998; Aubert et al., 2001; Ngwenyama and Bryson, 1999; Smith and Rupp, 2003). ASPs provide organizations with relief from industry pressures by delivering expertise at fixed costs, relieving the shortage of skilled IT staff, and allowing internal IT departments to focus on new applications. They also reduce initial capital outlay and controllable fixed monthly costs, and provide lease or rent options. This frees up capital that would normally be allocated to costly hardware upgrades.

The overall impact of transaction costs was previously found to have no effect on the degree of outsourcing (Ang and Straub, 1998). As part of transaction cost economics theory, transaction costs are involved in exchanges between firms. These may include coordination costs, monitoring costs, negotiating costs, governance costs, and so on. These costs act contrary to the benefits provided by the external vendor by highlighting the costs or risks that the organization must bear if it chooses to use an external provider for services. The costs negate the benefits of ASP adoption by creating concerns that lower the prospects of adoption.

Extending transaction costs, agency theory and the related incomplete contracts theory (ICT) focus on trust and risk while social exchange theory (SET) explores the relationships with vendors and their reputation/capability. Economic arguments that promote the adoption of ASPs cite cost savings as a key reason (Lacity and Willcocks, 1998; Smith and Rupp, 2003). Agency theory (Eisenhardt, 1989) extends the transaction costs notion by focusing on the actions of the parties in the relationship and the risks and motivations of each party. Trust and risk are significant to security; as the research on outsourcing matures, the focus shifts from "why to outsource" to "how to manage the relationship." Previous research has identified trust as a key factor in the outsourcing process (Sabherwal, 1999) and has shown that contracts are needed to protect parties due to the emergence of new technologies or changes in the relationship (Beulen and Ribbers, 2003). A key assumption of ICT is that contracts are always "incomplete." These contracts have not covered all contingencies and scenarios (Hart and Moore, 1999).

INFLUENCE OF TRANSACTION AND PRODUCTION COSTS

Previous research in information technology outsourcing has shown that a primary reason for using external providers is the potential for cost savings (Ang and Cummings, 1997; Aubert et al.,

1996; Lacity and Hirschheim, 1993; Lacity and Willcocks, 1998). In the classic "buy" or "build" decision from transaction costs theory (Coase, 1937; Williamson, 1991, 1996), hospitals have to weigh the costs of creating and supporting their own IT structure and applications against using ASPs to provide the services. The level of integration is determined by the relative costs of using the markets or employing resources within the firm (Rasheed and Geiger, 2001). ASPs have been projected to reduce production costs (of maintaining patient information and medical systems) in pure monetary terms for factors such as hardware, software, and personnel costs. The transaction cost approach has been the basis of previous research in the outsourcing of technology (Ang and Straub, 1998; Aubert et al., 2001; Ngwenyama and Bryson, 1999; Smith and Rupp, 2003). ASPs provide hospital IT departments with relief from industry pressures by delivering expertise at fixed costs, mitigating the shortage of skilled IT staff, and allowing internal IT departments to focus on new applications. They also reduce initial capital outlay and controllable fixed monthly costs, and provide lease or rent options. This frees up capital that would normally be allocated to costly hardware upgrades.

Production Costs

Production cost advantages play a dominant role in outsourcing decisions (Ang and Straub, 1998). In structuring the functions of an organization, the goal is profit maximization through the efficient production of outputs from inputs. The firm will produce the output when it has a cost advantage of market structures; similarly, the market will provide efficient production mechanisms in areas where the firm is not dominant. Organizations should seek ASPs based on their ability to provide cost-effective solutions. In the context of IS, a firm will choose to outsource or insource based on the comparative costs of internalizing IS versus the price it has to pay vendors for the same IS services (Ang and Straub, 1998). As the ASP market matures, ASP providers are able to increase client bases and achieve economies of scale. Research suggests that market-oriented structures can reduce costs from economies of scale and scope (Rasheed and Geiger, 2001). The growth of ASP vendors also allows them to negotiate lower costs with the major software providers; these lower costs can then be passed on to the end users. At some point, the costs of renting software from an ASP will be more beneficial than the costs of producing it internally. Higher internal productions costs will drive hospitals to seek alternatives in the current market. ASPs have been projected to reduce the production costs (of maintaining patient information and medical systems) in pure monetary terms for factors such as hardware, software, and personnel costs. Firms are more likely to outsource if the production cost advantages are high (Williamson, 1981). Production costs include the hardware, software, and IT labor resources needed to maintain internal production. ASPs operating with multiple clients can utilize their market-oriented structures to reduce costs and spread them over multiple clients. It is simpler for an ASP to maintain and update software packages than for a hospital IT department to keep up with frequent changes. As the software market becomes more skill-driven, the hospital may also have a difficult time attracting and retaining skilled IT employees.

> H_{1A}: Higher production costs will positively influence ASP model adoption.

Slack Resources

Organizations with high slack resources may choose to investigate the ASP model through the use of slack resources, regardless of the cost implications. Slack resources allow the organization to investigate new innovations in technology that may give the organization an advantage in the marketplace. Previous research has shown that slack resources positively affect adoption behavior; organizations are able to investigate new technologies with excess resources. Organizations with slack resources may also seek to establish themselves as industry leaders through direct investments in their technological infrastructure. The level of investment in specialized equipment or the skills required to yield value from an asset can influence its adoption (Ang and Cummings, 1997). Thus, the abundance of capital resources will allow organizations to investigate new technology and build internal IT capabilities. Organizations with high slack resources will also have lower production cost concerns. These organizations will tend to explore new technologies, ignoring production cost arguments that favor external production. Organizations' success may provide them with the flexibility to absorb more risk based on their abundant resources (Rai and Patnayakuni, 1996). Innovative management may seek to build on internal skills and improve internal operations by using slack resources to make the organization more efficient.

H_{1B}: High slack resources will negatively influence production costs.

Transaction Costs

Research in information technology outsourcing has shown that a primary reason for using external providers is the potential for cost savings (Ang and Cummings, 1997; Lacity and Hirschheim, 1993; Lacity and Willcocks, 1998). The overall impact of transaction costs was previously found to have no impact on the degree of outsourcing (Ang and Straub, 1998). As part of transaction cost economics (TCE), transaction costs are involved in exchanges between firms. These may include coordination costs, monitoring costs, negotiating costs, governance costs, and so on. These costs act contrary to the benefits provided by the external vendor by highlighting the costs or risks that the organization must bear if it chooses to use an external provider for services. They negate the benefits of ASP adoption by creating concerns that lower the prospects of adoption. In the classic "buy" or "build" decision from transaction cost theory (Coase, 1937; Williamson, 1991, 1996), hospitals have to weigh the costs of creating and supporting their own IT structure and applications against using ASPs to provide the services. The level of integration is determined by the relative costs of using the markets or employing resources within the firm (Rasheed and Geiger, 2001). Transaction costs capture the costs incurred in negotiating, maintaining, or modifying the ASP contract. These costs can pose a significant threat to the viability of the ASP option, eroding perceived benefits. If the ASP customizes hospital software, transaction costs will be significantly higher.

H_{2A}: High transaction costs will negatively influence ASP model adoption.

Asset Specificity

The uniqueness and specificity of an organization's information technology applications and assets can impact a firm's costs associated with the asset. Transaction costs, which later affect adoption behavior, are themselves increased by the limited nature and usage of the asset. A resource can be defined as asset specific if "it cannot readily be redeployed"; IT resources are proprietary by nature and are highly asset-specific (Oh and Gallivan, 2003). The level of investment in specialized equipment or the skills required to yield value from an asset can influence its adoption (Ang and Cummings, 1997; Nam et al., 1996). Legacy systems can be reduced or eliminated and old hardware can be sold for cash infusions to the hospitals (possibly even sold to the ASP). ASPs may have the greatest potential for organizations that are logistically or geographically disparate and/or administratively complex. Organizations with high asset specificity will seek to reduce their reliance on legacy systems and multiple platforms. Assets with high specificity can hinder redeployment of resources. Organizations with highly specific assets will seek more services from the ASP provider, thereby increasing transaction costs. The costs of deployment and maintenance of asset-specific resources can increase the negotiation costs and the service level costs from an ASP provider. Investments in specific assets lead to transaction costs (Aubert, Rivard, and Patry, 2004). The specificity of the organization's assets will increase the costs to adopters and create barriers to adoption by increasing the costs of changing over the legacy systems or redeploying assets. Trust permits greater flexibility in the selection of governance mechanisms when asset specificity is present (Jeffries and Reed, 2000).

H_{2B}: High asset specificity will positively influence transaction costs.

Supplier Presence

Hospitals are concerned with the long-term focus of their business. They need to be reassured that in turbulent times the vendors with whom they contract can guarantee that they will not disappear. Supplier presence reflects the paucity of available vendors in the marketplace. The lack of suitable suppliers can dissuade adopters (Ang and Straub, 1998). The presence of more suppliers reflects a growing industry with viable substitutes and new entrants willing to provide better services. The availability of reputable and trustworthy external IT service providers in the market can also be a concern to hospitals seeking to adopt ASPs (Ang and Cummings, 1997). The supply side of IT outsourcing remains underresearched in the academic literature (Seltsikas and Currie, 2002). The viability of the ASP model may dissuade potential adopters, and the business model remains immature and fundamentally flawed (Currie, 2003b). As the ASP model matures, the industry will see the emergence of more clearly defined enterprise ASP offerings from key players in the software and computing services industry (Ekanayaka, Currie, and Seltsikas, 2002). Larger outsourcing contracts are awarded to reputable vendors with track records (Hoecht and Trott, 2006).

H_{2C}: High supplier presence will negatively influence transaction costs.

MODERATING INFLUENCE OF TRUST AND PRIVACY PROTECTION

Moderators are important to the development of theory (Chin, Marcolin, and Newsted, 2003). The role of trust and privacy permeate the 1996 Health Insurance Portability and Accountability Act (HIPAA) guidelines. Considering the highly personal and potentially sensitive nature of medical data, there are significant risks to the confidentiality, integrity, and availability of such information (Zhang, Ahn, and Chu, 2002). The health care industry increasingly views IT as a fundamental asset in providing health-related information services and decision support on demand as well as in managing rising costs and changing organizational needs, improving the quality of health services and patient care, and fighting illness while promoting wellness (Raghupathi and Tan, 2002). With shrinking federal and state support for health care institutions, hospitals are forced to limit investments to proven technologies, and risk aversion has become an underlying obstacle to new technology adoption. This risk manifests itself as concerns over the privacy of patient information and trust for the vendor. IT represents a substantial investment for most corporations and constitutes a significant aspect of organizational work (Agarwal and Karahanna, 2000).

Vendor Trust

Trust is important in health care delivery because health care providers rely on collaboration to reduce complexity (Paul and McDaniel, 2004). Vendor trust has previously been identified as an antecedent in exchange relationships that involves risks and vulnerabilities (Barthélémy, 2003; Hart and Saunders, 1998; Sabherwal, 1999) and is often the most cited inhibiting factor (Heart and Pliskin, 2001) to the adoption of technology. Risks can be lowered in the presence of vendor trust. Trust in an organizational setting reduces complexity when new technology concerns emerge, which is especially important in health care delivery (Paul and McDaniel, 2004). With respect to the relationship between transaction costs and adoption, trust may play a moderating role: this can be explained by looking at the definition of transaction costs. Negotiation and monitoring costs can be lowered in the presence of vendor trust. Similarly, long-term governance will be reduced and trust may actually increase over time, thus minimizing transaction costs.

With respect to production costs, seeking vendors in the market to produce the services required exposes the organization to risk. The organization will be more likely to engage in external contracts in the presence of high trust. Production costs capture the costs of producing (hardware, software, and labor) service. We hypothesized that higher production cost concerns will positively influence the adoption of ASPs. If the costs of internal operations for hardware, software, and labor are rising, ASPs can provide a viable alternative. The reason hospitals would continue to operate their internal systems is to create a trustworthy internal network to protect patient data. Trust can affect the relationship between decisions to make or buy. The question then becomes whether this is a moderating, mediating, direct, or indirect role for trust. We tested the moderating and direct role of trust. Trust affecting adoption directly seems to address a simple question: Does trust affect my decision to adopt an ASP? Trust moderating the affect of production costs is more complicated. If the hospital decided that the concerns of higher internal production are significant, we may still not adopt because of concerns about trust. The level of trust in the third party or in the technology would moderate the relationship. If the hospital had significant issues with trust, ignoring high production costs, it would not adopt. The level of trust would play a role in their concerns.

H_{3A}: Vendor trust will moderate the relationship between transaction costs and ASP model adoption.

H_{3B}: Vendor trust will moderate the relationship between production costs and ASP model adoption.

Privacy Protection

Confidentiality and security of a patient's health information have always been important, even more so with the ease of electronic access (Huston, 2001). The adoption of technology must adequately protect patient privacy without exception. Privacy protections included improper access protections and unauthorized usage protections. Improper access protection refers to the protection of data at the organization or at the ASP vendor site, and encompasses both technological constraints and organizational policy (Smith, Milberg, and Burke, 1996). Health care workers are very cognizant of possible abuses in the form of unauthorized or inappropriate access to medical records that contain personal information (Baumer, Earp, and Payton, 2000). Unauthorized secondary usage refers to the inappropriate use of stored information at the ASP vendor site. The usage is specific to external concerns over data disclosed to third parties other than those included in the contract (Smith, Milberg, and Burke, 1996). ASP models that protect against unauthorized usage and improper access of information will be more likely to positively influence adoption. With respect to the relationship between transaction costs and privacy protection, privacy concerns may play a significant moderating role in the negotiation of data security, storage, information transfer, and privacy protection can be defined in the service level agreements. With respect to production costs, seeking vendors in the market to produce the services required exposes the organization to risk. The organization will expect to have privacy protection equivalent to or greater than the internally available protections.

The relationship between transaction costs and privacy is easily understood. Production costs capture the costs of producing the service. Higher production cost concerns will positively influence the adoption of ASPs. If the costs of internal operations for hardware, software, and labor are rising, ASPs can provide a viable alternative. The reason that hospitals would continue to operate their internal systems is to create a secure, private, internal network to protect patient data. In light of recent legislation, this concern over privacy and security is increased. The risk in outsourcing to lower production costs is related to the risk aversion of the hospital. Hence, privacy can affect the relationship of make versus buy. The question then becomes whether this is a moderating, mediating, direct, or indirect role for privacy. We tested a moderating and direct role of privacy. Privacy as a direct effect on adoption seems to address a simple question: Do privacy concerns affect my decision to adopt or not adopt an ASP model? Privacy moderating the affect of production costs is more complicated. If we (the hospital) decide that the concerns of higher internal production are significant, we may still not adopt because of concerns about privacy. If the hospital had significant concerns over privacy, ignoring high production costs, they would not adopt. The level of privacy protection would play a role in their concerns.

> H_{4A}: Privacy protection will moderate the relationship between transaction costs and ASP model adoption.
>
> H_{4B}: Privacy protection will moderate the relationship between production costs and ASP model adoption.

METHODOLOGY

Study Context and Sample

A mail survey was developed based on outsourcing literature (Ang and Straub, 1998; Lacity and Willcocks, 1998); content validity was established by the use of previously validated variables (see Table 9.1). Content validity was also established through individual interviews with IT professionals in the hospital industry. The survey instrument was developed from previous research and included various refinement procedures (Dillman, 2000). Initial survey constructs and questions were pretested with eight health experts, two MIS professors, and four Ph.D. candidates. This was done to review the survey instrument for clarity, completeness, and readability. A pilot test was conducted using a random sample of IT professionals. Eighty-four surveys were mailed resulting in twenty-nine usable responses with twelve surveys returned for incorrect information. The raw response rate was 34.5 percent while the adjusted rate was 40.3 percent. The internal consistency (Cronbach's alpha) of the pilot data was calculated with results ranging from 0.5903 to 0.9407. Factor analysis was used to verify discriminant validity; items with a factor rating below 0.5 were dropped.

The full survey was sent to 3,450 senior-level IT hospital executives. A five-week cutoff was established for the first wave of responses; a follow-up reminder card was mailed at the end of the five weeks to increase participation. The overall response rate calculation was 6.5 percent (223 surveys); this was low but not surprising considering the limitations of mail surveys and the

Table 9.1

Potential Application Service Provider (ASP) Applications

Service areas for ASPs	%
Accounting/payroll	49
Patient billing	63
Claims processing	65
Purchasing/inventory	48
Patient records	38
Personal applications	24
Other	28

nature of health care response rates. We further examined the mailing list that was provided to look for additional explanations for the low response rate. Of the 3,450 surveys, we eliminated 217 duplicates for hospital systems/groups. We also reviewed the list of titles. We eliminated all those non-IT (IT staff were considered to be recipients holding the title of chief executive officer [CEO], chief technology officer [CTO], chief information officer [CIO], director of IS, director of health IS, director of data processing, and vice president of IS); this resulted in the removal of another 481 names. Using the final list, we end up with:

223 / 3,450 = 6.5 percent (original count)
223 / 3,233 = 6.9 percent (less duplicates)
223 / 2,752 = 8.1 percent (less non-IT staff)

In studying IT in health care, a response rate of 30 percent in mail surveys is rare, and response rates between 5 percent and 10 percent are more common (Hikmet and Chen, 2003). Eighty-nine completed surveys were returned (fifty-three adopters, thirty-six nonadopters); an additional eighty-four surveys were returned indicating that the organization was "aware" of ASPs but had not advanced to that stage. These were NOT used in the calculations because the respondents had not completed a significant portion of the survey. Fifty excluded surveys with missing data were not used in the partial least squares (PLS) model. The low response could be attributable to lack of prenotification, lack of incentives, and the timing and length of the survey. Survey length has been found to have a negative influence on mail survey response rates in that the longer the survey, the more likely it is that the response rate will be lower (Sheehan, 2001; Yammarino, Skinner, and Childers, 1991). Recent studies have also indicated that samples in business-oriented studies were more sensitive. The survey was sent out toward the end of the year, which clashed with vacation time and traditional holidays. We did not include any advance notice or token incentive or prize drawing to increase participation as has been suggested in the survey design method (Dillman, 2000). Looking at the data, respondents indicated that they were using or would use an ASP for various functions (see Table 9.1). The sample (see Table 9.2) of hospitals varied in size (full-time employees [FTEs] and beds). Our sample represents the different sizes in the population of hospitals.

Further investigation of the low response rate was conducted. In addition to the reminder card that was mailed five weeks post survey mailing, we started calling a sample of CIOs. The original mailing list did not contain phone numbers. We used Web resources to locate a sample of fifty CIOs. Each was called to verify receipt of the survey or the card. We found that many (thirty-two) of the surveys had not been received by the CIO's office staff and a few (nine) had decided not to participate. The others (nine) asked us to resend the survey but we never heard back from them. This interception of

Table 9.2

Demographics of Responding Hospitals

Revenue range (in millions)	%	FTE range	%	Number of licensed beds	%
< 100	28	< = 500	28	< = 250	45
100–199	33	501–1,000	17	251–500	33
200–299	8	1,001–1,500	15	501–750	10
300–399	8	1,501–2,000	13	751–1,000	2
400–499	4	2,001–2,500	7	1,001–1,250	4
> = 500	19	2,501–3,000	2	1,251–1,500	5
		> 3,000	18	> 1,500	2

Table 9.3

Survey Response by Adoption Category

	Completed surveys	Incomplete surveys	Total
Adopters	53	0	53
Nonadopters	36	84*	120
Missing data	0	50	50
Total	89	134	223

*Awareness only.

Table 9.4

Survey Response by Adoption Level

	Completed surveys	Surveys with only adoption stages completed	Totals	Percentages
Awareness or other	17	84	101	58
Interest	12	0	12	7
Evaluation	4	0	4	2
Trial and reject or discontinuance	3	0	3	2
Commitment	16	0	16	9
Limited deployment	28	0	28	16
General deployment	9	0	9	5
Total	89	84	173	100

mail and the low response rate from senior officers has been a problem in previous research (Kearns and Lederer, 1999) Other factors that affected the low response rate include the length of the survey (eight pages) and the timing of the survey (see Tables 9.3 and 9.4). Due to timing issues, we had mailed our survey in the first week of December. This would mean that the surveys reached the desks of CIOs right before the holidays and were either low priority or discarded.

Construct Operationalization

Variables were selected from previously validated measures (see Table 9.5). Adopters can be found at various stages in the process of adoption of new technology. These stages include Ettlie's

Figure 9.1 **Conceptual Model: Transaction Cost Approach**

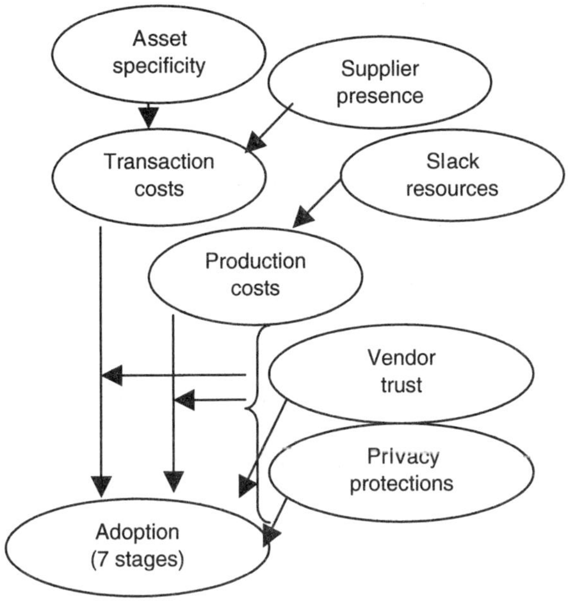

five-stage model (Ettlie and Vellenga, 1979), the common three-step adoption (initiation, adoption, implementation) (Rogers, 1995), and the six-step model (Fichman and Kemerer, 1997). For our research, we applied a seven-stage adoption model (Ettlie and Vellenga, 1979; Fichman and Kemerer, 1997). This model's stages included: awareness, interest, evaluation, trial and reject, commitment, limited deployment, and general deployment. The use of a seven-stage model allows for richer data analysis. The direct effects of transaction costs and production costs are not investigated at each stage but captured in a manner that reflects the concerns of the organization and the level of adoption at the time that the survey was completed. Respondents replied with their concerns at the level of current adoption stage. This gives us more data than a simple binary adoption variable. For example, a firm may decide to discontinue its operations based on transaction costs that become more transparent as the negotiation process progresses.

Bounded rationality may not have provided all the production or transaction costs to the organization at the time of adoption. Similarly, a firm that is cautious may be at a limited deployment stage while investigating the ASP process and building a relationship with the vendor. Vendor trust will then vary based on the level of adoption stage and experience with the vendor. Size has been linked to adoption behavior (Hoffman, Irwin, and Digman, 1996; Rai and Howard, 1993). While larger organizations are more innovative due to their flexibility to absorb risk (Sharma and Rai, 2003), research on outsourcing suggests that size is negatively correlated with the tendency to outsource (Chen and Soliman, 2002). We expect size to have no impact on adoption. Size was measured using the number of licensed beds reported (Irwin, Hoffman, and Geiger, 1998; Kimberly and Evanisko, 1981).

Data Analysis

Interaction analysis of moderators was the basis of recent research (Chin, Marcolin, and Newsted, 2003). PLS has been used previously in IS research (Agarwal and Karahanna, 2000; Chin, 1996; Compeau and Higgins, 1995; Gefen, Straub, and Boudreau, 2000; Venkatesh, 2000) and is

Table 9.5

Survey Items and Sources

List of survey variables		
Control	Size	Kimberly and Evanisko, 1981
Independent	Production costs	Ang and Straub, 1998
	Transaction costs	Ang and Straub, 1998
	Supplier presence	Ang and Straub, 1998
	Asset specificity	Ang and Straub, 1998
	Slack resources	Adapted from Miller and Friesen, 1992
	Privacy protections	Smith, Milberg, and Burke, 1996
	Vendor trust	Bharadwaj et al., 1999
Dependent	Adoption	Ettlie and Vellenga, 1979; Fichman and Kemerer, 1997

appropriate due to the minimal demands on sample size (Agarwal and Karahanna, 2000; Chin, 1996) and measurement scales. The stability of the estimates (the effect of noise) was tested via the bootstrap resampling method. Composite reliability and discriminant validity (average variance extracted; AVE) scores are reported (see Table 9.6). The square root of AVE and the correlations were checked and found to be within expected limits (see Table 9.7). The standardized coefficients represent the relative strength of the statistical relationship (Gefen, Straub, and Boudreau, 2000). The variables were reflective with size as the control variable. The number of licensed beds was chosen to represent size in the PLS model. The tax status of a hospital had previously been shown to correlate with the adoption of technology innovations (Hoffman, Irwin, and Digman, 1996); this was checked in our data and the correlation was found to be insignificant (correlation = 0.125, significance = 0.246). Eighty-nine surveys were used for the PLS calculations.

RESULTS

Results of Direct Effects

There were significant results ($R^2 = 0.135$) in the direct model—model 1 (see Table 9.8). Support was found for hypotheses (H_{1B}, H_{2A}, H_{2B}, and H_{2C}). No significant support was found for H_{1A}. Hospitals with slack resources were more likely to investigate ASPs and were less vulnerable to industry changes. The presence of a reputable supplier and the reliability of the supplier significantly affected transaction costs. With the introduction of privacy and trust as direct effects on adoption—model 2—the results (see Figure 9.2) did not change except that trust showed a slight significance. Slack resources contributed to production costs even though production costs were not significant ($R^2 = 0.198$); asset specificity and supplier presence were significant antecedents to both transaction costs ($R^2 = 0.239$); overall change in R^2 was 0.023. Transaction costs were significant while production costs, once again, did not show any significance in our sample. If you consider the ASP model as a variation of outsourcing, then the negotiating and coordination components of transaction costs were more important to health care organizations.

Vendor trust had a slightly significant impact on adoption behavior while privacy protections were not significant. This can be explained by the fact that adopters have service agreements that set protection guidelines; privacy protections can be implied in the contract and therefore are not as great a concern as trust. The minimal impact of trust (t-value –1.80) was unexpected. Trust was expected to play a significant role in adoption behavior. Trust limits the opportunistic behavior in interorganizational relationships (Sabherwal, 1999).

Table 9.6

Composite Reliability and Average Variance Extracted (AVE)

Variable	No. Items	Composite reliability (α)	Discriminant validity (AVE)
Vendor trust	8	0.958	0.743
Privacy protections	7	0.951	0.738
Slack resources	4	0.797	0.504
Transaction costs	3	0.873	0.696
Production costs	5	0.855	0.544
Asset specificity	5	0.910	0.672
Supplier presence	3	0.895	0.740

Table 9.7

Correlation Matrix and Square Root of Average Variance Extracted

	Supplier presence	Slack resources	Size	Adoption	Production costs	Transaction costs	Asset specificity	Trust	Privacy
Supplier presence	**0.860**								
Slack resources	–0.308	**0.711**							
Size	0.039	–0.068	**1.000**						
Adoption	0.156	0.085	–0.092	**1.000**					
Production costs	0.422	–0.359	–0.190	0.213	**0.748**				
Transaction costs	–0.424	0.329	0.062	–0.353	–0.442	**0.834**			
Asset specificity	–0.173	0.407	–0.001	–0.050	–0.173	0.289	**0.822**		
Trust	0.103	–0.180	–0.258	0.245	0.309	–0.244	–0.099	**0.863**	
Privacy	0.324	–0.041	–0.193	0.162	0.399	–0.413	–0.022	0.343	**0.860**

Results of Moderated Effects

Hypotheses 3 and 4 reflected the moderating effects of trust and privacy on both production and transaction costs, respectively. To assess the moderating effects of trust and privacy on transaction and production costs, three models were tested. The first model investigated all variables for interactions (see Figure 9.3); the second and third models investigated trust and privacy separately. PLS latent scores were used to calculate the interaction scores (see Table 9.9). The effects of privacy ($R^2 = 0.152$) and trust ($R^2 = 0.159$) separately were minimal and did not show any significant interactions in the results. Transaction costs were still the predominant significant variable while production costs did not change. Privacy and trust had no moderating effect on the cost variables. The full model with all of the interactions ($R^2 = 0.180$) reflected the direct model results with no moderation effects seen.

DISCUSSION

The results show that transaction costs are a key significant driver of ASP adoption in the health care industry. There was some support for the effects of vendor trust as a direct driver of the adop-

Figure 9.2 **Research Model Results for Direct Effects**

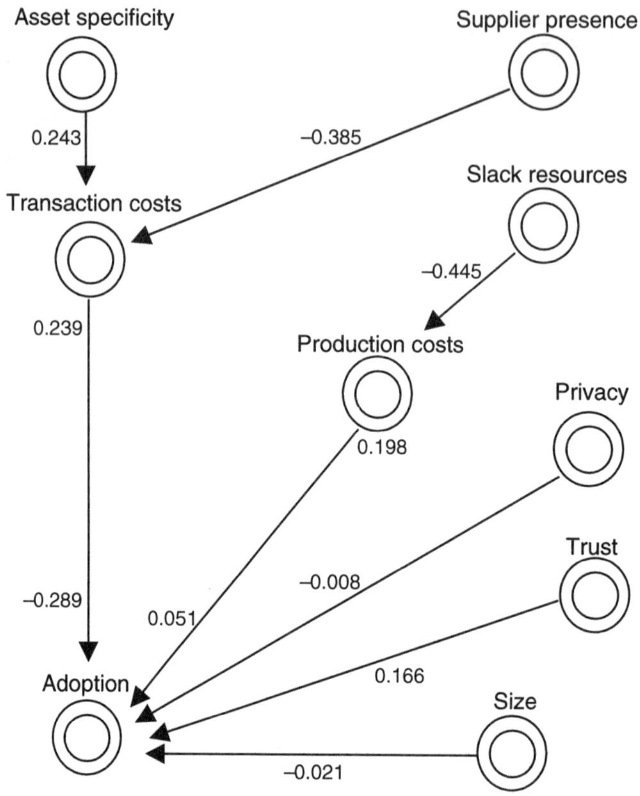

Table 9.8

Direct Model Using Partial Least Squares

	Model 1		Model 2	
	Coefficient	Results	Coefficient	Results
Production costs	0.084	No effect	0.051	No effect
Slack resources	–0.445****	Strong	–0.445****	Strong
Transaction costs	–0.310***	Strong	–0.289**	Strong
Asset specificity	0.243***	Strong	0.243***	Strong
Supplier presence	–0.385****	Strong	–0.385****	Strong
Size	–0.054	No effect	–0.021	No effect
Trust			0.166*	Support
Privacy			–0.008	No support
R^2	**0.135**		**0.158**	

*$p < 0.10$
**$p < 0.05$
***$p < 0.01$
****$p < 0.001$

Figure 9.3 **Research Model (Full Model) Results for Interaction Effects**

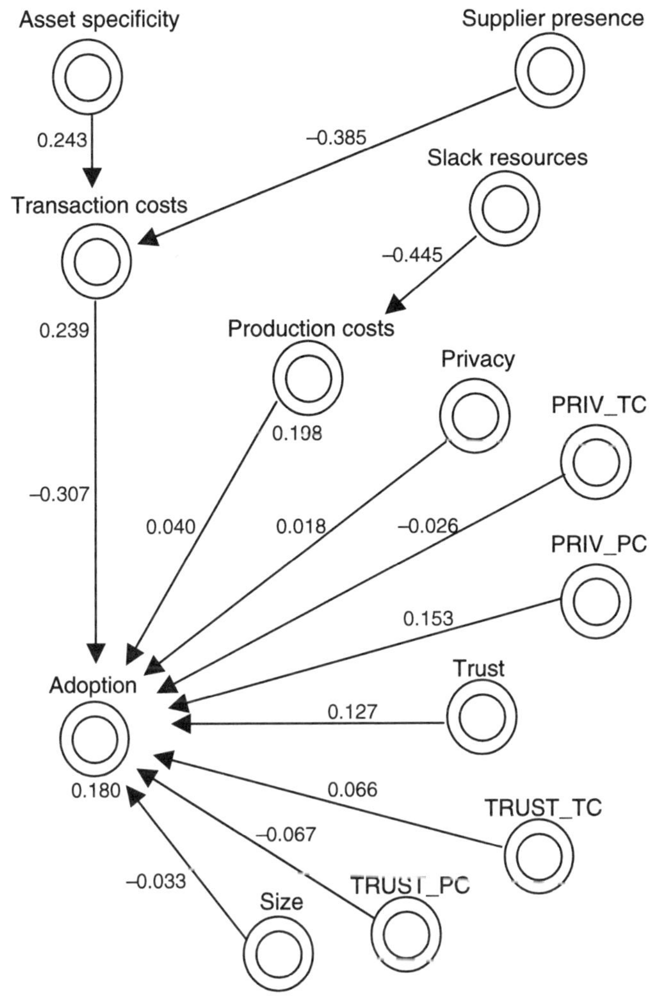

tion decision. Even though the results of this study show no significant moderating impact of trust and privacy, these variables continue to be of concern with adoption, and, more important, within the health care environment. Moderators may be included in the service level agreements affecting decisions prior to adoption. The HIPAA guidelines require that covered entities that use business associates must provide satisfactory assurances to safeguard protected health information. This provision may force privacy and security concerns to be addressed prior to adoption.

We expected to see significant interaction effects; the theory of transaction costs analysis implies that transaction costs reflect the risk and uncertainty within the market. Trust should have an impact on negotiation and coordination processes with ASPs. This impact shows up in the direct model on adoption. The overall size effect was calculated as 0.02 (between the full model and the direct) with 0.02 as small, 0.15 as moderate, and 0.35 as large (Chin, Marcolin, and Newsted, 2003); the effects of the interactions were small. Further examination of the data set showed numerous duplication of hospital systems with overlapping roles; the mailing list

Table 9.9

Interaction Model Using Partial Least Squares

	Full model	Privacy only	Trust only
	Coefficient	Coefficient	Coefficient
Production costs	0.040	0.024	0.073
Slack resources	–0.445****	–0.445****	–0.445****
Transaction costs	–0.307**	–0.330**	–0.279**
Asset specificity	0.243***	0.243***	0.243***
Supplier presence	–0.385****	–0.385****	–0.385****
Size	–0.033	–0.033	–0.016
Trust	0.127		0.146
Privacy	0.018	0.052	
Trust x production costs	–0.067		–.050
Trust x transaction costs	0.066		–0.001
Privacy x production costs	0.153	0.154	
Privacy x transaction costs	–0.026	0.063	
R^2	**0.180**	**0.152**	**0.159**

$**p < 0.05$
$***p < 0.01$
$****p < 0.001$

showed individuals who were part of the same system. This would further improve the response rate calculations.

Trust may not have shown up in the data because of the implied governance mechanisms in the contract. For initial adoption, prior negotiations between parties may have been proactive in creating benchmarking and reporting mechanisms together with acceptable performance levels. The concern of the vendor is to meet the levels agreed upon by the client. Trust may develop post adoption as the vendor and client interact and share information. Service levels may change and the client may have different needs; addressing these needs in a timely manner may improve the relationship and build interpersonal trust between the vendor employees and the client employees; this trust may spillover into organizational trust that solidifies the relationship as mutually beneficial.

IMPLICATIONS

An interesting result is the strength of transaction costs versus production costs. In earlier research by Ang and Straub (1998), production costs were more significant than transaction costs. The ASP model follows a similar pattern but transaction costs have a much greater impact in this study. The maturing outsourcing model may have shifted the focus from make-versus-buy concerns to transaction costs with the ASP. The use of a seven-stage adoption model is innovative and allows the results to reflect the concerns of the organization and the level of adoption at the time that the survey was completed. Building on the TCE concepts of uncertainty, bounded rationality, and information asymmetry, the seven-stage model provides stages of adoption that can be correlated with the response to the survey items. The lack of support for interaction effects may reflect the small data set. Future research will collapse the seven stages into four to improve the strength of the results and improve the research on adoption as a multilevel dependent variable. Trust and privacy may indeed be covered under service-level agreements with the vendor and may not be linked to transaction and production costs. The discussion of patient privacy and trust will continue to be the focus of future research; the prevalence of the Internet will drive more technology into the health care industry. Future research will also need to examine nonlinear effects of the predictor variables on adoption.

The study sample may be a key limitation with respect to causal implications of the results. The small sample size may have influenced the results. The composite reliability and discriminant validity results were not strong. Under small sample sizes, there is a known bias for PLS to overestimate the measurement loadings and underestimate the structural paths among constructs (Agarwal and Karahanna, 2000; Chin, Marcolin, and Newsted, 2003). Future research will need to reexamine the data once a significant sample has been achieved. The survey instrument was long and required various answers that may have led to low return rates. Some questions required actual financial data that may have been unavailable to the respondent, or data that were not something the hospital wanted to share. This could have caused survey recipients to forgo completing the survey or to return incomplete surveys. Another issue was the timing of the survey distribution; surveys were distributed in the middle of December and may have crossed many CIO desks during the holiday/vacation period. Organizations with no interest in adopting ASPs may have ignored the study (some justification comes from the numerous respondents that were aware of ASPs but failed to complete the survey).

The inclusion of traditional outsourcing hypotheses was shown to confirm that ASPs follow a similar adoption pattern. The statistical explanations are provided, and the theoretical explanations are interesting. While trust and privacy may affect transaction and production costs in our arguments, the data did not support the hypotheses. The direct effects of trust showed some significance. However, in the moderated model, the lack of effects of trust and privacy may be linked to other reasons. The role of service-level agreements (SLAs) between parties could alleviate the issues of trust and privacy. SLAs have evolved over time and vendors and clients have built relationships that can make concerns over trust and privacy standard. With both traditional outsourcing and ASP usage, the contract is the major definition of the relationship (Smith and Kumar, 2004). While legislation promotes security and privacy, vendors may have been using a higher level of performance with respect to these issues. Service providers in contractual relationships assume responsibility for providing contractual functions (Kishore et al., 2003) Certification of ASPs (Leem and Lee, 2004) may provide additional legitimacy to the ASP's reliability and reduce concerns about trust and privacy. Client relationship development builds over time and the concerns over trust and privacy may disappear as the relationship strengthens. The relationship may also require a balance between contractual management and trust (Barthélémy, 2003).

FUTURE RESEARCH

This in no way comprises the full set of possible variables that may explain adoption behavior. Interactions between several variables may account for more causality. Trust may have multiple influences (direct, moderating, or as an antecedent to other second order variables). This research focused on the direct and moderating influence of trust and privacy using a TCE approach. Testing the mediating effects could provide additional results. Future research should examine the interrelationships between the constructs and the various models for best fit. Trust requires work prior to outsourcing and during the relationship. Maintaining a long-term relationship will depend on the preparation that an organization makes before developing the relationship (Willcocks and Choi, 1995). Recent research has shown that trust-building mechanisms differ between vendor and client. Client senior management and project team members report that the fulfillment of promises is crucial to the development of trust, yet the outsourcing vendor does not share this view; for the outsourcer, fulfillment of promises is an artifact of a contractual relationship and both parties differ regarding what signals trust-building behavior (Lander et al., 2004). The study makes theoretical and empirical contributions to the outsourcing literature. Longitudinal research on trust after the adoption combined with pre-adoption data should be conducted to provide validity to the research.

APPENDIX 9.1. SURVEY ITEMS

Privacy Protections

Please answer the following questions based on your perceptions of the ASP vendor's likely behavior prior to the adoption of an ASP.

	Strongly disagree						Strongly agree
1. ASP vendors devote adequate time and effort in preventing unauthorized access to personal information.	1	2	3	4	5	6	7
2. Computer databases that contain personal information are protected by ASPs from unauthorized access—no matter how much it costs.	1	2	3	4	5	6	7
3. ASP vendors take adequate steps to make sure that unauthorized entities cannot access our information in their computers.	1	2	3	4	5	6	7
4. ASPs will not use our information for purposes other than that authorized by us.	1	2	3	4	5	6	7
5. When we give our information to an ASP for particular reasons, the ASP will never use the information for any other reason.	1	2	3	4	5	6	7
6. ASPs will never sell our information in their computer databases to others.	1	2	3	4	5	6	7
7. ASPs will never share our information with other entities unless it has been authorized by us.	1	2	3	4	5	6	7

Production and Transaction Costs

Please circle the *best* response to the following questions.

	Strongly disagree						Strongly agree
8. We have the scale and volume to justify internal data processing management and operations.	1	2	3	4	5	6	7
9. An ASP vendor would be able to reduce our *hardware* costs.	1	2	3	4	5	6	7
10. An ASP vendor would be able to reduce our *software* costs.	1	2	3	4	5	6	7
11. An ASP vendor would be able to reduce our *information systems personnel* costs.	1	2	3	4	5	6	7
12. It is cheaper to manage our own data processing facilities and services than to rely on an ASP vendor.	1	2	3	4	5	6	7
13. There would be significant problems associated with negotiating a contract or agreement (e.g., agreeing on conditions, prices, etc.) with an ASP vendor for our data processing services.	1	2	3	4	5	6	7
14. ASP vendors would have to be closely and constantly monitored to ensure that they adhere to our contractual terms and conditions.	1	2	3	4	5	6	7
15. It would be very difficult to modify our contracts or agreements with ASP vendors once a contract is signed.	1	2	3	4	5	6	7

Asset Specificity

Please circle the *best* response to the following questions.

	Strongly disagree						Strongly agree
16. Compared to our peer organizations, our IT facilities and services require technical skills that are relatively unique.	1	2	3	4	5	6	7
17. To process our data, ASP vendors would have to make substantial investments in equipment and software tailored to our needs.	1	2	3	4	5	6	7
18. Our data processing operations are more complex than the data processing operations of our peer organizations.	1	2	3	4	5	6	7
19. We use more hardware platforms and multiple systems configurations than most of our peer organizations.	1	2	3	4	5	6	7
20. Our organization software portfolio is more sophisticated and complex than those of peer organizations.	1	2	3	4	5	6	7

Supplier Presence

Please circle the *best* response to the following questions.

	Strongly disagree						Strongly agree
21. There are a sufficient number of reputable ASP vendors who potentially could provide IT facilities and services to our organization.	1	2	3	4	5	6	7
22. There are a sufficient number of trustworthy ASP vendors who potentially could provide IT facilities and services to our organization.	1	2	3	4	5	6	7
23. If we decide to terminate in-house IT operations, there are other ASP vendors who could provide us with the same level of IT facilities and services.	1	2	3	4	5	6	7
24. Services offered by ASP vendors can be adapted to the productivity goals of individual projects.	1	2	3	4	5	6	7
25. Services offered by ASP vendors can be adapted to suit the resources available to a project.	1	2	3	4	5	6	7

Vendor Trust

For the following areas, please rate the degree to which you trust the ASP vendor you may be considering to adopt.

	Extremely unimportant						Extremely important
26. The honesty and accuracy of deadlines set by the ASP vendor.	1	2	3	4	5	6	7
27. The follow-through in delivering on promises made by the ASP vendor.	1	2	3	4	5	6	7
28. The ASP vendor's honesty in business dealings.	1	2	3	4	5	6	7
29. The competency of the ASP vendor in accurately and efficiently processing paperwork.	1	2	3	4	5	6	7
30. The reliability of the computer system of the ASP vendor.	1	2	3	4	5	6	7
31. The willingness of the ASP vendor to share information.	1	2	3	4	5	6	7
32. The ASP vendor's adherence to agreements.	1	2	3	4	5	6	7
33. The ASP vendor's consistency in business dealings.	1	2	3	4	5	6	7

Slack Resources

Rate the internal abundance of the following resources for your firm.

	Very scarce and/or prohibitively expensive						Quite plentiful
34. Capital.	1	2	3	4	5	6	7
35. Skilled labor.	1	2	3	4	5	6	7
36. Material supplies.	1	2	3	4	5	6	7
37. Managerial talent.	1	2	3	4	5	6	7

REFERENCES

Agarwal, R. and Karahanna, E. 2000. Time flies when you're having fun: Cognitive absorption and beliefs about information technology usage. *MIS Quarterly*, 24, 4, 665–694.

Alborz, S.; Seddon, P.B.; and Scheepers, R. 2004. Impact of configuration on IT outsourcing relationships. In *Proceedings of the Americas Conference on Information Systems*, New York (August 6–8), 3551–3560.

Ang, S. and Cummings, L.L. 1997. Strategic response to institutional influences on information systems outsourcing. *Organization Science*, 8, 3 (May–June), 235–256.

Ang, S. and Straub, D.W. 1998. Production and transaction economies and IS outsourcing: A study of the U.S. banking industry. *MIS Quarterly*, 22, 4, 535–552.

Arino, A.; de la Torre, J.; and Ring, P.S. 2001. Relational quality: Managing trust in corporate alliances. *California Management Review*, 44, 1, 109–131.

Aubert, B.A.; Rivard, S.; and Patry, M. 1996. A transaction cost approach to outsourcing behavior: Some empirical evidence. *Information & Management*, 30, 2, 51–64.

———. 2004. A transaction cost model of IT outsourcing. *Information & Management*, 41, 7, 921–932.

Aubert, B.A.; Patry, M.; Rivard, S.; and Smith, H. 2001. IT outsourcing risk management at British Petroleum. In *Proceedings of the 34th Annual Hawaii International Conference on System Sciences*, vol. 8. Washington, DC: IEEE Computer Society, 3398–3407.

Barthélémy, J. 2003. The hard and soft sides of it outsourcing management. *European Management Journal*, 21, 5, 539–548.

Baumer, D.; Earp, J.B.; and Payton, F.C. 2000. Privacy of medical records: IT implications of HIPAA. *Computers and Society*, 30, 4, 40–47.

Beulen, E. and Ribbers, P. 2003. Managing an IT-outsourcing partnership in Asia. In *Proceedings of the Hawaii International Conference on System Sciences*. Hawaii: IEEE, 1–10.

Bharadwaj, A.S.; Sambamurthy, R.W.; and Zmud, R.W. 1999. IT capabilities: Theoretical perspectives and empirical operationalization. In *Proceedings of the 20th International Conference on Information Systems* (Charlotte, NC, December 12–15). Atlanta, GA: Association for Information Systems, 378–385.

Chen, L.-D. and Soliman, K.S. 2002. Managing IT outsourcing: A value-driven approach to outsourcing using application service providers. *Logistics Information Management*, 15, 3, 180–191.

Chin, W.W. 1996. The measurement and meaning of IT usage: Reconciling recent discrepancies between self-reported and computer recorded usage. In B.A. Aubert and W.W. Chin, eds., *Proceedings of the Administrative Sciences Association of Canada*. Montreal, PQ (May 25–28): 65–74.

Chin, W.W.; Marcolin, B.L.; and Newsted, P.R. 2003. A partial least squares latent variable modeling approach for measuring interaction effects. *Information Systems Research*, 14, 2, 189–217.

Choudhury, V. and Sabherwal, R. 2003. Portfolios of control in outsourced software development projects. *Information Systems Research*, 14, 3, 291–314.

Coase, R. 1937. The nature of the firm. *Economica*, 4, 16, 386–405.

Compeau, D.R. and Higgins, C.A. 1995. Application of social cognitive theory to training for computer skills. *Information Systems Research*, 6, 2, 118–143.

Currie, W.L. 2003a. A knowledge-based risk assessment framework for evaluating Web-enabled application outsourcing projects. *International Journal of Project Management*, 21, 3, 207–217.

———. 2003b. Value creation from application services provisioning: Lessons from four vendor firms. In *Proceedings of the 24th International Conference on Information Systems,* Seattle, WA (December 14–17), 143–154.

Dillman, D.A. 2000. *Mail and Internet Surveys: The Tailored Design Method.* New York: Wiley.

Eisenhardt, K.M. 1989. Agency theory: An assessment and review. *Academy of Management Review*, 14, 1, 57–74.

Ekanayaka, Y.; Currie, W.L.; and Seltsikas, P. 2002. Delivering enterprise resource planning systems through application service providers. *Logistics Information Management*, 15, 3, 192–203.

Ettlie, J.E., and Vellenga, D.B. 1979. The adoption time period for some transportation innovations. *Management Science*, 25, 5, 429–443.

Fichman, R.G. and Kemerer, C.F. 1997. The assimilation of software process innovations: An organizational learning perspective. *Management Science*, 43, 10, 1345–1363.

Friedman, L.H.; Goes, J.B.; and Orr, R. 2000. The timing of medical technology acquisition: Strategic decision making in turbulent environments. *Journal of Healthcare Management*, 45, 5, 317–331.

Gefen, D. 2002. Reflections on the dimensions of trust and trustworthiness among online consumers. *Database for Advances in Information Systems*, 33, 3, 38–53.

Gefen, D.; Karahanna, E.; and Straub, D.W. 2003. Trust and TAM in online shopping: An integrated model. *MIS Quarterly*, 27, 1, 51–90.

Gefen, D.; Straub, D.; and Boudreau, M.-C. 2000. Structural Equation Modeling and regression: Guidelines for research practice. *Communication of the Association for Information Systems*, 4, 7, 1–79.

Goo, J.; Kishore, R.; and Rao, H.R. 2000. A content-analytic longitudinal study of the drivers for information technology and systems outsourcing. In *Proceedings of the 21st International Conference on Information Systems*, Brisbane, Australia (December 10–13), 601–611.

Grabner-Kräuter, S. and Kaluscha, E.A. 2003. Empirical research in on-line trust: A review and critical assessment. *International Journal of Human-Computer Studies*, 58, 6, 783–812.

Gulati, R. 1998. Alliances and networks. *Strategic Management Journal*, 19, 4, 293–317.

Hart, O. and Moore, J. 1999. Foundations of incomplete contracts. *Review of Economic Studies*, 66, 226, 115–138.

Hart, P.J. and Saunders, C.S. 1998. Emerging electronic partnerships: Antecedents and dimensions of EDI use from the supplier's perspective. *Journal of Management Information Systems*, 14, 4, 87–111.

Heart, T. and Pliskin, N. 2001. Is E-commerce of IT application services (ASP) alive and well? *Journal of Information Technology Theory and Application*, 3, 4, 33–41.

Heart, T.; Pliskin, N.; and Tractinsky, N. 2004. Modeling intention to use an application service provider.

In *Proceedings of the 10th Americas Conference on Information Systems*, New York (August 6–8), 3534–3542.

Hikmet, N. and Chen, S.K. 2003. An investigation into low mail survey response rates of information technology users in health care organizations. *International Journal of Medical Informatics*, 72, 1–3, 29–34.

Ho, V.T.; Ang, S.; and Straub, D.W. 2003. When subordinates become IT contractors: Persistent managerial expectations in IT outsourcing. *Information Systems Research*, 14, 1, 66–86.

Hoecht, A. and Trott, P. 2006. Innovation risks of strategic outsourcing. *Technovation*, 26, 5–6 (May–June), 672–681.

Hoffman, J.J.; Irwin, J.G.; and Digman, L.A. 1996. Technological adoption in dynamic environments: The case of not-for-profit and for-profit hospitals. *Journal of Managerial Issues*, 8, 4, 497–507.

Hu, Q.; Saunders, C.; and Gebelt, M. 1997. Research report: Diffusion of information systems outsourcing: A reevaluation of influence sources. *Information Systems Research*, 8, 3, 288–301.

Huston, T. 2001. Security issues for implementation of e-medical records. *Communication of the ACM*, 44, 9, 89–94.

Ilie, V. and Parikh, M. 2004. A process view of information systems outsourcing research: conceptual gaps and future research directions. In *Proceedings of the 10th Americas Conference on Information Systems*, New York (August 6–8), 3561–3569.

Irwin, J.G.; Hofman, J.J.; and Geiger, S.W. 1998. The effect of technological adoption on organizational performance: Organizational size and environmental munificence as moderators. *International Journal of Organizational Analysis*, 6, 1, 50–64.

Jeffries, F.L. and Reed, R. 2000. Trust and adaptation in relational contracting. *Academy of Management Review*, 25, 4, 873–882.

Kavan, C.B.; Miranda, S.M.; and O'Hara, M.T. 2002. Managing the ASP process: A resource-oriented taxonomy. *Logistics Information Management*, 15, 3, 170–179.

Kearns, G.S. and Lederer, A.L. 1999. The influence of environmental uncertainty on the strategic use of information systems. *ACM SIGCPR Computer Personnel*, 20, 3, 40–68.

Kimberly, J.R. and Evanisko, M.J. 1981. Organizational innovation: the influence of individual, organizational, and contextual factors on hospital adoption of technological and administrative innovations. *Academy of Management Journal*, 24, 4, 689–713.

Kishore, R.; Agarwal, M.; and Rao, H.R. 2005. Determinants of sourcing during technology growth and maturity: An empirical study of e-commerce sourcing. *Journal of Management Information Systems*, 21, 3, 47–82.

Kishore, R.; Rao, H.R.; Nam, K.; Rajagopalan, S.; and Chaudhury, A. 2003. A relationship perspective on IT outsourcing. *Communication of the ACM*, 46, 12, 86–92.

Koh, C.; Ang, S.; and Straub, D.W. 2004. IT outsourcing success: A psychological contract perspective. *Information Systems Research*, 15, 4, 356–373.

Lacity, M.C. and Hirschheim, R. 1993. The information systems outsourcing bandwagon. *Sloan Management Review*, 35, 1, 73–87.

———. 1995. *Beyond the Information Systems Outsourcing Bandwagon: The Insourcing Response.* Chichester, UK: Wiley.

Lacity, M.C. and Willcocks, L.P. 1998. An empirical investigation of information technology sourcing practices: Lessons from experience. *MIS Quarterly*, 22, 3, 363–408.

Lander, M.C.; Purvis, R.L.; McCray, G.E.; and Leigh, W. 2004. Trust-building mechanisms utilized in outsourced IS development projects: A case study. *Information & Management*, 41, 4, 509–528.

Lee, J.-N.; Miranda, S.M.; and Kim, Y.-M. 2004. IT outsourcing strategies: Universalistic, contingency, and configurational explanations of success. *Information Systems Research*, 15, 2, 110–131.

Lee, S.-Y.D. and Alexander, J.A. 1999. Managing hospitals in turbulent times: Do organizational changes improve hospital survival? *Health Services Research*, 34, 4, 923–946.

Leem, C.S. and Lee, H.J. 2004. Development of certification and audit processes of application service provider for IT outsourcing. *Technovation*, 24, 1, 63–71.

Levina, N. and Ross, J.W. 2003. From the vendor perspective: Exploring the value proposition in information technology outsourcing. *MIS Quarterly*, 27, 3, 331–364.

Madden, C.W. 1999. Excess capacity: Markets, regulation, and values. *Health Services Research*, 33, 6, 1651–1668.

Mayer, R.C.; Davis, J.H.; and Schoorman, D. 1995. An integration model of organizational trust. *Academy of Management Review*, 20, 3, 709–734.

McKnight, D.H.; Cummings, L.L.; and Chervany, N.L. 1998. Initial trust formation in new organizational relationships. *Academy of Management Review*, 23, 3, 473–490.

Meyer, A.D. and Goes, J.B. 1988. Organizational assimilation of innovations: A multilevel contextual analysis. *Academy of Management Journal,* 31, 4, 897–923.

Miller, D. and Friesen, P.H. 1992. Structural change and performance: Quantum versus piecemeal-incremental approaches. *Academy of Management Journal*, 25, 4, 867–892.

Nam, K.; Rajagopalan, S.; Rao, H.R.; and Chaudhury, A. 1996. A two-level investigation of information systems outsourcing. *Communication of the ACM*, 39, 7, 36–44.

Natovich, J. 2003. Vendor related risks in IT development: A chronology of an outsourced project failure. *Technology Analysis and Strategic Management*, 15, 4, 409–419.

Ngwenyama, O.K. and Bryson, N. 1999. Making the information systems outsourcing decision: A transaction cost approach to analyzing outsourcing decision problems. *European Journal of Operational Research*, 115, 2, 351–367.

Oh, W. 2005. Why do some firms outsource IT more aggressively than others? The effects of organizational characteristics on IT outsourcing decisions. In *Proceedings of the Hawaii International Conference on System Sciences*, Hawaii, 1–9.

Oh, W. and Gallivan, M.J. 2003. An empirical assessment of transaction risks of IT outsourcing arrangements: An event study. In *Proceedings of the Hawaii International Conference on System Sciences*, Hawaii, 1–10.

Paul, D.L. and McDaniel, R.R., Jr. 2004. A field study of the effect of interpersonal trust on virtual collaborative relationship performance. *MIS Quarterly*, 28, 2, 183–227.

Raghupathi, W. and Tan, J. 2002. Strategic IT applications in health care. *Communication of the ACM*, 45, 12, 56–61.

Rai, A. and Howard, G.S. 1993. An organizational context for CASE innovation. *Information Resources Management Journal*, 6, 3, 21–34.

Rai, A. and Patnayakuni, R. 1996. A structural model for CASE adoption behavior. *Journal of Management Information Systems*, 13, 2, 205–234.

Rasheed, H.S. and Geiger, S.W. 2001. Determinants of governance structure for the electronic value chain: Resource dependency and transaction costs perspectives. *Journal of Business Strategies*, 18, 2, 159–176.

Ring, P.S. and Van de Ven, A. 1994. Developmental processes of cooperative interorganizational relationships. *Academy of Management Review*, 19, 1, 90–119.

Rogers, E.M. 1995. *The Diffusion of Innovations.* New York: Free Press.

Sabherwal, R. 1999. The role of trust in outsourced is development project. *Communication of the ACM*, 42, 2, 80–86.

Seltsikas, P. and Currie, W.L. 2002. Evaluating the application service provider (ASP) business model: The challenge of integration. In *Proceedings of the 35th Annual Hawaii International Conference on System Sciences*, 2801–2809.

Serva, M.A.; Sherer, S.A.; and Sipior, J.C. 2003. "When do you ASP?" The software life cycle control model. *Information Systems Frontiers*, 5, 2, 219–232.

Sharma, S. and Rai, A. 2003. An assessment of the relationship between ISD leadership characteristics and IS innovation adoption in organizations. *Information & Management*, 40, 5, 291–401.

Sheehan, K. 2001. E-mail survey response rates: A review. *Journal of Computer Mediated Communication*, 6, 2. http://jcmc.indiana.edu/vol6/issue2/sheehan.html.

Smith, A.D. and Rupp, W.T. 2003. Application service providers: An application of the transaction cost model. *Information Management & Computer Security*, 11, 1, 11–18.

Smith, H.J.; Milberg, S.J.; and Burke, S.J. 1996. Information privacy: Measuring individuals; concern about organizational practices. *MIS Quarterly*, 20, 2, 167–196.

Smith, M.A. and Kumar, R.L. 2004. A theory of application service provider (ASP) use from a client perspective. *Information & Management*, 41, 8, 977–1002.

Susarla, A.; Barua, A.; and Whinston, A.B. 2003. Understanding the service component of application service provision: An empirical analysis of satisfaction with ASP services. *MIS Quarterly*, 27, 1, 91–123.

Uzzi, B. 1997. Social structure and competition in interfirm networks: The paradox of embeddedness. *Administrative Science Quarterly*, 42, 1, 35–67.

Venkatesh, V. 2000. Determinants of perceived ease of use: Integrating control, intrinsic motivation, and emotion into the technology acceptance model. *Information Systems Research*, 11, 4, 342–365.

Walsh, K.R. 2003. Analyzing the application ASP concept: Technologies, economies, and strategies. *Communication of the ACM*, 46, 8, 103–107.

Willcocks, L. and Choi, C.J. 1995. Co-operative partnership and "total" IT outsourcing: From contractual obligation to strategic alliance? *European Management Journal*, 13, 1, 67–78.

Williamson, O.E. 1981. The modern corporation: Origins, evolution, attributes. *Journal of Economic Literature*, 19, 1537–1568.

———. 1991. Strategizing, economizing, and economic organization. *Strategic Management Journal*, 12, 75–95.

———. 1996. Economics and organization: A primer. *California Management Review*, 38, 2, 131–146.

Yammarino, F.J.; Skinner, S.J.; and Childers, T.L. 1991. Understanding mail survey response behavior: A meta-analysis. *Public Opinion Quarterly*, 55, 4, 613–639.

Zaheer, A.; McEvily, B.; and Perrone, V. 1998. Does trust matter? Exploring the effects of interorganizational and interpersonal trust on performance. *Organization Science*, 9, 2, 141–159.

Zhang, L.; Ahn, G.-J.; and Chu, B.-T. 2002. A role-based delegation framework for healthcare information systems. In *Proceedings of the ACM Symposium on Access Control Models and Technologies*. Monterey, CA (June 3–4), 125–134.

PART III

MANAGING THE OUTSOURCING RELATIONSHIP

CHAPTER 10

MANAGING THE IS OUTSOURCING RELATIONSHIP

KIM LANGFIELD-SMITH AND DAVID SMITH

Abstract: *The practice of outsourcing of information systems (IS) is a global phenomenon that has increased dramatically over the past twenty years. While there is a considerable body of literature devoted to whether or not IS should be outsourced and the benefits and pitfalls of outsourcing, less work has focused on identifying the factors that are important in managing the relationship between an organization and an outsourcer, and how control can be achieved when such a critical organizational function is outsourced. This chapter will draw on three case studies to focus on the key areas that need to be managed: inadequate contract specifications, unrealistic initial expectations of performance improvements, different organizational cultures, the loss of skills and knowledge, ineffective communication and information-sharing processes, inadequate performance measures and incentives, an absence of trust, and adverse reactions of employees.*

Keywords: *Information Systems, Management Control Systems, Outsourcing, Outsourcing Relationships, Supplier Relationships, Trust*

INTRODUCTION

Massive growth in outsourcing, in both the public and private sectors, occurred during the 1990s. Kern and Willcocks (2002) noted that information systems (IS) outsourcing has experienced a steady annual growth of approximately 20 percent, achieving a global market size of $US86 billion by 1996, and was estimated to reach $154 billion by 2004. Much has been written about the criteria that should guide decisions to outsource, and both successes and failures have been reported in the press. The financial press, in particular, tends to focus on the size of the contract and the identity of the successful bidder. Outsourcing "successes" and "failures" are often judged by whether the firm achieves cost savings, or experiences cost overruns. In the academic literature, IS outsourcing has been considered from several different perspectives. Aubert, Rivard, and Patry (2004, 921) summarized the perspectives that prior researchers have adopted when studying the outsourcing of IS (see Table 10.1).

This chapter focuses on the third category listed in Table 10.1, that is, on the relationship between the organization and the outsourcer. A mismanaged relationship may have serious implications for the firm's long-term strategy and continued competitiveness and profitability, even when the initial outsourcing decision was well conceived. On the other hand, a well-managed relationship can be highly beneficial to both the firm and the outsourcer.

Kern and Willcocks (2002) argued that IS outsourcing tends to be more complex than the outsourcing of other functions, due to the pervasive nature of information systems and technology

Table 10.1

Alternative Research Perspectives on Information Technology (IT) Outsourcing

Perspective	Source
Comparing outsourcing to insourcing	King and Malhotra (2000)
Evaluating how in-house services could be reorganized to provide benefits similar to outsourcing	Hirschheim and Lacity (2000); Lacity and Hirschheim (1995)
Examining characteristics of the client–supplier relationship and their impact on outsourcing success	Lee and Kim (1999); Lee (2001)
Examining the determinants of outsourcing	Lacity and Hirschheim (1993)
Analyzing IT outsourcing with a political or social lens to provide alternative explanations for outsourcing decisions	Loh and Venkatraman (1992); Nam et al. (1996); Aubert, Rivard, and Patry (2004)

Source: Adapted from Aubert, Rivard, and Patry (2004).

in modern organizations. Moreover, Willcocks, Fitzgerald, and Lacity (1996) noted a number of characteristics that make IS outsourcing distinctive:

- The IS function is not homogeneous, but rather it comprises a variety of IS-related activities;
- The pace of enhancements of IS capabilities makes IS outsourcing particularly uncertain;
- No simple basis exists for gauging the economics of IS outsourcing; and
- Large switching costs are associated with the IS outsourcing decision.

Costs and Benefits of Outsourcing

Many benefits underlie the increasing trend toward IS outsourcing. Outsourcers may provide wider access to specialist skills, being at the leading edge of practice and technology in their specialized area, and offer a level of expertise that a company cannot provide or develop in-house (Aubert, Rivard, and Patry, 2004). The emergence of rapidly changing specialist technologies has encouraged the development of specialist IS service companies, which can leverage economies of scale and scope to provide high value-added services. In addition, full utilization can be made of the outsourcer's investments, innovations, and capabilities that would be prohibitively expensive to duplicate within the firm. Outsourcing can allow firms to focus their resources and efforts on developing, or strengthening, their core competencies. This may provide a way to block competitors, by creating permanence in selected areas that competitors may find difficult to imitate (Quinn and Hilmer, 1994). Outsourcing may also create advantages through the creation of strategic coalitions with the world's best IS providers. IS outsourcing specialists should be able to operate more cost effectively through economies of scale.

Against these benefits, the potential limitations of outsourcing must be considered. A common criticism of outsourcing relates to the potential "hollowing out" of the firm. At its extreme, outsourcing may result in virtual organizations that consist of a small group of staff managing a vast network of external providers. This may lead to a loss of technological and human skills associated with the outsourced function, and can lead to a loss of competitiveness (Eroglu, 1994). However, there is limited evidence to support this claim. In fact, some virtual organizations operate quite successfully. For example, Benetton outsources nearly all of its manufacturing and retail operations and is considered successful. An outsourcing decision may be difficult to reverse when it involves a divestiture of physical and human assets, and any loss of in-house expertise may be difficult to reestablish if outsourcing is found to be a poor decision. Thus, outsourcing may lead to a loss of control over critical organizational functions and knowledge.

To realize some of the benefits outlined above and to avoid some of the potential problems, the choice of IS outsourcer is critical and there needs to be an awareness of the factors that are important in managing the outsourcing relationship. The outsourcing of IS can be problematic in comparison with some other outsourced functions—the strategic nature of IS is not always apparent to managers who are making the outsourcing decision. While many companies consider that only activities that are not critical to the firm's strategy should be outsourced, it has been suggested that activities integral to a strategy may also be outsourced, if sufficient controls and monitoring are introduced (Quinn, 1992; Lacity, Willcocks, and Feeny, 1995). However, there has been limited research addressing how outsourcing relationships involving IS can be managed to achieve control.

Is Control Different Under Outsourcing?

An important question when considering how to manage an outsourcing relationship is whether the management aspects and control issues are different for outsourced functions than for in-house functions. The most obvious difference arises from the legal separation between the buying organization and the outsourcer. Grabner (1993) uses the term *embedded firms* to describe the situation where various activities within the value chain take place across legally separate organizations. What forms of control are possible in embedded firms?

Outsourcing extends traditional organizational boundaries, creating a new organizational form. The relationship between an organization and an outsourcer resembles a partnership, rather than a traditional customer–supplier relationship (McHugh, Merli, and Wheeler, 1995), and developing close cooperative relationships can contribute significantly to the success of partnerships (Langfield-Smith and Greenwood, 1998). In some situations, outsourcers are located on site, and equipment and staff are transferred to the outsourcers. In other cases, the company and outsourcer own equipment jointly. These issues can create complex interdependencies between an organization and an outsourcer that do not usually arise in traditional customer–supplier relationships and may create new control issues for an organization. When the outsourced functions are critical to the effective operation of the firm, control becomes even more important. However, the design of traditional management control systems assumes that activities take place within the boundaries of an organization. There is limited research on how outsourcing relationships are managed to achieve organizational control.

Formal control within organizations may consist of direct controls over individual behavior (through direct supervision, ongoing oversight of staff, and detailed specifications of operating rules) and control over outcomes (through delegation of responsibilities, assigning of performance targets, and formal reporting and performance monitoring systems). These are behavior controls and outcome controls (Ouchi, 1979). In an embedded situation, it is not usually appropriate for an organization to impose direct supervision over activities performed by the outsourcer's employees. In addition, it cannot be assumed that a firm has direct and immediate access to information held by the outsourcer. Indirect controls, such as performance targets, may be used and included in outsourcing contracts. However, the degree of authority of a manager over an outsourcer may be quite different than that over his/her own employees. It is less likely that new systems for control can be imposed on an outsourcer without a fair degree of negotiation and coordination, and monitoring may be difficult if the outsourcer is an expert in a field in which the firm has little expertise.

Another barrier to control over an outsourcer relates to differences in the cultures of an organization and its outsourcer, such as different values, strategies, goals, and ways of operating. Within an organization, shared cultural values are an important source of control. However, divergent values may create difficulties in developing and managing the outsourcing relationship, lead to misunderstandings and mistrust, and force a greater reliance on formal controls.

The Focus of This Study

The purpose of this chapter is to focus on three outsourcing case studies to explore the management of IS outsourcing and the related issue of control. Specifically, the research question is: What are the key issues in managing an IS outsourcing relationship? A related question is also considered: Is it more difficult to control outsourced IS activities and responsibilities than in-house IS functions? The decision processes and experiences of three organizations that have outsourced IS activities and responsibilities provide the background to addressing these questions.

The three research case studies were identified from media reports of organizations that had undertaken major outsourcing of their IT functions.[1] Interviews were held with managers who were involved in the initial decision to outsource and in the initial and ongoing management of the outsourced function. Relevant company documents and media reports were also reviewed. The focus of the semistructured interviews was on understanding the background of the outsourcing activity and exploring important aspects in the management and control of the outsourcing relationship. Two researchers were present at each interview to enhance the reliability of analysis and conclusions. The interviews extended from one to two hours for each manager, and were recorded and transcribed to allow more accurate analysis. The transcripts were analyzed to extract themes and common issues.[2] The background to the outsourcing activities in each of the three case studies is presented in the following section. The third section identifies the management and control issues that emerged from the three case studies and the final section concludes the chapter.

THE THREE CASE STUDIES

Case 1. Central Energy

Central Energy (Central)[3] was formed through the merger of two electricity authorities: Hilton Energy (Hilton) and Woodside Electricity (Woodside). Central distributes and retails electricity and value-added energy services to more than a million people, sells major electrical contracting services throughout Australia, and retails energy services to major industrial and commercial clients throughout several states. The Australian electricity industry underwent considerable structural and regulatory changes in the 1990s, which led to increased competition and a greater emphasis on customer service and cost.

Immediately after the merger of Hilton and Woodside, the executive steering committee made a decision to outsource the information technology and telecommunications (IT&T) function.

Motivation for Outsourcing

At Central, the factors that motivated the decision to outsource IT&T included the problematic nature of merging two very different IS cultures; the need to improve cost management of IT&T;

greater access to technical knowledge and expertise; and the need to bring more discipline and control to the IT&T function.

The merger of the two electricity authorities brought together two IT&T functions that were very different in size and nature as well as in focus and direction. Developing a single, effective IT&T function was considered a major managerial issue and an important determinant of Central's ability to compete in the new contestable electricity environment. Hilton had 168 IT&T staff, was a mainframe environment with large-scale applications, and had frequent cost overruns. Woodside had 33 IS staff, a very low cost infrastructure with no mainframes, and limited funds for software development.

Before the merger, cost management of the IT&T function was poor, particularly at Hilton, and there were significant opportunities for achieving cost improvement and greater control over IS developments. Hilton's IT&T was strongly customer focused so a wide range of operating systems was supported and new applications were developed continually. Cost overruns were very common and there was little control over the initiation of new projects. The unrealistic transfer pricing that was used to charge internal users of IT&T services encouraged excessive and costly IS developments and a lack of accountability reflected an absence of commercial reality. Thus, a strong motivation for outsourcing was that the use, development, and cost of IS within Hilton, in particular, was considered by managers to be out of control. One senior IT manager described the situation that had existed at Hilton:

> In the past, electricity utilities were fairly wealthy organizations—cash rich and managed predominantly by engineers who like to build gold-plated systems. We now have redundant microwave links, multiple computer sites—you name it. It was technology gone mad.

In addition, some of the four business units of Central had started to develop their own IS groups. There was a strong need to bring IS planning and operations under central control.

Another reason for engaging in outsourcing was that Central needed to gain access to high levels of IS expertise. This was considered too difficult and impractical to develop in-house as Central believed that it should focus on its core business of delivering energy services. The competitive environment was placing greater demands on the business for "smarter systems," which would involve highly sophisticated IT and IS. Thus, there would be increasing reliance on the IT&T function, which was of critical importance for survival. Central's goal was to seek a partnership that would provide access to the specialized IT solutions that could only be provided by a global specialized outsourcer.

Criteria Used in the Outsourcing Decision

In mid-1996, Central called for tenders for the IT&T function. Bids from two large global companies were considered, along with an in-house bid. All bidders needed to demonstrate that they could offer value within the dynamic electricity environment. The criteria for assessing the tenders included the cost of providing the service, clear cost-reduction paths, management of IS staff transition issues, the approach to strategic planning of IS, the tenderer's experience and access to skills, plans for managing the contract, and the nature of the billing arrangements. The successful tenderer was Global Systems (Global) and the in-house proposal was "a clear third."

Case 2. ElectNet

ElectNet was formed to manage a high voltage electricity transmission network. It was previously part of a larger organization, PowerCo (Power), which was responsible for electricity generation and distribution. As with Central Energy, sophisticated IS systems would allow ElectNet to compete more effectively in the deregulated energy market.

Motivation for Outsourcing

When ElectNet split from Power, IS services continued to be provided by Power's IS department and other suppliers were engaged, as needed, to provide additional IS services. ElectNet took a cautious approach to outsourcing IS, as management was conscious of the problems that could accompany the appointment of an unsuitable outsourcer. After two years of research, a decision was made to outsource software support and hardware support to two separate outsourcers.

The three interrelated reasons for outsourcing the IS function were the desire to create a distinct IS strategy; the inability of the existing supplier to meet the changing IS needs; and the need to gain access to high caliber IS skills.

ElectNet had the option to retain Power as its IS service provider, but preferred to develop its own IS specific strategy and to have direct control over the service provision and outcomes it desired. Power's business was changing and they were unlikely to want to reconfigure their IS to manage the changing needs of ElectNet. While an in-house IS function could have been created, ElectNet's management wanted access to high-caliber IS skills and believed that was difficult to attract IS specialists to their firm because of the lack of a sufficiently attractive career path.

Criteria Used in the Outsourcing Decision

Over a two-year period, managers within ElectNet undertook a considerable amount of research to prepare for the tendering process. Several suppliers were approached and five criteria were used to assess the tenders: the skills of the specific individuals that would work on the project; the corporate experience in providing similar outsourcing services; the ability to draw on wider corporate resources to service ElectNet's requirements; appropriate quality control and delivery procedures; and cost. Two outsourcers were engaged, one to manage the operation of the hardware, and the other to provide software services.

Case 3. GHI

GHI is a large government department that outsourced all aspects of its IS management and operations in the late 1990s. This department processes sensitive information and relies on and develops large databases, so IS is a critical aspect of all operations. Prior to the outsourcing decision, all IS activities in GHI were managed in-house. This was costly and inefficient and there was an increasing need for the development of more sophisticated systems and applications. GHI was one of the first of many Australian government departments to outsource its IS function.

Motivation for Outsourcing

In the late 1990s, the Australian government decided that IS infrastructure services across all budget-funded agencies would be outsourced using a competitive tendering process. GHI was aware of this impending development and moved quickly to be one of the first government agencies to outsource IS, in the hope that they would have more control over the outsourcing process and obtain a better financial deal. Another motivation was to access IS skills and capabilities that were not available in-house. The information systems needed to undergo major reengineering, and a potential Y2K problem was emerging. There was a need for increased capabilities to support major future projects and there was awareness that the current systems were old and unsophisticated. GHI did not have the expertise to develop improved IS in-house and did not regard IS as part of its core competencies.

A decision was made to outsource all aspects of IS as a single tender, including mainframe and desktop hardware, applications development, help desk, applications maintenance and support, and strategic planning. Only a skeleton IS staff remained in GHI.

Criteria Used in the Outsourcing Decision

Tenders were called, but the size of the systems meant that only a few companies were large enough to submit a tender. Selection criteria included cost, capabilities, value for money, and track record. However, cost became a key driver for the selection insofar as the capabilities of the large companies were comparable. They were all multinational organizations with established records and could all easily fulfill the requirements of the contract. As this was one of the first of a series of large government outsourcing contracts, each tenderer wanted to gain an early foothold in the potentially large contract market, so the final two contenders competed fiercely on price. By outsourcing all of their IS activities and responsibilities to IS Experts, managers at GHI believed they had secured a very cost effective solution to their IS problem.

MANAGING THE OUTSOURCING RELATIONSHIP

In the first section, two questions were posed that relate to the management of the outsourcing relationship: What are the key issues in managing an IS outsourcing relationship? Is it more difficult to control outsourced IS activities and responsibilities than in-house IS functions? These questions will be addressed in this section.

Managing the Relationship

A range of issues emerged in the three cases that influenced the ability of the buying organizations to establish close and cooperative relationships with the outsourcers. These included the following:

- Inadequate contract specifications;
- Unrealistic initial expectations of performance improvements;
- Different organizational cultures;
- The loss of skills and knowledge;
- Ineffective communication and information-sharing processes;
- Inadequate performance measures and incentives;
- An absence of trust; and
- Adverse reactions of employees.

Table 10.2 provides a comparative summary of the issues for each of the three case studies and Table 10.3 outlines the causes of the issues, implications, and possible solutions.

Table 10.2

Summary of Issues for Each Case Study

Issue	Central	ElectNet	GHI
Inadequate contract specifications	• Contract formulated in haste after a merger • Inadequate specification of baseline services, no performance measures	• Extensive research undertaken prior to engaging outsourcers • Limited knowledge of cost base of in-house service	• Extensive research undertaken prior to engaging outsourcer • Comprehensive contract negotiated, including service-level agreements, performance measures, governance arrangements
	• Limited knowledge of the cost of in-house services and low performance provided inadequate base for the contract	• Lack of performance measures in contract	• Contract unable to be fully implemented due to insufficient IS skills at GHI
	• Considerable negotiations needed after the contract to determine cost of service and levels of service provision	• Included commitment to the vision of ElectNet	• GHI lost control over all aspects of IS function
Unrealistic expectations of performance improvements	• Managers' expectation of initial significant improvements in service levels and cost did not eventuate	• Short hand-over period to outsourcer made it impossible to convey the specialized IS knowledge required	• Constant referring to contract to resolve disputes
	• Improvements slow to emerge due to staff turnover and outsourcer's lack of knowledge of systems	• Hand-over period conducted using a "letter of the law" approach, rather than a value-adding approach	• Outsourcer did not tailor systems to suit GHI
	• Differing objectives of the two parties was a source of dissatisfaction • New use-pays approaches to information systems (IS) usage contributed to managers' dissatisfaction		• Many complaints about outsourcer from GHI staff • GHT did not implement governance processes to monitor outsourcer performance
			• GHI gradually took some major projects away from outsourcer and tendered to other parties
Different organizational cultures	• Central was a merger of two public sector organizations, whereas the outsourcer was commercial, profit seeking, and militaristic	• Close business alignment between ElectNet and outsourcers part of selection criteria	• Outsourcer focused on making profit on tightly costed project; GHI focused on delivering large government projects
	• Differences became less important over time as Central became more commercial and Global learned more about Central	• Some problems initially due to outsourcers' unfamiliarity with ElectNet's business cycles	• Outsourcers' unfamiliarity with GHI's core business impacted on quality of service delivery
The loss of skills and knowledge	• Not significant—some loss of staff and system-specific skills initially	• Not significant	• Loss of IS knowledge/skills persisted for a number of years
	• Access to specialized IS skills of outsourcer outweighed these problems	• Access to specialized IS skills of outsourcer outweighed any problems	• Scope of activities outsourced by GHI broader than in the other two cases

Table 10.2 *(continued)*

Ineffective communication and information-sharing processes	• Move from single to multiple points of contact between firm and outsourcer • As relationship evolved Central's information technology and telecommunications outsourcing manager focused on broader relationship issues	• Direct relationships between "owners" of systems in ElectNet, and the outsourcer • A single IS manager dealt with relationship management issues	• Contractual governance mechanisms not activated initially • Outsourcer unable to implement reporting and accountability systems
	• Emphasis on open communication issues and up-front resolution of issues	• Emphasis on open communication issues and up-front resolution of issues	• After three years, senior GHI IS manager appointed to coordinate contract; joint committees to set strategic direction for IS and oversee projects
	• Joint IS steering groups and working groups	• Ongoing communication needed to achieve business alignment • Monthly meetings to assess performance, identify issues, and resolve problems	
Inadequate performance measures and incentives	• No performance measures in initial contract	• Two types of service levels used to evaluate outsourcers' performance—core level (built into contracts) and specific level (outside contracts)	• Performance measures and targets built into original contract
	• Over first eighteen months, Central and outsourcer negotiated performance measures and targets • Risk/reward scheme implemented by Central to provide financial incentives to outsourcer	• Financial incentives not built into contracts • Flexibility built into contracts, allowing firm to renegotiate contracts if required	• Measures and targets ineffective due to lack of monitoring by GHI and insufficient staff resources at outsourcer • After renegotiation of contract, performance measures established and used appropriately
An absence of trust	• Outsourcer viewed as having high credibility prior to outsourcing	• Frequent communication between parties may have promoted perceptions of procedural fairness and enhanced trust	• Outsourcer viewed as having high credibility prior to outsourcing, may infer a level of trust
	• Frequent communication between parties may have promoted perceptions of procedural fairness • Where there was conflict, Global replaced key IS staff • Central retained ownership of IS infrastructure, limiting its exposure to risk • Some mistrust arose from the transition to "realistic" charging for IS services for the first time		• Trust assumed at start of contract but deteriorated when performance not achieved and conflicts arose
Adverse reactions of employees	• Some dissatisfaction among employees redeployed within Central	• No in-house IS staff pre-outsourcing	• Most IS staff from GHI joined the outsourcer, but did not stay long due to different ethos of outsourcer
	• Central chose a tenderer with an acceptable staff transition plan		

Table 10.3

Summary of Causes, Implications, and Solutions

Issue	Cause	Implications and solutions
Inadequate contract specifications	May be due to: • Inexperience of managers in engaging in information systems (IS) outsourcing • Lack of knowledge of the cost of in-house service • Lack of due diligence of the in-house function that is to be outsourced • Managers' inability to understand or specify the activity and responsibilities of the outsourced function • Difficulty in anticipating all contingencies and issues that may arise • Pressures to engage the outsourcer quickly	• May contribute to the failure of some outsourcing relationships • May be a barrier to establishing an initial smooth relationship • Complete contracts may not be possible due to ambiguity of IS functions • Contract needs to be revised over time to recognize specific needs and requirements of the parties, which were difficult to anticipate at the start of the relationship
Unrealistic initial expectations of performance improvements	Unrealistic expectations may be due to: • Initial overselling of the outsourcing concept rested on promises of improved performance • Managers may have false recollections of the performance of the in-house function • Increased accountability for in-house users of information technology (IT) services Initial low performance by outsourcers may be due to: • In-house IT staff with specialized skills leaving the organization • The outsourcer needing time to learn new skills and new systems • Lack of documentation of in-house systems and processes • Conflicts in the new relationship between the organization and the outsourcer • Contractual issues still under negotiation	• Need to consider the effect of cultural differences and the development of appropriate governance mechanisms when assessing initial performance expectations • Involving IS managers in the assessment of tenders may lead to more realistic expectations • Performance expectations as well as actual performance needs to be managed
Different organizational cultures	Globalized specialist IT outsourcing companies have different origins, objectives, expectations, and modes of operating compared with those of broad-based commercial or government organizations	• No obvious "solution" to managing cultural differences • An awareness of the issue and potential impact on the relationship can alert both parties to the danger of inappropriate assumptions about how either party will operate within the new relationship

The loss of skills and knowledge	Technical skills and knowledge may decrease in the buying firm due to: • Resignation of key IS staff just prior to outsourcing • IS staff who transferred to the outsourcer leaving within a short time frame • A lack of understanding that a certain level of technical expertise is needed to manage the relationship • Inadequate contract management skills	• The outsourcing firm needs to develop new skills in contract management, communication, and negotiation • Need to retain or develop a certain level of IS expertise and knowledge to effectively manage the outsourcer • Consider whether strategic IT areas or only operational areas should be outsourced
Ineffective communication and information-sharing processes	May be due to: • Lack of effective governance mechanisms in contracts • Governance mechanisms in place but not activated • Insufficient emphasis placed on maintaining open communication channels between firm and outsourcer	• Establish formal protocols for communicating with the outsourcer in early days of contract • Consider number of points of contact, frequency of meetings, problem-resolution processes • Protocol may change over time as relationship develops to establish more direct contact between the outsourcer and key service users
Inadequate performance measures and incentive systems	Performance measures and incentives may not be included in the initial contract due to: • Difficulty in specifying expectations and targets for service delivery • Lack of knowledge of the operations and performance of the IS function by the buying organization	• Performance measures may develop over time as both parties come to better understand the nature of the outsourced activity • Performance measures should focus on customer satisfaction, delivery responsiveness, product quality, and cost • The joint development of measures and incentives may contribute to developing positive relationships • Incentives may promote good relationships
An absence of trust	May be due to: • Lack of prior relationship between firm and outsourcer • Lack of communication and cultural differences • Loss of control of IS infrastructure	May be promoted through effective communication, repeated positive interactions, joint development of performance measures and incentives, and joint problem resolution
Adverse reactions of employees	• When IS is outsourced, employees may leave the firm, gain employment with the outsourcer, or be transferred to other functions within the firm • Adverse employee reactions to changes may influence the delivery of the IS function and the management of the relationship • Outsourced staff may be employed under conditions different from those of in-house staff, and this may lead to dissatisfaction on either side	The management of employee transitions should be included as a formal part of the outsourcing plan, and it may be the responsibility of both the buying firm and the outsourcer

Inadequate Contract Specifications

Outsourcing research has emphasized the importance of the contract in shaping the outsourcing relationship (Kern and Willcocks, 2002; Lacity and Willcocks, 1998) and inadequately specified contracts are cited as a major reason for the failure of some outsourcing ventures, particularly in IS (Domberger, 1998).

The contract between Central and Global related to the operation of the computer hardware, software development, and software support. Global retained ownership and ultimate responsibility for hardware. The contract allowed payment to Global for baseline services and additional payments for discretionary projects above that baseline. Baseline services were "the cost of maintaining all infrastructure and systems in the organization at the level at which they were at the point that the contract was signed." However, this definition was difficult to interpret, and, in the first year of the contract, conflicts between Central and Global arose as each had different ideas as to what constituted baseline services. A senior manager explained:

> People have to be very clear about their service level requirements. Not say "95 percent uptime" . . . none of this arbitrary nonsense. Be very specific about what those service level requirements are. Specify as much as you can get down. And people may say "Oh, it's not necessary because you're going to work these things out together." You can, but that means there needs to be extreme trust and that only occurs when you are really partners. But you do not start as partners. You start with the specifications; you work to it and the supplier/customer relationship. And that is where we came from. In the beginning it was an unhappy customer/supplier relationship.

Some managers believed that these problems could have been averted if more time had been spent negotiating the contract. However, at the time of the merger between Hilton and Woodside there were pressures to solve the IS problem quickly by getting an outsourcer on board. Once the contract was signed it was difficult to agree on which projects were to be included in the baseline and which were discretionary (and hence an extra cost to Central). During the first six months of the contract, Global and Central undertook an extensive verification of the cost of baseline services. A manager explains why this was the case:

> Redundancy programs were going on, and with the uncertainty there was a need to get some stability in the process. The cost of putting some trust in Global Systems during the 6 to 9 months was seen to be less than the cost of delaying the contract verification prior to final contract signing. This was the cost of provision of baseline services. We entered into a contract that said, "This is what we believe it is at the moment, but it will be subject to verification in the next six months." That should not have occurred. We should have spent more time as a business, chapter and verse, detailing what our expectations of service were, what the limitations were, what they were really going to get out of it.

ElectNet approached outsourcing differently to Central, with separate outsourcing of the software and hardware support. Ownership of the software and hardware stayed with ElectNet. The supplier of the software support contract was responsible for providing operational support, including operating ElectNet's helpdesk, maintaining desktop computers and providing software upgrades. The supplier of the hardware support contract provided facilities management and advice on hardware replacement.

The two contracts included a number of important provisions. First, the outsourcers needed to be committed to the vision and values of ElectNet. Second, the outsourcers needed to work cooperatively across the various contracts. Third, the outsourcers were to complete systems audits. Fourth, while initially the outsourcers were to deliver a range of discrete services, over time, a more holistic approach to service provision was desirable.

Two main elements were covered under these contracts—day-to-day operations and minor project work. Major IS projects were not included as ElectNet preferred to go to the market for this work. ElectNet also contracted with an external organization for financial software.

In GHI, as with ElectNet, research was undertaken prior to the formulation of the contract and legal specialists were engaged to formulate the contract. In this case all aspects of the IS operations, management, and strategy were outsourced. Managers in GHI believed that the contract was well written and very comprehensive, including service-level agreements, key performance indicators, and some aspects of governance arrangements. However, there were difficulties in implementing the contract as there were insufficient staff in GHI to monitor the contract and IS Experts' staff did not voluntarily initiate the required activities. It was some time before GHI found they had lost control over all of the IS functions, including IS strategy and planning. Ultimately, when the contract came up for renewal GHI management decided to take the management of the IS strategy back in-house and only allow the original outsourcer, IS Experts, to manage the software applications, while another outsourcer was engaged to manage the hardware.

The haste with which Central's contract was negotiated could explain why there was significant dissatisfaction with early performance. In contrast, ElectNet and GHI undertook considerable research before venturing into the outsourcing contract. There was a lack of performance measures in both Central and ElectNet, which were negotiated over the next few years. Managers at GHI saw the original contract as adequate and comprehensive. However, it could not be implemented effectively as internal governance arrangements within GHI had not been established. With the renegotiating of the contract at GHI came a need to increase the IS skills of GHI staff, to allow IS strategic planning and IS governance to be brought back in-house.

Clearly, there are many situations where organizations enter into contracts that are not comprehensive and need to be revised over time. This may be due to inexperience, a lack of due diligence in preparing the contract, or an inability to understand or to specify the nature of the activity and responsibilities of the outsourced function. It may also be due to the need to make a quick decision in times of crisis. As relationships develop, parties may come to recognize specific needs and requirements that were difficult to anticipate at the start of the relationship. IS, in particular, can be an area of high uncertainty and complete effective contracts can be difficult to formulate. In two case studies, there was limited knowledge as to the actual cost of the IS function prior to outsourcing and the performance of that function was not high. This provided an inadequate basis for establishing a realistic cost base and IS performance standards. Contracts were revised over time to resolve inadequacies and to incorporate more sophisticated provisions to cover areas such as performance measurement, cost, occupational health and safety, assigned responsibility for activities and costs, and specification of the sharing of the benefits from cost improvements.

Unrealistic Initial Expectations of Performance Improvements

Immediately after entering into an outsourcing arrangement, managers in the "buying" organization may have high expectations of achieving distinct improvements in service provision, often within a short time frame. This was the situation at Central and GHI, and to a lesser extent at ElectNet, but those high expectations were not realized.

The first twelve months of the outsourcing relationship at Central were described by one manager as "rocky," and it took about eighteen months for positive aspects to emerge. This disappointment followed an expectation among Central managers that Global would deliver massive improvements in service levels and costs. There were also memories of "how good things were" before outsourcing. Improvements were slow to emerge for a number of reasons. Some of the most valuable IT staff had left the company, and the staff who moved to Global did not have the skills to run some systems. As one manager explained, "specialized knowledge of the IT systems simply walked out the door." As in many situations, when redundancy packages are offered, the most talented staff with the best employment opportunities are the first to leave. Many of the IS applications at Central were custom-built and not well documented, so only a few employees knew how some of the applications operated. In addition, over the first year, some of Central's IS staff who had transferred to Global moved to other Global sites.

Conflicts arose from the differing objectives of the two parties: the outsourcer was trying to make a good financial return from the account, while Central was trying to manage the costs of the service. It took some time before the partners were able to work toward shared objectives for various projects and bonus systems that suited both parties. Another source of dissatisfaction was that Central's managers across the business units were now being charged the full cost for usage of IT&T services. Previously they had paid unrealistically low prices for IS services and development and had direct and almost uncontrolled access to IT&T service staff. The merger of the two electricity distributors, which was a difficult blending of two very different cultures, took managerial attention away from the details of the contract and from clarifying the advantages that might be gained from the new outsourcing relationship.

In contrast, ElectNet put considerable effort into developing the initial contracts with the outsourcers as it believed that this was crucial to managing the relationships. However, the first twelve months were difficult for all parties, partially because of the six-week hand-over period undertaken by Power. Essential IS skills were lost to ElectNet with the speedy departure of Power, and the hand-over time was too short to convey to the outsourcers the specialized IS knowledge needed to develop and operate a stand-alone IS function. Some ElectNet managers felt that Power took a "letter-of-the-law" approach and one ElectNet manager described it as "one of the most difficult times in my life."

At GHI, the first six months of the contract were described by one manager as the "honeymoon period." The majority of the IS staff had moved across to the employ of IS Experts. However, most of these staff left IS Experts over the next year. Problems began to emerge in the relationship after six months and there was constant reference to the contract and to lawyers to resolve disputes. GHI found that IS Experts took far too long to complete projects and activities, and seemed to be charging far too much where they detected opportunities for discretionary charges. GHI took some major projects away from IS Experts and tendered these to other suppliers. There was some doubt among GHI managers as to whether IS Experts was able to draw on sufficient skills or staff resources to deliver on some IS work. The international managers of IS Experts who had negotiated the contract had offered very low prices and the local office of IS Experts (who had to deliver the services) was unable to satisfy the agreement with its limited resources, and still make its own profit. These difficulties resulted in many complaints from GHI staff. While the basic routine systems and infrastructure were working with a high degree of reliability, IS Experts seemed to have limited capacity to enhance or tailor specific aspects of the IS functions. However, not all GHI managers were as critical, some remembering that the old in-house IS function was also problematic and the source of some problems that IS Experts was experiencing related to these prior systems.

Another driver of dissatisfaction was that GHI did not put in place any governance processes to monitor IS Experts' activities or to flag problems ahead of time. Because critical IS functions, such as strategic planning and policies, were outsourced, they were no longer managed by GHI staff, even indirectly. Staff satisfaction surveys were undertaken in GHI and while there were gaps between expectations and IS delivery, these began to narrow as parts of the contract were renegotiated.

It is very difficult to measure the benefits of outsourcing in the short term, as the introduction of an outsourcer is often accompanied by changes in systems, structures, operations, and new IS managers and staff. The move toward outsourcing is often accompanied by a significant internal marketing campaign to convince managers and staff of the need to change and of the benefits to be gained from engaging specialist IS firms, and in some cases "overselling" may raise expectations beyond a realistic level. The outsourcing companies themselves may contribute to these high expectations through the marketing of their skills, the benefits of outsourcing, and the success of their prior contracts.

The need for the outsourcer to learn new skills may slow improvements in service provision in the short term. In addition, the development of a good working relationship between the outsourcer and an organization's employees needs time to develop to realize those performance improvements. In the case studies, limitations in the contracts and in the implementation of the contracts influenced the initial experiences, and with the high stature and visibility of global outsourcing firms, there is naturally an expectation that service delivery will be high, and certainly higher than prior in-house service. In each of the three case studies, the prior in-house IS service had not been of high quality and was of uncertain cost. In Central and GHI, IS managers were not involved in the assessment of the tenders, which may have led to possibly unrealistic expectations. Other issues that need to be resolved in managing unrealistic expectations include managing different cultures and implementing appropriate governance mechanisms. These are discussed in the following sections.

Different Organizational Cultures

Much has been written about organizational culture and its impact on organizational functioning. Organizational culture is the shared values, meanings, and understandings that are specific to an organization and underlie how people construct reality and interpret particular events, actions, and situations (Morgan, 1986). An organization's culture encompasses specific knowledge, standard operating procedures, and "ways of doing things" (Langfield-Smith, 1995).

Central and Global had very different organizational cultures. Central resulted from the merger of two public-sector organizations, but was moving quickly to adopt commercial practices and principles. Global was highly commercial, profit seeking, and militaristic in its operations. One senior manager contrasted the two organizations.

> The way Central works is to have the process in place, but to empower people to do what they need to do. The account is probably worth 40 to 45 million dollars a year to Global Systems. My equivalent, the number one person in Global Systems, has signing authority to only $5,000—everything else goes up the line into the bureaucracy. You can talk about bureaucracy in the public service, but it is nothing to what you see in the way Global controls what you can and cannot do. That is the way they work. But having said that, they have introduced a rigor into this organization, which was far too free with its IT spending. That is a difficult thing to do with an internal IT shop.

After the first eighteen months these differences became less important, as Central came to adopt more commercial principles and Global came to learn "the Central way."

The achievement of a close business alignment between ElectNet and the outsourcers was a factor in creating a smooth working relationship, and a criterion in the selection of the outsourcers was the need for the outsourcers to gain an understanding of how the business operated and an appreciation of the values of ElectNet. ElectNet built into its contracts a requirement for the outsourcers to commit to the vision and values of the company. However, some managers at ElectNet underestimated how difficult it would be to achieve an alignment. Initial problems were experienced as the outsourcers were not familiar with the company's business cycles. One manager explained the difficulty of conveying the nature of the business to the outsourcers.

> The thing you realize is that the benefit of an internal in-house team is that they actually participate in the (routine) business processes. An internal group has to do its own budget so it realizes, as well as everyone else, that it is important to have the budget system available at a certain time. You do not need to tell them because they are doing it. Now the outsourcers obviously are not part of this process. And so it is important to focus on communication . . . while a lot of stuff is written down in documentation, you've really got to learn it through communication and experience.

Managers at GHI became very aware of the cultural differences that seemed to be driving some of the difficulties they experienced in the first year of outsourcing. The local office of IS Experts was under pressure to deliver a profit on a very tightly costed contract, while GHI was focused on delivering large programs that were critical to government operations and relied heavily on IS infrastructure. There was a realization in the first few years that IS Experts needed a good understanding of the business to solve IS problems. When IS problems arose in GHI, managers contacted customer service managers who worked for IS Experts, but the lack of understanding of the nature of GHI's business impeded the quality of the assistance that was provided.

Central, ElectNet, and GHI were former or current public-sector organizations that outsourced to specialist IS, globalized commercial entities. Given the different origins and the nature of the specialization, it is probably inevitable that the providers would have a culture different from that of the buying organizations and be unfamiliar with the nature of the organizations' business. Cultural differences and a lack of awareness of the buying organization's business model led to low service delivery, low satisfaction, and conflict.

While there is no easy solution to problems that arise from cultural differences, an awareness of the issue and its potential impact on the day-to-day operations and outsourcing relationship can alert both parties to the danger of making inappropriate assumptions about how either party will operate within the new relationship.

The Loss of Skills and Knowledge

The loss of skills and knowledge has been cited in the literature as being a major disadvantage of outsourcing. In addition, effectively managing the IS outsourcing relationship requires the development of new contract management skills, which also require a certain level of IS expertise and knowledge.

For Central and ElectNet, the loss of technical IS skills and knowledge was not significant. In both cases there was an initial period at the start of the outsourcing relationships where the transition to the outsourcers led to a loss of particular system-specific and organizational skills. However, this was of short duration. Both companies outsourced the IS functions, as they did not believe that it was possible or desirable to build up in-house expertise in the area. While Central had strong IS capabilities before outsourcing, the potential benefits of gaining the specialized expertise of the outsourcer were greater than any risk of exposure or dependence that might result from the loss of skills. For GHI, however, there was a clear loss of IS knowledge and skills that persisted for several years because the skeleton IS staff remaining in GHI was unable to effectively manage the IS contract. The activities that were outsourced by GHI were far broader than those of Central and ElectNet, who built up an in-house team of highly skilled IT staff to provide strategic and ongoing management of the IS function and outsourcing relationships. Senior management at GHI only realized the need to rebuild skills after IS performance had deteriorated and the relationship with IS Experts was damaged.

Managers in all case studies highlighted the need to develop new contract management skills as part of the outsourcing process. ElectNet's IS manager acknowledged that new skills had to be developed to manage the outsourcer, but believed that these skills should not only apply to the outsourcing situation—they were precisely the types of skills that should also be applied to manage in-house functions. This leads to the observation that the legal separation between a firm and its outsourcer heightens the importance of management and control issues in the eyes of some managers. Managers at both Central and ElectNet alluded to this, stating that the existence of an arm's-length monetary relationship between the two parties (as opposed to one involving internal transfer pricing) led to an increase in control.

Establishing cooperative relationships with outsourcers and their staffs may require managers to develop new skills in many areas, including communication and negotiation skills. In addition, the outsourcing of a function may require managers to learn how to relate to former staff who join the outsourcer, but nevertheless perform essentially the same functions as before the outsourcing took place.

Ineffective Communication and Information-Sharing Processes

Effective communication and information sharing are key determinants of the outsourcing relationship quality and outsourcing success (Lee and Kim, 1999; Lee 2001). In the three cases, protocols for effective communications between the organization and its outsourcers included the number of points of contact within the firm and the regularity of formal meetings.

The way in which Central related to Global changed over the first two years of the contract. Initially, Central's IT&T outsourcing manager was the sole contact point for Global, handling all day-to-day problems and working toward building strong relationships with Global. Over time, after more formal governance arrangements were put into place, Global assigned different service managers responsibility for each of those businesses, to handle specific day-to-day issues. This allowed the IT&T outsourcing manager to focus more on broader relationship matters. At Central, each of its four business units were customers for the service provided by Global, so there were direct contacts between the outsourcer and the four business areas. Each of the four business units of Central had a distinct focus and very different IS needs. A similar approach was taken by ElectNet, where a single IS manager managed the relationship, and then specific "owners" of each system within ElectNet developed direct relations.

A greater focus came to be placed on open communication channels and addressing issues up-front. Senior managers from both Central and Global met monthly as part of an IS steering group to work through the strategic plan, review performance, and discuss future plans and major projects and spending to date. There was also a working group to handle applications for new IT capital projects.

Managers at ElectNet considered ongoing communication with the outsourcers crucial to achieving the needed business alignment. ElectNet managers held monthly meetings with both outsourcers to review performance against service targets. These meetings provided the opportunity for feedback between the outsourcers and ElectNet, and allowed for the identification and resolution of issues. The software outsourcer conducted regular meetings with the systems' owners throughout ElectNet to ensure that services were appropriately delivered. The hardware outsourcer met ElectNet managers on each site to consider any infrastructure issues. ElectNet began with one staff member managing the interface between the company and the IS outsourcers, and then an IS team was gradually established within ElectNet to take on responsibility for IS strategy, contract management, IS purchasing, and training. ElectNet was also allowed some input into senior IS appointments employed by the outsourcing companies.

One of the initial problems experienced in implementing the IS contract at GHI was that while governance mechanisms were in the contract, they were not put into operation. Virtually no IS staff remained at GHI and the IS responsibilities transferred to IS Experts were extensive and critical to the effective operation of GHI. However, IS Experts were underresourced and were not able to implement their own reporting and accountability structures. One GHI manager claimed that at the time of the outsourcing, GHI managers trusted IS Experts to undertake the necessary reporting and performance management. For example, the original contract called for IS Experts to establish a performance improvement team, which was supposed to meet each quarter and to formulate innovative ways of doing business. However, even after the first two years, the team had never met or even formed. One manager described the difficult situation, which was exacerbated by the lack of technical IS staff remaining in GHI to monitor the performance of IS Experts.

> There was no governance structure put in place. So there was no meter to say it's time to start doing something. You knew something was bad when it blew up in your face . . . no one in GHI was asking questions like "where's your strategic plan, where's your disaster recovery plan, where's your business continuity plan, where's your enterprise architecture?" No one was asking those questions because no one knew that was the question to ask . . . they should have seen what was coming but didn't have the ability, or the experience as a mature purchaser and therefore didn't know what they should be doing.

After three years the contract with IS Experts was renegotiated. GHI limited the aspects of IS that were outsourced, contracted for more realistic (higher) fees, and put in place committees to provide adequate governance over IS operations. A Management Strategy Committee was formed, chaired by the chief executive officer (CEO) of GHI and consisting largely of second-tier managers of GHI. It met every six months to set the strategic direction of IS for GHI and to outline major projects. The senior management involvement highlights the high priority that had come to be given to IS. The Information Management Project Committee was formed to oversee all IS projects and to meet every six to eight weeks. Membership consisted of IS managers from both GHI and IS Experts. Strict project management and monitoring processes were put in place and steering committees were formed to manage individual projects.

Establishing formal communication protocols is a key aspect of governance and is important in helping establish ground rules and the expectations of each party. Protocols provide a way of solving problems as they arise, particularly in the early days of a contract, and establishing expectations in relation to service provision (Langfield-Smith and Greenwood, 1998). Single or multiple contact points may be used, depending on the characteristics of the function that is being delivered by the outsourcer and the complexity or critical nature of the service. At Central and ElectNet, communications with the outsourcers were managed during the earliest days by specialist active senior IS managers who remained in the buying organizations. At GHI there were no specialist IS managers responsible for overseeing the outsourced IS function, so controlling and monitoring through committees and meetings did not take place. It was only after the first three years of the contract that a senior IS manager was employed by GHI to determine why the outsourced relationship and the IS function were not satisfactory, to salvage the relationship, and to manage the governance process. As the IS expertise within GHI was rebuilt, stronger governance mechanisms became possible.

Inadequate Performance Measures and Incentives

It has been suggested that a firm may gain control over an outsourced function through ongoing monitoring of work performance as well as monitoring aspects of the outsourcing relationship (McFarlan and Nolan, 1995). This may be achieved by means of communications and meetings as outlined above as well as through performance measures and benchmarks, focusing on areas such as customer satisfaction, delivery responsiveness, product quality, and cost. These measures may be included in the contract or negotiated later.

Central did not include performance measures in the initial outsourcing contract, so over the first eighteen months, performance measures and targets were developed jointly by Central and Global to provide the most appropriate incentives for the outsourcers to deliver quality services. A risk/reward scheme was introduced to encourage Global to earn greater profits when undertaking a project, while also delivering cost savings and other outcomes to Central. The Central example emphasizes the way in which incentive systems can be structured to benefit both parties in the relationship. The first application was a new customer service system, a discretionary project. The system was developed after several weeks of negotiation between Central and Global. While Global once charged Central the direct costs, overhead, and profit margin for discretionary projects, under the risk/reward system, Global charged Central only for the direct costs and then bonuses were earned. These were based on weighted performance across three areas as follows:

- Cost: under or over budget (25 maximum)
- Quality: performance to plan (20), survey of end users (10), business continuity (20)
- Time: delivery to schedule (25)

Thus, a maximum score of 25 was awarded based on how prompt Global was in delivering the project on time. Depending on how the new system affected business continuity (which might be tested over several months), Global could receive a score of up to 20. (Business continuity was concerned with whether the new system resulted in interruptions to business, such as computer downtime, interrupted data access, and external customer problems.) The targets set for each of the performance measures were very challenging. The score that Global received was then linked to a profit multiplier. An overall score of 70 would return a normal profit for the project to Global, while a score of 90 to 100 would give it up to 150 percent of the normal profit. Global also conducted its own customer satisfaction surveys and these were shared with Central.

ElectNet used two types of service levels to evaluate the outsourcers' performance—core level and specific level. Core service levels were embedded into contracts (for example, hardware availability and reliability). Other specific measures were negotiated from time to time, but were not included in contracts. ElectNet's IS manager considered specific-level measures were not difficult to negotiate:

> We try to take a partnership approach with our service providers so that, for the majority of the time, both sides have the same interest in making the thing work and being successful.

Financial incentives were not built into contracts, with ElectNet instead preferring to provide nonfinancial incentives, such as offering to act as a reference site for the outsourcer. Furthermore, flexibility was factored into contracts, allowing ElectNet the opportunity to renegotiate contracts if required.

At GHI, service-level agreements, performance measures, and targets were built into the original contract, but were ineffective due to the lack of monitoring by GHI staff and due to IS Experts having limited staff resources. It was only when the contract was renegotiated after three years that comprehensive key performance indicators and reporting and management of projects through performance measures became established and used by the various project committees.

The implementation of performance measures to evaluate and control the work of outsourcers was a common development in all case studies. Only in the Central case were rewards tied explicitly to the achievement of targets. However, the development of performance indicators may serve several purposes. First, it provides a forum for interactions between the two parties, increasing the number of joint meetings and increasing familiarity. This may encourage high levels of trust between parties (Browning, Beyer, and Shetler, 1995; Chiles and McMackin, 1996). Second, performance indicators may provide an efficient means for communicating expectations between the two parties and assist in providing efficient forms of control (Jarillo, 1988). Third, the design of a risk/reward system allows both parties to share in the rewards and may contribute to the strengthening of a relationship of trust.

An Absence of Trust

It has been claimed that a high level of trust is a factor in establishing a close cooperative relationship between a firm and its outsourcer, and even for establishing a workable contract (Domberger, 1998; Langfield-Smith and Greenwood, 1998). It has been argued that certain minimum levels of trust are essential in all interfirm relationships, as trust reduces the possibility of opportunistic behavior (Axelrod, 1984; Bradach and Eccles, 1989). In addition, trust may increase the predictability of mutual behavior through each party honoring commitments and allowing partners to deal with unforeseen contingencies in mutually acceptable ways (Sako, 1992, 37). Contracts may not be needed to build up some forms of cooperative relationships; trust may act as a substitute for contracts and as an alternative control mechanism (Bradach and Eccles, 1989; Ring and Van de Ven, 1989). McAllister (1995) suggests that the development of trust may be inversely related to formal rules and monitoring.

However, the relationship between trust and cooperation is not entirely clear. Many researchers have argued that trust is critical for cooperation to take place (see, for example, Smith, Carroll, and Ashford, 1995). Gambetta (1988), while arguing that a positive association exists between trust and likelihood of cooperation, also suggests that trust may not always precede cooperation. Cooperation may occur because of shared interest in relationship outcomes. However, a variety of predictors of cooperation (including both psychological and structural factors) has been presented.[4]

In all three case studies, there were vast differences in the values of the buying organizations and the outsourcers. Managers at Central perceived Global as having high status and credibility as an outsourcing partner, and there is some evidence that this was an initial driver for GHI when they engaged IS Experts to manage all aspects of IS. In the Central and ElectNet cases, continual meetings and problem solving with the outsourcers may have promoted perceptions of procedural fairness, but as no prior relationships existed between the organization and its outsourcers, it is unclear whether initial perceptions of trust were high.

The managers at Central came to understand that Global was committed to the relationship and a growing trust developed between the two parties. A manager outlined this viewpoint:

> Central still bears by far the biggest risk in this relationship. If you assume the absolute worst, that Global Systems delivers a system late, over budget and with poor quality, sure it might lose out on a couple of million dollars profit, but the cost to Central would be significantly more. So there is an element of trust in this and the trust has to be that Global Systems has a reputation to sustain in the marketplace. It cannot afford to walk away from something like this—and it will not. These large organizations will not and there is a good enough relationship between our CEO and their CEO to ensure that it simply would not happen. There is too much win-win potential to come out of this.

Both parties worked toward building high levels of trust between the two organizations through meetings and other communications, including the development of the risk/reward scheme. Where there were incompatibilities, Global replaced some of its staff who were directly involved with Central.

The contract with Global was for the provision of management services, while Central continued to own the IS infrastructure. One reason for not giving total control to Global was related to the risk that if the relationship were to fail it would be difficult to recommence IS services in-house or with another outsourcer if ownership over IS assets had been lost. A senior manager explained the relationship between trust and risk.

> The more you trust, the more you are prepared to hand over. The more you feel "Hey things could break down. What recourse do we have? What backups do we have? How do we rebuild if there is a divorce?" There is some hesitancy in relation to the ownership of assets—but there is a gradual move away from that thinking.

At Central, some mistrust initially arose when managers within the four businesses were charged by the outsourcer for their use of IS services. This action was met with suspicion and claims of overcharging. The reaction was a result of the transition toward "realistic" charging for IS services, which had not been explained fully to Central managers at the start of the outsourcing. Clearly, effective communication may provide a way to encourage the development of trust, by clarifying expectations and encouraging repeated positive interactions.

Trust is a difficult aspect for any organization to assess in the initial days of an outsourcing relationship, and those initial perceptions are often based on the outsourcer's competence, which can be determined from its reputation and track record with respect to broad skills and expertise. However, trust is not based solely on competence. A key aspect of relationships arises from the need to assess a partner's intention to cooperate, sometimes known as goodwill trust (Sako, 1992). Perceptions of goodwill trust are assessed over time through repeated interaction and experience with the outsourcing partner.

Adverse Reactions of Employees

The reactions of outsourcing on employees must be considered carefully in the face of increased outsourcing. Outsourcing an in-house function may result in employees leaving the firm, gaining employment with the outsourcer, or being transferred to other functions within the firm, and adverse reactions of employees to outsourcing may influence the management of the relationship.

At Central, there was some dissatisfaction among IS staff who had chosen to be redeployed within the firm, rather than move to Global. This was managed carefully, so as not to spread unrest throughout the organization. Indeed, one criterion considered by Central when choosing a tenderer was how the outsourcers planned to manage transitional issues for staff. At ElectNet there was no in-house IS staff as the former IS function had been provided by Power. At GHI nearly all of the IS staff with technical skills chose to join IS Experts, to work in the outsourced operation. Only a few IS staff remained at GHI, and they were not technical IS staff. However, most of the staff who joined IS Experts did not remain with the outsourcers for long. One GHI manager suggested that this was because the ethos of IS Experts was so different from that of GHI.

Another potential management problem is that outsourced staff may be employed under working conditions different from those of in-house staff, which may lead to dissatisfaction. In all three case studies, the IS staff of the outsourcer were located on-site, within the organization, working alongside the organization's staff.

It is difficult to anticipate the impact of outsourcing on employees who remain with a firm, whether they are employees who are redeployed as a result of the outsourcing or those who believe that inequities have arisen with the introduction of outsourcing. The management of employee transitions should be included as a formal part of the outsourcing plan, and it may be the responsibility of both the firm and the outsourcer.

Summary

In this section, several factors were identified as important in the management of relationships between an organization and its outsourcers. The causes, implications, and possible solutions are summarized in Table 10.3. An emerging theme in the above discussions is that outsourcing can provide the means for achieving greater control within the organization. In the next section, the control implications of outsourcing will be explored in greater detail.

The Impact of Outsourcing on Control

A frequently cited disadvantage of outsourcing is a loss of control over knowledge, skills, and processes. The potential for this loss of control may depend on the nature of the function that is outsourced. Outsourcing some functions, for example, cleaning and catering, would not entail a high risk of loss of skills or knowledge for most firms. Outsourcing of other activities, such as in the areas of product design, manufacturing processing, or IS, is more likely to lead to a loss of knowledge and skills and possibly to a loss of control over those functions. The evidence relating to this issue in the case studies is not entirely consistent with this claim. In Central and ElecNet, managers believed that control, in terms of accountability for the IS activities, increased as a result of outsourcing. Improvements in control were cited as a benefit of outsourcing by managers interviewed, even at GHI.

Improvements in Control and Accountability

When outsourcing does not involve exchange of equity, control must be achieved through other means.[5] At Central, a variety of mechanisms served to create control. These were through specifications within the contract, the implementation of performance measures and incentives, the building of trust between the firm and the outsourcer, and the implementation of greater accountability systems within the firm.

In contrast to the criticism that outsourcing can lead to a loss of control, Central and ElectNet engaged in outsourcing as a way of improving control over IS activities and IS cost. At Central, when IS was performed in-house, management found it difficult to exercise effective control over spending by Central's businesses and to control new product development by IS staff. Transfer pricing systems did not create a sense of accountability or cost consciousness among internal buying and selling parties. The corporate boundary between Central and Global made the necessity for improved control more apparent. It could be argued that cost centers and profit centers are created within an organization to achieve the same type of outcomes. The control advantages of this form of internal structuring, however, did not seem to be effective within Central prior to outsourcing. We can only speculate as to why this was the case: Was it too difficult to impose more effective control through an internal pricing mechanism? Were the relationships between Central employees too close to allow for the implementation of effective control? Was outsourcing the only solution that could have been applied to improve control?

At Central, new practices that accompanied outsourcing encouraged greater cost management and accountability among the four internal business units. Before the outsourcing of IS, there had been little control over businesses' use of IS services. After outsourcing, managers were required to justify any requirements for IS development as part of the annual IS budget, and were charged for their usage of IS services. This provided an incentive for business managers to consider carefully their requirements and the way in which they were utilizing IS and IT. Managers at both Central and ElectNet stated that the outsourcer brought more discipline and accountability to the IS process. At ElectNet, similar issues of control arose. "Excessive" IS developments were curbed with the engagement of the IS outsourcer, as managers found they were now charged for new IS development. Greater accountability for IS costs ensued.

At GHI there was no improvement in control until several years into the relationship, when governance systems were activated. A GHI IS manager highlighted the relationship between trust and control.

> The emphasis now is on the relationship . . . a combination of trust and control. You go back to where it was [at] the start, we didn't have much control, but we had a lot of trust, but the trust soon withered away and where there's no increase in control (to compensate) we just had anarchy. We then tried to impose a lot of control but we didn't have any trust, and that didn't work either. So now we have a situation where we have a high level of trust, so we have a low level of formal controls. We have good governance arrangements. I don't call that more control. We were not in there inspecting them all the time because the governance arrangements are now working. Generally we don't impos[e] formal control unless the flags go up indicating problems.

Central, ElectNet, and GHI implemented both formal and informal controls to manage their relationships with outsourcers and control outcomes. Formal controls included performance measures, financial incentive systems, regular meetings, and systems for increased accountability over the use of the outsourcers' services. It appeared that these control systems were more rigorous than those that had been used within the organizations to control in-house IS activities. There may be a perception that stronger systems are needed to counter the potential loss of control that might occur when outsourcing a function. However, an ElectNet manager stated that the systems being used to manage the IS outsourcers were the same types of systems that *should* be used to manage in-house functions. The question remains: Was outsourcing the only solution to improving control over internal functions? Perhaps it was the easiest solution.

Is It More Difficult to Control an Outsourced Function?

Outsourcing changes the nature of control. The legal separation between an outsourcer and a firm may highlight to some managers that there is a need for greater control. However, it may also mean that control can be achieved only through limited means; direct supervision over staff and operations is not possible, so there must be greater reliance on indirect control mechanisms. Compared to the processes involved in implementing in-house controls, more negotiations will take place between an organization and an outsourcer when changing controls or imposing new controls. Cultural differences between a firm and outsourcer may make it difficult to implement formal controls and encourage the growth of informal controls.

This does not necessarily mean, however, that control must necessarily be weaker. The discipline of having to specify the nature of the service before going to tender may force a firm to identify, for the first time, its precise service needs, which may allow it to more easily develop performance measures and other controls over the service provided (Domberger, 1998). Also, by retaining ownership over key assets, firms may safeguard against creating situations of overdependency on an outsourcer. High levels of asset specificity are said to create increased dependence on an outsourcer and potentially to weaken control (Das and Teng, 2001). After control systems were put in place, managers in all three cases saw control as having strengthened under outsourcing. However, this may be dependent on the quality of the governance systems put in place as well as the caliber of the managers handling the processes in the buying organizations, and the low level of control associated with the prior in-house systems.

CONCLUSION

This chapter has focused on the IS outsourcing experiences of three organizations. The management of the outsourcing relationship and the related consideration of control were the focus of the study. While there is much literature on factors that influence the decision to outsource, limited attention has been given to important issues in managing the IS outsourcing relationship. The three cases in this chapter revealed a range of issues that are important in the management of the outsourcing relationship. These issues include inadequate contract specifications, initial expectations of performance improvements, different organizational cultures, the loss of skills and knowledge, ineffective communication and information-sharing processes, inadequate performance measures and incentives, an absence of trust, and adverse reactions of employees. A summary of these issues for each of the three cases is presented in Table 10.2. In addition to merely identifying and reporting these issues, the chapter has outlined the possible causes of each and has identified potential management solutions (see Table 10.3).

An often-cited disadvantage of outsourcing is the potential loss of control over the outsourced function and the loss of expertise and skills. However, the cases examined in this chapter do not support this contention. Over time, control increased due to the implementation of systems that were stricter than those in place prior to outsourcing. A question that remains unanswered is why the organizations were not able to implement similar strict controls when IS was provided in-house. It may be that the legal separation between a firm and the outsourcer creates a greater control consciousness. Outsourcing involves transactions in "real" money, which may be a more powerful motivation to establish tight controls than is an internal transfer pricing system. Also, it may be easier to enforce control over an outsourcer because there is usually a written contract and remedies for noncompliance. This reinforces the importance of contract specifications in managing and controlling the IS outsourcing relationship.

The findings of this study are of interest to managers who may be seeking to engage in outsourcing relationships and manage such relationships effectively, and to researchers who endeavor to understand control systems associated with new organizational forms. However, the limitations of the study must be also acknowledged. First, the evidence is based on only three case studies of IS outsourcing decisions and these were all former or current public-sector organizations. More extensive studies need to be undertaken to test the propositions that arose in this study. Second, the three organizations were all located in Australia. There may be some specific cultural factors that affect the applicability of the results to other settings. Third, in the cases presented in this chapter, the outsourcing decision had taken place within the previous five years. Lee and Kim (1999) found that outsourcing relationship quality was negatively associated with the age of the relationship. Thus, it may be useful to examine more mature outsourcing relationships to determine whether the management and control issues differ later in the relationship.

NOTES

1. Aspects of two of these case studies are also reported in Langfield-Smith, Smith, and Stringer (2000) and Langfield-Smith and Smith (2003).

2. These research methods are also discussed in Langfield-Smith, Smith, and Stringer (2000) and Langfield-Smith and Smith (2003).

3. The names of the organizations in the case studies have been disguised to preserve confidentiality.

4. Psychological determinants of cooperation include similarity in partner's values and norms that lead to shared expectations, perceived status and legitimacy of partners, and perceptions that interactive procedures are just (Bradach and Eccles, 1989; Chiles and McMackin, 1996). Structural determinants include the extent of prior social relationships (which may lead to perceptions of reliability and predicability), and the social context within which the relationships takes place (Browning, Beyer, and Shetler, 1995; Murnighan, 1994; Smith, Carroll, and Ashford, 1995).

5. Neither of the firms studied sought control through the purchase of equity in the outsourcer. Much empirical and normative research has considered the purchase of equity or shared ownership as a means of control. In fact, studies within the transaction cost economics framework classify alliances in terms of the extent of use of equity ownership (Gulati, 1995; Pisano, Russo, and Teece, 1988).

REFERENCES

Aubert, B.A.; Rivard, S.; and Patry, M. 2004. A transaction cost model of IS outsourcing. *Information and Management*, 41, 921–932.

Axelrod, R. 1984. *The Evolution of Co-operation.* New York: Basic Books.

Bradach, J.L. and Eccles, R.G. 1989. Markets versus hierarchies: From ideal types to plural forms. In W.R. Scott, ed., *Annual Review of Sociology* 15. Palo Alto, CA: Annual Reviews, 97–118.

Browning, L.D.; Beyer, J.M.; and Shetler, J.C. 1995. Building cooperation in a competitive industry: SEMATECH and the semiconductor industry. *Academy of Management Review*, 21, 113–151.

Chiles, T.H. and McMackin, J.F. 1996. Integrating variable risk preferences, trust and transaction cost economics. *Academy of Management Review*, 21, 73–99.

Das, T. and Teng, B. 2001. Trust, control and risk in strategic alliances: An integrated framework. *Organization Studies*, 22, 2, 251–283.

Domberger, S. 1998. *The Contracting Organization: A Strategic Guide to Outsourcing.* New York: Oxford University Press.

Eroglu, D. 1994. Global or domestic outsourcing of the "IS" function: Implications and recommendations. In S.A. Zahra and A.J. Ali, eds., *The Impact of Innovation and Technology in the Global Marketplace.* New York: International Business Press, 177–197.

Gambetta, D. 1988. Can we trust trust? In D. Gambetta, ed. *Trust: Making and Breaking Cooperative Relations.* Cambridge, MA: Basil Blackwell, 213–237.

Grabner, G. 1993. *The Embedded Firm.* London: Routledge.

Gulati, R. 1995. Does familiarity breed trust? The implications of repeated ties for contractual choice in alliances. *Academy of Management Review*, 21, 85–112.

Jarillo, J.C. 1988. On strategic networks. *Strategic Management Journal*, 9, 31–41.

Kern, T. and Willcocks, L. 2002. Exploring relationships in information technology outsourcing: The interaction approach. *European Journal of Information Systems*, 11, 3–19.

Lacity, M.C. and Willcocks, L.P. 1998. An empirical investigation of information technology sourcing practices: Lessons from experience. *MIS Quarterly*, 22, 363–408.

Lacity, M.C.; Willcocks, L.P.; and Feeny, D.F. 1995. IT outsourcing: Maximize flexibility and control. *Harvard Business Review* (May–June), 84–93.

Langfield-Smith, K. 1995. Organizational culture. In A. Berry, J. Broadbent, and D.T. Otley, eds., *Management Control Theories, Issues and Practices.* London: Macmillan, 179–200.

Langfield-Smith, K. and Greenwood, M. 1998. Developing cooperative supplier partnerships: A case study of Toyota. *Journal of Management Studies*, 35, 331–353.

Langfield-Smith, K. and Smith D. 2003. Management control and trust in outsourcing relationships. *Management Accounting Research*, 14, 281–307.

Langfield-Smith, K.; Smith, D.; and Stringer, C. 2000. *Managing the Outsourcing Relationship.* Sydney: University of New South Wales Press.

Lee, J-N. 2001. The impact of knowledge sharing, organizational capability and partnership quality on IS outsourcing success. *Information and Management*, 38, 323–335.

Lee, J-N. and Kim, Y-G. 1999. Effect of partnership quality on IS outsourcing success: Conceptual framework and empirical validation. *Journal of Management Information Systems*, 15, 29–61.

McAllister, D.J. 1995. Affect- and cognition-based trust as foundation for interpersonal cooperation in organization. *Academy of Management Review*, 21, 24–59.

McFarlan, F.W. and Nolan, R.L. 1995. How to manage an IS outsourcing alliance. *Sloan Management Review* (Winter), 9–23.

McHugh, P.; Merli, G.; and Wheeler, W.A. 1995. *Beyond Business Process Reengineering.* Chichester, UK: Wiley.

Morgan, G. 1986. *Images of Organization.* London: Sage.

Murnighan, J.K. 1994. Game theory and organizational behavior. In B.W. Staw and L.L. Cummings, eds., *Research in Organizational Behavior*, 16. Greenwich, CT: JAI Press, 82–124.

Ouchi, W. 1979. A conceptual framework for the design of organizational control mechanisms. *Management Science*, 25, 833–848.

Pisano, G.P.; Russo, M.V.; and Teece, D. 1988. Joint ventures and collaborate agreements in the telecommunications equipment industry. In D. Mowery, ed., *International Collaborative Ventures in US Manufacturing.* Cambridge, MA: Ballinger, 23–70.

Quinn, J.B. 1992. *Intelligent Enterprise: A Knowledge and Service Based Paradigm for Industry.* New York: Free Press.

Quinn, J.B. and Hilmer, F.G. 1994. Strategic outsourcing. *Sloan Management Review* (Summer), 43–55.

Ring, P.S. and Van de Ven, A. 1989. Formal and informal dimensions of transactions. In A. Van de Ven, H. Angle, and M.S. Poole, eds., *Research on the Management of Innovation: The Minnesota Studies.* New York: Ballinger, 71–192.

Sako, M. 1992. *Prices, Quality and Trust: Inter-Firm Relationships in Britain and Japan.* Cambridge: Cambridge University Press.

Smith, K.G.; Carroll, S.J.; and Ashford, S.J. 1995. Intra- and interorganizational cooperation: Towards a research agenda. *Academy of Management Review*, 21, 7–23.

Willcocks, L.; Fitzgerald, G.; and Lacity, M. 1996. To outsource IS or not? Recent research on economics and evaluation practice. *European Journal of Information Systems*, 5, 143–160.

CHAPTER 11

VENDOR COMMITMENT IN AN ASP OUTSOURCING CONTEXT

A Comparative Evaluation of the Roles of Power and Partnership

MATTHEW SWINARSKI, RAJIV KISHORE, AND H. RAGHAV RAO

Abstract: *De-escalation of commitment by service providers is a major risk in information technology (IT) outsourcing projects and it can lead to project failure. However, current research is still unclear about how best to maintain service provider commitment in IT outsourcing contexts. The goal of this research is to understand which of two alternative influence sources—power, a unilateral influence source, or partnership, a bilateral influence source—better explains service provider commitment in application service provider (ASP) outsourcing relationships. Data are collected through a controlled laboratory experiment to determine precisely the relative impact of these two variables on service provider commitment. The results of the study indicate that both power and partnership play critical roles in shaping service provider commitment in ASP outsourcing relationships, with partnership having a stronger influence. The findings suggest that client IT managers should seek a balance between the two control levers—power and partnership—as a means of managing their service providers more effectively to achieve outsourcing success.*

Keywords: *Application Service Providers (ASP), Client Power, Provider Dependence, Client–Provider Partnership, Experimental Methodology, Information Technology (IT) Outsourcing, Provider Commitment*

INTRODUCTION

Outsourcing has emerged as a key method for managing information technology (IT) in the current era. One of the critical issues associated with the success of IT outsourcing projects is the commitment of outsourcing providers to outsourcing relationships. Recent studies have shown that in IT outsourcing projects a major risk that can lead to project failure is vendor de-escalation of commitment to the outsourcing project (e.g., Natovich, 2003). If a current vendor withdraws from its commitments to a client contract owing to expected heavy losses, the client may have to switch to another vendor for ongoing operations or to get the outsourced project completed. However, switching IT providers generally undermines the economic and technical benefits of outsourcing due to the enormous start-up and learning costs associated with developing new relationships (Whitten et al., 2004). Thus, the issue of provider commitment to outsourcing relationships is very important to the success of outsourced IT projects. However, the IT outsourcing literature is quite silent about this particular vendor aspect as it has paid only scant attention to vendor issues in IT outsourcing relationships and has focused predominantly on client aspects (Dibbern et al., 2004; Lee et al., 2003).

The present research seeks to fill this void. In this chapter, we examine two alternate influence sources of vendor commitment that are under the control of clients to quite a large extent: (1) vendor perceptions of client power over them, and (2) vendor perceptions of the client–vendor partnership. These two constructs capture both unilateral (power) and bilateral (partnership) mechanisms that have the potential to shape vendor commitment toward the outsourcing relationship. While the notion of client–vendor partnership has been examined often in the IT outsourcing literature (e.g., Grover, Cheon, and Teng, 1996; Lee and Kim, 1999; Randeree, Kishore, and Rao, 2007 Sabherwal, 1999; see also chapter 9 in this volume), there are no studies that examine the influence of this construct on vendor commitment to the outsourcing relationship. Furthermore, to our knowledge, the notion of client power over vendor has not been studied directly in the IT outsourcing literature, although the notion of dependence, which is at the root of the power construct as discussed in later sections, has been studied in the interorganizational relationships (IOR) literature that considers variables from the transaction cost economics (TCE) theory (e.g., Bensaou and Anderson, 1999; Poppo and Zenger, 1998; Subramani and Venkatraman, 2003). Our focus in this research is vendor dependence over client insofar as it can lead to vendor perceptions of client power over vendor, which in turn can influence vendor commitment to the outsourcing relationship. While the early TCE literature focused predominantly on client dependence on vendor emanating from transaction-specific assets, recent TCE and IOR literatures acknowledge the presence of both vendor dependence on client and mutual dependence between vendor and clients in IORs (Rindfleisch and Heide, 1997). But as mentioned above, the impact of client power over vendor (emanating from vendor dependence on client) on vendor commitment to an outsourcing relationship has not been examined in previous IT outsourcing research.

We choose the application service provider (ASP) outsourcing paradigm for the present study as there are hardly any studies of partnership in the ASP outsourcing context in the IT outsourcing literature. The ASP model is a new outsourcing paradigm in which vendors generally provide access to predefined business application systems as an outsourcing service to multiple clients. As a result, services provided by ASP vendors are comparatively simpler and more straightforward and service levels are more clearly defined than those involved in traditional outsourcing relationships. Consequently, ASP relationships tend to be quite contractually based and it is not clear whether the notions of partnership will apply in this particular outsourcing context in a manner similar to more traditional outsourcing contexts.

We also take the alternate theoretical perspectives approach in this chapter and compare the two alternate influence sources—power and partnership—in a single model to understand which influence source better explains vendor commitment to an outsourcing relationship. Our approach is similar to the competing theoretical perspectives approach that is gaining currency in the organizational literature as it integrates and synthesizes knowledge in competing and often complementary theoretical paradigms and provides much deeper insights about the phenomenon of interest. Examples of recent papers that follow this approach include: Young, Charns, and Heeren (2004), comparing the structural contingency perspective with the professional autonomy perspective in the context of studying quality of and innovation in professional services; Ketokivi and Schroeder (2004), applying three different theoretical perspectives (strategic contingency, structural contingency, and institutional isomorphism) to investigate how innovative manufacturing practices diffuse in organizations; Wareham's paper (2003), synthesizing the competing theoretical perspectives of transaction cost economics and social networking theory in a study of interorganizational governance; Reuer and Koza (2000), applying arguments from the asymmetric information view and the indigestibility to joint venture formation; and Schroth and Shah (2000), comparing the group-value model and attribution theory as competing theoretical perspectives in examining the effects of procedural justice on an individual's self-esteem.

The chapter is organized as follows. First, we provide an introduction to the ASP outsourcing paradigm and discuss how ASP outsourcing differs from traditional IT outsourcing. We then discuss the relevant prior literature pertaining to the social and relational aspects of IT outsourcing. Next, we discuss the underlying theories, research models, and hypotheses pertaining to the impact of power and partnership on a service provider's commitment. We then describe the research method and analysis techniques. Finally, we discuss the results, the limitations of the study, implications for managers, and future directions for research. We use the terms service provider, provider, supplier, and vendor interchangeably in this chapter to refer to a vendor who provides IT services in the context of ASP outsourcing.

THE APPLICATION SERVICE PROVIDER PARADIGM

According to the ASP Industry Consortium, an ASP "manages and delivers application capabilities to multiple entities from a data center across a wide area network." The ASP model is a new form of IT outsourcing and it differs from the more traditional IT outsourcing relationships on four key dimensions: service customization, data location, asset ownership, and provider presence. First, ASP vendors generally offer their business applications as packaged solution services with little customization. Their intent is to mass serve multiple clients. In traditional IT outsourcing contexts, each customer is treated individually and solutions are designed to fit a client's unique needs. Second, the client data reside on the ASP platform in the ASP model whereas in the traditional IT outsourcing relationships, client data resides on the client's platform. Third, the client retains ownership of software applications in traditional outsourcing environments whereas software applications are rented/leased to the client on a recurring fee basis in the ASP context. Applications provided by the ASP are accessed by customers using browser windows through public and private networks, quite often the Internet. Finally, unlike traditional IT outsourcing contexts where providers may have employees stationed at client locations, or employees who at least make regular visits to client locations, the ASP model allows providers to service customers over greater distances using networks without maintaining any physical presence at client locations. As a result of these unique properties, the ASP model is geared predominantly toward providing application services that are relatively straightforward and can be well defined under service levels that can be easily specified and measured. Consequently, ASP relationships tend to be quite contractually based.

The unique properties of the ASP model discussed above allow clients to achieve such benefits as increased access to technical knowledge and wider breadth of applications, accelerated speed of deployment of IT applications, seamless connectivity and integration among diverse business partners through shared Web-based applications, scalability of IT infrastructure, and a lower and predictable total cost of ownership (Booker, 2000; Boyd, 2000; Johnson, 2000; Morgan, 2000). However, an important prerequisite for a client to reap these promised benefits is to have a high degree of vendor commitment toward the client relationship. As mentioned before, there is a paucity of research pertaining to vendor commitment in IT outsourcing in general and there is no research that examines vendor commitment, power, and partnership in the context of the contractually oriented application services arena. The ASP model, thus, provides an appropriate setting for testing the relative influences of power and partnership on vendor commitment in the context of IT outsourcing relationships.

RELEVANT PRIOR LITERATURE

Case studies on managing IT outsourcing relationships have found that the use of multiple service providers, detailed contracts, penalty clauses, short-term agreements, IT legal experts, and promises of contract extensions were effective mechanisms for establishing a client's power in the relationship in order to achieve successful outsourcing outcomes (e.g., Lacity and Hirschheim, 1993a, 1993b; Lacity and Willcocks, 1998; Lacity, Willcocks, and Feeny, 1995, 1996; Saunders, Gebelt, and Hu, 1997). These studies focused on how to efficiently structure the governance of an IT outsourcing engagement from a contractual viewpoint but generally ignored the relational dynamics involved in the outsourcing relationship. Concentrating on the contractual view and failing to incorporate the relational aspects may provide only a limited view of how to best manage IT outsourcing relationships. For example, researchers have argued that short-term contracts provide no incentive for service provider performance improvements (DiRomualdo and Gurbaxani, 1998); detailed contracts make less economic sense during the later years of the relationship (McFarlan and Nolan, 1995); exhaustive contracts may be impossible to construct for large and/or complex IS functions (Kishore et al., 2003); and trusting, cooperative relationships are often difficult to develop under conditions of tight governance control (Sabherwal, 1999). Therefore, as Macneil (1978a; 1978b) proposed, contracts are inherently incomplete and are not sufficient by themselves to ensure successful interorganizational relationships.

Recognizing the limitations of contracts as governance mechanisms for IT outsourcing relationships, researchers turned to relational exchange theories in order to identify additional factors critical to outsourcing success (e.g., Grover, Cheon, and Teng, 1996; Lee and Kim, 1999). In these studies, trust and partnership were considered as factors necessary for achieving better IT outsourcing relationships (Grover, Cheon, and Teng, 1996; Lee et al., 2002; Sabherwal, 1999). Further, these studies demonstrated that the intangible elements associated with IT outsourcing relationships (e.g., service quality, innovation, knowledge sharing, etc.) could be captured only through partnership-based outsourcing relationships (Lee et al., 2003). These studies show that win-win relationships can be developed only if the parties in an outsourcing foster an environment of trust, open communication, and cooperation. Evidence also supports the fact that both detailed and not-so-detailed contractual IT outsourcing relationships are more successful in partnership-based environments (Saunders, Gebelt, and Hu, 1997). As a result of these studies, the virtues of partnership are now generally accepted in the context of traditional IT outsourcing.

However, studies in the IT outsourcing area have not directly addressed the role of power as an alternate and/or complementary mechanism for managing IT outsourcing relationships, even though the literature on interorganizational relationships (IOR) has considered both power and partnership as constructs that play an important role in shaping relationships between interacting organizations. It is not unusual for a service provider's profit motives to run counter to the client's service needs, especially in situations when the client's service needs are dominated by the desire for cost efficiency (Lee et al., 2003), thereby making a partnership-based relationship less effective. In such situations of goal asymmetry, that is, when parties involved in the relationship have different and conflicting goals, power wielded by the client can play a key role in ensuring the continued commitment of the service provider to the relationship. Furthermore, power not only may provide an alternate relationship management mechanism but also may complement a partnership-style approach to relationship management by allowing the client to effectively resolve impasses that cannot be resolved with purely cooperative actions.

Therefore, we draw from literature on IT outsourcing, social and relational exchange, and interorganizational relationships to develop a research model that incorporates both power and

Figure 11.1 **Primary Research Model**

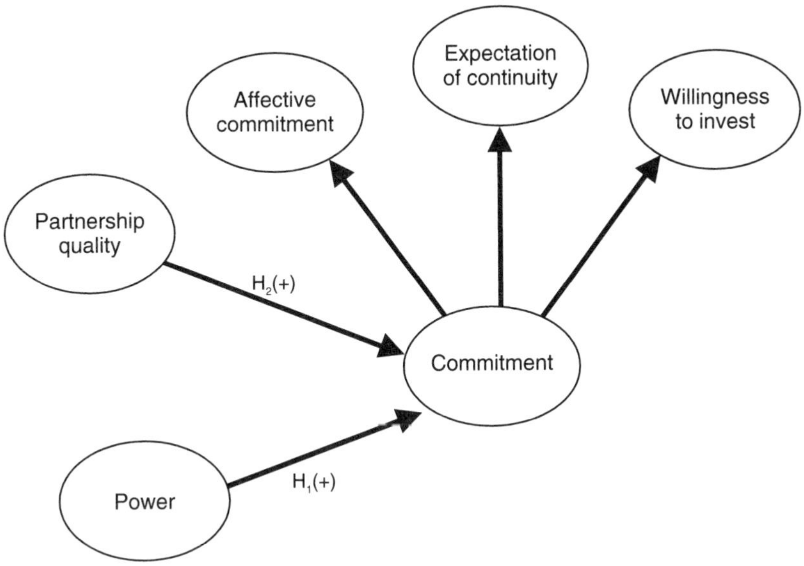

partnership as two distinct influence sources that may have an impact on service providers' commitment. As discussed above, the ASP model tends to be highly contractual and research on partnership and power in the context of ASPs may provide new insights about the importance of the social and relational aspects in this new form of IT outsourcing. The underlying theories and the research model are discussed next.

THEORY AND RESEARCH MODEL

The chapter presents two research models, as shown in Figures 11.1 and 11.2. In both models, the constructs of power and partnership are hypothesized to influence a service provider's level of commitment (consisting of three distinct dimensions). In the first model (the primary research model), commitment is conceptualized as a second-order construct with three distinct and non-related first-order constructs. This conceptualization is the traditional representation of the multidimensional nature of the commitment construct. In the second model (the alternate research model), commitment is represented as three distinct but interrelated constructs based on the work of Gundlach, Achrol, and Mentzer (1995). A detailed discussion of the underlying theories and arguments supporting these two research models is provided next.

Provider Commitment

Commitment is defined as a service provider's desire to remain in an IT outsourcing relationship and to continue to invest in the relationship to further its existence. The literature on IORs views commitment as a key factor in determining long-term relationships (Dwyer, Schurr, and Oh, 1987; Gundlach, Achrol, and Mentzer, 1995; Morgan and Hunt, 1994). Dwyer, Schurr, and Oh (1987) propose that "commitment represents the highest stage of relational bonding." Parties who are committed to an IOR work harder at handling problems and ensuring the achievement of both individual

Figure 11.2 **Alternate Research Model**

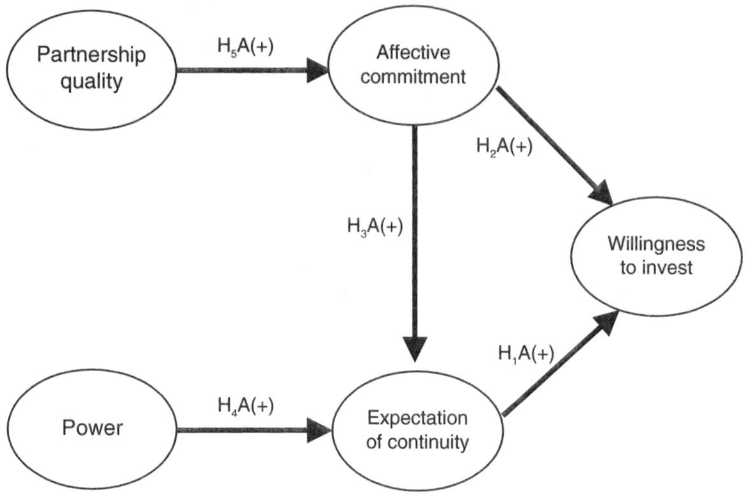

and joint goals (Mohr and Spekman, 1994) and they are more likely to accept or adhere to another party's requests (Morgan and Hunt, 1994). Research on IORs has considered commitment as the key dependent variable when viewing decisions in exchange relationships from the vendor's perspective (Andaleeb, 1996). Furthermore, as discussed earlier, vendor commitment is very important to achieving successful outcomes in IT outsourcing (Natovich, 2003). Therefore, following the IOR literature and the central role commitment plays in the IT outsourcing context, this study considers provider commitment as the dependent variable of interest in the research model.

Given the importance of commitment in IORs, it is not surprising to find diversity in the manner in which commitment has been conceptualized and defined. For example, *commitment* has been defined as:

- "an exchange partner's belief that an ongoing relationship with another is so important that it warrants maximum effort to maintain it" (Morgan and Hunt, 1994, 23).
- "an implicit or explicit pledge of relational continuity between exchange partners" (Dwyer, Schurr, and Oh, 1987, 19).
- "an enduring desire to maintain a valued relationship" (Moorman, Zaltman, and Deshpande, 1992, 316).

Commitment has also been associated with relational concepts such as motivation, loyalty, involvement, durability, consistency, pledges, idiosyncratic investments, and dedicated resources. Recently, there has been a growing perception that commitment is composed of three distinct dimensions (Gundlach, Achrol, and Mentzer, 1995; Kumar, Scheer, and Steenkamp, 1995). Kumar, Scheer, and Steenkamp (1995) classify these dimensions as willingness to invest, affective commitment, and expectation of continuity. Willingness to invest is the intention to become more deeply involved in the relationship through investments of capital and effort. Expectation of continuity is the firm's perceptions of both its own and its partner's intent to remain in the relationship. Affective commitment is the desire to continue the relationship because of positive affect toward the partner.

Determinants of Service Provider Commitment

Power as a Function of Dependence

Over the years there has been an increased interest in the study of power in the information systems (IS) domain (e.g., Jasperson et al., 2002). In order to facilitate the study of power in the IS domain, Jasperson and colleagues (2002) have provided a paradigm based in part on Bradshaw-Camball and Murray's (1991) power framework. Jasperson and colleagues' framework uses four power lenses to classify the various conceptual forms of power in IS: rational, pluralist, interpretive, and radical. This research uses the pluralist view of power, which assumes that parties involved in the relationship have different, often conflicting, goals. In this view, development, prioritization, and execution of organizational goals is an explicitly political process involving conscious negotiation based on control of resources and information. Power is viewed in terms of an objective reality in which there are objectively identifiable sets of optimal goals for each participant in an organization (Bradshaw-Camball and Murray, 1991). This view of power in the context of IT outsourcing relationships seems quite reasonable, since in most cases, a service provider's profit motives run counter to the client's service needs (Lacity, Willcocks, and Feeny, 1995). The pluralist view of power has been defined in a number of ways. Some of the key definitions are provided below:

- "The strength of power of O/P in some system A is defined as the maximum potential ability of O to influence P in A" (French and Raven, 1959, 152).
- "The power of actor A over actor B is the amount of resistance on the part of B which can be potentially overcome by A" (Emerson, 1962, 32).
- "If O has the capability of influencing P, we say that O has power over P" (Cartwright, 1965, 4).

The underlying theme of these conceptualizations of power is the potential ability of one party to influence another. Emerson (1962), who originally conceptualized the role of power in relationships, further proposed that the basis of one party's power over another party lies in the other party's dependence on the relationships; where "dependence of Actor A upon Actor B is (1) directly proportional to A's motivational investment in goals mediated by B and (2) inversely proportional to the availability of these goals to A outside the A-B relationship (Emerson, 1962)." El-Ansary (1975) later expanded and formalized the functional relationship between power and dependence as it pertains to IORs as follows:

Power: $P_{ij} = f(D_{ji})$
Dependence: $D_{ji} = f(G_{ij}, M_{ji}, A_{ji}, C_{ji})$

Where:

P_{ij} = power of *i* over *j*;
D_{ji} = dependence of *j* on *i*;
G_{ij} = goals mediated by *i* to *j*;
M_{ji} = motivational investment of *j* in goals mediated by *i*;
A_{ji} = alternatives available to *j* to substitute for *i*;
C_{ji} = cost to *j* of discontinuing relation with *i*.

While there are some other conceptualizations of power (e.g., Etgar, 1978; French and Raven, 1959), in this research we use El-Ansary's (1975) conceptualization of power as a function of dependence. We do so for a number of reasons. First, past interorganizational IS literature using the pluralist view of power (e.g., Hart and Saunders, 1997, 1998; Iacovou, Benbasat, and Dexter, 1995; Premkumar and Ramamurthy, 1995; Reekers and Smithson, 1996; Remus, 1986) has conceptualized power as a function of dependence. Further, the more one party is dependent on the other party in a relationship, the more the first party will be subject to the influence of the various powers exhibited and exercised by the second party (such as those exercised through rewards and coercion). This view is quite consistent with Emerson's (1962) conceptualization that the degree of a party's power in a relationship is a function of the other party's dependence on the relationship. Finally, in many cases in both the traditional and newer forms of IT outsourcing, such as the ASP model, a client's power over a service provider generally results from the service provider's dependence on the relationship with the client. This latter item is discussed next.

Based on El-Ansary's (1975) conceptualization, the dependence of a service provider on a client is theorized to be a function of the goals mediated by the client (G_{ij}), motivational investment of the service provider toward those goals (M_{ji}), availability of alternative clients (A_{ji}), and the costs associated with terminating the relationship (C_{ji}). This conceptualization of power and dependence seems to adequately explain some well-publicized outsourcing relationships, such as those between Xerox and EDS (Applegate and Davis, 1995), Kodak-IBM-DEC (Applegate, Montealegre, and Kodak, 1991), and USAA and IBM (Lasher, Ives, and Jarvenpaa, 1991). In each case the service provider was highly dependent on the outsourcing relationship at the time of the agreement. This is because each of these contractual relationships was substantial and made up a significant proportion of the service provider's IT outsourcing business. Further, these relationships involved the initial commitment of substantial capital and human and technical resources on the part of the service providers. In addition, at that time there were very few large businesses looking to outsource their IT departments, and these service providers needed big-name partners not only to promote but also to provide legitimacy to the then-fledgling IT outsourcing phenomenon. Finally, termination costs were very high at the onset of the relationships since service providers needed several years to see a return on their investments. Similar arguments for service provider dependence can also be made with respect to new forms of outsourcing such as ASPs. ASPs suffer from a very competitive environment with switching costs that are lower than those for traditional outsourcing; initial investments in technology and licensing are large and are recouped gradually over time through application lease agreements; and motivating client firms to adopt and continue to use this new and somewhat unproven outsourcing model has been difficult. Therefore, dependence represents an appropriate measure of a client's power in both traditional and new forms of IT outsourcing.

Social exchange theorists (Dwyer, Schurr, and Oh, 1987; Heide, 1994; Morgan and Hunt, 1994) have used power, conceptualized by dependence, as a means of explaining motivational forces for sustaining IORs. Their arguments for why parties choose to remain in IORs are grounded in economic theory. In this view, parties are committed to relationships that generate economic value or prevent economic losses (e.g., the cost of dissolving the relationship or of replacing the client). Others who have investigated the effect of asset specificity (one source of dependence) on industrial alliance from a transaction cost theory perspective have found empirical support for the concept that increased relationship-specific investments lead to increased levels of commitment in the relationship (Heide and John, 1990). Thus, the more dependent a service provider perceives itself to be in an outsourcing relationship, the more committed the service provider is expected to be to that relationship. Therefore, we hypothesize:

H_1: A service provider's perception of a client's power over the provider in terms of the provider's dependence on the client in an outsourcing relationship has a positive effect on the service provider's commitment to that particular relationship.

Partnership Quality

Drawing on the work of Grover, Cheon, and Teng (1996), partnership quality is defined in this study as consisting of four dimensions: trust, satisfaction, communication, and cooperation. A conscious effort was made to use a definition of partnership quality that did not imply any economic constructs, since profit motives of a service provider often run counter to the service desires of a client (Lacity, Willcocks, and Feeny, 1995). This definition of partnership quality is congruent with the concepts of relationship quality (Crosby, Evans, and Cowles, 1990) and relational norms (Macneil, 1978a, 1978b) in the IOR literature and does not include economic constructs.

The importance of partnership quality in IT outsourcing is predominantly based on Macneil's relational exchange theory (Macneil, 1978a, 1978b), which is founded on the notion that contracts alone are not enough for effectively managing the complexity inherent in IORs. It has been argued that the quality of the relationship between IT service providers and clients significantly impacts the success of IT outsourcing engagements (McFarlan and Nolan, 1995). According to McFarlan and Nolan (1995), if there is mutual interest in the relationship and if there are shared approaches to problem solving, IT outsourcing engagements have a greater chance of achieving their objectives. As IT outsourcing relationships become more complex and vendors take on ever-increasing portions of clients' IT infrastructures involving a high degree of strategic impact on clients' businesses, partnership-style relationships have become necessary to manage the outsourcing relationships effectively to achieve engagement goals (Kishore et al., 2003). In partnerships, parties develop an understanding of each others' organizational processes and engage in complementary activities to achieve mutual goals (Skinner, Gassenheimer, and Kelly, 1992). By working together they acquire much deeper knowledge about each others' unique needs and problems, and this may lead to relinquishing some control and forfeiting individual gains in favor of mutually compatible objectives (Goles and Chin, 2002). This leads to the development of trust in the relationship, instills confidence in the exchange partner's abilities, provides a feeling of security, and alleviates fears that the exchange partner will act opportunistically (Kim, 2000). Therefore, when the partnership quality in an outsourcing relationship is high, parties are more likely to be willing to make a commitment to the relationship because of the increased benefits to them and a decrease in behavioral uncertainty from the other party on account of opportunism. Thus, we hypothesize that:

H_2: A service provider's perception of partnership quality in an outsourcing relationship has a positive effect on the service provider's commitment to that particular relationship.

Alternate Model of Commitment

The research model discussed above treated commitment as a second-order construct comprised of three dimensions based on the work of Kumar, Scheer, and Steenkamp (1995). However, Gundlach, Achrol, and Mentzer (1995) provided some theoretical reasoning and empirical evidence of causal and temporal relationships among the three dimensions of commitment and referred to the influence of these dimensions on each other as a "self-enforcing cycle." Therefore we propose an alternate model, shown in Figure 11.2, in which the three dimensions of commitment are treated as three

Figure 11.3 **Commitment Cycle: Development of Long-term Relationships**

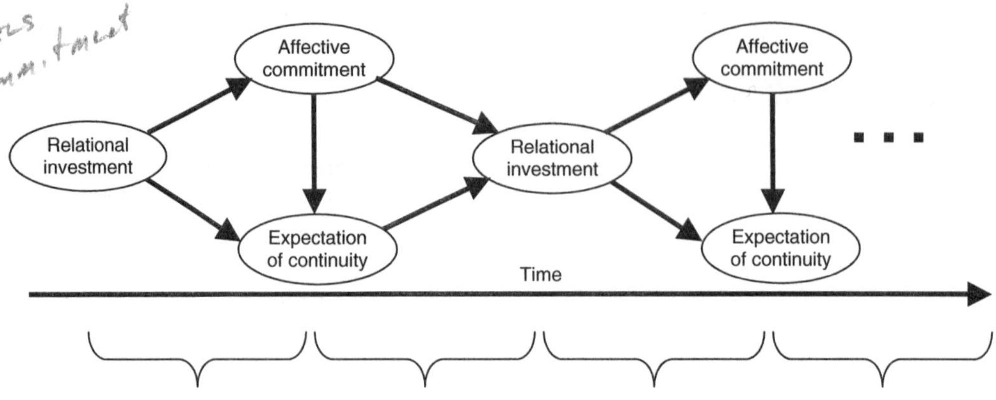

independent constructs. While there is little known about the individual impacts of partnership and power on the three dimensions of commitment, we propose a causal model based in part on the work by Gundlach, Achrol, and Mentzer (1995). Figure 11.3 shows a "self-enforcing cycle" between individual dimensions of commitment; it portrays two repeating phases, an economic phase, involving the investment of resources, and a relational phase, in which parties develop attitudes and expectations about the future of their relationship. A discussion of this figure will provide the basis for hypotheses 1 to 3 in our alternate model. As shown in Figure 11.3, long-term relationships start with parties making credible investments (Gundlach, Achrol, and Mentzer, 1995); this is consistent with the recent TCE view that idiosyncratic inputs by both parties lead to long-term relationships (Bensaou and Anderson, 1999; Williamson, 1988). In the context of IT outsourcing, such inputs may include dedicated technology resources, personnel, and stock options in the other organization. These inputs represent a vested interest in the relationship and perpetuate a belief that parties want to become more deeply involved with each other (Kumar, Scheer, and Steenkamp, 1995). Economic commitments are similar to a signaling mechanism, demonstrating to the other party that the relationship is valuable. These economic commitments help generate a sense of security as well as a sense of worth with respect to the relationship, thus enhancing the affective commitment of the parties. Such investments, especially if very specific to the outsourcing relationship, also create high switching costs and result in a greater desire to maintain and continue the relationship into the future (Heide and John, 1990). Gundlach, Achrol, and Mentzer (1995) provided empirical evidence that the commitment of credible inputs positively relates to long-term commitment intentions.

After credible investments in a relationship are made, a transition from the economic phase to the relational phase begins. In the economic phase, dedicated resources influence increased commitment; in the relational phase, both affective commitment and expectations of continuity begin their impact on increasing commitment levels. In service relationships, including ASP outsourcing, it is often more cost effective for the service provider to maintain current customers as opposed to continually acquiring and developing new ones, especially if the current services are satisfying their clients' needs. Having made credible investments in a relationship, the service provider now feels committed to the relationship, that is, the provider's affective commitment toward the relationship increases. These positive attitudes about the relationship further increase the provider's willingness to make additional investments in the relationship. A positive view of the relationship may make investments seem less risky and/or increase the perception that such investments will be adequately compensated by the other party. Additional investments in the relationship may also happen if the service provider believes the relationship will last long enough for sufficient returns to be realized. Thus, providers are more likely to invest in a relationship when they believe a relationship will continue into the future. Gundlach, Achrol, and Mentzer (1995) also provided some empirical support for these relationships among the three dimensions of commitment.

We model only the relational, and not the economic, phase of commitment in this research, as shown in Figure 11.2. We do this for several reasons. First, this study is focused on the social factors (power and partnership) impacting an IT service provider's commitment to an outsourcing relationship, making the relational phase of commitment more germane to this research. Second, the setting of this research is the ASP outsourcing model. The economic cycle of commitment in terms of credible investments by the ASP service providers has already taken place as the ASP model requires substantial up-front client-neutral investments by ASP service providers before they enter into any specific client contracts. Finally, this is not a longitudinal study, and thus Gundlach, Achrol, and Mentzer's complete self-enforcing cycle cannot be modeled here. Therefore we hypothesize that:

H_{1A}: A service provider's expectation about continuing an outsourcing relationship will have a positive effect on the service provider's willingness to invest further in that particular relationship.

H_{2A}: A service provider's affective commitment to an outsourcing relationship will have a positive effect on the service provider's willingness to invest further in that particular relationship.

H_{3A}: A service provider's affective commitment to an outsourcing relationship will have a positive effect on the service provider's expectation of continuity of that particular relationship.

As stated previously in the section on power as a function of dependence, parties are committed to IORs that generate economic value or prevent economic losses. This reasoning is well grounded in economic and power theories that posit that the more dependent one party is on another party, the higher the commitment of the former party will be to the relationship. As also discussed earlier, the power of a client over a vendor is conceptualized in this research as the dependence of the vendor on the client. Vendor dependence on the client is similar to the notion of relational investments in Gundlach, Achrol, and Mentzer's conceptualization (shown in Figure 11.3) in terms of the fact that one source of vendor dependence is the investments made by the vendor in the particular client relationship. However, there is a major difference between the notions of vendor dependence and relational investments. The notion of relational investments includes investments made by both a client and a vendor in the relationship. Thus, while relational investments are shown to impact both affective commitment and expectations of continuity in Gundlach, Achrol, and Mentzer's self-enforcing cycle shown in Figure 11.3, we expect client power over a vendor as a function of vendor dependence on the client to impact only the vendor's expectation of continuity but not its affective commitment. Arguably, a vendor's affective commitment toward the relationship with a client will increase with the client's increased investments in the relationship. Therefore, we hypothesize that:

H_{4A}: A service provider's perception of a client's power over the provider in terms of the provider's dependence on the client in an outsourcing relationship has a positive effect on the service provider's expectation of continuity of that particular relationship.

As mentioned before, past IS outsourcing research has examined the role of partnership quality on a client's perceptions but has not examined its influence from the service provider's viewpoint. As was also mentioned before, the previous literature is silent about the potential impact of partnership quality on the individual dimensions of the larger commitment construct. However, as we discussed in the section on partnership quality, partnership quality consists of trust, satisfaction, communication, and cooperation constructs, and these constructs have substantial affective aspects. Therefore, we expect partnership quality to have a direct impact on the affective commitment of the vendor, and the impact of partnership quality on the other two commitment constructs—expectation of continuity and willingness to invest—is expected to be mediated by the affective commitment construct through the mechanisms of Gundlach, Achrol, and Mentzer's self-enforcing cycle. Therefore, we hypothesize that:

> H_{5A}: A service provider's perception of partnership quality in an outsourcing relationship has a positive effect on the service provider's affective commitment to that relationship.

RESEARCH METHODOLOGY

We chose the research methodology for this research carefully, considering the state of knowledge in the field pertaining to this research and the goals of this particular study. As discussed in earlier sections, power, partnership, and commitment are well-developed and well-established constructs in the area of IOR and IT outsourcing literatures. However, the impact of power and partnership on vendor commitment has not been tested in prior research, particularly in the context of the highly contract-oriented ASP outsourcing paradigm. Therefore, the state of knowledge pertaining to these constructs and their relationships in this research can be best characterized as moderate. Further, the goal of this research is to establish the comparative influence of the two influence sources—one a unilateral source (power) and the other a bilateral source (partnership)—on vendor commitment. This goal can be characterized as theory testing rather than theory building.

McGrath's (1979) five-stage "theory of method" provides an excellent contingency framework for choosing appropriate research methods, dependent upon the state of knowledge and research goals. McGrath suggests using field studies for exploratory theory-building efforts in the earlier stages of the knowledge cycle and then for cross-validation of developed theories in real-life settings in the later stages of the knowledge cycle. He suggests using laboratory experiments for precise testing of key hypotheses during the intermediate stages of the knowledge cycle. Bonoma (1985) also provides a contingency model for choosing research methods and discusses the tradeoff between currency and integrity. Currency is more relevant in the context of exploratory theory-building studies whereas the integrity afforded by laboratory experiments, simulations, and models is more relevant when the goal is explanation and theory testing. Therefore, the laboratory experiment appears to be an appropriate choice for the current study, insfoar as the state of knowledge pertinent to the constructs and relationships of this research is somewhere in the middle of the knowledge continuum and our goal in this study is theory testing to assess the comparative impact of the two influence sources on vendor commitment.

Further, the experimental research methodology has been used frequently in past IS research dealing with decision making at the organizational and project levels of analysis, particularly in the context of IS project management and IS implementation research (e.g., Harrison and Harrell, 1993; Keil et al., 1994–95, 2000b, 2004; Smith, Keil, and Depledge, 2001; Tan et al., 2003). In addition, published studies in other management disciplines (Andaleeb, 1995,

1996; Gundlach and Cadotte, 1994) have used experimental methodology to test theoretical models involving similar relational and/or power constructs in the context of IOR. Therefore, we tested the hypothesized causal relationships in our proposed theoretical models (see Figures 11.1 and 11.2) using a controlled laboratory experiment. The experiment we conducted used a 2 × 2 factorial design in which the degree of partnership quality (strong/weak) and the level of dependence (high/low) were independently manipulated. We discuss the experimental design in detail in the following section.

Experimental Design

The experimental design involved a role-play exercise by subjects as client account mangers for an ASP company. Subjects were asked to read a brief scenario, similar to a mini-case, about a contractual service relationship between the ASP vendor and an individual client company. The same background information about the ASP–client relationship, such as the services contracted, the service-level agreements (SLAs), and the length of the contract were provided to each participant. Four treatments were created by manipulating the degree of partnership (strong/weak) and level of dependence (high/low). Partnership was manipulated by a letter given to the subjects in which they were told they had already written to the ASP's vice president of contract management. A similar approach was used by Andaleeb (1995, 1996), Schurr and Ozanne (1985), and Sullivan and Peterson (1982) to manipulate trust in the context of IOR. Based on the four dimensions of partnership relevant to outsourcing practices as defined by Grover, Cheon, and Teng (1996), the letter described the levels of communication, trust, cooperation, and satisfaction with the client. The four dimensions were portrayed favorably under the strong partnership treatment and unfavorably under the weak partnership treatment. The dependence manipulation was derived from El-Ansary's (1975) functional definition of power and dependence. The high dependence treatment was represented by stating that few potential clients exist in the current market segment; revenues from services provided to this particular client substantially contributed to the ASP's profits; a large portion of the ASP's manpower and equipment had been solely allocated to fulfilling this particular client's needs and it would be very difficult and costly for the ASP to reallocate these resources to other customers. For the low dependence treatment the statements were reversed. Based on the recommendations of Dennis and Valacich (2001), treatment levels were sufficiently differentiated in order to maximize effects. The case scenario template and the treatments are provided in the appendix.

Refinement of the case scenario was done in two stages. First, a group of seven management information systems (MIS) faculty and four MIS Ph.D. students, most of whom either had prior experience in managing IT outsourcing relationships or had worked for IT consulting firms or were currently doing research in the IT outsourcing area, evaluated the experimental material and provided feedback. After revising the experimental material based on their suggestions, a group of nineteen MBA and forty-four upper-level undergraduate students enrolled in MIS courses were selected for pretesting the experimental material and protocols. This pretest resulted in no changes in the experimental material and only minor adjustments to the experimental protocol.

Subjects

A total of 140 MBA and upper-level undergraduate students at a large state university in the northeastern United States were recruited as subjects for the actual experimental study; 48 were

Table 11.1

Sample Characteristics

Frequencies	All	Graduate	Undergraduate
Students	110	45	65
Males (Females)	83 (27)	34 (11)	49 (16)

Descriptive	Mean	Std. deviation	Mean	Std. deviation.	Mean	Std. deviation	Significance
Information technology (IT) work experience (months)	24.64	33.71	41.22	42.51	13.17	19.16	Yes
General management experience (months)	19.13	22.16	23.78	26.19	15.92	18.41	No
IT management experience (months)	8.11	20.39	14.33	29.07	3.82	9.00	Yes
GPA	3.37	0.39	3.63	0.21	3.24	0.40	Yes
Age	24.54	4.71	27.22	4.88	22.66	3.56	Yes

graduate students taking an MBA-level MIS course and 92 were undergraduate students taking a senior-level MIS course. The subject pool was familiar with the particular issues surrounding ASP outsourcing since it was an area recently covered in their MIS coursework. Of the 140 potential subjects, one declined to participate, and 29 were removed from the initial data set because they had no professional experience in information technology, general management, or information technology management. It was felt that subjects should have at least some relevant work experience in order to adequately assume the role of decision maker in the experiment. A total of 110 cases (45 graduate and 65 undergraduate) comprised the final data set, about which Table 11.1 provides demographic information.

There is some debate in the literature about the use of students as surrogates for managers. However, Remus (1986) provided empirical support for the use of students as surrogates in the context of managerial decision making. In addition, there are a number of precedents for using student subjects, both graduate and undergraduate, for high-level managerial decision-making tasks in organizational research, such as those dealing with business risk (Sitkin and Weingart, 1995), project management (Harrison and Harrell, 1993) including software projects (Keil et al., 1994–95, 2000a, 2000b, 2004; Keil, Mixon, and Truex, 1995; Smith, Keil, and Depledge, 2001; Tan et al., 2003); new product development (Schmidt, Montoya-Weiss, and Massey, 2001); and manufacturer and distributor exchange relationships (Andaleeb, 1995, 1996; Gundlach and Cadotte, 1994), including IT exchange channels (Gundlach, Achrol, and Mentzer, 1995). In these studies, student subjects have been asked to make organizational investment decisions in relation to corporate projects, software projects, new product development, manufacturer and distributor exchange relationships, including those in the IT domain. Further, to make these decisions students assumed the roles of company presidents (Keil, Mixon, and Truex, 1995; Keil et al., 2000b), upper-level managers (Gundlach, Achrol, and Mentzer, 1995; Gundlach and Cadotte, 1994), new product development managers (Schmidt, Montoya-Weiss, and Massey, 2001), system development project managers

(Keil et al., 2004), project managers (Harrison and Harrell, 1993), software project leaders (Tan et al., 2003), and lead systems analysts (Smith, Keil, and Depledge, 2001).

The experimental task in the present study does not involve executive decision making. Rather, it involves providing middle managerial level (client account manger) recommendations to executive management about workforce and technological investments needed to serve individual clients. The experimental scenario and the recommendation task are quite realistic from the viewpoint of the student subjects who have learned about the issues involved in ASP outsourcing in their programs and who may be expected upon graduation to perform duties similar to the recommendation task involved in the experiment. Therefore, student subjects are expected to act as effective surrogates for client account managers in this experimental research.

Decision Situation

As noted before, subjects were asked to imagine themselves in the role of the client account manger for the ASP company described in the scenario. The role of a client account manger was chosen in this research, as opposed to that of a chief information officer or chief executive officer, because a client account manager is expected to possess much better and direct information about the various study constructs. Further, as discussed above, student subjects are also expected to better relate to this position level and therefore to more easily project themselves into the experimental role. Subjects were told that in two weeks top executives of the ASP would meet to discuss plans for future workforce and technological investments needed to service current and future customers; and that their boss has asked them to write a report describing how best to service their individual clients. In order to efficiently measure and capture all independent and dependent variables in our research model, subjects were provided a list of items (measures) corresponding to each construct. They were told that the items were a series of possible recommendations on how to manage the client relationship, and they were asked to indicate the extent to which they agree or disagree with each recommendation.

Constructs and Measures

A conscious effort was made to adapt established and validated measures for the research constructs so as to facilitate comparison, replication, generalization, and validation. Measures were needed to (1) check whether treatment manipulations pertaining to the two independent constructs were properly administered and (2) capture all of the endogenous constructs. The individual items and their sources for each construct are provided in Tables 11.2 and 11.3. All items were measured using a seven-point Likert scale ranging from "strongly disagree" (1) to "strongly agree" (7).

Procedures

The subjects were randomly assigned to one of the four treatment groups: (1) strong partnership and high vendor dependence (i.e., high client power); (2) strong partnership and low vendor dependence (i.e., low client power); (3) weak partnership and high vendor dependence (i.e., high client power); and (4) weak partnership and low vendor dependence (i.e., low client power). Subjects were told before actually conducting the experiment that the case scenarios were developed using information from actual published ASP and IT outsourcing cases in order to simulate an actual situation an ASP may face. This was done to induce the feeling that the experimental conditions represented a real-world scenario. While the instructors who made their classes available for the

Table 11.2

Construct Measurement Items for Manipulation Checks

Constructs and source		Item code	Mean	Std. deviation	Item
Power (Dependence)-MPD (Heide, 1994)		MPD1	4.26	1.95	If your company decided to stop supplying application services to SouthBank, you could easily replace their profit contribution with application service supplied to other customers. (reverse scored)
		MPD2	4.75	1.86	If the relationship with SouthBank were terminated, it would not hurt our operations. (reverse scored)
		MPD3	4.28	1.78	Finding new buyers for the application services currently supplied to SouthBank would not have a negative impact on our costs. (reverse scored)
		MPD4	4.07	1.87	It would be relatively easy for us to find other buyers for the application services currently supplied to SouthBank. (reverse scored)
Partnership	Trust-MTR (Zaheer, McEvily, and Perrone,1998)	MTR1	4.09	1.64	SouthBank has always been even handed in its negotiations with us.
		MTR2	3.54	1.84	SouthBank may use opportunities that arise to profit at our expense. (reverse scored)
		MTR3	3.99	1.83	Based on past experience, we cannot with complete confidence rely on SouthBank to keep its promises. (reverse scored)
		MTR4*	3.24	1.60	We would be hesitant to conduct transactions with SouthBank when the specifications are vague. (reverse scored)
		MTR5	4.23	1.72	SouthBank is trustworthy.
	Satisfaction-MSF (Andaleeb, 1996)	MSF1	3.96	2.22	The relationship between our company and SouthBank does not seem to reflect a happy situation. (reverse scored)
		MSF2	4.09	1.97	The relationship between our company and SouthBank is very positive.
		MSF3	4.02	1.97	We are very satisfied with SouthBank.
	Communication-MCC (Morgan, 1994)	MCC1	4.07	1.59	SouthBank keeps us informed of new developments.
		MCC2	3.83	1.59	SouthBank provides us with frequent positive feedback on our performance.
		MCC3	4.35	1.71	SouthBank offers us very poor recognition programs. (reverse scored)
		MCC4	4.28	1.94	SouthBank communicates well their expectations for our company's service performance.
	Cooperation-MCO (Andaleeb, 1996 #58)	MC01	4.09	1.77	SouthBank collaborates with us in developing application services.
		MC02	4.21	1.74	SouthBank endeavors to work with us as a team.
		MC03	4.14	1.94	SouthBank has built and maintained a harmonious relationship with us.
		MC04	4.20	2.11	SouthBank does not cooperate with us. (reverse scored)

*Items dropped because of poor factor loading.

Table 11.3

Construct Measurement Items for Partial Least Squares Model

Constructs and source		Item code	Mean	Std. deviation.	Item
Commitment	Affective commitment-DCA (Kumar et al., 1995)	DCA1	4.11	1.78	Even if we could, our organization should not drop SouthBank as a customer because we like being associated with them.
		DCA2	3.95	1.85	We should remain a service provider to SouthBank because we genuinely enjoy our relationship with them.
		DCA3[a]	4.22	2.04	Our positive feelings toward SouthBank are a major reason we should continue working with them.
	Expectation of continuity-DCE (Kumar et al., 1995)	DCE1[a]	4.63	1.57	Our relationship with SouthBank should continue for a long time.
		DCE2	3.80	1.64	The renewal of our contractual relationship with SouthBank should be virtually automatic.
		DCE3	4.93	1.68	Our firm should not be doing business with SouthBank in the near future. (reverse scored)
	Willingness to invest-DCW (Kumar et al., 1995)	DCW1	4.52	1.32	If SouthBank requested it, we should be willing to make further investment to support their needs.
		DCW2	4.75	1.49	We should be willing to put more effort and investment into building our business with SouthBank.
		DCW3[b]	4.15	1.63	In the future we should work to link our firm with SouthBank.

[a]Items dropped to maintain an equal number of items in each of the first-order constructs for partnership. Modeling of second-order molecular constructs requires that all first-order constructs have the same number of items (Chin, 1995; Chin et al., 1996).

[b]Items dropped because of poor convergent and discriminant validity.

experiment had the option to offer their students extra credit for participating, no such rewards were offered and no other incentives were mentioned or given by anyone involved in conducting the experiment. Subjects were also informed that there were no right or wrong answers and participation was completely voluntary. All participants were required to sign a consent form before participating and after completing the experiment all participants were debriefed about the motivation and possible contributions of the research.

RESULTS

The research model was assessed using the partial least squares (PLS) technique and the PLS Graph Software Version 03.00 Build 1126. PLS is a component-oriented structural equation modeling technique (Chin, 1998a, 1998b; Gefen, Straub, and Boudreau, 2000; Lohmoller, 1989). It was selected for this research because it allows for modeling of second-order factors (Chin and Gopal, 1995; Chin, Marcolin, and Newsted, 1996), places minimal demands on sample sizes (Chin and Newsted, 1999; Gefen, Straub, and Boudreau, 2000), and is well suited for both exploratory and confirmatory research (Chin, 1998a, 1998b; Gefen, Straub, and Boudreau, 2000).

Table 11.4

Factor Analysis of Manipulation Checks

	Component		
Variable	1	2	3
MTR1	0.818	–0.018	–0.192
MTR2	0.636	0.004	0.508
MTR3	0.565	0.112	0.347
MTR4	0.302	0.230	0.375
MTR5	0.869	0.084	–0.160
MC01	0.728	–0.152	–0.271
MC02	0.869	0.013	–0.050
MC03	0.898	0.051	–0.064
MC04	0.785	–0.099	0.190
MSF1	0.815	0.054	0.310
MSF2	0.820	–0.125	–0.221
MSF3	0.926	0.018	–0.095
MCC1	0.749	–0.061	–0.320
MCC2	0.778	–0.172	–0.183
MCC3	0.619	0.088	0.439
MCC4	0.771	–0.151	–0.042
MPD1	0.106	0.826	–0.164
MPD2	0.033	0.819	–0.053
MPD3	0.113	0.777	–0.053
MPD4	0.022	0.860	–0.063

The results presented in the following sections are based on the final set of measurement items as indicated in Tables 11.2 and 11.3. Notes associated with the tables explain the reasoning for dropping selected items from further analysis. The tables also display the descriptive statistics for each item grouped by construct. Before addressing the reliability and validity process for the research model, the manipulation checks are examined.

Manipulation Checks

Following established procedures in the literature (e.g., Sitkin and Weingart, 1995; e.g., Smith, Keil, and Depledge, 2001), manipulation checks were conducted to ensure that the experimental treatments were successfully administered. This was done by comparing the treatment level for a particular construct with the average score for that construct measured through its individual items shown in Table 11.2. For example, the group of students who were administered a strong partnership treatment should report their instrument's high agreement with items pertaining to the partnership construct. High partnership scores on the individual items from this group would indicate that the strong partnership manipulation was successfully administered.

To perform these comparisons, or manipulation checks, we first factor analyzed the four items for the power construct and the sixteen items for the partnership construct (see Table 11.4). Three component factors were extracted with all but one item for the partnership constructs (MTR4) loading higher on the first factor and all the items for the power construct loading higher on the second measure. We dropped MTR4 from further analysis due to low loading on the partnership factor. Individual items for the four partnership subconstructs were averaged to produce single

Table 11.5

Manipulation Checks

Partnership		Low Power		High Power	
Strong	*N* = 27		*Mean*	*N* = 27	*Mean*
	Partnership		4.67	Partnership	4.85
	Power		3.84	Power	5.01
Weak	*N* = 27		*Mean*	*N* = 27	*Mean*
	Partnership		2.74	Partnership	2.69
	Power		3.77	Power	4.64
		Low	**Power**	**High**	

Note: Means are based on the final set of items for the power and partnership constructs; see Table 11.2.

partnership subconstruct scores. The four partnership subconstruct scores were further averaged to produce a single composite score for the partnership construct. The composite score for the power construct was similarly calculated by averaging the four items of the power construct.

Next, the group means for the four experimental treatment groups were calculated for the power and partnership constructs using their respective composite scores. These group means are shown in Table 11.5 in appropriate treatment cells. As Table 11.5 shows, the composite score for the power construct is larger (smaller) under the high (low) treatment level of power and the composite score for the partnership construct is larger (smaller) under the strong (weak) partnership treatment level. This indicates that the treatments were successfully administered.

To further verify the effectiveness of the treatments and to investigate any interactions, a 2 × 2 Type III MONOVA was run using the experimental treatments as the independent variables and the composite scores were calculated as described above for these variables as the dependent variables. The results of this MANOVA are given in Table 11.6. Again, as expected, the main effects for power and partnership are significant only for their respective composite scores. In addition, the interaction effect between the two manipulations was not found to be significant for either the power or the partnership composite scores, indicating the absence of any interaction between the two treatments. Based on the information presented in both Table 11.5 and Table 11.6, it is concluded that the manipulations (treatments) administered in the experiment were quite effective.

Measurement Model

The individual items for the partnership and power constructs shown in Table 11.2 were used only to assess the effectiveness of the four treatments[1] administered in this study. These items were not used any further to assess the impact of power and partnership on vendor commitment. The actual experimental treatment levels for the power (high and low) and partnership (strong and weak) were used as the values for the two independent variables for hypotheses testing in this research. Low and high power were coded as 0 and 1, respectively. Similarly, weak and strong partnership were coded as 0 and 1, respectively.

By using actual experimental treatments for the two independent variables instead of subject responses on items pertaining to these two independent variables, we eliminated any concerns about common method bias in this study. Common method bias generally occurs in survey/experimental data collection when respondents are asked to provide responses both to independent

Table 11.6

Results of the 2 × 2 Type III MANOVA

Independent variable	Dependent variable	Type III sum of squares	F-value	Significance
Intercept	Partnership	1,537.652	776.963	0.000
	Power	2,046.509	4,231.185	0.000
Main effect: Partnership manipulation	Partnership	115.905	58.464	0.000
	Power	1.370	2.833	0.095
Main effect: Power manipulation	Partnership	0.137	0.069	0.793
	Power	28.438	58.796	0.000
Interaction effect: Partnership × Power	Partnership	0.355	0.180	0.673
	Power	0.594	1.228	0.270

Notes: A Type III MANOVA was run because of the uneven number of observations in the manipulation cells (see Figure 11.4).

Means are based on the final set of items for the partnership and power constructs (see Table 11.2).

Table 11.7

Item Weights and Loadings

Construct	Item	Weight	Loading
Willingness to invest (DCW)	DCW1	0.55	0.89
	DCW2	0.57	0.91
Expectation of continuity (DCE)	DCE2	0.57	0.81
	DCE3	0.63	0.85
Affective commitment (DCA)	DCA2	0.54	0.95
	DCA3	0.52	0.94

and dependent variables on the same instrument. The concern is that respondents somehow see the relationship between independent and dependent variables and this colors their responses. We used actual experimental treatment levels as independent variable values. These were under the control of the researcher and were completely independent of subjects' responses on the items pertaining to the dependent variable. Thus, this study does not suffer from common method bias.

Because we used treatment levels for independent variables in the PLS model in this study, we performed the reliability and validity assessments only for the three subconstructs of the dependent variable. We assessed item reliability, convergent validity, and discriminant validity of the three constructs following procedures described in the literature (Chin, 1998b; Gefen, Straub, and Boudreau, 2000; Hulland, 1999). An item demonstrates good reliability if it has a loading greater than 0.70 on its respective construct (Chin, 1998b; Fornell and Larcker, 1981; Hulland, 1999). As Table 11.7 shows, loadings for all items are above the 0.70 threshold, and range from 0.84 to 0.95, thus demonstrating good item reliability for the three constructs. The convergent validity or internal consistency of the constructs was assessed using Fornell and Larcker's (1981) internal consistency measure. This measure is similar to Cronbach's alpha but without the assumption that all indicators are equally weighted (Chin, 1998b). Data in Table 11.8 show that composite reliabilities for the three dimensions of the commitment construct are above the 0.70 threshold limit, with the lowest being 0.82 for expectation of continuity (DCE). The discriminant validity was assessed using two methods. First, the average variance extracted (AVE) score for each construct

Table 11.8

Composite Reliabilities, Average Variance Extracted (AVE), and Interconstruct Correlations

Construct	Composite reliability	No. of items	DCW	DCE	DCA
Willingness to invest (DCW)	0.89	2	**0.90**		
Expectation of continuity (DCE)	0.82	2	0.45	**0.83**	
Affective commitment (DCA)	0.94	2	0.52	0.56	**0.94**

Notes: Diagonal elements in bold type are the square root of AVE, which should be larger than interconstruct correlations in the off-diagonal cells for discriminant validity. Fornell and Larcker's internal consistency measure shown in the composite reliability column is a measure for convergent validity and should usually be higher than 0.70. Signs for interconstruct correlations have been changed appropriately to account for negative signs for partial least squares weights. Composite reliability column is a measure for convergent validity and should usually be higher than 0.70. Negative signs for weights and loadings have been changed appropriately to aid interpretation and to be consistent with actual partial least squares outputs.

Table 11.9

Item Construct Loadings and Cross-Loadings

	Willingness to invest	Expectation of continuity	Affective commitment
DCW1	**0.90**	0.37	0.47
DCW2	**0.91**	0.44	0.47
DCE2	0.32	**0.81**	0.46
DCE3	0.42	**0.85**	0.47
DCA2	0.54	0.54	**0.95**
DCA3	0.44	0.52	**0.94**

Notes: Bold values are the self-loadings (loadings of items on their own construct) while other cells contain cross-loadings (loadings of items on constructs other than their own). Self-loadings should be higher than cross-loadings for convergent and discriminant validity. Signs for loadings and cross loadings have been changed appropriately to account for negative signs for partial least squares weights.

was calculated and compared with the minimal acceptable limit of 0.50. For each construct, the square root of the average variance extracted was compared to the correlations of the construct with all other constructs (Fornell and Larcker, 1981). Second, we also examined the loading and cross-loading of each item on different constructs. For good discriminant validity, items should load higher on their respective constructs than on other constructs. The cells in bold type along the diagonal in Table 11.8 contain the square root of the AVEs for the respective constructs and represent the variance shared between a construct and its measures. The off-diagonal cells in this table show interconstruct correlations and they represent the variance a construct shares with other constructs. As shown in Table 11.8, all AVEs are above the 0.50 minimum threshold and the square roots of all of the AVEs are greater than the respective interconstruct correlations. Table 11.9 is now used for the second test of discriminant validity. Moving across the rows in Table 11.9 and comparing the item loadings (cells in bold font) and cross-loadings (other cells), the values in the bold font cells should be and are greater than any other values in the row. Based on the data presented in Tables 11.8 and 11.9 all constructs demonstrate good discriminant validity. The results presented indicate that the measurement model displays good item reliability, conver-

Figure 11.4 **Partial Least Squares Results**

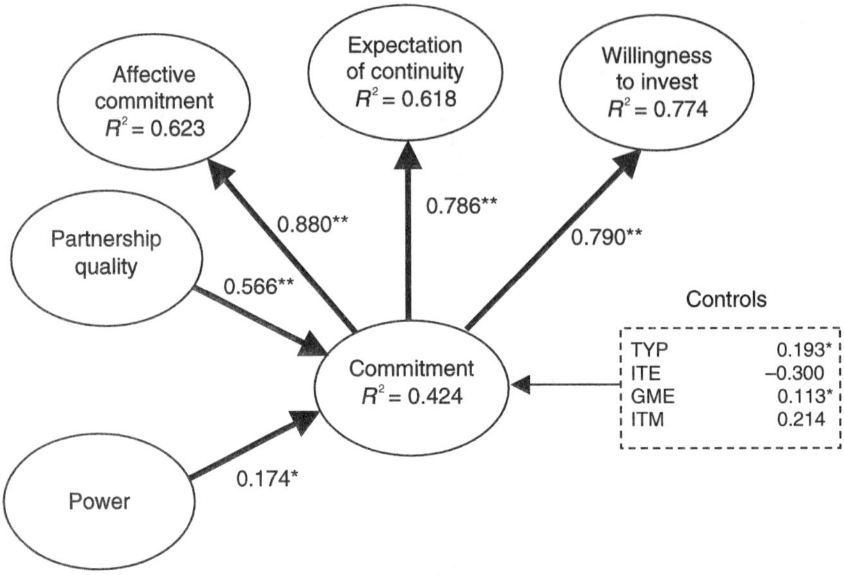

Notes: TYP— student type; ITE—IT work experience; GME—general management experience; ITM—IT management experience.

*p < 0.05

**p < 0.01

gent validity, and discriminant validity, and confirms that the three constructs associated with the multidimensional conceptualization of commitment are distinct constructs.

Hypothesis Testing

The research model was assessed using a PLS structural model following procedures suggested in the literature (Chin, 1998b; Gefen, Straub, and Boudreau, 2000; Hulland, 1999). In addition to the two independent variables, the PLS structural model also included controls for the direct effect of student type (TYP), IT work experience (ITE), general management experience (GME), and IT management experience (ITM). We examined the R^2 value for the endogenous construct, which indicates the amount of variance explained, as well as the coefficient and significance of each structural path in the model. As shown in Figure 11.4, the R^2 value for the dependent variable is sufficiently high with the model explaining 42.4 percent of the variance in the service provider's commitment.

After examining the R^2 values for the endogenous constructs, the coefficient and significance of each path were explored. Each structural path in the model corresponds to a testable hypothesis. Interpretation of the path coefficients is similar to simple regression (Chin, 1998b) with the caveat that the absolute value of the coefficients must be greater than the minimum threshold of 0.20 to eliminate the possibility of chance correlations (Chin, 1998a). In order to test the significance of each path, a bootstrapping procedure recommended in the literature was performed (Chin, 1998b, 2002) with 1,000 random subsamples. All path loadings for the three first-order constructs of the second-order molecular commitment construct were significant at the $p < 0.01$ level (see Figure

Table 11.10

Summary of Path Coefficients for Second-Order Constructs

Second-order construct	Dimensions	Path coefficient
Commitment	Willingness to invest	0.790**
	Expectation of continuity	0.786**
	Affective commitment	0.880**

Notes: The signs for path coefficients have been changed appropriately to account for negative signs for partial least squares weights used to calculate second-order construct scores.
*$p < 0.05$; **$p < 0.01$.

Table 11.11

Summary of Hypothesis Tests

Hypothesis	Path coefficient	Supported?
H_1: Power → Commitment	0.170*	Yes (weakly)
H_2: Partnership → Commitment	0.566**	Yes

Notes: The signs for path coefficients have been changed appropriately to account for negative signs for partial least squares weights.
*$p < 0.05$; **$p < 0.01$.

11.4 and Table 11.10). The path between power and commitment was significant at $p < 0.05$, but the path coefficient at 0.170 was slightly below the 0.20 threshold. The other path between partnership quality and commitment was significant at $p < 0.01$ with a path coefficient of 0.566 (see Figure 11.4 and Table 11.11). None of the control variables was found to have a significant coefficient over the minimum 0.20 threshold. Therefore, hypotheses 1 concerning the impact of client power on vendor commitment is weakly supported whereas hypothesis 2 concerning the impact of partnership quality on vendor commitment is strongly supported.

We also performed a 2 × 2 Type III ANOVA using the actual manipulations as independent variables and the composite scores for commitment, calculated by averaging the six commitment items specified in Table 11.3, as the dependent variable. Results for this ANOVA are shown in Table 11.12. As expected, the main effects of power and partnership on commitment were both significant. However, the ANOVA results also indicate that the interaction between power and partnership had a significant impact on vendor commitment. This interaction effect was not captured in our PLS model. These results indicate that while power may have a weak direct effect on vendor commitment (based on the PLS path coefficient from power to commitment), it does have a significant moderating influence on the impact of partnership quality on vendor commitment.

Alternate Model

The full alternate model shown in Figure 11.5 was tested using the same constructs and items as the PLS model described in the measurement model section. The results of PLS reliability and validation for the alternate model were very similar to those of the PLS models presented in Tables 11.7, 11.8, and 11.9. The alternate model measurement results again indicated that the measurement model displays good item reliability, convergent validity, and discriminant validity

Table 11.12

Results of the 2 × 2 Type III ANOVA of Commitment

Independent variable	Dependent variable	Type III sum of squares	*F*-value	Significance
Intercept	Commitment	2,040.249	2,130.287	0.000
Main effect: Partnership manipulation	Commitment	52.809	55.140	0.000
Main effect: Power manipulation	Commitment	4.517	4.716	0.032
Interaction effect: Partnership × Power	Commitment	7.540	7.873	0.006

Notes: A Type III MANOVA was run because of the uneven number of observations in the manipulation cells (see Table 11.5).

Means are based on the final set of six items for commitment (see Table 11.2).

and that the three subconstructs of the commitment construct are distinct. The alternate structural model PLS results are shown in Figure 11.5. As the figure shows, partnership quality significantly impacts affective commitment while power significantly impacts expectation of continuity, as hypothesized.

Further, both affective commitment and expectation of continuity are found to impact willingness to invest, which supports our conceptualization of the causal nature of the commitment construct discussed earlier. A modified alternate PLS model was also tested with paths to each commitment construct from both power and partnership quality constructs. The additional paths from the power and partnership quality constructs were not above the 0.20 coefficient threshold and were not significant. A 2 × 2 Type III MANOVA was also run using the actual manipulations as independent variables and the composite scores for the three commitment constructs, constructed by averaging the individual items for the three dimensions, as discussed in the manipulation checks section, as dependent variables. Results of this MANOVA analysis are given in Table 11.13. The main effects of partnership on each dimension of commitment were found to be significant. The main effect of power and the interaction effect of power and partnership were found to be significant only for the expectation of continuity construct. A discussion of all of the above results follows.

DISCUSSION

The goal of the research presented in this chapter was to perform a head-to-head comparison of the relative influence of a client's power conceptualized as provider dependence on the client and the quality of the client–provider partnership on service provider commitment to the ASP outsourcing relationship. The results presented provide good empirical support for the theoretical propositions, with the main PLS model explaining a significant amount of the variance in the service provider's commitment. Further, the coefficient for the path from power on commitment (H_1), while statistically significant, is rather low at 0.174 in the main model tested in this research with commitment as a second-order construct (see Figure 11.4). However, the coefficient for the path from power to expectation of continuity (which is one of the three dimensions of commitment) (H_{4A}) is greater at 0.231 and statistically significant in the alternate model in which the three dimensions of commitment are modeled as first-order constructs with an underlying causal structure. The coefficient for the path from the partnership quality construct to commitment (H_2) is quite high at 0.566 in

Figure 11.5 **Alternate Model Partial Least Squares Results**

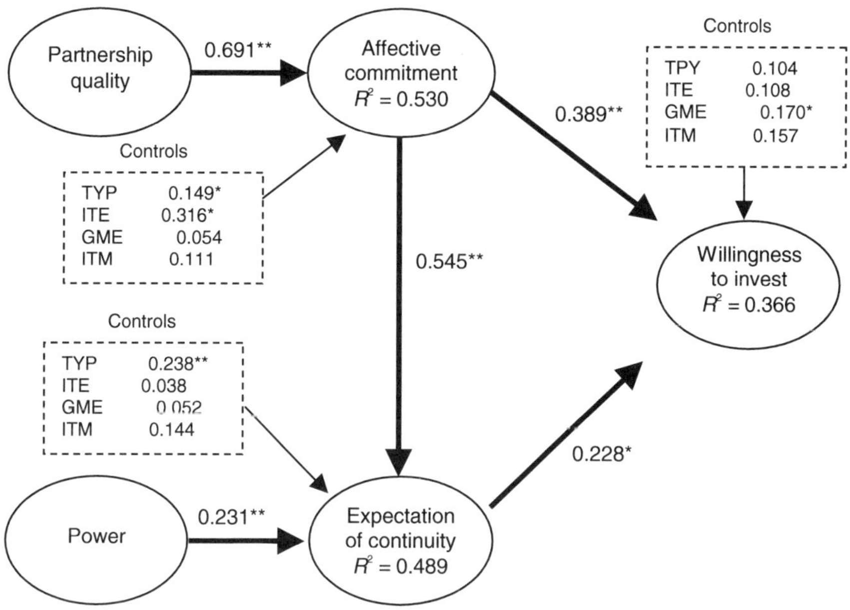

Notes: TYP— student type; ITE—IT work experience; GME—general management experience; ITM—IT management experience.

*p < 0.05

**p < 0.01

Table 11.13

Results of the 2 × 2 Type III MANOVA of Commitment Dimensions

Independent variable	Dependent variable	Type III sum of squares	*F*-value	Significance
Intercept	Willingness to invest	2,317.321	1,569.317	0.000
	Expectation of continuity	2,046.225	1,399.549	0.000
	Affective commitment	1,775.237	1,001.069	0.000
Main effect:	Willingness to invest	13.756	9.316	0.003
Partnership manipulation	Expectation of continuity	24.058	16.455	0.000
	Affective commitment	173.901	98.064	0.000
Main effect:	Willingness to invest	2.852	1.923	0.168
Power manipulation	Expectation of continuity	13.179	9.014	0.003
	Affective commitment	1.117	0.630	0.429
Interaction effect:	Willingness to invest	3.187	2.158	0.145
Partnership × Power	Expectation of continuity	17.101	11.696	0.001
	Affective commitment	5.371	3.029	0.085

Notes: A Type III MANOVA was run because of the uneven number of observations in the manipulation cells (see Figure 11.4).

Means are based on the final set of items for each commitment dimension (see Table 11.2).

the main model. Similarly, the coefficient for the path from the partnership quality construct to affective commitment (H_{5A}) is also quite high at 0.691 in the alternate model.

These results clearly indicate that partnership quality has a much greater impact on a service provider's commitment than does client's power over the provider. This is demonstrated in both the main model in which commitment is modeled as a second-order factor and in the alternate model in which the three dimensions of commitment are modeled as three independent constructs with an underlying causal structure. The finding that partnership plays a key role in influencing an IT service provider's commitment to the outsourcing relationship is consistent with findings about partnership quality in other IT outsourcing studies that have also found this construct to be positively related to various outsourcing success measures (Grover, Cheon, and Teng, 1996; Lee and Kim, 1999; Saunders, Gebelt, and Hu, 1997). While the impact of partnership on vendor commitment may not be surprising, it is interesting to note the size of the effect of partnership on vendor commitment given our definition of partnership, which did not include any reference to the economic incentives or benefit sharing that are typically found in traditional outsourcing partnerships.

Furthermore, based on transaction cost theory we would expect that a provider who is highly dependent on a client would continue to commit to the relationship (Heide and John, 1990; Rindfleisch and Heide, 1997). However, the client's power over the vendor in both the main and the alternate models had a significant but comparatively weaker relationship to commitment. While these results may indicate that client power emanating from provider dependence on the client may truly have a lower impact on provider commitment as compared with the influence of partnership quality on commitment, there another explanation for these results may be possible. The impact of client power on vendor commitment may in fact be a time-varying phenomenon with the impact of client power on provider commitment being much stronger in the earlier years of the outsourcing contract than in the later years. This may be because in the earlier years of the contract, the provider still has to recoup the specific investments it has made for the particular client (high provider dependence on client and thus high client power over the provider), and the provider may thus be more committed to the relationship. In contrast, in the later years of the contractual relationship, the provider has already recouped its client-specific investments and its commitment to the relationship may not be very high. In the experimental scenario used in this research, the provider is in the middle of a five-year contract, and, therefore, the lower degree of impact of the client's power on commitment may be an artifact of the experiment rather than a "true" effect. However, the reasoning about the moderation effect of the elapsed contractual duration on the relationship between vendor dependence (client power) and commitment is only intuitive and needs to be validated in future research.

Research Limitations

There are a few limitations associated with this study. First, as with any experiment, the variables under investigation were artificially manipulated so treatments could be adequately differentiated, and they represent only a limited set of the economic, social, and contractual factors involved in IT outsourcing relationships. Therefore, caution should be exercised in generalizing these results to real-world IT outsourcing situations. Second, the methodology involved using both graduate and undergraduate students as surrogates for actual mangers in IT service firms, and, therefore, the results of this study should be interpreted with caution. However, as we mentioned before, the student selection process targeted only specific student groups (those who had completed or were enrolled in appropriate MIS courses and those with appropriate professional experience in information technology, general management, and information technology management) to ensure that they had the necessary background to understand the outsourcing situation and to make appropriate and necessary recommendations. There is also a potential for systematically different responses from graduate and undergraduate students due to differences in education and experience levels but these factors were controlled for, as reported in the above discussion, and this difference was not found to be significant in any model. Third, the case provided to the students does not mention the profitability of the contract. It is quite possible that service providers may show more commitment when contracts are more profitable. Finally, the experimental scenario utilized only one kind of IT outsourcing model, that is, the ASP outsourcing model. While the newer ASP model of outsourcing is similar to the traditional forms of IT outsourcing in some ways, there are also several significant differences between the traditional and the ASP models of outsourcing, as discussed earlier. Future research with other forms of IT outsourcing should be conducted to validate the findings of this study.

Directions for Future Research

The intent of this research was to investigate how a client's power over a vendor and the partnership quality of their relationship impacts the service provider's level of commitment. While we believe this research has provided the theoretical groundwork and empirical support for the influence of unilateral and bilateral social controls (power and partnership) on vendor commitment, more work is needed to further develop this line of research. This research viewed power from the pluralist point of view; other views (e.g., rational or radical views) may be more appropriate in studying power in the context of IT outsourcing alliances or the working relationships between a client's and service provider's staff. An alternative view of power from the pluralist perspective was also taken. In this research, power was defined as a function of dependence; however, power may also be defined as a function of one's power bases (rewards, coercion, expert, legitimate, and referent) (French and Raven, 1959). The use of these social power bases in the form of detailed contracts (legitimate power), penalty clauses (coercive power), incentives (reward power), and IT legal experts (expert power) has been suggested by researchers as a means of effectively managing outsourcing relationships (Lacity and Hirschheim, 1993b; Lacity and Willcocks, 1998; Lacity, Willcocks, and Feeny, 1995, 1996). Future research should take these alternative conceptualizations of power and study their impact on vendor commitment.

Past literature (Grover, Cheon, and Teng, 1996; Lee and Kim, 1999; Saunders, Gebelt, and Hu, 1997) has typically used a client's strategic, technological, and economic benefits from outsourcing as success measures. However, as client firms engage in more selective outsourcing, split their IT functions among a greater number of IT service providers, and/or opt for more hybrid governance approaches (Kishore, Agarwal, and Rao, 2004–2005), intermediate variables become quite important as outsourcing and organizational success measures become further removed in the causal chain. Future IT outsourcing research may, therefore, wish to consider the use of vendor commitment as an important mediating construct in studies where the final outcome variables are organizational level success measures. In addition, commitment may be seen as a success measure from both a client and an IT service provider perspective, as opposed to the one-sided client view of success used in past research.

Future research may also look at how an outsourcing contract may be used as a mechanism for developing both partnership and power in the context of IT outsourcing relationships. Weitz and Jap (1995) state that elements of normative control and authoritative control are often contained in interorganizational contractual relations. The contract states each party's obligations and responsibilities; research on how the contract influences the development of relational norms and power would be of great interest.

Finally, this research focused solely on the ASP outsourcing model. Though, there are certain similarities between the ASP and the traditional models of outsourcing, as discussed earlier, there are certain major differences between these two models, such as service customization, data location, asset ownership, and provider presence. Future research should investigate the relative influences of power and partnership in other outsourcing models, including the traditional outsourcing model as well.

Theoretical Contributions and Managerial Implications

This study makes three major contributions. This is the first study to examine the phenomenon of vendor commitment in an IT outsourcing context, considering two major determinants of this construct. As discussed earlier, there is a paucity of research from the vendor perspective in the IT outsourcing literature and, to our knowledge, there is no study in the IS literature that deals with the notion of vendor commitment. Second, there is no study in the IT outsourcing literature that has considered power and partnership in an integrated manner. This study takes the alternate theoretical perspectives approach and compares the two alternate influence sources—power and partnership—for vendor commitment in a single model to understand which influence source better explains vendor commitment to an outsourcing relationship, thereby furthering our understanding of these two constructs. Finally, while partnership has been examined in a traditional outsourcing context, this study examines whether the notion of partnership remains applicable in the more contractually oriented ASP form of outsourcing. We indeed find that partnership remains a strong and significant determinant of vendor commitment.

This study also has implications for today's IT outsourcing managers. As was noted earlier, vendor commitment has been found to be a necessary prerequisite for successful outsourcing outcomes. While some researchers have advised practitioners to manage their IT service providers through the use of power (e.g., penalty clauses, short-term agreements, etc.) (Lacity and Hirschheim, 1993b; Lacity and Willcocks, 1998; Lacity, Willcocks, and Feeny, 1995, 1996), other researchers have advised practitioners to develop outsourcing relationships that are built less on contracts and more on trust (Lee and Kim, 1999; Sabherwal, 1999). This study finds that both power and partnership have a role to play in shaping vendor's commitment to an outsourcing relationship. Client IT managers, cognizant of the need for vendor commitment, should seek a balance between the two levers—power and partnership—that they have under their control for managing their IT vendors more effectively to achieve outsourcing success.

However, we would like to urge caution in interpreting the results of our study. These results certainly support Macneil's (1978a) proposition that contracts by their very nature are never complete and social mechanisms are therefore necessary to ensure the continuous commitment of the contracting parties to the relationship. However, our research in no way implies that social mechanisms are a replacement for contractual mechanisms in managing interorganizational relationships. A contract is necessary as the major mechanism for defining the structure and responsibilities of the parties in an interorganizational relationship. Therefore, client firms should apply due diligence in developing and enforcing contracts with their vendors and should not rely solely upon social mechanisms for managing relationships with their vendors.

Further, based on the results of the study, we recommend that clients consider developing flexible contracts that motivate their vendors' future commitment through contractual clauses that promote communication, knowledge sharing, and innovation while maintaining vendors' current commitment through contractual clauses that define arbitration and enforcement mechanisms. We believe that the contract can be used as the foundation for establishing and developing both power and partnership in an IT outsourcing relationship.

Parties in an IT outsourcing relationship should also consider creating interdependence in their relationship. In relationships that have a greater degree of interdependence, both parties possess power and they work together to foster a relationship of cooperation (Gundlach and Cadotte, 1994). Therefore, a higher degree of interdependence may also generate both power and partnership in an IT outsourcing relationship. Vendor and client firms may therefore wish to make mutual credible investments in their relationships to induce a higher degree of interdependence in their relationship, which could in turn lead to power and partnership in their relationship.

ACKNOWLEDGMENTS

The authors are grateful to the National Science Foundation (NSF) for providing funding for this research project under grant no. 9907325. Any opinions, findings and conclusions, or recommendations expressed in this material are those of the authors and do not necessarily reflect the views of the NSF.

The authors are also grateful to Shaila Miranda and the attendees of the IT outsourcing mini-track at the HICSS 2004 conference for providing valuable comments and suggestions during the course of development of this research.

NOTE

1. As discussed in the procedures section, these treatments are: (1) strong partnership and high vendor dependence (i.e., high client power); (2) strong partnership and low vendor dependence (i.e., low client power); (3) weak partnership and high vendor dependence (i.e., high client power); and (4) weak partnership and low vendor dependence (i.e., low client power).

REFERENCES

Andaleeb, S.S. 1995. Dependence relations and the moderating role of trust: Implications for behavioral intentions in marketing channels. *International Journal of Research in Marketing*, 12, 2, 157–172.

———. 1996. An experimental investigation of satisfaction and commitment in marketing channels: The role of trust and dependence. *Journal of Retailing*, 72, 1, 77–93.

Applegate, L.M. and Davis, K. 1995. Xerox: Outsourcing global information technology resources. Harvard Business School Case 195–158.

Applegate, L.M.; Montealegre, R.; and Kodak, E. 1991. Managing information systems through strategic alliances. Harvard Business School Case 192–030.

Bensaou, M. and Anderson, E. 1999. Buyer-supplier relations in industrial markets: When do buyers risk making idiosyncratic investments? *Organization Science*, 10, 4, 460–481.

Bonoma, T.V. 1985. Case research in marketing: Opportunities, problems, and a process. *Journal of Marketing Research*, 22, 2, 199–208.

Booker, E. 2000. ABCs of ASPs. *B to B*, 85, 12 (August 14), 29–30.

Boyd, J. 2000. Latest hosted service: Benefits administration. *Internetweek*, 825 (August 21), 19.

Bradshaw-Camball, P. and Murray, V.V. 1991. Illusions and other games: A trifocal view of organizational politics. *Organization Science*, 2, 4, 379–398.

Cartwright, D. 1965. Influence, leadership, control. In J.G. March, ed., *Handbook of Organizations*. Chicago, IL: Rand McNally, 1–47.

Chin, W.W. 1998a. Issues and opinion on structural equation modeling. *MIS Quarterly*, 22, 1, vii–xvi.

———. 1998b. The partial least squares approach to structural equation modeling. In G.A. Marcoulides, ed., *Modern Methods for Business Research*. Mahwah, NJ: Lawrence Erlbaum, 295–336.

Chin, W.W. and Gopal, A. 1995. Adoption intention in GSS: Relative importance of beliefs. *Database*, 26, 2 & 3, 42–64.

Chin, W.W. and Newsted, P.R. 1999. Structural equation modeling analysis with small samples using partial least squares. In R. Hoyle, ed., *Statistical Strategies for Small Sample Research.* Thousand Oaks, CA: Sage, 307–341.

Chin, W.W.; Marcolin, B.L.; and Newsted, P.R. 1996. A partial least squares latent variable modeling approach for measuring interaction effects: Results from a Monte Carlo simulation study and voice mail emotion/adoption Study. In *Proceedings of the Seventeenth International Conference on Information Systems.* Cleveland, OH (December 16–18): 21–41.

Crosby, L.A.; Evans, K.R.; and Cowles, D. 1990. Relationship quality in services selling: An interpersonal influence perspective. *Journal of Marketing*, 54, 3, 68–81.

Dennis, A.R. and Valacich, J.S. 2001. Conducting research in information systems. *Communications of the Association for Information Systems*, 7, 5, 1–41.

Dibbern, J.; Goles, T.; Hirschheim, R.; and Jayatilaka, B. 2004. Information systems outsourcing: A survey and analysis of the literature. *Database for Advances in Information Systems*, 35, 4, 6–102.

DiRomualdo, A. and Gurbaxani, V. 1998. Strategic intent for IT outsourcing. *Sloan Management Review*, 39, 4, 67–80.

Dwyer, R.F.; Schurr, P.H.; and Oh, S. 1987. Developing buyer-seller relationships. *Journal of Marketing*, 51, 2, 11–27.

El-Ansary, A.I. 1975. Determinants of power-dependence in the distribution channel. *Journal of Retailing*, 51, 2, 59–74.

Emerson, R. 1962. Power-dependence relationships. *American Sociological Review*, 27, 1, 31–41.

Etgar, M. 1978. Differences in the use of manufacture power in conventional and contractual channels. *Journal of Retailing*, 54, 4, 49–62.

Fornell, C. and Larcker, D.F. 1981. Evaluating structural equation models with unobservable variables and measurement error. *Journal of Marketing Research*, 18, 1, 39–50.

French, J.R.P. and Raven, B. 1959. The bases of social power. In D. Cartwright, ed., *Studies in Social Power.* Ann Arbor: University of Michigan Press, 150–167.

Gefen, D.; Straub, D.W.; and Boudreau, M.C. 2000. Structural equation modeling and regression: Guidelines for research practice. *Communications of the Association for Information Systems*, 4, 7, 1–77.

Goles, T. and Chin, W.W. 2002. Relational exchange theory and IS outsourcing: Developing a scale to measure relationship factors. In R. Hirschheim, A. Heinzl, and J. Dibbern, eds., *Information Systems Outsourcing: Enduring Themes, Emergent Patterns and Future Directions*. Berlin: Springer-Verlag, 221–250.

Grover, V.; Cheon, M.J.; and Teng, J.T.C. 1996. The effect of service quality and partnership on the outsourcing of information systems functions. *Journal of Management Information Systems*, 12, 4, 89–116.

Gundlach, G.T. and Cadotte, E.R. 1994. Exchange interdependence and interfirm interaction: Research in a simulated channel setting. *Journal of Marketing Research*, 30, 4, 516–532.

Gundlach, G.T.; Achrol, R.S.; and Mentzer, J.T. 1995. The structure of commitment in exchange. *Journal of Marketing*, 59, 1, 78–92.

Harrison, P.D. and Harrell, A. 1993. Impact of "adverse selection" on managers' project evaluation. *Academy of Management Journal*, 36, 3, 635–643.

Hart, P.J. and Saunders, C.S. 1997. Power and trust: Critical factors in the adoption and use of electronic data interchange. *Organization Science*, 8, 1, 23–41.

———. 1998. Emerging electronic partnerships: Antecedents and dimensions of EDI use from the supplier's perspective. *Journal of Management Information Systems*, 14, 4, 87–111.

Heide, J.B. 1994. Interorganizational governance in marketing channels. *Journal of Marketing*, 58, 1, 71–85.

Heide, J.B. and John, G. 1990. Alliances in industrial purchasing: The determinants of joint action in buyer supplier relationships. *Journal of Marketing Research*, 26, 1, 24–36.

Hulland, J. 1999. Use of partial least squares (PLS) in strategic management research: A review of four recent studies. *Strategic Management Journal*, 20, 2, 195–204.

Iacovou, C.L.; Benbasat, I.; and Dexter, A.S. 1995. Electronic data interchange and small organizations: Adoption and impact of technology. *MIS Quarterly*, 19, 4, 465–485.

Jasperson, J.; Bulter, B.S.; Carte, T.A.; Croes, H.J.P.; Saunders, C.S., and Zheng, W. 2002. Power and information technology research: A metatriangulation review. *MIS Quarterly*, 26, 4, 397–459.

Johnson, A.H. 2000. Breadth of expertise defines ASP start-up. *Computerworld*, 34, 31 (July 31), 60.

Keil, M.; Mixon, R.; and Truex, D.P. 1995. The effects of sunk cost and project completion on information technology project escalation. *IEEE Transactions on Engineering Management*, 42, 4, 372–381.

Keil, M.; Mixon, R.; Saarinen, T.; and Tuunainen, V. 1994–95. Understanding runaway information technology projects: Results for an international research program based on escalation theory. *Journal of Management Information Systems*, 11, 3, 65–85.

Keil, M.; Smith, J.H.; Pawlowski, S.; and Jin, L. 2004. "Why didn't somebody tell me?" Climate, information asymmetry, and bad news about trouble projects. *Database for Advances in Information Systems*, 35, 2, 65–84.

Keil, M.; Tan, B.C.Y.; Wei, K.-K.; Saarinen, T.; Tuunainen, V.; and Wassenaar, A. 2000a. A cross-cultural study on escalation of commitment behavior in software projects. *MIS Quarterly*, 24, 2, 299–325.

Keil, M.; Wallace, L.; Turk, D.; Dixon-Randall, G.; and Nulden, U. 2000b. An investigation of risk perception and risk propensity on the decision to continue a software development project. *Journal of Systems and Software*, 53, 2, 145–157.

Ketokivi, M.A. and Schroeder, R.G. 2004. Structural contingency and institutional explanations in the adoption of innovative manufacturing practices. *Journal of Operations Management*, 22, 1, 63–89.

Kim, K. 2000. On Interfirm power, channel climate, and solidarity in industrial distributor-supplier dyads. *Journal of the Academy of Marketing Science*, 28, 3, 388–405.

Kishore, R.; Agarwal, M.; and Rao, H.R. 2004–5. Determinants of information technology sourcing during technology growth and maturity: An empirical study of e-commerce sourcing. *Journal of Management Information Systems*, 21, 3, 47–82.

Kishore, R.; Rao, H.R.; Nam, K.; Rajagopalan, S.; and Chaudhury, A. 2003. A relationship perspective on IT outsourcing. *Communications of the ACM*, 46, 12, 86–92.

Kumar, N.; Scheer, L.K.; and Steenkamp, J.-B.E.M. 1995. The effects of perceived interdependence on dealer attitudes. *Journal of Marketing Research*, 32, 3, 348–356.

Lacity, M.C. and Hirschheim, R. 1993a. The information systems outsourcing bandwagon. *Sloan Management Review*, 35, 1, 73–86.

———. 1993b. *Information Systems Outsourcing: Myths, Metaphors and Realities*. New York: Wiley, 1993b.

Lacity, M.C. and Willcocks, L.P. 1998. An empirical investigation of information technology sourcing practices: Lessons from experience. *MIS Quarterly*, 22, 3, 363–408.

Lacity, M.C.; Willcocks, L.P.; and Feeny, D.F. 1995. IT outsourcing: Maximize flexibility and control. *Harvard Business Review*, 73, 3, 84–93.

———. 1996. The value of selective IT sourcing. *Sloan Management Review*, 37, 3, 13–25.

Lasher, D.R.; Ives, B.; and Jarvenpaa, S.L. 1991. USAA-IBM partnership in Information technology: Managing the Image Project. *MIS Quarterly*, 15, 4, 551–565.

Lee, J.-N. and Kim, Y.-G. 1999. Effect of partnership quality on IS outsourcing: Conceptual framework and empirical validation. *Journal of Management Information Systems*, 15, 4, 29–61.

Lee, J.-N.; Huynh, M.Q.; Kwok, R.C.; and Pi, S.-M. 2002. Current and future directions for IS outsourcing. In R. Hirschheim, A. Heinzl, and J. Dibbern, eds., *Information Systems Outsourcing: Enduring Themes, Emergent Patterns and Future Directions*. Berlin: Springer-Verlag, 451–473.

———. 2003. IT outsourcing evolution: Its past, present, and future. *Communications of the ACM*, 46, 5, 84–89.

Lohmoller, J. 1989. *Latent Variable Path Modeling with Partial Least Squares*. New York: Springer-Verlag.

Macneil, I.R. 1978a. Contracts: Adjusting of long-term economic relations under classical, neoclassical and relational contract law. *Northwestern Law Review*, 72, 5, 854–902.

———. 1978b. *The New Social Contract. An Inquiry into Modern Contractual Relations*. New Haven, CT: Yale University Press.

McFarlan, F.W. and Nolan, R.L. 1995. How to manage an IT outsourcing alliance. *Sloan Management Review*, 36, 2, 9–23.

McGrath, J.E. 1979. Toward a "theory of method" for research on organizations. In R.T. Mowday and R.M. Steers, eds., *Research in Organizations: Issues and Controversies*, Santa Monica, CA: Goodyear.

Mohr, J. and Spekman, R. 1994. Characteristics of partnership success: Partnership attributes, communication, behavior, and conflict resolution techniques. *Strategic Management Journal*, 15, 2, 135–152.

Moorman, C.; Zaltman, G.; and Deshpande, R. 1992. Relationships between providers and users of marketing research: The dynamic of trust within and between organizations. *Journal of Marketing Research*, 29, 3, 314–329.

Morgan, L. 2000. E-Mail service providers—More than e-mail. E-businesses are demanding a broad mix of value-added services from e-mail service providers—and they are getting it. *Internetweek*, 823 (July 31), 45.

Morgan, R.M. and Hunt, S.D. 1994. The commitment-trust theory of relationship marketing. *Journal of Marketing*, 58, 7, 20–38.

Natovich, J. 2003. Vendor related risks in IT development: A chronology of an outsourced project failure. *Technology Analysis & Strategic Management*, 15, 4, 409–419.

Poppo, L. and Zenger, T. 1998. Testing alternative theories of the firm: Transaction cost, knowledge-based, and measurement explanations for make-or-buy decisions in information services. *Strategic Management Journal*, 19, 9, 853–877.

Premkumar, G. and Ramamurthy, K. 1995. The role of interorganizational and organizational factors on the decision mode for adoption of interorganizational systems. *Decision Sciences*, 26, 3, 303–336.

Reekers, N. and Smithson, S. 1996. The role of EDI in inter-organizational coordination in the European automotive industry. *European Journal of Information Systems*, 5, 2, 120–130.

Remus, W. 1986. Graduate students as surrogates for managers in experiments on business decision making. *Journal of Business Research*, 14, 1, 19–25.

Reuer, J.J. and Koza, M.P. 2000. Lemons and indigestibility: Resource assembly through joint ventures. *Strategic Management Journal*, 21, 2, 195–197.

Rindfleisch, A. and Heide, J.B. 1997. Transaction cost analysis: Past, present, and future applications. *Journal of Marketing*, 61, 4, 30–54.

Sabherwal, R. 1999. The role of trust in outsourced IS development projects. *Communications of the ACM*, 42, 2, 80–86.

Saunders, C.; Gebelt, M.; and Hu, Q. 1997. Achieving success in information systems outsourcing. *California Management Review*, 39, 2, 63–79.

Schmidt, J.B.; Montoya-Weiss, M.; and Massey, A.P. 2001. New product development decision-making effectiveness: Comparing individual, face-to-face teams, and virtual teams. *Decision Sciences*, 32, 4, 575–600.

Schroth, H.A. and Shah, P.P. 2000. Procedures: Do we really want to know them? An examination of the effects of procedural justice on self-esteem. *Journal of Applied Psychology*, 85, 3, 462–471.

Schurr, P.H. and Ozanne, J.L. 1985. Influences on exchange processes: Buyers' preconceptions of a seller's trustworthiness and bargaining toughness. *Journal of Consumer Research*, 11, 4, 939–953.

Sitkin, S.B. and Weingart, L.R. 1995. Determinants of risky decision-making behavior: A test of the mediating role of risk perceptions and propensity. *Academy of Management Journal*, 38, 6, 1573–1592.

Skinner, S.J.; Gassenheimer, J.B.; and Kelly, S.W. 1992. Cooperation in supplier-dealer relations. *Journal of Retailing*, 68, 2, 174–193.

Smith, J.H.; Keil, M.; and Depledge, G. 2001. Keeping mum as the project goes under: Toward an explanatory model. *Journal of Management Information Systems*, 18, 2, 189–227.

Subramani, M.R. and Venkatraman, N. 2003. Safeguarding investments in asymmetric interorganizational relationships: Theory and evidence. *Academy of Management Journal*, 46, 1, 46–62.

Sullivan, J. and Peterson, R.B. 1982. Factors associated with trust in Japanese-American joint ventures. *Management International Review*, 22, 2, 30–40.

Tan, B.C.Y.; Smith, H.J.; Keil, M.; and Montealegre, R. 2003. Reporting bad news about software projects: Impact of organizational climate and information asymmetry in individualistic and collectivistic culture. *IEEE Transactions on Engineering Management*, 50, 1, 64–77.

Wareham, J.D. 2003. Information assets in interorganizational governance: Exploring the property rights perspective. *IEEE Transactions on Engineering Management*, 50, 3, 337–351.

Weitz, B.A. and Jap, S.D. 1995. Relationship marketing and distribution channels. *Journal of the Academy of Marketing Science*, 23, 4, 305–320.

Whitten, D.; Stephens, C.; Dwyer, S.; and Ellis, S. 2004. Discontinuation of application development outsourcing contracts. In *Proceedings of the Americas Conference on Information Systems*. New York: Association for Information Systems.

Williamson, O.E. 1988. The logic of economic organization. *Journal of Law, Economics, and Organization*, 4, 2, 65–93.

Young, G.J.; Charns, M.P.; and Heeren, T.C. 2004. Product-line management in professional organizations: An empirical test of competing theoretical perspectives. *Academy of Management Journal*, 47, 5, 723–734.

Zaheer, A.; McEvily, B.; and Perrone, V. 1998. Does trust matter? Exploring the effects of interorganizational and interpersonal trust on performance. *Organization Science*, 9, 2, 141–159.

APPENDIX 11.1 CASE INSTRUCTIONS

The scenario that follows is part of a research experiment that examines IT outsourcing decision-making. As part of this research experiment, you will be making an assessment of the amount of effort and resource that should be devoted to the relationship described in the IT outsourcing scenario. You will be asked to provide upper management with a series of recommendations on how to effectively manage this IT outsourcing relationship, including the amount of effort and resource that should be expended on the client's needs. Please take a few minutes to read over the scenario and to answer the questions that follow. Please respond to the questions in the order in which they are presented. Keep in mind that there are no right or wrong answers.

YOUR JOB

Imagine yourself to be a client account manager for E-SOFT, an application service provider (ASP) headquartered in Dallas, Texas. E-SOFT offers a set of wireless and web-based intranet and internet business applications to customers ranging from small to large enterprises. Your job as a client account manager is to decide on how to best manage these IT outsourcing relationships to ensure delivery of IT services which fit the current and future needs of E-SOFT's clients and E-SOFT's business objectives. You currently manage five IT outsourcing relationships. One of these accounts is SouthBank, a regional bank with several branches in and around the state of Texas.

E-SOFT'S APPLICATION SERVICE CONTRACT WITH SOUTHBANK

E-SOFT provides a Web and cellular interface to SouthBank's credit card payment and banking information system. The applications allow customers of SouthBank to access to their banking and credit card accounts through the Web or a cellular device. E-SOFT has just concluded its second year of a five-year IT outsourcing contract with SouthBank. This is an important time in the SouthBank and E-SOFT IT outsourcing relationship. SouthBank's contract contains several service escalation clauses that take effect at the end of the third year of their contract. These clauses target the following application service guarantees in the service level agreement (SLA):

Current service guarantees	**New service guarantees**
Servers will experience no more than 60 minutes unscheduled downtime per year.	Servers will experience no more than 30 minutes unscheduled downtime per year.
Applications will support 500 simultaneous users during peak hours.	Applications will support 1,000 simultaneous users during peak hours.
90% of users will have a response time of 2 seconds or less during peak hours.	95% of users will have a response time of 2 seconds or less during peak hours.
System restorations will take no more than 24 hours.	System restorations will take no more than 12 hours.

YOUR OPINION OF THE IT OUTSOURCING RELATIONSHIP WITH SOUTHBANK

A few weeks ago Steve Rice, the Vice President of Contract Management (your boss), asked you to describe the type of relationship E-SOFT has with SouthBank. You wrote the following memo:

Partnership: Strong

Steve,

"Regarding you query on the quality of our IT outsourcing relationship with SouthBank. I *have* many good things to say. Our working relationship with SouthBank *has been* a happy one. They *effectively* communicate their service needs and expectations. SouthBank's IT staff *has been very willing to cooperate* with us in implementing services and solving problems. *Both* organizations have developed a clear understanding of each other's behavior, policies and goals. SouthBank *always tries to keep* their promises and *never tries to take* advantage of us. I *am happy to say*, we *have developed* a very trusting relationship with SouthBank."

Partnership: Weak

Steve,

"Regarding your query on the quality of our IT outsourcing relationship with SouthBank. I *do not have* many good things to say. Our working relationship with SouthBank *has not been* a happy one. They *do not effectively* communicate their service needs and expectations. SouthBank's IT staff *has not been very willing to cooperate* with us in implementing services and solving problems. *Neither* organization has developed a clear understanding of each other's behavior, policies and goals. SouthBank *never tries to keep* their promises and *always tries to take* advantage of us. I *regret to say*, we *have not developed* a very trusting relationship with SouthBank."

How Important Is the IT Outsourcing Relationship With SouthBank to Your Company?

Information on the extent of your reliance on SouthBank, as a client, is presented below. You know that:

Power: High

- Currently, there are *few* companies in the market interested in outsourcing wireless and web-based intranet and internet business applications to ASPs.
- Services sold to SouthBank contribute to *more than 50%* of E-SOFT's total profits.
- A *large* portion of E-SOFT's manpower and equipment has been customized to fit SouthBank's application service needs. It would be *very difficult and costly* to reallocate and reconfigure these resources to service other customers.
- *Without incurring significant* costs, it would be rather *difficult* for E-SOFT to terminate its relationship with SouthBank.

Power: Low

- Currently, there are *many* companies in the market interested in outsourcing wireless and web-based intranet and internet business applications to ASPs.
- Services sold to SouthBank contribute to *less than 5%* of E-SOFT's total profits.
- A *small* portion of E-SOFT's manpower and equipment has been customized to fit SouthBank's application service needs. It would be *very easy and inexpensive* to reallocate and reconfigure these resources to service other customers.
- *Incurring only minimal* costs, it would be rather *easy* for E-SOFT to terminate its relationship with SouthBank.

Situation

In two weeks, E-SOFT is having its biannual review and assessment meeting. During the meeting, executives of E-SOFT discuss and plan the financial, workforce and technological investments needed to service E-SOFT's current and future customers. Steve Rice has asked you to write a report describing how to manage the SouthBank relationship and to present your recommendations at the meeting. You have decided to take a couple of hours out of your day to begin drafting the report.

CHAPTER 12

GOVERNANCE OF COMPLEX IT OUTSOURCING PARTNERSHIPS

ERIK BEULEN AND PIETER RIBBERS

Abstract: *Deciding whether to outsource information technology (IT) or to keep providing these services oneself is a key management responsibility. Once a decision to outsource has been made, relations with external providers have to be established and managed. IT outsourcing governance therefore encompasses those structures and processes that should ensure the delivery and utilization of IT services complying with the objectives of the participating organizations. The authors have carried out a study on governance practices in the management of complex IT outsourcing partnership relations. For this research, fourteen international case studies on European-based companies with pan-European or global operations were used. Working on the basis of the relevant socioorganizational, economic, and competition-based reference disciplines the practices found in these case studies were analyzed, and a framework was developed comprising ten governance factors. The major building blocks of this framework are the outsourcing company, the IT service suppliers, and the relations between them. The case studies used here all concern successfully managed complex IT outsourcing relations. Their yearly contract values varied from $0.4 million to $550 million. At the end of the contract period all contracts were renewed except for two, which were discontinued because of external market reasons. The very success of these outsourcing relationships provides an opportunity to analyze the problems and challenges met in such partnerships. As it turned out, any trouble that was experienced was always caused by a lack of attention paid to the governance factors of the framework.*

The conclusions drawn from this research work were supplemented with knowledge gained from interviews with experts from major consulting firms with international track records in IT outsourcing research and consulting.

Keywords: *Agency Theory, Corporate Governance, IT/IS Strategy, IT Governance, IT Outsourcing, Partnerships, Transaction Cost Theory*

PROBLEM DEFINITION

The question of how large organizations manage the complexity arising from global business operations and information technology (IT) infrastructures remains one of the most pressing issues currently facing managers (Brown and Magill, 1994; Doh, 2005; King, 2005; Sambamurthy and Zmud, 2000). And while this question is pertinent when IT and its department are legally part of the business organization, it is even more complex when the company's IT is largely outsourced. In the past, most literature on organizing IT has focused on the choice between centralization and decentralization, with federal models as an in-between option. Sambamurthy and Zmud (1999), for instance, focused on coordination, introducing the concepts of relational and integration architecture as building blocks of the organizational logic for IT activities. Recently, however, King (2005) once again stressed the complexity of outsourcing relations and Doh (2005) introduced the notion of complexity in offshore outsourcing relations.

Until recently, most research on IT outsourcing focused on its feasibility (Klepper, 1995; Lacity and Hirschheim, 1993, 1995; Lacity and Willcocks, 2001). Only limited attention was paid to the management of complex IT outsourcing partnerships (Cullen and Willcocks, 2003). The authors now propose a conceptual framework containing governance factors that apply to IT outsourcing partnerships. This framework is rooted in organization design theory and supported by a comparative analysis of case studies involving multinational European-based companies. The aim of our research work was to develop a better understanding of the management issues surrounding complex IT outsourcing partnerships, from the perspectives of both the outsourcing company and the IT service supplier.

The research work underlying this chapter concerned governance practices in managing complex IT outsourcing partnership relations in European-based companies with pan-European and global operations. In the sense used here, IT governance provides a specification of the decision rights and accountability framework meant to encourage desirable IT use behavior (Weill and Ross, 2004); in outsourcing relations it therefore encompasses the structures and processes that should ensure the delivery and utilization of IT services complying with the objectives of the participating organizations.

The structure of this chapter is as follows. In the next section the concept of IT governance is discussed in relation to basic reference disciplines. We then develop a conceptual framework to describe the complex issues that surround the governance of outsourcing relations. This is followed by an explanation of our research approach and a presentation of the case studies that form the basis of this study. In the next section, we discuss our conceptual framework, considering each of its building blocks from both case study and theoretical perspectives. Finally, we present and briefly discuss our conclusions.

IT GOVERNANCE: REFERENCE DISCIPLINES AND NEW DEVELOPMENTS

The governance of IT outsourcing relations must result in the realization of mutually set objectives. Since the partners in an outsourcing relationship are legally and economically independent of each other—meaning that there is no shared hierarchy—aligning such goals and working toward them is much more complex than is the case for insourcing. The cost-saving goal of the outsourcing company, for instance, conflicts with the IT service supplier's return-on-investment objectives.

In the literature on outsourcing relations a growing interest in IT governance may be observed (Sambamurthy and Zmud, 1999; Van Grembergen, 2002; Weill and Broadbent, 1998; Weill and Ross, 2004). IT governance processes describe the mechanisms that enable business and IT executives to integrate their business and IT decisions, to implement and monitor their decisions, and to learn from their effectiveness (Weill and Broadbent, 1998). IT governance should ensure that the IT services delivered add value to the business and that any IT risks are mitigated (Guldentops, 2004; ISACA, 2002). This involves the identification and detailed description of the IT business cases and the prioritization, selection, and (later) evaluation of the decisions taken (Luftman and Brier, 1999; Willcocks and Lester, 1996). At the conceptual core of all IT governance processes stands the organizational model of decision making, defined as the process of identifying and solving problems (Daft, 2001). Problem identification (monitoring external and internal environments to determine performance disturbances and diagnose deficiencies) and problem solution (developing, selecting, and implementing alternative courses of action) are the basic stages in any kind of organizational decision making (Daft, 2001; Mintzberg, 1979), including business decisions regarding IT (Luftman and Brier, 1999; Willcocks and Lester, 1996). This requires structured functions, principles, and decision processes with which to realize the flexibility and innovation needed.

Theories on Strategy: A Recapitulation

Basically, what all companies attempt to do is achieve a fit between their organization and their surroundings, in order to realize a maximum sustainable profit from that environment. This objective is the focus of their company strategy. Quite naturally, there are several kinds of such strategies. The governance of IT outsourcing relations may therefore be considered from the viewpoint of several different reference disciplines that have been adopted in the outsourcing literature, each with its own approach: socioorganizational, economic, and competition-based reference theories (Dibbern et al., 2004).

Socio-organizational Theories

Interorganizational relations may be viewed as a matter of negotiating and of building and breaking coalitions—processes in which every company attempts to achieve as many of its objectives as possible without actually hindering the realization of their partners' goals. This has sometimes been called a push-and-pull process (Cyert, March, and Clarkson, 1963). Such processes require trust between the participants or there will be no cooperation, let alone collaboration, to reach the win-win situations aimed at (Kumar and van Dissel, 1996). All stakeholders must understand one another's positions and must be willing to align their decision-making processes, control systems, and even their organizational cultures with those of their partners (Dyer and Singh, 1998). Then they can negotiate on sharing the risks and rewards involved in the partnership. The idea is that together the companies can generate more value than they would be able to realize independently, in another kind of partnership, or with a different partner. As long as they agree on this matter, they will be willing and able to deal with the wide variety of relational challenges facing them, such as new technologies and how or when to implement them; hidden costs; and sharing the cost savings that result from the collaboration. Even conflicts concerning their contracts and the financial results can be resolved if all parties have the will to make their partnership work (Earl, 1996). Use of the term *partnership* for such collaborative efforts was coined by Rothery, who defined it as a strategy to achieve higher performance or lower costs through the joint, mutually dependent action of independent organizations or individuals (Rothery and Robertson, 1995).

Economic Theories

Economic strategy theories focus on the way in which economic agents should coordinate their transactions and arrange for their governance. Of the two important schools in this field, agency theory considers companies the result of contracts between stakeholders, who may be groups inside the company but who also include external parties such as shareholders, suppliers, and customers. All parties play the role of either the principal (who pays for the products or services) or the agent (who delivers); and several of the parties involved may play a different role with respect to different partners. The essential difficulty in such situations is that no principal can ever fully judge the quality of the agent's work, which must therefore be monitored. This costs money, and if the parties do not really trust one another, these costs can be very high. The stated objective of agency theory is to define how such relations can best be organized, at the lowest cost, and with maximum profit for all (Earl, 1996).

From the work of Keil (2005), four basic assumptions on principal–agent relations may be derived: both parties behave rationally and have rational expectations; the principal's profit and success are directly influenced by the agent's actions; since the principal never knows everything there is to know about the agent (information asymmetry), the agent has a certain degree of freedom in prioritizing his own profit over that of the principal; and the principal's and agent's objectives are never the same. This means that money must be spent to assess and select the right agents, to establish which performance standards must be met, and to monitor whether they are actually met. Formal contracts are therefore needed to lead outsourcing relations in the right direction; but setting up such contracts means incurring further costs. All of these cost components must be analyzed in order to minimize their sum total and to enable the partners to recoup these investments from what should be increased profitability.

From another perspective, agency costs can be considered a particular type of transaction costs, which have been defined as the coordination costs associated with the various aspects of intercompany relations. These coordination costs are the subject of transaction cost theory (Williamson, 1975), which attempts to explain why companies insource or outsource the delivery of certain goods and services. Essentially, in transaction cost theory, coordination costs are balanced against production costs. If market conditions lead to a rise in production costs, the company will decide to outsource. But if, for example, there are too few suppliers or if there is a risk that they will serve their own purposes rather than those of their clients, companies will themselves produce what they need, using their internal structure rather than the market to govern the delivery. Transaction cost theory poses two basic questions: Which activities should be carried out by the company itself and which should be outsourced? And how should the company's relations with its business partners (including customers and suppliers) be managed?

Competition-based Theories

All profit organizations face competition. Starting from the inside out, this competition is for internal resources such as the competence of one's employees, for external resources (that is, resources that are essential but cannot all be supplied internally—raw materials, for instance), and finally for customers. Each of these resource types requires its own specific approach, and the customer resource requires a unique focus.

Internal resources are the subject of the resource-based view (Prahalad and Hamel, 1990), which looks at companies as collections of resources and competences that must be maintained and developed. If companies are so defined, it is obvious that they should focus on their core and unique competences in order to achieve a profitable and sustainable market position. Through analyzing the company's resources, it becomes clear which resources are critically important to its business performance—because it cannot deliver its products and services without them. Indications of the importance of certain resources are their uniqueness or rarity, and the complexity involved in imitating them or substituting for them. Essential resources should not be outsourced, while other resources may be treated as raw materials to be procured when needed.

This theory has given rise to the concept of focusing on core competences that is so important in many new business models. If all activities not belonging to the company's core competences are outsourced, the company can potentially focus on the activities that add the most value. Thus, companies are kept lean and are able to respond quickly to changes in their environment.

The resource dependency theory (Pfeffer and Salancik, 1978; Thompson, 1967) focuses on external resources: those resources that are not owned but regularly procured. The basic idea is that companies attempt to survive and therefore take action to keep their critical resources under control; but since it is impossible to own and exploit all the resources needed, their acquisition must somehow be ensured. In other words: the company's dependence on them must be managed. Hence, the name of the theory. Several aspects play a role here, and the company will strive for a situation in which it is as independent as possible, to be able to switch suppliers easily or use an alternative resource. Also, outsourcing remains attractive if the market is such that the buyer has substantial influence on the supplier, a general observation that holds for IT services as well (Grover and Teng, 1993). In resource dependency theory, the balance is again between contradictory forces, in this case certainty and autonomy (Davis and Powell, 1992).

Finally, there is the competition for customers. There are essentially two ways of attracting customers who prefer you above your competitors: your products or services are either the least expensive or of the highest quality—both in the customer's perception, of course. In either case, companies position themselves in their competitive environment according to their analysis of how, considering the external forces they face, they are best able to achieve a sustainable competitive position (Porter, 1980, 1985). Success thus depends on choosing the right competitive strategy. Once chosen, this strategy influences all other functional aspects of the organization, including human resources (HR) and IT: a clear business strategy contributes to a clear IT strategy.

New Developments in IT Governance

Many definitions of IT governance have been presented over the years. Traditionally, research has focused on the design of decision-making structures to control IT (Brown and Magill, 1994; Sambamurthy and Zmud, 1999), and the dominant model in contemporary enterprises was that of a federal IT governance structure, that is, a hybrid design of centralized infrastructure control and decentralized application control. However, in the current hypercompetitive environment and with the emergence of new electronic network organizations (El Sawy et al., 1999), classic, hierarchical IT governance designs are becoming obsolete and inadequate for dealing with the information processing and coordination needs experienced by many companies (Galbraith, 1993; Galbraith, Mohrman, and Lawler, 1998; Sambamurthy and Zmud, 2000). The orientation of IT governance is therefore shifting from the differentiation of IT decision-making structures to their integration in order to maximize IT value appropriation (Peterson, O'Callaghan, and Ribbers, 2000; Weill and Broadbent, 1998).

The latest development in IT governance thinking is the recognition of the importance of accountability (Weill and Ross, 2004). Financial scandals have caused authorities to issue stricter laws and regulations. A well-known example is the Sarbanes-Oxley Act issued in 2002. Its Section 404, for instance, focuses on the continuous improvement and development of a long-term financial architecture, and so directly influences IT governance. Other countries have adopted similar regulations and laws.[1]

A DESCRIPTIVE FRAMEWORK

The literature on outsourcing offers several contributions to the topic of how to manage IT outsourcing relations (Beulen, 2004; Beulen and Ribbers, 2003; Lacity and Willcocks, 2001; McKeen and Smith; 2001). According to Lacity and Hirschheim (1993) an IT outsourcing relation is characterized by:

Table 12.1

The Experience Needed to Manage Information Technology (IT) Outsourcing Relations

Relationship characteristics		Experience needed
IT sourcing decision types	Insourcing	Low
	Selective multiple sourcing	Medium
	Total sourcing	High
Service types	Information systems outsourcing	Low
	Processing outsourcing	Medium
	Business process outsourcing	High

Sources: Currie and Willcocks (1998); Lukacs (1998); Willcocks and Choi (1995).

- the outsourcing company;
- the IT service suppliers; and
- the relations between these parties.

The outsourcing company and the IT service suppliers are bound by a (contractual) agreement regarding the provision of IT services.

In outsourcing relations the outsourcing company is the party that decides to enter into a long-term contractual relation with one or more suppliers to provide it with all or part of its IT services. The IT service suppliers are responsible for the delivery of these services to the outsourcing company. When a supplier is selected, care must be taken that its profile fits the IT services requested (Lacity and Willcocks, 2001; Willcocks and Fitzgerald, 1994). It is important, for example, that the supplier be comparable in size to the outsourcing organization. If it is much larger, the outsourcing organization may not get all the attention it needs; and if it is much smaller, it may not be able to achieve the economies of scale from which the outsourcing company expects to benefit.

Relations between outsourcing companies and their IT service suppliers may take many different forms, depending on the outsourcing decisions and the type of services offered (Lukacs, 1998; Willcocks and Choi, 1995). With respect to the outsourcing decision, two choices must be made. First, between outsourcing all IT services and partial outsourcing, also called "total outsourcing" and "selective sourcing," respectively (Currie and Willcocks, 1998). (In the case of selective sourcing, part of the IT services will be provided by the company's internal IT department.) The second choice is between "single sourcing" and "multiple sourcing," that is, outsourcing to a single vendor or multiple vendors (Currie and Willcocks, 1998). Multiple sourcing obviously leads to increased coordination costs. For the type of services International Data Corporation (IDC) provides, the following differentiation has been suggested on the basis of the impact IT outsourcing has on the business organization (Lukacs, 1998): information systems outsourcing, processing outsourcing, and business process outsourcing.

Outsourcing relations differ with respect to their complexity and therefore the management attention they need. Complex IT outsourcing relations (multisite, multivendor, multiple-service, and often with contract values of more than $20 million) obviously must be much more closely monitored than small IT projects. Also, there is a relationship between the services needed and the sourcing types chosen, on the one hand, and the level of experience required for the relationship's management on the other (Currie and Willcocks, 1998; Willcocks and Choi, 1995). Generally, the higher the degree of client–supplier interdependence and the more complex the IT services involved, the higher the level of experience needed (Lukacs, 1998; Willcocks and Choi, 1995) (Table 12.1).

Figure 12.1 **A Conceptual Framework for the Governance of Complex Information Technology (IT) Outsourcing Relations**

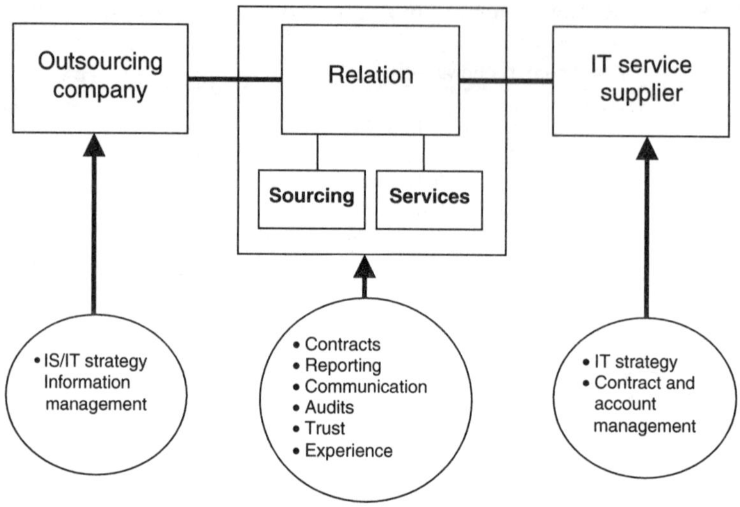

Developing the Framework

From this review of the essentials from the IT outsourcing literature, we can derive the building blocks for our conceptual framework, which is intended to provide guidance for the governance of complex outsourcing relations. The three main components of the framework are obvious: the outsourcing company, the IT service suppliers, and the relations between them. The reference theories now help us to identify the relevant governance factors for each of these three components. From the competition-based theories we have learned that companies need a positioning strategy that identifies their critical internal resources and capabilities and defines the external resources on which they depend. For the outsourcing company this means having a clear *IS/IT strategy* (including a sourcing strategy); for the IT service suppliers it means having a clear *IT strategy.*

Economic theory reveals that formal and efficient arrangements for managing and monitoring the relations are essential an both the recipient's and supplier's side of the relations, and also with respect to the relations themselves. In our opinion, this means that the outsourcing company should set up an information management (IM) function that represents its demand management, while the supplier needs a contract and account management (CAM) function to be the counterpart of its client's IM function. Formal arrangements regarding the relations involve contracts, reporting, communication, and audits.

Socioorganizational theories show that while formal arrangements are necessary they are not sufficient conditions for effective governance. To be successful, outsourcing relations should revolve around interpersonal and interorganizational relations based on shared understanding and commitment. We therefore propose that trust between the parties involved is an essential governance element. Some authors even consider trust an outcome measure of successful outsourcing relations (Barthélémy, 2003; Langfield-Smith and Smith, 2003; van der Zee and de Jong, 1999). And since we have seen that the success of outsourcing relations also depends on the experience of the partners involved, we feel that this, too, is an essential governance factor. The descriptive framework that we propose on the basis of these elements is presented in Figure 12.1.

THE CASE STUDIES AND THE INTERVIEWS

In order to corroborate our framework we analyzed fourteen case studies concerning European-based companies with pan-European or global operations that had (on the whole) successfully outsourced their IT services. For each case study, we investigated the effect of the attention paid to each of the framework's governance factors on the success of the outsourcing relationship. A note of caution: such research work is, naturally, explorative. Case studies can be used profitably in what is called analytical generalization, but not in statistical generalization (Yin, 1994). We used the case study methodology because it makes it possible to capture "reality" in considerably greater detail than other methods and it allows the analysis of a considerably greater number of variables.

For every case study, we interviewed representatives of both the outsourcing company and the service provider. In most cases four people were interviewed, which enabled us to cross-check their opinions; the minimum was two. In all interviews, the same research protocol was followed, the interviews were recorded, fully transcribed, and submitted to the interviewees for approval. Every interview started with open questions on the management of complex IT outsourcing partnerships. Then the framework's governance factors were verified and clarified by the interviewees.

Interviews were then conducted with experts from major consulting firms.[2] Each of these experts has an international track record of more than five years in research or consulting; all hold senior positions in their companies. These interviews enabled us to determine whether the case studies' results were influenced by the fact that all outsourcing organizations had used the same IT supplier: since these experts have access to information on a large number of complex IT outsourcing partnerships involving other IT services suppliers as well, talking to them helped us to avoid drawing conclusions on the basis of the best practices of only one supplier.

Finally, in addition to the interviews much time was spent gathering and analyzing supporting documentation for the case studies: corporate documents such as organization charts, requests for proposal, the minutes to relevant meetings, service-level agreements, contracts, and archival data, in addition to any information that was available in the public domain, such as annual reports and newspaper clippings. The purpose of cross-validating the documentary data, the interviews, and our own observations was to allow for "within method" data triangulation and to increase the interpretative validity of our research work (Jick, 1979).

All case studies included in our research concerned successfully managed, complex IT outsourcing relations. In order to determine whether a case was successful ten success criteria were applied (Table 12.2); at least eight out of ten had to be met for the relationship to be considered successful and the case study to be included in our work. One such criterion was contract renewal. All but two of the fourteen relationships studied were renewed after the contract period; and the two exceptions were discontinued not for business reasons but because of external market conditions. The homogeneity thus achieved in the outsourcing relations we investigated was necessary to ensure the internal validity of our conclusions (Myers and Avison, 2002).

The partnerships we investigated included a very broad scope of IT services because of the differences between the outsourcing companies studied (Table 12.3). They operated in different sectors and the contract values of their outsourcing relations varied from a total of $0.4 million to an annual $550 million. Some outsourcing companies (nos. 3, 4, and 6) belonged to the same parent company, but while companies no. 3 and no. 4 consisted of many divisions and ran complex IT outsourcing partnership relations, company no. 6 was involved in a partnership that was only just being set up. It had sold a substantial part of its IT department to an external IT supplier in return for a stake in the new company, and had agreed on a turnover guarantee for its supplier. Outsourc-

Table 12.2

Success Criteria of Outsourcing Relations

Measurable criteria	Soft criteria
Goals realized	Customer satisfaction
Service levels realized	Active communication
Expansion of the contract scope	Involvement
Renewal of the contract	Cultural fit
Absence of conflict escalation	Trust

ing company no. 5 had also sold its IT department to its supplier, but it had not taken shares in the resulting new company and had only signed service contracts for the years to come.

In all case studies, the IT supplier was Atos Origin, itself the result of the 2001 merger between the French computer services provider Atos and Origin, the Netherlands-based IT services subsidiary of Royal Philips Electronics. This group offers multinational clients a full range of IT services and solutions in forty countries around the world, including consulting, systems integration, and managed operations. The company has combined annual revenues in excess of 5 billion per annum (2005) and employs a staff of over 46,000 worldwide.[3]

A FRAMEWORK-BASED CASE STUDY ANALYSIS OF THE GOVERNANCE FACTORS

In this section all governance factors will be discussed: first, those that are considered important for the outsourcing company, then those for the service supplier, and finally the factors that apply specifically to the relation between them. Finally, a synthesis of these findings will be presented.

The Outsourcing Organization

We have proposed two governance factors that we consider of critical importance to the service recipient's side of an effective outsourcing relation: having an information systems/information technology (IS/IT) strategy and running a structured information management function.

The IS/IT Strategy

IS/IT strategies may be defined as follows: a company's long-term vision of how to optimize the use of information systems. They consist of two parts (Ward and Peppard, 2002): one for information systems and one for information technology. The IS strategy defines the organization's requirements for information and systems that are needed to support its business strategy; it is essentially concerned with demand management. Therefore, it is primarily based on the business and the translation of business requirements into information systems (alignment). But the way in which new systems and technologies may influence the company's existing business also plays an important role. An IS strategy defines the investments needed for the systems portfolio and the benefits expected from those systems. Closely related to it is the IT strategy, which delineates the way an organization's demand for information systems will be supported by technology: it is concerned with what can be called call "IT supply." This means it must anticipate new technological possibilities and market developments. The outsourcing company's combined IS/IT strategy

Table 12.3

The Case Studies: An Overview

Company	Industry (products and services)	Number of employees	Region	Total contract value (US$ million)	Contract starting date	Contract duration (years)
1	Discrete manufacturing (transport vehicles)	5,600	Europe	30	1992 (renewed 3 times)	5
2	Utilities (energy distribution)	1,500	Europe	23	1996 (renewed)	5
3[a]	Discrete manufacturing (hardware)	160,000	Asia	21	1998 (renewed)	5
4[b]	Services (consumer electronics, after-sales services)	160,000	Europe	40	1997 (renewed)	5
5	Process industry (chemicals)	64,000	Europe, Asia, North America	Confidential (yearly revenues over 75 million; initial transfer 750 employees; outsourcing partly offshore)	1999 onward	Purchase of internal IT division
6	Process industry (chemicals)	64,000	Asia	0.4	1999 (renewed)	3
7[c]	Telecommunications (connectivity)	31,500	Europe, Middle East, Asia	Confidential (> 20 million; outsourcing partly offshore)	1997	5
8	Media (newspapers)	6,100	Europe	4	1995 (renewed 2 times)	5
9[c]	Utilities (energy sales)	5,000	Europe	100	2000	5
10	Discrete manufacturing (various)	160,000	Europe, Asia, the Americas	Confidential (yearly revenues over 300 million; initial transfer 1,500 employees; outsourcing partly offshore)	1990 onward	Purchase of internal IT division (various contracts)
11	Consumer packaged goods (confidential)	100,000	Europe	2 (offshore)	2002	2
12	Consumer packaged goods (confidential)	60,000	Europe	Confidential (10,000 SAP seats)	2002	3
13	Telecommunications (mobile)	1,500	Europe	Confidential (full outsourcing of IT infrastructure services)	2003	3
14	Services (software)	1,000	Europe, Asia, the Americas	Confidential (over 35 FTEs; offshore)	1998 (renewed)	5

[a]This company is a subsidiary of company no. 6.

[b]This company is a subsidiary of company no. 6, but its activities are so different from those of company no. 3 that it is classified under services rather than discrete manufacturing.

[c]For these two case studies no interviews were conducted; only the outsourcing contracts were analyzed. The insights reported here are based on the personal involvement of one of the authors, and on written documents such as meeting reports and e-mails.

must pay focus explicitly on its sourcing strategy (Ward and Peppard, 2002). And even when the company decides to outsource its IS and IT, defining and implementing its IS/IT strategy always remains its own responsibility (Willcocks and Choi, 1995).

The importance of having an IS/IT strategy is corroborated by all of the case studies: every outsourcing company we investigated in the process of this study have such a strategy. Five companies (nos. 3, 4, 8, 9, and 10) had chosen to share their entire IS/IT strategy with their service provider. All companies except no. 1 had an IT board chaired by the company's chief information officer (CIO) expressly responsible for implementing its IS/IT strategy. This board always consisted of business managers (more specifically, general business unit managers) and the company's IT managers. The business managers' knowledge level and capabilities were usually sufficient (except in companies nos. 3, 6, and 10), as was their attention to the contract (except in companies nos. 9 and 12). Insufficiencies were found to have had a direct negative impact on the success of their companies' outsourcing relations, according to the companies' interviewees. The experts we interviewed, however, were generally very skeptical about the quality of the IS/IT strategies of most of the outsourcing companies. In their opinion, most IS/IT strategies were limited to the settlement of yearly IT budgets: "Quite often, IT strategy has very little to do with strategy. It is more like yearly budgets: save some money and there you go."

Information Management

Information management is a responsibility of the outsourcing company that cannot be outsourced; it constitutes the interface between the business processes and the IT suppliers. Generally, the IM function has a coordinating role. Its responsibility must therefore be separated from service delivery processes in order to avoid conflicts of interest. The IM function is headed by the company's CIO and further includes several dedicated information managers and business analysts for each of the various business processes or business units (Beulen 2004; Ward and Peppard, 2002). In most of today's outsourcing companies the CIO reports to a member of the board of directors (Potter, 2003; Remenyi, Grant, and Pather, 2005). Thus, the IM function's decisions usually carry sufficient authority to enable it to coordinate the company's IT outsourcing relations. Obviously, the IM function must have the business and IT knowledge to fulfill this delegated responsibility (Enns, Huff, and Higgins, 2003).

All case studies and experts confirmed our view that the information management function is a prerequisite to the effective management of complex IT outsourcing partnerships. There was general agreement on the need to implement IM independently from the internal IT department and to have it headed by the CIO. Of the case studies investigated, only company no. 1 still had a combined internal IT department and IM function, and according to the interviewees this combination did indeed hinder the governance of its outsourcing relations. Company no. 2 formerly had such a combination too, but had already begun to separate them for just this reason. In all other cases they were already separate. The importance of such a separation was explained by one of the experts: "Investments in hardware platforms and employee training made by IT departments really stop innovation. This limits the degree to which a company can utilize its IT. For this reason many companies originally began to outsource their IT services to external suppliers." In most cases, if the size of the company made it economically feasible, information management was organized per business unit. Company no. 5 is an excellent example of this structure: each division had a group information officer (GIO), who reported hierarchically to the group's business managers and functionally to the CIO. The company's divisions consisted of business units, each with its own information manager, who reported hierarchically to the unit's business managers and functionally to the GIO. Companies nos. 3, 4, 10, 11, and 12, the largest of the companies we investigated, had a similar structure. Such a structure helps to align business and IT. As for the knowledge base of the information managers, the general opinion was that it should include both business and IT knowledge. In fact, in the Asian IT outsourcing partnership (company no. 3) the outsourcing company replaced its IMs because they were lacking in business knowledge.

The IT Service Supplier

From the perspective of the IT supplier, too, we proposed two governance factors as prerequisites for a well-managed relation: having a well-defined IT strategy and running an adequate contract and account management function. These will be discussed next.

IT Strategy

In outsourcing partnerships the service provider needs an IT strategy too (Pinnington and Woolcock, 1997). Since it is its core business to provide IT services, its market approach and focus should be sparklingly clear as well as consistent and coherent (Grönroos, 1990). The purpose of the service provider's IT strategy has therefore been defined in the literature as one that enables it to provide the best possible supply of IT resources (Ward and Peppard, 2002).

The service provider in the case studies we investigated focused on large, European-based clients with subsidiaries all over the world, seeking growth opportunities both with existing clients and new clients. Market focus differed in each country and was based on a diversification strategy. Consequently, each business unit (one per country) had its own profit and loss responsibility, which made it somewhat difficult to align market focus across all countries. As one expert said: "A scattered market focus limits capabilities for developing one's knowledge of specific industries."

The representatives of the service recipients we interviewed indicated that their companies had a strong preference for "one-stop shopping." This made the service provider an interesting partner, since it offered end-to-end services. Nevertheless, the majority of the outsourcing companies studied here (nos. 1, 3, 4, 5, 7, 10, 12, and 14) had opted for multiple outsourcing, and their IT services were provided by several suppliers.

Contract and Account Management

In order to structure their relations with outsourcing companies, IT service suppliers must have a contract and account management function. Basically, it is responsible for realizing what has been agreed on; its orientation is customer satisfaction (Holden, 1990). This function monitors the fulfillment of the supplier's contractual obligations and maintains its relations with the outsourcing company. The CAM function, then, is the IT supplier's counterpart of the information management role in the outsourcing company. Its task is to function as the link, the main contact point between the service recipient's business functions (represented by their IM function) and the service provider. Contract and account managers must therefore have both business and IT knowledge (Grönroos, 1990).

All of the above factors were supported by the interviews. As the sales costs for expanding existing relations are substantially lower than for developing new leads, the service provider had already implemented a strong contract and account management. Regarding the structure of the CAM function, all experts agreed: it must mirror that of the outsourcing company. Indeed, in all case studies, the interviewees confirmed this point, and all felt that this mirrored structure contributes to the management of IT outsourcing partnerships. Only in the case of outsourcing company no. 4 was the CAM function part of a much larger CAM organization that was responsible for many such IT outsourcing partnership contracts. As a result, this particular partnership was not given the attention it needed and it did indeed suffer some damage as a result. The CA manager responsible for the provider's contacts with company no. 4 remarked: "Our CAM and service delivery responsibilities were merged into one role. This caused potential conflicts of interest since the contract manager should be responsible for customer satisfaction and the service delivery manager for the utilization of our service delivery capabilities."

Our interviews revealed an important aspect in this regard: the continuity of personnel in CAM positions. In the case of outsourcing company no. 2, the contract and account manager was replaced, which caused service delivery disruptions and a serious decline in the relationship between the outsourcing company and their supplier. Something similar happened with outsourcing company no. 6, which found that when several contract and account managers were replaced, and a (temporary) decrease in delivery continuity was noticed.

The Relationship

We will now discuss in some more detail the six governance factors proposed above as important to the maintenance and development of the outsourcing relationship itself: contracts, reporting, communication, audits, trust, and experience.

Contracts

Contracts are of key importance in managing IT outsourcing relations. Outsourcing contracts therefore require a proper contract structure that includes clearly described agreed upon service levels and penalties for not meeting them (Aubert, Rivard, and Patry, 2003; Kern and Blois, 2002). Somewhat surprisingly, perhaps, contracts must also be flexible (Shepherd, 1999) to be able to accommodate the inevitable changes in type, level, and quantity of the services to be delivered. Such flexibility, however, is not easily built into a contract (Domberger, Fernandez, and Fiebig, 2000).

The outsourcing relations we investigated all worked on the basis of comparable contract structures. This may be due to the fact that all partnerships were contracted by a single IT supplier. But our professional experience indicates that IT outsourcing partnerships with other IT suppliers have comparable structures, and the experts we interviewed confirmed this. This common structure is as follows. A corporate framework agreement (CFA) is set up, including the overall conditions and some general terms and conditions. Suspended from this CFA, as it were, are framework agreements, specifying which services are delivered to which of the client's organizational units. According to one expert: "The way the contracts are structured must reflect the way the outsourcing company is structured. Therefore, in centralized outsourcing companies all organizational units use service-oriented contract structures, whereas in decentralized outsourcing companies business-unit-oriented contract structures are used." This, too, is corroborated by the case studies: companies nos. 1 and 2 were centralized companies and indeed structured their contracts around the services they procured; and companies nos. 3, 4, 5, and 6 operated in a more decentralized manner and therefore structured their contracts on their organizational units.

One contract layer further down we find the service-level agreements (SLAs). These specify the levels at which specific services are to be delivered. Increasingly, balanced scorecards (BSCs) are used to allow parties to a contract to adapt their SLAs. One expert explained: "The balanced scorecard is a useful tool for discussions at both the tactical and strategic levels when contract changes have to be made. Balanced scorecards ensure that the discussion remains focused on the business instead of getting bogged down in technical details." However, in most of the cases investigated, BSCs were not actually used to manage the outsourcing relations; only companies no. 4, 8, and 12 did so.

Everyone involved observed that there is a strong need for flexibility in outsourcing contracts. Outsourcing relations can be quite dynamic because of constant changes in business and in the field of IT, and for the partners to be able to deal with these dynamics their contracts must be flexible. But only in the case studies involving companies nos. 2, 4, 5, and 8 was the service provider able to supply this flexibility, which shows that there is significant variation in how flexible a supplier can be. Maximum flexibility was found in the contract used for company no. 5: there, the outsourcing company had no purchasing commitments to its supplier at all. There were only a purchasing agreement, a CFA, and a service catalogue with the IT services offered and their prices. The outsourcing company's business units had no obligation to contract services from its preferred IT-supplier, which therefore had to prove its added value to each individual business unit. In all other cases the outsourcing company gave revenue guarantees. On the basis of our professional experience, however, we expect that future IT outsourcing partnerships will no longer include any turnover guarantees. Flexibility will be more important.

Reporting

In order for the outsourcing company to be able to track service delivery the IT supplier must report on a regular basis regarding the services delivered and their delivery level (Cullen and Willcocks, 2003; Palvia, 1995). For most outsourcing contracts, "regularly" means "monthly" (Wallace, 2000). Such reports are then used as input for discussions between the outsourcing company and its IT suppliers, which helps them to manage their relations. In five of the case studies (nos. 1, 2, 5, 7, and 10), a lack of such reporting was found to have hindered the relationship. Most problems were the result of reports that were overly technology oriented, instead of focused on business-related items, as they might have been if balanced scorecards or dashboards had been used (and as were used in case studies nos. 4, 8, and 12). For all outsourcing relations it is essential that the parties involved discuss their reporting practices; and indeed, we found that scheduled monthly meetings were held for this purpose in each relationship we analyzed. The importance of reporting is further emphasized by one of our experts, who said: "Service providers should also use reporting to take preventive measures, for example, to add extra storage facilities to the infrastructure in order to prevent incidents in the backup processes." And again, such future issues and suggestions were indeed found in the reports of all of the relationships studied.

Communication

Regular communication between the recipient and its suppliers is considered essential for establishing flexible partnership relations (Lee and Kim, 1999). However, communication has to be organized (Pollalis, 2003). Most of the IT outsourcing partnerships investigated showed similar communication structures that were organized into three management levels (Beulen, 2004): strategic, tactical, and operational. At the strategic level was a steering committee; among its members were the outsourcing company's general and IT managers and the IT supplier's general and account managers. Steering committee meetings typically took place once or twice a year. Service review meetings were held at the tactical level to monitor overall current performance and to anticipate the recipient's future requirements; these were held on a monthly basis. During these meetings the service provider's performance was discussed on the basis of their regular reports and in relation to the partnership's service-level management processes. Finally, the supplier's employees had daily operational discussions with their client's information managers.

The case studies that showed adequate communication structures were those in which the partners communicated with one another on the basis of a clear and layered setup. For each level the authorizations and topics to be discussed were detailed and described in the outsourcing contract. Nevertheless, in eight of our fourteen case studies the representatives interviewed felt that the communication in their outsourcing relation had been insufficient.

One of the experts interviewed shared an interesting observation with us: "In most IT outsourcing partnerships I have seen, the parties agreed on the communication structure and scheduled regular meetings. But the real issue, I feel, is what's on the agenda. Most discussions, even at the steering committee level, concern operational problems, which keeps the partnership from maturing. What they really should discuss is how they will work in the future." Our analysis of companies nos. 2 and 4 confirmed this view.

Audits

It is important for the outsourcing organization to formulate agreements about the conduct of audits (Sayana, 2004; Scott, 1996), that is, verifications of the supplier's processes. In addition, agreements must be made concerning regular benchmarks (Cullen and Willcocks, 2003; Lacity and Hirschheim, 1995, 1998): Is the price–quality ratio of the IT services provided in conformance with what is usual in the market?

IT suppliers who work in a process-oriented manner, for example, through International Organization for Standardization (ISO) certification or the implementation of Information Technology Infrastructure Library (ITIL) or Capability Maturity Model (CMM) procedures, are generally in a better position to provide the services contracted for. The experts interviewed considered this to be a critical success factor for the IT supplier. The service recipients interviewed felt that the absence or insufficiency of certification would disqualify prospective suppliers participating in the selection process for service provisioning relations with their companies. (This was explicitly mentioned by representatives of outsourcing companies nos. 1, 3, 4, 5, 9, 10, and 14). In all contracts investigated for this study, both audit and benchmark clauses were included. In most contracts there was a limit of one audit per year, since the costs to service providers for allowing their clients and their consultants to audit their work are substantial.

The most efficient way to provide for this kind of assurance is by third party statement. One expert added: "In some industries, such as the financial sector, third party statements are not sufficient. Regulations demand more assurance. Of course, these regulations are different for each country."

Trust

Trust is a particularly important criterion in the selection process used by outsourcing organizations (Earl, 1996; Lacity and Hirschheim, 1993; Willcocks and Fitzgerald, 1994). It must be maintained over the contract period (Beulen, 2004) because contracts cannot replace the trust between outsourcing companies and their suppliers (Lander et al., 2004). In other words: outsourcing contracts are signed on the basis of trust, but trust is also needed to maintain such relations. Mutual trust can be established and developed by exchanging strategy information with the objective of aligning the partners' business strategies: the complementarity of shared goals (Lacity and Hirschheim, 1995). In practice, this is not so easy, however. The parties are not always equals, as they should be in a true partnership, which significantly influences the way they feel about each other and thus the way that their governance relationship will be set up. Unequal relations can pose a problem; they were found, for example, in case studies nos. 3, 4, 10, 11, and 12. As one expert said: "Find an equal partner or forget the idea of a partnership." Nevertheless, in most of the case studies in our research the interviewees indicated that there was a high level of trust. The service provider usually invoices in advance, for example. The basis for such intercompany trust is usually found in the personal trust between the top people involved in the outsourcing relationship.

Experience

For the purposes of this chapter, we consider experience to be the level of capabilities of both the service recipient and the service providers in managing outsourcing partnerships (Bahli and Rivard, 2004; Lacity and Willcocks, 1998; Linder, 2004). Those interviewed for eight of our fourteen case studies felt that capabilities in managing the IT outsourcing relationship had been insufficient on both sides, which at times they felt had seriously threatened its success. In other case studies (nos. 1, 2, and 8), the interviewees stated that a significant positive contribution to the success of the relation was made by the fact that the team of representatives responsible for managing the outsourcing relationship remained unchanged.

Experience may be lacking for many reasons, and we found several examples. In case study no. 13, it was reported that a change of the provider's contract manager after five years was a threat to the relationship. In case study no. 3, the service recipient's information managers and business analysts were unable to manage their own company's needs because their focus was too narrowly technical. After one year and after consulting the service provider, they were therefore replaced by more business-oriented representatives. In case study no. 9, the representatives of both the service recipient and the service providers were replaced frequently, partly because the average project duration was less than eighteen months. Replacing them, however, was always a hot topic in the strategic-level discussions. Only after three years did this outsourcing relation stabilize, because both parties were then willing to commit to keeping the same people in their contract management roles for at least thirty-six months. Finally, the lack of capabilities in case study no. 6 was related to the inexperience of the provider's representatives and the limited value of the outsourcing contract. For the service recipient this outsourcing relationship was a regional pilot project, and the provider therefore made available people with only limited track records to manage their relations with the client.

Synthesis of the Case Findings

Summarizing the results of our analysis of the case studies from the perspective of reference disciplines reveals the following patterns. First, there was unanimous support for the need for the outsourcing company and its service provider to have, respectively, the *IS/IT strategy* and *IT strategy* called for by competition-based theories. If these are not clearly established, the outsourcing relationship is endangered. Furthermore, the provider's market approach is greatly improved by offering a consistent service portfolio based on its IT strategy.

Formal organizational arrangements to manage the outsourcing relationship were well established in all of the case studies investigated, in line with the economic theories approach. In every outsourcing company an information management function represented the company's business interests vis-à-vis their service provider; and these IM functions were organized independently of their companies' internal IT departments in order to avoid conflicts of interests. When economically feasible, the IM function was organized per business unit. On the providers' side, the IM functions were paired by contract and account management functions whose structures mirrored those of the outsourcing company. Everyone agreed that having as few personnel changes as possible in CAM positions is of key importance. Contracts with clearly described service levels and structured to reflect the organizational structure of the outsourcing company were found to be essential for successful outsourcing. However, all agreed that contracts should also offer flexibility. We expect that the need for flexibility is so strong that future contracts will cease to include turnover guarantees. In about a third of the case studies investigated, reporting proved to be a problem, mainly because the reports presented by the provider were too technical and therefore not sufficiently business oriented. Almost all of the outsourcing companies studied for this research had set up communication structures layered into strategic, tactical, and operational levels. The need for regular (yearly) audits was stipulated in the contracts of all the outsourcing relationships studied; a lack of certification on the part of the provider was considered a disqualifier in any selection process.

Trust and experience were proposed from a socioorganizational theory point of view. Both were recognized as essential factors in successful outsourcing relations. All recipients' and providers' representatives interviewed indicated they had experienced a high level of trust. Finally, a lack of experience in managing complex IT outsourcing relations was found to cause problems in more than half of our case studies. As with the CAM functions, personnel continuity was considered of prime importance.

CONCLUSIONS AND DISCUSSION

Managing complex IT outsourcing partnerships is not an easy task. Both the outsourcing company and the IT suppliers must do their utmost to turn their collaboration into a sustained success. The case studies we investigated and the interviews we conducted with experts in the field showed that having the best people available is not sufficient to manage complex IT outsourcing partnerships successfully.

In this chapter we therefore propose a descriptive framework identifying ten governance factors of critical importance to the success of complex IT outsourcing partnerships. These factors were derived from socioorganizational, economic, and competition-based theories. In addition we investigated a number of case studies and these provided additional support for this framework.

IT outsourcing governance requires substantial senior management attention. But to date most companies have only limited experience with such complex outsourcing relations (Beulen and Ribbers, 2002; De Haes and Van Grembergen, 2004; Lacity and Hirschheim, 1995). This is a problem for the implementation of IT governance in outsourcing relations, which is worsened by the increasing number of national laws and regulations concerning corporate and IT governance.[4]

What can we expect for the future? IT services will increasingly become commodities. Unit prices will be common practice not only for desktop seats but for ERP seats as well. Commercial off-the-shelf solutions will be the preferred option and their customization will be kept to a minimum. "On demand" and "utility" service provisioning are on their way (Ross and Westerman, 2004), and CSC, EDS, and IBM[5] are developing them. At present, these are mainly marketing concepts, but in the near future service recipients will likely have access to the required services in the required volumes, even though these fluctuate over the contract period, and they will only be charged for what they use. We therefore expect decreased complexity with respect to this type of outsourcing.

It is difficult to say what consequences the dramatic growth in business process outsourcing (BPO) will have for IT governance. The business literature provides only exploratory research (Willcocks et al., 2004). We expect business managers to pay increased attention when both IT services and actual business processes are outsourced to service providers. BPO requires much more frequent communication because the outsourced services are more directly linked to the recipient's primary business processes. On the other hand, this communication will be much more focused on the ratio of actual output versus contracted output, instead of on detailed technical discussions. Such communication is less complex. However, the governance of BPO relations must be investigated in more detail to formulate hard and fast conclusions.

NOTES

1. For an overview, see: www.ecgi.org.
2. CSC Research Services, Ernst & Young Consulting, GartnerGroup, International Data Corporation, and Nolan, Norton & Company.
3. See: www.atosorigin.com.
4. See: www.ecgi.org.
5. See: www.csc.com; www.eds.com; www.ibm.com.

REFERENCES

Aubert, B.; Rivard, S.; and Patry, M. 2003. A tale of two outsourcing contracts: An agency-theoretical perspective. *Wirtschaftsinformatik*, 45, 2, 181–190.

Bahli, B. and Rivard, S. 2004. Validating measures of information technology outsourcing risk factors. *Omega*, 33, 2, 175–187.

Barthélémy, J. 2003. The hard and soft sides of IT outsourcing management. *European Management Journal*, 21, 5 (October), 539–548.

Beulen E. 2004. Governance in IT outsourcing partnerships. In W. van Grembergen, ed., *Strategies for Information Technology Governance*. Hershey: Idea Group, 310–341.

Beulen, E. and Ribbers, P. 2002. Managing complex IT outsourcing partnerships. In *Hawaii International Conference on Systems Sciences 2002*. Hawaii: IEEE Computer Society Press.

———. 2003. A case study of managing IT outsourcing partnerships in Asia. *Communications of the AIS*, 11, 21 (March), 357–378.

Brown, C. and Magill, S. 1994. Alignment of the IS functions with the enterprise: Toward a model of antecedents. *Management Information Systems Quarterly*, 18, 4, 371–404.

Cullen, S. and Willcocks, L. 2003. *Intelligent IT outsourcing: Eight building blocks to success*. Oxford: Butterworth-Heinemann.

Currie W. and Willcocks, L. 1998. Analyzing four types of IT-outsourcing decisions in the context of scale, client/server, interdependency and risk migration. *Information Systems Journal*, 8, 2 (April), 119–143.

Cyert, R.; March, J.; and Clarkson, G. 1963. *Behavioral Theory of the Firm*. Englewood Cliffs, NJ: Prentice Hall.

Daft, R. 2001. *Organization Theory and Design*, 7th ed. Cincinnati, OH: South-Western.

Davis, G. and Powell, W. 1992. Organization-environment relations. In M. Dunnette and L. Hough, eds., *Handbook of Industrial and Organizational Psychology*, vol. 3. Palo Alto, CA: Consulting Psychologists Press, 315–375.

De Haes, S. and Van Grembergen, W. 2004. IT governance and its mechanisms. *Information Systems Control Journal*, 1, 27–33.

Dibbern, J.; Goles, T.; Hirschheim, R.; and Jayatilaka, B. 2004. Information systems outsourcing: A survey and analysis of the literature. *Database for Advances in Information Systems*, 35, 4 (Fall), 6–102.

Doh, J. 2005. Offshore outsourcing: Implications for international business and strategic management theory and practice. *Journal of Management Studies*, 42, 3, 695–704.

Domberger, S.; Fernandez, P.; and Fiebig, D. 2000. Modeling the price, performance and contract characteristics of IT outsourcing. *Journal of Information Technology*, 15, 2, 107–118.

Dyer, J. and Singh, H. 1998. The relational view: Cooperative strategy and sources of inter-organizational competitive advantage. *Academy of Management Review*, 23, 4, 660–679.

Earl, M. 1996. The risks of outsourcing IT. *Sloan Management Review*, 37, 2 (Spring), 26–32.

El Sawy, O.; Malhotra, A.; Gosain, S.; and Young, K. 1999. IT-intensive value innovation in the electronic economy: insights from Marshall industries. *Management Information Systems Quarterly*, 23, 3 (September), 305–335.

Enns, H.; Huff, S.; and Higgins, C. 2003. CIO influence behaviors: The impact of technical background. *Information & Management*, 40, 5 (May), 467–485.

Galbraith, J. 1993. *Organizing for the Future. The New Logic for Managing Complex Organizations.* San Francisco: Jossey-Bass.

Galbraith, J.; Mohrman, S.; Lawler, E. 1998. *Tomorrow's Organization. Crafting Winning Capabilities.* San Francisco: Jossey-Bass.

Grönroos, C. 1990. *Service Management and Marketing. Managing the Moment of Truth in Services Competition.* Lanham, MD: Lexington Books.

Grover, V. and Teng, J. 1993. The decision to outsource information systems functions. *Journal of Systems Management*, 44, 11 (November), 34–38.

Guldentops, E. 2004. Governing information technology through COBIT. In W. van Grembergen, ed., *Strategies for Information Technology Governance.* Hershey, PA: Idea Group, 269–309.

Holden, J. 1990. *Power Base Selling. Secrets of an Ivy League Street Fighter.* New York: Wiley.

ISACA. 2002. *IS Auditing Guideline, IT GOVERNANCE,* document # 060.020.050, 5.

Jick, T. 1979. Mixing qualitative and quantitative methods, triangulation in action. *Administrative Science Quarterly*, 24, 602–611.

Keil, P. 2005. Principal agent theory and its application to analyze outsourcing of software development. International Conference on Software Engineering. Session: Economics-Driven Software Engineering Research (EDSER), St. Louis, MO (May 16).

Kern, T. and Blois, K. 2002. Norm development in outsourcing relationships. *Journal of Information Technology*, 17, 1, 33–42.

King, W. 2005. IT strategy and innovation: Outsourcing becomes more complex. *Information Systems Management*, 22, 2, 89–90.

Klepper, R. 1995. The management of partnering development in IS outsourcing. *Journal of Information Technology*, 10, 4, 249–258.

Kumar, K. and van Dissel, H.G. 1996. Sustainable collaboration: Managing conflict and cooperation in interorganizational systems. *MIS Quarterly*, 20, 3 (September), 279–299.

Lacity, M. and Hirschheim, R. 1993. *Information Systems Outsourcing.* Chichester, UK: Wiley.

———. 1995. *Beyond the Information Systems Outsourcing Bandwagon.* Chichester, UK: Wiley.

Lacity, M. and Willcocks, L. 1998. An empirical investigation of information technology sourcing practices: Lessons from experience. *Management Information Systems Quarterly*, 22, 3 (September), 363–408.

———. 2001. *Global Information Technology Outsourcing: In Search of Business Advantage.* Chichester, UK: Wiley.

Lander, M.; Purvis, R.; McCray, G.; and Leigh, W. 2004. Trust-building mechanisms utilized in outsourced IS development projects: A case study. *Information & Management*, 41, 4 (March), 509–528.

Langfield-Smith, K. and Smith, D. 2003. Management control systems and trust in outsourcing relationships. *Management Accounting Research*, 14, 3, 281–307.

Lee, J.N. and Kim, Y.G. 1999. Effect of partnership quality on IS outsourcing success: Conceptual framework and empirical validation. *Journal of Management Information Systems*, 15, 4, 29–61.

Linder, J. 2004. Transformational outsourcing. *MIT Sloan Management Review*, 45, 2, 52–58.

Luftman, J. and Brier, T. 1999. Knowledge management: Achieving and sustaining business-IT alignment. *California Management Review*, 42, 1, 109–122.

Lukacs, M. 1998. *European Consulting and Management Services: European Outsourcing Markets and Trends 1996–2002.* London: International Data Corporation.

McKeen, J. and Smith, H. 2001. Managing external relationships in IS. In *Hawaii International Conference on Systems Sciences 2001*, Hawaii: IEEE Computer Society Press.

Mintzberg, H. 1979. *The Structuring of Organizations.* Englewood Cliffs, NJ: Prentice Hall.

Myers, M. and Avison, D. 2002. *Qualitative Research in Information Systems: A Reader.* London: Sage.

Palvia, P. 1995. A dialectic view of information systems outsourcing: Pros and cons. *Information & Management*, 29, 5 (November), 265–275.

Peterson, R.; O'Callaghan, R.; and Ribbers, P. 2000. Information technology governance by design: Investigating hybrid configurations and integration mechanisms. In *International Conference on Information Systems.* Atlanta: ICIS Administrative Office, 435–453.

Pfeffer J. and Salancik, G.R. 1978. *The External Control of Organizations.* New York: HarperCollins.

Pinnington, A. and Woolcock, P. 1997. The role of vendor companies in IS/IT outsourcing. *International Journal of Information Management*, 17, 3, 199–210.

Pollalis, Y. 2003. Patterns of co-alignment in information-intensive organizations: Business performance through integration strategies. *International Journal of Information Management*, 23, 6 (December), 469–492.

Porter, M.E. 1980. *Competitive Strategy.* New York: Free Press.

———. 1985. *Competitive Advantage.* New York: Free Press.

Potter, R. 2003. How CIOs manage their superiors' expectations. *Communications of the Association for Computing Machinery*, 46, 8, 74–79.

Prahalad, C.K. and Hamel, G. 1990. The core competence of the corporation. *Harvard Business Review*, 68, 3, 79–91.

Remenyi, D.; Grant, K.; and Pather, S. 2005. The chameleon: A metaphor for the chief information officer. *Journal of General Management*, 30, 3, 1–12.

Ross, J. and Westerman, G. 2004. Preparing for utility computing: The role of IT architecture and relationship management. *IBM Systems Journal*, 43, 1, 5–19.

Rothery, B. and Robertson, I. 1995. *The Truth About Outsourcing.* Aldershot, UK: Gower.

Sambamurthy, V. and Zmud, R. 1999. Arrangements for information technology governance: A theory of multiple contingencies. *MIS Quarterly*, 23, 2, 261–290.

———. 2000. Research commentary: The organizing logic for an enterprise's IT activities in the digital era—A prognosis for practice and a call for research. *Information Systems Research*, 11, 2 (June), 105–114.

Sayana, S. 2004. IT Audit basics: Audit of outsourcing. *Information Systems Control Journal*, 5, 11–14.

Scott, S. 1996. Audit and control of information services outsourcing. *IS Audit & Control Journal*, 6, 46–51.

Shepherd, A. 1999. Outsourcing IT in a changing world. *European Management Journal*, 17, 1, 64–84.

Thompson, J.D. 1967. *Organizations in Action: Social Sciences Bases of Administrative Theory.* New York: McGraw-Hill.

Van Grembergen W. 2002. Introduction to the mini track: IT governance and its mechanisms. In *Hawaii International Conference on System Science 2002.* Hawaii: IEEE Computer Society Press.

Wallace, W. 2000. Reporting practices: Potential lessons from Cendant Corporation. *European Management Journal*, 18, 3 (June), 328–333.

Ward, J. and Peppard, J. 2002. *Strategic Planning for Information Systems*, 3d ed. West Sussex, UK: Wiley.

Weill P. and Broadbent, M. 1998. *Leveraging the New Infrastructure: How Market Leaders Capitalize on Information Technology.* Boston, MA: Harvard Business School Press.

Weill, P. and Ross, J. 2004. *IT Governance.* Boston, MA: Harvard Business School Press.

Willcocks, L. and Choi, C. 1995. Co-operative partnerships and "total" IT-outsourcing: From contractual obligation to strategic alliance? *European Management Journal*, 13, 1 (March), 67–78.

Willcocks, L. and Fitzgerald, G. 1994. *A Business Guide to Outsourcing IT.* London: Business Intelligence.

Willcocks, L. and Lester, S. 1996. Beyond the IT productivity paradox. *European Management Journal*, 14, 3 (June), 279–290.

Willcocks, L.; Hindle, J.; Feeny, D.; and Lacity, M. 2004. IT and business process outsourcing: The knowledge potential. *Information Systems Management*, 21, 3 (Summer), 7–15.

Williamson, O. 1975. *Markets and Hierarchies.* New York: Free Press.

Yin, R. 1994. *Case Study Research: Design and Methods.* London: Sage.

van der Zee, J. and de Jong, B. 1999. Alignment is not enough: Integrating business and information technology management with the balanced business scorecard. *Journal of Management Information Systems*, 16, 2, 137–156.

CHAPTER 13

COORDINATION OF COMPLEX INFORMATION SYSTEM DEVELOPMENT PROJECTS

A Case Study of Finnish Universities

ANTTI NURMI, PETRI HALLIKAINEN, AND MATTI ROSSI

Abstract: *Coordination is considered critical for the success of large information system (IS) development projects. Generally, coordination focuses on managing the interdependencies among different organizational units within one organization. However, in IS outsourcing the interdependencies go beyond organizational boundaries into coordination of IS development between a software vendor and a client company. Our research focuses on the coordination of IS development in a setting where several vendors and client organizations develop a common information system. In this study, we investigate the characteristic features of system development in such a complex environment. We look especially at the coordination mechanisms and their evolution over time and the phases of system development. Our analysis shows that the coordination mechanisms become more formal and control oriented in the later stages of system development. This formality impedes the flexibility of the development process.*

Keywords: *Coordination Mechanisms, Complex Information System Development Projects, Outsourcing*

INTRODUCTION

As the software industry matures, less and less software is developed in-house (McFarlan and Nolan, 1995). Tighter information technology (IT) budgets force organizations to outsource their IT functions and system development, which are not their "core competence." Inevitably, some control over the development process is lost. Hence, the management of coordination between different parties involved in the development project becomes vital for the success of the project (Adler, 1995; Kraut and Streeter, 1995; Sabherwal, 2003).

We studied a consortium of Finnish universities developing a common student record system to find out what happens in practice in a multiple stakeholder outsourcing project. The common system development "process" has been going on for about ten years. Coordination between the different universities and vendors takes place through a mediating organization, that is, a consortium that has primary responsibility for system development. Hence, we sought to determine the primary coordination mechanisms used by the consortium organization with respect to clients and vendors. As this system development project has a relatively long history, we have also had a good opportunity to study the evolution of the coordination mechanisms over time. The consortium has evolved notably over the years. At the beginning of the project, the consortium consisted of five universities, but over the years it has expanded to thirteen. Decreased funding from the government in the mid 1990s and a scarcity of resources has forced the universities to cooperate.

We extended Sabherwal's (2003) analysis of coordination mechanisms to a complex setting with multiple stakeholders and studied the different coordination mechanisms applied. Sabherwal (2003) conducted multiple case studies and studied coordination mechanisms, factors affecting coordination mechanisms and their evolution in outsourced information systems development (ISD) projects. In addition, his analysis covers both client and vendor perspectives in outsourced system development projects. Following Sabherwal's reference model, we examined how the coordination mechanisms evolved during the system development process.

The structure of this chapter is as follows. In the next section we briefly review the existing theories on coordination in IS projects and discuss the theoretical implications of different sourcing strategies (simple dyadic, co-sourcing, multivendors, and complex). In the third section we introduce the research subject and methods. This is followed by our case description in the fourth section. In the fifth section, the coordination mechanisms and their evolution in our case setting are described. The results are discussed, and finally conclusions are drawn and future research directions are outlined.

COORDINATION THEORIES AND THE EVOLUTION OF COORDINATION MECHANISMS

Coordination problems have been studied in different scientific disciplines (Malone and Crowston, 1994). In information economics the research has focused on coordination costs (Bakos and Brynjolfsson, 1993; Gurbaxani and Whang, 1991). Coordination as a phenomenon has also been studied in organizational studies (Galbraith, 1973; Ring and Van de Ven, 1992, 1994) and in computer science. Each discipline has a different focus, but the basic phenomenon is the same: the process of managing dependencies among activities (Malone and Crowston, 1994). There are many different ways to categorize different coordination mechanisms. McCann and Galbraith (1981) proposed that coordination between organizational units can vary along three dimensions: cooperativeness, formality, and localization. According to these three dimensions, the endpoints of the organizational coordination mode continuum would be organic coordination (cooperative, informal, and decentralized) and mechanistic control (controlling, formal, and centralized). DeSanctis and Jackson (1994) proposed that the major mechanisms for facilitating interunit coordination of IT management are structural design approaches, functional coordination modes, and computer-based communication systems. Adler (1995) found five different coordination mechanisms (noncoordination, standards, schedules and plans, mutual adjustment, and teams) in electrical and mechanical engineering product development. Nidumolu (1996) saw coordination mechanisms as horizontal or vertical. Grant (1996) categorized coordination within a firm as rules and directives, sequencing, routines, and group problem solving and decision making. Crowston's (1997) categorization is based on dependencies of task versus task, task versus resource, and resource versus resource. Kim (2001) modeled inter- and intraorganizational coordination by three major components: object, actor, and process. In Kim's model all of the relations between organizational units can be modeled with these three components.

Van de Ven, Dahlbecq, and Koenig (1976) defined coordination as a mode of linking together different parts of an organization to accomplish a set of collective tasks. Malone and Crowston (1994) saw coordination as the process of managing dependencies among activities. However, these definitions are quite close to the concept of control (e.g., Kirsch 1997), and in general, coordination and control can be seen as different sides of the same coin. Both coordination and control have been studied extensively in the ISD literature, and they have crucial differences. While coordination focuses on managing interdependencies among multiple individuals or activities involved in the overall task, control focuses on improving performance relative to a certain overall goal when the goals of individual stakeholders differ from those of the larger overall entity (Sabherwal, 2003). It is also worth noting that if there is no dependency, then there will be no control and therefore both concepts are used in situations where there are dependencies among different intra- or inter-organizational units or among tasks.

Control can be exercised via formal or informal modes (Choudhury and Sabherwal, 2003; Kirsch, 1996, 1997; Kirsch et al., 2002). Furthermore, formal control modes can be divided into outcome control and behavior control; informal control modes can be divided into clan control and self-control. In outcome control, the controller is less interested in the process than in the outcome. In behavior control, on the contrary, the controller wants to control the process by issuing rules or procedures. Clan control is by definition a situation where there is a group of dependent people sharing common goals (Kirsch, 1996). Clan control is very close to the definition of coordination by Malone and Crowston (1994). Nevertheless, clan control is not a very useful concept in inter-organizational relationships where different organizations usually have different goals (Lacity and Hirschheim, 1993). Hence, the coordination theories offer a better match for our purposes.

Evolution of Coordination Mechanisms

Information system projects change and evolve during their life cycles. They usually start with a relatively vague idea of a system or the need for a solution to a specific business problem. Then a project is set up to solve the problem. As the project continues, the formality of the plans and the monetary effect of changes to the plans increases. As a consequence, different methods and tools are needed to manage system projects in different stages and in different circumstances. Evolutionary studies (Heiskanen, Newman, and Similä, 1996; Newman and Robey, 1992) aim at capturing the long-time development of certain issues. Sabherwal (2003) studied the evolution of coordination in outsourced system development projects and categorized the coordination mechanisms as

- standards;
- plans;
- formal mutual adjustment; and
- informal mutual adjustment.

Standards and plans are defined as a priori specifications of action, while informal mutual adjustment and formal mutual adjustment are regarded as more interactive, and mostly use information obtained during the project. Standards and plans differ on whether the mechanism specifies the rules performing the task (standard) or the goals to be achieved (plans). The distinction between formal and informal mutual adjustment is based on how the adjustments are made: formally or informally. Although setting up both standards and plans has high fixed costs, using these mechanisms involves low variable costs. In contrast, formal and informal mutual adjustment incur high variable costs and lower fixed costs. We see that coordination by standards and plans is more formal than formal or informal mutual adjustment, because standards and plans are based on a priori specifications. (Sabherwal, 2003)

Sabherwal's categorization of coordination mechanisms in outsourced information system

Figure 13.1 **Emergent Model of Evolution of Coordination Mechanisms**

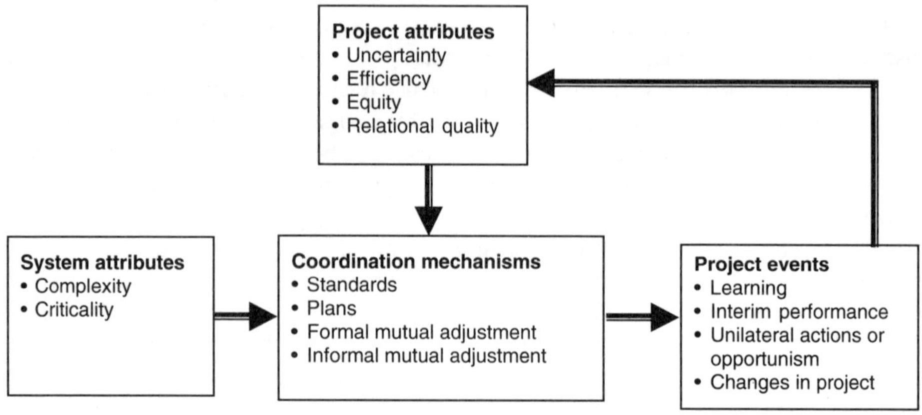

Source: Sabherwal (2003).

development projects is a synthesis of prior literature on coordination theories. He argues further that "coordination mechanisms have not been examined for either internal or outsourced IS development projects" (Sabherwal, 2003). Additionally, Sabherwal's categorization seems feasible for our purposes, because it employs quite similar, although simpler, interorganizational relationships than our case. Hence, we consider his categorization to be the best match for our purposes.

Sabherwal (2003) also presents an emergent model of evolution of coordination mechanisms (see Figure 13.1). The model is the result of a multiple case study involving twelve cases. According to the model, the coordination mechanisms are affected by project attributes (uncertainty, efficiency, equity, relational quality), system attributes (complexity, criticality), and project events (learning, interim performance, unilateral actions or opportunism, and changes in project) (Sabherwal, 2003). In this model, project events influence the coordination mechanisms indirectly via project attributes. Thus, something happens first in a project (event), which then changes the attributes of the project. The change in project attributes may change the coordination mechanisms that are used within the project.

Theoretical Implications of Different Sourcing Strategies

Outsourcing as a phenomenon has been researched extensively in the past few decades. Several different theoretical lenses have been used to study this issue. According to Klein (2002), the question of why to outsource has been studied extensively, using multiple methods. Other relevant questions for organizations considering outsourcing involve what to outsource and how to outsource. What to outsource refers to decisions about what parts of an organization or what parts of system development to outsource. How to outsource refers to building relationships between outsourcing stakeholders and how these kinds of relationships can be managed. As far as these three questions are concerned, our study focuses mainly on the "how" question, that is, how outsourcing relationships can be managed. We study this through the lenses of coordination theories.

In most cases, the research has focused on "dyadic relationships," that is, relationships between a single client and a single vendor (Gallivan and Oh, 1999). As a consequence, most theoretical and practical findings and implications from past research consider only dyadic relationships. For example, Gallivan and Oh (1999) analyzed and compared other possible options for the arrangement of information system sourcing (see Figure 13.2).

Figure 13.2 **Taxonomy of Four Classes of Outsourcing Relationships**

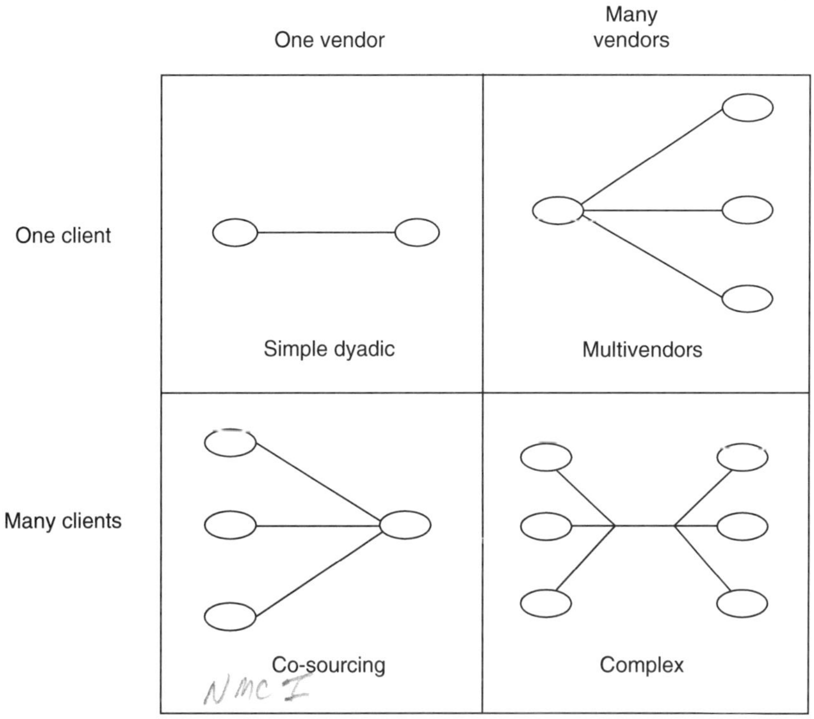

Source: Gallivan and Oh (1999).

Each of the four cells in Figure 13.2 represents a different sourcing option. Moreover, all of these different options have their own special characteristics, such as enabling and constraining forces (Gallivan and Oh, 1999). In the comparison between dyadic and multivendor relationships, they pointed out that the enabling forces include specialization of vendors, reduced transactional risk, and technical expertise of the vendors. The constraining forces for multivendor relationships would be increased coordination costs and contractual complexity. Furthermore, as the number of clients increases, (co-sourcing vs. dyadic outsourcing relationships) the main enabling forces are risk sharing and reduction among clients, increased relationship power toward vendors, and buyer economies of scale. Gallivan and Oh (1999) saw knowledge diffusion, strategic inflexibility, and client coordination costs as the key disadvantages of such settings.

In our case, the research setting is complex, that is, there are many vendors and many clients. The complexity in particular (the number of different stakeholders) leads to a situation where the outcome of the relationship is difficult to predict and is likely to be path dependent and influenced by the context in which these relationships take place (Gallivan and Oh, 1999). In other words, an in-depth analysis is needed to fully capture the essence of complex relationships.

RESEARCH SUBJECT AND METHOD

Software development in a university context has been studied to some degree in IS research (Heiskanen, Newman, and Similä, 2000; Newman and Noble, 1990; Newman and Robey, 1992;

Noble and Newman, 1993). Universities are considered a very challenging environment for system development. Weick (1976) described universities as loosely coupled systems, where each unit preserves its own identity and separateness. Academics are individualists who can and will act according to their own desires. This "academic way" is often reflected by support staff as well (Weick, 1976). In our study we looked at cooperation between several universities and a number of vendors. Considering the different organizational environments and climates of the institutions, the systems development process is even more challenging. Hence, coordinating would be a good word to describe this kind of environment, where little control is possible. Our research questions are therefore the following:

RQ_1: What are the coordination mechanisms used in the case setting?
RQ_2: What issues have had an effect on the coordination mechanisms used?
RQ_3: How does coordination evolve through different phases of system development?

As we analyze the data, our primary target is the coordination mechanisms that are used. Our case involves many stakeholders in several different organizations. Hence, it is not feasible to study all relationships among all of the organizations involved (the consortium, thirteen universities and three software vendors between 1995 and 2005). As a result, our primary interest is the coordination mechanisms used by the consortium organization for clients and vendors. Hence, our unit of analysis (Yin, 1994) is the consortium organization operating between the universities and the vendors, and the issue studied (Stake, 1995) is the coordination mechanisms. We seek to answer these questions by analyzing the case using the qualitative approach described in the next section.

Research Method

Given the small amount of prior research on such system development efforts, the qualitative research approach seems appropriate. We use an interpretive case study (Walsham, 1995) for this outsourced system development project. A single case study is an appropriate research design under several circumstances (Yin, 1994). The first rationale for using a single case study design is the criticality of the case, which can legitimate the use of a single case. In our study, criticality refers to a complex organizational environment that can capture the essence of the phenomenon studied, that is, coordination at a deep level. The second rationale for a single case study is the uniqueness of the case. A thorough review of the literature has not revealed any studies of this kind of research setting studying coordination. Nevertheless, the themes that we study are not idiosyncratic, but rather common in system development projects. Hence, our case is an example of outsourced system development in a complex and demanding organizational setting. The third rationale for a single case study is the revelatory power of the case. According to Yin (1994), a single case is revealing when the phenomenon has previously been inaccessible to scientific investigation. In practice, such revealing cases are rather scarce, but given our research setting there are also some revealing aspects. *Revealing* in our case refers to the organizational setting (i.e., a group of organizations developing a common information system), which can extend the scope of the current studies on coordination. The single case design can further be divided into holistic or embedded case studies (Yin, 1994). A holistic study focuses on the global nature of the phenomenon, whereas in an embedded case study design multiple units of analysis are selected. Our research setting could support both approaches, but given the nature of our research questions the holistic case study seems more interesting. Nevertheless, the coordination challenges are studied

Table 13.1

Other Background Material

Other written material (n)	Description
Internal proposals on how to develop the processes or organization (4)	Statements or studies
Master's theses written by key persons (3)	Historical information on the system development process
Budget information of consortium organization (2)	Financial data
Agreement documentation (4)	Between consortium organization and the member universities
Records from board meetings (2)	
Organizational charts (2)	From 2001 and from 2005
Facilitated group support system (GSS) session for strategy development (1)	Participants: Consortium staff, member universities staff (information technology managers, heads of Student Registrar Office) (for more detail, see Bragge et al., 2005)
Description of the system development process (3)	
Records from project group meetings (1)	Detailed specifications of certain feature
Status report of the consortium organization (1)	
Yearly plan (1)	Plans for the year 2004
Newspaper articles (2)	From campus magazines
Strategy for 2002–6 (1)	

through the subunits of the joint information system project, (i.e., universities, consortium, vendors), but our primary interest is in the coordination mechanisms used in communication between the consortium and the universities and between the consortium and the vendors.

Data Collection

Our main objective is to explore the coordination mechanisms and their evolution in the case setting. As the nature of the case leads to path dependency (Gallivan and Oh, 1999), it is important for us to understand the characteristic features of our case effort. The main focus of our data collection has been to gather data from the consortium organization. However, there are several opinions and interpretations on the same issues (Klein and Myers, 1999), depending upon which organization we ask; we also interviewed vendor representatives and people from member universities. We therefore interviewed people from several organizations and more than one person from each organization selected.

We conducted a total of ten semistructured interviews and one e-mail interview for background information. The interviews lasted from one hour to two hours. All interviews were recorded for later analysis.

The total number of interviewees was eleven. Six out of the eleven interviewees were involved in this system development project from the beginning, so we have information from all stages of the process. In addition, we had access to a lot of written material (theses, documents, manuals) and internal documentation (records, budget documentation, contracts, etc.) (see Table 13.1). Most of the testimonial material is also documented in theses written by people working for the consortium organization. As a result, the history of the project was studied using interviews as well as documented material.

Table 13.2

The Interviews

Organization	Interviews	Interviewees	Chief information officer	Project manager	Systems designer	Student administration	Administration
University 1 early adopter	4	2	2		2		
University 2 late adopter	1	3	1		1	1	
University 3 late adopter	1	2	1		1		
Consortium organization	3	2		2			1
Vendor	1	2		1	1		
Total	10	11	4	3	5	1	1

We conducted four interviews in one university that has been involved in the system development project from the beginning. The interviewees have been influential in the development of the consortium policies and structure and one of them is the current head of the consortium board. In contrast, we collected data from two universities that have recently joined the consortium in order to compare their views with the universities that have been in this consortium for a longer time. We interviewed two persons from the consortium because it has a key role in this kind of organizational structure. In addition, we interviewed two persons from one vendor company to capture the view of the vendor. A summary of the interviews can be seen in Table 13.2.

Data Analysis

After the interviews were conducted, the recordings were transcribed. The interviews produced over 180 pages of transcripts and dozens of pages of field notes. The interviewees had a chance to comment on our transcripts. In addition, we contacted interviewees for further information in case we had missed any details. From the transcripts a one-page summary was made of the interviews to capture the key points in each.

All of the data were analyzed iteratively to determine what actually happened over ten years of system development. Hence, we divided the system development process into stages (i.e., the negotiation stage, including the feasibility study, requirement analysis, detailed design, coding, first implementations, and maintenance and expansion of the consortium). This followed the phases of the actual system development process, which followed a waterfall life cycle. The division of system development into stages helped us to better identify and analyze the coordination mechanisms used in each system development phase.

As we analyzed the data, our first task was to identify the coordination mechanisms used (RQ_1). This was done primarily using the interview data, but written material was also used to support interview data. We searched the interview data for sentences and statements that discussed coordination and management issues. Then we did some "data triangulation" to see what could be found in the written material on the same topic. As a result, we listed the most influential coordination mechanisms used in each systems development phase in a table. At this point we used our own titles for the coordination mechanisms to better capture the nature of each. Later, after

Figure 13.3 **The Involved Organizations in 2005**

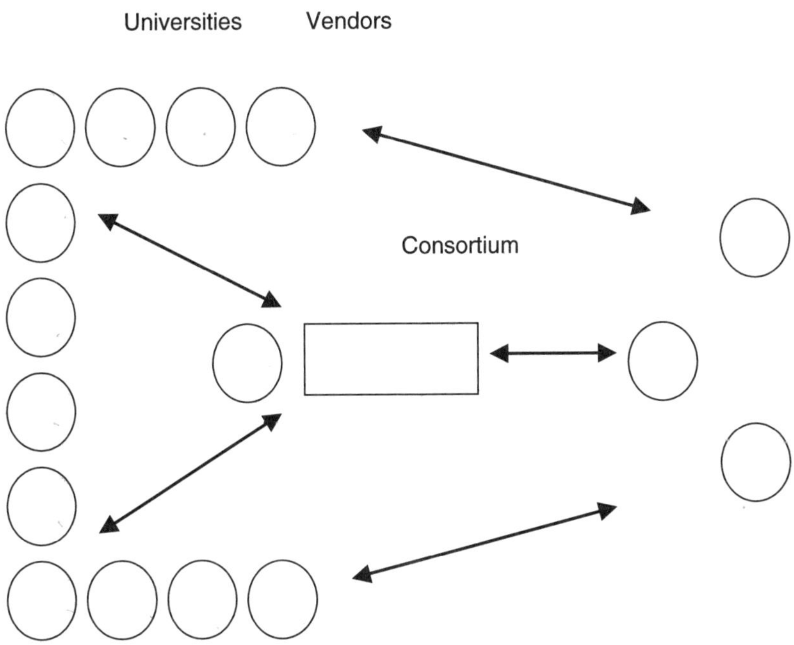

further analyzing the data, we categorized the coordination mechanisms with Sabherwal's (2003) categorization. This was done in order to better answer research question 3.

After identifying the most influential coordination mechanisms in each phase, we started to search for significant events that might have changed the course of actions (RQ_2). According to Sabherwal's (2003) emergent model of coordination mechanisms, the events in projects change the project attributes that may in turn change the coordination mechanisms. So, after identifying the significant events within our case, we further analyzed how these events had changed the project attributes and possibly the coordination mechanisms as well.

Research question 3 builds on research questions 1 and 2. Therefore, after identifying coordination mechanisms, events, and changes in attributes (RQ_1 and RQ_2), we can analyze how the coordination mechanisms actually evolved. As research questions 1 and 2 are mostly descriptive by nature, research question 3 is a synthesis of the results of questions 1 and 2. The analysis of evolution of coordination mechanisms in a complex (RQ_3) (multiorganizational) setting is therefore considered theory building. We used Sabherwal's (2003) theory as a reference model and extended it to complex settings.

CASE DESCRIPTION

Our case is a joint system development project, where thirteen Finnish universities (the total number of Finnish universities is twenty) have been developing a common student record system. The actual system development is outsourced. Although some of the vendors have changed over the years, the major one has been involved in the process from the beginning. The coordination between different universities and vendors is handled primarily by a mediating organization, that is, a consortium that has primary responsibility for system development. Different stakeholders from the universities participate in the system development process. IT staff and people from the student administrative office define the specifications in cooperation with staff from the other universities and people from the consortium. Then the agreed features are frozen and the vendors develop those features. Although the organizational structure of university cooperation has changed over the years, a "high-level" illustration of the case effort (in 2005) is shown in Figure 13.3. The consortium described in the middle acts as an intermediary between the universities and the vendors.

In Figure 13.3, one university is placed in the center of the university "network" because it plays a crucial role in this development project. First, this university has been involved in the project from the beginning and it is the largest university in Finland. Second, this university provides premises to the consortium organization. Third, it runs a service center that provides outsourcing services to other universities in terms of IT infrastructure, that is, hardware, IT support, and user training.

System development was started in 1995 by two vendors that formed a so-called vendor alliance in working very closely together. In 1999, the larger vendor bought the smaller one and then there was only one vendor involved. Later, in 2001, two new software vendors were chosen to further develop the system. So, Figure 13.3 describes the organizations involved in 2005 (thirteen universities, the consortium, and three software vendors). A more detailed description of the consortium organization can be found in Bragge and colleagues (2005).

Development of the new student record system was begun in 1995 by five universities. There were different reasons that these five different universities joined the consortium. In one university, the old system was too person-centric, and in another the old system was out of date, but basically all the universities were in need of a new system. As a consequence, these five universities made an agreement to develop the system jointly in order to cut costs and to be able to develop a better and more functional system. Another factor that pushed universities to cooperate was decreased funding from the government. The first step in the joint-development process was the foundation of the consortium, which is the coordinating organ between the universities and vendors. Five universities made the first "consortium agreement" in 1995. Before that, all five universities developed and maintained their own information systems for student information purposes. There were some informal negotiations among the universities' IT personnel, and the consensus was that a joint effort would be a reasonable way to develop a new system and a way to cut costs. So, in 1996 a feasibility study and risk analysis were done to evaluate the principal risks and prospects for joint system development. System development in an outsourced multiorganizational environment was considered challenging, but under the circumstances it was the most feasible solution. Through the joint effort, some development costs could be cut and a more up-to-date system could be developed. After the feasibility study, a requirements analysis was done in cooperation with the vendors chosen. At this point coordination among different organizations seemed to work well because specifications were made at such a high level of abstraction that it was easy for every party to agree. However, with the benefit of hindsight, the university consortium did not document the requirements accurately enough, which caused difficulties in the later stages of system development. The actual coding started somewhat later, after the requirements analysis stage. Consequently, there were delays in the first releases of the software. There were some difficulties with both the application development environment and the work of the vendors. The first client implementations of the software were done in the late 1999.

Over the years, other Finnish universities have joined the university cooperation system and as of 2005, there were thirteen member universities. As a consequence, the original consortium universities and the late adopters are in a different position in terms of learning the organizational and technological environment of the system. The original members of the consortium have been

Figure 13.4 **The Stages of System Development in Our Case Effort**

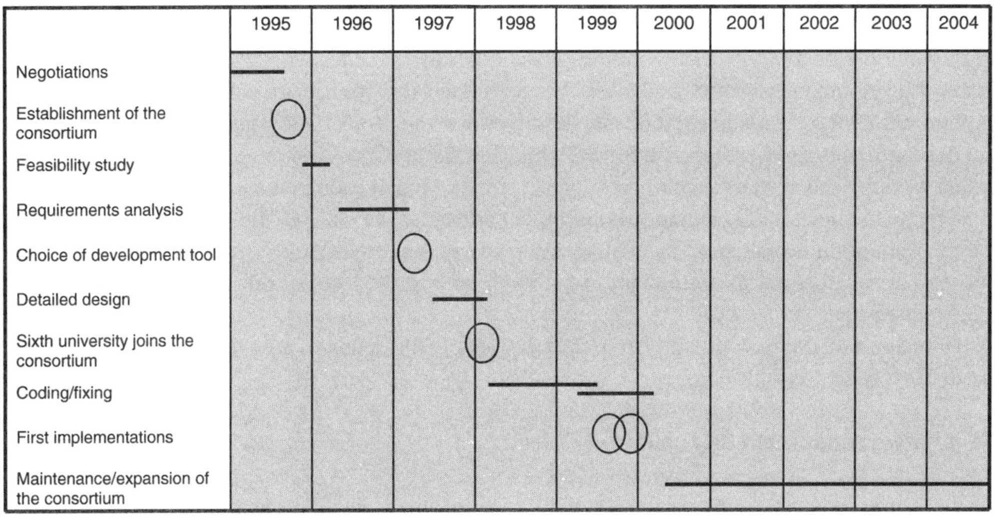

Source: Partly adapted from Saarinen (2001).

Notes: Horizontal lines are different phases of system development. Circles refer to certain events during the different phases of system development.

involved in the system development from the beginning, that is, the system is tailored to their needs. From the late adopters' point of view, the student record system is a parameterized software package and they can procure extra components for it.

The architecture of the jointly developed information system is twofold (in 2005): the administrative staff and the students have their own user interface to the system. Originally, the system was planned to serve the needs of the administrative staff (student register, exam schedule, course results), but over the years the system has expanded to serve different stakeholders and different purposes. Since the diffusion of the Internet in the late 1990s, increasing numbers of student services have been available in the system. Students register for courses and exams, cancel their registration, enroll, order their academic records, edit their contact information, and plan their studies via the system. One significant advantage of joint-system development is its ability to facilitate student mobility between universities. As the two universities (one where a student is enrolled and the other where a student is visiting) have the same information system, data interchange should be smoother. Recently, there has been growing interest in integrating the system with other systems used in different universities. The system provides interesting information on student performance and this is useful to the management of the universities, and, for example, to the Ministry of Education. One university has an ongoing project whereby the system is integrated with the calendar program so that information can be imported to personal calendars from the system. System development has been going on for a long time (about ten years now). The system is improved all the time and new features are added to it constantly. The major stages in system development are illustrated in Figure 13.4.

The number of system users is rather difficult to specify, but according to one estimate there are about 600–700 administrative users and tens of thousands of student users all over Finland. In this sense, our case system is a rather widely diffused information system.

EVOLUTION OF COORDINATION OVER THE SYSTEM DEVELOPMENT LIFE CYCLE

In this section we analyze the evolution of the coordination mechanisms in different phases of system development and the issues that have affected the coordination mechanisms used. We explain influential events in each phase, describe how the project attributes have changed across the life cycle of the project (see Table 13.3), and identify the most influential coordination mechanisms used in each system development phase. By looking at each phase of system development, the events that occur, and changes in the project attributes we can see the long-time evolution of the coordination mechanisms. To avoid excessively long case descriptions, we describe only the events that we interpret as significant to our study and to the level of our analysis (coordination mechanisms).

The nature of this particular system development effort leads to a development process with six distinct stages as follows.

Negotiations and Feasibility Study

At the negotiation stage, the parties develop joint (not individual) expectations about their motivations, possible investments, and the perceived uncertainties of a business deal that they are exploring to undertake jointly (Ring and Van de Ven, 1994). In our case, the early stages of system development were very informal. There was no suitable packaged software available for these kinds of purposes, so the IT managers of the five universities decided to create a dedicated system. Interestingly, at this stage the possibility of expansion of the consortium was not considered or systematically studied.

For the purpose of a feasibility study, a joint project was set up. The feasibility study costs were split by the participating universities. The main idea was to determine how to develop an information system jointly and to establish some kind of "rules" for cooperation. At this point, the aim was to identify the key processes within each university and try to incorporate them at a high level. The consortium was formed to act as a client of the system vendors because it was obvious early on that the universities lacked the resources to develop the new system internally.

Completed somewhat behind schedule, the feasibility study suggested that the system be implemented by prototyping (Saarinen, 2001). However, this approach was soon dropped because it was considered too costly. The most critical risk identified in the feasibility study was "disagreement between different stakeholders."

The idea to start developing the new student record system jointly emerged through informal relations among staff in different universities. In addition, the coordination mechanisms used during the feasibility study were very informal. However, a general agreement, that is, the consortium agreement, was needed to provide a framework for the forthcoming cooperation. Hence, the coordination mechanisms used in the negotiation phase were informal meetings and the consortium agreement. In Sabherwal's (2003) terms, these mechanisms would be informal mutual adjustments (i.e., informal meetings, personal contacts, see the quote below) and formal mutual adjustment (i.e., consortium agreement).

> There was a need for a new system in many universities. Then we informally discussed the possibility to develop [a] new student record system jointly with colleagues from the other universities.—Project Director from the consortium organization

Requirements Analysis

A ten-member project team was responsible for the requirements analysis. This group had participants from all five member universities, consortium organization, and the vendors' representatives. The requirements analysis stage started in fall 1996 and was finished in February 1997. The specifications were made, but they were too general to be useful in implementing the system. This was because the specifications were made on a level of abstraction that made it easy for all parties to agree. Because the processes within each university were fairly different, very detailed specifications were not even possible. Another issue that caused ambiguity later was the unsystematic documentation of the requirements. Many issues were discussed and agreed upon with the vendors, but left undocumented, so that it was difficult later to recall what had been agreed on. Third, end-user participation was neglected, but this was partly due to the tight schedule. However, all the stakeholders were happy with the results of the requirements stage at this point.

The main coordination mechanism in this system development phase was the ten-member project team, which held weekly meetings to design the requirements. A general agreement specifying cooperation mechanisms preceded the requirements analysis phase. In this phase there were no major coordination problems because all the universities worked toward a common goal and were dependent on each other to be able to build the new system. However, different organizational climates in different organizations made requirements analysis difficult.

The coordination mechanisms used in this phase were informal mutual adjustment (i.e., project group) and formal mutual adjustment (i.e., consortium agreement). It might be argued that the project group could be categorized as a formal mutual adjustment, but in our opinion, the project group worked informally on the whole, as the following excerpts demonstrate:

> We formed a project group which had members from all five member universities and representatives from vendors.—Project manager from the consortium organization

> The requirements analysis was generally ok, but it was made on too general a level.—Project manager from the consortium organization

> The documentation was deficient, especially for the functionality of the system.—Project manager from the consortium organization

> In the beginning there were no end-users involved.—Vendor project manager

Detailed Design

The choice of development tools was made in 1997 after requirements analysis. Tool selection was necessary in order to be able to continue the process. The new system's life cycle was estimated to be at least ten years, so the development tools could not be old-fashioned, but on the other hand, overly novel technology was to be avoided as well. There were some differences in the technological architectures of the universities' old systems, and, therefore, the development tool was chosen to support data independence at the database level. In fact, only one university had a different database technology, and because of this, a certain development tool was chosen. Diffusion of the Internet at that time also had an effect on the system development. The development tool did not work in Web-based development and had to be changed. Therefore, the system is presently twofold: a client system for the administrative staff at universities and a Web application for students. The choice of development tools is a characteristic feature in system development of such multiorganizational systems where compromises will always be necessary. Heterogeneous organizational and technological environments bring features to system development that are absent in a system within one organization. In addition, it is worth noting that if this university had joined the consortium at the later stages of the development process, it would have been very unlikely for these requirements to have had any weight in the decision.

In Sabherwal's (2003) coordination categorization, the most influential mechanisms in the detailed design phase were informal mutual adjustments (i.e., project group) and formal mutual adjustment (i.e., consortium agreement). Both the formal and informal adjustments are visible in the interviews:

> Third Consortium agreement was signed in 1997 for designing and implementing the system. —Project manager from the consortium organization

> The development tool might have been different if one university had not needed a database-independent development tool.—Project director from the consortium organization

> There were a limited number of large-scale Internet-based systems in those days.—Project director from the consortium organization

Coding

Coding of the system began in spring 1998. The coding was done according to the documents created in the detailed design phase. There were some difficulties in the coding phase and a delay in the first release of the software. The client (i.e., the consortium) was under the impression that the vendors would ask further information about the system features, but the vendor coded the system according to the available documentation despite the fact that the documents were vague, and the requirements were too general. This was due to differences in the requirements of the consortium members. Furthermore, the development tool made the system unstable and the module testing was not sufficient. Therefore, implementation of the new student record software was postponed.

In this system development phase the most influential coordination mechanisms were coordination by plans (i.e., requirements documentation) and formal mutual adjustment (i.e., consortium agreement).

> The customer thought that the vendor would ask for more precise specifications, but the system was coded according to the original documents.—Project manager from the consortium organization

First Implementations

One university joined the consortium after the coding had started (at the beginning of 1998) because they thought that they had a millennium problem. This further complicated the development process. The detailed design was already finished, so the sixth university was in a different situation compared with the five original universities—it would buy a software package rather than a tailored information system. In addition, the coding phase lasted a year longer than it was supposed to because of insufficient documentation and communication between the vendor and the client. In spite of this, the first implementation was made before the millennium. The system was somewhat unfinished at this stage, but nevertheless it had to be implemented as the millennium approached. Two universities implemented the system just before the millennium. The system was not ready, and hence, the system development had to be continued in order to improve its functionality.

There were also some changes in the vendor setting in 1999. There had been two main vendors up to this point, but in the summer of 1999 the larger vendor bought the smaller one, making development of the system the responsibility of a single vendor. However, in the maintenance phase new vendors were chosen to further develop the system. Altogether, the consortium faced difficult times: the development process was behind schedule, the millennium was approaching, and the system did not meet the level of functionality sought by the client. Some of the functionality problems were solved by the vendor free of charge.

> The first implementations were several months behind from the original schedule and the system was not even ready.—Chief information officer (CIO) from of one the universities

> In 1999 the bigger vendor bought the smaller vendor.—CIO from of one of the universities

Additionally, there were some difficulties in the conversions of data in the first implementations. Having joined the consortium during the development project the sixth university faced the biggest problems. The other five universities implemented the system one by one during 2000 and 2001.

In this phase, several different and somewhat incompatible coordination mechanisms were used. The consortium agreement was used to coordinate cooperation at a general level, while requirements documentation and required code inspections (Kraut and Streeter, 1995) were to guide actual system development. Hence, the coordination mechanisms used (Sabherwal, 2003) were formal mutual adjustment (i.e., consortium agreement and code inspections) and plans (i.e., requirements documentation).

Maintenance and the Expansion of the Consortium

After the first implementations, system development continued in order to improve system functionality. Between 2001 and 2004, seven more universities joined the consortium. The information on implementations accumulated gradually. As the system became more and more functional, more universities joined the consortium cooperation, which, on the other hand, made coordination more difficult. This is also supported by earlier research stating that the more complex the system, and the more parties involved, the more coordination is needed (Koushik and Mookerjee, 1995; Kraut and Streeter, 1995). At this point, the system was at an adequate technological level but the number of consortium universities made the organizational issues challenging. At the same time, coordinating issues have become more important for the consortium's work. The consortium as well as the member universities have recognized that new mechanisms are needed to make cooperation work. This is reflected in the increased depth and scope of strategic planning concerning the further development of the system (Bragge et al., 2005). The general agreement, that is, the consortium agreement, has been the basis for cooperation between the universities throughout the system development process. In the maintenance and expansion phase, the consortium started to make yearly plans and strategies for further system development. As the student registration system became more functional, different project/user groups were set up to further develop the different modules of the system.

As the system development process has advanced, the coordination mechanisms have become more formal (i.e., concerning standards and plans) and the number of coordination mechanisms has increased, as can be seen from the quotes below. In the maintenance phase, the coordination mechanisms used (Sabherwal, 2003) were formal mutual adjustment (i.e., consortium agreement), standards (i.e., development bank), plans (i.e., strategy for further development, yearly plans), and informal mutual adjustments (i.e., user groups).

> Yearly plans are made for further development of the system.—Project director from the consortium organization

> We have a strategy for years 2002–2006.—Project manager from the consortium organization

> We have user development groups for different modules.—Project manager from the consortium organization

> About 200 active users are able to contribute to [the] development bank.—Project manager from the consortium organization

> There is an endless need for compromising.—Project manager from one of the universities

> When you have thirteen universities together, it is quite a jungle. . . . And to reach mutual understanding is sometimes really difficult.—Project manager from one of the universities

DISCUSSION

In Table 13.3 we synthesize our analysis of the case effort. Following Sabherwal's (2003) reference model we have identified the significant project events, the changes in project attributes, and the key coordination mechanisms in each system development phase. In the last row of Table 13.3 we gather influential project events that have taken place during each system development phase. We also present the changes in project attributes with two different concepts. We first analyzed the project attributes with our own concepts (the second to last row in Table 13.3). Then we categorized the changes found in the project attributes using Sabherwal's (2003) terms (second row) in Table 13.3. The top row of Table 13.3 shows the most influential coordination mechanisms in each system development phase.

From Table 13.3 several observations can be made. System development started with informal coordination mechanisms such as informal mutual adjustments. As the process advanced, more control-oriented (i.e., standards and plans) coordination mechanisms were introduced. Even though there were some technological difficulties in coding and implementation, the coordination mechanism did not change radically. Only after several new members joined the consortium, thus increasing organizational complexity, did coordination become a relevant issue. As a result, it can be observed that the number of coordination mechanisms and the formality of coordination have increased over time. So, coordination mechanisms are also becoming more and more formal and close to control. This can be seen as a direct result of the expansion of the consortium and the diverging needs of the consortium members (see Table 13.3). Our system development phase "Maintenance and Expansion of the Consortium" is a characteristic feature of this project in which the number of clients increased, and it may be absent in other system development projects that have fewer stakeholder organizations. On the other hand, we can speculate that in the future these kinds of cooperative settings will be more common and thus similar problems can appear in other contexts.

One issue that has changed the project attributes is the need for constant compromise and ne-

Table 13.3

The Evolution of Coordination Mechanisms in Our Case Example

System development phase	Negotiation	Requirements analysis	Detailed design	Coding	First implementation	Maintenance and the expansion of the consortium
The most influential coordination mechanisms used (in Sabherwal's terms)	• Informal mutual adjustment • Formal mutual adjustment	• Informal mutual adjustment • Formal mutual adjustment	• Informal mutual adjustment • Formal mutual adjustment	• Formal mutual adjustment • Plans	• Formal mutual adjustment • Plans	• Informal mutual adjustment • Formal mutual adjustment • Standards • Plans
Changes in project attributes (in Sabherwal's terms)		• Increased uncertainty	• Increased compromise	• Efficiency issues • Relational quality issues	• Efficiency issues • Relational quality issues	• Increased compromise
Changes in project attributes		• Too vague analysis of requirements • Lack of sufficient documentation • Lack of end-user participation	• Compromise	• Delayed schedule • Insufficient communication with the vendor	• Unfinished system • Delayed schedule	• Compromise
Project events (issues affecting coordination mechanisms)	• The first consortium agreement		• The selection of development tools • Diffusion of the Internet	• Sixth university joined the consortium	• Changes in vendor setting	• Increase the number of participants in the consortium • Technical improvement of the system

gotiation on the most mundane details. All of the participating universities must agree on future system specifications. Hence, in the maintenance phase, some universities have started to develop the system by themselves without having to negotiate with other consortium universities. Most interviewees commented that the greatest challenges of multiorganizational system development are organizational, that is, coordination issues. Clearly, the economic constraints have forced universities to cooperate. At the same time, however, coordination of system development has been a challenge. Furthermore, there was serious disagreement among the organizations about the "readiness" of the system. In some universities the system was seen to be ready and some interviewees saw the system as incomplete. All these issues made organizing and coordinating system development even more challenging.

As the system has become more functional, the interdependence of the consortium members has decreased. This decreased interdependence might also have forced them to adopt tighter control mechanisms. At the beginning of the development project the universities were much more dependent on each other as they all needed the new information system and no one was able to do it completely alone. In other words, the incompleteness of the system made the organizations dependent on each other. However, as the system was implemented and became more functional, the interdependency decreased. As a consequence, if one university decided to leave the consortium, it might be able to survive on its own. This would not have been possible at the early stages of joint system development. On the other hand, as coordination by definition is work by dependent parts toward a common goal, control is needed when the goals of the parts are not shared. As interdependence decreases and the goals of different stakeholders spread, coordination mechanisms become more formal and more control oriented.

CONCLUSION AND FURTHER RESEARCH

In this chapter we have discussed coordination in a complex environment. In our research setting, the coordination mechanisms varied across the phases of system development. At the formal level a cooperation agreement was needed to make coordination possible. This consortium agreement was a vehicle for setting a common goal and thus the key coordination mechanism.

The actual system development decisions were made in the project/user group meetings. The different project/user groups were the primary forum of actual system development at its early and late stages. As the system became more functional and more universities joined the cooperation, some universities also started their own system development activities outside the consortium structure.

The need to compromise is the most characteristic feature of this kind of system development in which several stakeholders participate. This was seen as the most challenging aspect of the development process, especially in the later stages of the system life cycle. Different organizational and technological environments caused decision making and reaching mutual understanding to be difficult. As the number of universities in the consortium increased, more compromise was needed. Compromise was present in all stages of system development. The choice of development tools was the most visible instance of this phenomenon. Sabherwal's (2003) does not include the project attribute "compromise," in his model because it focuses on dyadic relationships between vendor and client. Hence, our concept can be seen as an extension of Sabherwal's model in complex settings.

Compromise affected coordination mechanisms in two ways. First, it made system development more difficult and therefore increased coordination needs. Second, compromise forced the consortium to formalize its decision making, which can be seen in the increasing number of coordination mechanisms used. This formality, together with the large current number of members in the consortium, has made it nearly impossible for the consortium to reach any consensus agreements on development issues, which has caused the system to evolve quite slowly.

Given the organizational context, that is, a consortium of universities, the study has its limitations. First, we studied only one case, which limits the scope for broad generalizations. Second, the university environment is rather different from the business environment, although large consortium market places, such as Covisint, exhibit similar patterns and problems. And third, given the large number of different stakeholders, the large number of different views cannot be captured by a limited number of interviews and formal documentation. However, we believe that we were able to obtain a fairly good picture of this kind of multiclient multivendor outsourcing situation through the conducted interviews and other background material.

In the future, we will be interested in studying the differences between coordination and control mechanisms in other settings. Questions like how and when control should be practiced are of great importance in all system development projects and we will study this issue in other contexts with similar settings. The consortium as an organizational form has its own implications for system development. Determination of advantages and challenges will also be part of future research. Because we have a case example with a relatively long history, we can study more in depth the evolution of coordination in terms of how and why development coordination goes in a particular direction (e.g., control ← → coordination ← → chaos). Concepts such as compromise and dependency need more clarification of their roles in complex system development projects.

Furthermore, the political and social aspects of system development in such a setting are of great interest to us. The most interesting aspect for our future study is the maintenance of balance among control, coordination, and chaos in development in a manner that allows for the agile development of new features while maintaining control and consensus among consortium participants.

REFERENCES

Adler, P.S. 1995. Interdepartmental interdependence and coordination: The case of the design/manufacturing interface. *Organization Science*, 6, 2, 147–167.

Bakos, J.Y. and Brynjolfsson, E. 1993. Information technology, incentives, and the optimal number of suppliers. *Journal of Management Information Systems*, 10, 2, 37–54.

Bragge, J.; Merisalo-Rantanen, H.; Nurmi, A.; and Tanner, L. 2005. GSS-enabled strategy development in a multiorganization environment. In *Proceedings of the Group Decision and Negotiation Conference*, Vienna. (July 10–13).

Choudhury, V. and Sabherwal, R. 2003. Portfolios of control in outsourced software development projects. *Information Systems Research*, 14, 3, 291–314.

Crowston, K. 1997. A coordination theory approach to organizational process design. *Organization Science*, 8, 2, 157–176.

DeSanctis, G. and Jackson, B.M. 1994. Coordination of information technology management: Team-based structures and computer-based communication systems. *Journal of Management Information Systems*, 10, 4, 85–111.

Galbraith, J.R. 1973. *Designing Complex Organizations*. Reading, MA: Addison Wesley.

Gallivan, M.J. and Oh, W. 1999. Analyzing it outsourcing relationships as alliances among multiple clients and vendors. In *Proceedings of the Thirty-second Annual Hawaii International Conference on System Sciences (HICSS-32)*, Maui, 1–13.

Grant, R.M. 1996. Toward a knowledge-based theory of the firm. *Strategic Management Journal*, 17 (Winter Special Issue), 109–123.

Gurbaxani, V. and Whang, S. 1991. The impact of information systems on organizations and markets. *Communications of the ACM*, 34, 1, 59–73.

Heiskanen, A.; Newman, M.; and Similä, J. 1996. Software contracting: A process model approach. In *Proceedings of the International Conference on Information Systems*. Cleveland, OH, 51–62.

———. 2000. The social dynamics of software development. *Accounting, Management and Information Technologies*, 10, 1, 1–32.

Kim, H-W. 2001. Modeling inter- and intra-organizational coordination in electronic commerce deployments. *Information Technology and Management*, 2, 3, 335–354.

Kirsch, L.J. 1996. The management of complex tasks in organizations: Controlling the systems development process. *Organization Science*, 7, 1, 1–21.

———. 1997. Portfolios of control modes and Is project management. *Information Systems Research*, 8, 3, 215–239.

Kirsch, L.J.; Sambamurthy, V.; Ko, D.G.; and Purvis, R.L. 2002. Controlling information systems development projects: The view from the client. *Management Science*, 48, 4, 484–498.

Klein, H.K. and Myers, M.D. 1999. A set of principles for conducting and evaluating interpretive field studies in information systems. *MIS Quarterly*, 23, 1, 67–93.

Klein, K. 2002. On the theoretical foundations of current outsourcing research. In R. Hirschheim, A. Heinzl, and J. Dibbern, eds., *Information Systems Outsourcing Enduring Themes, Emergent Patterns and Future Directions.* Berlin: Springer, 24–44.

Koushik, M.V. and Mookerjee, V.S. 1995. Modeling coordination in software construction: An analytical approach. *Information Systems Research*, 6, 3, 220–255.

Kraut, R.E. and Streeter, L.A. 1995. Coordination in software development. *Communications of the ACM*, 38, 3, 69–81.

Lacity, M.C. and Hirschheim, R. 1993. The information systems outsourcing bandwagon. *Sloan Management Review* (Fall), 73–86.

Malone, T.W. and Crowston, K. 1994. The interdisciplinary study of coordination. *ACM Computing Surveys*, 26, 1, 87–119.

McCann, J.E. and Galbraith, J.R. 1981. Interdepartmental relations. In P. Nystrom and W. Starbuck, eds., *Handbook of Organization Design.* New York: Oxford University Press, 60–84.

McFarlan, F.W. and Nolan, R.L. 1995. How to manage an it outsourcing alliance. *Sloan Management Review*, 36, 2, 9–24.

Newman, M. and Noble, F. 1990. User involvement as an interaction process: A case study. *Information Systems Research*, 1, 1, 89–113.

Newman, M. and Robey, D. 1992. A social process model of user-analyst relationships. *MIS Quarterly*, 16, 2, 249–266.

Nidumolu, S.R. 1996. A comparison of the structural contingency and risk-based perspectives on coordination in software-development projects. *Journal of Management Information Systems*, 13, 2, 77–113.

Noble, F. and Newman, M. 1993. Integrated system, autonomous departments, organizational invalidity and system change in a university. *Journal of Management Studies*, 30, 2, 195–219.

Ring, P.S. and Van De Ven, A.H. 1992. Structuring cooperative relationships between organizations. *Strategic Management Journal*, 13, 7, 483–499.

———. 1994. Developmental processes of cooperative interorganizational relationships. *Academy of Management Review*, 19, 1, 90–119.

Saarinen, V. 2001. Kohti valtakunnallista opintotietojärjestelmää-tapaustutkimus kuuden yliopiston yhteistyöstä. Master's thesis. University of Helsinki.

Sabherwal, R. 2003. The evolution of coordination in outsourced software development projects: A comparison of client and vendor perspectives. *Information and Organization*, 13, 3, 153–202.

Stake, R.E. 1995. *The Art of Case Study Research.* Thousand Oaks, CA: Sage.

Walsham, G. 1995. Interpretive case studies in is research: Nature and method. *European Journal of Information Systems*, 4, 74–81.

Van de Ven, A.H.; Dahlbecq, A.L.; and Koenig, R. 1976. Determinants of coordination modes within organization. *American Sociological Review*, 41, 2, 322–338.

Weick, K.E. 1976. Educational organizations as loosely coupled systems. *Administrative Science Quarterly*, 21, 1, 1–19.

Yin, R.K. 1994. *Case Study Research: Design and Methods.* Newbury Park, CA: Sage.

PART IV

HOLISTIC VIEW OF IT OUTSOURCING

CHAPTER 14

MANAGEMENT OF OUTSOURCED IS DEVELOPMENT PROJECTS

The Role of Social Capital and Intellectual Capital

RAJIV SABHERWAL

Abstract: *The importance of outsourced information system development (OISD) for contemporary organizations is well recognized. However, effective and efficient management of OISD projects continues to be an arduous task. Arguing that this may be due to a somewhat narrow focus on project effectiveness and efficiency and on short-term goals, this chapter examines the role of social capital and intellectual capital in the management and success of OISD projects. It develops an integrative model including project management mechanisms, social capital, intellectual capital, traditional project performance, and contingency factors. The relationships among these dimensions are examined, and the associated feedback paths are discussed. Some implications for the management of OISD projects are also identified. Empirically, the chapter is rooted in eighteen primary case studies of OISD projects.*

Keywords: *Outsourcing of System Development, Social Capital, Intellectual Capital, Project Management Mechanisms, Project Performance*

INTRODUCTION

Outsourced information system development (OISD) has become a pervasive and important phenomenon in business organizations (e.g., Aubert, Rivard, and Patry, 1996; Feeny, Lacity, and Willcocks, 2005; Lacity, Willcocks, and Feeny, 1996). OISD involves cooperative, "partnership-based" relationships among several groups, including: the users and the IS department from the client organization, marketing personnel (who obtain the initial order) and programmers from the vendor, and the top managers and project managers from both organizations. However, it is difficult to make the concepts of cooperation and partnership work. Several problems may arise during the project, including hidden costs, reduced flexibility, loss of control, and reduced innovativeness (Earl, 1996). Such problems are largely ignored in the IS literature, which portrays "an overly optimistic view of IS outsourcing" (Lacity and Hirschheim, 1993, 256). McFarlan and Nolan compare outsourcing alliances to marriage: "Like marriage, however, these arrangements are much easier to enter than to sustain or dissolve (1995, 9)."

To some extent, the problems during OISD projects may be addressed, and sometimes prevented, through cautious vendor selection and flexible contracts (Lacity, Willcocks, and Feeny, 1996; McFarlan and Nolan, 1995). In fact, the response is often to try minimizing such problems by tightening the contract. However, the problems encountered in OISD are often social or intellectual in nature, and require careful attention during the project. For example, the lack of personal contact may inhibit trust for the individuals from the other firm as well as knowledge about that firm. Creating additional structures to control the partner's performance may not help alleviate such problems.

Information system development (ISD) project teams in general, and OISD teams in particular, commonly focus on the traditional project goals of completing the project so as to meet the scope, schedule, and budget requirements. Members of OISD project teams often focus on the short-term demands of the project, without recognizing the long-term implications of the events during the project. With a few exceptions, such as the consideration of psychosocial outcomes for project teams (Hackman, 1990; Pinto, Pinto, and Prescott, 1993), literature on project management has also concentrated on these traditional goals without considering the other important impacts that project management practices might produce. Tom Peters disagrees with this approach: "On time. On budget. Who cares?" (1999, 25).

In attempting to address these issues, this chapter examines the role of social capital (e.g., Cohen and Prusak, 2001; Nahapiet and Ghoshal, 1998; Putnam, 1995) and intellectual capital (e.g., Grant, 1996a, 1996b; Nahapiet and Ghoshal, 1998) in the management and success of OISD projects. It develops an integrative model including project management mechanisms, social capital, intellectual capital, traditional project performance, and contingency factors. The relationships among these dimensions are examined, and the associated feedback paths are discussed. This chapter draws upon the literature from social psychology, traditional IS development, outsourcing, and knowledge management. The relevant literature is mentioned in describing the emergent model. Empirically, the chapter is rooted in eighteen primary case studies of outsourced IS development projects, which I have used earlier to examine other aspects related to the management of OISD projects, namely, trust (Sabherwal, 1999), coordination (Sabherwal, 2003), and control (Choudhury and Sabherwal, 2003).

The rest of this chapter is organized as follows. The next section summarizes the empirical foundations underlying the chapter. It is followed by sections describing the roles of project management mechanisms, social capital, and intellectual capital within the context of OISD projects. The subsequent sections examine feedback paths and identify some contingency factors that affect the management of OISD projects. The chapter concludes by identifying some implications for the management of OISD projects. The empirical basis for the chapter is summarized in Appendix 14.1. More details on these aspects are given in three other studies (Sabherwal, 1999, 2003; Choudhury and Sabherwal, 2003).

PROJECT MANAGEMENT MECHANISMS

In studying the management of IS development projects, several scholars (e.g., Beath, 1987; Henderson and Lee, 1992; Kirsch, 1996, 1997) have focused on the issue of *control.* These authors have generally viewed control in terms of ensuring that individuals act consistently with the objectives being pursued. For example, Kirsch (1997, 215) states: "In this paper, control is viewed broadly, encompassing all attempts to ensure individuals in organizations act in a manner that is consistent with meeting organizational goals and objectives." Control in the context of OISD projects differs from control in internal IS development in two ways, as noted by Choudhury and Sabherwal (2003): (1) controllers and controllees belong to different organizations; and (2) controllers and controllees may not be single individuals but groups within or across organizations.

Coordination[1] has been defined as "Managing dependencies between activities" (Malone and Crowston, 1994, 90). The following is more specific to coordination in software development.

> In software development, it [coordination] means that different people working on a common project agree to a common definition of what they are building, share information, and mesh their activities. . . . To build the software efficiently, they must share detailed design specifications and information about the progress of software modules. In sum, they must coordinate their work so that it gets done and fits together, so that it isn't done redundantly, and so that components of the work are handed off expeditiously (Kraut and Streeter, 1995, 69).

Coordination differs from control. Whereas control focuses on improving performance relative to certain overall goals, such as organizational goals, coordination focuses on managing interdependencies among individuals or activities (Crowston, 1997; Kraut and Streeter, 1995). Moreover, the importance of control derives from the need to ensure performance with respect to certain overall goal when the goals of the individual stakeholders (e.g., the employees) differ from the goals of the larger overall entity (e.g., the organization), whereas coordination is important because the overall task consists of multiple activities or individuals that depend upon each other. More specifically, coordination of OISD projects is difficult because the project teams tend to be made up of diverse individuals across two or more organizations, with each organization having its own goals, shared language, and belief systems.

Despite these differences, control and coordination are interrelated, and they affect the overall performance of the IS development project. Since most organizational processes involve goals as well as multiple participants, both coordination and control are required, and problems and successes in one area affect the other as well. Improved coordination among the stakeholders involved in IS development would help in monitoring and controlling the project. On the other hand, control over the IS development activities may improve coordination among them as well. As Kirsch puts it, "managers exercise control to coordinate specific activities" (1997, 236).

Prior research has pointed out that control in IS development may be exercised by the project manager or by the team members (Henderson and Lee, 1992). Moreover, control may be performed formally based on behavior or outcomes, or informally based on clan control at the group level or self-control at the individual level (Kirsch, 1996, 1997). The specific mechanisms for implementing these modes of control, for example, rules and procedures, budgets and schedules, socialization, and so on, have been studied (Kirsch, 1997). Similarly, prior research on coordination in IS development has examined alternative coordination mechanisms (Crowston, 1997). Several ways of classifying coordination have also been proposed. These include task–task, task–resource, and resource–resource coordination (Crowston, 1997), vertical and horizontal coordination (Nidumolu, 1995), and coordination by programming and coordination by feedback (March and Simon, 1958; Van de Ven, Delbecq, and Koening, 1976). Several specific coordination mechanisms have been identified (DeSanctis and Jackson, 1994; Keil and Carmel, 1995; Kraut and Streeter, 1995; Nidumolu, 1995), including standards, hierarchy, plans, slack resources, vertical information systems, direct contact, liaison roles, task forces, and integrating roles.

Coordination and control are often supported through similar mechanisms. Several of the control mechanisms discussed by Kirsch (1997) are similar to those discussed by DeSanctis and Jackson (1994), including meetings, reports, and organizational roles. The relationship between coordination and control may therefore be extended using the common classifications of the mechanisms used to achieve them. One dimension that has been used to classify both coordination and control is the *formalization* of the mechanisms used. Kirsch (1995, 1996) has distinguished between formal control (output control, behavior control) and informal control (self-control, clan control), while Kraut and Streeter (1995) have differentiated between formal and informal coordination.

Figure 14.1 **Coordination and Control Mechanisms**

Degree of formalization (Low → High)	Low degree of interpersonal interaction	High degree of interpersonal interaction
High	**Output control; Formal, Impersonal coordination** • Project milestones (Henderson and Lee, 1992; Kirsch, 1996, 1997; Kraut and Streeter, 1995) • Modification request and error tracking procedures (Kraut and Streeter, 1995) • Standards (Adler, 1995) • Exception resolution plans (Adler, 1995) • Sign-offs (Adler, 1995)	**Behavior control; Formal, Interpersonal coordination** • Walk-throughs (Kirsch, 1997) • Status review meetings (Kraut and Streeter, 1995) • Design review meetings (Adler, 1995; Kraut and Streeter, 1995) • Code review meetings (Kraut and Streeter, 1995) • Mutual adjustment (Adler, 1995)
Low	**Self-control; Noncoordination** • Self-monitoring (Kirsch, 1996, 1997) • "Over the wall" exchange (Adler, 1995) • "Work-arounds" (Adler, 1995) • Self-management (Kirsch, 1997)	**Clan control; Informal, Interpersonal coordination** • Socialization (Kirsch, 1996, 1997; Ouchi, 1980) • Rituals and ceremonies (Kirsch, 1997; Ouchi, 1980) • Teams (Adler, 1995) • Colocation of staff (Kraut and Streeter, 1995)

Low → High

Degree of interpersonal interaction

A second common dimension that has been used to classify both coordination and control is the *degree of interpersonal interaction* involved. Kraut and Streeter (1995) distinguish between interpersonal and impersonal coordination mechanisms. A similar distinction may be applied to control mechanisms. Both behavior control and clan control require that the party exercising the control be able to observe the behavior of the agent—these forms of control may, therefore, be viewed as interpersonal. Outcome and self-controls, on the other hand, require less interpersonal interaction between the controller and the controlled and may, therefore, be classified as impersonal. These two dimensions—formalization and degree of interpersonal interaction—lead to the classification of project management mechanisms into four types, as shown in Figure 14.1. The informal–impersonal, informal–interpersonal, formal–impersonal, and formal–interpersonal cells correspond to self, clan, output, and behavior control (Kirsch, 1995, 1996), respectively. They also directly represent the three types of coordination discussed by Kraut and Streeter (1995)—formal impersonal, formal interpersonal, and informal interpersonal, with a fourth type (noncoordination) being included to reflect the situation in which coordination is neither formal nor interpersonal (Adler, 1995). Figure 14.1 presents some of the specific mechanisms that may be used in each cell.

The Effect of Project Management Mechanisms on Project Performance

Figure 14.2 summarizes the emergent model of management of OISD projects. The individual paths comprising this model are labeled on the figure, and discussed below. The effect of project management mechanisms on project performance, represented using path P1 in Figure 14.2, includes two components: the effect of the *extent of use of project management mechanisms*, and the effect of the *forms of project management mechanisms*. Instead of using the label "project success" in Figure 14.2, we use a more general term—*project deliverables.* Project deliverables

Figure 14.2 **Management of Outsourcing: Emergent Model**

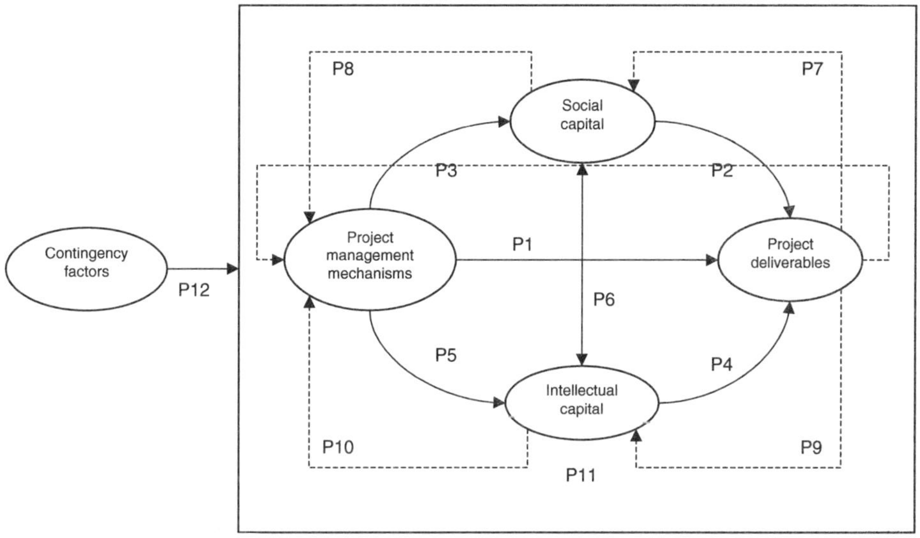

can be either final deliverables that represent project success or interim deliverables that might have feedback effects on social capital, intellectual capital, and project management mechanisms. Such feedback effects are discussed later.

As discussed earlier, the use of project management mechanisms enables coordination and control of the OISD project, thereby facilitating efficiency (due to reduced redundancy, improved turnaround, etc.) as well as effectiveness (e.g., due to reduced miscommunication of specifications, increased collaboration, etc.). Thus, the extent of use of project management mechanisms may be expected to facilitate project success. However, it is important to recognize the possibility of overuse of project management mechanisms. Project management mechanisms involve a certain cost in terms of physical resources (such as the demands on communication media) as well as the time spent by the concerned individuals. Thus, the use of project management mechanisms leads to saving in production costs, but, as the use of these mechanisms increases, the saving in production costs may be more than offset by increased coordination costs associated with these mechanisms. Moreover, effectiveness benefits from project management mechanisms are also limited beyond a certain point. We therefore propose a curvilinear relationship between the extent of use of project management mechanisms and project deliverables.

In addition to the above effect of the extent of use of project management mechanisms, the form of coordination and control mechanisms also affects project deliverables. Prior research has examined the effects of different types of control (e.g., Henderson and Lee, 1992) and coordination mechanisms (e.g., Nidumolu, 1996) on project performance.

A shift from impersonal mechanisms to interpersonal mechanisms implies increased coordination costs, and hence, reduced efficiency. However, this drop in efficiency should be viewed in conjunction with the potential increase in effectiveness, partly through increased social or intellectual capital, as discussed later in this chapter. Similarly, a shift from formal to informal mechanisms implies less use of routines, and therefore increased coordination costs and reduced efficiency, but a potential for increased social and intellectual capital, and consequently greater effectiveness.

SOCIAL CAPITAL

Broadly defined, *social capital* is an inherent asset in social relations and networks, including features of social organizations such as networks, norms, and social trust that facilitate coordination and cooperation for mutual benefit (Putnam, 1995). Social capital is primarily embedded within networks of mutual acquaintance and recognition. Through the contacts or connections within networks, other resources become available. For example, through "friends of friends" (Boissevain, 1974) or "weak ties" (Granovetter, 1973), network members can gain privileged access to information and opportunities.

Social capital is a multidimensional construct. Cohen and Prusak (2001) consider social capital as consisting of the active connections among people: the trust, mutual understanding, and shared values and behaviors that bind the members of human networks and communities and make cooperative action possible. Other studies of social capital examine the more or less dense interlocking networks of relationships between individuals and groups (e.g., Putnam, 1993). This relates to the discussion of weak ties and strong ties in social networks, although such ties have traditionally been examined in contexts that do not involve contractual obligations (Granovetter, 1973). The commonly considered components of social capital are: reciprocity, which is viewed as a combination of short-term altruism and long-term self-interest (Taylor, 1982); trust, which reflects a sense of confidence that others will respond as expected and act in mutually supportive ways and arises within a community of regular, honest, and cooperative behavior; and social norms, which provide a form of informal social control that obviates the need for more formal, institutionalized sanctions (Coleman, 1988; Putnam, 1993).

Aspects of social capital have been examined in several articles on IS development. Attention has frequently focused on such social factors as commitment, involvement, conflict, motivation, and trust, although largely within the context of internal IS development. These social factors assume even greater importance in OISD projects. OISD projects frequently bring together individuals who are total strangers, may not even meet during the project, and are expected to work together in a tough, high-stress environment. This is especially true in international outsourcing. "Trust and commitment are imperiled when organizations with different cultures must communicate and work together" (Badaracco, 1991).

In a temporary setting (an OISD project's contractual period) and an international context, knowledge-based trust is difficult to achieve.[2] Members might never have worked together before and do not expect to work together again. The team's setting is not conducive to activities that will build more traditional and long-lasting forms of trust. Lacking the traditional sources of social capital, such as familiarity, shared experience, reciprocal disclosure, threats and deterrents, fulfilled promises, and demonstrations of nonexploitation of vulnerability (Meyerson et al. 1996), team members may be expected to demonstrate low levels of trust. However, in their study, Jarvenpaa and Leidner (1999) observed high initial trust among members of some of the teams. They argue that there is also a social dimension of trust that is complementary to the rational one. Lacking sufficient time to build proper expectations from prior interactions, individuals in temporary virtual settings tend to use expectations built on categories reflecting roles, or stereotypes based on occupation and/or identity.

The Effect of Social Capital on Project Performance

Social capital literature identifies the efficiency and effectiveness benefits of cohesive, or strong ties (i.e., network closure) (Coleman, 1988; Friedkin, 1982), and the flexibility benefits of dispersed or weak ties (Burt, 1992, 1997). In managing OISD projects, a combination of strong and weak ties is needed to simultaneously achieve the benefits associated with these two kinds of ties. Social capital thus helps enhance the performance of OISD projects in terms of traditional efficiency and effectiveness. Social capital enhances the efficiency of action and helps actors to coordinate critical interdependencies (Gulati, 1995), thereby leading to greater project efficiency. Moreover, by facilitating creativity and innovations (e.g., Putnam, 1993) and improving access to information, resources, and opportunities (e.g., Granovetter, 1973), social capital can lead to greater effectiveness of OISD projects. Path P2 in Figure 14.2 depicts the effect of social capital on project performance.

In several cases, aspects of social capital, including trust in the other organization's motives, confidence in its capabilities, and a high level of identification with the overall OISD group, led the participants to work together on the OISD project rather than find ways to assign blame. A senior executive implicitly attributed the success of a large domestic project, which went through ups and downs, to social capital.

> There was never any discussion about stopping, we were always full force ahead . . . people cared and continue to care about this project. . . . If you have 20 people no matter what the mixture you are not going to get everyone to get along with everyone else. But what is important is that the vast majority of people actually get along . . . *that is what made it work, people getting along.*

In several cases, participants emphasized the importance of the commitment of one or both of the organizations. In fact, in a few cases, commitment to the project seemed to be the single most important factor driving the project. In one large project, a senior executive from the client organization commented about the vendor's commitment:

> They were very focused on us. They were very intent on doing a good job, on time. They hired their best programmers or put their best programmers on this. They wanted it very much to be successful. They were trying very hard . . . They had a lot at stake and they really wanted it to work. I don't know if anybody else would have performed any better.

The cases clearly indicated the importance of social capital in OISD projects. This is not surprising according to Limerick and Cunnington (1993, 95–96):

> Trust reduces uncertainty about the future and the necessity for continually making provisions for the possibility of opportunistic behavior among participants. . . . Trust lubricates the smooth, harmonious functioning of the organization by eliminating friction and minimizing the need for bureaucratic structures that specify the behavior of participants who do not trust each other.

On the other hand, a lack of social capital, characterized by low group identification, distrust for the other organization, and conflict among the two organizations, led to a lot of finger pointing. Focusing on self-interests, each organization sought to identify ways in which the other organization may have hurt the project. In one large project, for example, a vendor executive blamed the client and an intermediary organization for the project's problems:

> Whatever we committed was to our contractor there. But what the contractor signed with the local vendor, we were not aware. It was totally transparent as far as we were concerned.

> . . . Customer was having so much expectation from us as per his contracts, which we were not aware. . . . When we submit the requirement study, it has to be translated. If I go for customer meeting, I have to go with an interpreter. Whatever I record in English has to be translated, feedback has to be again translated into English. . . . So there was going to be time delay. Due to that the complete thing got delayed by 6 to 8 months in all . . . and suddenly the customer forced us to the development there. They came up with their own reason of security and all other things . . . they forced us to do the development there. So the whole thing was there. In fact we were forced to send six more people from India to finish the development in time. It was then delayed by 6–8 months.

The Effect of Project Management Mechanisms and Social Capital

Careful use of project management mechanisms helps build social capital, as shown using path P3 in Figure 14.2. Limerick and Cunnington (1993, 96) continue: "But trust does not come naturally. It has to be carefully structured and managed." Explicit efforts to build social capital are needed in OISD projects, especially when the client lacks prior outsourcing experience or the vendor is located in another country. A senior manager at one of the vendor organizations remarked:

> At least the first time when something is going off-shore, we feel that the client's perception is that they may be losing control—that they are not going to manage it anymore. So the fear of not being physically present during the development process seems to be a factor. . . . We try to go out of our way to address this feeling by specifically, for example, talking [about] reporting mechanisms. The communication set-up also seems to be [a] very critical factor in terms of [the] client feeling that [they can] communicate with us.

However, project management mechanisms differ in their effects on social capital. The project management mechanisms that are interpersonal in nature lead to the development of social capital. But impersonal mechanisms do not involve the kind of rich interactions needed to develop social capital. In the case of one large project, the lack of interpersonal communication combined with some problems with interim deliverables adversely affected the client's confidence in the vendor's abilities. A change in the vendor's project manager, followed by the use of monthly dinner meetings of senior executives from the client and vendor, helped in addressing this decrease in social capital, and eventually in improving project performance. A senior vendor executive remarked:

> [T]hey were afraid that they were not getting attention. That was not the case but they did not know it and we were not communicating it effectively. [The new project manager] got in and convinced [the client] that in fact we were working on this and not sitting here and opening up the communication and got little pieces that had not been looked after and . . . by the next meeting there was an improvement in attitude and that continued steadily improving for several months until it got to where basically both sides [were] comfortable about the system's chances.

Whereas interpersonal mechanisms enable the development of social capital, formal mechanisms can sometimes prevent a decrease in social capital. For example, the use of standards for communication can prevent conflict that might hurt social capital. The following comment by a vendor executive is illustrative:

> It happens once in 20 or 30 cases for whatever reason, the fax did not reach the particular place. . . . What happened instead is that, the sender assumed the fax had reached [us] and is waiting for response. . . . And then he sends the next fax and assumes the previous fax was received. And he says, "as I mentioned in the previous fax." What happens is, this guy, who is receiving it, he's receiving this fax, and he's missed one fax and he's received the earlier fax. So he's referring to the earlier fax. Because this guy is unaware of the immediately previous fax. There is a total miscommunication. This kind of thing over thousands of miles, believe me, although [it] looks so simple, can be so irritating, so problematic . . . you know, these people who are in software development, are pretty sensitive people. . . . How is this customer writing to me like that? . . . Why is he having such a strong tone? You know, you can't really seem to work for the next two [or] three days.

INTELLECTUAL CAPITAL

Economists have traditionally viewed physical and human capital as key resources that enable productive and economic activity, but they also recognize knowledge as a valuable resource. For example, according to Marshall (1965, 115), "capital consists in a great part of knowledge and organization. . . . [K]nowledge is our most powerful engine of production." More recently, Quinn (1992, 241) has expressed a similar view, arguing that "the economic and producing power of the firm lies more in its intellectual and service capabilities than its hard assets—land, plant and equipment. . . . [V]irtually all public and private enterprises—including most successful corporations—are becoming dominantly repositories and coordinators of intellect."

In this chapter, we use the term *intellectual capital* consistently with the definition of Nahapiet and Ghoshal (1998, 245) to refer to "the knowledge and knowing capability of a social collectivity, such as an organization, intellectual community, or professional practice." Specifically in the context of OISD projects, *intellectual capital* refers to the knowledge and knowing capability that resides across the organizations involved in the project, including the client, the vendor, and potential intermediaries. Moreover, it incorporates: (a) tacit knowledge, which includes insights, intuitions, and hunches, is difficult to express and formalize, and therefore difficult to share, as well as explicit knowledge, which can be expressed in numbers and words and shared formally and systematically in the form of data, manuals, and the like (Polanyi 1966); and (b) the capability to create, share, and utilize knowledge, which depends on processes such as internalization, externalization, socialization, and combination processes[3] for creating and transferring knowledge (Nonaka, 1994; Nonaka and Konno, 1998), exchange of explicit knowledge (Nahapiet and Ghoshal, 1998), and direction[4] and routines[5] in applying knowledge (Conner and Prahalad, 1996; Grant, 1996a, 1996b).

The Effect of Intellectual Capital on Project Performance

Intellectual capital can facilitate project performance in terms of effectiveness as well as efficiency, as shown using path P4 in Figure 14.2. The importance of intellectual capital is reflected in prior suggestions that distinctive thought worlds, unfamiliar language, and disparate verbal skills among participants are key obstacles in the performance of interorganizational, multidisciplinary, or multifunctional teams (Carlile and Rebentisch, 2003; Dougherty, 1992; Okhuysen and Eisenhardt, 2002; Szulanski, 1996).

Knowledge sharing across the members of the project team facilitates efficiency by reducing redundancy or "reinvention of the wheel." It can also facilitate effectiveness, as indicated by previous arguments that prior knowledge determines the organization's absorptive capacity, that is, the ability to evaluate and utilize outside knowledge (Cohen and Levinthal 1990), and combinative capability, that is, the ability to generate new combinations of existing knowledge (Kogut and Zander 1992). Knowledge creation capability also enhances the effectiveness of the project by enabling the use of innovative development approaches and solutions during the OISD process. Finally, knowledge application ability contributes to efficiency by enabling the utilization of the client's or the vendor's prior knowledge. The following comment by a client senior executive highlights the effect of the utilization of the vendor's knowledge.

> As we saw the system develop, we wanted to add some things . . . but in most of the cases . . . they convinced us that we didn't need [to]. Most of the cases, they were right. [T]he system that they had was pretty flexible and it . . . could [be] customized for particular needs. They did, they were flexible. They would add anything we wanted; [sometimes] they tried to convince us that [we] shouldn't but they would add it anyway.

The cases also indicated that gaps in intellectual capital have a negative effect on project performance. Gaps in intellectual capital surfaced in three forms: vendor's inadequate knowledge of the client's business, client's users' inadequate knowledge of information systems, and client's IS staff's inadequate knowledge of the functional area. Such lack of intellectual capital led to multiple, conflicting interpretations about system specifications and system development processes.

The Effect of Project Management Mechanisms on Intellectual Capital

Project management mechanisms can facilitate intellectual capital, as shown using path P5 in Figure 14.2. Project management mechanisms affect intellectual capital in two broad ways. First, by providing information on the potential participants' knowledge domains, they enable the creation of teams such that intellectual capital will be enhanced and also facilitate the utilization of the appropriate team members' knowledge during the project. Such a connection between project management and intellectual capital is related to the characterization of control during initial project stages, called "collective sense making" in a recent study of global software development (Kirsch, 2004). In several of the OISD projects I studied, client executives examined the résumés of the vendor's personnel who might participate in the OISD project and influenced the assignment of appropriate individuals. In one case, the client's senior executives were actively involved in interviewing individuals when the vendor was trying to hire a new project manager.

Second, by facilitating interactions among project participants, project management mechanisms provide forums for individuals to create, share, or apply knowledge. Mechanisms involving greater interpersonal interaction enable socialization, thereby facilitating the creation and sharing of tacit knowledge (Nonaka and Takeuchi, 1995), whereas the more formalized mechanisms facilitate the sharing of explicit knowledge through exchange (Nahapiet and Ghoshal, 1998), and the utilization of both tacit and explicit knowledge through the use of direction or routines (Grant, 1996a, 1996b).

Consistent with the above arguments, the cases revealed that the lack of intellectual capital might be caused by inadequate interpersonal interaction early in the project. In two cases, the focal vendor was not involved from the beginning of the project, thus being asked to work with requirements developed by another vendor or the client, and consequently had inadequate understanding of the client's business. In another project, the client's IS department was not involved during requirements specifications, which led to some ambiguity in specifications.

THE RELATIONSHIP BETWEEN SOCIAL CAPITAL AND INTELLECTUAL CAPITAL

Social capital and intellectual capital are mutually interdependent. They affect each other, as shown using path P6 in Figure 14.2, and discussed below.

Social capital leads to greater intellectual capital by enhancing individuals' motivation to share knowledge (Nahapiet and Ghoshal, 1998). Aspects of social capital, such as trust, commitment, and identification, lead OISD project participants to believe that sharing their knowledge with others will eventually provide value to themselves (Moran and Ghoshal, 1996). For example, the integration of engineering knowledge across different functional areas has been argued to benefit from "a bond or social connection between the engineers derived from the commonality of their core experiences, education, and professional socialization" (Thomas-Hunt, Ogden, and Neale, 2003, 465).

Intellectual capital also affects social capital. OISD team members often trust other participants based on the recognition of their abilities and knowledge. Indeed, one form of trust identified in the literature (Lewicki and Bunker, 1996; Sabherwal, 1999), called "knowledge-based trust," is based on the involved parties' knowing each other well.

In some cases, the vendor had developed previous systems for the client, and in several other cases, the client asked the vendor (and maybe some other vendors) to demonstrate ability by developing a small system. Demonstration of knowledge and expertise was clearly used by some vendors as a way of gaining the client's confidence. One senior vendor executive remarked:

> Initially we had to gain . . . credibility with the client. The best way . . . is to put some of our people to work with the clients. Then he sees them in operation. Then he gets some [indication of] the[ir] capabilities. . . . We had some of our people work there. Those people were pretty much convinced about our capabilities.

FEEDBACK PATHS

The above discussion focuses on the effect of project management mechanisms on social capital and intellectual capital, and the effect of project management mechanisms, social capital, and intellectual capital on project performance. However, the reverse effects are also important, and may take place during the evolution of the OISD project.

Interim project performance affects social capital (path P7). Successful accomplishment of project goals seemed to improve trust, whereas performance problems sometimes caused conflict and distrust. In some projects, jointly celebrating the completion of interim deliverables through a party or a cruise improved the participants' mutual trust. Demonstrating the completed portion of the system also helps. A senior executive thus described a successful pilot:

> Instead of just "trust me" it was something tangible to show. So, to be honest that was the big motivation. We wanted to put something out there to show we had some result[s]. That was a shot in the arm. Not only did it buy us some management time but it helped people internally who were getting burned out, feeling demoralized, despondent.

Several vendors recognized the importance of ensuring successful performance, especially through meticulous quality assessments.

> Each interim deliverable that you submit . . . [you] have to make it reflect the organization's ability to deliver. So before you deliver it's always good to take feedback if possible within the development organization. If there are basic flaws, there can be some input taken from people with experience in similar areas. These are continuously incorporated into the project . . . you need to have regular reviews and things like that.

The feedback path from project performance to social capital is especially important when the client and the vendor are remotely located; the client's inability to observe the vendor's behavior places greater importance on the timeliness and quality of deliverables. One vendor's project manager remarked:

> The client is not able to see how people are working, and how much time we are spending on each activity. They may get the time sheet, but they may not know whether the person is actually spending time, 8 hours or 6 hours. It will only be on paper. Problem[s] happen . . . only when there is a delay in delivering. The client may not see.

Moreover, social capital may affect the use of project management mechanisms (path P8). One common effect we observed is that a high level of social capital leads to reduced emphasis on project coordination and control. For example, a senior executive of a large client organization thus explained the lack of attention to project management mechanisms:

> I think in this case, we are lucky with the vendor because [it is to our] mutual benefit to continue working and we both [made] efforts to deliver and to be very flexible. But [this] is a more special relationship, [a] strategic relationship. [Were it] not, I would say that I would be much more formal in the time when things are going to be delivered.

Indeed, a high level of social capital may sometimes lead to an almost complete lack of attention to project management mechanisms (path P8), which, in turn, can cause performance problems (path P1, discussed earlier), and those performance problems could then diminish social capital (path P7). The following comment illustrates this possibility, as a vendor, realizing the lack of control by the client (which had a high level of trust for the vendor) abdicated its system-testing responsibilities, leading to problems and erosion of trust.

> One of the lessons learned is [that] they didn't test very well, and I found so many issue[s] that had to be sent back. I think [the vendor's] programmers developed the sense of "let's program it and give it to them to test." Because I'm going to find it anyway, it may have been faster for them to just develop and send me codes to test. [T]he problem with that was I would spend more and more of my time testing as opposed to finding requirements for installation. So the developers thought that I was doing such a good job at testing that they decided to let me continue doing that. I think they stopped their emphasis on going in and checking for things [themselves]. That is when [the client's vice president for IS] became involved and really insisted that they [pay] for testing software.

Some projects indicated that a high level of social capital does not obviate the need for project control. In a few cases, the client and the vendor began the project with such confidence in their own (and partner's) abilities and so much trust in each other that they neither established any project management mechanisms (path P8) nor identified potential obstacles. They were rudely surprised somewhat later when problems surfaced.

Feedback paths similar to paths P7 and P8 for social capital seemed apparent for intellectual capital as well. Interim deliverables seemed to affect intellectual capital (path P9), such as in the use of demos and prototypes to learn about the system specifications. Moreover, the sharing of knowledge led to changes in project management mechanisms (path P10), as seen, for example, when the client relaxes controls upon believing that the vendor personnel had acquired the information and knowledge needed to successfully complete the project.

In some cases, the two organizations started the project well, establishing coordination and control mechanisms. However, upon encountering initial success, they became complacent and relaxed. Project management mechanisms were therefore either ignored or discarded altogether, and minor problems, which were symptomatic of larger issues, were not given adequate attention (reflects the feedback path, P11, from project performance to project management mechanisms). In such cases also, problems inevitably escalated, and affected the project significantly.

THE EFFECTS OF CONTINGENCY FACTORS

Prior research on coordination and control has examined the factors influencing control (Beath, 1987; Kirsch, 1996, 1997) and coordination (Koushik and Mookerjee, 1995; Kraut and Streeter, 1995). Path P12 in Figure 14.2 depicts the effect of contingency factors on the relationships among project management mechanisms, social capital, intellectual capital, and project deliverables. This path is discussed below, although a detailed discussion of the effects of the contingency factors on individual paths (P1 to P11) is beyond the scope of this chapter.

The context-dependent nature of processes associated with social capital (e.g., Jarvenpaa, Shaw, and Staples, 2004) and intellectual capital (Becerra-Fernandez and Sabherwal, 2001) has also been highlighted. Four contingency factors—structural arrangement, interorganizational differentiation, project complexity, and project criticality—emerged from the cases as prominently affecting the need for coordination. Of these factors, which are briefly discussed below, two (project complexity and criticality) are attributes of the IS project, while the other two (structural arrangement and interorganizational differentiation) are attributes of the outsourcing arrangement.

Before I discuss the contingency factors, a brief discussion of the *structural arrangement* of the OISD project is in order. I found five broad types of structural arrangements, depicted in Figure 14.3, to be used in the cases. One of these involved no intermediary between the client and the vendor. Such direct relationship between the client and the vendor was found in nine of the eighteen cases.

In another form of structural arrangement—internal mediation—the vendor had, and utilized, a local (i.e., located in the same city as the major group of project participants from the client) unit. This local unit was either a subsidiary firm or simply a local office. Such *internal mediation* was used in seven projects. It was especially helpful in two projects, where individuals from the vendor's local unit played an important role in project management, and in facilitating the communication between the client and the Colombia-based programmers and analysts. The importance of the vendor's local unit has been highlighted in some previous studies of IS outsourcing (e.g., Continental Bank, as discussed by Huber, 1993, p. 129).

Two types of structural arrangements involved an external party. In one type, a third party was

Figure 14.3 **Types of Structural Arrangements**

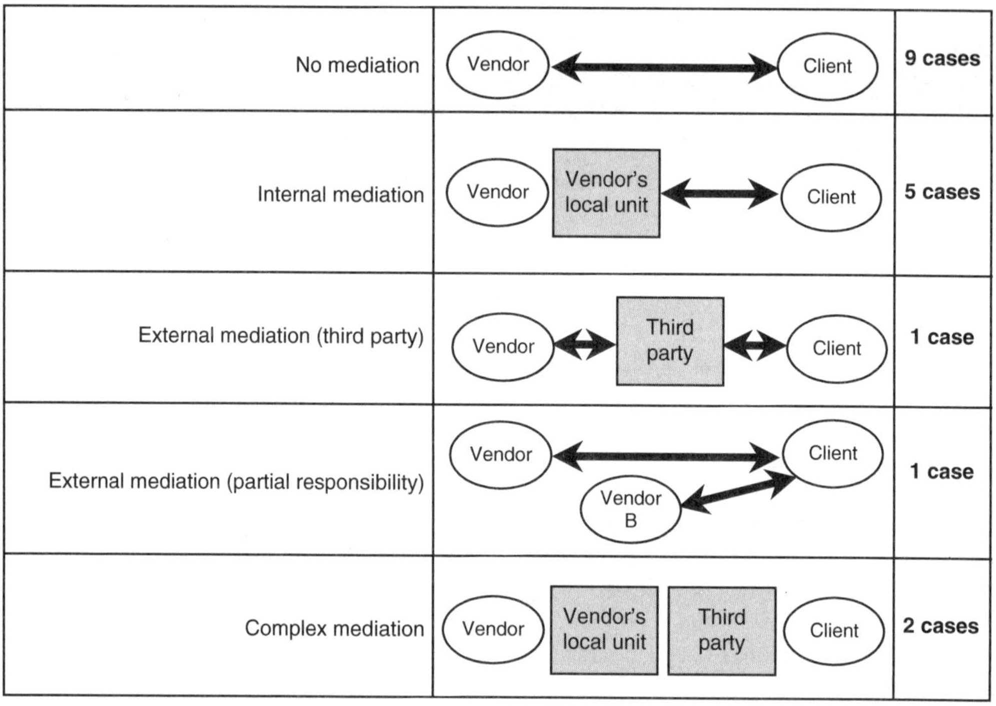

present between the client and the vendor. In the other type of *external mediation,* two vendors (including the one responsible for system development) were jointly responsible for delivering the complete information system. Each of these forms of external mediation was used in one project. Finally, two cases involved *complex mediation,* as the vendor used a local unit (internal mediation), and another organization (external mediation—third party) was also involved. Including these two cases, internal mediation was present in seven cases, identified earlier, whereas external mediation (third party) was present in three cases. In two cases, the third party was a consultant hired by the client to manage the process, while in one case the third party was a turnkey system vendor, which integrated the software developed by the focal vendor with hardware and system software and delivered the complete package to the client.

External mediation between the client and the vendor increased the need for project management mechanisms. In the one case involving external mediation (partial responsibility), the focal vendor not only had to coordinate with the other vendor and the client regarding the development and delivery of modules of software, but it also spent considerable time tracking and discussing with the client the delays and additional expenses that might have arisen due to problems with the other vendor's performance. In the cases involving external mediation (third party), the presence of the consultant or the turnkey vendor, as expected, led to the need for the client as well as the focal vendor to coordinate activities with the intermediary. What was less obvious was the need for the client and the focal vendor to maintain coordination with each other as well. Where the client and the focal vendor did not do so, depending entirely on the intermediary party for coordination, misunderstandings and conflict resulted, adversely affecting social capital.

That external mediation led to greater need for project management mechanisms seemed to be because the presence of the third party increased the uncertainty in the relationship between the client and the focal vendor. Uncertainty explained the effect of another contingency factor, *project complexity,* on the need for project management mechanisms. Interviewees characterized ten of the projects as complex. Several of the interviewees in these cases mentioned the greater need for coordination and control in complex projects. In one highly complex project, two executives from the client visited the vendor for a period of four weeks during the middle of the project. This visit addressed the uncertainty (especially with respect to specifications) arising from project complexity. The vendor's project manager remarked:

> The specifications were not clearly laid out. During the development process we found that specifications of lots of things were still evolving. So they also felt that maybe a face-to-face meeting should help in clearing out all specifications-related issues.

In another complex project, a variety of mechanisms, including the use of e-mail follow-ups for faxes, regular conference calls, a liaison person from the vendor being present at the client site, an executive from the client visiting the vendor early in the project, and a detailed project plan prepared by the client, were used to facilitate coordination and control.

The above two contingency factors were related to uncertainty (external mediation and project complexity), which has been highlighted in the organizational information processing literature (Daft and Lengel, 1986: Egelhoff, 1991). The next two contingency factors—interorganizational differentiation and project criticality—relate more to differentiation and interdependence, respectively. Differentiation and interdependence, along with uncertainty, are considered to be key determinants of potential for intergroup conflict, which may be addressed using integrating mechanisms (Daft, 1992; Lawrence and Lorsch, 1967; Pondy, 1967; Walton and Dutton, 1969).

Interorganizational differentiation between the client and the vendor enhanced the need for communication. In seven cases, the vendor and the client differed significantly in terms of their cultures, languages, and formality. One common difference, mentioned by vendors as well as clients, was that the vendors desired greater formalization of expectations regarding the system and the process, whereas the clients wanted things to remain somewhat flexible. Consequently, client and vendor had different expectations regarding the details to be provided in requirements specification. In some cases, this difference between the perceptions of vendors and clients was exacerbated by cultural differences. Language differences also increased the need for coordination, especially in the case of one project. Another component of interorganizational differentiation—which required greater coordination and control—was the time difference that existed between the client and the vendor in several cases. The personnel involved in software development not only were not in the same office, but also were not in their offices at the same time, and greater effort was consequently needed to ensure adequate coordination of activities.

Project criticality led to the need for greater project management mechanisms in eight cases. Projects that were expected to significantly impact organizational performance increased the client's feeling of dependence on the vendor. This was due mainly to the inherent importance of the system, but also to some extent because these projects attracted close attention from the client's top managers. Vendors also felt more dependent on inputs from the client's users and IS personnel, due to the greater pressure to develop the system and the belief that successful development of such an important system would help them in obtaining future contracts with the same client as well as other clients. Project criticality can be related to interdependence because not only is the client's dependence on the vendor higher when the project is more critical, but also the vendor is more likely to benefit (in overall reputation and future relations with the vendor) from success with critical projects. On the other hand, project management mechanisms received less emphasis in noncritical projects, as illustrated by the following remark of a senior client executive:

> I think we were flexible because it wasn't a time critical project. It was something that was not of critical need or business critical needs so we slipped a month or two, nothing really happened. So, we were able to [do] that but I would not do it in a critical project. I would be much more formal and tie the vendor to their dates more. In this case, it slipped many times.

In Case 7, where the project was relatively simple but so important that its announcement caused the client's share price to increase, there was continuous pressure on timely software development; personnel from the client and the vendor visited each other frequently, and one interviewee felt that the programmers sometimes found the pressure to be too much. The effect of project criticality on need for coordination and control was also observed in Case 3, where the more critical modules of the system were developed at the client site, and Case 1, where the vendor's programmers were moved to the client site for a two-week period.[6] In addition, project criticality exacerbates the focus on short-term project demands in critical projects.

The four contingency factors seemed to influence the need for project management mechanisms. Consequently, greater use of project management mechanisms would lead to greater project success under certain circumstances. In addition, the contingency factors also had a moderating effect on some of the other relationships (e.g., interorganizational differentiation and structural arrangements moderated the effect of project management mechanisms on knowledge capital). Moreover, over the course of the OISD project, these contingency factors were themselves affected by project management mechanisms, changes in social and intellectual capital, and project performance. Most notably, through the enhanced intellectual capital arising from the project management mechanisms, knowledge inadequacy would be decreased. Similarly, through the enhanced social capital arising from the project management mechanisms, interorganizational differentiation might be decreased as the personnel involved in the project developed a better understanding of the culture and goals of the other organization. The bidirectional path P11 in Figure 14.2 represents the moderating effects of the contingency factors on the other relationships in the model and the feedback path from the other constructs to the contingency factors, but a more detailed consideration of these relationships is beyond the scope of this chapter.

CONCLUSIONS

This chapter has examined the impacts of project management mechanisms on two infrequently examined but important aspects—social capital (e.g., Cohen and Prusak, 2001; Nahapiet and Ghoshal, 1998; Putnam, 1995) and intellectual capital (e.g., Grant, 1996a, 1996b; Nahapiet and Ghoshal, 1998). Social capital and intellectual capital were proposed as additional benefits from project management that affect the traditional criteria of project success in either the short term or the long term. Thus, it is argued that project management mechanisms affect project success either directly or indirectly through their effects on social and intellectual capital.

Overall, this chapter has sought to make four specific contributions by adopting a macro view of OISD project management and examining how project management affects social and intellectual capital within the project team as well as externally. First, by employing a broader view of project objectives—development of social capital and intellectual capital in addition to traditional project performance—this chapter provides insights into ways in which project managers can embed the

Figure 14.4 **Effects of Project Management Mechanisms**

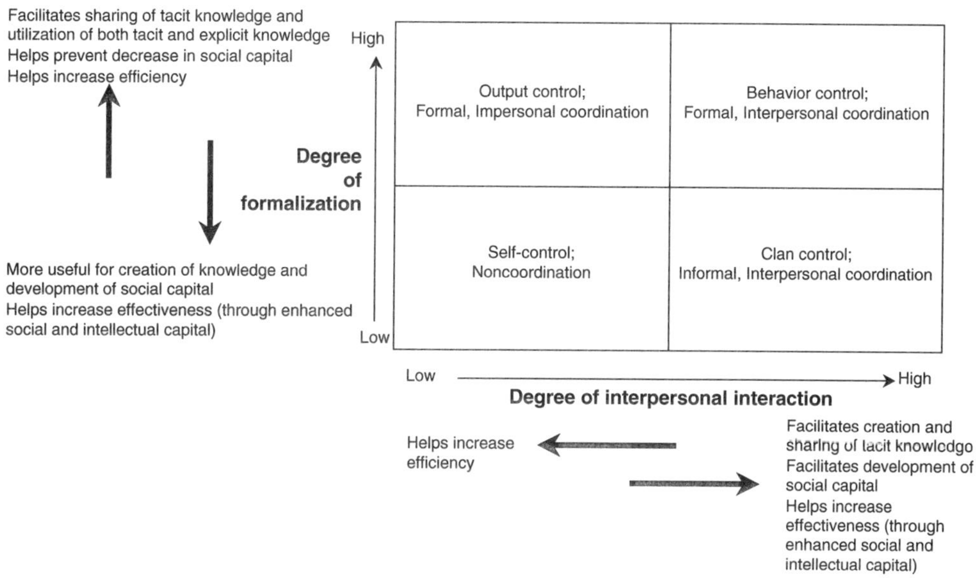

development of social capital and intellectual capital within normal project management rather than viewing them as developing either through luck or through actions considered peripheral to the project. The development of intellectual and social capital, in turn, would help improve project performance in terms of the deliverables.

Second, the chapter has highlighted the need for OISD project managers and project team members to address the contradictory demands of short-term project considerations and long-term organizational objectives. For example, in assigning the best possible people to an OISD project team, the emphasis is on that focal project rather than on the broader implications. When a vendor's project manager instead seeks to replace an experienced individual on a team comprising several experienced individuals with a less experienced individual, it can potentially have an adverse effect on the project. It might also have an adverse short-term impact on the social capital if the client views this as an unexpected opportunistic move by the vendor. However, it can produce long-term benefits by helping an inexperienced employee acquire knowledge and develop ties with the client, which could be helpful in future projects. Thus, project management mechanisms not only have short-term impacts on the project by directly affecting efficiency and effectiveness, but, through their effects on social capital and intellectual capital, they also have long-term impacts both on that project and future projects.

Third, this chapter has highlighted the importance of viewing project management mechanisms as a portfolio rather than individually. Figure 14.4 summarizes the effects of different kinds of mechanisms, as discussed earlier in the chapter. For example, a shift from impersonal to interpersonal mechanisms can potentially lead to increased effectiveness, partly by enhancing social capital and facilitating the creation and sharing of tacit knowledge, but it can also lead to reduced efficiency. Each kind of project management mechanism thus provides certain benefits, and, consequently, a judicious combination of different types of mechanisms is needed.

Fourth, this chapter has examined the dynamics of management of OISD projects by highlighting the direct and indirect (through social capital and intellectual capital) effects of project management mechanisms on project performance as well as the associated feedback paths. Project managers can benefit from being sensitive to these dynamics, for example, the potential impacts that poor-quality interim deliverables might have on the project management mechanisms that may need to be used later in the project.

The broad focus of the chapter as well as space limitations inhibited a more in-depth examination of certain aspects. For example, the specific effects of the contingency factors could not be examined. Moreover, the theoretical foundations for various effects could not be detailed further. Further research on OISD projects is needed to address these topics. Hopefully, this chapter has raised some important issues related to the role of social capital and intellectual capital in OISD projects, which can be further pursued in such future research. Management of OISD projects continues to be an important yet difficult task, and further understanding of its effects is clearly needed, as illustrated by the following remark of one senior executive at a client firm:

> One of the things that I look back at is vendor management. I have got to believe there was a better way to do that. The targets were more than what they were really capable of . . . yet we were angry and trying to make them do it. I would come back and sit in my office and think "we are killing these people." It is not like they were bad guys, they weren't going back and not working. They were trying to do the[ir] best.

ACKNOWLEDGMENTS

I am grateful to Joyce Elam and Vivek Choudhury, with whom I have worked on research in this area. I also acknowledge insightful comments from Suzanne Rivard and an anonymous reviewer on an earlier version of this chapter. These comments have helped to improve the chapter considerably. Finally, I am deeply indebted to all of the informants and organizations that participated in this research effort.

NOTES

1. Scholars in several areas, including organization theory (e.g., Adler, 1995; Galbraith, 1974), computer science, economics, and biology have investigated the topic of coordination. See Malone and Crowston (1994) for an excellent review of discussion of coordination in these diverse fields.
2. I am grateful to an anonymous reviewer for highlighting this point.
3. *Externalization* involves the expression of tacit knowledge and its conversion into comprehensible forms that others can understand. *Combination* involves converting explicit knowledge into more complex sets of explicit knowledge (Nonaka, 1994; Nonaka and Konno, 1998; Nonaka and Takeuchi, 1995). *Socialization* is the sharing of tacit knowledge between individuals, usually through joint activities rather than written or verbal instructions (Nonaka, 1994). Finally, *internalization* is the conversion of explicit knowledge into the organization's tacit knowledge.
4. *Direction* refers to a mechanism whereby an individual possessing certain knowledge directs the action of another individual without transferring the underlying knowledge to that individual (Grant, 1996b). It involves the transfer of instructions but not the transfer of knowledge, and has therefore been labeled as knowledge substitution (Conner and Prahalad, 1996).
5. Routines also support knowledge substitution, but involve the use of standards, policies, or automation to store and communicate direction (Grant, 1996a, 1996b).
6. They returned once the client and vendor's top management recognized that their productivity was being adversely affected by their being away from their home, family, and so on.

REFERENCES

Adler, P.S. 1995. Interdepartmental interdependence and coordination: The case of the design/manufacturing interface, *Organization Science*, 6, 2, 147–167.

Aubert, B.A.; S. Rivard, S.; M. Patry. 1996. A transaction cost approach to outsourcing behavior: Some empirical evidence. *Information and Management*, 30, 2, 51–64.

Badaracco, J.L. 1991. *The Knowledge Link.* Boston: Harvard Business School Press.

Becerra-Fernandez, I. and Sabherwal, R. 2001. Organizational knowledge management: A contingency perspective. *Journal of Management Information Systems*, 18, 1, 23–55.

Beath, C.M. 1987. Managing the user relationship in information systems development projects: A transaction governance approach. In *Proceedings of the Eighth International Conference on Information Systems*, Pittsburg, PA, December 6–9, 415–427.

Boissevain, J. 1974. *Friends of Friends.* Oxford: Blackwell.

Burt, R. S., 1992. *Structural Holes: The Social Structure of Competition.* Cambridge: Harvard University Press.

———. 1997. A note on social capital and network content. *Social Networks*, 19, 4, 355–373.

Carlile, P.R. and E.S. Rebentisch. 2003. Into the black box: The knowledge transformation cycle. *Management Science*, 49, 9, 1180–1195.

Choudhury, V. and Sabherwal, R. 2003. Portfolios of control in outsourced software development projects. *Information Systems Research*, 14, 3, 291–314.

Cohen, D. and Prusak, L. 2001. *Good Company: How Social Capital Makes Organizations Work.* Boston: Harvard Business School Press.

Cohen, W.M. and Levinthal, D.A. 1990. Absorptive capacity: A new perspective on learning and innovation. *Administrative Sciences Quarterly*, 35, 128–152.

Coleman, J. 1988. Social capital in the creation of human capital. *American Journal of Sociology*, 94, 95–120.

Conner, K.R. and C.K. Prahalad. 1996. A resource-based theory of the firm: Knowledge versus opportunism. *Organization Science*, 7, 5, 477–501.

Crowston, K. 1997. A coordination theory approach to organizational process design. *Organization Science*, 8, 2, 157–175.

Daft, R.L. 1992. *Organization Theory and Design*, 4th ed. New York: West.

Daft, R.L. and Lengel, R.H. 1986. Organization information requirements, media richness, and structural design. *Management Science*, 32, 5, 554–571.

DeSanctis, G. and Jackson, B.M. 1994. Coordination of information technology management: Team-based structures and computer-based communication system. *Journal of Management Information Systems*, 10, 4, 85–110.

Dougherty, D. 1992. A practice-centered model of organization renewal through innovation. *Strategic Management Journal*, 13, 77–92.

Earl M. J. 1996. The Risks of Outsourcing IT. Sloan Management Review, 37, 3, 26–32.

Egelhoff, W.G. 1991. Information processing theory and the multinational enterprise. *Journal of International Business Studies* (Third Quarter), 341–368.

Feeny, D.; Lacity, M.; and Willcocks, L.P. 2005. Taking the measure of outsourcing providers. *Sloan Management Review*, 46, 3, 41–48.

Friedkin, N. 1982. Information flow through strong and weak ties in intra-organizational networks. *Social Networks*, 3, 273–285.

Galbraith, J.R., 1973. *Designing Complex Organizations.* Reading, MA: Addison-Wesley.

Granovetter, M.S. 1973. The strength of weak ties. *American Journal of Sociology*, 78, 1360–1380.

Grant, R.M. 1996a. Prospering in dynamically-competitive environments: Organizational capability as knowledge integration. *Organization Science*, 7, 4, 375–387.

———. 1996b. Toward a knowledge-based theory of the firm. *Strategic Management Journal*, 17, 109–122.

Gulati, R. 1995. Does familiarity breed trust? The implications of repeated ties for contractual choice in alliances. *Academy of Management Review*, 38, 1, 85–112.

Hackman, J.R. 1990. *Groups that Work (And Groups that Don't).* San Francisco: Jossey-Bass.

Henderson, J.C. and Lee, S. 1992. Managing I/S design teams: A control theories perspective. *Management Science*, 38, 6 (June), 757–777.

Huber R. L.1993. How Continental Bank outsourced its "crown jewels" *Harvard Business Review*, 71, 1, 121–130.

Jarvenpaa, S. and Leidner, D., 1999. Communication and Trust in Global Virtual Teams, *Organization Science*, 10, 6, 791–815.

Jarvenpaa, S.L.; Shaw, T.R.; and Staples, D.S. 2004. Toward contextualized theories of trust: The role of trust in global virtual teams. *Information Systems Research*, 15, 3, 250–267.

Keil, M. and Carmel, E. 1995. Customer-developer links in software development. *Communications of the ACM*, 38, 5, 33–44.
Kirsch, L.J. 1996. The management of complex tasks in organizations: Controlling the systems development process. *Organization Science*, 7, 1, 1–21.
———. 1997. Portfolios of control modes and IS project management. *Information Systems Research*, 8, 3, 215–239.
———. 2004. Deploying common systems globally: The dynamics of control. *Information Systems Research*, 15, 4, 374–395.
Kogut, B. and Zander, U. 1992. Knowledge of the firm, combinative capabilities, and the replication of technology. *Organization Science*, 3, 3, 383–397.
Koushik, M.V. and Mookerjee, V.S. 1995. Modeling coordination in software construction: An analytical approach. *Information Systems Research*, 6, 3, 220–254.
Kraut, R.E. and Streeter, L.A., 1995. Coordination in software development. *Communications of the ACM*, 38, 3, 69–81.
Lacity, M.C. and Hirschheim, R. 1993. The information systems outsourcing bandwagon. *Sloan Management Review* (Fall), 73–86.
Lacity, M.C.; Willcocks, L.P.; and Feeny, D.F. 1996. The value of selective IT outsourcing. *Sloan Management Review* (Spring), 13–25.
Lawrence, P.R. and Lorsch, J.W. 1967. New management job: The integrator. *Harvard Business Review*, 45 (November–December), 142–151.
Lewicki, R.J. and Bunker, B.B. 1996. Developing and maintaining trust in work relationships. In R.M. Kramer and T.R. Tyler, eds., *Trust in Organizations*. Thousand Oaks, CA: Sage, 114–139.
Limerick, D. and Cunnington, B. 1993. *Managing the New Organization*. San Francisco: Jossey-Bass.
Malone, T.W. and Crowston, K. 1994. The interdisciplinary study of coordination. *ACM Computing Surveys*, 26, 1, 87–119.
March, J.G. and Simon, H.A. 1958. *Organizations*. New York: Wiley.
Marshall, A. 1965 [1890]. *Principles of Economics*. London: MacMillan.
McFarlan, F.W. and Nolan, R.L. 1995. How to manage an outsourcing alliance. *Sloan Management Review* (Winter), 9–23.
Meyerson, D.; Weick, K.E.; and Kramer, R.M. 1996. Swift trust and temporary groups. In R.M. Kramer and T.R. Tyler (eds.). *Trust in Organizations: Frontiers of Theory and Research*, pp. 165–195. Thousand Oaks, CA: Sage.
Miles, M.B. and Huberman, A.M. 1990. *Qualitative Data Analysis*, 10th printing. Newbury Park, CA: Sage.
Moran, P. and Ghoshal, S. 1996.Theories of economic organization: The case for realism and balance. *Academy of Management Review,* 21, 1, 58–72.
Nahapiet, J. and Ghoshal, S. 1998. Social capital, intellectual capital, and the organizational advantage. *Academy of Management Review*, 23, 2, 242–266.
Nidumolu, S. 1995. The effect of coordination and uncertainty on software project performance: Residual performance risk as an intervening variable. *Information Systems Research*, 6, 3, 191–219.
Nonaka, I. 1994. A dynamic theory of organizational knowledge creation. *Organization Science*, 5, 1, 14–37.
Nonaka, I. and Konno, N. 1998. The concept of "ba": Building a foundation for knowledge creation. *California Management Review*, 40, 3, 40–54.
Nonaka, I. and Takeuchi, H. 1995. *The Knowledge-Creating Company*. New York: Oxford University Press.
Ouchi, W.G. 1980. Markets, bureaucracies, and clans. *Administrative Science Quarterly*, 25, 129–141.
Okhuysen, G.A. and Eisenhardt, K.M. 2002. Integrating knowledge in groups: How formal interventions enable flexibility. *Organization Science*, 13, 4, 370–386.
Peters, T. 1999. *The Project 50 (Reinventing Work): Fifty Ways to Transform Every "Task" Into A Project That MATTERS!* New York: Knopf.
Pinto, M.B.; Pinto, J.K.; Prescott, J.E. 1993. Antecedents and consequences of project team cross-functional cooperation. *Management Science*, 39, 10, 1281–1297.
Polanyi, M.1966. *The Tacit Dimension.* London: Routledge and Kegan Paul.
Pondy, L.R. 1967. Organizational conflict: Concepts and models. *Administrative Science Quarterly*, 12, 2, 296–320.
Putnam, R.D. 1993. The prosperous community: Social capital and public life. *American Prospect*, 13, 35–42.
———. 1995. Bowling alone: America's declining social capital. *Journal of Democracy*, 6, 1, 65–78.
Quinn, J.B. 1992. *Intelligent Enterprise.* New York: Free Press.

Sabherwal, R. 1999. The role of trust in managing outsourced IS development projects. *Communications of the ACM*, 42, 2, 80–87.
———. 2003. The evolution of coordination in outsourced software development projects: A comparison of client and vendor perspectives. *Information and Organization*, 13, 153–202.
Strauss, A. L. 1987. *Qualitative Analysis for Social Scientists*. Cambridge: Cambridge University Press.
Szulanski, G. 1996. Exploring internal stickiness: Impediments to the transfer of best practice within the firm. *Strategic Management Journal*, 17 (Winter Special Issue), 27–43.
Taylor, M. 1982. *Community, Anarchy and Liberty*. Cambridge: Cambridge University Press.
Tesch, R. 1990. *Qualitative Research: Analysis Types and Software Tools*. New York: Falmer Press.
Thomas-Hunt, M.C.; Ogden, T.Y.; and Neale, M.A. 2003. Who's really sharing? Effects of social and expert status on knowledge exchange within groups. *Management Science*, 49, 4, 464–477.
Van de Ven, A.H.; Delbecq, A.L.; and Koening, R. 1976. Determinants of coordination modes within organizations. *American Sociological Review*, 41, 2, 322–338.
Walton, R.E. and Dutton, J.E. 1969. The management of interdepartmental conflict. *Administrative Science Quarterly*, 14, 1, 73–84.

APPENDIX 14.1. SUMMARY OF RESEARCH METHODS

Data Collection

Eighteen case studies of OISD projects, conducted through interviews with a number of participants in each project, constitute the data underlying the theoretical model developed here. The research methodology and the contexts of the cases are summarized below. Thirteen projects were studied primarily through interviews with multiple individuals at the vendors (these were five large vendors, located in India); three projects were studied through interviews at the client as well as the vendor; and two projects were studied through interviews at the client organization. This strategy enabled me to examine the phenomenon from both perspectives, and in a number of projects, while keeping the research costs reasonable.

Each project included the delivery of a product to the client, with the vendor being responsible for that product. In no project did the vendors' programmers work on a number of different systems for the client with the vendor being paid for hours of programming service provided. Within these broad boundaries, the projects differed considerably. They differed in size and functionality, including a system with a budget of $25 million, several other systems with budgets exceeding $1 million, and some projects with budgets of around $0.1 million. They included some highly complex systems as well as simpler systems, such as the conversion from one platform to another. Eight clients were located in United States, five in the UK, and the rest were spread across the Netherlands, Thailand, and Oman. The vendors were located in the United States, India, and Colombia. Overall, the projects were quite heterogeneous in terms of clients, vendors, and systems. This variety enabled examination of the social factors in a broad set of projects.

A total of forty-five interviews (twenty-two at clients and twenty-three at vendors) lasting seventy-two hours (twenty-nine at clients and forty-three at vendors) were conducted with forty-seven informants (twenty-one at clients and twenty-seven at vendors). I conducted all of the interviews, except one, which was done by a research associate. I used interview protocols but allowed the interviewees to develop their own views instead of forcing them to fit their experiences into pre-established categories. Each interview was tape-recorded, with additional notes being taken when necessary, and then transcribed.

Data Analysis

Interviews for the eighteen cases produced over 900 pages of transcripts and over 100 pages of field notes. I conducted the data analysis in a systematic and comprehensive, but not rigid, fashion, as described in Sabherwal (2003). The analysis began with examination of the interview transcripts, and was performed in two broad steps.

The first step involved the preparation of case-wise summaries of concepts. The initial theoretical perspective was open-ended, with the project management mechanisms (coordination and control mechanisms) and the project context representing the starting point. However, these concepts were provisional; in an attempt "to produce concepts that seem to fit the data" (Strauss, 1987, 28), further concepts were developed and refined as the analysis of the transcripts progressed.

Most of the interview transcripts had been read during data collection, but all the transcripts were read carefully following the completion of the fieldwork. While reading the transcripts, I made extensive use of a highlighter to identify and delineate interviewee comments, which helped segment the data into relevant and meaningful pieces of text, or units (Tesch, 1990). Most of these pieces of text described an underlying concept—such as trust—in an interviewee's words, but some of them represented the interviewee's perceptions of relationships among two or more concepts. I also wrote analytical comments, or "memos," in the margins adjacent to each piece of text. By identifying the concept or the relationship implicit in each piece of text, memos "help the analyst to move easily from data to a conceptual level, . . . developing key categories and showing their relationships, and building toward a more integrated theory of events, processes, and outcomes in the site" (Miles and Huberman, 1990, 71). The process of writing memos and identifying the concepts and their interrelationships followed an iterative approach, which characterizes grounded theory building; as refinements occurred in the underlying concepts over the course of the analysis, I occasionally reverted to the transcripts read earlier and modified some of the memos in light of these refined concepts.

Once all of the transcripts had been read and the constructs refined, I constructed a one-page form for summarizing the key aspects of each case. This form was completed for each project by going through the transcripts and examining the memos. The form for each project summarized the type of project management mechanisms used and the contingency factors, and provided links to the memos in the transcripts in terms of the interview and the page number of the transcript.

Together, the four analytical devices—highlighting to segment data into pieces of text, memos identifying the nature of each piece of text, the summary form for each case, and the links between forms and memos—enabled me to decontextualize the interviewee comments and then recontextualize them (Tesch, 1990). In other words, they helped me to take the interviewee comments out of their original context (i.e., an interview) and present them in a different context (i.e., the coordination mechanisms and the various contingency factors in each case).

The second step of the analysis involved cross-case comparison, which was done by examining similar concepts across the cases. Using the links to memos, indicated on each form, I went back to the transcripts to view similar concepts across cases from the interviewees' perspectives. These comparisons helped me to understand the cross-case variations in each concept. To examine the relationships among concepts, I used the links on the forms to go back to the transcripts and read the cross-concept comments made by the interviewees. These comments were supplemented by combining cross-case comparisons for multiple concepts (such as for the context and the project mechanisms). The resulting insights into the relationships among the various concepts were further examined in the light of prior literature.

CHAPTER 15

CONTRACTING IN IT OUTSOURCING

Hierarchical and Psychological Contractual Elements as Key Managerial Governance Mechanisms

CHRISTINE KOH AND SOON ANG

Abstract: *Drawing predominantly from organizational economics, current research on outsourcing contracts has focused on designing contract structures to align the incentives of outsourcing parties, and address the issues of adverse selection and moral hazard. This perspective of information technology (IT) contracting is unnecessarily narrow, as it fails to acknowledge the valuable role of contracts as a managerial governance mechanism. In this chapter, we propose a conceptual framework that adds hierarchical and psychological contractual elements to existing contract structures. Hierarchical elements emulate the social structures underlying hierarchical governance mechanisms and provide a useful means to address the limitations of market exchanges. The psychological contract, representing the client's and vendor's beliefs and expectations about their mutual obligations in outsourcing, governs the behaviors of and interactions between the parties.*

Keywords: *IT Outsourcing Success, IT Outsourcing Management, Legal Contracts, Psychological Contracts*

INTRODUCTION

Information technology (IT) outsourcing remains one of the most enduring trends in the management of IT resources (Ang and Beath, 1993; Ang and Cummings, 1997; Ang and Slaughter, 2001; Ang and Straub, 1998; Lacity and Willcocks, 2001; Slaughter and Ang, 1996). It is estimated that the worldwide outsourcing market will grow from US$191 billion in 2004 to US$267 billion by 2009 (Gartner Forecast, 2005). Newer forms of outsourcing are becoming more popular. The advent and widespread use of the Internet has propelled a rapid growth in application service provider (ASP) outsourcing (Currie and Seltsikas, 2001). Another new form of outsourcing, business process outsourcing (BPO), is the fastest-growing market, projected to reach US$133.7 billion in 2005 (Gartner Press Release, 2005).

Despite the growth of outsourcing, empirical results on outsourcing success remain mixed (Lee, Miranda, and Kim, 2004; Levina and Ross, 2003). While there are some success stories (e.g., Lacity and Willcocks, 1998), persistent evidence remains of contract cancellations and early terminations (e.g., Bahli and Rivard, 2003; Kern, Willcocks, and van Heck, 2002; Lacity and Willcocks, 2000b; Michell and Fitzgerald, 1997) and lawsuits (e.g., Ang and Toh, 1998).

One major contributing factor to low success rates in IT outsourcing is the relative lack of attention to the implementation and management of IT outsourcing. To date, outsourcing research has focused more on the decision and contracting for outsourcing. Drawing predominantly from organizational economics, research on outsourcing has focused on designing contract structures to align the financial incentives of outsourcing parties (e.g., see Bryson and Sullivan, 2003; Bryson and Ngwenyama, 2000; Chaudhury, Nam, and Rao, 1995; Gopal et al., 2003; Richmond and Seidmann, 1993; Wang, Barron, and Seidmann, 1997; Whang, 1992). Research on strategies for managing outsourcing remains relatively scarce (Dibbern et al., 2004). Perhaps the assumption is that once a careful strategic analysis is made of the sourcing decision, outsourcing success should occur. Typically, in strategic analysis, a legal contract is drawn that narrowly specifies the exchange of goods and services in return for certain levels of financial consideration. Yet, as in any managerial task or the management of complex projects, careful and thorough strategic analysis does not naturally translate into a successful execution of the sourcing decision (Mintzberg, 2004).

In this chapter, we propose that outsourcing success requires the contracting process to extend beyond strategic analysis and legal contracting. Rather, outsourcing projects require that both parties in the outsourcing arrangement implement appropriate managerial governance mechanisms in the structure of the contract. We begin the chapter by describing legal contracting and its relation to outsourcing. Then, we present an expanded perspective on contracting. The expanded perspective infuses managerial governance mechanisms in the form of hierarchical and psychological contractual elements into existing legal contract structures. Hierarchical elements emulate the social structures underlying hierarchical governance mechanisms and provide a useful means to address limitations of market exchanges. The psychological contract, representing the client's and vendor's beliefs and expectations about their mutual obligations in outsourcing, governs the behaviors of and interactions between the parties. We conclude with directions for future research on the value of such an expanded perspective in IT contracting.

CONTRACTS AS A LEGAL PROMISE FOR THE EXCHANGE OF GOODS AND SERVICES

Research on outsourcing management has emphasized the importance of the contract structures embedded in the legal contract. In the classical view of contracting (Macneil, 1980), a contract represents a promise enforceable by law, involving the exchange of a promise for consideration. The required elements in all contracts are, therefore, a clear definition of what is being promised and the price at which the promise will be fulfilled.

IT outsourcing is a form of legal contracting. A provider makes a promise to deliver certain products/services to a client, in exchange for payment or financial consideration. The outsourcing contract, being essentially a legal document, must therefore stipulate the terms of the exchange between the client and the vendor, embodied in the products/services exchange and the financial exchange (Kern and Willcocks, 2000; Whang, 1992).

Adopting a legal view of contracting, outsourcing research has examined four key elements of contract structures:

- *Products/services specifications*—The ability to define the products/services exchanged is an essential condition for market exchanges. It provides the basis for assessing contract performance (Williamson, 1979). In IT outsourcing, the products/services are usually specified in service-level agreements defining the service being contracted for, and where and when it is delivered (Larson, 1998). The service-level agreement typically includes detailed metrics related to areas such as volume of work (e.g., the number of service calls or maintenance requests to be handled per unit of time), quality (e.g., defect rates, service availability), and responsiveness (e.g., time taken to handle a service request) (Hayes, 2004; Misra, 2004). To ensure that the metrics set are realistic, firms should baseline their current performance, and benchmark against the industry (Hayes, 2004; Lacity and Willcocks, 1998; Rubin, 1997).

- *Pricing structure*—The choice of pricing structure has attracted much research. Research has either adopted an empirical or analytic methodology to understand how pricing structure can influence the effectiveness of a contract (e.g., see Bryson and Sullivan, 2003; Bryson and Ngwenyama, 2000; Chaudhury, Nam, and Rao, 1995; Gopal et al., 2003; Richmond and Seidmann, 1993; Wang, Barron, and Seidmann; Whang, 1992). The most commonly adopted pricing structures in IT outsourcing are fixed-fee contracts, time-and-materials contracts, and cost-plus or hybrid contracts (Kalnins and Mayer, 2004; Slaughter et al., 2005). These pricing structures differ in how risks are allocated between the parties and, therefore, they provide different financial incentives that can promote or discourage opportunistic behaviors. For example, a fixed-price contract places risks predominantly with the vendor, and the vendor may thus be motivated to cut costs to enhance its profits, especially where product quality is hard to assess.
- *Payment schedule*—Although relatively less studied, the payment schedule is also an important aspect of the financial exchange. Payment schedules have a direct effect on the vendor's project finances and profitability, and clients can use progressive payments linked to project milestones as an incentive to ensure schedule compliance by the vendor (e.g., Dayanand and Padman, 2001).
- *Contract duration*—This defines the duration of the exchange, and is an important contract choice, in addition to the pricing structure (Cheung, 1969). A principal limitation of long-term contracts is their inflexibility in the face of uncertainty (Coase, 1937), and firms can use contract length as a means to achieve efficient low-cost adaptation to change (Crocker and Masten, 1988, 1991). Similarly, IT outsourcing research suggests that short-term contracts are more successful, because shorter contracts enable the parties to more accurately assess their requirements and analyze the cost implications, provide greater motivation for vendors to perform, and allow clients to recover faster from mistakes (Lacity and Willcocks, 1998).

From a theoretical perspective, much of the work on contract structures is motivated by agency theoretic principles and the inherent need to design an effective contract structure to address issues of adverse selection and moral hazard (Grossman and Hart, 1983; Holmstrom, 1979; Milgrom and Roberts, 1992).

IT outsourcing involves essentially an agency relationship between the client and vendor, typified by goal incongruence between the parties (Lacity and Hirschheim, 1993). Agency theory holds that individuals act through self-interest and, therefore, the goals of the principal and the agent often diverge. Consequently, the agent may not always behave in the principal's best interests, resulting in the danger of adverse selection and moral hazard (Jensen and Meckling, 1976; Ross, 1989). These risks may be particularly acute in complex exchanges such as IT outsourcing, where difficulties often exist in specifying and verifying product quality attributes, and information asymmetry between the client and vendor, giving rise to the classic "lemons" problem described by Akerlof (1970). Therefore, contract theory and agency theory suggest that the choice of an appropriate contract structure is crucial; the contract structure should be designed to provide incentives to align the goals of the client and vendor, and address issues of adverse selection and moral hazard (Grossman and Hart, 1983; Holmstrom, 1979; Milgrom and Roberts, 1992).

While we acknowledge the importance of this stream of work, the limited focus on the contract structure ignores the wider role of the contract as a governance mechanism. The contract not only defines the terms of the exchange, but also forms the foundation for daily interactions between the parties (Kern and Willcocks, 2000). Yet, there is little emphasis in the literature on the use of the contract to actually manage the postcontract process. We believe that research needs to move beyond the emphasis on legal contract elements, examine managerial governance mechanisms, and incorporate them explicitly into IT contracts. To that end, we propose a conceptual framework that incorporates both hierarchical and psychological contractual elements into the contract structures of an IT contract.

HIERARCHICAL ELEMENTS IN IT

Stinchcombe (1985, 1990) developed the idea of hierarchical elements in contracts as a means of addressing the limitations of market exchanges in handling complex and uncertain transactions, such as IT outsourcing. Transaction costs theory predicts that firms should refrain from outsourcing when they experience difficulty in specifying requirements in advance; when they are uncertain about prices, costs, or quantities; when they require specific assets; or when they cannot control the behavior of agents. Outsourcing in such situations is less efficient than internal hierarchical governance, since firms incur higher transactions costs in negotiating and enforcing such contracts (Williamson, 1979). However, Stinchcombe proposes that firms can address these market limitations by emulating the social structures underlying hierarchical governance mechanisms. In essence, the hierarchical elements framework proposes that firms can incorporate into the contract elements that are commonly found when the activity is governed internally or hierarchically (Stinchcombe, 1985, 1990).

Based on parallels to the social structures underlying hierarchical intrafirm transactions, Ang and Beath (1993) identified five hierarchical elements as they relate to IT outsourcing (see Table 15.1 for a summary). These are:

- *Command structures and authority systems* where rights and responsibilities are assigned to either the client or vendor to make discretionary decisions, issue orders, or demand performance. The authority structure must clearly specify the person who is authorized to make certain decisions and the appropriate communication and approval process. For example, in software projects where requirement changes are often frequent, the contract should identify the client personnel who is authorized to issue such change requests, how such changes should be communicated to the vendor, and the vendor personnel who is authorized to accept or reject the changes. In large outsourcing projects, the contract may also designate certain key vendor personnel and require the vendor to obtain client approval before any changes can be made.
- *Rule-based incentive systems* where rewards and punishments are tied to vendor performance, and not to the market. Rule-based incentive systems are appropriate for transactions with high uncertainty, where it is difficult to specify performance contingencies in advance. In such situations, the incentive system must provide inducements for future performance rather than simply serve as a reward for past performance. This can be achieved through rule-based incentive systems that tie the compensation level to the level of performance achieved, instead of based on market-determined forces. For example, if timely delivery is vital, the contract may include penalties for delays beyond an agreed-upon completion date and bonuses for early completion. Similarly, operations and network outsourcing

contracts may specify penalties to be imposed if the vendor fails to meet prespecified service levels.

- *Standard operating procedures* where routines are followed by parties in the contract to ensure that the contract progresses as planned. Such standard operating procedures define the specific actions or behaviors that vendors are supposed to follow and are important as a basis for behavior and outcome controls. Common examples include requiring the vendor to produce formal progress reports; to conduct regular face-to-face meetings with clients; and to bring the client's attention to potential IT operational problems and project delays.
- *Non–market-based pricing systems* where pricing algorithms are designed to accommodate cost uncertainties in long-term IT contracts. Non–market-based systems use the market price established by competitive bidding but modified by cost-recovery procedures. A combination of market pricing and cost-recovery algorithms is designed to ensure a reasonable balance between price risk for the client and compensation risk for the vendor. Examples include a time-and-materials contract as well as reimbursements for costs incurred by the vendor.
- *Informal dispute resolution mechanisms* where procedures are developed to settle conflicts without direct referral to court sanction. Disputes are inevitable in most outsourcing contracts, and parties should aim to resolve the disputes with minimal damage to the relationship. Because of the potential damage to business relationships, legal recourse should be sought only as a last-resort measure. Rather, firms should use private grievance procedures to handle disputes as far as possible. When a dispute first arises, project managers from the client and vendor organizations should work together to try to resolve the dispute. If this fails, the dispute can be referred higher to senior management from both organizations, who will then intervene and negotiate the dispute directly. If the dispute still cannot be resolved by the senior management teams, the client and vendor may agree to submit the dispute to nonbinding mediation by a mutually agreed-upon party, or to seek arbitration to reach a final and binding solution. Formal legal redress should be used as a last resort only after all of these private grievance mechanisms have been exhausted.

Hierarchical elements help firms meet two important objectives: control and coordination (Gulati and Singh, 1998). Reflecting its roots in transaction costs theory, hierarchical elements are often viewed as a response to appropriation concerns, based on their ability to assert control by fiat, provide monitoring, and align incentives. Incentive systems and nonmarket pricing, in particular, highlight attempts to achieve control by aligning the interests of the parties. Besides control, outsourcing parties also need to coordinate their tasks and make mutual adjustments during the contract in response to other parties' actions as well as changes in the environment. Hierarchical elements, such as command structure and authority systems, and standard operating procedures make it easier to coordinate tasks between the partners by clarifying decision-making procedures and anticipating issues before they arise. Similarly, dispute resolution procedures help to reduce the scope of disputes and allow parties to discover joint solutions to more effective coordination (Gulati, Lawrence, and Puranam, 2005; Gulati and Singh, 1998).

In sum, the hierarchical elements framework argues that firms can achieve the flexibility and necessary control functions afforded by hierarchies by incorporating such hierarchical governance mechanisms into their contracts. Research has demonstrated the usefulness of the hierarchical elements framework in the context of IT outsourcing. Firms can use hierarchical elements to address the high appropriation risks associated with software outsourcing contracts, which are typically characterized by high asset specificity and uncertainty (Ang and Beath, 1993). Failure to incorporate such hierarchical elements into the contract often contributes to outsourcing failures

Table 15.1

Hierarchical Elements in Outsourcing Contracts

Hierarchical elements	Examples	Illustrative statements
1. Command structures and authority systems	Explicit assignment of responsibilities	"Any changes in the functional specification must be specifically approved in writing by both client's project manager and vendor's vice president of programming."
	Explicit assignment of authority for authorizing changes Authority over price adjustments Authority over assignment/change of personnel Right to audit work in progress and final performance Right to cancel project	"Vendor shall not replace the vendor project manager for reasons other than death, disability, resignation, or termination of employment, or upon request by client. In the event that the vendor project manager must be replaced, vendor will give client at least thirty days' notice prior to assigning a new vendor project manager, and client will have the right to interview and reject the new assigned vendor project manager."
2. Rule-based incentive systems	Rules for penalties for delay	"In the event of a delay in delivery . . . vendor shall pay to client the sum of $X for each day of delay in delivery as liquidated damages."
	Rules for rewards for early completion Right to change incentive structure during the contract	"Vendor will be responsible for meeting the service level agreements specified in Attachment A. . . . In the event vendor fails to meet these service-level agreements, and total unplanned outages exceeds X percent for any week, a penalty of $Y will be imposed, and offset as a credit against vendor's fees for that week."
3. Standard operating procedures	Formal progress reports Regular meetings to discuss problems	"Vendor will develop, verify, and submit for review and approval each item listed in Attachment A for client. Vendor will provide client with weekly status reports outlining accomplishments, problems/issues, upcoming tasks, and project resource requirements."
4. Non–market-based pricing systems	Pricing based on cost recovery consideration	"For optional services, client will reimburse vendor for the number of hours spent, computed based on vendor's standard charges for such services at the time they are provided."
5. Informal dispute resolution mechanism	Private grievance procedures involving project managers at the first level and senior management at the second level Provision for third-party mediation/arbitration	"In the event of any dispute, controversy, or disagreement with respect to performance under this Agreement, the parties agree to first submit the dispute in writing to the designated client and vendor project managers. If the project managers cannot resolve the dispute within ten days of receipt of the dispute, the dispute shall be submitted in writing to the Project Executive Committee, comprised of at least two senior management members from both the client and vendor, to negotiate the dispute directly. If the Project Executive Committee cannot resolve the dispute within twenty days of receipt of the dispute, the dispute will be submitted to arbitration."

Source: Adapted from Ang and Beath (1993).

(Ang and Toh, 1998). As such, firms should design and incorporate these hierarchical elements into the contract.

THE CLIENT–VENDOR PSYCHOLOGICAL CONTRACT

In addition to the hierarchical elements, effective managerial governance of IT outsourcing also requires a clear and explicit understanding of the contracting parties' psychological contract. Unlike legal contracts that are made explicit, a psychological contract refers to people's *mental* beliefs and expectations about their mutual obligations in a contractual relation (Rousseau, 1995). These mental beliefs can be shaped by explicit obligations incorporated into the written contract. More critically, psychological contracts reflect implicit obligations that exist only in the parties' minds. Understanding the psychological contract is important because the parties' behaviors are driven by their beliefs and perceptions of these obligations, regardless of whether these obligations are incorporated into the written contract. Ultimately, "all contracts, whether written or unwritten, are fundamentally psychological, existing in the eye of the beholder" (Rousseau and Parks, 1993, 19), and it is the parties' subjective interpretations that govern their day-to-day interactions. It is important, therefore, to look beyond the written contract to understand the psychological contract between the parties. This is particularly critical in IT outsourcing, since it involves multiple stakeholders from both the client and vendor organizations (Lacity and Willcocks, 2000a), and the parties involved in negotiating and drafting the contract are often different from the parties involved in its day-to-day execution. Further, the written contract in large IT outsourcing deals is usually so long and complex that it is impractical to distribute the contract to all parties involved, leaving individuals to rely on their set of beliefs about the contract only.

Recent research by Ho, Ang, and Straub (2003) and Koh, Ang, and Straub (2004) demonstrates the critical role that the psychological contract plays in determining the success of IT outsourcing. IT outsourcing involves essentially a contract and a set of mutual obligations between a client and a vendor, whereby the vendor agrees to make specific contributions to the client in return for certain benefits from the client. Research shows six client obligations and six vendor obligations, and fulfillment of these obligations has a significant positive effect on outsourcing success, over and above the effects of project characteristics such as project type, duration, and size. Table 15.2 summarizes these obligations.

Client project managers expect their vendor to fulfill six vendor obligations:

- *Vendor obligation for accurate project scoping.* Clients expect vendors to define precisely the nature and range of services covered in the outsourcing contract and to be flexible in handling requests for changes. This is important because the project scope directly affects the price the client pays. If the vendor underestimates the project scope and ends up in a loss situation, he is likely to be disproportionately concerned with reducing costs, and this may lead to declining service quality and additional costs for the client as well as contract inflexibility and adversarial relationships, as is often exhibited in a "winner's curse" situation (Kern, Willcocks, and van Heck, 2002). Flexibility in handling scope changes is also important because outsourcing costs can escalate significantly if the vendor exercises very tight project control and levies additional charges for every minor change.
- *Vendor obligation for clear authority structures.* Clients expect vendors to delineate clearly the decision-making rights and reporting structures in the project in terms of the roles and responsibilities of all parties involved. This is essential for clients to maintain control over

Table 15.2

Client–Vendor Psychological Contract Obligations in Information Technology Outsourcing

	Definition	Sample quotes
A. Vendor obligations		
1. Accurate project scoping	Define precisely the nature and range of services covered in the outsourcing contract and be flexible in handling vendors' requests for changes in these services.	"I think not many of them [vendors] are good at scoping. There was this contract that we awarded to this vendor, because he was the lowest bidder. But it's quite clear that he underbid on the tender. I think they were just too new to the game. They had to honor the contract, even though they ended up losing money on it. But we were concerned with the quality of work and deliverables." "A major problem we face is that vendors tend to exercise too tight control over the project scope. Any small change, they will insist on additional charges. The vendor must recognize that there will always be changes in scope during the project."
2. Clear authority structures	Delineate the decision-making rights and reporting structures in the project in terms of the roles and responsibilities of all parties involved.	"We have this contract with this vendor who, in turn, subcontracted parts of the project to two other vendors, one for hardware and another for software. I'm not sure they know what they're doing, or who's responsible for what. He (the primary vendor) seems to be having lots of trouble coordinating and integrating the services of his subcontractors."
3. Taking charge	Complete the job and solve problems independently with minimal client involvement.	"We contracted with this vendor to develop a software system for us. But he just kept coming back to us with all the problems he encountered. It was very frustrating, we felt like we're doing the job for him."
4. Effective human capital management	Assign high-quality staff to work on the project and minimize staff turnover during the project.	"We were very upset with the vendor. They had assigned a non-IS staff on their project team. We thought he would be value-adding with his other expertise but he just didn't perform." "The vendor was facing very high attrition, and many of the vendor staff resigned half-way during the project. The worst case was when the [vendor] project manager left. This affected the project schedule and quality of work, and the project ended up being delayed."
5. Effective knowledge transfer	Educate client in terms of the necessary skills, knowledge, and expertise associated with using the outsourced system or service.	"We recently contracted a vendor to develop a system that interfaces with our current financial system. It was only during the project that we realized that our own staff were not able to answer their questions about the financial system. We realized too late that the previous vendor responsible for implementing the financial system failed to transfer adequate knowledge to your staff."

Table 15.2 *(continued)*

6. Building effective interorganizational teams	Invest time and effort to foster a good working relationship between the client and vendor staffs working on the project.	"This is really a multicultural project. We have people from different backgrounds and nationalities. The vendors put in quite a bit of effort bringing the team together. They organized social activities and brown-bag lunches."
B. Client obligations		
1. Clear specifications	Understand and articulate explicitly and comprehensively the requirements for the services covered by the outsourcing project.	"There was this software development project that we were working on. The client wanted us to generate a whole list of reports, but when we asked for details, he didn't seem to know what he wanted at all! Worse, when we asked him why he needed those reports, he couldn't give us any valid business reasons, other than the fact he had always had them."
2. Prompt payment	Pay vendors on time and do not withhold payments unreasonably.	"Payment is usually not a problem for us. But sometimes, if the client is not happy with us, he will not sign off on the project deliverables, and this delays the payment process." "You have to understand this, no matter what happens, we still have to pay our staff on the first day of every month. If the client is late in his payments to us, we end up carrying his financial cost."
3. Close project monitoring	Be actively involved in overseeing the project progress and attend all project meetings and discussions regularly.	"It was so frustrating. We sent this interim report to the client manager a month ago, but until today, he still hasn't read it yet! We have to keep chasing him, because we need his approval on it before the development process can move to the next phase."
4. Dedicated project staffing	Assign key employees who possess the required skills and knowledge to work with vendor staff on the project.	"Like in this recent case, the client assigned two resource persons to work with us on the project. But whenever we approached them for help or information, they always claimed to be busy with other work, and in the end, nothing gets done! They just did not have the commitment to the project at all!"
5. Knowledge sharing	Provide information required by vendor and educate vendor with the industry and firm-specific knowledge necessary to build or operate the system.	"We had trouble getting information from them about their company. We wanted to know more . . . their culture, operating procedures, business goals, and so on. But we're quite disappointed. Usually they are quite supportive but not in this." "Many times, we also learn from our clients, the way their business runs. This helps us build up our industry expertise."
6. Project ownership	Ensure that senior management provides strong leadership, support, and commitment toward the project.	"We expect senior management to be committed to the project, be willing to pump in their resources and time to see the project through to the end." "They need to own the project. We can't make the decisions for them. They must decide and lead."

Source: Adapted from Koh, Ang, and Straub (2004).

the project and ensure proper accountability, especially in large projects that involve multiple vendors and/or subcontractors, given the difficulty of coordinating roles and responsibilities of the different parties involved.

- *Vendor obligation for taking charge.* Clients expect vendors to complete the job and solve problems independently with minimal client involvement. Clients typically view vendors as the technical experts, and thus expect vendors to be able to make quick decisions to resolve any issues that arise. Consequently, clients expect vendors to go beyond their contractual roles and take charge during the project to solve any arising problems independently in order to avoid delays to the project.
- *Vendor obligation for effective human capital management.* Clients expect vendors to assign high quality staff to work on the project and to minimize staff turnover during the project. Clients expect vendor staff to possess all the requisite skills for the project; these include technical skills, change-management and project-management skills, as well as business knowledge and industry experience. Clients also expect vendors to minimize personnel changes during the project; when changes are inevitable, vendors should provide sufficient notice and ensure prompt replacements, so that the quality of services will not be affected.
- *Vendor obligation for effective knowledge transfer.* Clients expect vendors to educate them on the necessary skills, knowledge, and expertise associated with using the outsourced system or service. Knowledge transfer is crucial for most projects, and clients expect vendors to put in place procedures such as project documentation and training programs to facilitate such knowledge transfer.
- *Vendor obligation for building effective interorganizational teams.* Clients expect vendors to invest time and effort in fostering a good working relationship between the client and vendor staffs working on the project. Clients recognize the importance of a good client–vendor relationship, and expect vendors to make special efforts to build a cohesive project team and ensure that the team can work amicably together.

Vendor managers, on the other hand, expect their client to fulfill the following obligations:

- *Client obligation for clear specifications.* Vendors expect clients to understand and articulate explicitly and comprehensively the requirements for the services covered by the project. Clear specifications are important in software projects, given the need to capture business needs and requirements accurately; however, other outsourcing contracts similarly require clear specifications to accurately define project baselines and service level agreements. Vendors expect clients to understand and articulate their business requirements and project specifications clearly, and minimize project changes and rework that will drive up the vendor's costs in the process.
- *Client obligation for prompt payment.* Vendors expect clients to pay them on time and not withhold payments unreasonably. While it is common practice for clients to link payments to project milestones, vendors expect clients not to unreasonably withhold payment to protest over other unresolved issues or dissatisfaction with the vendor, since such delayed payments can adversely affect the vendor's project finances and profitability.
- *Client obligation for close project monitoring.* Vendors expect clients to be actively involved in overseeing the project progress and to attend project meetings and discussions regularly. This is important so that issues can be identified and resolved promptly between the parties.
- *Client obligation for dedicated project staffing.* Vendors expect clients to assign key employees with the required skills and knowledge to work with their staff on the project. Vendors often lack a complete understanding of their client's requirements, and must rely on the client

employees' tacit knowledge and intimate understanding of the firm. Consequently, vendors expect clients to assign sufficient staff to the project, and ensure that they dedicate sufficient time to work on the project.

- *Client obligation for knowledge sharing*. Vendors expect clients to provide any information required and to educate them with the industry- and firm-specific knowledge necessary to build or operate the system. Vendors need to learn the details of the client's business processes and applications, especially in software projects where a keen knowledge of the specific context of the organization's business processes is required. Such learning also helps vendors to build up industry expertise.
- *Client obligation for project ownership*. Vendors expect client senior management to provide strong leadership, support, and commitment toward the project. Vendors expect clients to have a strong sense of psychological ownership of the project, and to treat the project as their own. Otherwise, clients may wrongly think that they are outsourcing all their problems, thus leaving the vendor to resolve all issues that arise.

In sum, the concept of a psychological contract draws our attention to the fact that not all promises are incorporated into a typical legal written contract. Ambiguous promises are more likely to lead to perceived breaches of a psychological contract. Therefore, the more firms work toward clarifying mutual promises and making these obligations explicit, the greater the likelihood of success in IT outsourcing. Further, the psychological contract's emphasis on mutual obligations between the parties highlights the duality of the outsourcing relationship. This addresses the dire need for outsourcing research to move beyond its dominant focus on the client perspective (Dibbern et al., 2004) to provide a balanced view that incorporates the views of both parties involved.

RELATIONSHIP BETWEEN HIERARCHICAL AND PSYCHOLOGICAL CONTRACTUAL ELEMENTS

While we have discussed the hierarchical and psychological contractual elements separately in the sections above, in reality, the ideas and concepts of both overlap. Table 15.3 shows how the two are related to each other.

Some clear overlaps exist—for example, client obligation for close project monitoring is similar to the hierarchical element of standard operating procedures; and vendor obligation for clear authority structures is similar to the hierarchical element of command structures and authority system. Other psychological contract obligations are partially reflected in the hierarchical elements. For example, vendor obligation for effective human capital management reflects a client's expectation that the vendor will assign high-quality staff to work on the project and to minimize staff turnover during the project. The client can try to address this by designating key vendor personnel on the project (e.g., the project manager), and requiring explicit approvals for key personnel changes—both of these reflect the hierarchical element of command structures and authority systems. However, this alone is insufficient to ensure high-quality staff (the client will not be able to designate *all* of the vendor staff assigned to the project or to effectively evaluate the quality of their skills ex ante) or low turnover in the first place. The same applies to client obligation for dedicated project staffing. Similarly, while clear specifications and accurate project scoping are crucial client and vendor obligations, in reality, these cannot be easily captured in the contract. Rather, command structures and authority systems can be used to minimize the effects of uncertainty in project specifications and scoping (e.g., through authority for price adjustments

Table 15.3

Relationship Between Hierarchical and Psychological Contractual Elements in Information Technology Outsourcing

Psychological contractual elements	Hierarchical elements (1) Command structures and authority systems	(2) Rule-based incentive systems	(3) Standard operating procedures	(4) Non–market-based pricing systems	(5) Informal dispute resolution mechanisms
Client obligations for:					
Clear specifications	X			X	
Prompt payment	X				
Close project monitoring			X		
Dedicated project staffing	X				
Knowledge sharing					
Project ownership					
Vendor obligations for:					
Accurate project scoping	X			X	
Clear authority structures	X				
Taking charge					
Effective human capital management	X				
Effective knowledge transfer					
Building effective interorganizational teams					

and project change), and non–market-based pricing systems (e.g., cost-plus contracts) may be employed where such uncertainty is expected to be high.

In sum, while there are some overlaps between the psychological contract obligations and the hierarchical elements, the two are not synonymous. Table 15.3 highlights the fact that not all psychological contract obligations are reflected in the hierarchical elements, and vice versa. For example, the hierarchical element "dispute resolution mechanism" is missing from the list of psychological contract obligations. This may reflect, in part, the parties' emphasis on the relationship (e.g., vendor obligation on building effective interorganizational teams) and, therefore, their reluctance to recognize the likelihood that disputes will arise. Further, the hierarchical elements reflect primarily the client's perspective only. This can be attributed to its roots in transaction costs economics, with its emphasis on controls to safeguard against opportunism and contractual hazards. As such, the hierarchical elements are designed to "achieve purposes of dealing with uncertainties that rational *clients* will often want to deal with" (Stinchcombe, 1990, 232; emphasis added). The vendor's perspective is grossly missing in this framework. The psychological contract perspective, with its emphasis on mutuality, provides a balanced view of both parties to the contract.

In summary, we believe that the hierarchical and psychological contractual elements complement each other, and successful outsourcing management requires an integrative framework that incorporates both these elements to the legal elements in contract structures.

EXPANDING THE VIEW OF IT CONTRACTUAL ELEMENTS

Figure 15.1 summarizes our conceptual framework. We propose that outsourcing research needs to move beyond the emphasis on legal contract structures in order to understand the wider role of the contract

Figure 15.1 **Expanded View of Contractual Elements in Information Technology (IT) Outsourcing**

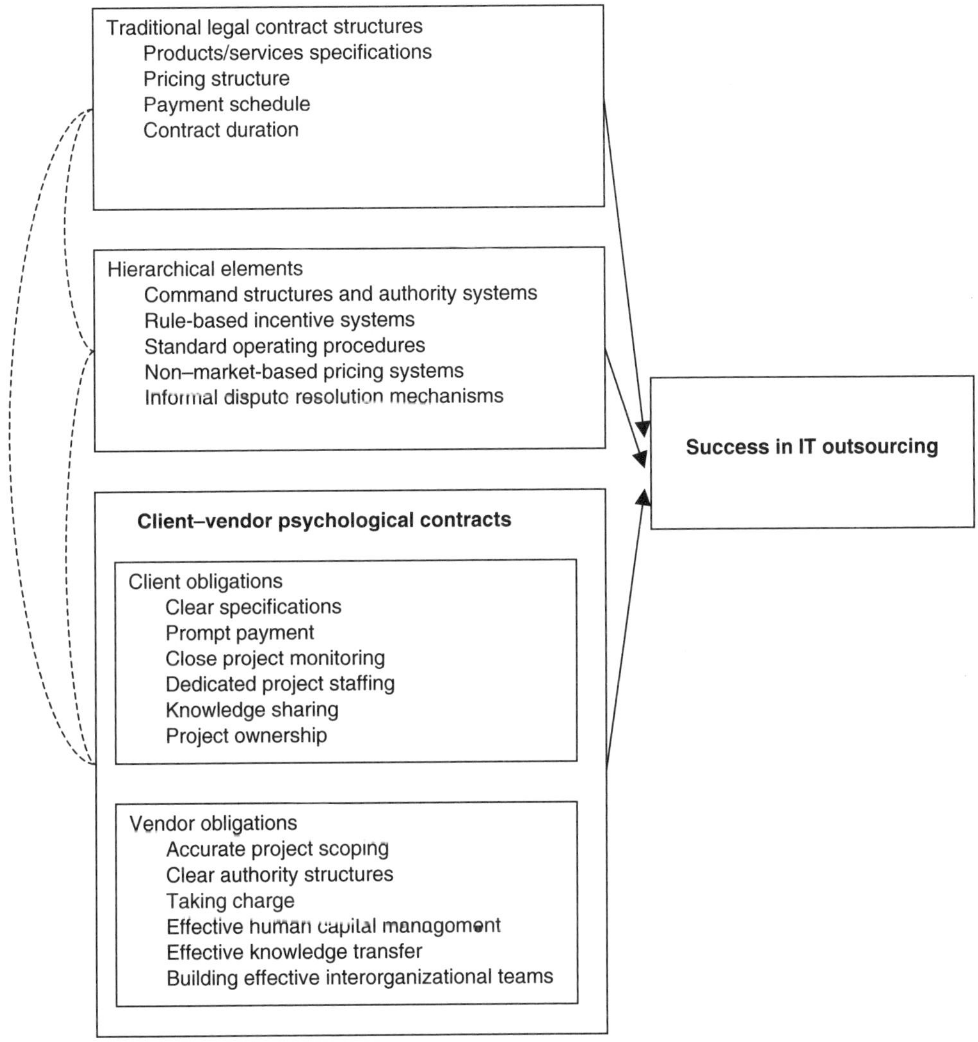

as a governance mechanism in the day-to-day interactions between the parties. This requires an integrative perspective that incorporates the written contract as well as the hierarchical and psychological contractual elements. We strongly advocate that firms should make these hierarchical and psychological contractual elements explicit and incorporate them into the contract, as far as possible.

From a research perspective, our stream of work represents only the beginning of a journey toward understanding the critical role hierarchical and psychological contractual elements play in determining success in IT outsourcing. First, we urge more research into understanding the fundamental nature of hierarchical and psychological contractual elements as it applies to new forms of outsourcing. With the changing landscape of IT outsourcing, it would be interesting to explore how the model applies to newer forms of outsourcing, such as ASPs, BPOs, and offshore outsourcing contracts. Research could examine underlying differences in the alternative forms of outsourcing, and the corresponding differences in managerial governance mechanisms required.

Second, research could explore how the different hierarchical and psychological contractual elements complement each other. We believe that more work should be done to understand how the different hierarchical and psychological contractual elements can be configured together—that is, how to design effective "bundles" of elements to ensure comprehensiveness combined with efficiency in embedding managerial governance mechanisms in IT outsourcing contracts.

Third, recall that we used transaction cost and psychological contracting theoretical frameworks to develop the hierarchical and psychological elements as managerial governance mechanisms. However, each hierarchical and psychological element in itself requires further theoretical and empirical scrutiny. For example, on the psychological obligation for knowledge transfer, future research could leverage on the wider body of knowledge on knowledge-transfer and learning, to determine how they can be applied to designing more managerial governance mechanisms in IT outsourcing as it pertains to knowledge-transfer between the client and the vendor. Similarly, research could draw on organizational behavior concepts such as psychological ownership (Pierce, Kostova, and Dirks, 2001) for conceptual grounding in understanding the determinants of stronger project ownership on the part of clients for IT outsourcing contracts.

Finally, we believe that research should examine how IT contracts evolve over time. Contracts, being legal documents, do not change easily. Contract renegotiations and revisions are often lengthy and expensive endeavors. As such, contract changes tend to be only incremental over time, and firms usually make adjustments in their subsequent contracts only after they have experienced persistent actual problems during the course of the interactions (Mayer and Argyres, 2004). While the written contract is an ex ante device (Dekker, 2004) and often hard to revise ex post, the parties need to continually adapt and fine-tune the organizational governance mechanisms as they interact with each other. Further, the psychological contract is not a static concept, and research has shown that the parties' perceptions of obligations change over time (Robinson, Kraatz, and Rousseau, 1994). More work is needed to understand how the different contractual elements evolve over time and gain knowledge about the antecedents to and consequences of such changes.

CONCLUSION

In this chapter, we propose an expanded conceptual framework of the elements that will be necessary for successful outsourcing. We suggest additional managerial governance mechanisms in the form of hierarchical and psychological contractual elements to complement existing legal contract structures that have formed the primary focus of IT outsourcing. Hierarchical elements emulate the social structures underlying hierarchical governance mechanisms and provide a useful means to address limitations of market exchanges. The psychological contract, representing the client's and vendor's beliefs and expectations about their mutual obligations in outsourcing, governs the prescribed roles and behaviors of parties to the IT outsourcing contract. Our intent is to encourage more research that will focus on managerial governance mechanisms beyond the traditional legal contract structures in our quest toward enhancing our understanding and management of IT outsourcing.

REFERENCES

Akerlof, G.A. 1970. The market for "lemons": Quality uncertainty and the market mechanism. *Quarterly Journal of Economics*, 84, 488–500.

Ang, S. and Beath, C.M. 1993. Hierarchical elements in software contracts. *Journal of Organizational Computing*, 3, 3, 329–361.

Ang, S. and Cummings, L.L. 1997. Strategic response to institutional influences on information systems outsourcing. *Organization Science*, 8, 3, 235–256.
Ang, S. and Slaughter, S. 2001. Work outcomes and job design for contract versus permanent information systems professionals on software development teams. *MIS Quarterly*, 25, 3, 321–350.
Ang, S. and Straub, D.W. 1998. Production and transaction economies and IS outsourcing: A study of the U.S. banking industry. *MIS Quarterly*, 22, 4, 535–552.
Ang, S. and Toh, S. 1998. Failure in software outsourcing: A case analysis. In L.P. Willcocks and M.C. Lacity, eds., *Strategic Sourcing of Information Systems*. New York: Wiley, 351–368.
Bahli, B. and Rivard, S. 2003. The information technology outsourcing risk: A transaction cost and agency theory-based perspective. *Journal of Information Technology*, 18, 211–221.
Bryson, K. and Sullivan, W.E. 2003. Designing effective incentive-oriented contracts for application service provider hosting of ERP systems. *Business Process Management*, 19, 6, 705–721.
Bryson, N. and Ngwenyama, O.K. 2000. Structuring IS outsourcing contracts for mutual gain: An approach to analyzing performance incentive schemes. *Journal of the Association for Information Systems*, 1, 9, 1–41.
Chaudhury, A.; Nam, K.; and Rao, H.R. 1995. Management of information systems outsourcing: A bidding perspective. *Journal of Management Information Systems*, 12, 2, 131–160.
Cheung, S.N.S. 1969. Transaction costs, risk aversion, and the choice of contractual arrangements. *Journal of Law and Economics*, 12, 1, 23–42.
Coase, R.H. 1937. The nature of the firm. *Economica*, 4, 16, 386–405.
Crocker, K.J. and Masten, S.E. 1988. Mitigating contractual hazards: Unilateral options and contract length. *Rand Journal of Economics*, 19, 3, 327–343.
———. 1991. Pretia ex machina? Prices and process in long-term contracts. *Journal of Law and Economics*, 34, 1, 69–99.
Currie, W. and Seltsikas, P. 2001. Exploring the supply-side of IT outsourcing: Evaluating the emerging role of application service providers. *European Journal of Information Systems*, 10, 3, 123–134.
Dayanand, N. and Padman, R. 2001. Project contracts and payment schedules: The client's problem. *Management Science*, 47, 12, 1654–1667.
Dekker, H.C. 2004. Control of inter-organizational relationships: Evidence on appropriation concerns and coordination requirements. *Accounting, Organizations and Society*, 29, 27–49.
Dibbern, J.; Goles, T.; Hirschheim, R.; and Jayatilaka, B. 2004. Information systems outsourcing: A survey and analysis of the literature. *Database for Advances in Information Systems*, 35, 4, 6–102.
Gartner Forecast: IT Outsourcing, Worldwide, 2004–2009. 2005. August 31. Available at www.gartner.com/it/products/research/asset_129169_2395.jsp.
Gartner Press Release. 2005. Gartner says increased demand for business process outsourcing to create a seller's market in 2005, March 29. Available at www.gartner.com/press_releases/asset_123795_11.html.
Gopal, A.; Sivaramakrishnan, K.; Krishnan, M.S.; and Mukhopadhyay, T. 2003. Contracts in offshore software development: An empirical analysis. *Management Science*, 49, 12, 1671–1683.
Grossman, S.J. and Hart, O.D. 1983. An analysis of the principal-agent problem. *Econometrica*, 51, 1, 7–56.
Gulati, R. and Singh, H. 1998. The architecture of cooperation: Managing coordination costs and appropriation concerns in strategic alliances. *Administrative Science Quarterly*, 43, 4, 781–814.
Gulati, R.; Lawrence, P.R.; and Puranam, P. 2005. Adaptation in vertical relationship: Beyond incentive conflict. *Strategic Management Journal*, 26, 415–440.
Hayes, I.S. 2004. Metrics for IT outsourcing services level agreements. Available at www.clarity-consulting.com/metrics_article.htm.
Ho, V.T.; Ang, S.; and Straub, D.W. 2003. When subordinates become IT contractors: Persistent managerial expectations in IT outsourcing. *Information Systems Research*, 14, 1, 66–87.
Holmstrom, B. 1979. Moral hazard and observability. *Bell Journal of Economics*, 10, 74–91.
Jensen, M. and Meckling, W.H. 1976. Theory of the firm: Managerial behavior, agency costs and ownership structure. *Journal of Financial Economics*, 3, 4, 305–360.
Kalnins, A. and Mayer, K.J. 2004. Relationships and hybrid contracts: An analysis of contract choice in information technology. *Journal of Law Economics & Organization*, 20, 1, 207–229.
Kern, T. and Willcocks, L.P. 2000. Exploring information technology outsourcing relationships: Theory and practice. *Journal of Strategic Information Systems*, 9, 4, 321–350.
Kern, T.; Willcocks, L.P.; and van Heck, E. 2002. The winner's curse in IT outsourcing: Strategies for avoiding relational trauma. *California Management Review*, 44, 2, 47–69.

Koh, C.; Ang, S., and Straub, D.W. 2004. IT outsourcing success: A psychological contract perspective. *Information Systems Research*, 15, 4, 356–373.

Lacity, M.C. and Hirschheim, R. 1993. The information systems outsourcing bandwagon. *Sloan Management Review*, 35, 1, 73–86.

Lacity, M.C. and Willcocks, L.P. 1998. An empirical investigation of information technology sourcing practices: Lessons from experience. *MIS Quarterly*, 22, 3, 363–408.

———. 2000a. Relationships in IT outsourcing: A stakeholder perspective. In R.W. Zmud, ed., *Framing the Domains of IT Management: Projecting the Future Through the Past*. Cincinnati, OH: Pinnaflex Educational Resources, 355–384.

———. 2000b. Survey of IT outsourcing experiences in US and UK organizations. *Journal of Global Information Management*, 8, 2, 5–23.

———. 2001. *Global Information Technology Outsourcing: In Search of Business Advantage*. Chichester, UK: Wiley.

Larson, K.D. 1998. The role of service level agreements in IT service delivery. *Information Management & Computer Security*, 6, 3, 128–134.

Lee, J.-N.; Miranda, S.M.; and Kim, Y.-M. 2004. IT outsourcing strategies: Universalistic, contingency, and configurational explanations of success. *Information Systems Research*, 15, 2, 110–131.

Levina, N. and Ross, J.W. 2003. From the vendor's perspective: Exploring the value proposition in information technology outsourcing. *MIS Quarterly*, 27, 3, 331–364.

Macneil, I.R. 1980. *The New Social Contract: An Inquiry into Modern Contractual Relations*. New Haven, CT: Yale University Press.

Mayer, K. J. and Argyres, N.S. 2004. Learning to contract: Evidence from the personal computer industry. *Organization Science*, 15, 4, 394–410.

Michell, V. and Fitzgerald, G. 1997. The IT outsourcing market-place: Vendors and their selection. *Journal of Information Technology*, 12, 223–237.

Milgrom, P.R. and Roberts, J. 1992. *Economics, Organization and Management*. Englewood Cliffs, NJ: Prentice Hall.

Mintzberg, H. 2004. *Managers, not MBAs: A Hard Look at the Soft Practice of Managing and Management Development*. San Francisco: Berrett-Koehler.

Misra, R.B. 2004. Global IT outsourcing: Metrics for success of all parties. *Journal of Information Technology Cases and Applications*, 6, 3, 21–34.

Pierce, J.L.; Kostova, T.; and Dirks, K.T. 2001. Toward a theory of psychological ownership in organizations. *Academy of Management Review*, 26, 2, 298–312.

Richmond, W.B. and Seidmann, A. 1993. Software development outsourcing contract: Structure and business value. *Journal of Management Information Systems*, 10, 1, 57–72.

Robinson, S.L.; Kraatz, M.S.; and Rousseau, D.M. 1994. Changing obligations and the psychological contract: A longitudinal study. *Academy of Management Journal*, 37, 1, 137–153.

Ross, M. 1989. Relation of implicit theories to the construction of personal histories. *Psychological Review*, 96, 341–357.

Rousseau, D.M. 1995. *Psychological Contracts in Organizations: Understanding Written and Unwritten Agreements*. Thousand Oaks, CA: Sage.

Rousseau, D.M. and McLean Parks, J. 1993. The contracts of individuals and organizations. In L.L. Cummings and B.M. Staw, eds., *Research in Organizational Behavior*, vol. 15. Greenwich, CT: JAI Press, 1–47.

Rubin, H.A. 1997. Using metrics for outsourcing oversight. *Information Systems Management* (Spring), 7–14.

Slaughter, S. and Ang, S. 1996. Employment outsourcing in information systems. *Communications of the ACM*, 39, 7, 47–54.

Slaughter, S.; Harter, D.E.; Ang, S.; and Whitaker, J. 2005. Contracts and quality in software development outsourcing: An empirical study. Working paper.

Stinchcombe, A.L. 1985. Contracts as hierarchical documents. In A. Stinchcombe and C. Heimer, eds. *Organization Theory and Project Management*. Bergen: Norwegian University Press, 121–171.

———. 1990. *Information and Organizations*. Berkeley: University of California Press.

Wang, E.T.G.; Barron, T.; and Seidmann, A. 1997. Contracting structures for custom software development: The impacts of informational rents and uncertainty on internal development and outsourcing. *Management Science*, 43, 12, 1726–1744.

Whang, S. 1992. Contracting for software development. *Management Science*, 38, 3, 307–324.

Williamson, O.E. 1979. Transaction cost economics: The governance of contractual relations. *Journal of Law and Economics*. 22, 2, 233–261.

CHAPTER 16

THE OFFSHORE OUTSOURCING LANDSCAPE

Historical Development and Challenges for the IS Discipline

BEENA GEORGE AND RUDY HIRSCHHEIM

Abstract: *Because of the importance of offshore outsourcing as one of the key business developments of the twenty-first century, this chapter explores its historical roots in information technology (IT) outsourcing and the evolution of the IT service industry in India. The chapter also discusses some of the challenges posed by offshore outsourcing, mostly from the perspective of the West. In particular, the chapter aims to open a dialogue on some of the possible implications of offshore outsourcing for the information systems (IS) discipline.*

Keywords: *Offshore Outsourcing, IS Discipline, IT Outscoring, Outsourcing*

INTRODUCTION

The notion of outsourcing—making arrangements with an external entity for the provision of goods or services to supplement or replace internal efforts—has been around for centuries. Kakabadse and Kakabadse (2002) track one of the earliest occurrences of outsourcing to the ancient Roman Empire, where tax collection was outsourced. Closer to home, in the early years of American history, the production of wagon covers was outsourced to Scotland, where they used raw material imported from India in the production process (Kelly, 2002). Outsourcing remained popular in the manufacturing sector, with part of the assembling in many industries being subcontracted to other organizations and locations where the work could be done more efficiently and cheaply (Vaze, 2005). Commenting on this unstoppable trend, Pastin and Harrison (1974) wrote that such outsourcing of manufacturing functions was creating a new form of organization, the "hollow corporation,"[1] which would require considerable changes in the way organizations were managed. While they limited their research to the role of management in the hollow corporation, they comment on the substantial (and unpleasant) social and economic changes that the outsourcing of manufacturing was causing. It was just a harbinger of things to come.

It was not long before the idea of outsourcing was also applied to the procurement of information technology (IT) services. While the current wave of IT outsourcing can be traced back to the deal of Electronic Data Systems (EDS) with Blue Cross in the early 1960s, it was the landmark Kodak deal in 1989 that won acceptance for IT outsourcing as a strategic tool. Many large and small outsourcing deals were inked in the years that followed. From its beginnings as a cost-cutting tool, IT outsourcing has evolved into an integral component of a firm's overall information systems strategy (Linder, 2004). Still, reducing costs is an idea that never loses its appeal, and the opportunity to meet the IT demands of the organization with a less-expensive but well-trained labor pool has led organizations to look for such resources beyond national borders, at locations both far and near. Recent statistics vouch for the continued acceptance and popularity of IT outsourcing as well as this trend toward outsourcing to different global locations. A Gartner study conducted in 2004 placed global IT outsourcing[2] at $176.8 billion in 2003, and forecasted that its grow to $235.6 billion in 2007, and to $253.1 billion in 2008 (Souza et al., 2004). While outsourcing has grown beyond the domain of decisions embodying IT, such as where and how to source IT, to a much wider set of business functions, IT outsourcing still leads the pack with 67 percent of all global outsourcing deals in 2004 being related to IT (Pruitt, 2004). This inexorable trend toward outsourcing and offshoring[3] brings unique sets of challenges to all parties involved. Western organizations have to walk a tightrope between the savings and efficiencies that offshoring could provide and the adverse reactions from a society increasingly disenchanted by the job displacement and loss that outsourcing brings. Tales of unemployment in IT and related fields have concomitantly led to a decline in enrollment in computer science and information systems programs, raising concerns about the future of the IS discipline.

This paper offers a brief overview of IT outsourcing and the trend towards offshore outsourcing. It explores how and why offshore outsourcing is growing, as well as the challenges that it poses. We believe that taking an IT outsourcing lens helps one to understand the evolution of outsourcing to include other business functions as well as the growing prominence of offshore outsourcing. Lastly, the paper explores some of the issues that offshore outsourcing presents to the academic information systems (IS) discipline in the West.

IT OUTSOURCING MOTIVATION AND HISTORY

Although organizations outsource IT for many reasons, the growth of IT outsourcing can be attributed to two primary phenomena: (1) a focus on core competencies, and (2) a lack of understanding of IT value (Lacity, Hirschheim, and Willcocks, 1994). First, motivated by the belief that sustainable competitive advantage can be achieved only through a focus on core competencies, the management of organizations has chosen to concentrate on what an organization does better than anyone else while outsourcing the rest. As a result of this strategy, IT came under scrutiny. The IT function has been viewed as a noncore activity in organizations; further, senior executives believe that IT vendors possess economies of scale and technical expertise to provide IT services more efficiently than internal IT departments. Second, the growth in outsourcing may also be due to a lack of clear understanding of the value delivered by IT (Lacity and Hirschheim, 1993). Though senior executives view IT as essential to the functioning of the organization,[4] it is viewed as a cost that needs to be minimized. Believing that outsourcing will help meet the IT needs of the organization less expensively, organizations have chosen to outsource. Interestingly, some researchers (e.g., Hirschheim and Lacity, 2000) have found that outsourcing has not always yielded the benefits that organizations had hoped for. This has led to numerous normative strategy proposals to help organizations achieve success (Cullen, Seddon, and Willcocks, 2005; Lacity and Hirschheim, 1993; Linder, 2004).

Initially, when organizations looked to external sources for the provision of IT services, the vendor provided a single basic function to the customer, exemplified by facilities management arrangements where the vendor assumed operational control over the customer's technology assets, typically a data center. The agreement between Blue Cross and Electronic Data Systems in 1963 for the handling of Blue Cross's data processing services was different from previous "facilities management" contracts. EDS took over the responsibility for Blue Cross's IT people extending the scope of the agreement beyond the use of third parties to supplement a company's IT services. EDS's client base grew to include customers such as Frito-Lay and General Motors in the 1970s, and Continental Airlines, First City Bank, and Enron in the 1980s. Other players entered the outsourcing arena as well, the most noteworthy being the ISSC division of IBM. ISSC's deal with Kodak in 1989 heralded the arrival of the IT outsourcing mega-deal and legitimized the role of outsourcing for IT. Following the success of the Kodak deal, well-known companies around the world quickly followed suit—General Dynamics, Xerox, and McDonnell Douglas in the United States; Lufthansa in Germany; Rolls Royce and British Aerospace in Britain; KF Group in Sweden; Canada Post in Canada; Telestra, LendLease, and the Commonwealth Bank of Australia in Australia; and ABN Amro in the Netherlands (Dibbern et al., 2004).

IT outsourcing has evolved from the sole-sourcing and total-sourcing arrangements of yesteryears, where one vendor provides all IT services to its client, to complex arrangements involving multiple vendors and multiple clients (Clemons, Hitt, and Snir, 2000; Gallivan and Oh, 1999). According to Mears and Bednarz (2005), companies are also outsourcing on a much more selective basis than ever before. The tools and resources available today make it easier for IT executives to manage their IT portfolios and achieve the economies they need without outsourcing everything. (Of course, a key challenge is to determine which pieces of the IT portfolio to outsource and which to keep internal.) Outsourcing also now embraces significant partnerships and alliances, referred to as co-sourcing arrangements, where client and vendor share risk and reward. These co-sourcing arrangements build on the competencies of the client and vendor to meet the client's IT needs. Kaiser and Hawk (2004) provide recommendations to organizations considering co-sourcing arrangements with offshore vendors. They note that organizations should avoid total dependency on the vendor by maintaining their IT competencies in-house.

IT outsourcing as it was practiced through the turn of this century was primarily domestic outsourcing. While it had considerable impact on the way organizations structured and managed their IT, and to some extent, redefined the roles of IT managers, the impacts were largely limited to the client and vendor firms' boundaries with the possible exception of the creation of some new intermediary organizations (e.g., outsourcing consulting firms). Domestic IT outsourcing barely created a stir in the public press perhaps because no one foresaw that the outsourcing of a critical knowledge–work function (i.e., IT) might have more dramatic effects if these tasks could be performed not domestically but globally. In some way, this is surprising because most U.S. firms were hiring numerous foreign IT people, and importing people from places like the Philippines and India on staff augmentation contracts. Indeed, according to Sheshabalaya (2004) and Friedman (2005), while major changes were already taking place in IT in the late 1980s and throughout the 1990s in the United States, they went unnoticed, mostly because of the dot.com boom and Y2K remediation needs. We will return to this theme later in the chapter.

OFFSHORE OUTSOURCING

A prominent change in the outsourcing arena is the growth in offshore outsourcing (Lacity and Willcocks, 2001; Morstead and Blount, 2003; Robinson and Kalakota, 2004). Driven by the pressures of globalization and the ensuing need to address opportunities and threats from global competition, companies are increasingly looking at the less expensive resources available in offshore locations. And these less expensive resources are readily available in countries like India, China, and the Philippines.

An outsourcing arrangement is considered "offshore outsourcing" when the responsibility for management and delivery of information technology services is delegated to a vendor who is located in a country different from that of the client (Sabherwal, 1999). While the three leading countries in the offshore outsourcing arena are India, Israel, and Ireland (Carmel, 2003b), nearshore providers in Canada and Mexico are also popular among U.S. clients because of geographic proximity. Some clients find the nearshore scenario more attractive because these locations facilitate continuous monitoring (Rao, 2004). China is also quickly gaining popularity because of its low labor costs.

As in domestic outsourcing, a primary driver of offshore outsourcing is the continued pressure organizations face to cut costs associated with IT while simultaneously maintaining and improving processes (Nicholson and Sahay, 2001; McFarlan, 1995; Rajkumar and Dawley, 1998). The time differences between the client and the offshore vendor locations create extended workdays that can contribute to increased IT productivity. With efficient distribution of work between the client and vendor locations, projects can theoretically be finished faster (Apte, 1990; Carmel and Agarwal, 2001, 2002; Morstead and Blount, 2003; Rajkumar and Dawley, 1998; Ramanujan and Lou, 1997).

Organizations also turn to offshore outsourcing because of the lack of IT resources to perform the required tasks. Faced with the unavailability of trained professionals, organizations look to foreign shores to gain access to knowledgeable IT personnel and valuable IT assets (Apte et al., 1997; Morstead and Blount, 2003; Rottmann and Lacity, 2004; Sahay, Nicholson, and Krishna, 2003; Terdiman, 2002). Offshore vendors typically have well-trained IT personnel with the requisite technical knowledge and skills. These vendors have also recognized the need to train their staff not only in the latest technologies, but also in management and communication skills, and they have established numerous world-class facilities to do so (Khan et al., 2002). Such technical expertise and staff qualifications make these vendor firms very attractive to clients, since clients look to outsource activities that involve high-level technical skills (Aubert, Rivard, and Patry, 2004).

In addition, offshore vendors have obtained certifications to prove their ability to execute and deliver quality work. These certifications assure the client organizations that the vendor is following quality practices in the management of the project and they are also important in gaining the client's trust and developing the client–vendor relationship (Heeks and Nicholson, 2004). Vendors aim to align their practices with standards in different areas including software development processes (e.g., CMM), workforce management (e.g., PeopleCMM), and security (e.g., ISO 17779) (Hirschheim, George, and Wong, 2004). Qu and Brocklehurst (2003) find that client organizations pay particular attention to these certifications in the vendor evaluation and selection process. However, Coward (2003) comments that while large organizations look toward certifications for quality assurance and success in offshore projects, small and medium enterprises focus on personal connections in the selection of vendors.

Finally, as in domestic outsourcing, the bandwagon effect (Lacity and Hirschheim, 1993) comes into play in offshore outsourcing as well. The sheer fact that these offshore choices are available and that other organizations are taking advantage of those options prompt additional organizations to consider offshore outsourcing (Carmel and Agarwal, 2001, 2002; Gopal, Mukhopadhyay, and Krishnan, 2002; Overby, 2003; Qu and Brocklehurst, 2003). With such drivers, offshore outsourcing is growing at a faster rate than domestic outsourcing in the United States. While outsourcing within the United States is growing at a rate of 10–15 percent annually, offshore outsourcing is growing at a rate greater than 20 percent and will grow from $7 billion in 2003 to $10 billion in 2005 (EBusiness Strategies, 2004). Meta Group (2004) predicts that by 2009, an average organization will be sending 60 percent of its applications work offshore.

Offshore arrangements come in a variety of flavors to match the client's desire for ownership and control: conventional offshore outsourcing arrangements, joint ventures, build-operate-transfer arrangements, and captive centers. These arrangements span the continuum from complete handover of the project to an offshore vendor in conventional offshore outsourcing arrangements to establishment of a captive center in the foreign country. While the client usually has a low to medium level of control on the operation and delivery services in conventional offshore outsourcing, the client retains full ownership and control of the assets, personnel, management, and operations of a captive center. Such captive center arrangements are not strictly outsourcing arrangements, since in outsourcing the responsibility for the management of the IT services is handed off to an external vendor. These captive center arrangements fit under the umbrella of "offshoring" (Robinson and Kalakota, 2004). In joint ventures and build-operate-transfer arrangements, the client is able to take advantage of the vendor's knowledge of the local market, while retaining a certain amount of control. Such shared ownership can reduce the risk of offshore outsourcing. A build-operate-transfer is an arrangement where a domestic client contracts with an offshore vendor to set up an offshore center, with the goal of taking over the ownership and management of the center once it is established (Khan et al., 2002; Kumar and Willcocks, 1996; Morstead and Blount, 2003).

A related development has been the offshore outsourcing of IT-enabled services and business processes. Many offshore IT vendors have produced offshoots to manage business process outsourcing (BPO) deals. Examples are Wipro's Spectramind and Infosys's Progeon. The BPO market is making giant strides; it is estimated that the offshore BPO market will grow at a rate of 79 percent annually to reach a size of $24.2 billion, while the offshore IT outsourcing market is expected to grow at a rate of 43 percent to $56 billion by 2008 (EBusiness Strategies, 2004). Currently, IT outsourcing dominates offshore outsourcing; the numbers cited for offshore outsourcing of IT services range from 28 percent (Offshore IT Outsourcing, 2004) to 50 percent (NeoIT, 2004) of all offshore outsourcing. Among the various IT services, applications development, maintenance, and support are most likely to be outsourced to offshore locations (ibid.).

In the domain of offshoring, India is by far the dominant force. In 2004, India's growth rate was 34.5 percent and its revenues were $17.2 billion (siliconindia.com, 2005). Because of its dominant position, it is important to explore how it achieved this position.

EVOLUTION OF OFFSHORE OUTSOURCING IN INDIA

While the concept of offshoring started gaining attention when organizations like Texas Instruments and Motorola discovered India as a source of qualified professionals at costs significantly less than at home, the origins of offshore outsourcing can be traced back to the 1970s and Tata Consultancy Services (TCS). TCS, the first domestic software firm in India, was created by pooling together the IT talent of the Tata group to serve the needs of its member companies. In the mid-1970s, F.C. Kohli (chief executive officer of TCS) visited Burroughs on his visit to the United States as a director of the Institute of Electrical and Electronics Engineers (IEEE). TCS entered into an agreement with Burroughs[5] whereby Burroughs would obtain contracts from clients and TCS would develop applications for them (Khanna and Palepu, 2004).

In 1977, a policy decision by the Indian government limiting foreign investment forced IBM (which had been in India since 1952), to pull out of the country. IBM's departure opened the computer market to domestic manufacturers and foreign companies such as Burroughs and ICL. Consequently, there was a need for software conversion programs so that the IBM applications could be run on these new computer systems. In addition, the public sector programs like nuclear and space research required software applications (Athreye, 2005). Two factors facilitated the growth of India's technical capability: (1) the exposure to a variety of programming environments and projects, and (2) the need to be creative in software development so that they could extract the most from the aging systems that remained and the limited computer systems that could be put together internally (Desai, 2003; Rapoport, 1996). Meanwhile, with the acknowledgment of the "cost–quality advantage of Indian programmers" and the subsequent demand from foreign markets, some entrepreneurs saw the advantage in adopting the staff augmentation model. These opportunities encouraged firms like Wipro and Satyam to enter the IT market.

By the early 1980s, there was global recognition of the programming manpower available in India. Lacking the communication infrastructure to support offshore work, many of the IT firms focused on staff augmentation. Other companies became quite inventive in their use of offshore resources. An example was Data General.[6] In the early 1980s, Jag Dalal,[7] director of Management Information Systems at Data General (a manufacturer of information systems storage systems and open systems servers) entered into an agreement with an Indian firm called Data Conversion Inc.[8] (now known as Patni Computer Systems). Data Conversion Inc. would provide software development services for Data General in exchange for which Data Conversion would receive and market equipment from Data General. The requirements and other information for the projects were sent to India "in a pouch" on an Air India flight. Development work was done in India and code was sent back on the next day's return flight, and comments and corrections were then sent to India by the same method. Through continued exchanges, the projects were completed. While the first project was a failure primarily because of miscommunication, later projects produced satisfactory results.

In 1985, Texas Instruments (TI) established a captive offshore development center in India to take advantage of the labor arbitrage. Many other multinationals followed in TI's footsteps including Motorola and General Electric (GE), and established captive centers in India. With the same goal in mind, during the 1990s, IT departments of Fortune 500 companies began offshoring low-level IT work such as mainframe maintenance. Economic liberalization in the early 1990s had changed the landscape yet again, and foreign firms—including those that had previously left India because of unfavorable government policies—arrived in India to find "a home-grown expertise in elegant, economical software writing" (Rapoport, 1996) and the "India brand" was born. As Heeks (1999) comments, India's success was the culmination of a shared vision and efforts by policymakers and industrialists to be leaders in export of IT services.

But most likely, the current wave of offshore outsourcing got its impetus from the Y2K phenomenon (Reingold, 2004). Faced with a lack of professionals to complete the Y2K remediation work, many U.S. organizations looked to foreign shores for professionals capable of doing this work. Offshore vendor organizations, which were biding their time to get into foreign and more lucrative markets, saw this as their opportunity to get the proverbial "foot in the door." Concomitantly, the telecommunications infrastructure developed to a level where it was practical and cheaper to do work remotely. Yet, when examining the total amount of software exports from India, it can be seen that Y2K contracts were more of a one-time bonus[9] to an industry growing steadily at a rate of over 50 percent for the greater part of the 1990s—emphasizing that the growth of India's IT industry was not just due to "millennium luck," but the result of years of effort to develop as a world power in the IT industry (Sheshabalaya, 1999).

Today offshore outsourcing is an entrenched part of business. There are many strong contenders in the offshore IT outsourcing industry in addition to India, for example, Israel, Ireland, China, the Philippines, Vietnam, and the former Eastern bloc countries of Europe. In fact, offshore resources have been so well recognized that many U.S. and European IT firms have opened their own centers in India, as well as in China, the Philippines, and other locations. The offshore outsourcing industry has also evolved in this process with mergers and acquisitions across and within national borders. Foreign firms are trying to strengthen their foothold in the U.S. market by acquiring U.S. firms, while U.S. firms are trying to gain access to resources available elsewhere by entering into agreements with local firms in those locations (Currie, 2000) .

SUCCESS FACTORS OF OFFSHORE OUTSOURCING COUNTRIES

The sustained success of India and of Ireland and Israel (together known as the 3I countries) in the offshore outsourcing arena has stimulated the interest of researchers and practitioners alike (e.g., Carmel, 2003b; Heeks and Nicholson, 2002). Certainly, the competitive advantage enjoyed by a country in the IT services sector is a function of the skills and technology that has been developed in that country (Porter, 1990). The foundation for such competitiveness lies in the effectiveness and efficiency of the cultural, economic, and social institutions in the country. In turn, the success of these institutions lies in the capabilities of individuals and their strong emphasis on formal education. As Heeks (1999) notes, in the case of India, success in the IT services industry was realized by the efforts of individuals with far-reaching vision and entrepreneurial spirit. Thus, the key to the advancement of these countries (India, Ireland, Israel, etc.) lies in the capabilities developed in the institutions and the human capital of the countries. The identification of these success factors is of great interest to the leadership of other countries who would like to repeat the success of these countries.

A shared vision at the national level to become a strong competitor in the IT services arena appears to be a common factor in countries that have achieved success (Arora and Gambardella, 2005; Carmel, 2003b; Heeks and Nicholson, 2002; Heeks and Nicholson, 2004). This vision gets implemented through government policies; for example, the Israeli government's support of the industry through subsidies for research and development and support for start-ups helped Israel achieve its leadership position in new technology product development. Further, the provision of tax breaks and subsidies and other inducements to IT services companies by the government promoted the growth of the industry in the country. The government has also been willing to put into place new laws that provide intellectual property protection and data security, making these locations more attractive as offshore destinations (Heeks and Nicholson, 2004). Additionally, the government provides support through reform plans and allocation of funds for development of the infrastructure required for the industry (Heeks and Nicholson, 2004; NASSCOM, 2005).

Heeks and Nicholson (2002, 2004) examined the composition of the software industry in the 3I countries and identified certain common characteristics such as concentration, clustering, competition, and collaboration. One reason that these countries have been recognized as leaders in this industry is the presence of a number of sizable companies in the industry in each country creating the "concentration" necessary to establish a brand image for the country. The software industry in these three countries is characterized by clustering in select locations in the country (Carmel, 2003a). In fact, the government encourages such "clustering" because it facilitates the efficient provision of physical infrastructure; a good example is the development of technology parks in India. Interfirm "competition" within the industry is weak, because global demand is so high and entry barriers are low.[10] Another characteristic of the firms in the IT services industry in the three leading countries has been their ability to *collaborate;* organizations such as NASSCOM in India, Industrial Development Authority and the National Software Directorate in Ireland, and the Israeli Association of Software Houses lead and support their member companies by influencing government policy, heading marketing efforts, and disseminating research (Arora and Gambardella, 2005; Heeks and Nicholson, 2004). These organizations play a key role in maintaining and enhancing the reputation of the IT services industry in the country; for example, these associations encourage and advertise the achievement of certifications (e.g., CMM levels) by their member companies, showing that they subscribe to and meet global standards in the provision of IT services. Another example is NASSCOM's recent efforts to develop a national database of IT and BPO workers, which is aimed at quenching anxiety regarding data theft by individuals employed by Indian companies (NASSCOM, 2005). Such efforts at the national level are important to establishing and sustaining relationships with client organizations in other countries.

However, the most significant factor in the development of the IT services industry in the 3I countries has been the availability of vast numbers of English-speaking trained individuals (Carmel, 2003a; Heeks and Nicholson, 2004). These countries have invested heavily in education and training, particularly in the science and engineering disciplines, and they produce a large number of graduates every year. Yet, the industries in these countries were not able to absorb this capacity, which created an excess supply at the time when global demand for these skills was high—certainly a propitious situation for the countries (Arora and Gambardella, 2005). The opportunities offered by the IT services industry in the United States and Europe were quite attractive to this labor pool, especially given the higher remuneration and rewards this industry could offer (Heeks and Nicholson, 2004; Tessler, 2003). Yet these remuneration rates were much less than those paid in the United States and other client countries and contributed to the appeal of the 3I countries as offshore outsourcing locations.

As the stories of Dalal and Kohli earlier in this chapter illustrate, establishing a connection to an offshore firm—a required first step in offshore outsourcing—often happens through the personal efforts of individuals from a country. The emigration of professionals was decried as "brain drain" in earlier decades in countries like India and Israel. Today, these expatriates help create and sustain linkages between client companies in their country of domicile and vendor companies in their country of origin. Many of these expatriates have also returned to their native land to spearhead new organizations or manage the offshore efforts of their employers. These personal ties contribute not only to the development of trust between organizations that are geographically separate but also to the exchange of information (Arora and Gambardella, 2005; Carmel, 2003b; Carmel and Agarwal, 2001, 2002; Heeks and Nicholson, 2004).

Thus, it can be seen that factors at the national, industry and enterprise, and individual levels have contributed to the success of these countries in the IT services industry (Heavin, Fitzgerald, and Trauth, 2001; Heeks and Nicholson, 2002, 2004). Researchers examining the success of the 3Is—India, Ireland, and Israel—have identified similar sets of factors, but have categorized these factors differently. Heeks and Nicholson (2002), for example, placed these success factors into the categories of demand, national vision and strategy, international linkages, software industry characteristics, and supply factors and infrastructure in their software export success model. Carmel (2003b) presented an "oval" model that built on Heeks and Nicholson's model and incorporated additional factors such as quality of life and wages. While these classifications aid further study in this area, the question remains whether the success can be replicated elsewhere or whether the success factors were particular to these three countries. Examining the Indian success story in depth in his thought-provoking book *Rising Elephant*, Seshabalaya (2004) contends that India's success is built on attributes that are specific to India and difficult for others to emulate. Studies on different countries (the Caribbean—Abbot [2005]; Indonesia—Bruell [2003]; Vietnam—Chidamber [2003]; Ukraine—Gengler [2003]; Russia—Hawk and McHenry [2005]; Russia and China—Heeks and Nicholson [2004]; Iran—Nicholson and Sahay [2003]) based on a framework presented by Heeks and Nicholson (2002)[11] support this view. Other countries aspiring to succeed in the IT services arena would have to blaze their own path based on their particular strengths, while guided by the overarching lesson offered by the 3I countries.

MANAGEMENT CHALLENGES IN OFFSHORE OUTSOURCING

There are a number of concerns associated with the management of offshoring that organizations considering such a move would be well advised to pay attention to, especially in light of reports of high failure rates in offshoring. For instance, a recent Gartner survey of offshore outsourcing arrangements in 2003 reported a failure rate of more than 50 percent (cited in Ante, 2004). The concerns related to offshoring can be placed into four categories: cultural factors, geographical distance, infrastructure and security issues, and morale and public opinion issues. These factors can impact the knowledge transfer between the client and the offshore provider, which is necessary for the successful completion of an outsourcing project.

Cultural Factors

National cultures and values contribute to the molding of organizational cultures and thus could lead to differences in practices within the client and offshore vendor organizations. These differences can lead to problems in the relationship between the two organizations in areas integral to the success of an outsourcing arrangement (Karamouzis, 2002; Overby, 2003; Qu and Brocklehurst, 2003; Ramarapu, Parzinger, and Lado, 1997). Communication issues are a prominent item on this list of problems, with differences in nuances and accents hindering exchange of ideas and resolution of problems (Apte et al., 1997; Davison, 2004; Krishna, Sahay, and Walsham, 2004; Morello, 2003; Patrick, 2004). The superior–subordinate relationship and the handling of issues in different organizations are also affected by the embedded attitudes of the employees and vary across national cultures.

Nicholson and Sahay's (2001) description of the relationship between a UK-based software development company—Sierra—and its Indian subsidiary illustrate these problems. Differences in accent and differences in meanings attached to words caused considerable problems in communication. Additionally, the deference to hierarchy practiced by the Indian employees did not sit well with the employees at the Sierra UK location, who were used to an environment where people shared and shot down ideas regardless of their position in the organization. While the Indian employees did not see any problems in working overtime as long as the work was delivered on time, the UK-based employees considered it inefficient.

To alleviate problems stemming from cultural differences, offshore vendor firms typically invest in cultural training for employees who will be interfacing with clients from other nations. Krishna, Sahay, and Walsham (2004) exhort client firms to do the same to create an environment of mutual understanding that will support all the activities required to complete the delivery of the outsourced IT service. Another solution is to place individuals who bridge cultures, such as expatriates, in liaison positions; these individuals should be familiar with the cultures in both settings (Carmel and Nicholson, 2005). Leading offshore vendors have also invested in hiring qualified individuals to be on the management team from the countries client organizations are located in. This facilitates a smoother relationship with the client and the vendors see it as a worthwhile investment, even though the costs are high (*Times of India*, 2005). Many of the senior executives of the offshore vendor organizations have gained experience studying in higher education institutions or working in organizations in countries where their clients are now located. This sensitization of the vendor representatives to the client's management practices provides an additional level of comfort for the client (Khanna and Palepu, 2004).

Geographical Distance

The physical distance between the client's location and the vendor's location can lead to considerable challenges in the management of the offshore projects (Gopal et al., 2003; Herbsleb and Moitra, 2001). The travel and relocation costs associated with managing an offshore project can cut into the expected savings from the project. Organizations depend on information and communication technologies to address management and communication needs, though these cannot match the efficacy of face-to-face meetings. Moreover, conferencing facilities are not usually available at every location, and thus even electronic conferencing may involve some travel. Client and vendor representatives believe that face-to-face meetings are important, especially when problems arise. Most vendor firms, therefore, supplement communication using IT with face-to-face meetings on a regular basis (Carmel and Agarwal, 2002).

While the time zone difference between client and vendor organizations that provides for development around the clock is considered to be one of the advantages of offshore outsourcing, the handling of time differences is a touchy issue in offshore outsourcing management (Apte et al., 1997; Goolsby, 2002). Interviews conducted by the authors with Indian vendors and U.S. client representatives indicated that this is one of the problems in the day-to-day management of outsourcing relationships. Vendor firm employees were more vociferous believing that they are forced to bend over backward to set meetings at times convenient to client firm employees. The vendor firm employees commented how these long hours added to the work pressure, creating an untenable situation. A manager at an offshore vendor firm in Mumbai, India, described how she had to stay after work for five to six hours just to take calls at a time convenient to the client. While she agreed that some disruption to one's personal schedule is inevitable with the time zone difference, she resented the fact that the client expected the vendor employees to make all the adjustment.[12] Client representatives have also not been immune to this problem. We conducted interviews at one organization that had outsourced its applications development work to an Indian firm. There we were told by one outsourcing manager how he was awakened by telephone calls from a vendor representative to his cell phone in the middle of the night, sometimes three or four times a night. Clearly, individuals in client and vendor organizations need to be sensitive to the time difference in scheduling conferences, meetings, and so on.

Infrastructure and Security

There is no question that the infrastructure available in the vendor's home country will affect the quality of the outsourced service (Apte et al., 1997; Morstead and Blount, 2003; Rajkumar and Dawley, 1998). Telecommunication services in these offshore locations may not be as reliable as in the client's location, compounding the problems associated with managing a long-distance relationship. Even basic utility services such as uninterrupted power supply can be a problem in some parts of the world. However, in many countries, the government recognizes the need to provide the adequate infrastructure for the growth of the IT services industry. For example, in India, "technoparks"[13] that rival facilities available anywhere in the world have been set up to house high-technology ventures. The Indian government also has plans for power reforms and some locations have achieved power surplus status. Deregulation opens doors to foreign companies (NASSCOM, 2005).[14]

Organizations looking to offshore locations to meet their outsourcing needs are troubled by news reports of security breaches, and theft of code and sensitive data from the vendor's offices (Davison, 2004; Morstead and Blount, 2003; Ribeiro, 2005). While U.S. firms face more stringent laws for ensuring the integrity of records and safe handling of data (e.g., Sarbanes-Oxley), they find that ensuring security in vendor locations is a challenge. Rao (2004) points out that since intellectual property protection is often governed by the laws of the country where the work is taking place, clients need to ensure that they have adequate safeguards in place. According to Murthy (2004), organizations should weigh the importance and specificity of the intellectual property that would need to be transferred when making offshore outsourcing decisions. To assuage clients' concerns, vendor firms are improving their security measures and obtaining certifications that prove they adhere to accepted standards. In India, for example, previously it was difficult to obtain a background check on an employee (Cooney, 2004). Recently, NASSCOM has proposed that a third-party organization be formed to create and maintain a national database of IT and BPO employees (*Economic Times*, 2005). Gartner Inc. suggests that risks offshore are not particularly different from those faced onshore; but the client does need to be mindful of the hurdles posed by the local legal and government systems when working with a vendor from another country (Willoughby, 2003).

Employee Morale and Public Opinion

The client organization may face resistance from within when employees are confronted with the loss of their jobs through offshore outsourcing (Baruch and Hind, 2000; Karamouzis, 2002; Morstead and Blount, 2003; Wade, 2004). While some contend that the U.S. economy as a whole would benefit from offshore outsourcing (ITAA, 2004), that is of small consolation to the employee who has to train his replacement before being terminated. Such tales fuel the opposition from employees and labor unions and bring negative publicity to offshoring (DiamondCluster, 2004). This may also lead to the occurrence of a "survivor syndrome" among remaining employees that affects their morale, performance, and productivity (Baruch and Hind, 2000; DiamondCluster, 2004; Elmuti and Kathawala, 2000; Karamouzis, 2003; Karamouzis et al., 2002; Morello, 2002; Morstead and Blount, 2003;). In addition, organizations are also concerned about their customers' (J. King, 2004; Patrick, 2004) and stockholders' opinions (Furlonger et al., 2003) about offshore outsourcing because negative evaluations may result in reduced market share or declining stock prices (J. King, 2004).

IMPLICATIONS FOR THE IS DISCIPLINE

Although there is disagreement about how easy such challenges will be to overcome, few seem to have considered the implications of offshoring on the discipline of IS; especially given that the majority of the IS discipline has traditionally been housed in the West. This seems somewhat surprising to us, as there would appear to be the potential for significant consequences for the discipline. For example, is there a possibility that external stakeholders and influences could undermine the economic base on which IS research and teaching depends? What would these external influences look like and how would they affect the discipline? Would the locus of the discipline shift from the West to the East? And if so, would the research directions change? So far, little discussion has ensued (but see Davis et al., 2004 and Hirschheim and Klein, 2003). What is particularly worrisome to us is the lack of regard being given to the rather alarming drop in student numbers in both IS and computer science (Datz, 2004; Fraunenheim and Yamamoto, 2004; Vegso, 2005).

So what does this mean for the discipline of IS? Even if the move toward the offshoring of IT work turns out to be inexorable, this does not necessarily spell the demise of the discipline (in the West). We believe that if the IS field recognizes the fact that most coding, support, infrastructure, and operations jobs will likely be offshored to the East,[15] there is still a key area where IS can prosper in the West, namely, in the IT enablement of organization/business processes. These are the so-called customer-facing jobs. This appears to be a fruitful avenue for IS academics in the West to focus on as it might help differentiate Western IS from what develops in the East, at least in the short term. In the longer term, there is no reason to believe this function might not find its way to the East as well.[16] But at least in the short term, it appears that most organizations in the West will likely rely on local talent to undertake such IT process enablement.

Of course, this begs the question of whether the notion of business process enablement through the application of IT is an overlooked IS core competence or whether other functional units could also perform this function. We believe that it is—or should be—an IS core competence. Consider that in the past, information systems development involved studying existing business processes, identifying new opportunities and/or restructuring the processes, and then building systems that would support the rationalized new business processes/model. In the past, for political and other reasons, the restructuring often turned out to be minor, thus anchoring the new system firmly to the old way of doing things. Many of the so-called business process reengineering exercises suffered this fate. The reengineering efforts simply did not accomplish the hoped-for changes. However, this has begun to change, and in fairly dramatic fashion. One need only look at enterprise resource planning systems (ERP) and related approaches that have reversed the old systems development model. New software modules embracing industry best practices are implemented allowing organizations to change their business processes. Usually this requires both organizational process and structure redefinitions to be prepared and then adopted for this alignment with best practices to take place. IS seems particularly well suited to perform this function since IS *has* studied information systems development (and its associated methods and tools) for decades and the new business process redesign is a logical extension of the earlier emphasis on methods of information requirements analysis, information systems design, and implementation. So we believe Western IS academics should focus their attention on this key core competence.

To be sure, IS as a discipline will have to evolve. For the West, the focus could be primarily on process redesign and the IT enablement of these processes as well as the implementation of the system when it is complete. The actual coding and maintenance of the modules will be done in the East. So what we see is more a growing division of labor between the West and the East, at least in the short term.[17] A yet to be determined issue is: where will IS research be located? As much of IS training moves to the East, presumably the growth of IS faculty in these countries will spur new research. This in turn is likely to reduce the funding base for IS research in the West to match its reduced faculty ranks. Not only have the organizations that have gone to offshore locations established their own research and development centers there (which often operate at higher quality assurance ratings (e.g., CMM) than their centers in the home country, (cf. Mohnot, 2003), they have also sponsored research at leading educational institutions in these countries. For example, in India, Intel Corp. is funding research at the Indian Institute of Technology (IIT) in Chennai to discover appropriate applications and usage models for wireless Internet in rural environments. IBM's India Research Laboratory has set up a technology center at the Indian Institute of Technology–Delhi that focuses on advanced IT applications in the areas of bioinformatics, grid computing, and knowledge management. Similarly, the Indian Institute of Technology–Kharagpur is doing research work in collaboration with multinationals such as Motorola, Hewlett-Packard, Oracle, and GE Capital. As research moves from the West to the East, it might change its character and we wonder how such research will fit with the research that remains in the West? And if the differences between the research in the West and the East surpass the differences that exist between North American and European IS research, then this is likely to fuel a new identity and legitimation debate. At this time it is hard to know if and to what extent the IS issues studied in the East will be different from those considered "core" in the West, although there is reason to believe it might not be as different as some think. For example, because a large number of IS researchers/academics in India have received their Ph.D.s from the United States or Europe, the current wave of research being carried out in India appears to be in line with what is going on in the West, as is demonstrated by numerous international collaborations (e.g., Krishna, Sahay, Nicholson, and others). (Of course, the Indian diaspora no doubt has much to do with this fact.)

Another reason for the similarity of teaching and research interests could be the establishment of the Association for Information Systems (AIS) divisions in Asia. We have noticed the increased participation of researchers from Indian institutions, such as the IITs and the Indian Institutes of Management at AMCIS, ICIS, ECIS, and IFIP TC8 events.

Last, but not least, is the issue of adjusting courses and degrees to the new realities. It could be of critical importance for U.S. universities to step up to the challenge and prepare their IS graduates for work in the new IT-enabled global economy both onshore and offshore (Ferguson, 2004; Schuldt and Davis, 2005). Some IS academics have stepped up to the challenge and offered recommendations. W. King (2004), for instance, suggests that the IS curriculum be revamped so as to focus on three core areas: software interfacing, contract management, and strategic technology assessment. Davis and colleagues (2004) contend that the IS curriculum should be revised to include offshoring management as a key component, and that new specializations should be added to the curriculum, namely, offshore infrastructure management, offshore system development management, offshore operations management, and offshore outsourcing management. Revising IS programs to be more attuned to the changing global nature of the discipline and the new realities of offshoring would make its students more relevant and employable, and might help reverse the trend of declining enrollments in the United States. Additionally, by preparing our students for the offshoring world, we would in effect be "taking the lead." This might be something the field could build upon and use in teaching students from other disciplines about the nature of offshoring (which presumably will affect them in whatever business functional area they major in). In essence, just as IT outsourcing was the precursor to business process outsourcing, IT offshoring is the precursor to business process offshoring. The field should capitalize on its early adopter status and apply its learning in other disciplines.

CONCLUSIONS

Tracing the evolution of outsourcing and offshore outsourcing, it is evident that these business practices are here to stay. It is also clear that the increasing popularity and acceptance of outsourcing and offshore outsourcing have brought new challenges to IT management, and, consequently, to the IS discipline. An awareness of the implications of these changes is vital to the future of the IS discipline, particularly in academic institutions in countries that are leading consumers of offshore outsourcing services, namely, the industrialized nations of the Western hemisphere. While it is not easy to prescribe a solution to the dilemma facing educators in the IS discipline, it is clear that curricular changes are necessary. IS academics in the West should focus on areas that would enable our graduates to compete successfully in the new IT-enabled global economy. We believe that the Association for Information Systems can and should play a key role in the future of the discipline, especially as it relates to offshoring. And indeed, this is already happening. For example, the AIS has taken a leadership role in helping to spearhead a change in IS education. Recognizing the need to promote courses that reflect the new social and technical trends in IS globally, the AIS sponsored a competition to recognize courses in the area of software development innovations and offshore outsourcing (Markus 2005). Such efforts that recognize and encourage the creation of courses and changes in curricula need to be applauded and extended.

Further, many of the research issues that need to be addressed in this global economy cannot be studied in isolation in one region of the world. Such research requires the collaboration and efforts of researchers from different countries. Similar to its developmental role in IS education, another role that AIS could play might be in helping to establish virtual research centers allowing researchers from countries such as India and China to enter into collaborative ventures with their counterparts in the West. As an example, we are in the process of setting up a collaborative virtual outsourcing/offshoring research center with some Indian and Australian colleagues. More of these kinds of collaborative efforts could prove highly useful for the discipline.

In conclusion, we believe the discipline needs to embrace the set of changes to which we have alluded. We further believe that the AIS is a good vehicle for fostering the necessary changes the field will need to make to be successful in the future.

ACKNOWLEDGMENTS

We are indebted to Heinz Klein and Siew Fan Wong for their thoughts and assistance on this chapter.

NOTES

1. An organization that designs and distributes, but does not produce anything
2. The term *global outsourcing* is used to refer to all outsourcing deals across the world, and includes both outsourcing to vendors in the same country and outsourcing to vendors in other countries. The former is referred to as domestic outsourcing and the latter as offshore outsourcing.
3. *IT offshoring* refers to the "migration of all or part" of the development and maintenance of IT services to another location and encompasses the offshore outsourcing of IT services.
4. Davis and colleagues (2004) make the interesting observation that while IT was indeed not a core competence for most organizations, it was nevertheless "special," that is, a critical success factor that was necessary but not sufficient for the success of a firm. Initially it was thought that such functions could not be outsourced, but either (a) IT was not "special," or (b) the logic that "special" functions could not be outsourced was a fallacy. In either case, the outsourcing of IT has continued to grow.
5. Now part of Unisys.
6. Data General was acquired by EMC in 1999.
7. Data Conversion Inc. was the distributor for Data General in India at that time.
8. Email from Dalal to the author, August 11, 2004.
9. Y2K contracts accounted only for 23 percent of Indian software exports in 1998 (Sheshabalaya, 1999).
10. Of course, there is a downside to this lack of competition. Without competition, low-quality vendors can enter the market producing substandard work that could end up being the subject of pejorative media reports, thus diluting the nation's reputation.
11. Heeks and Nicholson's (2002) software export success model categorizes the success factors into the categories of demand, national vision and strategy, international linkages, software industry characteristics, and supply factors and infrastructure.
12. Some commentators have noted that the need for Indians to work at night to be available for their clients in the United States is creating significant problems for the Indian family lifestyle where parents work normal daytime hours, but their school-leaving children work evening shifts. The problem becomes even more acute in young families, where one adult is forced to work during the evenings while the other works during the day.
13. The development of software technology parks—technoparks—is a project of the Indian Ministry of Information Technology. These parks offer several advantages to high-tech companies, including zero import duty on the import of all capital goods, a special ten-year income tax rebate, and availability of infrastructure facilities such as high-speed data communication links (NASSCOM 2005).
14. NASSCOM is India's National Association of Software and Service Companies, the premier trade body and the chamber of commerce of the IT software and services industry in India.
15. And even if these jobs are outsourced/offshored, would it not still be necessary for students to have some knowledge of these areas so that they could interface with the vendors and manage these activities? How can one manage something that one does not know? Indeed, students need more technology knowledge, not less. This also suggests to us (as it has for many commentators) that the key will be to instill an attitude and desire for lifelong learning and to ensure that the discipline possesses the capability to support this. Technology and the need to teach technology skills are not going away. We simply cannot conceive of a society in which technology skills are not valued or are perceived as unnecessary.
16. Indeed, some suggest there really is little if any difference in what IS students in the East and West study, and thus ultimately what functions and tasks they can and cannot perform.

17. But as we already suggested, there is no reason to believe that this can be sustained in the longer term as offshore companies move up the value chain and actually execute many/most of the activities on the value chain themselves. See also the discussion in Gopal, Beaubien, and Marcon (2002).

REFERENCES

Abbot, P.Y. 2005. Software-export strategies for developing countries: A Caribbean perspective. *Electronic Journal of Information Systems in Developing Countries*, 20.

Ante, S. 2004. Shifting work offshore? Outsourcer beware. *BusinessWeek Online*, January 12.

Apte, U. 1990. Global outsourcing of information systems and processing services. *Information Society*, 7, 4, 287–303.

Apte, U.M.; Sobol, M.G.; Hanaoka, S.; Shimada, T.; Saarinen, T.; Salmela, T.; and Vepsalainen, A.P.J. 1997. IS outsourcing practices in the USA, Japan, and Finland: A comparative study. *Journal of Information Technology*, 12, 4, 289–304.

Arora, A. and Gambardella, A. 2005. From underdogs to tigers. In A. Arora and A. Gambardella, eds., *The Rise and Growth of the Software Industry in Some Emerging Economies*. Oxford: Oxford University Press.

Athreye, S. 2005. The Indian software industry and its evolving service capability. *Industrial and Corporate Change*, 14, 3, 1–26.

Aubert, B.; Rivard, S.; and M. Patry. 2004. A transaction cost model of IT outsourcing. *Information & Management*, 41, 921–932.

Baruch, Y. and Hind, P. 2000. "Survivor syndrome"—A management myth? *Journal of Managerial Psychology*, 15, 1, 29–45.

Bruell, N. 2003. Exporting software from Indonesia. *Electronic Journal of Information Systems in Developing Countries*, 13.

Carmel, E. 2003a. Taxonomy of new software exporting nations. *Electronic Journal of Information Systems in Developing Countries*, 13.

Carmel, E. 2003b. The new software exporting nations: Success factors. *Electronic Journal of Information Systems in Developing Countries*, 13.

Carmel, E. and Agarwal, R. 2001. Tactical approaches for alleviating distance in global software development. *IEEE Software* (March/April), 22–29.

———. 2002. The maturation of offshore sourcing of information technology work. *MIS Quarterly Executive*, 1, 2, 65–78.

Carmel, E. and B. Nicholson. 2005. Small firms and offshore software outsourcing: High transaction costs and their mitigation. *Journal of Global Information Management*, 13, 3, 33–54.

Chidamber, S.R. 2003. An analysis of Vietnam's ICT and software services sector. *Electronic Journal of Information Systems in Developing Countries*, 13.

Clemons, E.K.; Hitt, L.M.; and Snir, E.M. 2000. A risk analysis framework for IT outsourcing. (October 31). Draft manuscript available at http://tecom.cox.smu.edu/esnir/Outsourcing.pdf.

Cooney, M. 2004. Assessing the offshore outsourcing security risk. (June 18). Southborough, MA: Network World Inc. Available at www.networkworld.com/weblogs/outsourcing/005444.html.

Coward, Christopher T. 2003. Looking beyond India: Factors that shape the global outsourcing decisions of small and medium sized companies in America. *Electronic Journal of Information Systems in Developing Countries*, 13.

Cullen, S.; Seddon, P.; and Willcocks, L. 2005. Managing outsourcing: The lifecycle imperative. *MIS Quaterly Executive*, 4, 1, 229–246.

Currie, W. 2000. The supply-side of IT outsourcing: The trend towards mergers, acquisitions and joint ventures. *International Journal of Physical Distribution & Logistics Management*, 30, 3/4, 238–254.

Datz, T. 2004. Degrees of change. *CIO Magazine* (October 15). Available at www.cio.com/archive/101504/school.html.

Davis, G.; Ein-Dor, P.; King, W.; and Torkzadeh, R. 2004. IT offshoring: History, prospects and challenges. Paper presented at ICIS2004, Senior Scholars Session, Washington.

Davison, D. 2004. Top 10 risks of offshore outsourcing. *SearchCIO.com* (February 16). Available at http://searchcio.techtarget.com/originalContent/0,289142,sid19_gci950602,00.html.

Desai, A. 2003. The dynamics of the Indian information technology industry. DRC Working Paper no. 20, Centre for New and Emerging Markets, London Business School.

DiamondCluster. 2004. Global IT outsourcing study. DiamondCluster International.

Dibbern, J.; Goles, T.; Hirschheim, R.; and Jayatilaka, B. 2004. Information systems outsourcing: A survey and analysis of the literature. *Database*, 35, 4, 6–102.

EBusiness Strategies. 2004. Offshoring statistics-dollar size, job loss, and market potential, (August 10). Available at www.ebstrategy.com/Outsourcing/trends/.

Economic Times. 2005. BPO fraud: Nasscom wants 3rd party to keep database. *Economic Times*, May 5.

Elmuti, D. and Kathawala, Y. 2000. The effects of global outsourcing strategies on participants' attitudes and organizational effectiveness. *International Journal of Manpower*, 21, 2, 112–128.

Ferguson, E. 2004. Impact of offshore outsourcing on CS/IS curricula. In *Proceedings of the Central Plains Conference of the Consortium for Computing Science in Colleges*, 68–77.

Frauenheim, E. and M. Yamamoto. 2004. Reforms, not rhetoric, needed to keep jobs on U.S. soil. c|net news.com. Available at http://news.com.com/Offshoring+U.S.+needs+reforms%2C+not+rhetoric/2009-1070_3-5198156.html.

Friedman, T. 2005. *The World Is Flat: A Brief History of the Twenty-First Century*. New York: Farrar, Straus and Giroux.

Furlonger, D.; Cournoyer, S.; Collins, K.; and Redshaw, P. 2003. White-collar job loss due to offshore outsourcing inflated. ID number: QA-20–2590 (June 16). Stamford, CT: Gartner Inc. Available at www.gartner.com/DisplayDocument?doc_cd=115628&ref=g_fromdoc.

Gallivan, M.J. and Oh, W. 1999. Analyzing IT outsourcing relationships as alliances among multiple clients and vendors. In *Proceedings of the Thirty-Second Annual International Conference on System Sciences* (January).

Gengler, E. 2003. Ukraine and success criteria for the software exports industry. *Electronic Journal of Information Systems in Developing Countries*, 13, 8, 1–18.

Goolsby, K. 2002. Offshore is not offhand: Recommendations for effective offshore outsourcing. White paper, The Outsourcing Center. Dallas, TX: The Everest Group. Available at http://www.c-trade.org/files/clusters/ICT/Effective%20Offshore%20Outsourcing%20White%20Paper.pdf.

Gopal, A.; Beaubien, L.; and Marcon, T. 2002. Old wolf, new wool suit: India, IT, and the legacy of colonialism. In *Proceedings of the Twenty-third International Conference on Information Systems* (Barcelona, December 15–18), 525–532.

Gopal, A.; Mukhopadhyay, T.; and Krishnan, M.S. 2002. The role of software processes and communication in offshore software development. *Communications of the ACM*, 45, 4, 193–200.

Gopal, A.; Sivaramakrishnan, K.; Krishnan, M.S.; and Mukhopadhyay, T. 2003. Contracts in offshore software development: An empirical analysis. *Management Science*, 49, 12, 1671–1683.

Hawk, S. and McHenry, W. 2005. The maturation of the Russian software industry. *Journal of Information Technology for Development*, 11, 1, 31–57.

Heavin, C.; Fitzgerald, B.; and Trauth, E.M. 2001. Factors influencing Ireland's software industry: Lessons for economic development through IT. In M. Korpela and R. Montealeagre, eds., *Information Systems Perspectives and Challenges in the Context of Globalization.* Boston, MA: Kluwer Academic.

Heeks, Richard. 1999. Software strategies in developing countries, development informatics. Working Paper Series, Paper no. 6, Institute for Development Policy and Management, University of Manchester, June. Available at http://unpan1.un.org/intradoc/groups/public/documents/NISPAcee/UNPAN015540.pdf.

Heeks, R. and Nicholson, B. 2002. Software export success factors and strategies in developing and transitional economies. Paper no. 2002–12, University of Manchester, Institute for Development Policy and Management. Available at http://unpan1.un.org/intradoc/groups/public/documents/NISPAcee/UNPAN015604.pdf.

Heeks, R. and Nicholson, B. 2004. Software export success factors and strategies in follower nations. *Competition and Change*, 8, 3, 267–303.

Herbsleb, J.D. and Moitra, D. 2001. Global software development. *IEEE Software*, 18, 2, 16–20.

Hirschheim, R. and Klein, H. 2003. Crisis in the IS field? A critical reflection on the state of the discipline. *Journal of the Association of Information Systems*, 4, 5, 237–293.

Hirschheim, R. and M. Lacity. 2000. Information technology insourcing: Myths and realities. *Communications of the ACM*, 43, 2, 99–107.

Hirschheim, R.; George, B.; and Wong, S. 2004. Information systems outsourcing: The move towards offshoring. *Indian Journal of Economics and Business*, Special Issue on Offshore Outsourcing (Fall).

ITAA. 2004. *Executive Summary: The Comprehensive Impact of Offshore IT Software and Services Outsourcing on the U.S. Economy and the IT Industry.* Prepared by: Global Insight, Inc., Massachusetts, 2004.

Kaiser, K. and Hawk, S. 2004. Evolution of offshore software development: From outsourcing to co-sourcing. *MISQ Executive*, 3, 3, 69–81.

Kakabadse, A. and Kakabadse, N. 2002. Trends in outsourcing: Contrasting USA and Europe. *European Management Journal*, 20, 2, 189–198.
Karamouzis, F. 2002. Debunking the myths of offshore IT service offerings. ID number DF-15–5315 (March 21). Stamford, CT: Gartner Inc.
———. 2003. The impact on people when going offshore for IT services. ID number TG-20–4757 (July 18), Stamford, CT: Gartner Inc.
Karamouzis, F.; Young, A.; Young, C.; and Sinha, D. 2002. Understanding the "human cost" of cost savings. ID number COM-18–9808 (December 23). Stamford, CT: Gartner Inc.
Kelly, T. 2002. A brief history of outsourcing. *Global Envision*. Available at www.globalenvision.org/library/3/702/ (accessed May 9, 2004).
Khan, N.; Currie, W.L.; Weerakkody, V.; and Desai, B. 2002. Evaluating offshore IT outsourcing in India: Supplier and customer scenarios. In *Proceedings of the Thirty-sixth Hawaii International Conference on System Sciences* (January 6–9). Washington, DC: IEEE Computer Sciences.
Khanna, T. and Palepu, K. 2004. The evolution of concentrated ownership in India: Broad patterns and a history of the Indian software industry. NBER Working Papers 10613. Cambridge, MA: National Bureau of Economic Research.
King, J. 2004. Damage control: How to combat offshore outsourcing backlash, *Computerworld* (July 12). Available at www.computerworld.com/managementtopics/outsourcing/story/0,10801,94404,00.html?nas=AM-94404.
King, W. 2004. Outsourcing and the future of IT. *Information Systems Management*, 21, 4, 83–84.
Krishna, S.; Sahay, S.; and Walsham, G. 2004. Managing cross-cultural issues in global software outsourcing. *Communications of the ACM*, 47, 4, 62–66.
Kumar, K. and Willcocks, L. 1996. Offshore outsourcing: A country too far? In *Proceedings of the Fourth European Conference on Information Systems* (Lisbon, July 2–4), 1309–1325.
Lacity, M. and Hirschheim, R. 1993. *Information Systems Outsourcing: Myths, Metaphors and Realities*. Chichester, UK: Wiley.
Lacity, M.C. and Willcocks, L.P. 2001. *Global Information Technology Outsourcing: In Search of Business Advantage*. Chichester, UK: Wiley.
Lacity, M.; Hirschheim, R.; and Willcocks, L. 1994. Realizing outsourcing expectations: Incredible expectations, credible outcomes. *Information Systems Management*, 11, 4, 7–18.
Linder, J. 2004. *Outsourcing for Radical Change*. New York: AMACOM.
Markus, L. 2005. Introduction to the 2004 AIS award papers on innovation in information systems education. *Communications of the Association for Information Systems*, 15, 16.
McFarlan, F.W. 1995. Issues in global outsourcing. In P. Palvia, S. Palvia, and E. Roche, eds. *Global Information Technology and Systems Management: Key Issues and Trends*, Nashua, NH: Ivy League, 352–364.
Mears, J. and Bednarz, A. 2005. "Take it all" outsourcing on the wane. Networkworld.com, May 30. Available at http://napps.networkworld.com/news/2005/053005outsourcing.html.
Mohnot, N. 2003. Why "India inside" spells quality? *Dataquest*, October. Available at www.dqindia.com/content/advantage/103102703.asp.
Morello, D. 2002. Offshore outsourcing rattles IT profession in U.S., Europe. ID number SPA-18–9278 (December 5). Stamford, CT: Gartner Inc.
———. 2003. The organizational implications of offshore outsourcing. ID number AV-21–1610 (October 24). Stamford, CT: Gartner Inc. Available at www.gartner.com/DisplayDocument?ref=g_search&id=413700&subref=advsearch.
Morstead, S. and Blount, G. 2003. *Offshore Ready: Strategies to Plan & Profit from Offshore IT-Enabled Services*. Houston, TX: ISANI Press.
Murthy, S. 2004. The impact of global IT outsourcing on IT providers. *Communications of the AIS*, 14, 553–557.
NASSCOM. 2005. GE looks to India for growth. Available at www.nasscom.in/Nasscom/templates/NormalPage.aspx?id=26041.
NeoIT. 2004. The captive ownership option in offshoring: Challenges and opportunities. San Ramon, CA: NeoIT. www.NeoIT.com.
Nicholson, B. and Sahay, S. 2001. Some political and cultural issues in the globalization of software development: Case experience from Britain and India. *Information and Organization*, 11, 25–43.
———. 2003. Building Iran's software industry: As assessment of plans and prospects. *Electronic Journal of Information Systems in Developing Countries*, 13, 1–19.

Offshore IT Outsourcing.com. 2004. IT leading as most active area of outsourcing. http://offshoreitoutsourcing.com/Pages/outsourcing_statistics.asp. (August 10).

Overby, S. 2003. The hidden costs of offshore outsourcing. *CIO Magazine*.(September 1)

Pastin, M. and Harrison, J. 1974. Social responsibility in the hollow corporation. *Business & Society Review*, 54.

Patrick, R.B. 2004. Signs of offshore backlash growing. *Computerworld Canada* (January 5).

Porter, M. 1990. *The Competitive Advantage of Nations*. New York: Free Press.

Pruitt, S. 2004. Survey: 275,000 telecom jobs to go offshore by 2008. *Computerworld*. Available at http://napps.networkworld.com/news/2004/0324surve2750.html.

Qu, Z. and Brocklehurst, M. 2003. What will it take for China to become a competitive force in offshore outsourcing? An analysis of the role of transaction costs in supplier selection. *Journal of Information Technology*, 18, 1, 53–67.

Rajkumar, T.M. and Dawley, D.L. 1998. Problems and issues in offshore development of software. In L.P. Willcocks and M.C. Lacity, eds., *Strategic Sourcing of Information Systems*. Chichester, UK: Wiley.

Ramanujan, S. and Lou, H. 1997. Outsourcing maintenance operations to off-shore vendors: Some lessons from the field. *Journal of Global Information Management*, 5, 2, 5–15.

Ramarapu, N.; Parzinger, M.; and Lado, A. 1997. Issues in foreign outsourcing. *Information Systems Management*, 14, 2, 27–31.

Rao, M.T. 2004. Key issues for global IT outsourcing: Country and individual factors. *Information Systems Management* (Summer), 17–21.

Rapaport, R. 1996. Bangalore. *Wired*, Issue 4.02 (February). Available at www.wired.com/wired/archive/4.02/bangalore.html.

Reingold, J. 2004. A brief (recent) history of offshoring. *FastCompany*, 81 (April). Available at www.fastcompany.com/magazine/81/offshore_extra.html.

Ribeiro, J. 2005. Indian call center workers charged with Citibank fraud. April 7. www.infoworld.com. Available at www.infoworld.com/article/05/04/07/HNcitibankfraud_1.html.

Robinson, M. and Kalakota, R. 2004. *Offshore Outsourcing: Business Models, ROI and Best Practices*. New York: Milvar Press.

Rottman, J. and Lacity, M. 2004. Offshore sourcing: Twenty practices offshore sourcing. *MISQ Executive*, 3, 3, 117–130.

Sabherwal, R. 1999. The role of trust in outsourced IS development projects. *Communications of the ACM*, 42, 2, 80–86.

Sahay, S.; Nicholson, B.; and Krishna S. 2003. *Global Software Work: Micro-Studies Across Borders*. Cambridge: Cambridge University Press.

Schuldt, B. and Davis, B. 2005. Offshore outsourcing: A new driver for university curriculum change? Southeastern Louisiana University, Working Paper.

Sheshabalaya, A. 1999. India's software success down to more than just millennium luck. *Financial Times*, March 18.

———. 2004. *Rising Elephant: The Growing Clash with India over White Collar Jobs and Its Challenge to America and the World*. Monroe, ME : Common Courage Press.

siliconindia.com. 2005. IT-ITES export revenues up 34.5%. Available at www.siliconindia.com/shownewsdata.asp?newsno=28331&newscat=Technology (accessed June 2, 2005).

Souza, R.D.; Goodness, E.; Young, A.; Silliman, R.; and Caldwell, B.M. 2004. IT outsourcing market forecast: Worldwide, 2002–2007. ID number ITNI–WW–MS–0126 (March 9). Stamford, CT: Gartner Inc.

Terdiman, R. 2002. Offshore outsourcing can achieve more than cost savings. ID number: CS-16–3520 (May 24). Stamford, CT: Gartner Inc.

Tessler, S.; Barr, A.; and Hanna, N. 2003. National software industry development: Considerations for government planners. *Electronic Journal of Information Systems in Developing Countries*, 13.

Times of India. 2005. Indian firms get a phoren touch. *Times of India*, February 23.

Vaze, S. 2005. The politics (and economics) of outsourcing. *Express Computer*, March 7. Available at www.express-computer.com/20050307/technology02.shtml.

Vegso, J. 2005. Interest in CS as a major drops among incoming freshmen. *Computing Research News*, 17, 3 (May). Available at http://www.cra.org/CRN/articles/may05/vegso.

Wade, W. 2004. Offshoring grows, along with a backlash. *American Banker*, 169, 4 (January 7), 13.

Willoughby, M. 2003. Offshore security: Considering the risks. *Computerworld*, September 15.

EDITORS AND CONTRIBUTORS

Soon Ang is Goh Tjoei Kok Chair Professor in management and executive director of the Center for Cultural Intelligence (CCI) at the Nanyang Business School, Nanyang Technological University of Singapore. She holds a Ph.D. in MIS from the Carlson School of Management at the University of Minnesota. She is a world authority on outsourcing, cultural intelligence, and the management of global talent, and has an outstanding record of research and teaching in management. Internationally, Soon Ang has won numerous prestigious best paper awards at the U.S. Academy of Management Meeting at San Diego, at the Hawaiian International Conference on Systems Sciences (HICSS), and at the Association of Computing Machinery (ACM) in Computer Personnel Research (SIGCPR) conference. She was awarded the Researcher of the Strategy, Management and Organization Division Award in 2004 for the quality of her research at the Nanyang Business School, and was awarded the first of three endowed chair professorships by Nanyang Technological University in 2005.

Benoit A. Aubert is professor of information systems at HEC Montreal and President and Chief Executive Officer of the CIRANO (Centre inter-universitaire de recherche en analyse des organisations). He currently co-chairs the Outsourcing Track of the Hawaii International Conference on Systems Sciences (since 1997). His main research areas are outsourcing, risk management, and new organization forms. He has published several articles, book chapters, and conference proceedings on these topics. He has also published papers on trust, ontology, and health care information systems. He is senior editor of *Database*.

Bouchaib Bahli is an associate professor at John Molson School of Business, Concordia University. He has published more than twenty papers in MIS journals and conference proceedings of refereed and recognized international conferences. His publications have appeared in the *Journal of Information Technology, Information and Management, OMEGA,* and *Communications of AIS.* He has been selected as the recipient of the 2005 JMSB Distinguished Junior Researcher Award. His research interests are in the areas of IT outsourcing, IS risk management, and maturity of IS development processes. He was nominated twice for the JMSB Distinguished Teaching Award.

Jérôme Barthélémy is an associate professor of strategic management at ESSEC (France). He holds a Ph.D from HEC (France) and has been a visiting research scholar at the University of California at Berkeley. His research has appeared in journals such as *Information & Management, MIT Sloan Management Review, Economics Letters,* and *Academy of Management Executive.*

Erik Beulen is a senior manager with Accenture, and is associated with Tilburg University in the Netherlands. He has written widely on the subject of outsourcing and offshore outsourcing, including co-authored publications with Wendy Currie and Erran Carmel. In 2006, his book on managing IT outsourcing with Pieter Ribbers and Jan Roos was published by Routledge.

Anne-Marie Croteau is an associate professor of MIS at the John Molson School of Business at Concordia University. She holds a Ph.D. from Université Laval. Her research focuses mainly on strategic information technology alignment and the impact of information technology on business performance. Her research has been published in *Journal of Strategic Information Systems, Journal of Information Technology,* and *Canadian Journal of Administrative Sciences* as well as in various national and international conference proceedings.

Beena George is a visiting professor in the Department of Management Information Systems at the Cameron School of Business of the University of St. Thomas, Houston, Texas. She completed her graduate studies in business administration at the Indian Institute of Management, Calcutta, India, and her doctoral studies at the University of Houston, Texas. Her primary research focus and teaching interests are in the area of outsourcing of information systems and information technology enabled services. Her graduate course on sourcing management was awarded the distinction of excellence in the 2004 AIS-sponsored awards competition for innovation in IS education. Her other research interests include the management of IS and technology acceptance.

Abhijit Gopal holds a Ph.D. from the University of Georgia, and is an associate professor at the Richard Ivey School of Business at the University of Western Ontario, Canada. His interests lie in the interstitial and peripheral locations of information systems use with particular emphasis on the manner in which information technologies shape and are shaped by political and social conditions and considerations. He has published in leading journals in the field.

Petri Hallikainen is an assistant professor at the Helsinki School of Economics. He holds a Ph.D. (2003) in information systems science from the Helsinki School of Economics. His research interests include the evaluation processes of information systems, developing processes for managing IS projects throughout their life cycles, and investigating ERP system adoption processes. He has publications in the *Journal of Global Information Management* and in *IEEE Transactions on Professional Communication*, and in several conference proceedings, including the Hawaii International Conference on System Sciences.

Rudy Hirschheim is the Ourso Family Distinguished Professor of Information Systems at the E.J. Ourso College of Business at Louisiana State University. He has previously been on the faculties of the University of Houston, University of Oxford (UK), University of London (UK), and McMaster University (Canada). He has held visiting appointments at Monash University (Australia), University of New South Wales (Australia), and University of Bayreuth (Germany). He and Richard Boland are the consulting editors of the John Wiley Series in Information Systems. He is senior editor for the *Journal of the Association for Information Systems* and on the editorial boards of the journals: *Information and Organization, Information Systems Journal, Journal of Strategic Information Systems,* and *Journal of Information Technology,* and has previously been on the boards of *European Journal of Information Systems* and *MIS Quarterly.* He was vice president for publications for the Association for Information Systems.

William R. King holds the title of university professor in the Katz Graduate School of Business at the University of Pittsburgh. He has served as president of TIMS (now INFORMS), founding president of the Association for Information Systems (AIS), and editor-in-chief of the *MIS Quarterly.* He is a fellow of AIS, the American Association for the Advancement of Science and DSI, and was named an inaugural fellow of INFORMS—as one of about 100 people who had the greatest impact on management science over fifty years. He originated the modern concept of IS strategic planning. After his concept and methodology were adopted by IBM and incorporated into its Business Systems Planning (BSP) methodology, it was applied in firms all over the world. He has published more than 300 papers in leading journals on information systems, strategic planning, and management science. In 2004, he received the Leo Lifetime Exceptional Achievement Award from AIS.

Rajiv Kishore is an associate professor in the School of Management at the State University of New York at Buffalo. His primary research interest is in how organizations can improve their IT services delivery capabilities, particularly through IT outsourcing and globally distributed work, use of innovative systems analysis and design methods and techniques, and adoption of advanced technological innovations. His papers have been published or accepted for publication in *Journal of Management Information Systems, Communications of the ACM, Decision Support Systems, Information Systems Frontiers, Journal of Database Management,* and *Journal of Healthcare Information Management.* He has presented his research at ICIS, HICSS, AMCIS, SIM, and others. He received a best paper award at AMCIS 2001 and was nominated for a best paper award at AMCIS 2003 and HICSS 2004. He is also the recipient of a multiyear National Science Foundation research grant as a co-principal investigator in the area of IT outsourcing.

Christine Koh is an assistant professor of information technology and management at the Nanyang Business School, Singapore. She holds a master of science (IS) from Claremont Graduate School, and is currently completing her Ph.D. Her research interests are in IT outsourcing, specifically on managing client–vendor relationships. She also conducts research on managing IT professionals, and cultural intelligence. Her papers have been published in *Information Systems Research, Journal of IT Cases and Applications,* and *Journal of Global IT Management.* Her papers have also been accepted for presentation at international conferences including the International Conference in Information Systems, Academy of Management Meeting, and Society of Industrial and Organizational Psychology.

Kim Langfield-Smith is a professor of management accounting in the Department of Accounting and Finance at Monash University, Melbourne, Australia. She has a bachelor of economics from the University of Sydney, a master of economics from Macquarie University, and a Ph.D. from Monash University. She has published in a variety of local and international journals in the accounting, management, and psychology fields, and has received two prizes for her contribution to management accounting from the International Federation of Accountants (IFAC). Her research interests are in the area of management control systems and behavioral management accounting. She has published articles in leading journals including *Accounting, Organizations and Society, Journal of Management Accounting Research, Management Accounting Research, Behavioral Research in Accounting, Journal of Accounting Literature, Journal of Management Studies,* and *Journal of Operational Research Society.*

Kalle Lyytinen is Iris S. Wolstein Professor at Case Western Reserve University. He received his Ph.D. from the University of Jyväskylä, Finland. He currently serves on the editorial boards of several leading IS journals including, *Journal of AIS* (editor-in-chief), *Journal of Strategic Information Systems, Information & Organization, Requirements Engineering Journal, Information Systems Journal, Scandinavian Journal of Information Systems,* and *Information Technology and People,* among others. He is an AIS fellow (2004). He has published more than 150 scientific articles and conference papers and edited or written eleven books on topics related to system design, implementation, software risk assessment, computer-supported cooperative work, standardization, and ubiquitous computing. He is currently involved in research projects that study IT-induced innovation in software development, architecture, and the construction industry, design and use of ubiquitous applications in health care, high-level requirements models for large scale systems, and the development and adoption of broadband wireless standards and services.

Teresa Marcon is a doctoral candidate at the Richard Ivey School of Business, the University of Western Ontario, Canada. Her interests fall at the intersection of contemporary theory and information technologies in society. Her dissertation recounts a history of the interplay of language and practices in offshore information technology outsourcing from the Foucauldian perspective. Her work has been accepted for publication in *Information Systems Journal* and has also been published in a book chapter and in conference proceedings.

Pankaj Nagpal is a Ph.D. candidate at Case Western Reserve University. He holds an undergraduate degree in mechanical engineering from the Indian Institute of Technology (formerly University of Roorkee), an M.B.A. from JBIMS, Bombay, and an M.S. from Boston University. His research interests include sourcing of information technology services, business value of IT, and technology usage in the health care sector. His work has been published in leading IS conference proceedings. He has served as an invited discussant at the International Conference on Information Systems (ICIS). Before entering academia, he worked for ten years in business and industry. As an executive in a major global firm, he was part of the founding team that started a highly successful venture designing and executing large, complex, global projects.

Antti Nurmi is a Ph.D. candidate and a teaching assistant at the Helsinki School of Economics. He holds an M.Sc. (economics) from the Helsinki School of Economics with a major in information systems science. His doctoral dissertation focuses on managing multiorganizational information systems development projects. His research interests include sourcing of information systems, project management, and virtual teams. His research has been presented at several conferences including the Hawaii International Conference on System Sciences (HICSS).

Wonseok Oh is an assistant professor of information systems at McGill University. He received his Ph.D. in information systems from the Stern School of Business, New York University. His research interests include the business value of information systems, network theory, economic aspects of e-commerce, and IT outsourcing. His work has been published or is forthcoming in *Information Systems Research*, *Management Science*, *Journal of Management Information Systems*, *International Journal of Electronic Commerce*, and *Journal of Information Systems*. He has also won several best paper awards at major IS conferences such as the International Conference on Information Systems (ICIS) and the Hawaiian Internal Conference on System Science (HICSS).

Ebrahim Randeree is a Ph.D. candidate in the School of Management at the State University of New York at Buffalo. His primary research focus is in the area of outsourcing and is combined with his interests in information assurance, strategic IT, and knowledge management, specifically in the area of health care. He has worked in physician management and continues to function as an instructor in the capstone undergraduate strategic management course at the University at Buffalo. His papers have been published or accepted for publication in the *Journal of Healthcare Information Management, International Journal of Electronic Healthcare,* and the *Journal of Knowledge Management.* He has presented his research at HICSS, AMCIS, and EAM. He was nominated for a best paper award at HICSS 2005.

H. Raghav Rao is a professor in the School of Management at the State University of New York at Buffalo. His interests are in the areas of management information systems, decision support systems, outsourcing, and information assurance. He has authored or co-authored more than 100 technical papers, of which more than 70 are published in archival journals. His work has received best paper and best paper runner-up awards at AMCIS and ICIS. He has received funding for his research from the National Science Foundation, the Department of Defense, and the Canadian Embassy, and he has received the university's prestigious teaching fellowship. He also received a Fulbright fellowship in 2004. He is a co-editor of a special issue of the *Annals of Operations Research*, the *Communications of ACM*; he is associate editor of *Decision Support Systems*, *Information Systems Research*, and *IEEE Transactions in Systems, Man and Cybernetics*; and co-editor-in-chief of *Information Systems Frontiers*.

Pieter Ribbers is a professor of information management at Tilburg University (the Netherlands). His interests span management and governance of information technology. His most recent book, co-authored with Mike Papazoglou, is *e-Business: Organizational and Technical Foundations* (Wiley, 2006). He is a member of the editorial board of *Information & Management*. He co-authored, with Erik Beulen and Jan Roos, a book on managing IT outsourcing partnerships (Routledge, 2006).

Suzanne Rivard is a professor of information technology and chair of strategic management of information technology at HEC Montréal. She is a fellow of the Canadian Royal Society. Her research interests are in the areas of enterprise systems implementation, outsourcing of information systems services, software project risk management, IS outsourcing risk management, and strategic alignment. Her work has been published in such journals as *Communications of the ACM, Database, Information and Management, Interfaces, Journal of Information Technology, Journal of Management Information Systems, MIS Quarterly, Organization Science,* and others. She has served as an associate editor for *Information Systems Research* and *MIS Quarterly*. She is currently a member of the editorial board of the *Journal of Management Information Systems,* and an associate editor of the *Journal of the Association for Information Systems.*

Matti Rossi is an acting professor of information systems and director of the electronic business program for professionals (Muuntokoulutus) at the Helsinki School of Economics. He has worked as a research fellow at Erasmus University Rotterdam and as a visiting assistant professor at Georgia State University, Atlanta. He received his Ph.D. degree in business administration from the University of Jyväskylä in 1998. He has been the principal investigator on several major research projects funded by the technological development center of Finland and Academy of Finland. His research papers have appeared in journals such as *CACM, Journal of AIS, Information and Management*, and *Information Systems*, and more than thirty of them have appeared in conference proceedings such as ICIS, HICSS, and CAiSE.

Rajiv Sabherwal is a University of Missouri System Curators' Professor, the Emery C. Turner Professor of Information Systems at the University of Missouri, St. Louis, and director of the Ph.D. program in business administration (with an emphasis on information systems). He is a senior editor of *MIS Quarterly,* departmental editor (information technology) for *IEEE Transactions on Engineering Management,* and serves on the editorial boards for *Information Systems Research* and *Journal of AIS.* His research focuses on knowledge management, information systems strategy, and social aspects of systems development. It has been published in journals such as *Information Systems Research, Journal of Management Information Systems, MIS Quarterly, California Management Review, Communications of the ACM, IEEE Transactions on Engineering Management, Organization Science,* and *Decision Sciences.* Some of his research has been funded by the Advanced Practices Council of the Society for Information Management. He received a Ph.D. in business administration from the University of Pittsburgh, and a postgraduate diploma in management from the Indian Institute of Management, Calcutta.

David Smith is a senior lecturer in the Department of Accounting and Business Information Systems at the University of Melbourne, Australia, having held prior academic appointments at La Trobe and Monash Universities. He has a bachelor of commerce (honors) from La Trobe University, and a Ph.D. from Monash University. He has published in refereed journals including *Behavioral Research in Accounting, Journal of Accounting Literature,* and *Management Accounting Research.* His current research interests include management control of interfirm relationships.

Matthew Swinarski is assistant professor of management information systems at the Sam and Irene Black School of Business (Penn State). He completed his Ph. D. at the State University of New York at Buffalo. His research interests include IS outsourcing and IT services delivery capabilities. His teaching interests are in database management systems, IS strategy and IT management. He has served as issue managing editor for the *Journal of Information Technology Theory & Application* and as an IT consultant for small and medium-sized companies in the Buffalo, New York, area.

SERIES EDITOR

Vladimir Zwass is the Distinguished Professor of Computer Science and Management Information Systems at Fairleigh Dickinson University. He holds a Ph.D. in computer science from Columbia University. He is the founding editor-in-chief of the *Journal of Management Information Systems*, one of the three top-ranked journals in the field of information systems; the journal is in its twenty-fourth year in publication. He is also the founding editor-in-chief of the *International Journal of Electronic Commerce*, ranked globally as the top journal in its field. Dr. Zwass is the founding editor-in-chief of the monograph series *Advances in Management Information Systems*, the objective of which is to codify the field's knowledge and research methods. He is the author of six books and several book chapters, including entries in the *Encyclopaedia Britannica*, as well as a number of papers in various journals and conference proceedings. He has received several grants, consulted for a number of major corporations, and is a frequent speaker to national and international audiences. He is a former member of the professional staff of the International Atomic Energy Agency in Vienna, Austria.

INDEX

D

R

Anthony
Mr. Edwards
MARGARET GC - 504-628-1366 /

784-0334 . Schleffer c61